Pro .NET 1.1 Remoting, Reflection, and Threading

TOBIN TITUS, SYED FAHAD GILANI, MIKE GILLESPIE, JAMES HART,
BENNY K. MATHEW, ANDY OLSEN, DAVID CURRAN, JON PINNOCK,
ROBIN PARS, FABIO CLAUDIO FERRACCHIATI, SANDRA GOPIKRISHNA,
TEJASWI REDKAR, SRINIVASA SIVAKUMAR

apress®

Pro .NET 1.1 Remoting, Reflection, and Threading

Copyright © 2005 by Tobin Titus, Syed Fahad Gilani, Mike Gillespie, James Hart, Benny K. Mathew, Andy Olsen, David Curran, Jon Pinnock, Robin Pars, Fabio Claudio Ferracchiati, Sandra Gopikrishna, Tejaswi Redkar, Srinivasa Sivakumar

All rights reserved. No part of this work may be reproduced or transmitted in any form or by any means, electronic or mechanical, including photocopying, recording, or by any information storage or retrieval system, without the prior written permission of the copyright owner and the publisher.

ISBN: 1-59059-452-5

Printed and bound in the United States of America 9 8 7 6 5 4 3 2 1

Trademarked names may appear in this book. Rather than use a trademark symbol with every occurrence of a trademarked name, we use the names only in an editorial fashion and to the benefit of the trademark owner, with no intention of infringement of the trademark.

Lead Editor: Ewan Buckingham
Technical Reviewers: Rick Delorme, Don Reamey
Editorial Board: Steve Anglin, Dan Appleman, Ewan Buckingham, Gary Cornell, Tony Davis, Jason Gilmore, Jonathan Hassell, Chris Mills, Dominic Shakeshaft, Jim Sumser
Assistant Publisher: Grace Wong
Project Manager: Beckie Stones
Copy Manager: Nicole LeClerc
Copy Editor: Julie McNamee
Production Manager: Kari Brooks-Copony
Production Editor: Kelly Winquist
Compositor: Kinetic Publishing Services, LLC
Proofreader: Patrick Vincent
Indexer: Michael Brinkman
Artist: Kinetic Publishing Services, LLC
Cover Designer: Kurt Krames
Manufacturing Manager: Tom Debolski

Distributed to the book trade in the United States by Springer-Verlag New York, Inc., 233 Spring Street, 6th Floor, New York, NY 10013, and outside the United States by Springer-Verlag GmbH & Co. KG, Tiergartenstr. 17, 69112 Heidelberg, Germany.

In the United States: phone 1-800-SPRINGER, fax 201-348-4505, e-mail orders@springer-ny.com, or visit http://www.springer-ny.com. Outside the United States: fax +49 6221 345229, e-mail orders@springer.de, or visit http://www.springer.de.

For information on translations, please contact Apress directly at 2560 Ninth Street, Suite 219, Berkeley, CA 94710. Phone 510-549-5930, fax 510-549-5939, e-mail info@apress.com, or visit http://www.apress.com.

The information in this book is distributed on an "as is" basis, without warranty. Although every precaution has been taken in the preparation of this work, neither the author(s) nor Apress shall have any liability to any person or entity with respect to any loss or damage caused or alleged to be caused directly or indirectly by the information contained in this work.

The source code for this book is available to readers at http://www.apress.com in the Downloads section.

For my wife, Carol for being a solid rock and support in my career. For my parents, who continue to teach their sons, no matter how old they get. To my brother, Rick, for showing me that happiness isn't achieved, it's a choice. To my grandparents, for their sacrifices to get us where we are today, their stories of life in a better time, their bear hugs that seem to get stronger every year, and baked goods that my mouth waters for at the very thought of them. My aunts and uncles, cousins, and nieces for always making room in their schedules for me at a moment's notice when I come home to visit.

Contents at a Glance

About the Author xv
About the Technical Reviewers xvii
Acknowledgments xix
Introduction xxi

CHAPTER 1	Introducing .NET Remoting	1
CHAPTER 2	Remoting Basics	15
CHAPTER 3	Custom Remoting	43
CHAPTER 4	Configuration and Deployment	99
CHAPTER 5	Asynchronous Remoting	127
CHAPTER 6	Debugging and Error Handling	159
CHAPTER 7	Flexible Programming	209
CHAPTER 8	Examining Assemblies, Objects, and Types	223
CHAPTER 9	Using Objects	251
CHAPTER 10	Creating Objects	279
CHAPTER 11	Attributes	301
CHAPTER 12	The .NET Component Model	343
CHAPTER 13	Defining Threads	397
CHAPTER 14	Threading in .NET	421
CHAPTER 15	Working with Threads	469
CHAPTER 16	Threading Models	519
CHAPTER 17	Scaling Threaded Applications	535
CHAPTER 18	Debugging and Tracing Threads	563
CHAPTER 19	Networking and Threading	593

INDEX 619

Contents

About the Author... xv
About the Technical Reviewers... xvii
Acknowledgments... xix
Introduction.. xxi

CHAPTER 1 **Introducing .NET Remoting**................................. 1

    Distributed Systems... 1
        Client-Server Models... 2
        Evolution of Distributed Systems............................... 4
    Using .NET Remoting... 6
        Remote Object Types.. 7
        Context.. 8
        Managing Remote Objects.. 9
        The Remoting Process.. 10
    Summary.. 14

CHAPTER 2 **Remoting Basics**.. 15

    .NET Remoting Classes.. 15
        Classes Associated with Marshaling............................ 16
        Channel Classes... 17
        .NET Remoting Code Example.................................... 19
    Marshaling User-Defined Objects.................................... 22
        Marshaling User-Defined Objects by Value...................... 22
        Marshaling User-Defined Objects by Reference.................. 25
    MBR Activation Modes... 26
        Server-Activated Objects...................................... 26
        Client-Activated Objects...................................... 30
        Dynamically Publishing Server-Activated Objects............... 31
    MBR Lifetime Management.. 36
        A Closer Look at Leased-Based Lifetimes....................... 36
        Manipulating Leases... 38
        Renewing Leases... 39
    Summary.. 42

CHAPTER 3 Custom Remoting 43

A Closer Look at the Sink Chain 43
    Formatter Classes 44
    Channel Sink Interfaces and Classes 45
    Client Channel Sink Providers 47
Customizing the Sink Chain 48
    The Basic Invert Example 48
    Adding a New Client Channel Sink 52
    Replacing the Formatter Sink 59
    Adding a Custom Formatter 62
Custom Serialization 71
    Defining a Custom Serialization Format 72
Channels with Custom Transport Protocols 83
    Channel Interfaces 83
    Implementing a Custom TCP/IP Socket Channel 84
Summary 98

CHAPTER 4 Configuration and Deployment 99

Configuration 99
    Standard Configuration File Types 100
    Configuration File Structure 100
    Loading a Configuration File 105
Deploying Metadata 110
    Using Interface-Only Assemblies 111
    Using Soapsuds 113
Hosting 115
    Hosting in a Windows Service 115
    Hosting in IIS 119
Versioning 123
    Assigning a Version Number 123
    Determining the Version to Use 124
    Other Versioning Issues 124
Summary 125

CHAPTER 5 Asynchronous Remoting 127

Simple Asynchronous Remoting 127
    Implementing a Slow Synchronous Process 128
    Implementing a Slow Asynchronous Process 130
    Implementing a Slow Asynchronous Remote Process 135

Using Events with Asynchronous Remote Processes 138
    Generating Events in a Single Application Domain 139
    Passing Events Between Remote Applications 141
    Multiuser Asynchronous Remote Applications 149
Using Call Contexts with Asynchronous Remoting.................. 154
    Using Call Contexts in the Teleconference Application 154
Summary 157

CHAPTER 6 Debugging and Error Handling 159

Common Exceptions in Remoting Applications 159
    Illustrating Common Remoting Exceptions 160
Diagnosing and Preventing Errors in Remoting Applications.......... 169
    Implementing the Bank Application 170
    Dealing with Errors in the Client 183
    Dealing with Errors in the Remote Object 185
    Improving the Bank Application............................. 189
Defining Custom Exception Classes for Remote Objects 191
    Defining Exception Classes in the Exception Inheritance
      Hierarchy... 191
    Exceptions and Serialization 192
    Defining Constructors 194
    Defining Informational Properties and Methods................ 197
Logging Error Information at the Server 198
    Logging Errors to a File.................................... 198
    Logging Errors to a Database 200
    Logging Errors to the Windows Event Log.................... 203
Summary 207

CHAPTER 7 Flexible Programming 209

Reflection Defined.. 209
    What Is Reflection For?.................................... 210
Type Terminology.. 212
Binding 213
    Early (Static) Binding...................................... 213
    Runtime Binding.. 214
    Object-Orientation 214
    Late Binding 215
Metadata... 218
Accessing .NET Metadata 219
    Attributes... 220

	Reflection in .NET	221
	Examining Objects	221
	Manipulating Objects	221
	Creating Objects	221
	Summary	221
CHAPTER 8	**Examining Assemblies, Objects, and Types**	**223**
	Examining Assembly Metadata	223
	The Assembly Class	225
	Examining Type Metadata	230
	Retrieving Types	230
	Type Class Members	231
	Examining Class Member Metadata	234
	The MemberInfo Class	235
	The FieldInfo Class	238
	The PropertyInfo Class	240
	The MethodBase Class	242
	The MethodInfo Class	243
	The ConstructorInfo Class	245
	The EventInfo Class	246
	The ParameterInfo Class	247
	Summary	250
CHAPTER 9	**Using Objects**	**251**
	Why Invoke Members Using Reflection?	251
	Invoking Members Dynamically	252
	Invoking Class Members Using the Info Classes	252
	Invoking Class Members Using InvokeMember()	256
	Reflective Invocation at a Price	272
	Reflection or Delegates?	273
	Summary	278
CHAPTER 10	**Creating Objects**	**279**
	Dynamic Assembly Loading	279
	Creating Assembly References	280
	Methods Used for Dynamic Assembly Loading	282
	Instantiating Classes Dynamically	283

Abstract Factory Pattern..285
    Implementing the Abstract Factory Pattern with Dynamic
    Assembly Loading in VB .NET 289
Summary 300

CHAPTER 11   Attributes 301

Understanding Attributes 302
    Syntax for Using Attributes...................................304
    Testing a Data Type for Standard Attributes 311
Using Predefined .NET Attributes 315
    Understanding Attribute Class Definitions 316
    Using Attributes to Control the Compiler 322
    Defining and Using Assembly Attributes 327
Defining New Custom Attributes.....................................332
Summary 340

CHAPTER 12   The .NET Component Model 343

Investigating the .NET Component Model..........................344
    Components, Controls, and Classes 344
    Using Reflection with the Component Model 345
Creating New Components 358
    Defining a Component Class 359
    Storing Components in a Container 364
    Using Components in VS .NET...............................372
    Defining Properties and Events for a Component...............375
    Defining Converter Classes for Components...................381
    Testing the Final Employee Component Class 392
Summary 395

CHAPTER 13   Defining Threads 397

Threading Defined...397
    Multitasking 398
    Processes 399
    Threads 400
Thread Support in Visual Basic .NET 410
    System.AppDomain..411
    Thread Management and the .NET Runtime...................418
Summary 419

CHAPTER 14 Threading in .NET 421

System.Threading Namespace 421
    Thread Class. 422
    Creating a Thread 424
    ThreadStart and Execution Branching 427
    Thread Properties and Methods 429
    Thread Priorities. 431
    Timers and Callbacks 434
    Spinning Threads with Threads. 436
Life Cycle of Threads. 442
    Putting a Thread to Sleep 443
    Interrupting a Thread. 445
    Pausing and Resuming Threads 447
    Destroying Threads 453
    Joining Threads 455
Why Not Thread Everything?. 457
Threading Opportunities. 458
    Background Processes 458
    Accessing External Resources. 461
Threading Traps 462
    Execution Order Revisited 463
    Threads in a Loop 465
Summary 468

CHAPTER 15 Working with Threads 469

Why Worry About Synchronization? 469
    Synchronize Critical Sections 470
    Making the Account Object Immutable 471
    Using a Thread-Safe Wrapper 472
.NET Synchronization Support. 472
.NET Synchronization Strategies 473
    Synchronized Contexts 473
    Synchronized Code Regions. 474
    Manual Synchronization 488
    Synchronization and Performance 498
Beware of Deadlocks 498
End-to-End Examples 501
    Writing Your Own Thread-Safe Wrappers 501
    A Database Connection Pool 510
Summary 518

CHAPTER 16 Threading Models 519

Multiple Threads in Applications 519
STA Threading Model 520
MTA Threading Model 521
    Specifying the Threading Model 522
    Designing Threaded Applications 522
    Threads and Relationship 524
Summary 533

CHAPTER 17 Scaling Threaded Applications 535

What Is Thread Pooling? 535
    The Need for Thread Pooling 536
    The Concept of Thread Pooling 536
The CLR and Threads 537
    The Role of the CLR in Thread Pooling 537
    Glitches Involved in Thread Pooling 538
    The Size of a Thread Pool 538
Exploring the ThreadPool Class 539
Programming the Thread Pool in VB .NET 542
Scalability in .NET 547
    A Thread Pool Manager 548
Summary 561

CHAPTER 18 Debugging and Tracing Threads 563

Creating the Application Code 564
Debugging Your Code 564
    Visual Studio .NET Debugger 565
    Stepping Through the Code 568
    Setting Breakpoints 568
    Debugging Threads 570
Code Tracing 570
    The System.Diagnostics.Trace Class 571
    Using Different Listener Applications 574
    Tracing Switches 579
    The Debug Class 583
The DataImport Example 584
    The Code 584
    Testing the Application 589
    Logical Errors 589
Summary 591

CHAPTER 19 Networking and Threading ... 593

Networking in .NET ... 593
- System.Net Namespace ... 594
- System.Net.Sockets Namespace ... 595

Creating the Sample Application ... 595
- Design Goals ... 596
- Building the Application ... 597
- Running the Applications ... 615

Summary ... 618

INDEX ... 619

About the Author

Beginning at the age of 10, programming BASIC on an ATARI 800XL, **TOBIN TITUS** has seen more than his fair share of technologies come and go. His most recent experiences have been designing and implementing solutions for the .NET platform. Holding MCAD and MCSD "Early Achiever" certifications, he was asked by Microsoft to help design the next generation developer certification track. He has previously co-authored three books for Wrox Press and served as technical editor for countless others. Currently, Tobin is a senior developer/analyst for T*i*BA Solutions (http://www.tibasolutions.com), a Greenville, South Carolina-based technology firm that provides customized information technology solutions to meet mission-critical business needs. T*i*BA Solutions offers a full line of services: business consulting, project management, and customized software application design and development. He can be reached at authorresponse@titus.to.

About the Technical Reviewers

RICK DELORME works as a consultant in Ottawa, Ontario, and currently spends much of his time working with Microsoft .NET technologies as an MCSD for Microsoft.net.

When not working he enjoys running, golfing, and spending time with his young son.

DON REAMEY is a program manager for Microsoft Corporation working on business intelligence tools. He has been in the industry for 17 years and holds a bachelor's degree in Computer Information Systems.

Acknowledgments

I want to thank the kind folks who have been tremendous resources in this project in one fashion or another. To the many contributors to this book who wrote the first drafts for version .NET 1.0 before many people even had a grasp of the basics, you guys deserve the lion's share of the credit. Beckie Stones and Ewan Buckingham, you guys are awesome to work with and I admire your tremendous work ethic. Eric Eicke at Net Tool Works (http://www.nettoolworks.com) has always been a great friend and is always willing to provide a wealth of information. Chris Boar at Microsoft has always had the hook up when it was needed—and always listened when I had some complaint about certification! Jack Bradham at Microsoft: thanks a million for your help and friendship. Lastly, thanks to the team at T*i*BA Solutions that brought me on board: Ken, Kirk, Dave, Phil, and Pierre. You guys really understand the value of designing and building great software—not just slapping a rag-tag team together and making a quick buck.

Introduction

When reading the title of this book, you might ask yourself "Why did they put remoting, reflection, and threading together in one book?" The answer might not seem obvious at first, but after reading this introduction you should understand why these three technologies belong in a developer's toolkit and in a single book. These three technologies share the following benefits:

- **Flexibility**: Today's business needs demand that applications have the capability to grow with the business. All three of these technologies bring that flexibility to the table in a variety of ways.
- **Power**: Although .NET has brought about a highly powerful development platform by itself, the inclusion of these three core technologies gives .NET developers the ability to create powerful solutions with minimal effort.
- **Ease of Use**: Flexibility and power are great features to have, but they don't mean anything if they come at the price of complex APIs and increased development time.

Remoting

Today's applications demand to be scalable. One of the many ways to make an application scalable is to separate your application into logical and physical tiers. This is often referred to as distributed computing. The distributed programming model has been implemented in many ways throughout the years. In the .NET world, this is done most often with remoting. The "power" of remoting allows two processes—on the same computer or a networked computer—to communicate as though they were in the same process. The programming model for remoting is not complex providing that "ease of use" credential listed earlier. Furthermore, remoting can be programmed without regard to where the logical components will physically reside. Both the caller (client) and the receiving component (server) can be configured long after the application has been compiled. If your business needs currently only require a single server for all tiers of your application, remoting can be configured to do so. If later, your business requires more processing power, remoting can be configured to move your tiers to another or multiple servers—now that's "flexibility."

Reflection

When describing the need for flexibility in programming, you need look no further than reflection. When a piece of .NET code is successfully compiled, you typically create an assembly that contains the compiled code, data, and metadata. Metadata is information about what is contained in the assembly such as classes, class members, and other types. Reflection provides the capability of a .NET application to read the metadata in an assembly, including itself.

The capability to read data about itself is what gives the technology the name "reflection." Several methods in .NET allow you to determine what assembly is currently running, what assembly called in to the current method, and what assembly was the starting assembly for the current process. This capability provides a great deal of flexibility in runtime decision-making. Code can now make decisions based on how it is being called. For instance, you could make a method behave differently if it was called by one of your own assemblies as opposed to when it was called by a third-party assembly. Reflection also provides a great deal in power through the use of attributes. Attributes are special decorations that you can add to your assemblies, classes, and members, which add metadata to the compiled assembly. You can use these attributes to control the way security is handled in .NET, the way components are handled at designtime, and more. With all this power, reflection still provides a very simple API through the `System.Reflection` namespace.

Threading

Even the most simple of applications often have more than one operation to perform at a time. For instance, the application may be connecting to a database to perform a query, while also responding to user input on the user interface (UI). By default, .NET applications perform these operations synchronously—that is, they execute them one at a time. This makes your application appear unresponsive. By assigning operations to different threads, you give your application the capability to share processor execution time with more than one operation. Threading refers to the capability of an application to spawn a new thread and control its execution lifecycle. By allowing you to control the thread's execution, you are given a great amount of power. A computer system can execute multiple threads simultaneously if more than one processor is installed. If a computer system has two processors, two threads can execute simultaneously. Likewise, four threads can be executed in unison if the system has four processors. By default, the operating system decides which threads go to which processor. However, .NET provides the flexibility for the application programmer to decide which processors the application threads can be assigned to and at what priority they are run. The power of the thread and its associated configuration comes in a very easy-to-use object and configuration models.

Now the Bad News

So far you've heard all the good news about these technologies. If you stopped reading right now, you would come away feeling that anyone could write applications using these technologies without a care in the world. In some ways, we want to give you that impression. We want to get you excited about these technologies because after they are mastered, they provide an invaluable set of skills to you, your development team, and more importantly, your end users.

However, as the uncle of a famed masked superhero once said, "With great power comes great responsibility." While I'm not one to take wisdom from fictional characters as a rule, I think this is sound. The power of these technologies does come at a price. That price is the responsibility to understand the limits and best practices of each of these technologies before haphazardly including them in your design documents.

Looking ahead in our book, we are going to cover these three topics one by one, and mostly as separate topics. In those sections, we'll cover the power and pitfalls involved in these premium technologies. We highly suggest you use this book as you practice these concepts as often as you can. As with any skill, the more time you spend using it, the more familiar you make yourself with the limits, restrictions, and tricks needed to use it effectively.

CHAPTER 1

Introducing .NET Remoting

This chapter explains the basic concepts behind .NET Remoting. We'll start by examining distributed systems in general and client-server systems in particular. You'll see how they have evolved over the past few years, and what peculiar issues remote object systems must contend with.

After we cover the basics, we'll discuss .NET Remoting itself, including the various remote object types available and how they are managed. You'll see the entire remoting process and how .NET Remoting makes it all work.

Distributed Systems

Shortly after World War II, the government in Britain decided that two computers would be adequate for its needs. Things have changed a little since then, and dealing with entire networks of computers is routine. Before we look at what remoting involves, let's consider why networking systems are used. There are essentially three types of networked, or *distributed*, system:

- Cooperative systems
- Peer-to-peer systems
- Client-server systems

All these systems are made up of several independent processes—generally running on separate computers—interacting with each other. I say "generally" because any system that is made up of several processes working together within a single machine could be regarded as a miniature distributed system. In fact, as you'll see, it doesn't actually matter to the .NET Remoting model whether the various processes are running in the same machine or different ones. In fact, remoting is merely two processes or application domains talking to each other.

Cooperative systems are networks in which the various tasks are allocated to different processing units with a common, shared goal. It may be distributed for several different reasons. First, there might be a number of specialized functions that can only be carried out in one specific place; a typical example of this is the system that controls how an automobile works. Second, it might be more efficient to distribute the processing across several machines. Finally, it might be effective from a development point of view to distribute the tasks between different teams, each working on their own module.

Peer-to-peer systems are more loosely linked networks, where computers exchange information with each other but are not necessarily working toward a common goal. For example, an automatic financial trading system might communicate with several other systems to establish best prices before executing a trade through another one.

Client-server systems are more asymmetric, in that one kind of computer (a client) is initiating the process, while the other computers in the network (the servers) are effectively slaves. Generally (but not necessarily), the ultimate client end of such a system is a human user. Arguably, all peer-to-peer systems are actually client-server systems, because at any one time, one specific computer (the client) is driving the process forward. In fact, it's possible for one application to be a server of another as well as being a client of a third.

The .NET Remoting model is very much a client-server model. Before we look at it in any detail, however, we should examine the different variants of the client-server model.

Client-Server Models

In client-server systems, a client application talks to a server over a network using a *protocol*. A protocol consists of a number of message types that can be used to transmit information in either direction. It can either be standard (such as HTTP) or proprietary (such as MSMQ). It can also be *synchronous* or *asynchronous*. In a synchronous protocol, every message exchange involves a request going one way and a response coming back. HTTP is such a protocol. In an asynchronous protocol, however, there is no requirement for the sender to wait for a response. Indeed, there may be more than one response to a single initial request. Examples of this abound in the protocols used in the finance industry.

The type of protocol has a significant impact on the nature of the system that uses it. Any system built on top of an asynchronous protocol needs to have a connection open continuously between the client and the server. In other words, it needs to have a *session*. With a synchronous protocol, there is no such necessity.

Systems are divided into *session-oriented* and *session-less* categories. In a session-oriented system, a link is established between the client and the server and maintained while a number of messages are exchanged. While this link is in place, the server retains some idea of the client's *state*. In this sense, state refers to a set of data associated with the client that persists for the duration of the session. In a session-less system, a new logical link is established with every message exchange, and then destroyed afterwards. The server has no concept of state in between messages. In fact, for efficiency's sake, the physical link between the client and the server may still be maintained (simply because establishing it may take time and resources), but *logically*, it is broken every time. If such a system were a living organism, it would be something with an ultra-low attention span, such as a goldfish.

The World Wide Web (WWW) is probably the most famous session-less system. That's the reason it scales so well, because there is no need for all the servers involved to keep track of all the users that fly in and out of their Web pages. It's also why Web-based reservation systems are such a nightmare, because making a reservation intrinsically involves keeping track of your state as you go through the process, and you end up making extensive use of cookies as a sort of pseudo-session. Most proprietary reservation systems are, incidentally, highly session-oriented.

The following diagram shows a typical session-less distributed system. Each time the client sends a request to the server, a new connection is established and then broken as soon as the response is received.

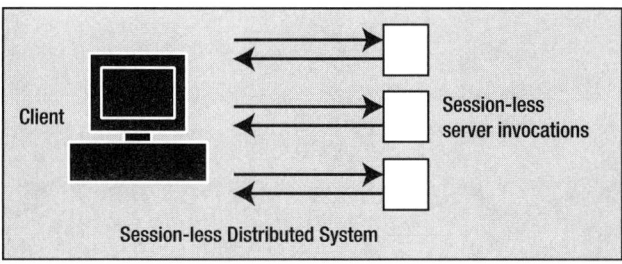

The next diagram shows a synchronous, session-oriented system. Again, each request gets a single, immediate response, but the server retains information about the client session and hence the client's state.

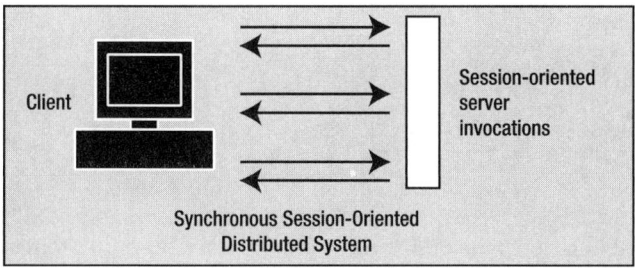

The final diagram in this sequence shows an asynchronous, session-oriented system. Here, a single request from the client can provoke several responses from the server, each pertaining to the current session.

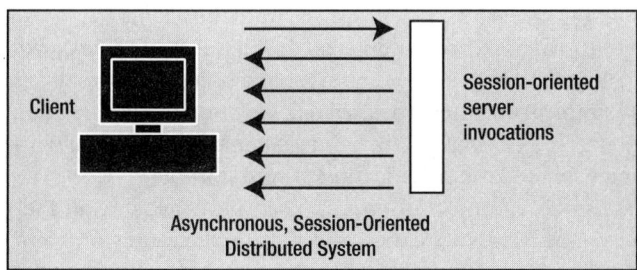

There is also a distinction between *single-user systems* and *multiuser systems*. A multiuser system in this sense involves multiple clients interacting with each other simultaneously in real time via a central server. Multiuser systems are intrinsically session-oriented because some kind of state must be held by the server on behalf of the various clients for any interaction between them to be meaningful. They are also typically asynchronous in nature. A typical example of such a system is a teleconference as shown in the following diagram.

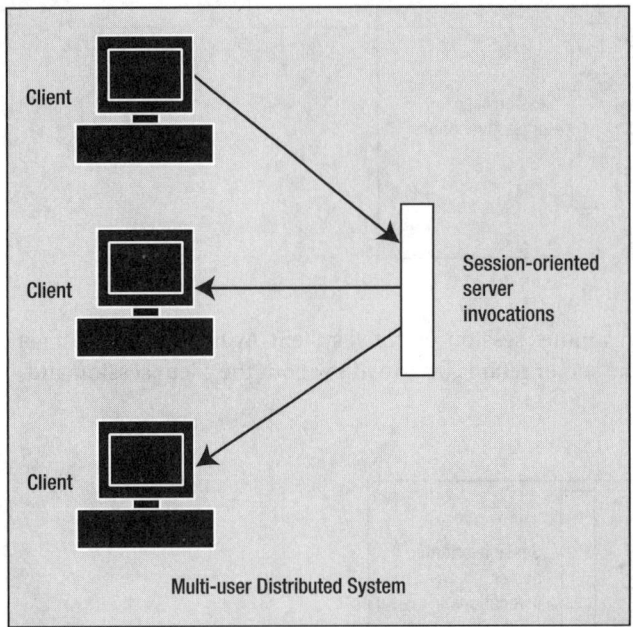

Multi-user Distributed System

In this kind of system, one client talks to all the others via a central server. Such a system is asynchronous and session-oriented. In fact, any system in which users can interact with each other in real time is session-oriented.

Evolution of Distributed Systems

Now that we've established the kinds of distributed systems you need to develop, the next question to ask is what sort of underlying technology can be used to implement them. Basically, you need some software sitting on the server that receives incoming calls from the clients.

During the late seventies and eighties, a lot of work was done on the idea of *Remote Procedure Calls* (*RPCs*). The idea was that you could effectively code your server as a set of library routines, and then code your client as if it was simply using those locally. Well, yes and no. Yes if you had the bandwidth, no—well, almost all the time, in fact. There was also a massive problem with versioning. What happened when you extended the specification of your library?

Around the start of the nineties, however, object orientation suddenly became all the rage, and someone spotted that *encapsulation* might be the answer to the versioning problem. Encapsulation is one of the central concepts in object-oriented programming, expressing the principle that you can make whatever changes you like to the underlying implementation of an object, provided that the methods and properties it presents to the world remain constant. So the idea of isolating the remote software behind rigidly defined language-independent object interfaces arose. Two alternative solutions rapidly emerged: the Object Management Group's CORBA (Common Object Request Broker Architecture) (in 1992) and Microsoft's COM (Component Object Model) (in 1993). COM was a general component model, which could be used for communication with in-process objects as well as remote objects. Distributed COM (DCOM) came as part of the COM package.

> **Tip** Actually, a third solution also emerged at about this time: Java Remote Method Invocations (RMI). However, because RMI was restricted to Java implementations, it was ruled out of any discussions of language-independent mechanisms.

However, this separation had a number of crucial problems. First, you needed a significantly higher skill level to develop these distributed systems (which didn't please those in charge of the project budget). In fact, the solutions were difficult to work with, and it wasn't until Microsoft brought out Visual Basic 6 (which hid all the really horrible stuff under the surface) that COM really came into the mainstream. The crucial difference with .NET is that the component model is built into the framework from the word go, in all the languages from C# to VB .NET, and remoting is just another .NET area to learn about—you don't have to get a grip on a completely new technology.

Secondly, CORBA failed to attain mass acceptance because it wasn't endorsed by Microsoft. DCOM, however, was only available on Microsoft systems. There was an initiative to port it to other systems, but this never really caught on.

Finally, and most importantly, all these solutions used a proprietary, binary protocol for client-server communication. That is perfectly acceptable when you have an in-house system, but not when you're dealing with clients that are outside your firewall and sometimes behind their own firewall.

Unfortunately, just when it was ripe for distributed object systems to take over the world, the Web became prime-time news, and they didn't.

SOAP and Web Services

However, distributed objects didn't go away. They simply went under cover, and reemerged several years later under the banner of SOAP. *SOAP (Simple Object Access Protocol)* essentially involves the client encoding object method calls in XML (Extensible Markup Language) and inserts them in packets of a standard protocol (such as HTTP). These packets are then sent to the server through—in the case of HTTP—whichever port the Web server is listening on (generally port 80). SOAP disposed of any firewall problems, and was immediately hailed as the best thing since—well, the last best thing. Not only could you now carry on complex interactions through a firewall, but it also didn't matter what technology you were using on the client or the server, as long as they both understood SOAP. Also, all the interactions were carried out using a transparent plain-text format (XML), which made debugging easier.

The SOAP movement led to the next big thing, *Web Services*. With Web Services, you can define your service using the *Web Services Definition Language* (WSDL). This is essentially a generalization of the old *Interface Definition Languages* (IDLs) used by CORBA and DCOM, and gives a client everything it needs to know about the method calls in the interface. You can then use SOAP to invoke those methods. The next stage of this process is to store the WSDL file in a *UDDI registry* (Universal Description, Discovery, and Integration registry) on the Web so that interested parties can locate your service automatically (as shown in the following diagram). Web Services set out to make distributed objects the programmatic equivalent of Web sites, with client programs using UDDI registries as search engines. However, in the same way that not all applications are best delivered through a Web browser, not all distributed objects are best delivered through a Web Service.

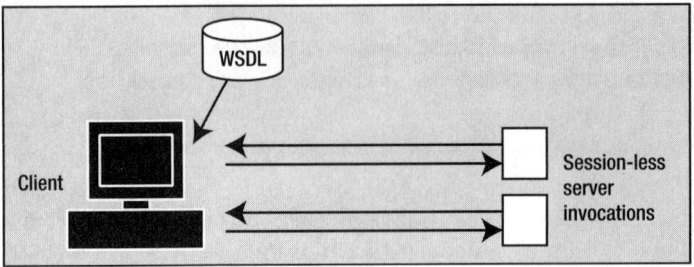

The strange thing about SOAP is that despite its name, it really doesn't have anything to do with objects. There is absolutely no reason why the piece of software at either end needs to be object oriented, as long as it handles the incoming calls correctly. You could program a light bulb to understand a certain format of SOAP request and turn itself off or on by command; the light bulb doesn't need to be object-oriented. SOAP's great advantage is that it can be used by almost any kind of networked computer system. However, if you know that your client and server are both similar systems, bringing SOAP into things just introduces a massive, unnecessary protocol overhead, and it would be easier to use an old fashioned binary DCOM-style protocol. Bandwidth is certainly less of an issue these days than it used to be, but it still isn't unlimited.

As an illustration, consider this snippet from the SOAP specification, which shows how invoking a single method (GetLastTradePrice), passed in a single parameter (the symbol DIS), gets encoded as a SOAP message:

```
<SOAP-ENV:Envelope
  xmlns:SOAP-ENV=_http://schemas.xmlsoap.org/soap/envelope/_
  SOAP-ENV:encodingStyle=_http://schemas.xmlsoap.org/soap/encoding/">
    <SOAP-ENV:Body>
        <m:GetLastTradePrice xmlns:m="Some-URI">
            <symbol>DIS</symbol>
        </m:GetLastTradePrice>
    </SOAP-ENV:Body>
</SOAP-ENV:Envelope>
```

That's a total of 316 bytes to encode a simple 3-byte parameter. Clearly a tradeoff must be made between generality and efficiency. As you'll see, .NET Remoting offers the enticing possibility of being able to choose whichever is appropriate without making massive application-level changes to accommodate both alternatives.

Using .NET Remoting

.NET Remoting might be the best solution currently available for distributed computing. In Microsoft's white paper, *An Introduction to Microsoft .NET Remoting Framework* (available at http://msdn.microsoft.com/library/en-us/dndotnet/html/introremoting.asp), .NET Remoting is described as providing a "rich and extensible framework for objects living in different AppDomains, ..." An AppDomain (application domain) is an isolated environment where applications execute. Within such an environment, an application can't be independently stopped, directly access code in applications in other AppDomains, or cause other applications to crash.

Multiple `AppDomains` can run in a single process, although there isn't a one-to-one correlation between `AppDomains` and threads. In fact, several threads can belong to a single `AppDomain`. At any one time, a thread executes in a single `AppDomain`, although it isn't permanently confined to one. The central principle behind .NET Remoting, then, is that it facilitates the development of object-oriented systems where objects exist in more than one `AppDomain`.

.NET Remoting offers several big gains:

- Writing remote applications does not require you to learn an entire new technology, because .NET Remoting is just one more facet of .NET as you'll see in Chapter 2.

- You can develop applications that are both efficient for internal clients and accessible for external ones (you'll see this later on in this chapter, as we look at the different alternatives available for channels and formatters).

- You can support non-.NET clients using a standard protocol (SOAP).

Remote Object Types

There are three main remoting scenarios, each of which has a corresponding .NET remote object type. The objects fall into two main categories: *server-activated* objects and *client-activated objects*. Server-activated objects can be subdivided further into *single call objects* and *singleton objects*. We'll briefly look at all these three types, and then take a more detailed look at how object lifetimes are managed.

Single Call Objects

The single call object handles one and only one incoming request at a time, and doesn't hold any state information between calls. Each method call is treated as independent of every other one, and there's no concept of a session for the object. This is a slightly weird type of object when you first encounter it, because it seems to cut right across the usual idea of an object being equivalent to logic + data. So you have to think more in terms of an object as being simply a repository for a set of related functionality. This type of object is useful in satisfying session-less requirements, and is particularly appropriate to hold the business logic in classic n-tier applications.

Singleton Objects

As its name suggests, this type of object is useful in circumstances where a single instance of an object is required. This is used in both session-oriented and session-less applications. A suitable session-oriented application is a multiuser scenario, in which state is held across a number of connected clients, such as the teleconferencing system mentioned earlier. Another scenario where this type of object might be used is when a single client receives asynchronous events back from the server. We'll be looking at asynchronous remoting in more detail in Chapter 5.

In a session-less application, a single call object can be used, but the process of instantiating such an object is time-consuming or resource-consuming. This is a massively scalable solution, but if you use this type of object in a session-less application, you must be 100% sure that you never hold any state between calls.

A single call object is instantiated with every call, and then eventually destroyed by the garbage collector, so there's no issue with state. However, a singleton object is instantiated by the first call, and stays there until the last client releases it.

Client-Activated Objects

Finally, the *Client-Activated Object* (*CAO*) is the closest that .NET Remoting gets to the classic COM. CAO is used in highly session-oriented applications. A separate instance is created for each client, and remains in existence until released by the client. As far as the client is concerned, it's the same as if the object in question was local rather than remote.

Context

Context is the remoting topic that has tremendous potential to cause confusion because it actually has two separate and different uses in .NET. The first use, which has direct relevance to remoting, is in "call context." The second use, which is not specifically relevant to remoting, is in "context-bound objects."

Call Context

When designing a class to be used for a remoted application, you generally want to make the method calls as elegant and concise as possible. This isn't always as simple as it might seem, however. Imagine that your application does some kind of multistage order entry, but that you want the scalability of a single-call object. You must decide what to do with all that session information. One option is to insert everything into a database as you go along, but that creates all sorts of rollback and recovery issues. Another option is to simply extend your method calls so that each one has input arguments representing every part of the order entered so far, but that's horribly inelegant.

The neatest solution is to put everything in a special object, called the *call context*, which is automatically serialized along with every single method call as shown in the following diagram.

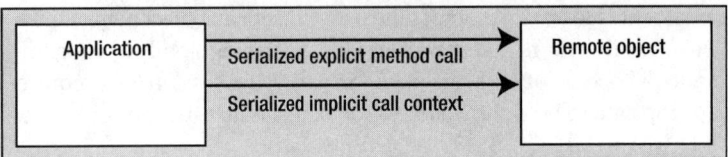

You should understand, however, that just because the call context is not passed across explicitly in every single method call doesn't mean that it has no impact on bandwidth. For a future medical application, for example, we would try to avoid the temptation to put the patient's entire DNA structure into the call context, because we would be waiting a long time for the response to come back.

You'll see the call context in action in Chapter 5, where it turns out to be particularly useful in asynchronous multiuser applications.

Context-Bound Objects

The other use of the term context in .NET is slightly more complex. The idea is that in certain applications, you might want to have a set of objects within an AppDomain that obeys certain rules. Such objects are bound to the same context. The concept is a kind of extension of the transaction context idea introduced with Microsoft Transaction Server (MTS), where if you create a series of objects within the same transaction context, they are all treated as part of the same transaction. Confusingly, MTS context is still an entirely separate thing in .NET, and uses an entirely separate mechanism from .NET context-bound objects.

With regard to remoting, the main thing you need to understand is that how access to objects within another context is controlled is very similar to how access to objects in another `AppDomain` is managed. The context rules need to be enforced, so if you're outside the context in question, the only way you can access an object inside the context is via a proxy—just like remoting. The proxy is responsible for enforcing the rules of the context. For example, thread synchronization is one attribute that can be controlled like this. If you specify your object to be context-bound with the synchronization attribute, the framework makes sure that only one thread can access your object at any one time.

The context principle is also extensible (although this is not particularly well documented officially), so that you can specify your own context rules.

Managing Remote Objects

When looking at the question of managing remote objects, two central issues must be resolved: where to put them (in other words, hosting) and when to dispose of them (in other words, lifetime).

Hosting

Let's start by looking at where to host these objects. After all, they need to be available in a runnable program that is capable of receiving the remote invocations. There are three basic alternatives.

- Host them in any ordinary .NET EXE or managed Windows Service.
- Host them in Internet Information Server (IIS), which effectively exposes your objects to the world as Web Services.
- Host them in the .NET component services infrastructure. If you do this, the objects can be incorporated into transactions, and you can use COM+ concepts such as just-in-time (JIT) activation and object pooling.

Leased-Based Lifetime

After a system is distributed across more than one machine, the question of knowing when to release resources immediately becomes a lot more complex than within a single machine. In .NET, the lifetimes of objects are managed according to a process called *leased-based lifetime*. A *lease* is created for every object that also has a reference created outside its host `AppDomain`. Each `AppDomain` has a *lease manager*, which periodically checks the status of all outstanding leases. Each lease has a *lease time* associated with it, and when this time expires, the lease manager releases the object to be destroyed by the garbage collector.

Each lease time begins with a standard default value. However, the lease's behavior can be changed by the client or the server object itself. For example, the server object can set its lease time to infinity, which means that it never expires; this means that the object will never be destroyed. The client can simply renew the lease by making a call on the lease manager. The lease can also be set so that each call to the object extends the lease by a preset amount.

Finally, the client can register a *sponsor* for the lease. A sponsor is simply an object that implements a particular interface that can be called by the lease manager. If a lease is about to expire, the lease manager asks the sponsors if they are interested in renewing the lease. A timeout is associated with this request to ensure that if contact is lost with the sponsor, the sponsor is dropped from the list.

The topic of leased lifetimes is covered in more detail in Chapter 2.

The Remoting Process

Now let's turn our attention to how the clients and servers talk to each other to facilitate method calls on remote objects. Any form of remoting needs a transport mechanism. Given its ubiquity, there's no other option but TCP/IP as the base protocol. All you need to do now is define an application-level protocol to go on top. However, as you've seen, a number of conflicting demands must be satisfied when choosing such a protocol.

A proprietary binary protocol such as DCOM is not firewall-friendly. SOAP goes some way to resolving this, but it's a much looser, general-purpose heavyweight protocol, which isn't the best solution if you're looking for efficiency. One of the neat things about .NET Remoting is that you can choose your own transport mechanism.

Using Channels

In .NET Remoting, a transport mechanism is referred to as a *channel*. By default, you get a choice of two channels: TCP and HTTP. This is a great concept, but *terrible* terminology, because HTTP, of course, also uses TCP as its underlying transport mechanism. What Microsoft really means by "TCP channel" is "TCP/IP with proprietary binary protocol on top." What it means by "HTTP channel" is "TCP/IP with HTTP on top." Of these two alternatives, the TCP channel is more compact and efficient, and ideal for use inside a firewall. The HTTP channel is more useful if your clients are outside your firewall.

It gets better. If neither of these channel types suits your needs, then you can roll your own, which makes .NET Remoting infinitely extensible. We'll look at the issues involved in providing your own channel type in Chapter 2.

Formatters and Serialization

The issue of formatting objects for transmission between clients and servers is intimately linked with the underlying channel technology. The essential problem is that although it's easy to format a single number into a message for transmission from a client to a server, squashing a whole object into a stream of bytes is a different matter. The squashing of an object into a byte stream is called *serialization*, and the reconstruction of the object from the byte stream at the other end is called *deserialization*. The software that carries out the process of serialization and deserialization is called a *formatter*, and a similar choice is available with channels.

Out of the box, .NET Remoting comes with two formatters:

- Binary

- SOAP

The binary formatter is a natural partner for the TCP channel, and the SOAP formatter is a natural partner for the HTTP channel, but you can use the binary formatter with the HTTP channel or vice versa. Remember, however, that the binary formatter carries far less overload than the SOAP formatter because the SOAP formatter uses XML elements to wrap all your data in a SOAP envelope. Again, if you want, you can even provide your own formatter—there's an example in Chapter 2.

Marshaling

Now that we've covered serialization, let's discuss marshaling. To *marshal* an object means to make it available to be used, either remotely or locally. If you specify an object as being of type marshal by reference (MBR), that means all you're interested in remotely is a reference to it. You don't want an actual copy of the object to be made on your client. You just want it to be sitting there on the server awaiting your method calls. So any object that is to be invoked remotely should be designated as being of type MBR.

So far, so good. But if you want to actually pass an object from the server to the client, or vice versa, the object itself is reinstantiated in a different `AppDomain` from where it started. As you've just seen, you need to use your formatter on the object to serialize it. But you can only do that if the object is of type marshal by value (MBV), which means that it must be *serializable*.

Metadata and Configuration

Now let's consider how the client finds out what methods are available in the server object. To access remote objects, a client needs to get the metadata information for the object. This can occur in three ways:

- The server can create and distribute a metadata assembly.
- The server can create and distribute a WSDL file.
- The client can generate a metadata assembly from a running server.

The most straightforward way is to create a metadata assembly for the server object, which can be distributed to the clients. The metadata can then be extracted from the assembly as if it were for a local object. However, this isn't always possible; for example, if the clients are Web-based, the server object can provide a WSDL file describing its methods. The client can then generate SOAP requests using this WSDL in the standard Web services manner. We covered this briefly in the evolution of .NET Remoting discussion. A standard utility called Soapsuds can generate WSDL files from server objects. Finally, clients can also use Soapsuds to generate a metadata assembly from a running server.

As well as finding out how to invoke methods on the object, a client also needs information on how to access its remote objects. This is held in a configuration file, separately from the client application, to make it easy to change as the system configuration changes without having to rebuild the client process. A configuration file contains information on things like the URI (Uniform Resource Identifier) of the objects, the channels being used, the lease time settings, and so on. This configuration file resides on the client, and might be set up completely by the end user, or perhaps downloaded from the server prior to use. Chapter 4 includes much more information on deployment.

The following diagrams provide a couple of typical examples of how remoting might work in practice. First, this is how an IIS-hosted object might be accessed as a Web service using the HTTP channel with the SOAP formatter.

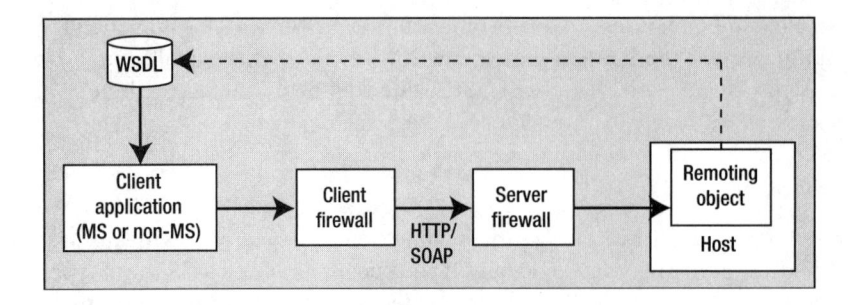

In this case, the client application obtains the WSDL file in some manner, perhaps from an entry in a UDDI table or maybe as part of a distribution kit. It then uses this to generate SOAP messages to send through its firewall and that of the server to the remoting object. The remoting object is invoked with the specified method and arguments, returning a value. The return message is also encoded as a SOAP message.

Next, the following diagram shows how a remoting object might be accessed within an organization's internal network using the TCP channel with the binary formatter.

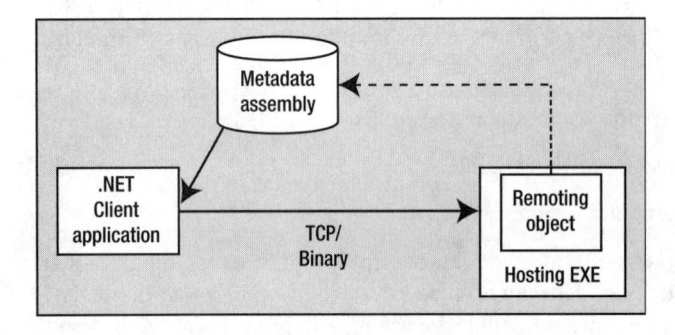

Here, the metadata assembly is created by the remoting object, and either distributed to the clients as part of the distribution kit or made available in some central download area. The client application then uses this assembly to determine how to communicate with the remoting object. All interactions in this case use the binary formatter and TCP/IP, because this is the most efficient protocol when no firewalls are present. This mechanism is also restricted to .NET clients, because other clients are unable to make use of metadata assembly. This contrasts with the previous picture, in which using WSDL opens up the application to both MS and non-MS clients.

The Whole Picture

Now let's look at a more complete picture of how .NET Remoting works. We'll look at the whole process as shown in the following diagram, and then discuss each of the elements in turn.

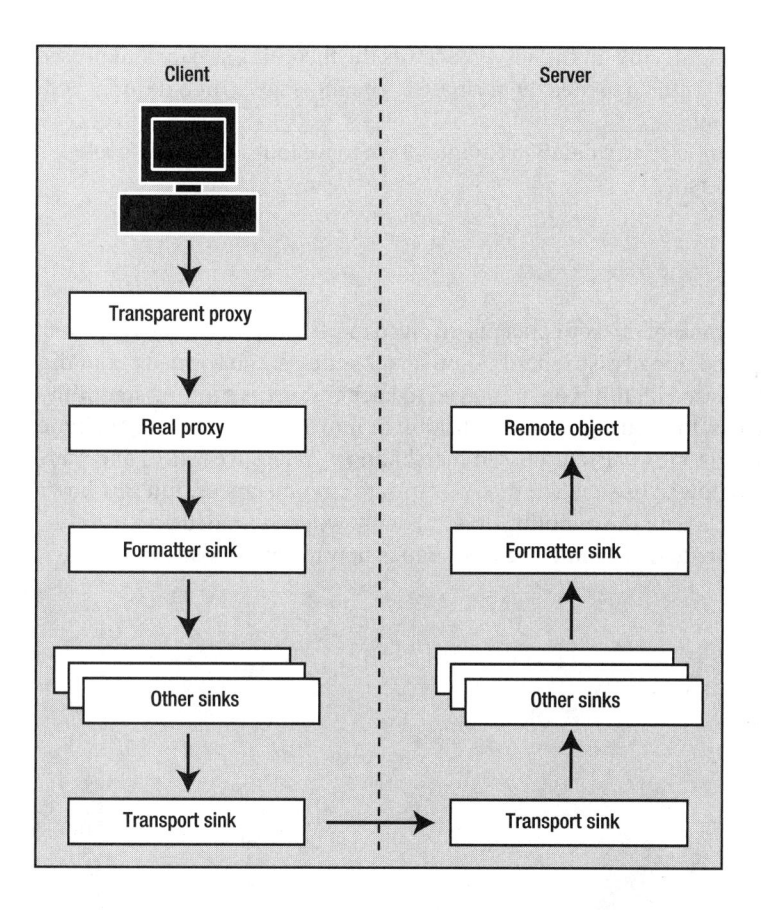

Whenever a client activates a remote object, two *proxy objects* are created in the client. As its name suggests, a proxy object is a substitute for the real, remote object in the local domain. It has the same methods and properties as the remote object; the only difference is that it doesn't actually do anything. The real work is being done by the machine at the other end of the line.

Two proxies are involved: the *transparent proxy* and the *real proxy*. The transparent proxy is an exact copy of the remote object, in that it has all the method calls available that the remote object has. The transparent proxy intercepts all the method calls directed to the remote object, and passes these on to the real proxy. The real proxy is never accessed directly, but it handles all outbound communication. The real proxy interface is in fact public, and can be extended and customized to do things such as custom load balancing and failover, for instance.

The real proxy then passes the message on to the channel sink chain. A *sink*, in this context, is an element of software that can receive something. This chain of sinks carries out further processing on the method calls before they get sent out to the server. The first sink in the chain might carry out formatting according to whatever mechanism has been registered, whereas the final sink in the chain is the transport sink that sends the byte stream out.

At the other end, the transport sink on the server receives the incoming stream and passes it back through the sink chain until it reaches the formatter. The message is then deserialized and passed in to the remote object.

You'll see this process in much more detail in Chapter 3 when we look at how to develop custom channels and formatters.

Summary

In this chapter, we've covered most of the key concepts involved in .NET Remoting. We've looked at where it fits into the long tradition of distributed client-server systems. You learned about the three object types, and how leased lifetimes are managed to keep resources running smoothly. You've also seen how channels, formatting, and serialization fit into .NET remoting to facilitate method calls on remote objects. We've also discussed marshaling by reference (MBR) and marshaling by value (MBV), and how to use each in the appropriate circumstances. You saw how a client gets ahold of the metadata for the remoting object. Finally, we've examined how proxies and channel sinks work together to make remoting work. You're now ready to try some serious remote programming.

CHAPTER 2

Remoting Basics

In the previous chapter, we introduced most of the concepts you'll need to know when you make remotable applications. This chapter now shows you how to implement these concepts in VB .NET code.

In this chapter, we'll take the basic .NET Remoting concepts and show you how to implement them in some simple remotable applications. After you've mastered this chapter together with Chapter 3, you'll be able to produce real-world systems that use the enormous potential of .NET Remoting.

We'll implement solutions to demonstrate how to do the following with .NET Remoting:

- Directly publishing remote objects
- Marshaling by value
- Marshaling by reference
- Creating server-activated objects (singleton and single call)
- Creating client-activated objects
- Manipulating leases and creating sponsors–lifetime management
- Implementing an MBR object tracking handler

First you need to get familiar with many of the classes and methods you'll use to create remotable applications.

.NET Remoting Classes

In the previous chapter, we reviewed the basic remoting concepts you need to understand to use .NET Remoting. This section begins to explain how you can implement .NET Remoting using VB .NET code.

Let's begin by reviewing the .NET namespaces, classes, and methods you'll encounter the most when you use remoting in your applications.

Classes Associated with Marshaling

In the previous chapter, you met the concept of *marshaling*, which is nothing more than data crossing processing boundaries. As noted in that chapter, you can marshal a remote object either by *value* (MBV), in which case the remote object is serialized, passed to the client, and then reinstantiated; or by *reference* (MBR), which means an object is controlled remotely by passing messages between the client and the remote object via proxy objects.

The `MarshalByRefObject` Class

You can control whether a particular object can be MBR or MBV. If the object inherits from the `System.MarshalByRefObject` class, it is MBR; if it doesn't inherit from the `MarshalByRefObject` class, the object is implicitly MBV.

■**Note** Many issues regarding MBV objects will be addressed later. These issues revolve around serialization of the object, the object's type, and the assembly that the type is in.

Whenever you need to implement remoting between applications in different application domains, you should make the object being remoted an MBR object. However, you can also use MBR classes locally, within the same application domain as the MBR class (in this scenario, a proxy object doesn't need to be created; instead, you get a reference to the MBR object itself).

The `ObjRef` Class

Looking more closely at the process of MBR, we also noted in the previous chapter that the following steps take place:

1. A serializable version of the remote object is created on the host.
2. The serializable version is passed along the remoting channel to the client.
3. The serializable version of the object is deserialized and parsed to create a transparent proxy (a copy of the remote object), housed inside a real proxy (which handles outbound communication).

The serializable version of an object—created in Step 1—is represented by the `System.Runtime.Remoting.ObjRef` class. An `ObjRef` object stores all the relevant information needed to create remote object proxies on the client side, including for example its URL and type information. In fact, another way of defining "marshaling" and "unmarshaling" is the creation and deserialization of an `ObjRef` object.

The `RemotingServices` Class

To actually perform marshaling and unmarshaling, we use a couple of methods from the `System.Runtime.Remoting.RemotingServices` class: `Marshal()` and `Unmarshal()`. `RemotingServices` also contains the `Connect()` and `Disconnect()` methods, which are used by a client to connect to and disconnect from a remote object proxy, given the type and URL of the object.

Channel Classes

Channel objects are used to transport messages between remote applications. You saw in the previous chapter that messages are passed through channel sink chains before and after they are passed between client and host via a channel.

All channel objects implement the `System.Runtime.Remoting.Channels.IChannel` interface. Channels that send information implement the `IChannelSender` interface, whereas channels that receive information implement the `IChannelReceiver` interface; both of these interfaces are derived from `IChannel`. When creating your own custom channels, you must implement the appropriate interface on your class. This allows you to register your class as a channel type in remoting configuration. We'll discuss custom channels further in the next chapter.

TCP Channel Classes

In Chapter 1, we noted that .NET Remoting provides a choice of two predefined channels: TCP and HTTP. The `System.Runtime.Remoting.Channels.Tcp` namespace contains channels that use TCP/IP to transport messages. Although TCP channels encode messages in binary format for transmission by default, you can configure them to use other types of encoding.

The main class we'll use from this namespace is `TcpChannel`, which is a basic TCP sender-receiver channel implementation. This class is actually a combined channel, which combines the classes `TcpServerChannel` (used to transmit messages via TCP) and `TcpClientChannel` (used to receive them via TCP) for convenience. `TcpChannel` implements three interfaces: `IChannel`, `IChannelSender`, and `IChannelReceiver`. Here are some examples of how to create a `TCPChannel`:

```
Dim channel1 As New TcpChannel()
Dim channel2 As New TcpChannel(10000)
```

As you can see, there are actually several overloads of the `TcpChannel()` constructor. The no-argument constructor creates a new `TcpChannel` instance, activating a *client* channel. In the second overload, we pass the constructor a port number (10000) where a *server* channel will be activated.

In fact, there is another overload that takes three arguments. You'll need to use this overload if you want to define multiple channels in the same application domain:

```
Dim prop1 As New Hashtable()
prop1("name") = "FirstTcpChannel"
prop1("port") = "1001"
Dim channel3 As New TcpChannel( _
    prop1, Nothing, Nothing)
```

Note that the first parameter passed to the constructor is a `Hashtable` containing the name we give to the channel and the port. We need to use this constructor when using multiple channels to define the channel name, or else all the channels we create will be given the same name by default:

```
Dim prop2 As New Hashtable()
prop1("name") = "SecondTcpChannel"
prop1("port") = "1002"
Dim channel4 As New TcpChannel( _
    prop2, Nothing, Nothing)
```

The second and third parameters passed to the constructor here are the *client channel sink provider* and the *server channel sink provider*, respectively. These parameters allow you to choose which formatter the channel should use for serializing data. We've passed Nothing for these parameters to allow the channel to choose its own formatter for serialization (the default formatter for HttpChannel is SoapFormatter, and the default formatter for TcpChannel is BinaryFormatter). We'll discuss channel sink providers and formatters in more depth in the next chapter.

Finally, you should note that the port numbers used in these examples are arbitrary. Generally, the Internet Assigned Numbers Authority (IANA) divides port numbers into three groups:

- **Well-known ports (port numbers 0 through 1023)**: These ports are predefined by IANA. For example, port 80 is the ubiquitous HTTP port, and port 21 is the FTP port. You must not register your remoting objects on ports 0 through 1023!

- **Registered ports (port numbers 1024 through 49151)**: These ports are also listed by IANA for use by common third-party software products such as Microsoft SQL Server (port 1433) and IBM MQSeries (port 1414). You can register your remoting objects on ports 1024 through 49151, as long as you are sure the port isn't already in use by another application.

- **Private ports (port numbers 49152 through 65535)**: These ports are not assigned by IANA. Feel free to use these ports for your remoting objects.

For a full list of port assignments, see http://www.iana.org/assignments/port-numbers.

HTTP Channel Classes

The System.Runtime.Remoting.Channels.Http namespace is, as you would expect, the HTTP channel equivalent of System.Runtime.Remoting.Channels.Tcp. It contains channels that use TCP/IP with HTTP on top to transport messages between remoted objects. By default, these channels encode messages in SOAP format for transmission, although as with TCP, the encoding is configurable.

A basic implementation of an HTTP channel is provided by the HttpChannel class. Like TcpChannel, HttpChannel is a combination of classes (HttpServerChannel and HttpClientChannel), and it implements IChannel, IChannelSender, and IChannelReceiver. Here's an example of how to create an HttpChannel:

```
Dim channel5 As New HttpChannel()
Dim channel6 As New HttpChannel(6001)
```

As with TcpChannel(), there is a pair of overloads for the HttpChannel() constructor. The first activates a new client channel, whereas the second activates a server channel on port 6001.

The ChannelServices Class

The most commonly encountered class from the System.Runtime.Remoting.Channels namespace is the ChannelServices class, which contains methods to control channel registration, resolution, and URL discovery (we'll take a closer look at these concepts later). For example, its RegisterChannel() method (strangely enough) registers a channel:

```
ChannelServices.RegisterChannel(channel1)
```

As you can see, the only parameter we need to pass into the method is the TcpChannel or HttpChannel we created earlier.

The RemotingConfiguration Class

We can use the methods of the System.Runtime.Remoting.RemotingConfiguration class to modify configuration settings. For instance, the Configure() method allows you to use XML configuration files to configure remoting. The class also contains several methods used to register remotable objects with the client or host.

.NET Remoting Code Example

Now that we've discussed the basic classes you need to know to use .NET Remoting, it's time to start playing around with code. For the first code example, let's dive in and build a simple client-server (host) solution. In this example, the server will marshal a simple integer in response to a client request, incrementing the value of the integer by one with each client request.

You'll create two console applications—ExchangeClient and ExchangeHost (representing the client and the host respectively)—and one shared class library called ExchangeObjects.

Creating the Shared Class Library

The library will contain just one class, and the simple logic is implemented in this class, including console messages that inform you of what's happening:

```
Public Class Exchange
  Inherits System.MarshalByRefObject
  Private mNextIndex As Integer
  Public Sub New()
    Console.WriteLine("Exchange Started")
    mNextIndex = 1000
  End Sub
  Public Function NextOrder() As Integer
    mNextIndex = mNextIndex + 1
    Console.WriteLine( _
        "Exchange NextOrder : " & mNextIndex)
    Return mNextIndex
  End Function
End Class
```

This class can be instantiated and the function NextOrder() called directly by a client in the same application. However, to allow the object to be run outside the client application domain requires the infrastructure provided by .NET Remoting; in particular, we need our Exchange class to inherit from MarshalByRefObject.

Creating the Host Process

We need to create an instance of our Exchange class within a process (the host) and then inform the .NET infrastructure that it can pass a reference to the object to remote clients and accept calls on the object's methods made remotely.

The code for this host console application looks like this:

```
Imports System.Runtime.Remoting
Imports System.Runtime.Remoting.Channels
Imports System.Runtime.Remoting.Channels.Tcp
```

```
Imports ExchangeObjects
Module Module1
  Sub Main()
    Console.WriteLine("ExchangeHost started")
    ' Create and register a channel
    Dim channel As New TcpChannel(10000)
    ChannelServices.RegisterChannel(channel)
    ' Create and publish an Exchange object
    Dim exchange As New Exchange()
    RemotingServices.Marshal(exchange, "Exchange")
    ' Wait
    Console.ReadLine()
  End Sub
End Module
```

Let's take a closer look at the code. We create and register a remoting channel to use TCP:

```
Dim channel As New TcpChannel(10000)
ChannelServices.RegisterChannel(channel)
```

Here we specified that port 10000 will be used to listen for incoming messages. Any unused port could be chosen, although the first 1024 are reserved for system use. We then create an instance of our Exchange class with New, and use the RemotingServices.Marshal() method to register the instance with the .NET Remoting infrastructure, associating the URI "Exchange" with our Exchange object:

```
Dim exchange As New Exchange()
RemotingServices.Marshal(exchange, "Exchange")
```

Creating the Client Process

The client code looks like this:

```
Imports System.Runtime.Remoting
Imports ExchangeObjects
Module Module1
  Sub Main()
    ' Create URL, assuming local machine
    Dim url As String = _
        "tcp://localhost:10000/Exchange"
    ' Create proxy to remote object
    Dim exchange As Exchange = _
        CType(RemotingServices.Connect( _
        GetType(Exchange),url), Exchange)
    ' Call remote function
    Dim index As Integer = exchange.NextOrder()
    Console.WriteLine( _
        "Client: NextOrder returned: " & index)
    Console.ReadLine()
  End Sub
End Module
```

> **Note** When compiling this code or using it in a Visual Studio project, make sure to add a reference to the `System.Runtime.Remoting.dll` assembly.

You'll notice that the first thing we do is create a URL, used to specify the location of the remote object. The general URL format looks like this:

`scheme://server:port/uri`

Each part of the format is described here:

- `scheme`: Specifies the protocol to be used to access the resource (TCP or HTTP).
- `server`: Specifies the name (or IP address) of the computer where the resource is located. `localhost` denotes that it's located on the local machine, but it could be any accessible computer on the LAN or Internet.
- `port`: The port on which the remote computer is listening.
- `uri`: Specifies the target resource.

In our example, the location of our server object is

`tcp://localhost:10000/Exchange`

The subsequent call to `RemotingServices.Connect()` that uses the URL looks ugly because of the casting requirements:

```
Dim exchange As Exchange = _
    CType(RemotingServices.Connect(
    GetType(Exchange),url), Exchange)
```

It returns a proxy object that supports the same public methods as our original, and looks to our client very much like the real object that is running on the server. You'll find that the client also needs a reference to our `ExchangeObjects` class library so that it has access to the description of `Exchange`'s methods—the class metadata—even though the underlying `Exchange` implementation code is not running as part of our client application.

Finally, having connected to the remote `Exchange` object, we can call the `NextOrder()` method on it:

```
Dim index As Integer = exchange.NextOrder()
```

At runtime, the call is converted via the proxy and remoting infrastructure to a call on the remote object running on our server. The return value of the function is similarly routed back to our client.

Running the Example

Add the necessary references to the `ExchangeObjects` project and `System.Runtime.Remoting.dll` assembly and then build them. Start the host process running in a separate console window as shown in the following diagram. After this server is started, it will continue running until you press Enter.

```
Command Prompt - ExchangeHost
C:\Documents and Settings\christianp\My Documents\Visual Studio Projects
\ExchangeHost\bin>ExchangeHost
ExchangeHost started
Exchange Started
```

Now if you run the client repeatedly in another console, you can see that a different, sequential number is returned each time. The console output generated within the NextOrder() method appears on the console running the server (see the following diagram), confirming that the code is running where you want it and that each client call is being directed to the same single object.

```
Command Prompt - ExchangeHost
C:\Documents and Settings\christianp\My Documents\Visual Studio Projects
\ExchangeHost\bin>ExchangeHost
ExchangeHost started
Exchange Started
Exchange NextOrder : 1001
Exchange NextOrder : 1002
```

Curiously, if you wait some minutes before running the client again, an exception occurs (on the client), indicating that the remote object has not been found. This happens because the remoting infrastructure decides at some stage that the marshaled object is no longer required and removes the object from its table of published objects—this is the leased-based lifetime mechanism mentioned in the previous chapter. We'll look a little more closely at this mechanism later in this chapter in the section regarding leased-based lifetimes.

Marshaling User-Defined Objects

In a real distributed solution of any complexity, the client and server are likely to exchange data that is more complex than just the integer returned in the introductory example. Such data would typically appear in a UML (Unified Modeling Language) analysis model as an *entity class* and subsequently be implemented in VB .NET as a class (or perhaps a group of related classes). .NET Remoting provides rich functionality to support the exchange of these potentially complex objects. .NET Remoting allows you to marshal these objects using either MBR or MBV.

The first code example showed one way in which MBR can be explicitly invoked for an object by deriving its class from System.MarshalByRefObject, and then publishing the object directly with the remoting infrastructure by calling RemotingServices.Marshal(). Let's now consider MBV by looking at the other approaches that can be used to invoke MBR.

Marshaling User-Defined Objects by Value

To illustrate MBV for user-defined objects, we'll extend the earlier example so that the NextOrder() function returns a copy of an object of class Order. Add this new Order class to the ExchangeObjects project:

```vb
<Serializable()> Public Class Order
  Private mIndex As Integer
  Public Sub New(ByVal Index As Integer)
    Console.WriteLine("Order: New: " & Index)
    mIndex = Index
  End Sub
  Public ReadOnly Property Index() As Integer
    Get
      Console.WriteLine("Order: Index: " & mIndex)
      Return mIndex
    End Get
  End Property
End Class
```

As you can see, the Order class that we have created will encapsulate the order data. For the purpose of this demonstration, this is just an index, initialized via a constructor and retrievable via a Get property method.

Passing Object State

An object is thought of as consisting of state and behavior. We need to consider how to transfer the state of the marshaled object between application domains when using MBV.

The object state is represented by the values of its member variables, is likely to be different for each object instance, and may change from time to time. To pass a copy of a remote object by value, the current contents of its member variables actually need to travel from one location to another via the chain of proxies and sinks. As you've seen, the stage of converting the object state into a form that can be written to disk or copied to another location is referred to as serialization, and in VB .NET, Remoting is performed by the formatter sink. The converse stage (which occurs at the other end of the remoting channel) of creating a copy of the object from this serialized form is described as deserialization.

It doesn't always make logical sense to serialize an object; for example, the data may be dependent on its location or on the time, or perhaps specific to the application domain or computer hardware it is running on. VB .NET does not assume that an object can be serialized; instead, the developer must explicitly allow this feature by using an attribute as follows:

```vb
<Serializable()> Public Class Order
```

In most cases, VB .NET can then automatically perform serialization when required, including serializing any objects that may be held as member variables, provided they are of a class that is also marked with the <Serializable()> attribute. Even complex data structures (known as *graphs*) can be handled provided that all the objects in the graph are from classes that have the <Serializable()> attribute; an exception is thrown if this is not the case.

Note There are many rules about serialization that are beyond the scope of this book. For instance, since version 1.1 of the .NET Framework, serialization of an object may fail if the object's type exposes public events. It would be wise to research serialization at MSDN.

The serialized data can be represented either in a binary form or in XML-based SOAP. Binary is significantly more efficient, as it limits the overhead of converting an object into the longer SOAP message, transporting this longer message, and then converting it back at the other end. However, XML does have the advantage of being much more readable and being understood by platforms other than .NET. Like much in the VB .NET environment, the algorithm used to serialize/deserialize a class can be customized and formats other than binary and SOAP employed. This is explored further in the next chapter.

Accessing Object Behavior

Although we can pass object state using serialization, we haven't considered how to pass object behavior yet. With VB .NET, the behavior is implemented by the methods defined for a class.

An important implication of this is that the assembly containing this class must be deployed so that it can be accessed wherever the object is. Another way of looking at this is that an object can only sensibly be copied during MBV to where the class code is accessible. In our example, this is achieved by making the class library DLL available to both the client and server applications. For the client and server to run on different machines, this DLL must be accessible to both machines.

Modifying Our Example to Pass an MBV Object

To complete the sample, you now need to modify the Exchange class so that the NextOrder() method creates and returns our Order object rather than just an integer as before:

```
Public Function NextOrder() As Order
   mNextIndex = mNextIndex + 1
   Console.WriteLine("Exchange NextOrder : {0}", _
       mNextIndex)
   Return New Order(mNextIndex)
End Function
```

You also need to modify the client to retrieve the Order object and then to output the index to the console, implicitly calling the Get property method:

```
' Call remote function
Dim order As Order = exchange.NextOrder()
Console.WriteLine( _
   "Client: NextOrder returned: {0}", order.Index)
```

When ExchangeHost and then Client are run in separate console windows, it is apparent from the console output messages that the constructor for the Order class is run in the ExchangeHost window but that its Index property Get method is run in the Client window. This is an impressive achievement considering how little code we have written.

Tightly and Loosely Coupled Solutions

Our sample solution now includes two classes contained within one assembly. They are both created on and have code that is run on the server, but they are accessed and used differently by our client:

- **Exchange:** An MBR object. This inherits from `MarshalByRefObject`; the remote client takes a reference to it, the client calls its `NextOrder()` method, and the code runs in the server.

- **Order:** An MBV object. This is serializable; the client accepts a copy of it, the client calls a `Get` property method, and the code runs in the client. Note that there is no `MarshalByValueObject` base class; the object need only be marked as `<Serializable()>`.

The code of the MBV object actually runs in the client, requiring its assembly to be accessible to the client. The client does not need the code of the MBR object because it doesn't run there. However, the client needs to know about the public properties and methods of both classes. The client must know this interface metadata. Fortunately, this information is also contained within the class library assembly.

This pattern of client and server sharing an assembly, with shared object code for MBV objects running in both locations, is typical of tightly coupled solutions. Usually, this is the appropriate architecture for enterprise solutions running wholly within a single organization.

The interface metadata can be made available at runtime in other ways as well as you'll see in Chapter 3; however, it's likely that in the majority of object-oriented enterprise solutions built using .NET Remoting, at least one remote MBV object will require its assembly to be deployed on the client. Besides that, it also makes sense—for anything other than the most trivial application server—to split the application logic into component assemblies, and to limit the number that need to be deployed to the clients.

A loosely coupled pattern, where only simple data types are passed between client and server is more likely to be used between different organizations, perhaps even where the client has no prior relationship with the service provider. This is firmly the domain of Web Services and SOAP.

Marshaling User-Defined Objects by Reference

To demonstrate the ease with which we can switch from marshaling our user-defined `Order` object by reference rather than by value, we can simply change the `Order` class definition in our sample as follows:

```
Public Class Order
  Inherits System.MarshalByRefObject
```

Now when we run the `ExchangeHost` and then the client, the trace shows that the `NextOrder()` method runs in the server host application rather than in the client application. To explain the program flow further, the `Order` object is created on the host by our call to `New` and then returned to the client by reference. Subsequently, the client calls the `Index` property's `Get` method on the object, which, because the client holds only a reference, is passed back to the host where the method is run and the result is marshaled back to the client.

Classes that access system resources on the remote machine, such as databases, files, and message queues, are usually defined as MBR types. These resources are often only accessible to objects that physically reside on the remote machine, or include information that only makes sense in the context of the remote machine. A class that implements the `IDisposable` interface often tends to be an MBR type; the `Dispose()` method releases resources owned by this class.

When you write an MBR class, you should pay particular attention to how you design the programming interface to the class. In particular, you should define the methods in such a way as to maximize their efficiency and reduce chattiness. Here are some guidelines:

- Avoid providing a myriad of property getters and setters. Every time the client application accesses a property, it involves a round-trip to the server to call the appropriate property procedure. This can lead to extremely poor performance. Instead, provide methods that return a set of related data items all at once; the client application now only needs to make a single method call to retrieve all this information.

- Think carefully about the types of data passed into and out of remoting methods. If you can get by with passing or returning a string rather than a complete object, then do so.

- When you do need to pass objects to or from remoting methods, consider defining a custom serialization format for these objects (we'll discuss how in the next chapter). You might be able to reduce the amount of data that is serialized and deserialized when the object is passed across a remoting boundary.

Finally, it's possible, although unusual, to have an object that both inherits `MarshalByRefObject` and also has the `<Serializable()>` attribute. In a .NET Remoting method call, the `MarshalByRefObject` behavior takes precedence, but in other situations, for example when saving the object state to disk, the object is serialized normally. Be sure to use this scenario with care! Serialization and use of `MarshalByRefObject` each comes with their own set of complexities. Mixing them means you have to abide by both sets of rules within the same class.

MBR Activation Modes

In our samples so far, we have explicitly created MBRobjects by calling `New`. We then directly published one on the server as a remotable object by calling `RemotingServices.Marshal()`, and also returned a reference to one from a remote function call.

This straightforward approach is appropriate in many situations, but the .NET Remoting Framework includes several additional mechanisms that can be used to directly control the activation of an MBR object. These activation mechanisms allow for remote objects that are not explicitly created in host code, but rather are created automatically by the .NET Remoting infrastructure in response to client activity. Confusingly, these activated objects are subdivided into *server activated* and *client activated*, although in both cases activation actually occurs on the server in response to client activity.

Server-Activated Objects

Server-activated objects are also referred to in the .NET documentation as *well-known objects*. These remote objects are only first created when a client calls one of their methods, not when a client proxy is created, reducing the number of messages that need to be exchanged. There are two types of server-activated objects:

- singleton
- single call

In the singleton case, once the remote object is created, all clients calling any of the object's methods use the same single object instance (as long as the lifetime lease does not expire); on the other hand, a new single-call object is created and destroyed for every method call made by a client.

Singleton server activation is appropriate for remote objects that need to retain shared state between method calls; that is, client applications that can (or need to) share information among themselves, because each client application is connected to the same remote object and has access to the same shared information. Clearly, the remote object has to take measures to synchronize access to nonthreadsafe resources to prevent several clients from accessing the same resource simultaneously.

Single-call server activation is appropriate for stateless remote objects, where the remote object doesn't need to hold any information between method calls.

Registering Server-Activated Objects

A server-activated object must be registered with the server where it is to be published and also must be registered with any clients that are to consume its service. This registration can be carried out through configuration files or programmatically. In this section, we'll slightly modify our earlier example to register a server-activated singleton object programmatically.

To register a server-activated object with the server, we call the RegisterWellKnownServiceType() method from the RemotingConfiguration class on a RemotingConfiguration object, associating the server object type with a URI and choosing singleton or single call. You can adapt our example host code to do this:

```
Imports System.Runtime.Remoting
Imports System.Runtime.Remoting.Channels
Imports System.Runtime.Remoting.Channels.Tcp
Imports ExchangeObjects

Module Module1
  Sub Main()
    Console.WriteLine("ExchangeHost started")
    ' Create and register a channel
    Dim channel As New TcpChannel(10000)
    ChannelServices.RegisterChannel(channel)

    ' register an Exchange Service
    RemotingConfiguration.ApplicationName = _
      "ExchangeApplication"
RemotingConfiguration.RegisterWellKnownServiceType( _
      GetType(Exchange), "Exchange", _
      WellKnownObjectMode.Singleton)
    ' Wait
    Console.ReadLine()
  End Sub
End Module
```

Here you specified that the remote object should have type Exchange, should have the URI "Exchange", and should be in singleton mode (specified via the WellKnownObjectMode enumeration).

The remote server-activated object is registered on any clients by calling the RegisterWellKnownClientType() method on a RemotingConfiguration object, associating the object type with a URL. You can do this in our example client code:

```
Imports System.Runtime.Remoting
Imports ExchangeObjects

Module Module1
  Sub Main()
    ' Create URL, assuming local machine
    Dim url As String =_
"tcp://localhost:10000/ExchangeApplication/Exchange"

    ' Create proxy to remote object
RemotingConfiguration.RegisterWellKnownClientType( _
    GetType(Exchange), url)
    Dim exchange As New Exchange()
    Console.WriteLine( _
      "Client: Exchange proxy created")
    ' Call remote function
    Dim order As Order = exchange.NextOrder()
    Console.WriteLine( _
      "Client: NextOrder returned: {0}", order.Index)
  End Sub
End Module
```

> **Note** Notice the use of a URI that registers the location of the object: `"tcp://localhost:10000/ExchangeApplication/Exchange"`. Do not confuse this with a Web server URL.

When this example is run, you'll see that the server object is not created until after a client calls the `NextOrder()` method as shown in the next diagram.

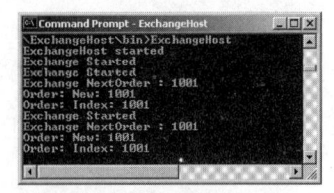

However, the object remains active and services subsequent client requests, and the index value increases each time a client is run (see the following diagram).

```
C:\Documents and Settings\Tobin\Desktop\books\APress\RemotingCh2_Client\Exchange
Client
Client: NextOrder returned 1001

C:\Documents and Settings\Tobin\Desktop\books\Apress\RemotingCh2_Client\bin>Exch
angeClient
Client: Next Order returned: 1002
```

To change to use single call mode, you just need to change the value of the `WellKnownObjectMode` enumeration in the `RegisterWellKnownServiceType()` call:

```
RemotingConfiguration.RegisterWellKnownServiceType( _
GetType(Exchange), "Exchange", _
    WellKnownObjectMode.SingleCall)
```

If we repeatedly rerun the client, as we did previously, the trace shows that the index doesn't increment (see the following diagram).

```
\ExchangeHost\bin>ExchangeHost
ExchangeHost started
Exchange Started
Exchange Started
Exchange NextOrder : 1001
Order: New: 1001
Order: Index: 1001
Exchange Started
Exchange NextOrder : 1001
Order: New: 1001
Order: Index: 1001
```

This is because the `Exchange` object is repeatedly destroyed and reactivated for each method call, so the value of the index is repeatedly initialized in the constructor.

The client code included the following line that requires further explanation:

```
Dim exchange As New Exchange()
```

Ordinarily, we would expect this call to create a local instance of the `Exchange` class, but because `Exchange` inherits `MarshalByRefObject` and had previously been registered using `RegisterWellKnownClientType()`, only a proxy is actually created locally and subsequent method calls are routed to the remote object. To confirm this distinction, we can easily revert to "ordinary" local behavior by commenting out the registration call, and then building and rerunning just the client—everything happens within the client application!

There is an alternative way to create the proxy object (instead of using `RegisterWellknown➥ClientType()` and calling `New`):

```
Dim exchange As Exchange = _
    Activator.GetObject(GetType(Exchange), url)
```

The `Activator` class contains methods that we can use to create or access objects of a specific type. Its `GetType()` method simply creates a proxy for a remote object, given its type and URL. This style has the advantage of being more explicit than a call to `RegisterWellKnownClientType()`; it's clear that the purpose of the code is to create a proxy to a remote well-known object.

Client-Activated Objects

Client activation allows each client to create its own instance of a server object. A new and distinct instance is created on the activated server at the time that the client creates a proxy. Subsequently, when the client makes multiple method calls on the proxy, they are all directed to the same instance. The instance lifetime is managed by the leased-lifetime mechanism. One client can create multiple proxies with each one resulting in a distinct object instance being created on the server.

Client activation is appropriate in situations where the remoting object needs to retain client-specific state between method calls. Each client gets its own remoting object, so the remoting object can hold information that is unique to that client.

Registering Client-Activated Objects

We can easily modify the earlier example to use a client-activated object. On the server, the object now needs to be registered using `RemotingConfiguration`'s `RegisterActivatedServiceType()` method as follows:

```
Sub Main()
  ' Create and register a channel
  ChannelServices.RegisterChannel( _
      New TcpChannel(10000))
  ' register a client activated Service
RemotingConfiguration.RegisterActivatedServiceType( _
      GetType(Exchange))
  ' Wait
  Console.ReadLine()
End Sub
```

Notice how the `RegisterActivatedServiceType()` method requires you to specify the remote object type. Also note that we've combined the `TcpChannel` object declaration with the call to `RegisterChannel()` for brevity.

On the client, the object is registered using `RemotingConfiguration`'s `RegisterActivated➥ClientType()` method, like this:

```
Sub Main()
  ' Create URL, assuming local machine
  Dim url As String = "tcp://localhost:10000"
  ' Create proxy and activate remote object
RemotingConfiguration.RegisterActivatedClientType( _
      GetType(Exchange), url)
  Dim exchange As New Exchange()
  ' Wait
  Console.WriteLine( _
```

```vbnet
      "Client: proxy created. " + _
      "Hit <enter> to continue")
    Console.ReadLine()
    ' Call remote function repeatedly
    Do
      Dim order As Order = exchange.NextOrder()
      Console.WriteLine( _
        "Client: NextOrder returned: {0}", order.Index)
      ' Wait
      Console.WriteLine("Hit <enter> to continue")
      Console.ReadLine()
    Loop
End Sub
```

As you can see, the `RegisterActivatedClientType()` method requires the URL of the remote object as well as its type.

Running this example, you can see that the remote object is created on the server when the proxy is created on the client, rather than being deferred until the first method call, as was the case with the well-known objects in the previous section. In this example, we have also added code to repeatedly call the `NextOrder()` method. When the code is run, the `Order` object returned by each call to `NextOrder()` holds an index value that is one greater each time. This shows that each call is being directed to the same instance of the `Exchange` object. By running another copy of the client in yet another console window, you can see that the second client has activated a different instance of the `Exchange` class, as the index values returned are again starting from 1001. Similarly, if the first client is restarted, the index values returned again start from 1001 because a new instance of the `Exchange` class has been activated.

Finally, you may have noted another distinction between well-known remote objects and client-activated ones. Well-known remote objects typically have explicitly defined URIs, whereas the URI of the client-activated objects are generated on-the-fly by the remoting infrastructure.

Dynamically Publishing Server-Activated Objects

To finish this section, let's consider a slightly more advanced topic concerning remote object activation: dynamic publishing.

The .NET Remoting infrastructure always calls a parameterless constructor to instantiate server-activated remotable types. If you want a parameterized constructor to be called, you must write some extra code in the server application to create the object programmatically. You must also write code to publish the object dynamically.

This actually gives the server-side programmer a great deal of flexibility, because you can dynamically publish and disconnect remote objects whenever you like. For example, you can write application logic to determine when an object should be available or unavailable to remoting clients. This decision might be based on production environment conditions, such as the availability of databases, message queues, and application/Web servers. You can even limit the availability of remoting objects based on the time of day; for example, you might make a remoting object available between midnight and 6 AM, to allow quiet-time processing while most applications are shut down.

In the next few pages, we'll look at a simple example of dynamic publication.

Defining the Remoting Class

We'll define a simple remoting class named `MonitorTimespan`. This class has a parameterized constructor, and a function named `GetInfo()` that can be called by client applications.

```
Imports System
Namespace MyRemoteNamespace
  Public Class MonitorTimespan
    Inherits MarshalByRefObject
    ' Date and time we were created,
    ' plus an ID for this object
    Dim mCreationTime As DateTime
    Dim mID As String
    ' Parameterized constructor,
    ' must be called manually by server
    Public Sub New(ByVal ID As String)
      mCreationTime = DateTime.Now
      mID = ID
    End Sub
    ' Simple function
    Public Function GetInfo() As String
      Dim Elapsed As TimeSpan = _
        DateTime.Now.Subtract(mCreationTime)
      Dim Seconds = CInt(Elapsed.TotalSeconds)
      Return String.Format( _
        "{0} was created {1} seconds ago.", _
        mID, Seconds)
    End Function
  End Class
End Namespace
```

Defining the Host Application

Now let's look at the server application. The server application creates a couple of `MonitorTimespan` objects using the parameterized constructor, and dynamically publishes and disconnects these objects using the `Marshal()` and `Disconnect()` methods on the `RemotingServices` class. The `Marshal()` method registers an object with the remoting infrastructure, and the `Disconnect()` method stops an object from receiving messages through the registered remoting channels.

```
Imports System
Imports System.Runtime.Remoting
Imports System.Runtime.Remoting.Channels
Imports System.Runtime.Remoting.Channels.Tcp
Imports MyRemoteNamespace

Public Class DynamicPublishingServer
  Public Shared Sub Main()
    ' Register a TcpChannel on port 6000
    Dim aChannel As New TcpChannel(6000)
    ChannelServices.RegisterChannel(aChannel)
```

```vb
    ' Create some remotable objects, using
    ' parameterized constructor
    Dim monitor1 As New _
       MyRemoteNamespace.MonitorTimespan("Monitor1")
    Dim monitor2 As New _
       MyRemoteNamespace.MonitorTimespan("Monitor2")
    Try
      ' Dynamically publish the monitor1 object
      Dim ref1 As ObjRef = _
         RemotingServices.Marshal(monitor1, _
         "MonitorTimespan.rem")
      Console.WriteLine("Currently published: {0}", _
         ref1.URI)
      Console.WriteLine( _
         "Press Enter to disconnect monitor1")
      Console.ReadLine()
      ' Now dynamically disconnect monitor1
      RemotingServices.Disconnect(monitor1)
      Console.WriteLine( _
         "No object currently published")
      Console.WriteLine( _
         "Press Enter to publish monitor2")
      Console.ReadLine()
      ' Now dynamically publish the monitor2 object
      Dim ref2 As ObjRef = _
         RemotingServices.Marshal(monitor2, _
         "MonitorTimespan.rem")
      Console.WriteLine("Currently published: {0}", _
         ref2.URI)
      Console.WriteLine( _
         "Press Enter to disconnect monitor2")
      Console.ReadLine()
      ' Now dynamically disconnect monitor2
      RemotingServices.Disconnect(monitor2)
      Console.WriteLine( _
         "No object currently published")
    Catch ex As Exception
      Console.WriteLine(_
         "DynamicPublishingServer error: {0}", _
         ex.Message)
    End Try
  End Sub
End Class
```

Compile the class, remembering to reference the appropriate namespaces and classes, and then run the server application in a command-prompt window. The server application displays the following message initially, to indicate that the monitor1 object is currently published.

```
Command Prompt
C:\Documents and Settings\books\DynamicsPublishingServer\bin>DynamicPublishingSe
rver
Currently published: /389280cd_a70f_426f_875d_b907b1e221269/MonitorTimespan.rem
Press Enter to disconnect monitor1
```

Defining the Client Application

To illustrate what it means to dynamically publish and disconnect remotable objects, consider the following simple client application.

```
Imports System
Imports MyRemoteNamespace

Public Class DynamicPublishingClient
  Public Shared Sub Main()
    ' Get a reference to (proxy for) remote object
    Dim obj As Object = Activator.GetObject( _
      GetType(MyRemoteNamespace.MonitorTimespan), _
      "tcp://localhost:6000/MonitorTimespan.rem")
    ' Convert to actual type of remote object
    Dim aRemoteObject As _
      MyRemoteNamespace.MonitorTimespan = _
      CType(obj, MyRemoteNamespace.MonitorTimespan)
    ' Invoke method on remote object
    Console.WriteLine(aRemoteObject.GetInfo())
  End Sub
End Class
```

Compile the client application, remembering to include the appropriate references during compilation.

Testing the Sample Application

The first time you run the client application in a command-prompt window, a message like this is displayed in the client's console window. This message indicates that the monitor1 object is currently published at the server.

```
Command Prompt
C:\Documents and Settings\books\DynamicsPublishingClient\bin>DynamicPublishingCl
ient
Monitor1 was created 289 seconds ago.
```

If you switch to the server application's console window and press Enter, the server application disconnects the `monitor1` object. This means there is no object currently published at the server (see the following diagram).

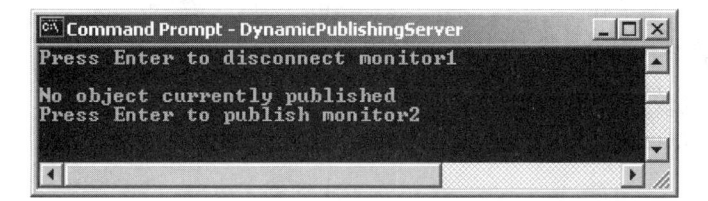

```
Command Prompt - DynamicPublishingServer
Press Enter to disconnect monitor1

No object currently published
Press Enter to publish monitor2
```

If you run the client application again, you get an exception because there is no object currently published at the server (see the following diagram).

```
Command Prompt
C:\Documents and Settings\christianp\My Documents\Visual Studio Projects
\DynamicPublishingClient\bin>DynamicPublishingClient

Unhandled Exception: System.Runtime.Remoting.RemotingException: Object <
/MonitorTimespan.rem> has been disconnected or does not exist at the ser
ver.
Server stack trace:
   at System.Runtime.Remoting.Channels.ChannelServices.CheckDisconnected
OrCreateWellKnownObject(IMessage msg)
   at System.Runtime.Remoting.Channels.ChannelServices.DispatchMessage(I
ServerChannelSinkStack sinkStack, IMessage msg, IMessage& replyMsg)

Exception rethrown at [0]:
   at System.Runtime.Remoting.Proxies.RealProxy.HandleReturnMessage(IMes
sage reqMsg, IMessage retMsg)
   at System.Runtime.Remoting.Proxies.RealProxy.PrivateInvoke(MessageDat
a& msgData, Int32 type)
   at MyRemoteNamespace.MyRemoteNamespace.MonitorTimespan.GetInfo() in C
:\Documents and Settings\christianp\My Documents\Visual Studio Projects\
MonitorTimespan\MonitorTimespan.vb:line 19
   at MyRemoteNamespace.DynamicPublishingClient.Main() in C:\Documents a
nd Settings\christianp\My Documents\Visual Studio Projects\DynamicPublis
hingClient\DynamicPublishingClient.vb:line 15
```

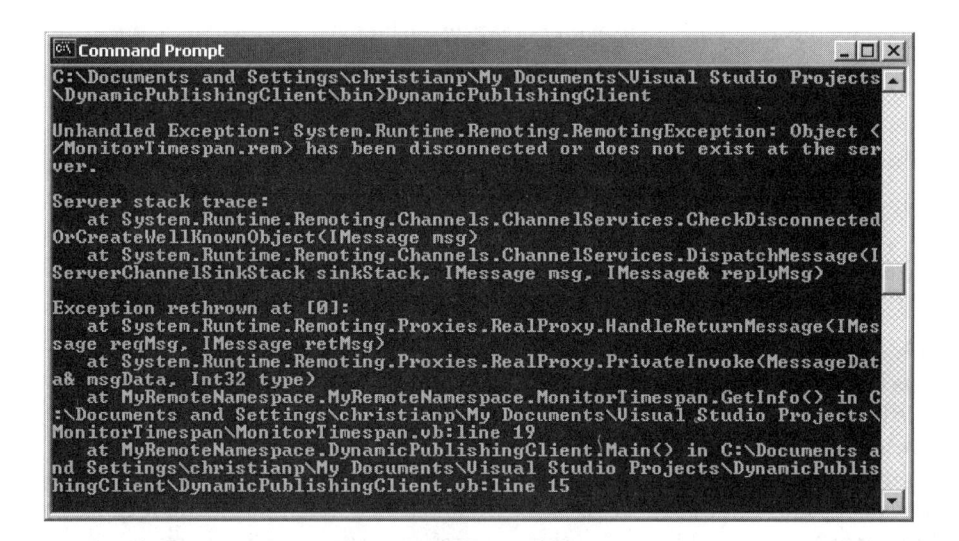

Switch back to the server application's console window and press Enter again. This causes the server application to publish the second remotable object, `monitor2`. If you run the client application now, you'll get a connection to the `monitor2` object that is currently published at the server as shown next.

```
Command Prompt
C:\Documents and Settings\christianp\My Documents\Visual Studio Projects
\DynamicPublishingClient\bin>DynamicPublishingClient
Monitor2 was created 531 seconds ago.

C:\Documents and Settings\christianp\My Documents\Visual Studio Projects
\DynamicPublishingClient\bin>
```

Finally, switch back to the server application's console window and press Enter. The server application disconnects `monitor2`, and then terminates as shown here.

```
Command Prompt
Press Enter to disconnect monitor2
No object currently published
C:\Documents and Settings\christianp\My Documents\Visual Studio Projects
\DynamicPublishingServer\bin>_
```

In other words, you've just published (and disconnected) two remote objects dynamically.

MBR Lifetime Management

.NET provides a sophisticated mechanism for managing the lifetime of MBR objects (*lifetime* refers to the time during which the object can be accessed remotely). It works efficiently and scales well when compared with other mechanisms used in the past for distributed garbage collection. The mechanism applies to any remoted MBR object, regardless of how it was activated and of how its clients first received a proxy reference to it. For example, it could have been

- directly published
- client or server activated
- passed as a parameter in, or returned from, a method call

The only case where it isn't relevant is for single-call server-activated objects, which only survive for as long as an individual method call.

After the lifetime has expired, clients that attempt to call methods on a proxy to the remote object will result in a `RemotingException`.

Although this mechanism is referred to as *distributed garbage collection*, after an object has been disconnected, it may not necessarily be available for garbage collection because it may still be referenced locally. This could occur with a reference to an explicitly created object directly published by calling `RemotingServices.Marshal()` or passed in a method call.

A Closer Look at Leased-Based Lifetimes

The aim of lifetime management is to release server resources that are no longer needed using a mechanism that uses minimal resources. In Chapter 1, we saw that the mechanism used by .NET is *lease-based lifetimes* where each MBR object can have an associated lease object. When MBR objects are first marshaled, their lease is activated with an initial lease time (the default is five minutes). The application domain has a *lease manager* that periodically checks for leases that have expired. Before disconnecting the associated MBR object, the lease manager gives any registered *sponsors* an opportunity to renew the lease.

Microsoft has provided a *tracking handler* that can be used to notify you when an MBR object has been disconnected, perhaps following the expiry of its lease. Let's take a closer look at this now, using the `Exchange` example we created earlier.

Implementing a Tracking Handler

A tracking handler can be used to see when the remoting infrastructure marshals, unmarshals, and disconnects an object. You can add one to our ExchangeHost project by creating a new Tracker class, as in the following example, and then registering it:

```
Imports System.Runtime.Remoting
Imports System.Runtime.Remoting.Services

Public Class Tracker
  Implements ITrackingHandler
  Public Sub MarshaledObject( _
    ByVal obj As Object, ByVal oref As ObjRef) _
    Implements ITrackingHandler.MarshaledObject

    Console.WriteLine( _
       "Tracker: Marshaled: {0}", obj.ToString())
    If (oref.URI <> Nothing) Then
      Console.WriteLine( _
         "Tracker: URI: {0}", oref.URI)
    End If
  End Sub

  Public Sub UnmarshaledObject( _
    ByVal obj As Object, ByVal oref As ObjRef) _
    Implements ITrackingHandler.UnmarshaledObject
    Console.WriteLine( _
       "Tracker: Unmarshaled: {0}", obj.ToString())
  End Sub
  Public Sub DisconnectedObject(ByVal obj As Object) _
    Implements ITrackingHandler.DisconnectedObject
    Console.WriteLine( _
       "Tracker: Disconnected: {0}", obj.ToString())
  End Sub
End Class
```

The point to note here is that our Tracker class needs to implement the ITrackingHandler interface from the System.Runtime.Remoting.Services namespace. This interface contains the methods MarshaledObject(), UnmarshaledObject(), and DisconnectedObject(), which are called when an MBR object is marshaled, unmarshaled, or disconnected from its proxy.

Because the TrackingServices class that is needed to register the tracking handler resides in the same namespace, the following statement also needs to be added prior to the Main() subroutine of ExchangeHost:

```
Imports System.Runtime.Remoting.Services
```

The tracking handler can then be registered by calling the RegisterTrackingHandler() method on the TrackingServices class in Main():

```
' Create and register a channel
Dim channel As New TcpChannel(10000)
ChannelServices.RegisterChannel(channel)
' Register a tracking handler
TrackingServices.RegisterTrackingHandler(New Tracker())
' Register an Exchange Service
RemotingConfiguration.RegisterActivatedServiceType( _
  GetType(Exchange))
```

When running this version of the server and then the client, it's interesting to see the URI that is internally generated for the marshaled objects.

If you allow the client to request several Order objects and than terminate (by pressing Enter several times and then Ctrl+C), we see the Order objects on the server being marshaled, as shown here.

If the host is then allowed to remain running, after about five minutes, the Tracker will report that the Order instances have been disconnected (see the following diagram). This occurs because their leases have expired, (assuming we have not overridden the InitializeLifetimeService() method of the Order class, which we'll discuss in a moment).

Manipulating Leases

As mentioned earlier, each MBR object has, by default, an associated lease object. This object contains properties that define the lease's policies, and methods that can be used to set and retrieve the lease time. These properties and methods are inherited from the ILease interface that lease objects must implement.

An MBR object can be given an infinite lifetime by overriding its InitializeLifetimeService() method (inherited from its base class MarshalByRefObject) to initialize it without a lease:

```
Public Overrides Function _
  InitializeLifetimeService() As Object
    Return Nothing
End Function
```

The `InitializeLifetimeService()` method can also be used to initialize the values mentioned for the lease properties if you want them to be different from the defaults. These properties include

- `CurrentLeaseTime`: The amount of time remaining on the lease.
- `CurrentState`: The current state of the lease (one of `Null`, `Initial`, `Active`, `Renewing`, or `Expired`).
- `InitialLeaseTime`: The initial time assigned to `CurrentLeaseTime`.
- `RenewOnCallTime`: When the MBR object's methods are called, the `CurrentLeaseTime` is set to this value if it is greater than the current value.

The default value for `InitialLeaseTime` is 5 minutes and for `RenewOnCallTime` is 2 minutes. These values can be changed by code. Let's now modify our sample application so that we can control the leases associated with our MBR objects. Change the values for our `Exchange` object to 40 seconds for the `InitialLeaseTime` and to 10 seconds for the `RenewOnCallTime`.

First, the `ILease` interface comes from the `System.Runtime.Remoting.Lifetime` namespace, so you must import it:

```
Imports System.Runtime.Remoting.Lifetime
```

Next, modify the overridden `InitializeLifetimeService()` method:

```
Public Overrides Function _
   InitializeLifetimeService() As Object
  Dim lease As ILease = _
    CType(MyBase.InitializeLifetimeService(), ILease)
  If lease.CurrentState = LeaseState.Initial Then
    lease.InitialLeaseTime = TimeSpan.FromSeconds(40)
    lease.RenewOnCallTime = TimeSpan.FromSeconds(10)
  End If
  Return lease
End Function
```

Notice that this code checks that the lease is in its initialization state, `LeaseState.Initial`, before attempting to change the time settings.

Renewing Leases

Leases are renewed (the `CurrentLeaseTime` is increased) in one of the following ways:

- One of the MBR object's methods is called
- The lease's `Renew()` method is called
- A registered sponsor renews the lease when prompted

Let's now take a closer look at the latter scenario.

Creating Sponsors

A server might receive no requests from its clients for some time. Because of this, the server object might expire before the client is done with it, unless some other object acts on behalf of the client. .NET uses the sponsor mechanism to allow periodic checks to test that the client applications are still active, so the server should remain active too.

The sponsor mechanism works in the following way. After the lifetime manager detects a lease where the CurrentLeaseTime has fallen to zero, the lease will expire unless one or more sponsors have been registered for the lease. Registered sponsors are then given an opportunity to renew the lease before it expires. Sponsors are allowed a finite time to respond to renewal requests; this time is defined by the SponsorshipTimeout property from the LifetimeServices class in the System.Runtime.Remoting.Lifetime namespace. This namespace also contains the ISponsor interface that sponsors must implement. This interface contains a method, Renewal(), which is called to get the sponsor to request a lease renewal.

In the following example, you can further modify our client application to register a sponsor for the lease associated with the remote client-activated Exchange object, and output a console message when the sponsor renews the lease. First, create the new ExchangeSponsor class:

```
Imports System
Imports System.Runtime.Remoting
Imports System.Runtime.Remoting.Lifetime

Public Class ExchangeSponsor
   Inherits MarshalByRefObject
   Implements ISponsor
   Public Function Renewal(ByVal lease As ILease) _
     As TimeSpan Implements ISponsor.Renewal
     Console.WriteLine("Lease renewal requested")
     Return TimeSpan.FromSeconds(10)
   End Function
End Class
```

Note that our ExchangeSponsor class inherits from MarshalByRefObject, allowing a reference to it to be passed to the server so that the server may call its Renewal() method when it needs to request the lease to be renewed. The Renewal() method implements ISponsor.Renewal() and returns a TimeSpan value used to refresh the CurrentLeaseTime property of the lease.

Next you need to modify the client to register the ExchangeSponsor. The sponsor mechanism relies upon the server using the remoting infrastructure to send messages to the client to ask the sponsor object to renew the lease. Therefore, you need to register a channel on which the client can listen for and receive these messages using the RegisterChannel() method. Specify a TCP channel with a port number of zero to allow the infrastructure to allocate its choice of port:

```
Imports System.Runtime.Remoting
Imports System.Runtime.Remoting.Lifetime
Imports System.Runtime.Remoting.Channels
Imports System.Runtime.Remoting.Channels.Tcp
Imports ExchangeObjects
```

```vbnet
Module Module1
  Sub Main()
    Dim channel As New TcpChannel(0)
    ChannelServices.RegisterChannel(channel)
    ' Create proxy to remote object
RemotingConfiguration.RegisterActivatedClientType( _
        GetType(Exchange), "tcp://localhost:10000")
    Dim exchange As New Exchange()
```

Next, you need to retrieve the lease associated with the `Exchange` object using the `RemotingServices.GetLifetimeService()` method, create an `ExchangeSponsor` object, and then register it using `ILease`'s `Register()` method:

```vbnet
    ' Get lease, create and register sponsor
    Dim lease As ILease = CType( _
      RemotingServices.GetLifetimeService(exchange), _
      ILease)
    Dim sponsor As New ExchangeSponsor()
      lease.Register(sponsor)

    Do
      ' Call remote function repeatedly
      Console.WriteLine( _
        "Lease time before call: {0}", _
        lease.CurrentLeaseTime.Seconds)
      Dim order As Order = exchange.NextOrder()
      Console.WriteLine( _
        "Lease time after call: {0}", _
        lease.CurrentLeaseTime.Seconds)
      ' Wait
      Console.WriteLine("Hit <enter> to continue")
      Console.ReadLine()
    Loop
  End Sub
End Module
```

In this sample, you've also added a trace to output the current lease time before and after calling a method on the exchange object. This allows you to see the `CurrentLeaseTime` being reset to the `RenewOnCallTime` as shown here.

```
C:\Command Prompt - ExchangeClient
C:\Documents and Settings\christianp\My Documents\Visual Studio Projects
\ExchangeClient\bin>
C:\Documents and Settings\christianp\My Documents\Visual Studio Projects
\ExchangeClient\bin>ExchangeClient
Lease time before call: 39
Lease time after call: 39
Hit <enter> to continue
Lease renewal requested

Lease time before call: 8
Lease time after call: 9
Hit <enter> to continue
```

Summary

In this chapter, we demonstrated how to implement simple remoting in VB .NET code. We started by looking more closely at marshaling remotable objects by value (MBV) or by reference (MBR). MBV requires an object to be serializable and requires the object's code to be accessible wherever it is to be used. To make an object available for MBR, you must make the class of the object inherit from `MarshalByRefObject`. Both types of marshaling occur implicitly whenever an object is passed to or returned from a method call made on a remote object.

You saw that MBR objects can be directly published by a host or can use one of the built in activation modes:

- server activated
- client activated

We also noted that server-activated objects can be singleton or single call. Singleton implies that every method call from any client is directed to the same single object instance. Single call allows a new remote object to be created for each method call made by any client, the object being discarded immediately after the method has completed. In both of the server cases, there is only one active server object. The client-activated model allows each client to create and use its own instance of a server object.

After discussing remote object marshaling in some depth, we moved on to look at how you can control remote object lifetimes. An MBR object has an associated lease that is used by the application's lease manager to determine when the object is no longer required remotely; the object can then be disconnected from its proxies. We demonstrated how to add a tracking handler to a host application to monitor MBR objects being marshaled, unmarshaled, and disconnected.

We noted that a lease gradually expires with time but is renewed when a method of the MBR object is called. It can also be renewed explicitly by calling the lease's `Renew()` method, or through sponsors. Sponsors provide a mechanism through which checks can be made to ensure that a remote server object is still required. We rounded the chapter off by creating a sponsor class capable of renewing the lease on a remote object.

CHAPTER 3

Custom Remoting

Exploring the hinterlands of complex software technologies can be scary, and generally shouldn't be undertaken lightly. Some of you might recall the journey into the heart of darkness that constituted the inner workings of DCOM. Some are probably still there trying to come to grips with custom marshaling.

The truly extraordinary thing about .NET Remoting, however, is how astonishingly *flexible* the whole thing is. Almost every single significant part of it can have the standard mechanism replaced by a suitable plug-in, and Microsoft has gone to great lengths to make it as easy as possible to do just that. In this chapter, we'll explore the inner workings of remoting, to see how you can use these techniques to

- Insert a custom sink into the sink chain
- Provide your own formatter sink
- Implement a custom formatter and use custom serialization
- Provide your own custom transport mechanism for a channel

In the process, you'll learn about all the underlying mechanisms of .NET Remoting.

A Closer Look at the Sink Chain

In Chapter 1 we introduced the idea of a chain of channel sinks with the following diagram.

Within an AppDomain, each sink calls the next one in turn via a method invocation. Between AppDomains, transport sinks send a message to each other via TCP/IP (or some other appropriate mechanism).

Let's now look beneath the surface of the sink chain, and consider the classes that are associated with it.

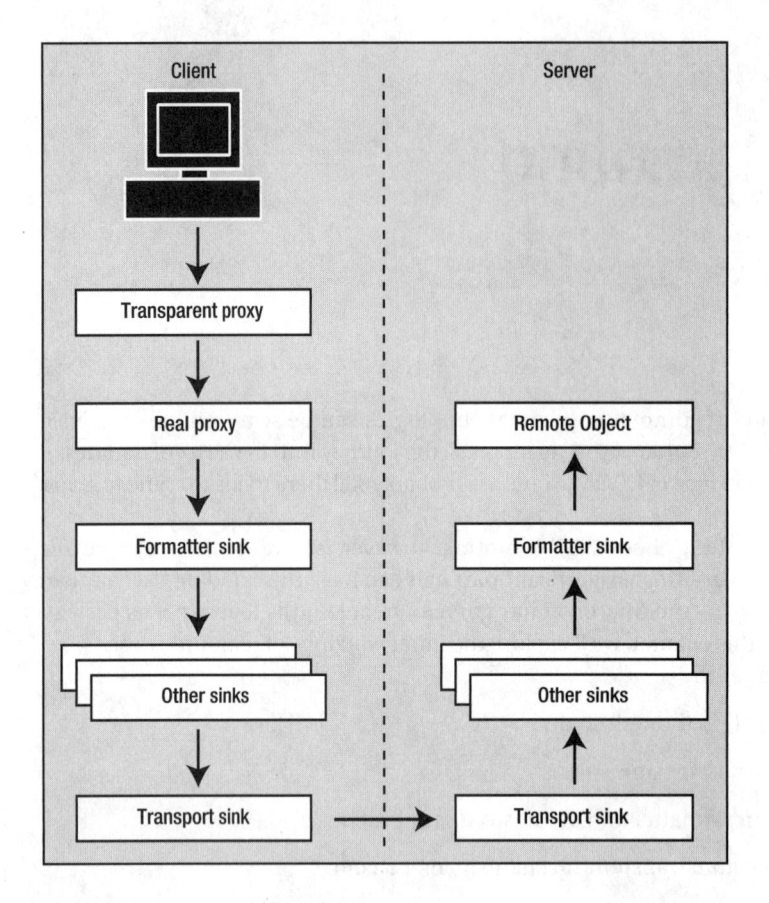

Formatter Classes

In Chapter 1, we noted that .NET provides two predefined formats for serializing the data in the formatter sink: binary or SOAP format.

Any class that is to be used to format this data must implement the `IFormatter` interface and override the `Serialize()` and `Deserialize()` methods. The three predefined classes that implement this interface are

- `System.Runtime.Serialization.Formatter`
- `System.Runtime.Serialization.Formatters.Binary.BinaryFormatter`
- `System.Runtime.Serialization.Formatters.Soap.SoapFormatter`

As you might expect, `Formatter` provides a basic formatter implementation. We'll generally use the `BinaryFormatter` and `SoapFormatter`, which serialize and deserialize objects in binary and SOAP format, respectively.

Choosing Channels and Formatters

Because you can choose which channel (TCP or HTTP) and which formatter (binary or SOAP) to use, it's useful to know some guidelines about making these choices:

- If speed is important to you, use a binary formatter. The binary formatter serializes the data into a much more condensed format than the SOAP formatter, which results in quicker data transfer because it reduces the payload traveling over the wire. This is particularly relevant if the remoting object is hosted by a different machine, but it can also be beneficial if the remoting object is hosted by a different app domain on the same machine. Serializing and deserializing data in binary format is more efficient than in SOAP format.

- If you want the data to be human readable or you want to perform XML processing on the data, use a SOAP formatter.

- If your remotable object executes within a secured environment, such as behind a firewall or on a secure intranet, use a `TcpChannel` for maximum performance. TCP is a lower-level and more efficient communication protocol than HTTP.

- If security is important to you, host your remotable object in IIS and use an `HttpChannel` to communicate with the object. This allows IIS to take care of all the security issues, rather than you having to write security-related code. For more information about IIS hosting, see Chapter 4.

- For maximum interoperability, use an `HttpChannel`. In this case, use a SOAP formatter unless you have large amounts of data to transfer or a low-bandwidth network connection; in these cases, consider using a binary formatter instead.

A server must register at least one channel, but it can define several channels if more flexibility is required. For example, a server application can register a SOAP-format `HttpChannel` on one port; a binary-format `HttpChannel` on a second port; and a binary-format `TcpChannel` on a third port (obviously each channel must use a different port). By providing all these channels, you allow clients to choose which channel to use, to suit their particular needs. For example, intranet clients can use a binary-format `TcpChannel` because speed is necessary. Business partners over the Web would use the same object over a SOAP-format `HttpChannel` hosted in IIS, because flexibility and security are more important than speed.

Obviously, there may be situations where you feel that the predefined channels and/or formatters do not provide the functionality you need. Luckily, .NET allows you to create custom channels and formatters and use these instead. Later in the chapter, we'll take a closer look at how to do this.

Channel Sink Interfaces and Classes

Many interfaces and classes from the `System.Runtime.Remoting.Channels` namespace are worth a look if you want to understand more about the sink chain.

The base interface for all channel sinks is `IChannelSinkBase`. However, the important functions and properties for sinks are provided by two interfaces that are derived from this interface:

- `IClientChannelSink`
- `IServerChannelSink`

Obviously, the first provides the functionality for client channel sinks, and the second for server channel sinks. Finally, there are two interfaces used with formatter sinks:

- `IClientFormatterSink`
- `System.Runtime.Remoting.Messaging.IMessageSink`

Let's take a closer look at these interfaces.

The `IClientChannelSink` Interface

Here are the public property and methods in the `IClientChannelSink` interface:

- `NextChannelSink`: This property should return the next channel sink in the client sink chain.
- `AsyncProcessRequest()`: This method gets invoked when an asynchronous method call is to be processed.
- `AsyncProcessResponse()`: This method gets invoked when an asynchronous response is to be processed.
- `GetRequestStream()`: This method is a request for the stream object onto which the request is to be serialized.
- `ProcessMessage()`: This method gets invoked when a synchronous method call is to be processed.

The `IServerChannelSink` Interface

Here are the properties and methods of the `IServerChannelSink` interface:

- `NextChannelSink`: This should return the next channel sink in the server sink chain.
- `AsyncProcessResponse()`: This gets invoked when an asynchronous response is to be processed.
- `GetResponseStream()`: This is a request for the stream object onto which the response is to be serialized.
- `ProcessMessage()`: This gets invoked when a synchronous method call is to be processed.

In other words, `NextChannelSink`, `AsyncProcessResponse()`, and `ProcessMessage()` are analogous to the corresponding property and methods in the `IClientChannelSink` interface. Obviously, methods to process the request are not needed on the server side.

The `IMessageSink` Interface

The first sink in the chain is where the messages are serialized. Therefore, it is slightly different from the others in the chain, in that it also has to implement the `IMessageSink` interface in the

`System.Runtime.Remoting.Messaging` namespace as well as `IClientChannelSink`. This sink is therefore often known as a *message sink*. A message sink passes a raw message object on to the next one in the chain. Often when we refer to a "channel sink," we actually mean a sink that passes a serialized representation of a message on to the next sink in the chain. This is why the formatter is always the first link in the channel sink chain. Here are some methods and properties from the `IMessageSink` interface:

- `NextSink`: This should return the next message sink in the client sink chain.
- `AsyncProcessMessage()`: Invoked when an asynchronous message (a method call) is to be processed.
- `SyncProcessMessage()`: Invoked when a synchronous message (a method call) is to be processed.

In our example, we're using the TCP channel as the transport mechanism. By default, the formatter that this uses is the binary one, and on the client side, the `BinaryClientFormatterSink` class implements the binary formatter. In our next example, we'll interpose a new sink in between this and the transport sink.

The IClientFormatterSink Interface

As you've seen, to mark a client sink as a formatter sink, you make it implement `IClientChannelSink` and `IMessageSink`. An alternative to this is to implement the `IClientFormatterSink` interface, which combines these two interfaces.

The `IClientFormatterSink` interface is implemented by two concrete classes. `BinaryClientFormatterSink` is the implementation class for a client formatter sink that uses the `BinaryFormatter`. Similary, `SoapClientFormatterSink` provides a client formatter sink that uses `SoapFormatter`.

Client Channel Sink Providers

Before we dive into an example, let's consider the concept of a *channel sink provider*, which we mentioned briefly in Chapter 2. The channel sink provider is a kind of factory class that is used to generate the channel sinks themselves. Scarily, these can also be chained together. By default, the TCP channel uses its own internal implementation, but you can also request it to use yours as well. On the client side, channel sink providers are objects that implement the interface `IClientChannelSinkProvider` in the `System.Runtime.Remoting.Channels` namespace. On the server side channel, sink providers implement the interface `IServerChannelSinkProvider`.

Here are the public property and method in the `IClientChannelSinkProvider` interface:

- `Next`: This should return the next sink provider in the client sink provider chain.
- `CreateSink()`: This gets invoked when a sink is to be created.

Here are the properties and methods from `IServerChannelSinkProvider`:

- `Next`: This should return the next sink provider in the client sink provider chain.
- `CreateSink()`: This gets invoked when a sink is to be created.

Again, `CreateSink()` and `Next` should be familiar from `IClientChannelSinkProvider`.

As with sink classes, you get differentiation between "normal" channel sinks and formatter (message) sinks. There are two interfaces for formatter sink providers:

- `IClientFormatterSinkProvider`
- `IServerFormatterSinkProvider`

Each of these inherits from its corresponding channel sink provider interface, and each interface is implemented by two concrete classes as you might expect:

- `BinaryClientFormatterSinkProvider`
- `SoapClientFormatterSinkProvider`
- `BinaryServerFormatterSinkProvider`
- `SoapServerFormatterSinkProvider`

You can use the constructors for these classes to select formatters for a channel. Although you would usually use this technique to specify a nondefault formatter for a channel, you can also use this technique to explicitly specify the default formatter—in case the default formatter is changed in some later version of .NET, for example:

```
Dim channel1 As New HttpChannel( _
    prop1, New BinaryClientFormatterSinkProvider(), _
      New BinaryServerFormatterSinkProvider())
```

Here `prop1` contains the name and port selected for the HTTP channel (as you saw in Chapter 2). We've obviously specified here that we want to use a binary formatter on the client and server sides.

Customizing the Sink Chain

Let's stop skirting around the issue and start playing around with some code. In this and the following sections, you'll customize the sink chain.

First, you'll interpose an "other sink" in between the formatter sink and the transport sink. After you've done this, you'll look at what is coming through from the formatter sink by dumping out the contents of the transport headers and serialized request stream to the command line.

That should give you enough of an idea of what is necessary to write our own formatter sink. We'll do this in two stages: first we'll use a standard formatter and then we'll implement our own.

So the first step is to create a new client channel sink. However, we first need a sample application to use the new sink with.

The Basic Invert Example

We'll use a simple example as a vehicle for our activities: a single-call object with an interface called `IInvert`. To keep things ordered, we'll create a solution called `Invert1`, and create three projects in this: a class library called `Invert`, and two console applications called `InvertClient` and `InvertServer`, respectively.

Implementing the `Invert` Class Library

`Invert` contains the interface definition for `IInvert`:

```
<Serializable()> Public Class InvertibleObject
  Public _string1 As String
  Public _string2 As String
End Class

Public Interface IInvert
  Function InvertString( _
    ByVal input As String) As String
  Function InvertDouble( _
    ByVal input As Double) As Double
  Function InvertObject( _
    ByVal input As InvertibleObject) _
    As InvertibleObject
End Interface
```

The idea is that each of the three methods carries out some kind of inversion on its input. To make things just a little bit more interesting, we've introduced the concept of an `InvertibleObject`. You'll see what that means in a little while, but the main reason for this is to force the issue of object serialization.

Implementing `InvertServer`

`InvertServer` is the host. As ever, it's in two parts: the implementation of `IInvert`, `MyInvert` (our remotable class), and the main startup module. Here's the implementation of `IInvert`:

```
Imports System.Runtime.Remoting
Imports System.Runtime.Remoting.Channels
Imports System.Runtime.Remoting.Channels.Tcp
Imports Invert

Class MyInvert Inherits MarshalByRefObject
  Implements IInvert
  Public Function InvertDouble( _
    ByVal input As Double) As Double _
    Implements Invert.IInvert.InvertDouble
    Dim output As Double
    If (input = 0.0) Then
      output = 0.0
    Else
      output = 1 / input
    End If
```

```vbnet
      Console.WriteLine( _
        "InvertServer: Input <{0}>, output <{1}>", _
        input, output)
      Return output
    End Function

    Public Function InvertString( _
      ByVal input As String) As String _
      Implements Invert.IInvert.InvertString
      Dim output As String
      Dim length As Integer
      Dim iChar As Integer
      length = input.Length
      For iChar = 0 To length - 1
        output += input.Chars(length - iChar - 1)
      Next iChar
      Console.WriteLine( _
        "InvertServer: Input <{0}>, output <{1}>", _
        input, output)
      Return output
    End Function
    Public Function InvertObject( _
      ByVal input As Invert.InvertibleObject) As _
      Invert.InvertibleObject _
      Implements Invert.IInvert.InvertObject

      Dim output As New InvertibleObject()
      output._string2 = input._string1
      output._string1 = input._string2
      Console.WriteLine( _
        "InvertServer: Input <{0}, {1}>, output <{2}, _
        {3}>", input._string1, input._string2, _
        output._string1, output._string2)
      Return output
    End Function
End Class
```

So, InvertDouble() returns the inverse of the incoming value and InvertString() reverses the order of the incoming string. InvertObject() swaps the two strings making up an invertible object around, so that the object {"Hello", "world"} becomes {"world", "Hello"}.

Here's the main module:

```vbnet
Module InvertServer
  Sub Main()
    Dim channel As TcpChannel
    Console.WriteLine("Server started")
    channel = New TcpChannel(8086)
    ChannelServices.RegisterChannel(channel)
```

```vb
    RemotingConfiguration.RegisterWellKnownServiceType( _
      GetType(MyInvert), "MyInvert.rem", _
      WellKnownObjectMode.SingleCall)
      Console.ReadLine()
  End Sub
End Module
```

Again, this is fairly straightforward. Strictly speaking, for a production system, we should make the TCP channel number configurable, but to keep things simple we won't deal with additional details. We've chosen 8086 here as an homage to the early days of microprocessors.

Implementing InvertClient

Finally, InvertClient is the client:

```vb
Imports System.Runtime.Remoting
Imports System.Runtime.Remoting.Channels
Imports System.Runtime.Remoting.Channels.Tcp
Imports Invert
Module InvertClient
  Sub Main()
    Dim url As String
    Dim invert As IInvert
    Dim dblValue As Double
    Dim strValue As String
    Dim objInValue As InvertibleObject
    Dim objOutValue As InvertibleObject
    url = "tcp://localhost:8086/MyInvert.rem"
    invert = CType(Activator.GetObject( _
      GetType(IInvert), url), IInvert)
    objInValue = New InvertibleObject()
    objInValue._string1 = "Hello"
    objInValue._string2 = "world"
    dblValue = invert.InvertDouble(1.234)
    strValue = invert.InvertString("ABCDE")
    objOutValue = invert.InvertObject(objInValue)
    Console.WriteLine( _
      "InvertClient: dblValue = <{0}>, _
      strValue = <{1}>, objValue = <{2}>, <{3}>", _
      dblValue, strValue, objOutValue._string1, _
      objOutValue._string2)
    Console.ReadLine()
  End Sub
End Module
```

Once again, this type of thing should be familiar to you after Chapter 2. All we're doing is instantiating our local version of the object, and passing a double, a string, and an invertible object to it in turn. Here's what happens on the server when we run it:

```
>InvertServer
Server started
InvertServer: Input <1.234>, output <0.810372771474878>
InvertServer: Input <ABCDE>, output <EDCBA>
InvertServer: Input <Hello, world>, output
<world, Hello>
```

The following looks about right on the client:

```
>InvertClient
InvertClient: dblValue = <0.810372771474878>,
strValue = <EDCBA>, objValue = <world>, <Hello>
```

Adding a New Client Channel Sink

Now let's get back on track. We want to create a new channel sink to use with this example. The first step toward this goal is to implement and configure an appropriate channel sink provider on the client and server side. For this example, however, we only need to develop the client side, because the server side will remain standard. Therefore, we'll create a new client sink provider implementation called InvertClientChannelSinkProvider, and then we'll create a new client channel sink implementation called InvertClientChannelSink.

Implementing the Invert Client Channel Sink Provider

Let's add a new class library project to the solution called InvertFormatter. We're going to put the new channel sink provider in the new InvertFormatter project.

We start by importing some namespaces, and then we define a member variable to hold a reference to the next channel sink provider in the chain. You'll see that this ends up being the TCP channel's default sink provider. Incidentally, because the relationship between each sink provider in the chain and the next one is a method invocation, we don't need a reference to the previous sink provider.

```
Imports System.Runtime.Remoting.Channels
Imports System.IO

Public Class InvertClientChannelSinkProvider
   Implements IClientChannelSinkProvider
   Dim _next As IClientChannelSinkProvider
```

As noted earlier, the next method, CreateSink(), is called by the TCP channel implementation when it wants a new sink created. We first create an instance of our own sink class. In the process of constructing this, we need to pass in a reference to the next sink in the chain. So we ask the next provider in the chain to create a sink. As this is the TCP channel's own provider, the sink created will be a TCP transport sink. So the next sink after our new sink will be the TCP transport sink, which is exactly what we wanted. Finally, we create an instance of the binary client formatter sink, passing in a reference to our own sink as *its* next sink, and return this back to the caller.

```
  Public Function CreateSink( _
    ByVal channel As IChannelSender, _
    ByVal url As String, _
    ByVal remoteChannelData As Object) _
    As IClientChannelSink _
    Implements IClientChannelSinkProvider.CreateSink
    Console.WriteLine( _
      "InvertClientChannelSinkProvider: CreateSink")
    Dim sink As New _
      InvertClientChannelSink(_next.CreateSink( _
      channel, url, remoteChannelData))
    Return New BinaryClientFormatterSink(sink)
  End Function
```

So the one call to `CreateSink()` actually instantiates three channel sinks, linked together as shown in the next figure.

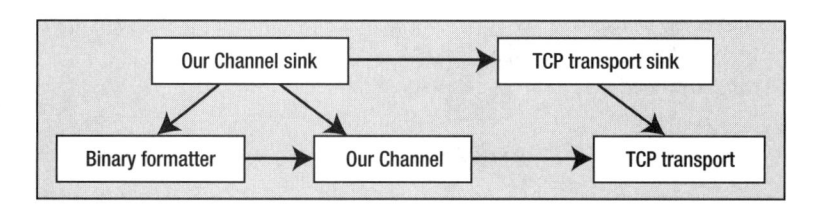

The next property is simply used for accessing the next sink provider in the chain. Note that the name given by VS.NET by default, Next(), is invalid for Visual Basic (because it's a reserved word), so you'll have to substitute your own.

```
  Public Property NextSinkProvider() _
    As IClientChannelSinkProvider _
    Implements IClientChannelSinkProvider.Next
    Get
     Console.WriteLine( _
      "InvertClientChannelSinkProvider: " & _
      " Get NextSinkProvider")
     Return _next
    End Get
    Set(ByVal Value As IClientChannelSinkProvider)
      Console.WriteLine( _
        "InvertClientChannelSinkProvider: " & _
        Set NextSinkProvider")
      _next = Value
    End Set
  End Property
End Class
```

Implementing the Invert Client Channel Sink

We'll implement the channel sink in the `InvertFormatter` project as well. First of all, we need a member variable to hold a reference to the next channel in the chain. We'll also have a constructor that takes that reference in as its argument:

```
Public Class InvertClientChannelSink
  Implements IClientChannelSink
  Dim _next As IClientChannelSink
  Public Sub New( _
    ByVal nextSink As IClientChannelSink)
    _next = nextSink
  End Sub
```

Next, we need a couple of methods to handle asynchronous requests and responses. As this is a single-call object, we don't need to add any functionality here, although we do need to provide an implementation, as they are part of the interface `IClientChannelSink`:

```
Public Sub AsyncProcessRequest(ByVal sinkStack _
  As IClientChannelSinkStack, ByVal msg As _
  System.Runtime.Remoting.Messaging.IMessage, _
  ByVal headers As ITransportHeaders, _
  ByVal stream As System.IO.Stream) _
  Implements IClientChannelSink.AsyncProcessRequest
  Console.WriteLine( _
    "InvertClientChannelSink: AsyncProcessRequest")
End Sub
Public Sub AsyncProcessResponse(ByVal sinkStack _
  As IClientResponseChannelSinkStack, _
  ByVal state As Object, ByVal headers _
  As ITransportHeaders, ByVal stream _
  As System.IO.Stream) Implements _
  IClientChannelSink.AsyncProcessResponse
  Console.WriteLine( _
    "InvertClientChannelSink: AsyncProcessResponse")
End Sub
```

Then we have the `ProcessMessage()` method that handles synchronous message exchanges. The principal input to this method is a reference to a stream of data, and the principal output is also a reference to a stream. Remember what we said about the data having been serialized by this point?

```
Public Sub ProcessMessage(ByVal msg _
  As System.Runtime.Remoting.Messaging.IMessage, _
  ByVal requestHeaders As ITransportHeaders, _
  ByVal requestStream As System.IO.Stream, _
  ByRef responseHeaders As ITransportHeaders, _
  ByRef responseStream As System.IO.Stream) _
  Implements IClientChannelSink.ProcessMessage
  Console.WriteLine( _
    "InvertClientChannelSink: ProcessMessage")
```

Now here are the transport headers:

```
Dim entry As DictionaryEntry
For Each entry In requestHeaders
  Console.WriteLine( _
   "    Header key: <{0}>", entry.Key)
  Console.WriteLine( _
   "    Header value: <{0}>", entry.Value)
Next
```

Next we'll dump out the serialized request stream by using a private method for this (we'll define it a little later):

```
DumpStream(requestStream)
```

Now we pass the message on to the next sink in the chain (which, as we know, is the transport sink), and get the response back. Unfortunately, the response stream doesn't support the Length property, so we can't dump that out.

```
  _next.ProcessMessage(msg, requestHeaders, _
    requestStream, responseHeaders, responseStream)
End Sub
```

Next, we need to implement the GetRequestStream() method that responds to an enquiry for the request stream, which we pass on to the next sink in the chain:

```
Public Function GetRequestStream(ByVal msg _
  As System.Runtime.Remoting.Messaging.IMessage, _
  ByVal headers As ITransportHeaders) _
  As System.IO.Stream _
  Implements IClientChannelSink.GetRequestStream
  Console.WriteLine( _
    "InvertClientChannelSink: GetRequestStream")
  Return _next.GetRequestStream(msg, headers)
End Function
```

We also need an implementation of the NextChannelSink property, which returns a reference to the next sink in the chain:

```
Public ReadOnly Property NextChannelSink() _
  As IClientChannelSink _
  Implements IClientChannelSink.NextChannelSink
  Get
   Console.WriteLine( _
     "InvertClientChannelSink: Get NextChannelSink")
   Return _next
  End Get
End Property
```

We'll pass all requests for properties to the next sink in the chain:

```vb
    Public ReadOnly Property Properties() _
      As System.Collections.IDictionary _
      Implements IClientChannelSink.Properties
      Get
        Console.WriteLine( _
          "InvertClientChannelSink: Get Properties")
        Return _next.Properties()
      End Get
    End Property
```

Finally, here's the implementation of our private `DumpStream()` method that dumps out a stream as raw hex data:

```vb
    Private Sub DumpStream(ByVal strm As Stream)
      Dim length As Integer
      Dim buffer As Byte()
      Dim iByte As Integer
      length = strm.Length
      ReDim buffer(length)
      strm.Read(buffer, 0, length)
      For iByte = 0 To length - 1
        If iByte Mod 20 = 0 Then
          Console.WriteLine()
          Console.Write("     ")
        End If
        If buffer(iByte) <= 15 Then
          Console.Write(" {0}", Hex$(buffer(iByte)))
        Else
          Console.Write(" {0}", Hex$(buffer(iByte)))
        End If
      Next
      Console.WriteLine()
      For iByte = 0 To length - 1
        If iByte Mod 20 = 0 Then
          Console.WriteLine()
          Console.Write("     ")
        End If

        Console.Write("  {0}", Chr(buffer(iByte)))
      Next
      Console.WriteLine()
      strm.Seek(0, IO.SeekOrigin.Begin)
    End Sub
End Class
```

Modifying the Invert Client Code to Use the Invert Client Channel Sink

We need to do one more thing before we can try out the new sink. We need to tell the client to use our adapted TCP channel rather than the standard one. So we need to register the new channel. Here's what we do to the client:

```vb
Imports System.Runtime.Remoting
Imports System.Runtime.Remoting.Channels
Imports System.Runtime.Remoting.Channels.Tcp
Imports Invert
Imports InvertFormatter

Module InvertClient
  Sub Main()
    Dim url As String
    Dim invert As IInvert
    Dim dblValue As Double
    Dim strValue As String
    Dim objInValue As InvertibleObject
    Dim objOutValue As InvertibleObject
    Dim provider As InvertClientChannelSinkProvider
    Dim channel As TcpChannel
    provider = New InvertClientChannelSinkProvider()
    channel = New TcpChannel(Nothing, _
        provider, Nothing)
    ChannelServices.RegisterChannel(channel)
    url = "tcp://localhost:8086/MyInvert.rem"
    invert = CType(Activator.GetObject( -
        GetType(IInvert), url), IInvert)
    objInValue = New InvertibleObject()
    objInValue._string1 = "Hello"
    objInValue._string2 = "world"
    dblValue = invert.InvertDouble(1.234)
    strValue = invert.InvertString("ABCDE")
    objOutValue = invert.InvertObject(objInValue)
    Console.WriteLine( _
       "InvertClient: dblValue = <{0}>, " & _
       "strValue = <{1}>, objValue = <{2}>, <{3}>", _
       dblValue, strValue, objOutValue._string1, _
       objOutValue._string2)
    Console.ReadLine()
  End Sub
End Module
```

We're using a special constructor for TcpChannel so that we can specify a reference to a client channel sink provider. Incidentally, the first argument can hold a dictionary object that contains parameters, such as—as you'll see on the server side—the port number. The third argument is a reference to a server channel sink provider—again, you meet this later.

Running the Example

The server side remains unchanged, so let's try it out and see what happens by running the client program. The following figure shows what you'll see on the client.

CHAPTER 3 ■ CUSTOM REMOTING

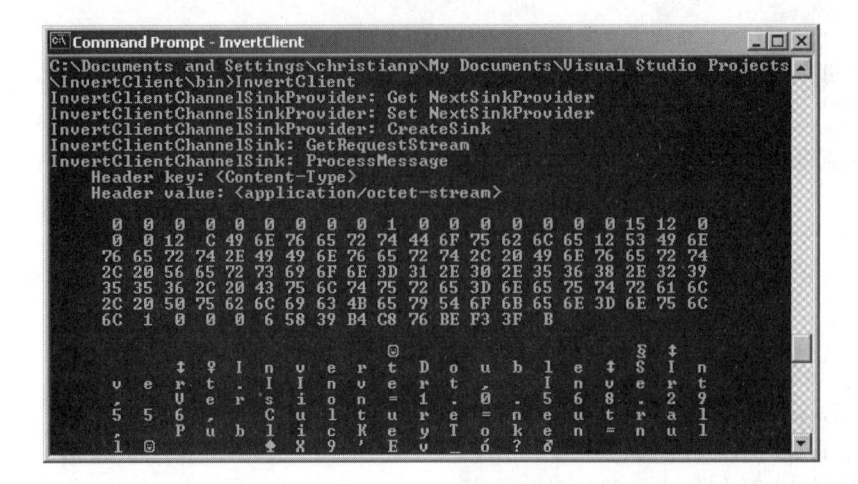

```
Command Prompt - InvertClient
C:\Documents and Settings\christianp\My Documents\Visual Studio Projects
\InvertClient\bin>InvertClient
InvertClientChannelSinkProvider: Get NextSinkProvider
InvertClientChannelSinkProvider: Set NextSinkProvider
InvertClientChannelSinkProvider: CreateSink
InvertClientChannelSink: GetRequestStream
InvertClientChannelSink: ProcessMessage
    Header key: <Content-Type>
    Header value: <application/octet-stream>

    0  0  0  0  0  0  0  0  1  0  0  0  0  0  0 15 12  0
    0  0 12  C 49 6E 76 65 72 74 44 6F 75 62 6C 65 12 53 49 6E
   76 65 72 74 2E 49 49 6E 76 65 72 74 2C 20 49 6E 76 65 72 74
   2C 20 56 65 72 73 69 6F 6E 3D 31 2E 30 2E 35 36 38 2E 32 39
   35 35 36 2C 20 43 75 6C 74 75 72 65 3D 6E 65 75 74 72 61 6C
   2C 20 50 75 62 6C 69 63 4B 65 79 54 6F 6B 65 6E 3D 6E 75 6C
    6C  1  0  0  0  6 58 39 B4 C8 76 BE F3 3F  B

                         ☻ ♀ I  n  v  e  r  t  D  o  u  b  l  e ‡ ♫ S  I  n
          v  e  r  t  .  I  I  n  v  e  r  t  ,     I  n  v  e  r  t
             V  e  r  s  i  o  n  =  1  .  0  .  5  6  8  .  2  9
          5  5  6  ,     C  u  l  t  u  r  e  =  n  e  u  t  r  a  l
                P  u  b  l  i  c  K  e  y  T  o  k  e  n  =  n  u  l
          l  ☺          ♠  X  9  '  E  v  _  ó  ?  δ
```

The first thing that happens is that our provider is asked what its next provider is; at first, this is nothing. The next provider gets set; this is the TCP formatter's own provider. We are then asked to create a sink, and all the action transfers there. The sink is asked for the request stream, and then this is filled with the serialized message.

If you look at the message, you can discern some recognizable data in the midst of all the mess. Despite the fact that this is the more efficient binary formatter at work here, there's still a substantial overhead (although it's nothing compared to what you get if you choose to use the SOAP formatter instead).

You can try a little interpretation on what the formatter is doing to serialize the message going over the wire. For example, if you look at the first message in the previous figure, you can see a counted string of the 12 bytes of InvertDouble (which is clearly the name of the method being invoked) followed by 83 bytes of Invert.IInvert, Invert, Version=1.0.891.29380, Culture=neutral, and PublicKeyToken=null (which identifies the assembly containing the method). Finally, you can see 8 bytes at the end, 58 39 B4 C8 76 BE F3 3F, which—curiously enough—turn out to be the binary representation of the double-precision, floating-point number 1.234.

We get a similar message for InvertString() as shown in the following figure.

```
Command Prompt - InvertClient
InvertClientChannelSink: GetRequestStream
InvertClientChannelSink: ProcessMessage
    Header key: <Content-Type>
    Header value: <application/octet-stream>

    0  0  0  0  0  0  0  0  1  0  0  0  0  0  0 15 12  0
    0  0 12  C 49 6E 76 65 72 74 53 74 72 69 6E 67 12 53 49 6E
   76 65 72 74 2E 49 49 6E 76 65 72 74 2C 20 49 6E 76 65 72 74
   2C 20 56 65 72 73 69 6F 6E 3D 31 2E 30 2E 35 36 38 2E 32 39
   35 35 36 2C 20 43 75 6C 74 75 72 65 3D 6E 65 75 74 72 61 6C
   2C 20 50 75 62 6C 69 63 4B 65 79 54 6F 6B 65 6E 3D 6E 75 6C
    6C  1  0  0  0 12  5 41 42 43 44 45  B

                         ☻ ♀ I  n  v  e  r  t  S  t  r  i  n  g ‡ ♫ S  I  n
          v  e  r  t  .  I  I  n  v  e  r  t  ,     I  n  v  e  r  t
             V  e  r  s  i  o  n  =  1  .  0  .  5  6  8  .  2  9
          5  5  6  ,     C  u  l  t  u  r  e  =  n  e  u  t  r  a  l
                P  u  b  l  i  c  K  e  y  T  o  k  e  n  =  n  u  l
          l  ☺          ♣  ♠  A  B  C  D  E  δ
```

Of somewhat more interest is the serialization of our invertible object, which we can see in the third block of data:

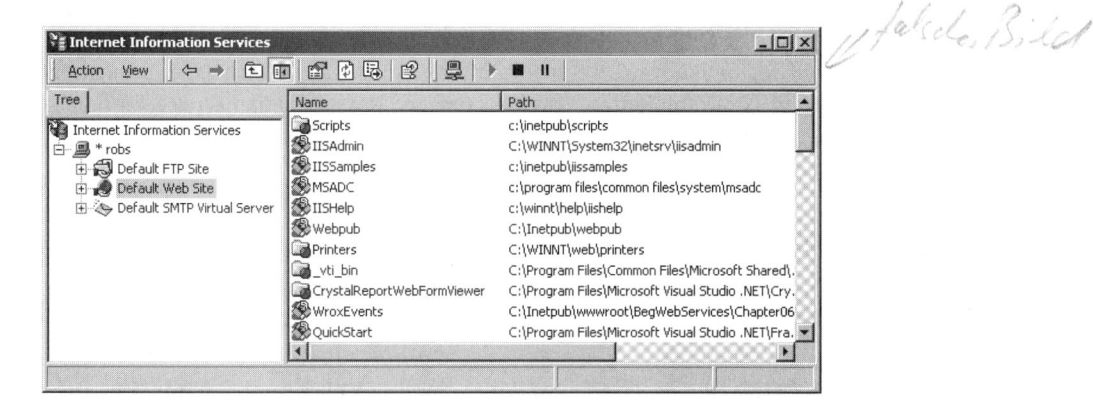

[Screenshot of Internet Information Services window showing Default Web Site contents with Name and Path columns listing items such as Scripts, IISAdmin, IISSamples, MSADC, IISHelp, Webpub, Printers, _vti_bin, CrystalReportWebFormViewer, WroxEvents, QuickStart.]

We can see that, by default at any rate, the names of the underlying objects and their values get sent across the wire. There is clearly some scope for improvement here, and we'll look at this later.

There's one important point that we almost overlooked. Why would we do this? Why would we interpose another sink channel between the formatter and the transport? One answer is *security*. If you want to encrypt, that's precisely the place where you'd want to do it, because that's the point at which the outgoing message is first serialized, and therefore open to encryption. Another process that could be carried out at this point might be data *compression*.

Replacing the Formatter Sink

Let's delve a little further, and replace the standard binary formatter sink with our own formatter sink (which will be a modified version of our custom channel sink from the previous section). We'll still keep the binary formatter at this stage, but we'll provide our own formatter sink implementation. In order to do this, we're going to have to put our sink at the head of the chain, which means that we'll have to implement `IMessageSink` as well as `IClientChannelSink`. Let's forge on.

We don't need to make any changes at all to either the client or the server. However, we'll need to make a small change to the sink provider to ensure that our formatter sink is the head of the sink chain, not the binary formatter. This is what we need to do:

```
Public Function CreateSink(ByVal channel _
   As IChannelSender, ByVal url _
   As String, ByVal remoteChannelData As Object) _
   As IClientChannelSink _
   Implements IClientChannelSinkProvider.CreateSink
  Console.WriteLine( _
    "InvertClientChannelSinkProvider: CreateSink")
  Return New InvertClientChannelSink( _
    _next.CreateSink( channel, url, _
    remoteChannelData))
End Function
```

Just to refresh our memories, what we're doing here is instantiating our formatter sink, and passing it a reference to a newly created transport sink as the next one in the chain.

Implementing the Formatter Sink

It's now time to turn our custom sink into a true formatter sink. To do this, we need to implement the `IMessageSink` interface, from the `System.Runtime.Remoting.Messaging` namespace. We'll need to add this namespace to our project as well as `System.Runtime.Serialization.Formatters.Binary`, which will be needed later on:

```
Imports System.Runtime.Remoting.Messaging
Imports System.Runtime.Remoting.Channels
Imports _
 System.Runtime.Serialization.Formatters.Binary
Imports System.IO
```

We'll also need to change the declaration of our channel sink class so that it implements the `IMessageSink` interface:

```
Public Class InvertClientChannelSink
  Implements IClientChannelSink
  Implements IMessageSink
```

Next, we need to add the methods that this interface requires. First of all, here's the method that receives asynchronous messages. Again, we'll leave this empty:

```
Public Function AsyncProcessMessage(ByVal msg _
   As IMessage, ByVal replySink As IMessageSink) _
   As IMessageCtrl _
     Implements IMessageSink.AsyncProcessMessage
  Console.WriteLine( _
    "InvertClientChannelSink: AsyncProcessMessage")
End Function
```

The next one handles synchronous messages, and this is where the serious work is going to be done. Notice that the incoming argument is a structured message object, not a stream. Our challenge is to turn this into a stream for passing onwards down the channel sink chain. For the time being, we're going to do exactly what the standard, off-the-shelf, binary formatter sink does, and use the standard, off-the-shelf, binary formatter to serialize our message:

```
  Public Function SyncProcessMessage( _
    ByVal msg As IMessage) As IMessage _
    Implements IMessageSink.SyncProcessMessage
    Console.WriteLine( _
      "InvertClientChannelSink: SyncProcessMessage")
    Dim outHeaders As New TransportHeaders()
    Dim outStream As New MemoryStream()
```

```
Dim inHeaders As ITransportHeaders
Dim inStream As Stream
Dim formatter As New BinaryFormatter()
formatter.Serialize(outStream, msg)
```

It's as simple as that. After we have our stream, we can pass it on to the next channel sink in the chain, into its `ProcessMessage()` method. This is what the binary formatter sink was doing to our custom sink in the previous example. Notice that the returned objects are instantiated by the called sink.

```
_next.ProcessMessage(msg, outHeaders, _
    outStream, inHeaders, inStream)
```

Now that we have our returned stream, all we need to do is deserialize it back into a message to pass up to our caller:

```
Return formatter.Deserialize(inStream)
End Function
```

The last property we need to add is one to handle a request for the next sink in the chain:

```
Public ReadOnly Property NextSink() As IMessageSink _
    Implements IMessageSink.NextSink
    Get
        Console.WriteLine( _
            "InvertClientChannelSink: Get NextSink")
        Return _next
    End Get
End Property
```

Our own implementation of `ProcessMessage()` is no longer called now, so we can remove all the logging code from it, and dispose of our `DumpStream()` private method:

```
Public Sub ProcessMessage(ByVal msg _
    As IMessage, ByVal requestHeaders _
    As ITransportHeaders, ByVal requestStream _
    As System.IO.Stream, ByRef responseHeaders _
    As ITransportHeaders, ByRef responseStream _
    As System.IO.Stream) _
    Implements IClientChannelSink.ProcessMessage
    Console.WriteLine( _
        "InvertClientChannelSink: ProcessMessage")
    _next.ProcessMessage( msg, requestHeaders, _
        requestStream, responseHeaders, responseStream)
End Sub
```

Our sink chain has now reduced to this (see the following figure).

```
┌─────────────────────────────────────────────────────┐
│   ┌──────────────────┐        ┌──────────────────┐  │
│   │ Our formatter sink│───────▶│ TCP transport sink│  │
│   └──────────────────┘        └──────────────────┘  │
└─────────────────────────────────────────────────────┘
```

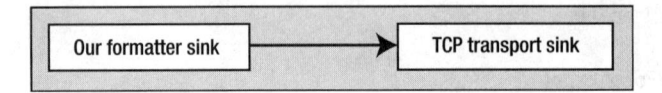

Running the Example

This is what you'll see at the client when we run our new version:

```
>InvertClient
InvertClientChannelSinkProvider: Get NextSinkProvider
InvertClientChannelSinkProvider: Set NextSinkProvider
InvertClientChannelSinkProvider: CreateSink
InvertClientChannelSink: SyncProcessMessage
InvertClientChannelSink: SyncProcessMessage
InvertClientChannelSink: SyncProcessMessage
InvertClient: dblValue = <0.810372771474878>,
strValue = <EDCBA>, objValue = <world>, <Hello>
```

Now let's write our own formatter. To do this, we have to make some changes to the server end of things, because that's where the new way of serializing data will be decoded. Let's extend our solution and define a new serialization.

Adding a Custom Formatter

Writing your own formatter isn't something you'd generally want to do because of all the transmitting, serializing, and deserializing that must be done to get remoting to work. Unless you're *really* strapped for bandwidth and you can see opportunities for compressing large objects, the standard binary formatter is as efficient as you're likely to get. Some gains might be made by implementing custom serialization at the object level (as you'll see later); however, there usually isn't much point in implementing your own formatter. We'll implement our own formatter here to complete our implementation by adding in the server side.

For the purposes of this example, we'll implement a new serialization called *time-stamped binary*. As its name suggests, this involves inserting a timestamp at the beginning of each message. The message itself will be binary formatted in the usual manner.

Before we move on to implementing our custom formatter, we need to change the server to be ready to use custom formatting as well. To do this, we need to define a couple of classes that implement IServerChannelSinkProvider and IServerChannelSink, respectively. We'll add these to our InvertFormatter project.

Implementing the Invert Server Channel Sink Provider

Let's look at the code we need to add on the server side, starting with the provider. It's very similar to the client side, so we won't waste any more time discussing it any further:

```vb
Public Class InvertServerChannelSinkProvider
  Implements IServerChannelSinkProvider

  Dim _next As IServerChannelSinkProvider

  Public Function CreateSink( _
    ByVal channel As IChannelReceiver) _
    As IServerChannelSink _
    Implements IServerChannelSinkProvider.CreateSink
    Console.WriteLine( _
      "InvertServerChannelSinkProvider: CreateSink")
    Return New InvertServerChannelSink( _
      _next.CreateSink(channel))
  End Function

  Public Sub GetChannelData( _
    ByVal channelData As IChannelDataStore) _
 Implements IServerChannelSinkProvider.GetChannelData
    Console.WriteLine( _
    "InvertServerChannelSinkProvider: GetChannelData")
    If Not (_next Is Nothing) Then
      _next.GetChannelData(channelData)
  End If
End Sub
Public Property NextSinkProvider() _
    As IServerChannelSinkProvider _
    Implements IServerChannelSinkProvider.Next
    Get
      Console.WriteLine( _
        "InvertServerChannelSinkProvider: " & _
        " Get NextSinkProvider")
      Return _next
    End Get
    Set(ByVal Value As IServerChannelSinkProvider)
      Console.WriteLine( _
        "InvertServerChannelSinkProvider: " & _
        Set NextSinkProvider")
      _next = Value
    End Set
  End Property
End Class
```

Implementing the Invert Server Channel Sink

The server sink class itself is different, however. First, it doesn't have to implement IMessageSink. Message sinks are a client-side concept, and they don't appear on the server side at all. Partly because of this, there tends to be more arguments to most of the methods, as they are effectively doubling up on both interfaces. This is at its most spectacular in the ProcessMessage() method, as you'll see soon.

However, the class starts off the same as on the client side:

```
Public Class InvertServerChannelSink
  Implements IServerChannelSink
  Dim _next As IServerChannelSink
  Public Sub New( _
    ByVal nextSink As IServerChannelSink)
    _next = nextSink
  End Sub
```

The first difference we encounter is that there's no AsyncProcessRequest() method because it won't ever be needed by a server (the client is doing the requesting). However, we still need an AsyncProcessResponse() method:

```
  Public Sub AsyncProcessResponse(ByVal sinkStack _
    As IServerResponseChannelSinkStack, _
    ByVal state As Object, ByVal msg As IMessage, _
    ByVal headers As ITransportHeaders, _
    ByVal stream As System.IO.Stream) _
    Implements IServerChannelSink.AsyncProcessResponse
    Console.WriteLine( _
      "InvertServerChannelSink: AsyncProcessResponse")
  End Sub
```

ProcessMessage() is where things get interesting. There are effectively two sets of arguments to this method, the first of which gets used when the message is in serialized form, and the second of which gets used when the message is in object form. The following arguments are used for serialized messages as shown in the following table.

Argument	Type	In/Out	Description
requestHeaders	ITransportHeaders	In	Headers associated with incoming request stream
requestStream	Stream	In	Incoming request stream
responseHeaders	ITransportHeaders	Out	Headers associated with outgoing response stream
responseStream	Stream	Out	Outgoing response stream

The arguments in the following table are used for messages in object form.

Argument	Type	In/Out	Description
requestMsg	IMessage	In	Incoming request message
responseMsg	IMessage	Out	Outgoing response message

In this implementation, as you'll see, both forms are used. As this is a formatter sink on the server side, the data arrives in serialized form in the requestStream argument, supported by requestHeaders. The goal is to invoke the required method and return the correct response in the responseStream argument:

```
Public Function ProcessMessage(ByVal sinkStack _
  As IServerChannelSinkStack, ByVal requestMsg _
  As IMessage, ByVal requestHeaders _
  As ITransportHeaders, ByVal requestStream _
  As System.IO.Stream, ByRef responseMsg _
  As IMessage, ByRef responseHeaders _
  As ITransportHeaders, ByRef responseStream _
  As System.IO.Stream) As ServerProcessing _
  Implements IServerChannelSink.ProcessMessage
  Console.WriteLine( _
    "InvertServerChannelSink: ProcessMessage")
  Dim formatter As New InvertFormatter()
```

We start by declaring a new formatter object of type InvertFormatter (the name of our custom formatter class that we will define later in this section). Then we deserialize our incoming stream into a fully constituted message object:

```
requestMsg = formatter.Deserialize(requestStream)
```

The next thing we have to do is pass across the URI associated with the object. Confusingly, this is known by different names, depending on whether it's one of the transport headers or whether it's one of the message properties:

```
requestMsg.Properties("__Uri") = _
    requestHeaders("__RequestUri")
```

Finally, before we pass the message on to the next sink, we need to clear the request stream. If we don't do this, the next sink will throw an exception.

```
requestStream = Nothing
```

Now we can pass our message object through to the next sink. Note that this time around, requestMsg is the critical input argument, and responseMsg is the output argument.

```
_next.ProcessMessage( sinkStack, requestMsg, _
    Nothing,Nothing,responseMsg, Nothing, Nothing)
```

After we get our response, we need to serialize it to send it back to the client, so we create a memory stream and serialize the message to it:

```
responseStream = New MemoryStream()
formatter.Serialize(responseStream, responseMsg)
```

Finally, we instantiate an empty transport headers object and return a "processing complete" status back to the calling sink:

```
responseHeaders = New TransportHeaders()
Return ServerProcessing.Complete
End Function
```

The remaining methods and properties are similar to their client-side counterparts, so we won't discuss them any further here:

```vb
    Public Function GetResponseStream(ByVal sinkStack _
      As IServerResponseChannelSinkStack, _
      ByVal state As Object, ByVal msg As IMessage, _
      ByVal headers As ITransportHeaders) _
      As System.IO.Stream _
      Implements IServerChannelSink.GetResponseStream
      Console.WriteLine( _
        "InvertServerChannelSink: GetResponseStream")
      Return _next.GetResponseStream( _
        sinkStack, state, msg, headers)
    End Function
    Public ReadOnly Property NextChannelSink() _
      As IServerChannelSink _
      Implements IServerChannelSink.NextChannelSink
      Get
        Return _next
      End Get
    End Property
    Public ReadOnly Property Properties() _
      As System.Collections.IDictionary _
      Implements IServerChannelSink.Properties
      Get
        Console.WriteLine( _
          "InvertServerChannelSink: Get Properties")
        Return _next.Properties()
      End Get
    End Property
End Class
```

Implementing the Custom Invert Formatter

It's time to write our formatter class. A formatter class has to implement the class `IRemotingFormatter` in the `System.Runtime.Remoting.Messaging` namespace. Following are the properties and methods of the interface (which inherits from `IFormatter`):

- **Binder**: Gets or sets the serialization binder.
- **Context**: Gets or sets the streaming context used for serialization and deserialization.
- **SurrogateSelector**: Gets or sets the surrogate selector used by the current formatter.
- **Deserialize()**: Gets invoked when an object is to be deserialized from a stream.
- **Serialize()**: Gets invoked when an object is to be serialized into a stream.

Let's now add our implementation to our `InvertFormatter` project. First, we need to import another namespace:

```
Imports System.Runtime.Remoting.Messaging
Imports System.Runtime.Remoting.Channels
Imports _
   System.Runtime.Serialization.Formatters.Binary
Imports System.IO
Imports System
```

We need this for a `DateTime` structure later.

Here's how the class starts. Two alternative serialization methods are available, depending on whether or not the information in the transport headers is to be used. In our example, we're only using the first one, so we'll focus on that. All we do is get the current time, and serialize that ahead of the rest of the object in question:

```
Public Class InvertFormatter
  Implements IRemotingFormatter

  Public Sub Serialize( _
    ByVal serializationStream As System.IO.Stream, _
    ByVal graph As Object) _
    Implements IRemotingFormatter.Serialize
    Console.WriteLine( _
      "InvertFormatter: Serialize (1)")
    Dim formatter As New BinaryFormatter()
    Dim timeStamp As DateTime
    timeStamp = DateTime.UtcNow
    formatter.Serialize( _
       serializationStream, timeStamp)
    formatter.Serialize(serializationStream, graph)
  End Sub
```

The alternative serializer is left as an exercise for you:

```
Public Sub Serialize( _
  ByVal serializationStream As System.IO.Stream, _
  ByVal graph As Object, ByVal headers() _
  As Header) _
  Implements IRemotingFormatter.Serialize
  Console.WriteLine( _
    "InvertFormatter: Serialize (2)")
End Sub
```

Deserializing is obviously the inverse of the serialization process:

```
Public Function Deserialize( _
  ByVal serializationStream As System.IO.Stream) _
  As Object _
  Implements IRemotingFormatter.Deserialize
```

CHAPTER 3 ■ CUSTOM REMOTING

```
    Console.WriteLine( _
      "InvertFormatter: Deserialize (1)")
    Dim formatter As New BinaryFormatter()
    Dim timeStamp As DateTime
    Dim msg As Object
    timeStamp = formatter.Deserialize( _
        serializationStream)
    msg = formatter.Deserialize(serializationStream)

    Console.WriteLine( _
      "    Deserialized at <{0}>", timeStamp)
    Return msg
  End Function
  Public Function Deserialize( _
    ByVal serializationStream _
    As System.IO.Stream, ByVal handler _
    As HeaderHandler) As Object _
    Implements IRemotingFormatter.Deserialize
    Console.WriteLine( _
      "InvertFormatter: Deserialize (2)")
  End Function
```

The remaining properties are used for more specialized purposes, and we won't be looking at them in any detail. First, the property `Context` would be used to specify a streaming context. This essentially describes the source or destination of the stream, along with any application-specific context information:

```
  Public Property Context() _
    As System.Runtime.Serialization.StreamingContext _
    Implements IRemotingFormatter.Context
    Get
      Console.WriteLine( _
        "InvertFormatter: Get Context")
    End Get
    Set( ByVal Value As
      System.Runtime.Serialization.StreamingContext)
      Console.WriteLine( _
        "InvertFormatter: Set Context")
    End Set
  End Property
```

The property `Binder` allows us to specify a different *serialization binder*. This is a reference to an object that controls how a serialized object is bound to a particular type:

```
Public Property Binder() As _
  System.Runtime.Serialization.SerializationBinder _
  Implements IRemotingFormatter.Binder
    Get
      Console.WriteLine( _
        "InvertFormatter: Get Binder")
    End Get
```

```
    Set( ByVal Value As _
    System.Runtime.Serialization.SerializationBinder)
      Console.WriteLine( _
          "InvertFormatter: Set Binder")
    End Set
  End Property
```

Finally, the property SurrogateSelector would allow us to specify a *surrogate selector*. This is a reference to another object that handles the serialization of a given object or class of objects. Usually, objects contain whatever information they need to serialize themselves, either by specifying the attribute <Serializable>, or by implementing the interface ISerializable (which we'll look at in the next section). However, they may also use a surrogate to do the serialization for them; such a surrogate object implements the interface ISerializationSurrogate, which bears a remarkable resemblance to ISerializable. We'll look at this briefly when we discuss custom serialization later in this chapter.

```
Public Property SurrogateSelector() _
 As System.Runtime.Serialization.ISurrogateSelector _
 Implements IRemotingFormatter.SurrogateSelector
    Get
    Console.WriteLine( _
       "InvertFormatter: Get SurrogateSelector")
    End Get
    Set( ByVal Value As _
 System.Runtime.Serialization.ISurrogateSelector)
       Console.WriteLine( _
          "InvertFormatter: Set SurrogateSelector")
    End Set
  End Property
End Class
```

Modifying InvertServer

To use the new server channel sink, we also have to change the server code itself by using the same constructor for TcpChannel that we used on the client side:

```
Module InvertServer
  Sub Main()
    Dim channel As TcpChannel
    Dim properties As New Hashtable()
    Dim provider As _
        New InvertServerChannelSinkProvider()
    Console.WriteLine("Server started")
    properties("port") = 8086
    properties("name") = "jon"
    provider = New InvertServerChannelSinkProvider()
    channel = New TcpChannel( _
        properties, Nothing, provider)
    ChannelServices.RegisterChannel(channel)
```

```
RemotingConfiguration.RegisterWellKnownServiceType( _
    GetType(MyInvert), "MyInvert.rem", _
    WellKnownObjectMode.SingleCall)
  Console.ReadLine()
  End Sub
End Module
```

Notice that this time around, we need to pass in some properties to the constructor. First, we need to specify the port, and then we need to specify a name for the channel, something that we haven't had to do before. This is massively important because if you leave this out, your implementation will be confused as to which version to use, and it won't work correctly. Finally, you'll need to import the InvertFormatter project, so add the following line to the top of InvertServer:

```
Imports InvertFormatter
```

Modifying the Message Sink

Finally, to use the new formatter, we also need to make a change to InvertClientChannelSink. SyncProcessMessage():

```
Public Function SyncProcessMessage( _
  ByVal msg As IMessage) As IMessage _
  Implements IMessageSink.SyncProcessMessage
  Console.WriteLine( _
    "InvertClientChannelSink: SyncProcessMessage")
  Dim outHeaders As New TransportHeaders()
  Dim outStream As New MemoryStream()
  Dim inHeaders As ITransportHeaders
  Dim inStream As Stream
  Dim formatter As New InvertFormatter()
  formatter.Serialize(outStream, msg)
  ...
End Function
```

Running the Example

If we run all this, here's what we see on the server side (see the following figure).

Look closely, and you can see our server channel sink provider being hooked into the provider chain, and our formatter sink being created. You also can see a message containing a method invocation arriving at our sink's `ProcessMessage()` method. This is then passed on to our formatter for deserialization into a message object, and we can see the timestamp extracted from it. This message object is then passed into the server-side sink chain, where it eventually ends up invoking our server object with input argument 1.234. The return value is calculated to be 0.810372771474878. We receive this back in our channel sink, which passes it on to the formatter again to serialize into a stream to be sent back to the client. The process is repeated twice more for the text `"ABCDE"` and the object `{"Hello", "world"}`.

The following figure shows what we see on the client.

Again, we see the sink provider being created and fit into the chain of providers, followed by the creation of our formatter sink. The initial method invocation results in a message arriving at our sink's `SyncProcessMessage()` method, which serializes it and sends it on to the transport sink. We receive the message back, deserialize it into a message object, and pass it back to the caller. This happens three times, before the client finally outputs all the results, which look the same as they did before, indicating that everything's still working fine.

Custom Serialization

We can improve on the standard serialization provided by simply adding the `<Serializable>` attribute to our class definition. The most obvious reason to do this is to cut down on bandwidth requirements. Before we move on to implementing a custom channel implementation, it's worth taking a brief detour to look at this.

To define a custom serialization format, our class must implement the `ISerializable` interface, so that it can define its own serialization and deserialization rules. Here's how we might do this for a class called `MyMBVType`:

```
Imports System
<Serializable> _
Public Class MyMBVType
  Implements ISerializable
  Public Sub GetObjectData( _
    ByVal info As SerializationInfo, _
```

```
        ByVal context As StreamingContext) _
    Implements ISerializable.GetObjectData
      ' Serialize the object in a special format...
    End Sub
    Public Sub New(ByVal info As SerializationInfo, _
                ByVal context As StreamingContext) _
      ' Deserialize the object from
      ' the special format...
    End Sub
    ' Plus other members of our MBV type...
End Class
```

You'll notice that we've had to add some extra code on top of implementing ISerializable.

The GetObjectData() method is originally defined in the ISerializable interface. We must override this method, and write some code to serialize our object in our special format.

The New() method is a deserialization constructor, called implicitly when the object is deserialized. In this constructor, we write some code to deserialize the data that we serialized in the GetObjectData() method.

Now that we know the basics, let's see how we might implement a custom serialization format.

Defining a Custom Serialization Format

In this section, we'll see an example of an MBV class that would benefit from having a custom serialization format. This will allow instances of the class to be marshaled more efficiently to and from remote methods. In our example, we'll examine a class called Equation. As its name suggests, the class represents a mathematical equation such as the following:

$$y = 3x^2 + 2x + 10$$

Implementing a Serializable MBV Class

The Equation class stores the coefficients of x^2, x, and units. The class also calculates the results of this equation, for values of x ranging from 0 to 50. These values will be stored in an array of Points, to allow the equation to be plotted efficiently in a Windows Form (without having to be recalculated each time the form is repainted). To make our application even more exciting, the Equation class will also store a Color, so we can plot each equation in a nice color.

Here's an initial version of the Equation class, without custom serialization:

```
Imports System
Imports System.Drawing
Namespace MyRemoteNamespace
  <Serializable()> _
  Public Class Equation
    ' The (x, y) points for this equation
    Public Const mNumPoints As Integer = 50
    Private mPoints(mNumPoints - 1) As Point
    ' The coefficients of X-squared, X, and units
    Private mX2, mX1, mX0 As Integer
    ' The color to use when the equation is plotted
```

```vb
      Private mLineColor As Color
      ' Constructor, called by the application
      ' to create a new Equation
      Public Sub New(ByVal LineColor As Color, _
        ByVal X2 As Integer, _
        ByVal X1 As Integer, _
        ByVal X0 As Integer)
        ' Store the equation coefficients
        ' and line color
        mX2 = X2
        mX1 = X1
        mX0 = X0
        mLineColor = LineColor
        ' Calculate all the points for the equation
        Dim X As Integer
        For X = 0 To mNumPoints - 1
          mPoints(X) = _
          New Point(X, (mX2 * X ^ 2) + (mX1 * X) + mX0)
        Next
      End Sub
      ' Property to get the equation's points
      Public ReadOnly Property Points() As Point()
        Get
          Return mPoints
        End Get
      End Property
      ' Property to get the equation's color
      Public ReadOnly Property LineColor() As Color
        Get
          Return mLineColor
        End Get
      End Property
    End Class
End Namespace
```

Create a new class library called EquationStore and add the class to it. If we use this version of the Equation class in our application, the serialized format for Equation objects will be quite wasteful. For every Equation object, we'll serialize 50 Point objects, 3 integers (mX2, mX1, and mX0), and a Color object. In a simple benchmark test that serialized an ArrayList of 5 equations, the serialized data is 5,201 bytes in size. We can dramatically improve this situation by defining a custom serialization format for the Equation class.

Specifically, there's no reason to serialize the 50 Point objects. The Points help us plot the equation efficiently on the screen, but they're not essential when we serialize the equation. All we need to serialize are the coefficients and the color; the Points can be recalculated when the Equation object is deserialized. This significantly reduces the amount of data we need to serialize; in the same benchmark test, the size of a serialized ArrayList of 5 equations is reduced from 5,201 bytes to 653 bytes. In other words, we can achieve an order of magnitude reduction in the amount of data marshaled over the network when Equation objects are passed to or from a remote method.

The easiest way to prevent particular fields from being serialized is by using the `<NonSerialized()>` attribute as shown next. In this example, the `mPoints` array will not be serialized when `Equation` objects are passed across remoting boundaries:

```
<Serializable()> _
Public Class Equation
   Public Const mNumPoints As Integer = 50
   ' Non-serialized fields
   <NonSerialized()> _
   Private mPoints(mNumPoints - 1) As Point
   ' Serialized fields
   Private mX2, mX1, mX0 As Integer
   Private mLineColor As Color
   ' Plus methods, etc...
End Class
```

The `<NonSerialized()>` attribute is ideal in simple situations, where we just want to inhibit particular fields from being serialized. In more complex situations, we might want to take more control over the serialization format. For example, we might want to serialize a summary of our object's state, or serialize the state using different data types. In these scenarios, we can implement the `ISerializable` interface and define specialized methods to perform the serialization and deserialization. The following code shows how to define the custom serialization format for the `Equation` class:

```
Imports System
Imports System.Drawing

Namespace MyRemoteNamespace
  <Serializable()> _
  Public Class Equation
    Implements ISerializable
    ' The (x, y) points for this equation
    Public Const mNumPoints As Integer = 50
    Private mPoints(mNumPoints - 1) As Point
    ' The coefficients of X-squared, X, and units
    Private mX2, mX1, mX0 As Integer
    ' Store the color to use when the
    ' equation is plotted
    Private mLineColor As Color
    ' Custom serialization method
    Public Sub GetObjectData( _
       ByVal info As SerializationInfo, _
       ByVal context As StreamingContext) _
       Implements ISerializable.GetObjectData
       ' Just serialize the equation's
       ' coefficients and color
```

```vb
            info.AddValue("X2", mX2)
            info.AddValue("X1", mX1)
            info.AddValue("X0", mX0)
            info.AddValue("LineColor", _
                mLineColor, GetType(Color))
        End Sub
        ' Deserialization constructor
        Public Sub New(ByVal info As SerializationInfo, _
                       ByVal context As StreamingContext)
            ' Deserialize the equation's
            ' coefficients and color
            mX2 = CInt(info.GetValue("X2", _
               GetType(Integer)))
            mX1 = CInt(info.GetValue("X1", _
               GetType(Integer)))
            mX0 = CInt(info.GetValue("X0", _
               GetType(Integer)))
            mLineColor = CType( _
               info.GetValue("LineColor", _
               GetType(Color)), Color)
            ' Calculate all the points for the equation
            Dim X As Integer
            For X = 0 To mNumPoints - 1
               mPoints(X) = New _
                 Point(X, (mX2 * X ^ 2) + (mX1 * X) + mX0)
            Next
        End Sub
        ' New() constructor, Points() and
        ' LineColor() as before...
    End Class
End Namespace
```

Note that the <NonSerialized()> attribute has been removed. Also note the following points about the Equation class:

- The Equation class implements the ISerializable interface.

- The GetDataObject() method serializes the equation's coefficients and color, but not the equation's Points. To serialize a data item, we call AddValue() on the SerializationInfo object; note that we must provide a textual name for each piece of data to assist the deserialization process:

    ```vb
    info.AddValue("X2", mX2)
    info.AddValue("X1", mX1)
    info.AddValue("X0", mX0)
    info.AddValue("LineColor", mLineColor, _
        GetType(Color))
    ```

- The deserialization constructor deserializes the equation's coefficients and color, but not the equation's Points (because these weren't serialized). To deserialize data, we call GetValue() on the SerializationInfo object; we use the textual name to identify which item of data we are deserializing:

```
mX2 = CInt(info.GetValue("X2", GetType(Integer)))
mX1 = CInt(info.GetValue("X1", GetType(Integer)))
mX0 = CInt(info.GetValue("X0", GetType(Integer)))
mLineColor = CType(info.GetValue("LineColor", _
    GetType(Color)), Color)
```

- The deserialization constructor then recalculates the Points for the equation using the coefficient values. Note that the extra time spent recreating the points during deserialization is not nearly as costly as marshaling the data; the bottleneck here is the data marshaling, not the computational effort to recreate the mPoints array:

```
Dim X As Integer
For X = 0 To mNumPoints - 1
  mPoints(X) = New Point(X, (mX2 * X ^ 2) + _
        (mX1 * X) + mX0)
Next
```

Implementing the Remoting Class

The source file EquationStore.vb also defines an MBR class named EquationStore, which is the remotable class in this example. Here's the code for the EquationStore class. This code is located in the same file as the Equation class:

```
Imports System
Imports System.Drawing
Imports System.Collections
Imports System.IO
Imports _
  System.Runtime.Serialization.Formatters.Binary
Imports System.Runtime.Serialization

Namespace MyRemoteNamespace
  ' This is the Remoting class in this example
  Public Class EquationStore
    Inherits MarshalByRefObject
    ' Receive an ArrayList from the client
    ' app, and write to a file
    Public Sub WriteEquations(_
      ByVal equations As ArrayList)
      Dim stream As FileStream = Nothing
      Try
        stream = File.Create("Equations.dat")
        Dim formatter As New BinaryFormatter()
        formatter.Serialize(stream, equations)
```

```vb
      Finally
        If Not stream Is Nothing Then
          stream.Close()
        End If
      End Try
    End Sub
    ' Load an ArrayList from a file, and
    ' return to client app
    Public Function ReadEquations() As ArrayList
      Dim stream As FileStream = Nothing
      Dim equations As ArrayList = Nothing
      Try
        stream = File.OpenRead("Equations.dat")
        Dim formatter As New BinaryFormatter()
        equations = _
          CType(formatter.Deserialize(stream), _
          ArrayList)
      Finally
        If Not stream Is Nothing Then
          stream.Close()
        End If
      End Try
      Return equations
    End Function
  End Class
  ...
End Namespace
```

Note the following points about the `EquationStore` class:

- The `WriteEquations()` method receives an `ArrayList` (of `Equation` objects) from the client application, and writes the data to a file named `Equations.dat`. We've used a `BinaryFormatter` to serialize the data, but we could have chosen any file-storage mechanism (for example, SOAP serialization, comma-separated values, and so on). Binary serialization seems the best option in this case, because we can take advantage of the efficient serialization format for `Equation` objects.

- The `ReadEquations()` method loads an `ArrayList` (of `Equation` objects) from the file `Equations.dat`, and returns the `ArrayList` to the client application. This will cause the `ArrayList` (and each of its `Equation` objects) to be serialized in transit.

■**Note** If you want to use SOAP formatting rather than binary formatting to save and reload the `ArrayList` to disk, create a `SoapFormatter` rather than a `BinaryFormatter`. Then import `System.Runtime.Serialization.Formatters.Soap` rather than `System.Runtime.Serialization.Formatters.Binary`.

Compile the `EquationStore` and `Equation` classes, including the appropriate references.

Implementing the Host

Let's write a simple server application, `CustomSerializationServer`, to host the remotable object. The server program registers a TCP channel on port 6000, and registers the `EquationStore` class as a singleton remoting service type:

```vb
Imports System
Imports System.Runtime.Remoting
Imports System.Runtime.Remoting.Channels
Imports System.Runtime.Remoting.Channels.Tcp

Public Class CustomSerializationServer
    Public Shared Sub Main()
      Dim aChannel As New TcpChannel(6000)
      ChannelServices.RegisterChannel(aChannel)
      Try
RemotingConfiguration.RegisterWellKnownServiceType( _
          GetType(MyRemoteNamespace.EquationStore), _
          "EquationStore.rem", _
          WellKnownObjectMode.Singleton)
        Console.WriteLine( _
          "CustomSerializationServer running. " & _
          "Press Enter to quit.")
        Console.ReadLine()
      Catch ex As Exception
        Console.WriteLine( _
          "CustomSerializationServer error: {0}", _
          ex.Message)
      End Try
    End Sub
End Class
```

Compile this server application, remembering to include any necessary references, and then start the server application in a command prompt window.

Implementing the Client

Now let's write a simple client application, `EquationPlotterForm`, to create and plot equations. When the user closes the Windows Form, we call `WriteEquations()` on a remote `EquationStore` object to store the equation data on the remote machine. When the application is reopened, we call `ReadEquations()` on a remote `EquationStore` object to reload the equation data; we then plot the equations on the form. The following figure shows how the form looks.

Here's the full source code for the client application. The relevant parts relating to custom serialization and remoting are highlighted; we'll discuss these sections after the code listing (for more information about the graphics-related code, see Visual Studio .NET help).

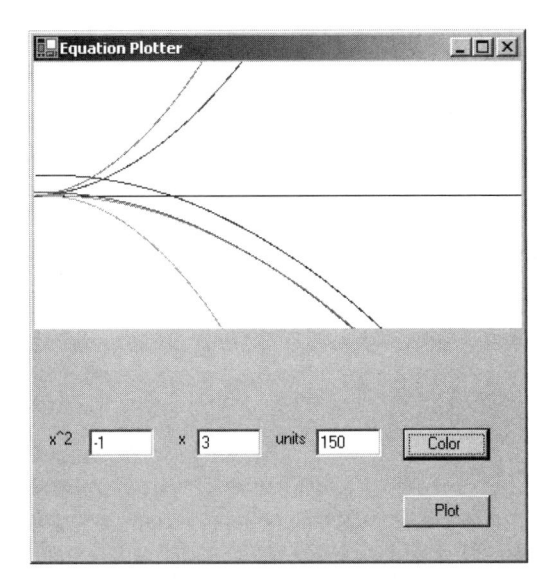

We start by importing some namespaces that we'll need later. Then we begin the definition of the `EquationPlotterForm` form class by declaring a couple of member fields:

```
Imports System
Imports System.Runtime.Serialization
Imports System.Runtime.Remoting
Imports MyRemoteNamespace
Imports System.Drawing
Imports System.Windows.Forms
Public Class EquationPlotterForm
  Inherits System.Windows.Forms.Form
  ' The collection of Equation objects to plot
  Private mEquations As ArrayList
  ' The plotting area on the form
  Private mRect As Rectangle
```

The next method loads an `ArrayList` of `Equation` objects from the remote object when the form loads:

```
Private Sub EquationPlotterForm_Load( _
    ByVal sender As Object, _
    ByVal e As EventArgs) Handles MyBase.Load
    ' Set the plottable area on the form
    mRect = New Rectangle( _
        0, 0, CInt(Width), CInt(Height / 2))
```

```vb
    ' Get a proxy for the remote object
    Dim obj As Object = Activator.GetObject( _
      GetType(MyRemoteNamespace.EquationStore), _
      "tcp://localhost:6000/EquationStore.rem")
    ' Convert to actual type of remote object
    Dim aRemoteEquationStore As _
      MyRemoteNamespace.EquationStore = _
      CType(obj, MyRemoteNamespace.EquationStore)
    ' Read ArrayList of Equations (use
    ' empty ArrayList if errors)
    Try
      mEquations = _
        aRemoteEquationStore.ReadEquations()
    Catch Ex As Exception
      mEquations = New ArrayList()
      MessageBox.Show(Ex.Message, _
      "Couldn't load equations from Remoting server", _
        MessageBoxButtons.OK, _
        MessageBoxIcon.Error)
    End Try
  End Sub
```

Next we add a method that passes an `ArrayList` of `Equation` objects to a remote object when the form closes:

```vb
  Private Sub EquationPlotterForm_Closed( _
    ByVal sender As Object, _
    ByVal e As EventArgs) Handles MyBase.Closed
    ' Get a proxy for the remote object
    Dim obj As Object = Activator.GetObject( _
      GetType(MyRemoteNamespace.EquationStore), _
      "tcp://localhost:6000/EquationStore.rem")
    ' Convert to actual type of remote object
    Dim aRemoteEquationStore As _
      MyRemoteNamespace.EquationStore = _
      CType(obj, MyRemoteNamespace.EquationStore)
    ' Write ArrayList of Equations
    ' (display message if any errors)
    Try
      aRemoteEquationStore.WriteEquations(mEquations)
    Catch Ex As Exception
      MessageBox.Show(Ex.Message, _
        "Remoting server could not save equations", _
        MessageBoxButtons.OK, _
        MessageBoxIcon.Error)
    End Try
  End Sub
```

Next we handle the Click events for the buttons:

```vb
Private Sub btnColor_Click( _
  ByVal sender As System.Object, _
  ByVal e As System.EventArgs) _
  Handles btnColor.Click
  Dim dlgColor As New ColorDialog()
  dlgColor.ShowDialog(Me)
  btnColor.BackColor = dlgColor.Color
End Sub
Private Sub btnPlot_Click( _
  ByVal sender As System.Object, _
  ByVal e As System.EventArgs) _
  Handles btnPlot.Click
  ' Are any text fields blank?
  If txtX2.TextLength = 0 Or _
    txtX1.TextLength = 0 Or _
    txtX0.TextLength = 0 Then
    ' Display an error message, and
    ' return immediately
    MessageBox.Show( _
      "Please fill in all text boxes", _
      "Error", MessageBoxButtons.OK, _
      MessageBoxIcon.Error)
    Return
  End If
  ' Get the coordinate values entered in
  ' the text fields
  Dim X2 As Integer = Integer.Parse(txtX2.Text)
  Dim X1 As Integer = Integer.Parse(txtX1.Text)
  Dim X0 As Integer = Integer.Parse(txtX0.Text)
  mEquations.Add( _
    New Equation(btnColor.BackColor, X2, X1, X0))
  Me.Invalidate(mRect)
End Sub
```

We have not included the Windows Form Designer-generated code for brevity, so you should note that txtX2, txtX1, and txtX0 refer to the text boxes on the form (left to right), while btnColor and btnPlot refer to the Color and Plot buttons respectively.

Finally we handle the Paint event for the form:

```vb
Public Overloads Sub EquationPlotterForm_Paint( _
  ByVal sender As Object, _
  ByVal e As PaintEventArgs) _
  Handles MyBase.Paint
  ' Display a white rectangle for the
  ' plottable area
```

```vbnet
      e.Graphics.FillRectangle( _
        New SolidBrush(Color.White), mRect)
      ' Draw a horizontal line for the X axis
      Dim horizAxis = CInt(mRect.Height / 2)
      e.Graphics.DrawLine(New Pen(Color.Black), _
        0, _
        horizAxis, _
        CInt(Width), _
        horizAxis)
      ' Graphics-related code, to plot the
      ' equations nicely :-)
      e.Graphics.SetClip(mRect)
      e.Graphics.TranslateTransform(0, horizAxis)
      e.Graphics.ScaleTransform( _
        mRect.Width/Equation.mNumPoints, -0.1)
      ' Loop through the equations in the ArrayList
      Dim I As Integer
      For I = 0 To mEquations.Count - 1

        ' Get next Equation, and call DrawLines
        ' to plot its Points
        Dim eq As Equation = _
          CType(mEquations(I), Equation)
        e.Graphics.DrawLines( _
          New Pen(eq.LineColor), eq.Points)
      Next
    End Sub
End Class
```

Note the following points about the `EquationPlotterForm` class:

- `EquationPlotterForm` has an `ArrayList` field named `mEquations`, which is initialized in the `EquationPlotterForm_Load()` method when the form loads. Here, we call the `ReadEquations()` method on the remote `EquationStore` object to try to reload an `ArrayList` of previously stored equations. Remember, the `ArrayList` (and its `Equation` objects) will be implicitly serialized when returned from the `ReadEquations()` method, and then implicitly deserialized when received by our client application.

- If the `ReadEquations()` method throws an exception (maybe because there is no `Equations.dat` file on the remote machine), our client application creates an empty `ArrayList` instead.

- When the form is closed, we call the `WriteEquations()` method on the remote `EquationStore` object, to save the `ArrayList` on the remote machine. The `ArrayList` (and its `Equation` objects) will be implicitly serialized when we call `WriteEquations()`, and then implicitly deserialized when received by the remote method.

- The `btnPlot_Click()` method plots a new equation using the coefficients and color specified by the user. We create a new `Equation` object to remember the equation's coefficients and color, and then call `Me.Invalidate(mRect)`. This raises a `Paint` event on the form to cause the form's plottable area to be repainted.

> **Note** When we create a new `Equation` object here, we are *not* using the deserialization constructor. We are using the other constructor in the `Equation` class, which initializes the equation's coefficients and color using the values we pass into the constructor. The constructor also calculates all the points for the equation to avoid having to recalculate the points every time the form is repainted.

- The `EquationPlotterForm_Paint()` method handles the `Paint` event on the form. The method loops through all the `Equation` objects in the `ArrayList`, and calls `DrawLines()` on each `Equation` object. `DrawLines()` is a standard method in the `Graphics` class, and draws lines joining all the `Points` in a `Point` array.

Running the Example

Compile the client application, including all the required references during compilation. Then run the client application in a command prompt window (make sure the `CustomizedSerializationServer` application is running before you start `EquationPlotterForm`).

The client application displays an empty form initially. Enter some coefficients, and click Plot to plot the equation on the form. Repeat this exercise several times to plot a number of equations. When you are happy with your work, close the form. Then reopen the form immediately; the equations should be plotted the same as before.

This confirms that the `ArrayList` of `Equation` objects has been successfully serialized and deserialized to and from the remote object. It also confirms that the data was persisted to `Equations.dat` using the same serialization mechanism. In both cases, the `GetObjectData()` method was called to serialize each `Equation` object, and the deserialization constructor was called to deserialize each `Equation` object. We have optimized the behavior of our application by reducing the amount of data that is passed over the network and written to disk.

Channels with Custom Transport Protocols

We're on the final stage of our journey now, as we look into custom transport protocols. In this section, we'll implement a custom transport sink. This could take a number of forms; for example, it might use MSMQ (Microsoft Message Queuing), or named pipes, or any number of alternative transport mechanisms. Why would you want to do this? In the case of MSMQ, you might want to use its reliable transport mechanism to provide a higher level of service, particularly if using one-way methods.

Channel Interfaces

Implementing a custom channel involves putting together a class that implements the standard interfaces `IChannel`, `IChannelSender` (on the client side), and `IChannelReceiver` (on the server side), and hooking it into the .NET remoting infrastructure. All these interfaces can be found in the `System.Runtime.Remoting.Channels` namespace. Here are the properties and methods of the `IChannel` interface:

- `ChannelName`: Gets the name of the channel.
- `ChannelPriority`: Gets the channel priority.
- `Parse()`: Gets invoked to break up an incoming URL into an object URI and a channel URI.

Here's the same for `IChannelReceiver`:

- `ChannelData`: Gets the channel data store, containing channel-specific data.
- `GetUrlsForUri()`: Gets invoked to get an array of all the possible URLs for a given URI.
- `StartListening()`: Gets invoked to start listening for incoming calls.
- `StopListening()`: Gets invoked to stop listening for incoming calls.

Finally, here's the lone method for `IChannelSender`:

- `CreateMessageSink()`: Gets invoked to create the initial message sink as the head of the chain.

On the client side, we need to provide a transport sink as the final link in the chain; whereas on the server side, it's the first link in the chain. On the server side, we also need to actually create the sink chain. Let's see how it all fits together with a simple example.

Implementing a Custom TCP/IP Socket Channel

For our custom channel implementation, we'll implement a simple TCP/IP socket channel. Although one exists already, we don't want to clutter up the discussion by introducing some alien technology at this stage. If we concentrate on something essentially simple like sockets, we'll be able to focus on the methodology.

Our protocol will be really simple. Each message consists of the serialized method call message, preceded by its length as a 2-byte integer. Our server will be sitting listening on a socket. When it receives a connection, it will spawn a new socket to receive the incoming message. After processing the message, the socket will die. The client will simply establish a connection, send the message, and await the response. When it receives the response, it will drop the connection. As you'll see, it's not a particularly industrial-strength implementation either, but the point is to focus on the surrounding framework that allows us to do this.

Implementing the Invert Channel Class

The first thing we need to do is add a new project to our Invert example, called `InvertChannel`. This project will contain the following classes associated with our new channel:

- The channel class
- The server transport sink
- The client transport sink
- The client transport sink provider

In the grand tradition of `TcpChannel`, we'll implement both the client and server sides within the same class, so the channel class has to implement the three interfaces `IChannel`, `IchannelReceiver`, and `IChannelSender`.

Here's how it starts. The constructor has the same signature as the "with properties" version of the `TcpChannel` constructor. If you want, you can get a default implementation of this by inheriting from the `BaseChannelWithProperties` class. By the way, there are similar base classes for channel sinks, and so on, if you want to use them.

We'll need to import some namespaces to handle the sockets, and the memory streams that we're going to use:

```
Imports System.Net.Sockets
Imports System.Net
Imports System.IO
```

We begin by saving the references to the client or sink providers, and establish whether we're on the client or server side:

```
Public Class InvertChannel
  Implements IChannel
  Implements IChannelReceiver
  Implements IChannelSender
  Dim _clientProvider  As IClientChannelSinkProvider
  Dim _serverProvider  As IServerChannelSinkProvider
  Dim _isServer As Boolean
  Dim _channelURIs As String()
  Dim _channelDataStore As ChannelDataStore
  Dim _transportSink As InvertServerTransportSink
  Dim _sock As Socket
  Dim _port As Integer

  Public Sub New(ByVal properties As IDictionary, _
    ByVal clientSinkProvider _
    As IClientChannelSinkProvider, _
    ByVal serverSinkProvider _
    As IServerChannelSinkProvider)
    Console.WriteLine("InvertChannel: New")
    _clientProvider  = clientSinkProvider
    _serverProvider  = serverSinkProvider
    If _serverProvider Is Nothing Then
      _isServer = False
    Else
      _isServer = True
    End If
```

The remainder of the constructor is purely for the benefit of the server side. We need to instantiate the channel data store, and populate it from the current sink provider chain.

```
    If _isServer Then
      ReDim _channelURIs(1)
      _channelURIs(0) = "MyChannel.rem"
      _channelDataStore = New _
        ChannelDataStore(_channelURIs)
        Dim prov As IServerChannelSinkProvider
```

```
    While Not (prov Is Nothing)
      prov.GetChannelData(_channelDataStore)
      prov = prov.Next
    End While
```

Next, we use a helper method from `ChannelServices` to create our server sink chain. This provides the dispatch channel sink at the far end, and also invokes the server provider to create the formatter sink in the middle, as well as any other sinks that we may have specified. The helper method returns a reference to the head of the chain:

```
    Dim sink As IServerChannelSink
    sink = _
      ChannelServices.CreateServerChannelSinkChain( _
        _serverProvider, Me)
```

Having done that, we need to insert our transport sink at the head of the chain. This is the first time we've actually had to do this with a sink, because previously we've just been inserting sinks in the middle or at the end of the chain. This new head sink is implemented in a completely new class that we'll come to in a minute, `InvertServerTransportSink`. Finally, we extract the TCP/IP port number from the incoming property dictionary and start listening. The methods `StartListening()` and `StopListening()`, despite being defined as part of the IChannelReceiver interface, are not—surprisingly—nvoked by the framework. Instead, we have to call them:

```
    _transportSink = _
        New InvertServerTransportSink(sink)
    _port = properties("port")
    StartListening(Nothing)
  End If
End Sub
```

The next couple of properties return the name and priority of the channel, respectively:

```
Public ReadOnly Property ChannelName() As String _
  Implements IChannel.ChannelName
  Get
    Console.WriteLine( _
      "InvertChannel: Get ChannelName")
    Return "jon"
  End Get
End Property
Public ReadOnly Property ChannelPriority() _
  As Integer _
  Implements IChannel.ChannelPriority
  Get
    Console.WriteLine( _
      "InvertChannel: Get ChannelPriority")
    Return 1
  End Get
End Property
```

The next property returns the channel store on the server side:

```
Public ReadOnly Property ChannelData() As Object _
  Implements IChannelReceiver.ChannelData
  Get
    Console.WriteLine( _
      "InvertChannel: Get ChannelData")
    If _isServer Then
      Return _channelDataStore
    Else
      Return Nothing
    End If
  End Get
End Property
```

The next two methods don't actually get invoked in this implementation, although we have to provide an empty implementation to complete the interface. The first one, Parse(), breaks up an incoming URL into an object URI and channel URI:

```
Public Function Parse(ByVal url As String, _
  ByRef objectURI As String) As String _
  Implements IChannel.Parse
  Console.WriteLine("InvertChannel: Parse")
  Return Nothing
End Function
```

The other one, GetUrlsForUri(), returns an array of possible URLs for a given object URI:

```
Public Function GetUrlsForUri( _
  ByVal objectURI As String) As String() _
  Implements  IChannelReceiver.GetUrlsForUri
  Console.WriteLine("InvertChannel: GetUrlsForUri")
  Return Nothing
End Function
```

The next method is used to create the message sink at the head of the client channel sink chain. In fact, the first thing we do is add a new sink provider—the transport sink provider—at the *end* of the client-side sink provider chain. So on the client side, we allow the standard provider mechanism to create the transport sink, as opposed to the server side, where we instantiate it directly. This makes perfect sense, because on the client side, it's right at the end of the chain, whereas on the server side, it's at the beginning. After we've added our transport sink provider, we invoke the client sink provider at the head of the sink provider chain to create the message sink. If you recall, this sink provider was passed to us at channel instantiation time, and so is the formatter sink provider, and the formatter sink also has a message sink:

```
Public Function CreateMessageSink( _
    ByVal url As String, _
    ByVal remoteChannelData As Object, _
    ByRef objectURI As String) As IMessageSink _
    Implements IChannelSender.CreateMessageSink
```

```vb
      Console.WriteLine( _
        "InvertChannel: CreateMessageSink")
      Console.WriteLine( _
        "    url <{0}>, objectURI <{1}>", _
        url, objectURI)
      If _isServer Then
        Return Nothing
      Else
        Dim nextProv As IClientChannelSinkProvider
        nextProv = _clientProvider
        While Not (nextProv.Next Is Nothing)
          nextProv = nextProv.Next
        End While
        nextProv.Next = _
          New InvertClientTransportSinkProvider()
        Return _clientProvider.CreateSink( _
          Me, url, remoteChannelData)
      End If
    End Function
```

On the server side, we need to listen for incoming connections by instantiating a server-side socket. We use the port number that was passed in with the constructor, and our local address. After it's bound and listening, we watch for asynchronous events that indicate that a new connection has been accepted. We're not actually using the StopListening() method here, so we'll leave it empty.

```vb
    Public Sub StartListening(ByVal data As Object) _
      Implements IChannelReceiver.StartListening
      Console.WriteLine( _
        "InvertChannel: StartListening")
      Dim endPoint As IPEndPoint
      _sock = New Socket( _
        AddressFamily.InterNetwork, _
        SocketType.Stream, ProtocolType.IP)
      endPoint = New _
        IPEndPoint(Dns.Resolve( _
        Dns.GetHostName()).AddressList(0), _port)
      _sock.Bind(endPoint)
      _sock.Listen(5)
      _sock.BeginAccept(New AsyncCallback( _
        AddressOf AcceptCallback), _sock)
    End Sub

    Public Sub StopListening(ByVal data As Object) _
      Implements IChannelReceiver.StopListening
      Console.WriteLine("InvertChannel: StopListening")
    End Sub
```

Before we look at the acceptance callback, let's recap what we're doing with each method call. The client will establish a connection to the server, send over its method call data, wait for a response, and then drop the connection. The server completes the asynchronous acceptance process, so that the incoming connection is established:

```
Private Sub AcceptCallback( _
  ByVal result As IAsyncResult)
  Console.WriteLine( _
    "InvertChannel: AcceptCallback")
  Dim newSock As Socket
  Dim buffer As Byte()
  Dim length As Integer
  newSock = _sock.EndAccept(result)
```

Next, we get the length of the incoming stream. Remember how we specified the structure of our messages? We elected to encode the length of the message in raw form in a pair of bytes:

```
ReDim buffer(2)
newSock.Receive(buffer, 2, SocketFlags.None)
length = buffer(0) * 128 + buffer(1)
Console.WriteLine( _
  "    {0} bytes received", length)
```

Now that we know how many bytes to receive, we can get the actual method call data. After we get it, we put it into a memory-based stream:

```
ReDim buffer(length)
length = newSock.Receive( _
  buffer, length, SocketFlags.None)
Dim requestStream As New MemoryStream( _
  buffer, 0, length)
requestStream.Seek(0, SeekOrigin.Begin)
```

Now we just pass the stream on to the first sink in the server side of the chain, which is the transport sink that we instantiated back in the constructor. We need to pass in the URI of the object in the transport headers as well:

```
Dim requestHeaders As New TransportHeaders()
Dim responseStream As Stream
Dim responseHeaders As ITransportHeaders
requestHeaders("__RequestUri") = "/MyInvert.rem"
_transportSink.ProcessMessage(Nothing, _
  Nothing, requestHeaders, requestStream, _
  Nothing, responseHeaders, responseStream)
```

From here on, we simply take the response stream, encode its length as a byte pair, and send this back to the client, followed by the response data:

```
responseStream.Seek(0, SeekOrigin.Begin)
length = responseStream.Length
Console.WriteLine( _
  "    {0} bytes to be sent back", length)
```

```
        ReDim buffer(2)
        buffer(0) = (length - 64) / 128
        buffer(1) = length Mod 128
        newSock.Send(buffer, 2, SocketFlags.None)
        ReDim buffer(length)
        responseStream.Read(buffer, 0, length)
        newSock.Send(buffer, length, SocketFlags.None)
```

Now we're ready for another one:

```
        _sock.BeginAccept(New AsyncCallback( _
            AddressOf AcceptCallback), _sock)
    End Sub
End Class
```

So that's what our custom channel looks like. We introduced one or two new classes in the process, so let's take a look at them before we try running it. Apart from anything else, we haven't seen what the client side of the connection looks like yet.

Implementing the Invert Server Transport Sink

The transport sink on the server side is *very* boring. As you can see, it passes everything on to the next sink in the chain, so we don't need to spend any more time discussing it, especially as we've seen channel sinks already.

```
Public Class InvertServerTransportSink
    Implements IServerChannelSink
    Dim _next As IServerChannelSink
    Public Sub New( _
        ByVal nextSink As IServerChannelSink)
        _next = nextSink
    End Sub

    Public Sub AsyncProcessResponse(ByVal sinkStack _
        As IServerResponseChannelSinkStack, _
        ByVal state As Object, ByVal msg As IMessage, _
        ByVal headers As ITransportHeaders, _
        ByVal stream As System.IO.Stream) Implements _
        IServerChannelSink.AsyncProcessResponse
        Console.WriteLine( _
        "InvertServerTransportSink: AsyncProcessResponse")
    End Sub

    Public Function ProcessMessage(ByVal sinkStack _
        As IServerChannelSinkStack, ByVal requestMsg _
        As IMessage, ByVal requestHeaders _
        As ITransportHeaders, ByVal requestStream _
        As System.IO.Stream, ByRef responseMsg _
```

```vb
      As IMessage, ByRef responseHeaders _
      As ITransportHeaders, ByRef responseStream _
      As System.IO.Stream) As ServerProcessing _
      Implements IServerChannelSink.ProcessMessage
      Console.WriteLine( _
        "InvertServerTransportSink: ProcessMessage")
      Return _next.ProcessMessage(sinkStack, _
        requestMsg, requestHeaders, _
        requestStream, responseMsg, _
        responseHeaders, responseStream)
    End Function

    Public Function GetResponseStream(ByVal sinkStack _
      As IServerResponseChannelSinkStack, _
      ByVal state As Object, ByVal msg As IMessage, _
      ByVal headers As ITransportHeaders) _
      As System.IO.Stream _
      Implements IServerChannelSink.GetResponseStream
      Console.WriteLine( _
        "InvertServerTransportSink: GetResponseStream")
      Return _next.GetResponseStream( _
        sinkStack, state, msg, headers)
    End Function

    Public ReadOnly Property NextChannelSink() _
      As IServerChannelSink _
      Implements IServerChannelSink.NextChannelSink
      Get
        Return _next
      End Get
    End Property

    Public ReadOnly Property Properties() _
      As System.Collections.IDictionary _
      Implements IServerChannelSink.Properties
      Get
        Console.WriteLine( _
          "InvertServerTransportSink: Get Properties")
        Return _next.Properties()
      End Get
    End Property
  End Class
```

Implementing the Invert Client Transport Sink Provider

This bears a distinct resemblance to our earlier `InvertClientChannelSinkProvider`. In fact, it's identical apart from the substitution of `TransportSink` for `ChannelSink`:

```vbnet
Public Class InvertClientTransportSinkProvider
  Implements IClientChannelSinkProvider
  Dim _next As IClientChannelSinkProvider
  Public Function CreateSink(ByVal channel _
    As IChannelSender, ByVal url As String, _
    ByVal remoteChannelData As Object) _
    As IClientChannelSink _
    Implements IClientChannelSinkProvider.CreateSink
    Console.WriteLine( _
      "InvertClientTransportSinkProvider: CreateSink")
    Return New InvertClientTransportSink(url)
  End Function

  Public Property NextSinkProvider() _
    As IClientChannelSinkProvider _
    Implements IClientChannelSinkProvider.Next
    Get
      Console.WriteLine( _
        "InvertClientTransportSinkProvider: " & _
        "Get NextSinkProvider")
      Return _next
    End Get
    Set(ByVal Value As IClientChannelSinkProvider)
      Console.WriteLine( _
        "InvertClientTransportSinkProvider: " & _
        Set NextSinkProvider")
      _next = Value
    End Set
  End Property
End Class
```

Implementing the Invert Client Transport Sink

The client transport sink is, as you might expect, a little more exciting because this is where the serialized stream containing the remote method call gets sent out to the server. Let's look at the constructor first. The important thing we have to do here is extract the address and port number of the server:

```vbnet
Public Class InvertClientTransportSink
  Implements IClientChannelSink

  Dim _host As String
  Dim _port As Integer

  Public Sub New(ByVal url As String)
    Console.WriteLine( _
      "InvertClientTransportSink: New")
```

```vb
    Dim iHost As Integer
    Dim iSlash As Integer
    Dim iColon As Integer
    Dim port As String

    iHost = url.IndexOf("//") + 2
    iColon = url.IndexOf(":", iHost)
    iSlash = url.IndexOf("/", iHost)

    _host = url.Substring(iHost, iColon - iHost)

    If _host = "localhost" Then
       _host = Dns.GetHostName
    End If

    port = url.Substring(iColon + 1, _
       iSlash - iColon - 1)
    _port = CInt(port)
End Sub
```

We're right at the end of the sink channel chain here, so we return nothing from each of the following methods and properties:

```vb
Public Function GetRequestStream(ByVal msg _
   As IMessage, ByVal headers _
   As ITransportHeaders) As System.IO.Stream _
   Implements IClientChannelSink.GetRequestStream
   Console.WriteLine( _
      "InvertClientTransportSink: GetRequestStream")
   Return Nothing
End Function

Public ReadOnly Property NextChannelSink() _
   As IClientChannelSink _
   Implements IClientChannelSink.NextChannelSink
   Get
     Console.WriteLine( _
        "InvertClientTransportSink: " & _
        "Get NextChannelSink")
     Return Nothing
   End Get
End Property

Public ReadOnly Property Properties() _
  As System.Collections.IDictionary _
  Implements IClientChannelSink.Properties
```

```
    Get
      Console.WriteLine( _
        "InvertClientTransportSink: " & _
        "Get Properties")
        Return Nothing
    End Get
End Property
```

We're not dealing with asynchronous requests here, so the next two methods are blank:

```
Public Sub AsyncProcessRequest(ByVal sinkStack _
  As IClientChannelSinkStack, ByVal msg _
  As IMessage, ByVal headers _
  As ITransportHeaders, ByVal stream _
  As System.IO.Stream) _
  Implements IClientChannelSink.AsyncProcessRequest
    Console.WriteLine( _
      "InvertClientTransportSink: " & _
      "AsyncProcessRequest")
End Sub

Public Sub AsyncProcessResponse(ByVal sinkStack _
  As IClientResponseChannelSinkStack, _
  ByVal state As Object, ByVal headers _
  As ITransportHeaders, ByVal stream _
  As System.IO.Stream) _
  Implements _
  IClientChannelSink.AsyncProcessResponse
    Console.WriteLine( _
      "InvertClientTransportSink: {0}", _
      AsyncProcessResponse")
End Sub
```

We're now at the point where the client side goes into action. Here's how the transport sink's ProcessMessage() method starts. We need to establish our connection to the correct port on the correct server:

```
Public Sub ProcessMessage(ByVal msg _
  As IMessage, ByVal requestHeaders _
  As ITransportHeaders, ByVal requestStream _
  As System.IO.Stream, ByRef responseHeaders _
  As ITransportHeaders, ByRef responseStream _
  As System.IO.Stream) _
  Implements IClientChannelSink.ProcessMessage
    Console.WriteLine( _
      "InvertClientTransportSink: ProcessMessage")
    Dim length As Integer
    Dim sock As Socket
    Dim endPoint As IPEndPoint
```

```
    Dim buffer As Byte()
    sock = New Socket(AddressFamily.InterNetwork, _
      SocketType.Stream, ProtocolType.IP)
    endPoint = New _
     IPEndPoint(Dns.Resolve(_host).AddressList(0), _
      _port)
    sock.Connect(endPoint)
```

Having done that, we get the length of the outgoing stream, and send it to the server; this should look familiar from the equivalent code on the server side:

```
    length = requestStream.Length
    Console.WriteLine( _
    "   {0} bytes to be sent", length)
    ReDim buffer(2)
    buffer(0) = (length - 64) / 128
    buffer(1) = length Mod 128
    sock.Send(buffer, 2, SocketFlags.None)
```

Next, we send over the data from the stream itself:

```
    ReDim buffer(length)
    requestStream.Seek(0, SeekOrigin.Begin)
    requestStream.Read(buffer, 0, length)
    sock.Send(buffer, length, SocketFlags.None)
```

Then we wait for the response:

```
    sock.Receive(buffer, 2, SocketFlags.None)
    length = buffer(0) * 128 + buffer(1)
    Console.WriteLine( _
    "   {0} bytes received", length)
    sock.Receive(buffer, length, SocketFlags.None)
```

After we've received the response, we encode it in a memory-based stream to return to the calling sink, and close the socket:

```
    responseStream = New MemoryStream(buffer, _
       0, length)
    sock.Close()
    sock = Nothing
  End Sub
End Class
```

The response stream will then go back to the formatter sink, which will reconstitute it as a method return message, and pass it back to the caller. Incidentally, you might have noticed that our code is sitting waiting on a socket Receive(), and could be left indefinitely if, say, the wire had fallen out of the back of the computer. So a more industrial-strength implementation would probably use BeginReceive(), and be prepared to time out the call and throw an exception. An even more industrial-strength implementation would use BeginSend() instead of Send() as well.

Modifying InvertServer to Use InvertChannel

Our last task is to modify the server and client to use our new InvertChannel. To do this, we need to replace calls to TcpChannel with calls to InvertChannel:

```
Imports System.Runtime.Remoting
Imports System.Runtime.Remoting.Channels
Imports System.Runtime.Remoting.Channels.Tcp
Imports Invert
Imports InvertFormatter
Imports InvertChannel
Module InvertServer
  Sub Main()
    Dim channel As InvertChannel.InvertChannel
    Dim properties As New Hashtable()
    Dim provider As _
       New InvertServerChannelSinkProvider()
    Console.WriteLine("Server started")
    properties("port") = 8086
    properties("name") = "jon"
    provider = New InvertServerChannelSinkProvider()
    channel = _
      New InvertChannel.InvertChannel( _
      properties, Nothing, provider)
    ChannelServices.RegisterChannel(channel)
RemotingConfiguration.RegisterWellKnownServiceType( _
    GetType(MyInvert), "MyInvert.rem", _
    WellKnownObjectMode.SingleCall)
    Console.ReadLine()
  End Sub
End Module
```

Modifying InvertClient to Use InvertChannel

As with InvertServer, to modify the client, we just need to replace any references to TcpChannel with references to InvertChannel:

```
Imports System.Runtime.Remoting
Imports System.Runtime.Remoting.Channels
Imports System.Runtime.Remoting.Channels.Tcp
Imports Invert
Imports InvertFormatter
Imports InvertChannel
Module InvertClient
  Sub Main()
    ...
    Dim provider As InvertClientChannelSinkProvider
    Dim channel As InvertChannel.InvertChannel
    provider = New InvertClientChannelSinkProvider()
```

```
    channel = _
      New InvertChannel.InvertChannel ( _
        Nothing, provider, Nothing)
    ChannelServices.RegisterChannel(channel)
    url = "tcp://localhost:8086/MyInvert.rem"
    invert = CType(Activator.GetObject( _
      GetType(IInvert), url), IInvert)
    ...
  End Sub
End Module
```

Running the Example

Let's finish this off by running the complete system for the last time. The following figure shows the server side.

```
Command Prompt - InvertServer
C:\Documents and Settings\christianp\My Documents\Visual Studio Projects
\InvertServer\bin>InvertServer
Server started
InvertChannel: New
InvertServerChannelSinkProvider: Get NextSinkProvider
InvertServerChannelSinkProvider: Set NextSinkProvider
InvertServerChannelSinkProvider: CreateSink
InvertServerChannelSinkProvider: Set NextSinkProvider
InvertChannel: StartListening
InvertChannel: Get ChannelName
InvertChannel: Get ChannelName
InvertChannel: Get ChannelName
InvertChannel: Get ChannelPriority
InvertChannel: Get ChannelData
InvertChannel: Get ChannelData
InvertChannel: AcceptCallback
    194 bytes received
InvertServerTransportSink: ProcessMessage
InvertServerChannelSink: ProcessMessage
InvertFormatter: Deserialize (1)
    Deserialized at (22/07/2001 18:58:29)
InvertServer: Input (1.234), output (0.810372771474878)
InvertFormatter: Serialize (1)
    91 bytes to be sent back
InvertChannel: AcceptCallback
    192 bytes received
InvertServerTransportSink: ProcessMessage
InvertServerChannelSink: ProcessMessage
InvertFormatter: Deserialize (1)
    Deserialized at (22/07/2001 18:58:29)
InvertServer: Input (ABCDE), output (EDCBA)
InvertFormatter: Serialize (1)
    89 bytes to be sent back
InvertChannel: AcceptCallback
    347 bytes received
InvertServerTransportSink: ProcessMessage
InvertServerChannelSink: ProcessMessage
InvertFormatter: Deserialize (1)
    Deserialized at (22/07/2001 18:58:29)
InvertServer: Input (Hello, world), output (world, Hello)
InvertFormatter: Serialize (1)
    248 bytes to be sent back
```

We start off by creating our new channel. Then we create our channel sink provider and insert it in the sink provider chain, before creating our server channel sink. The channel starts listening, the framework interrogates it for various parameters, and then we see the acceptance callback firing to indicate an incoming call. We receive a 194-byte message that we process in the manner shown earlier to get our result. As a result of the serialization process, we end up with a 91-byte message to send back. This process is repeated three times. Note that the last time, we also see the serialization interface on the invertible object being used.

The next figure shows the client.

```
Command Prompt - InvertClient
C:\Documents and Settings\christianp\My Documents\Visual Studio Projects
\InvertClient\bin>InvertClient
InvertChannel: New
InvertChannel: Get ChannelName
InvertChannel: Get ChannelName
InvertChannel: Get ChannelName
InvertChannel: Get ChannelPriority
InvertChannel: Get ChannelData
InvertChannel: Get ChannelData
InvertChannel: CreateMessageSink
     url <tcp://localhost:8086/MyInvert.rem>, objectURI <>
InvertClientChannelSinkProvider: Get NextSinkProvider
InvertClientChannelSinkProvider: Set NextSinkProvider
InvertClientChannelSinkProvider: CreateSink
InvertClientTransportSinkProvider: CreateSink
InvertClientTransportSink: New
InvertClientChannelSinkProvider: CreateSink
InvertClientTransportSink: New
InvertClientChannelSink: SyncProcessMessage
InvertFormatter: Serialize (1)
InvertClientTransportSink: ProcessMessage
    194 bytes to be sent
    91 bytes received
InvertFormatter: Deserialize (1)
    Deserialized at <22/07/2001 18:58:29>
InvertClientChannelSink: SyncProcessMessage
InvertFormatter: Serialize (1)
InvertClientTransportSink: ProcessMessage
    192 bytes to be sent
    89 bytes received
InvertFormatter: Deserialize (1)
    Deserialized at <22/07/2001 18:58:29>
InvertClientChannelSink: SyncProcessMessage
InvertFormatter: Serialize (1)
InvertClientTransportSink: ProcessMessage
    347 bytes to be sent
    248 bytes received
InvertFormatter: Deserialize (1)
    Deserialized at <22/07/2001 18:58:29>
InvertClient: dblValue = <0.810372771474878>, strValue = <EDCBA>, objVal
ue = <world>, <Hello>
```

Here, we again start off by creating our new channel, which the framework then interrogates to get its parameters. We set up the channel sink provider chain, and then the channel sink chain, including the transport sink at the end. Then we get our first synchronous method invocation coming into our formatter sink. We serialize this using our formatter, and pass it on to the transport sink, which sends it off as a 194-byte message. We get a 91-byte response, which we pass back to the formatter sink for deserialization, and therefore back to the caller. Again, this is repeated three times.

Summary

In this chapter, we went on a journey into the interior of .NET Remoting, a journey made possible by the "pluggability" of its architecture. We began by inserting our own custom channel sink into the chain. Then we modified that into a client-side formatter (message) sink, before implementing our own formatter. We also implemented our own serialization on a simple object to use with the formatter sink. Finally, we implemented our own custom TCP/IP socket-based channel.

CHAPTER 4

Configuration and Deployment

In this chapter, we'll look at some of the configuration and deployment options that the .NET Framework provides for remotable applications.

We'll look at the options for configuring channels and distributed objects on both clients and servers because this can be done either programmatically or via XML configuration files. You'll also learn about the .NET Framework Configuration Tool that allows an administrator to change some of the properties in configuration files.

Previous chapters showed that for remoting to work, client proxy objects require access to metadata that describes the remote object. This chapter discusses various approaches to providing clients with the metadata they need. You'll consider whether the client and server should share the same assembly, whether you should replace the remote class implementation in a client assembly with an interface, or whether to use the Soapsuds tool to generate an assembly containing the metadata needed on the client.

The examples we've developed so far in the book have had server objects hosted in console applications. Other mechanisms are also available for hosting that provide advantages for unattended operation of the server objects. We look at hosting in Windows Services and Internet Information Server (IIS).

Finally, you'll learn how to use versioning to ensure that the version of an object running remotely on a server is compatible with the clients attempting to use it. The versioning infrastructure allows a version number to be assigned to an assembly and can be used to specify which versions can interoperate.

Configuration

In the code examples so far we've set various remoting options such as port numbers and lease timeouts through code. This approach has allowed you to clearly see the values that need to be set, and has the added advantage that only the EXE and DLL files need to be distributed. Programmatic configuration is also useful if you need to amend the configuration dynamically as the program is executing, based on runtime conditions. For example, you can use application logic to determine which port number, channel, and activation mode you want to use for a particular remoting type.

Typically, however, there are situations where the appropriate values for some options should not be hard-coded because they cannot be determined during the development phase but only later during deployment. The appropriate values may vary from situation to situation—they may need to be set differently on separate machines and they may need to be changed over time—and to do this through programmatic configuration, you would have to change and rebuild the source code after each modification.

For example, because only one application at a time can listen on a port, it's important to allow the port number used by a server to be configurable so that clashes can be avoided. Another example is to distribute load among multiple server machines, by each running copies of the server objects and configuring groups of clients to use different servers by having different URLs.

You should note, however, that in some situations, it's essential to define the configuration information programmatically, such as when you dynamically publish server-activated types. However, most of the time, file-based configuration is the best option.

.NET provides a flexible configuration infrastructure based around XML configuration files.

Standard Configuration File Types

.NET configuration files have, by convention, the extension `.config`. They are used to configure various subsystems within .NET. Although a single XML schema is defined to hold the configuration data, the configuration data can be split across multiple files, with each file holding a subset of the data.

The standard configuration files are

- **Application configuration file**: By default, these should reside in the startup directory for the assembly and have the same name as the assembly but with the extension `.config`; for example, `ExchangeHost.exe.config`. You may specify a different path or file name programmatically if you want. However, the framework will probe for the configuration file in the same directory as the assembly, with the naming rules as defined here.

- **Machine configuration file**: This is named `machine.config` and resides in a subdirectory of the .NET runtime named `\CONFIG`. For a typical Windows 2000 or Windows NT installation, this directory would be similar to `C:\WINNT\Microsoft.NET\Framework\v1.0.3705\CONFIG`. On Windows XP, where the `SystemRoot` environment variable is `\Windows`, this file would typically be installed at `C:\Windows\Microsoft.NET\Framework\v1.0.3705\CONFIG`.

- **Security configuration file**: This file resides within the same directory as `machine.config`. It controls access to resources used by assemblies. This file is not used directly by .NET Remoting.

Configuration File Structure

So what does a configuration file look like? A configuration file used to register a well-known singleton using HTTP on port 10000, looks like this:

```xml
<?xml version="1.0" encoding="utf-8" ?>
<configuration>
  <system.runtime.remoting>
    <application>
      <channels>
        <channel ref = "http" port= "10000"/>
      </channels>
      <service>
```

```
      <wellknown
        mode = "Singleton"
        type = "ExchangeObjects.Exchange,ExchangeObjects"
        objectUri = "exchangeuri.soap"
      />
    </service>
  </application>
  </system.runtime.remoting>
  <customErrors mode="off" />
</configuration>
```

We'll be using this configuration file a little later. For now, let's take a closer look at the XML elements and attributes present in this file.

The `<configuration>` and `<system.runtime.remoting>` Elements

The `<configuration>` element is the root element of every .NET configuration file. The `<system.runtime.remoting>` element indicates that this is a remoting configuration file with four child elements:

- `<application>`: Contains information about the remote objects used or exposed by the application. We'll take a closer look at this element in a moment.

- `<channels>`: Contains channel template information. Its child element `<channel>` provides a channel template that can be referenced elsewhere in the file. You should note that a default channel implementation is provided in machine.config so you don't need to worry about creating templates for the default HTTP and TCP channels.

- `<channelSinkProviders>`: Contains templates for client channel sink provider (under the `<clientProviders>` child element) and server channel sink provider (under the `<serverProviders>` child element).

- `<debug>`: When present, this element requires the system to load all types on startup, so that it's easy to catch typing errors present in the configuration file.

You can only have a single instance of each of these inside `<system.runtime.remoting>`. Let's take a closer look at the `<application>` element. For more information about other elements used in XML configuration files, refer to the MSDN documentation.

The `<application>` Element

The `<application>` element contains one optional attribute (name, the name of the application, as used in the activation URL) and five child elements, most of which are discussed in the following sections.

The `<service>` Element

Server objects to be activated by the remoting infrastructure are configured within the `<service>` element. They can be `<wellknown>` (server-activated) or `<activated>` (client-activated). Well-known objects have the mode attribute, which can be either Singleton or SingleCall, and the objectUri attribute, which registers the object's URI. The type attribute is the full type name of the object and the name of the assembly containing its implementation.

The `<service>` element can also define objects as client-activated, in which case only the object type and assembly name are required. If our example were client-activated, it would look like this:

```
<service>
  <activated
    type = "ExchangeObjects.Exchange,ExchangeObjects"
      />
</service>
```

It's important to note that the `<service>` node is used to register objects with the remoting framework where the objects are to be created and marshaled automatically by the framework. Other objects that are marshaled by explicitly calling `RemotingServices.Marshal()` or that are passed as parameters or return values in method calls should not be registered in the configuration file.

An object that is explicitly published by a host that calls the `RemotingServices.Marshal()` method from code is, as far as client configuration is concerned, identical to a well-known singleton. The operational difference is that the object does not have to be created when a client first tries to use it (it already exists), so the initial delay that occurs with server-activated objects is reduced.

The `<client>` Element

An application can be configured as a consumer of remote objects by using the `<client>` element. As with the `<service>` element, remote objects configured within the `<client>` node can be `<wellknown>` (server-activated), or `<activated>` (client-activated).

The client configuration for a well-known object requires `type` and `url`. The configuration for a client of the well-known server shown in the earlier example is as follows (we'll see how to actually call and use this file a little later):

```
<?xml version="1.0" encoding="utf-8" ?>
<configuration>
  <system.runtime.remoting>
    <application>
      <client>
        <wellknown
          type = "ExchangeObjects.Exchange,ExchangeObjects"
          url = "http://localhost:10000/exchangeuri.soap"
        />
      </client>
    </application>
  </system.runtime.remoting>
  <customErrors mode="off" />
</configuration>
```

The assembly name used here should be the name of the assembly containing the object metadata deployed on the client. This might not always be the same assembly that is used on the server; the "Deploying Metadata" section later in this chapter explores some of the reasons why you might want them to be different.

The equivalent configuration for a client-activated object is

```
<client url = "http://localhost:10000">
  <activated
    type = "ExchangeObjects.Exchange,ExchangeObjects"
  />
</client>
```

In this case, one URL is defined for a client with potentially many client-activated objects.

You should note that you don't need to use the same registration method on both client and server. For example, an object could be registered as a server in code using `RegisterWellKnownServiceType()`, and then consumed by a client that simply calls New in code to get a proxy, having used a configuration file to register the object as `<wellknown>`.

The `<channels>` Element

The `machine.config` configuration file installed with the .NET Framework includes channel templates that associate ID strings (`tcp` and `http`) with the classes providing channel implementations (`TcpChannel` and `HttpChannel`). An application can be configured to use one or more of the standard channels by setting the `ref` attribute of the `<channel>` child element of `<channels>` to the appropriate template ID.

A port can be associated with a channel using the `port` attribute of `<channel>`: for HTTP, this defaults to the standard port 80. Note, however, that if IIS is running on the same machine, it will have already allocated port 80 for its own use. If you attempt to use the same port for your server, initialization will fail.

This code configures a server to use HTTP on port 10000:

```
<application>
  <service>
    <wellknown
      mode="Singleton"
      type="ExchangeObjects.Exchange,ExchangeObjects"
      objectUri="exchangeuri.soap"
    />
  </service>
  <channels>
    <channel ref="http" port="10000" displayName="channel1" />
  </channels>
</application>
```

In this configuration example, the channel attribute `displayName` is used to associate a name with the channel/port combination. Only the .NET Framework Configuration Tool, which is described later in this chapter, uses this `displayName`.

When using TCP, a `port` must be specified for the server.

A client-side port is required where the server calls methods on client objects (including sponsors for lifetime leases). A port of zero on the client side indicates to the framework that it can allocate a free port to the channel, thus avoiding clashes between applications.

By default, the TCP channel uses the binary formatter and the HTTP channel uses the SOAP formatter, although you can configure the client to use the binary formatter with the HTTP channel. The required configuration, matching the server listed previously is

```
<application>
  <client>
    <wellknown
      type = "ExchangeObjects.Exchange,ExchangeObjects"
      url = "http://localhost:10000/exchangeuri.soap"
    />
  </client>
  <channels>
    <channel ref="http">
      <clientProviders>
        <formatter
          ref = "binary"
        />
      </clientProviders>
    </channel>
  </channels>
</application>
```

This allows the significantly more efficient binary formatter to be used, while still retaining the advantages of HTTP (many firewalls will allow HTTP to pass through on port 80 and the messages can be secured using SSL by IIS).

The `<lifetime>` Element

Lifetime settings can be specified in the `<lifetime>` element. For example:

```
<application>
  <lifetime
    leaseTime="30S"
    renewOnCallTime="30S"
    leaseManagerPollTime="10S"
  />
</application>
```

In this example, we've specified an initial `leaseTime` and a `renewOnCallTime` of 30 seconds, with a `leaseManagerPollTime` (the amount of time the lease manager sleeps between checking for expired leases) of 10 seconds.

These lifetime settings apply to all MBR objects within the application, so there may be occasions when it's still appropriate to override these settings in code for an individual class by using the `InitializeLifetimeService()` method (as described in Chapter 2).

The `<customErrors>` Element

The `<customErrors>` element is new to .NET version 1.1. Exceptions in .NET are serializable, meaning that they can propogate from the server back to the client caller. However, new security changes in version 1.1 of the .NET Framework do not allow this to occur by default when the client caller and remoting server are on the same physical machine. This setting works exactly the same as the `<customErrors>` tag the `<system.web>` configuration section uses in ASP.NET. When this tag's mode attribute is set to `Off`, the remote server can send exceptions to the client over remoting channels. Otherwise, remote callers will receive a `System.Runtime.Remoting.RemotingException` with the text `Server encountered an internal error`. For more information, turn on `customErrors` in the servers `.config` file.

> **Note** Take notice that the exception message is wrong. When you receive this notice, do not turn the `customErrors` mode to `on`. Instead, set them to `off`.

Loading a Configuration File

So how do you actually load configuration files in your code? The `machine.config` file (as distributed with .NET) contains configuration for the default channels used by .NET Remoting, and the Framework reads this file automatically. Additional application-specific configuration can be read from a file by explicitly calling the `Configure()` method of the `System.Runtime.Remoting.RemotingConfiguration` class. This method call takes a string containing the name of the configuration file to be read as its argument; usually this is the application configuration file.

Next we'll illustrate how to use configuration files by modifying a simple version of the Exchange example from Chapter 2 to configure the host and client from files.

Creating the `ExchangeObjects` Class Library

Here are the contents of the `ExchangeObjects` class library, which contains the implementation of the remote MBR `Exchange` class and the MBV `Order` class. Recall that the `Exchange` class contains the `NextOrder()` method that returns an `Order` object when called by the client.

```
Imports System.Runtime.Remoting.Lifetime
Public Class Exchange
  Inherits System.MarshalByRefObject

  Private mNextIndex As Integer

  Public Sub New()
    Console.WriteLine("Exchange Started")
    mNextIndex = 1000
  End Sub

  Public Function NextOrder() As Order
    mNextIndex = mNextIndex + 1
    Console.WriteLine("Exchange NextOrder : " & mNextIndex)
    Return New Order(mNextIndex)
  End Function

  Public Overrides Function InitializeLifetimeService() As Object
    Dim lease As ILease = _
      CType(MyBase.InitializeLifetimeService(), ILease)
    If lease.CurrentState = LeaseState.Initial Then
      lease.InitialLeaseTime = TimeSpan.FromSeconds(40)
      lease.RenewOnCallTime = TimeSpan.FromSeconds(10)
    End If
    Return lease
  End Function

End Class
```

```vb
<Serializable()> Public Class Order

  Private mIndex As Integer

  Public Sub New(ByVal Index As Integer)
    Console.WriteLine("Order: New: " & Index)
    mIndex = Index
  End Sub

  Public ReadOnly Property Index() As Integer
    Get
      Console.WriteLine("Order: Index: " & mIndex)
      Return mIndex
    End Get
  End Property

End Class
```

Creating the ExchangeHost

The host application looks like this:

```vb
Imports System.Runtime.Remoting
Imports ExchangeObjects

Module Main
  Public Sub Main()
    Console.WriteLine("Host started")

    'Configure using file
    RemotingConfiguration.Configure("ExchangeHost.exe.config")

    ' Wait
    Console.ReadLine()
  End Sub
End Module
```

Note how we're using the `Configure()` method to read from a configuration file called ExchangeHost.exe.config, and how this file follows our naming scheme for application configuration files of `<application name>.config`.

Creating the ExchangeClient

The `ExchangeClient` reads its remoting configuration from a file named ExchangeClient.exe.config:

```vb
Imports System.Runtime.Remoting
Imports ExchangeObjects
Module Main
```

```
  Public Sub Main()
    ' Create proxy to remote object
    RemotingConfiguration.Configure("ExchangeClient.exe.config")
    Dim exchange As New Exchange()

    ' Call remote function
    Dim order As Order = exchange.NextOrder()
    Console.WriteLine("Client: NextOrder returned: " & order.Index)
  End Sub
End Module
```

Creating the `ExchangeHost.exe.config` File

Here's the configuration file for the host application:

```
<?xml version="1.0" encoding="utf-8" ?>
<configuration>
  <system.runtime.remoting>
    <application>
      <channels>
        <channel ref = "http" port= "10000"/>
      </channels>
      <service>
        <wellknown
          mode = "Singleton"
          type = "ExchangeObjects.Exchange,ExchangeObjects"
          objectUri = "exchangeuri.soap"
        />
      </service>
    </application>
  </system.runtime.remoting>
</configuration>
```

We've already discussed the contents of both this file and the client configuration file in-depth earlier, so we won't cover it again here. Place this file in the same directory as `ExchangeHost.exe`, along with a copy of `ExchangeObjects.dll`.

Creating the `ExchangeClient.exe.config` File

Finally, here's the configuration file for the client:

```
<?xml version="1.0" encoding="utf-8" ?>
<configuration>
  <system.runtime.remoting>
    <application>
      <client>
        <wellknown
          type = "ExchangeObjects.Exchange,ExchangeProxy"
          url = "tcp://localhost:1000/exchangeuri.rem"
        />
```

```
        </client>
      </application>
    </system.runtime.remoting>
</configuration>
```

Again, you'll need to place this file in the same directory as the executable (`ExchangeClient.exe`) along with a copy of `ExchangeObjects.dll`.

Running the Example

Now let's run the example. First, start up the host. You'll see a message indicating that the server has started, which also means that the host has read its remote object configuration from the file.

Start the client in a separate console window. You should see another message appear in the host window telling you that the client has called the `NextOrder()` method, and what the order number is. If you run the client again, you'll see that the order number hasn't changed (remember that we defined the remote object to be a singleton in the host configuration file). Again, because the client application is running smoothly, the remote object configuration must have been read correctly from the client configuration file.

.NET Framework Configuration Tool

The Microsoft-supplied .NET Framework Configuration Tool includes support for administering .NET Remoting settings in configuration files. The tool is based on the Microsoft Management Console and is available from the `Start` menu by choosing `Programs` ➤ `Administrative Tools` ➤ `Microsoft .NET Framework Configuration`.

This tool allows some of the key remoting configuration settings to be changed through a user-friendly interface, avoiding the need to understand and modify the underlying XML. This is good because directly changing XML often introduces errors to the remoting configuration that could easily stop a solution from working.

XML configuration files should be treated as part of the source of a solution and managed alongside the VB .NET code, perhaps using source code management tools. The .NET Framework Configuration Tool can then be used at the deployment stage to adjust settings for the particular environment. Remember, however, that the tool actually changes the underlying configuration files, so be careful when upgrading an application because local configuration file changes may be lost.

The tool supports remoting configuration settings in both the machine configuration file and application configuration files.

To view and modify an application configuration file, follow these steps:

1. Add the application to the tool by selecting `My Computer` ➤ `Applications` from the tree view and then choosing the `Add an Application to Configure` task.

2. The `Configure an Application` dialog box lists applications that have previously been run. Select one of the console `Host` assemblies from the list and click `OK` to add it.

3. Alternatively, you can click the `Other` button to browse through the directory structure to find the assembly. You can repeat these steps to also add a client assembly.

You can then find the host application under the `Application` node in the tree view and expand the node by clicking the + symbol as shown here.

CHAPTER 4 ■ CONFIGURATION AND DEPLOYMENT

[Screenshot of .NET Framework Configuration tool showing Remoting Services node selected under ExchangeHost.exe application, with Tasks panel showing "View Remoting Services Properties".]

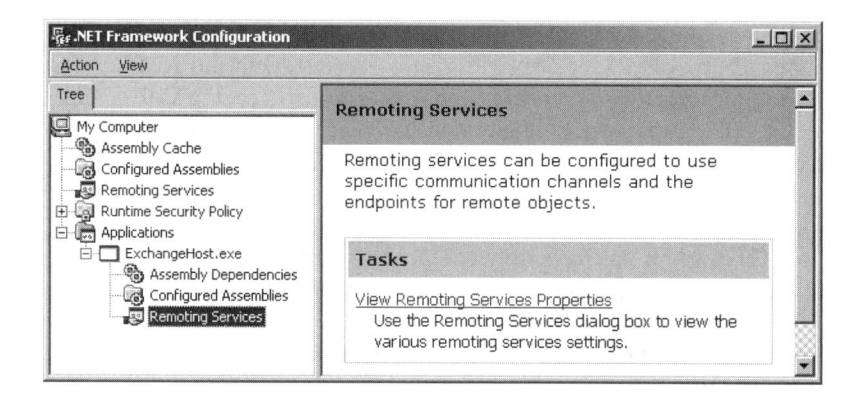

To view and modify the remoting configuration for the application, you select `View` ➤ `Remoting Services` ➤ `Properties`. The `Remoting Services Properties` dialog box appears. To view the well-known (server-activated) objects that have been configured for the application, choose the `Exposed Types` tab. An example of this (for the Exchange example from the previous section) is shown here.

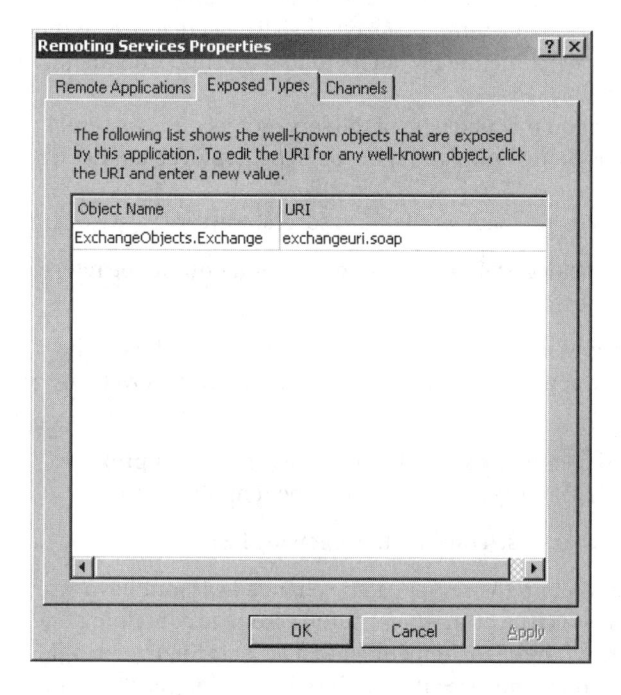

[Screenshot of Remoting Services Properties dialog on Exposed Types tab showing a table with Object Name "ExchangeObjects.Exchange" and URI "exchangeuri.soap".]

The `Remote Applications` tab displays the URL of remote applications and objects that have been registered in the configuration file. These can be modified through the tool. Where well-known objects are being consumed, the whole URL is shown. In the case of client-activated objects, only the protocol, machine, and port of the listening server application are shown.

The `Channels` tab allows attributes associated with a channel, such as the port number, to be displayed and modified.

The machine-wide settings can be accessed by selecting My Computer ➤ Remoting Services from the tree view and then the View Remoting Services Properties task. Only the .NET Remoting configuration within the `<application><channels>` node of the `machine.config` XML configuration files is visible to the .NET Framework Configuration Tool. The only visible configuration installed within `machine.config` as part of the default installation of .NET is used to provide for the default TCP and HTTP channels. These can be seen in the Channels tab of the Remoting Services Properties dialog box.

The default TCP and HTTP channels have only one property that can be changed: `delayLoadAsClientChannel`. This property, when True, indicates that the channel can be chosen by default by the .NET Framework. It will be used for client requests when no channel has been registered for the client (provided that the channel supports the protocol specified in the URL of the request made by the client).

Deploying Metadata

In the .NET Remoting community, *metadata* is usually used to describe the methods of a particular class; this is sometimes also known as class type information. The metadata of an MBR server object is needed when its clients are being built because it allows strong type checking or *early-binding*—the preferred approach with .NET because it allows many coding errors to be detected at the compilation stage rather than at runtime. The clients also need access to the metadata at runtime because the proxies examine the metadata to marshal and unmarshal method calls to and from the remote server object.

This means an assembly needs to contain the metadata of the server object. This assembly needs to be referenced when the client is being built, and it needs to be deployed so that it's available to the client at runtime.

This metadata assembly can be created and made available in several ways:

- The assembly containing the server object definition and implementation can be referenced by clients at build time and deployed on client machines.

- An assembly can be created that contains only the interface of the server object. The client can be built against this interface-only assembly and the assembly deployed on the client.

- The Soapsuds tool can be used to create an assembly containing the client proxy by running the tool against the server assembly or against a running remoting server.

Each approach has benefits and drawbacks, so consider the following factors:

- In all these cases, the implementation on the server can be changed without having to make any changes on the client. This is true even when the full assembly containing the server implementation is deployed on the client; remember that it's only there to provide the metadata, the implementation code is not executed on the client. As long as the methods used by the clients are still available, changes to the server-side code will not stop the client code from running. The .NET Remoting Framework will, however, throw an exception at runtime if the client calls a method that has been removed from the server. So, if you anticipate making significant changes to the server code after deployment, deploying the interface on the client or using Soapsuds may be the preferred options.

- MBV objects are passed in method calls between client and server, and their code is executed in both; they therefore require the assembly containing their implementation, rather than just metadata, to be available to the client.

- Deploying the assembly containing the implementation on the client is the simplest approach and imposes no limitations on client object code.

- Using interfaces, the proxy cannot be created using new because this constructor will not run against an interface.

Next, let's explore the interface and Soapsuds approaches.

Using Interface-Only Assemblies

In the version of the Exchange example we created earlier, the ExchangeObjects assembly would have to be deployed on both client and server. In this section, we'll split the code to create two projects, ExchangeObjects and ExchangeInterface, so that only the new ExchangeInterface assembly needs to be deployed on the clients.

We'll end up with one solution containing four projects:

- **ExchangeHost**: This is the generic console host described in the configuration section. The object to be remoted is defined by the configuration file.

- **ExchangeInterface**: This class library project builds the assembly that needs to be deployed to both the client and server. It contains an interface definition for the Exchange class and the implementation of the MBV Order class.

- **ExchangeObjects**: This class library project builds the assembly that needs to be deployed only on the server. It contains the implementation of the Exchange class and references the ExchangeInterface project.

- **ExchangeClient**: This console project uses the remote Exchange object, but only the ExchangeInterface project is referenced.

Creating the ExchangeInterface Class Library

This project contains the interface that the client will use to retrieve an Order object from the server, as well as the implementation of the Order class (as this is an MBV object, its code is actually run on the client):

```
Public Interface IExchange
  Function NextOrder() As Order
End Interface

<Serializable()> Public Class Order
  ' contents of Order class
End Class
```

Modifying the ExchangeObjects Project

This project implements the IExchange interface used by the client; it also includes methods that are not made visible to the client, in this case a constructor and an override for the InitializeLifeTimeService() method.

We first add a reference to the `ExchangeInterface` project and then the code as follows:

```
Imports ExchangeInterface

Public Class Exchange
  Inherits System.MarshalByRefObject
  Implements IExchange
  Private nextIndex As Integer

  Public Sub New()
    nextIndex = 1000
  End Sub

  Public Function NextOrder() As Order _
    Implements IExchange.NextOrder
    nextIndex = nextIndex + 1
    Return New Order(nextIndex)
  End Function

  Public Overrides Function InitializeLifetimeService() As Object
    ' ... etc
```

This is the code we had before except that the `Exchange` class implements `IExchange` and the method `NextOrder()` implements `IExchange.NextOrder()`. Remember that we also moved the implementation of `Order` to `ExchangeInterface`.

Modifying the Host and Client Applications

We don't need to change any of the code for the `ExchangeHost` application, but we need to include a copy of `ExchangeInterface.dll` (that we get when the solution is built) with the host project.

We do, however, have to modify the `ExchangeClient` code a little. It now uses only the `IExchange` interface rather than the `Exchange` class:

```
Imports System.Runtime.Remoting
Imports ExchangeInterface

Module Main
  Sub Main()
    ' Create proxy to remote object
    RemotingConfiguration.Configure("ExchangeClient.exe.config")
    Dim url As String = "http://localhost:10000/exchangeuri.soap"
    Dim exchange As IExchange = _
      Activator.GetObject(GetType(IExchange), url)

    ' Call remote function
    Dim order As Order = exchange.NextOrder()
    Console.WriteLine _
      ("Client: NextOrder returned: " & order.Index)
  End Sub
End Module
```

This version of the client code imports the `ExchangeInterface` namespace rather than `ExchangeObjects`, and consequently the `Client` project needs to have a reference to the `ExchangeInterface` project.

The other change is that we used `Activator.GetObject()` to create a proxy implementing the `IExchange` interface. We can't create a new object using `New` anymore because it won't work for interfaces.

Finally, we also need to add a copy of `ExchangeInterface.dll` to the client project.

Advantages and Limitations of the Interface Approach

A significant advantage of this approach is that by going to the trouble of defining an interface for the MBR object, the designer has made the intentions clear. The designer is indicating to anyone subsequently working with the solution that there are only certain methods that they intended the client to call.

A limitation is that because a constructor cannot be called directly on an interface, `New` cannot be used on the client to create the local proxy from the interface-only assembly. One implication of this is that client-activated objects can only be constructed with default parameters. This can be worked around by using the Class Factory approach, which means coding a server-activated object with a single method that creates and returns a reference to the object the client needs. The method call can include parameters that are passed to the object's constructor.

Using Soapsuds

An alternative way of avoiding the need to deploy the full server assembly on the client is to use the Soapsuds tool. In a typical Visual Studio .NET installation, the `Soapsuds.exe` file can be found at:

`C:\Program Files\Microsoft Visual Studio .NET\FrameworkSDK\Bin`

Soapsuds can create the proxy assembly that the client uses at runtime. To generate the client proxy assembly directly from the server assembly, you can use Soapsuds with the `-ia` (input assemblyfile) and `-oa` (output assemblyfile) options. For example:

`>Soapsuds -ia:ExchangeObjects -oa:ExchangeProxy.dll`

This creates an assembly called `ExchangeProxy.dll` containing the metadata. The client project needs to reference this at build time and then the metadata assembly is used at runtime by modifying the client configuration file to use `ExchangeProxy` rather than `ExchangeObjects`:

```
<application>
  <client>
    <wellknown
      type = "ExchangeObjects.Exchange,ExchangeProxy"
      url = "tcp://localhost:10000/exchangeuri.rem"
    />
  </client>
</application>
```

Be careful with naming, however, because typically the proxy and real server assemblies have different file names, although the namespaces and types they contain are the same. The preceding highlighted line of XML identifies the file name of the assembly as `ExchangeProxy`, but the name of the object as `ExchangeObjects.Exchange`.

Retrieving Metadata from a Running Server

Soapsuds generates the metadata assembly in a two-stage process. The first stage is to obtain an XML-encoded description of the server object's methods, and the second stage is to generate the assembly from the XML description. The XML description can be encoded as either Web Services Description Language (WSDL) or Services Description Language (SDL). WSDL is an increasingly used standard together with SOAP and has largely replaced the proprietary SDL; WSDL is the default for Soapsuds.

The WSDL metadata description can be requested dynamically from a running .NET Remoting server configured to support SOAP. You can see this WSDL in Internet Explorer by running one of our server-activated examples configured to use HTTP and SOAP, and then requesting a URL of the form:

```
http://localhost:<port>/<class>?WSDL
```

For example:

```
http://localhost:10000/exchangeuri.soap?WSDL
```

Assuming the server is running correctly, the browser displays an XML document describing the `Exchange` server object—precisely the metadata that is needed to construct the client proxies. This screenshot shows only a small part of the WSDL document.

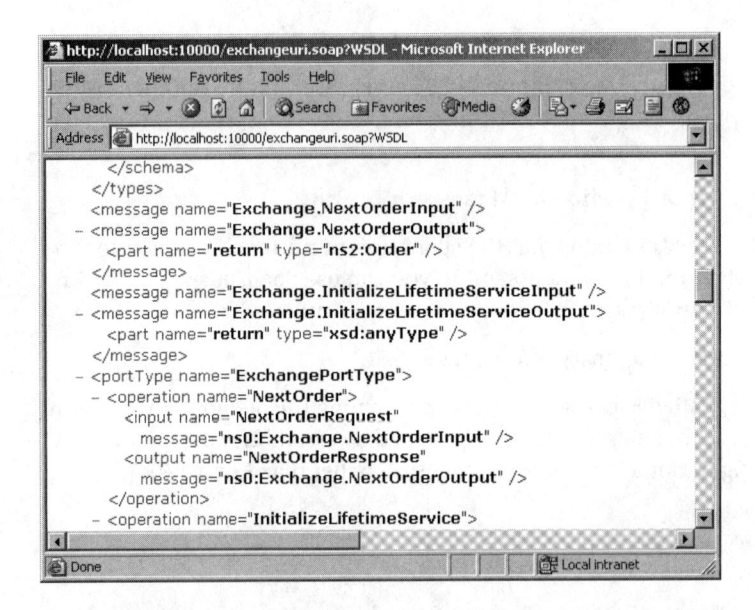

This approach of requesting the WSDL document from a remote object is a useful diagnostic for checking availability.

The Soapsuds tool can use this mechanism to retrieve the WSDL metadata and then create an assembly that you can reference from our client project and deploy with the client assembly. To use Soapsuds in this way, try running it with the following options:

```
>Soapsuds -url:http://localhost:10000/Exchangeuri.soap?WSDL
-oa:ExchangeProxy.dll
```

This is another way of creating the same proxy assembly as in the earlier example, except that in this case, it's generated from a running object rather than from the assembly containing the object.

Hosting

In Chapter 2 we used a console application to host the server objects. This is a great approach for testing and debugging software during the development cycle, but you need something more industrial strength for hosting a commercial solution.

Several alternative common approaches to hosting are available, which we'll look at in a moment First, however, let's consider the requirements (always a good idea when building software) of our host. What do you need from the host application?

- **Administrative control**: A mechanism is necessary for starting the service—making the service available for use, perhaps automatically when the machine it is running on restarts. You might even want to change characteristics of the service while it's running, so the ability to send operator commands could be helpful.

- **Visibility**: There's unlikely to be a need for a user interface because users interact with the client applications, but an administrator wants the comfort of being able to check that the server objects are available.

- **Logging**: Things do go wrong, so a mechanism for recording problems or just significant events is helpful.

- **Security**: You might not want just any client to have access to your production server, not just because there are malicious or dishonest people, but also to avoid accidental misuse.

- **Availability**: Disks break, machines crash, network cables get disconnected, power fails, and much more, so you might want to have alternative servers available to limit disruption to your users.

- **Scalability**: One machine might not be powerful enough to service all your clients, so you might want to spread the load across multiple machines.

- **Ease of development**: You want to avoid doing any more development work than is necessary by using the Microsoft infrastructure.

Now that you know the issues to be addressed when choosing an appropriate host, let's look at hosting using Windows Services and IIS, because both environments address many of the issues raised in the preceding list.

Hosting in a Windows Service

Windows Services (previously known as NT Services) has the infrastructure necessary to host our server object. It provides a process for our object to run within and allows for unattended operation by automatically starting this process when Windows starts. There is a Services utility that shows the service is running and through which you can send commands to control the service. This utility can be started on Windows 2000 by choosing Start ➤ Programs ➤ Administrative Tools ➤ Services.

To create and install a Windows Service, you need to do a little development; fortunately, Visual Studio .NET provides tools that simplify this procedure. The bad news, however, is that the Standard Edition of Visual Studio does not include this feature so an investment in one of the more expensive editions is required.

The extra development work required beyond that needed for the console application can be broken down into several stages:

1. Create a Windows Service project.
2. Register your MBR object with the .NET Remoting Framework.
3. Add installation components.
4. Report status to the Windows Event Log.
5. Install the Windows Service project manually or via an installation project.

We'll now use the Exchange example to work through these stages. Start by copying the directory containing the Exchange solution to a new directory called `WindowsService`, and also rename the solution file within this directory to the new solution name, also `WindowsService`. The `ExchangeObjects` project code remains unchanged. To keep things clear and simple, we'll use programmatic configuration for the host and client, so we'll need to modify the client a little. We're using a Windows Service to host the remote objects, so we don't need the `ExchangeHost` project anymore.

Modifying the Client

Following is the client code. We'll perform our client configuration programmatically this time:

```
Imports System.Runtime.Remoting
Imports ExchangeObjects

Module Module1

  Sub Main()
    ' Create URL, assuming local machine
    Dim url As String = _
      "tcp://localhost:10000/ExchangeApplication/Exchange"

    ' Create proxy to remote object
    Dim exchange As Exchange = Activator.GetObject( _
      GetType(Exchange), url)

    ' Call remote function
    Dim order As Order = exchange.NextOrder()
    Console.WriteLine("Client: NextOrder returned: " & order.Index)
  End Sub

End Module
```

Creating a Windows Service Project

Now that we've opened the existing console-based solution, choose File ➤ Add Project ➤ New Project ➤ Visual Basic Projects, and select the Windows Service template to create a project named ExchangeWSHost.

The project that is created contains a class that inherits from System.ServiceProcess.ServiceBase. This class has a default class name of Service1; you can change this class name and the associated VB file name to something more meaningful, say ExchangeService. In the Properties window, you also need to change the ServiceName property to ExchangeService, and the Name property to ExchangeService.

This name change also needs to be made in the code. Expand the Component Designer-generated code region, and in the Main() method, change the New Service1() call to New ExchangeService().

The template also creates empty OnStart() and OnStop() methods. These methods are called when the service is started and stopped via the Windows Services tools.

Registering the Server Object

You need to add a reference to the ExchangeObjects class library before you can use it within the Windows Service. You also need to add a reference to the .NET component System.Runtime.Remoting.

You need to edit the ExchangeService code to add the appropriate remoting and ExchangeObjects namespaces and then to register the server object from the OnStart() code:

```vb
Imports System.ServiceProcess
Imports System.Runtime.Remoting
Imports System.Runtime.Remoting.Channels
Imports System.Runtime.Remoting.Channels.Tcp
Imports ExchangeObjects

Public Class ExchangeService
  Inherits System.ServiceProcess.ServiceBase

#Region " Component Designer generated code "
...
#End Region

Protected Overrides Sub OnStart(ByVal args() As String)
    ' Add code here to start your service. This method should set things
    ' in motion so your service can do its work.

    ' Create and register a channel
    Dim channel As New TcpChannel(10000)
    ChannelServices.RegisterChannel(channel)
```

```
' Register an Exchange Service
RemotingConfiguration.ApplicationName = "ExchangeApplication"
RemotingConfiguration.RegisterWellKnownServiceType( _
   GetType(Exchange), "Exchange", WellKnownObjectMode.Singleton)

End Sub

Protected Overrides Sub OnStop()
  ' Add code here to perform any tear-down necessary
  ' to stop your service.
End Sub

End Class
```

The highlighted sections of code are changes from the standard template.

Adding the Installation Components

Visual Studio .NET can assist with adding the installation components. To display the property browser for the service, select the background of the `ExchangeService.vb [Design]` tab as shown here.

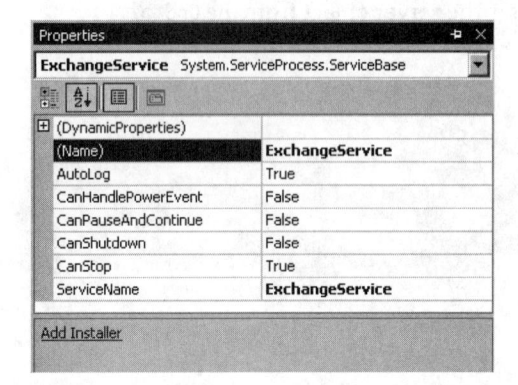

Properties	
ExchangeService System.ServiceProcess.ServiceBase	
(DynamicProperties)	
(Name)	**ExchangeService**
AutoLog	True
CanHandlePowerEvent	False
CanPauseAndContinue	False
CanShutdown	False
CanStop	True
ServiceName	**ExchangeService**
Add Installer	

Near the bottom of this property browser window is a hyperlink called `Add Installer`. When you select this hyperlink, a new `ProjectInstaller` class is created with two components: `ServiceInstaller1` and `ServiceProcessInstaller1`.

Selecting the `ServiceProcessInstaller1` component displays the component's properties in the property browser. One of these properties is `Account`, which controls the account and therefore the security privileges under which the service process runs. You can choose one of the listed values as appropriate for the resources that our object required. If `User` is chosen, a username and password must be entered at installation time and the process will run with the security rights of the chosen user. Alternatively, you can choose one of the predefined accounts: `LocalService`, `NetworkService`, or `LocalSystem` as appropriate.

For this example, choose `LocalSystem` and then build the solution.

Installation

The service we've created must now be installed. You can do this by running `installutil.exe` at the command line. To install at the command line, open a Visual Studio .NET command prompt and change directory to the `bin` directory of the `ExchangeWSHost` project we've just created. Enter the following:

```
>Installutil ExchangeWSHost.exe
```

Once installed, the service becomes visible in the list of services shown by the `Services Administrative Tool`. This tool can then be used to start the service manually by selecting the service from the list and choosing `Action` ➤ `Start` from the menu.

You can now run the client to demonstrate that the server is operating as expected.

The `Properties` dialog box can be used to control the `startup mode` so that, for example, the service is started automatically following a system reboot. The `Recovery` tab provides options that will restart the service following a failure. The service can also be stopped, started, and paused manually.

To uninstall the service at the command line, you can use:

```
>Installutil /u ExchangeWSHost.exe
```

Hosting in IIS

IIS services requests using HTTP and has the facility to host .NET Remoting objects. These can be configured programmatically or by using configuration files. In this section, we'll look at both approaches.

Let's work through the steps needed to host the simple `Exchange` example in IIS. Start by creating a new solution in Visual Studio .NET and name the solution `DeploymentIIS`. Create a new class library project called `ExchangeObjects` with one class called `Exchange`. We'll keep things simple and have the `NextOrder()` method return an integer rather than an MBV `Order` object:

```vb
Public Class Exchange
  Inherits System.MarshalByRefObject
  Private nextIndex As Integer

  Public Sub New()
    nextIndex = 1000
  End Sub

  Public Function NextOrder() As Integer
    nextIndex = nextIndex + 1
    Return nextIndex
  End Function

  Public Overrides Function InitializeLifetimeService() As Object
    Dim lease As ILease = _
      CType(MyBase.InitializeLifetimeService(), ILease)
```

```
    If lease.CurrentState = LeaseState.Initial Then
       lease.InitialLeaseTime = TimeSpan.FromSeconds(40)
       lease.RenewOnCallTime = TimeSpan.FromSeconds(10)
    End If
    Return lease
  End Function

End Class
```

IIS Configuration

IIS automatically reads the configuration for server objects it is to host from a file called `web.config`. This configuration can be defined using the same XML schema you saw in the earlier examples. You can configure the object as follows:

```
<?xml version="1.0" encoding="utf-8" ?>
<configuration>
  <system.runtime.remoting>
    <application>
      <service>
        <wellknown
          mode = "Singleton"
          type = "ExchangeObjects.Exchange,ExchangeObjects"
          objectUri = "exchangeuri.soap"
        />
      </service>
    </application>
  </system.runtime.remoting>
</configuration>
```

You should note that the URIs for IIS-hosted well-known server objects must end with `.rem` or `.soap` to distinguish them from other types of objects hosted by IIS. Only the HTTP channel can be used with IIS, although clients can choose to use either the binary formatter or SOAP. The port to be used by HTTP cannot be specified by the remoting configuration but rather by setting properties on the Web site using Internet Services Manager. The default port of 80 is normally used.

Administering IIS

To host a .NET Remoting object through IIS, a virtual directory must be created for a Web site. You can use Internet Services Manager to create one for an existing Web site. The manager can be started on Windows 2000 using Start ➤ Programs ➤ Administration Tools ➤ Internet Services Manager. Then select the Web site from the tree view; here the local machine is named `robs` and the `Default Web Site` has been chosen.

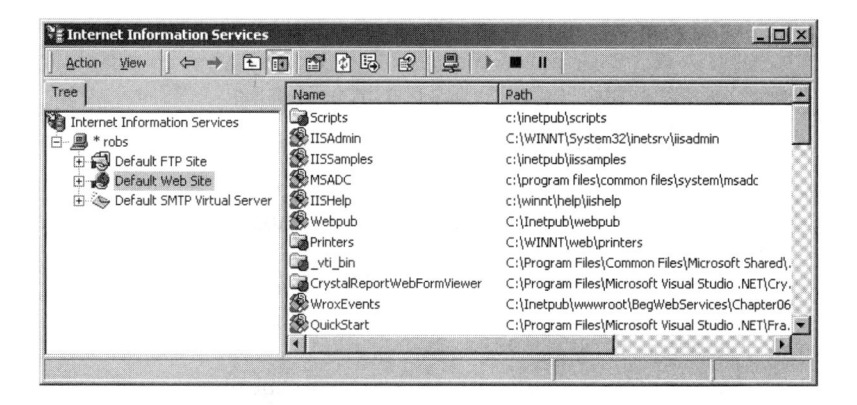

You then select Action ➤ New ➤ Virtual directory. A wizard starts, which prompts in turn for an alias, a directory, and permissions as shown here.

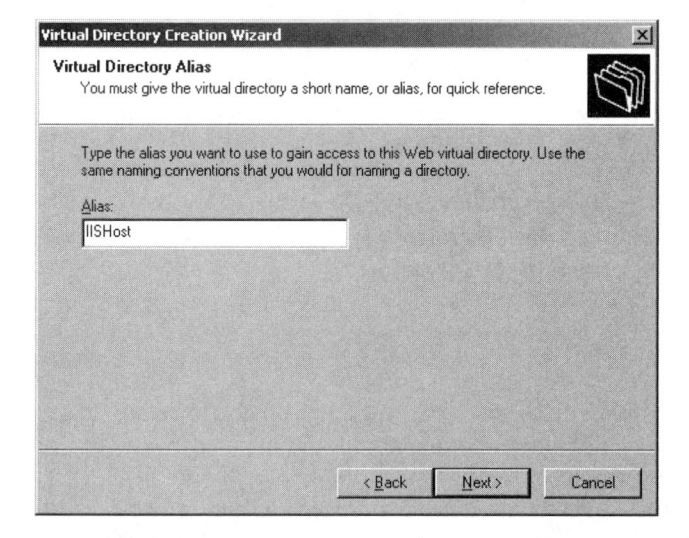

The virtual directory alias becomes part of the URL needed by the client to locate a remote object; the full URL syntax is

http://<server>:<port>/<alias>/<resource>

In this case, we choose the alias IISHost, giving our Exchange object the following URL:

http://localhost/iishost/exchangeuri.soap

The directory that you enter in the wizard becomes the root of the virtual directory and is the location where the web.config configuration file needs to reside. The assembly DLL containing the object to be hosted needs to reside in a subdirectory of the root called /bin.

The default permissions offered by the wizard are correct for our sample.

After you've finished with the wizard, copied the web.config file to the virtual directory root, and copied exchangeobjects.dll to the bin subdirectory, the object is ready to use. You can test that the object is available simply by requesting the WSDL in a browser using

http://localhost/iishost/exchangeuri.soap?WSDL

Client-activated objects do not have a well-known URI, but their availability can still be checked by retrieving the metadata for all objects configured for the virtual directory:

http://<server>:<port>/<alias>/RemoteApplicationMetadata.rem?WSDL

Registering Objects Programmatically Using Global.asax

As an alternative to using the web.config configuration file, you can use the Global.asax file to register objects programmatically by adding code to the Application_Start() subroutine. The Global.asax file is also located in the root of the virtual directory. The following code could be used instead of the configuration file in the previous example:

```
<%@ Import Namespace="System.Runtime.Remoting" %>
<%@ Import Namespace="ExchangeObjects" %>

<script language="VB" runat="server">

  Sub Application_Start(Sender As Object, E As EventArgs)
    ' Do application startup code here
    Dim exch As New WellKnownServiceTypeEntry(GetType(Exchange), _
      "exchangeuri.soap",WellKnownObjectMode.Singleton)
    RemotingConfiguration.RegisterWellKnownServiceType(exch)
  End Sub

</script>
```

Why would you want to use this rather than web.config? Although objects to be hosted by IIS using the .NET Remoting Framework are registered automatically if configured in web.config, the same is not true for objects consumed in IIS by ASP.NET pages. If you want to write an ASP.NET page as a client of a remoting object, then the object needs to be registered explicitly in Global.asax, either by calling RegisterActivatedClientType() or RegisterWellKnownClientType(), or by calling RemotingConfiguration.Configure() to read a configuration file.

Advantages of Using IIS

Many of the advantages of using IIS as a host relate to the use of HTTP rather than IIS itself. IIS does not support the TCP channel, so if the performance of TCP is required, IIS is not an option. However, because IIS allows the efficient binary formatter to be used instead of SOAP, it should be possible to meet most performance needs using IIS with the HTTP channel and the binary formatter.

A major advantage of using HTTP is that Internet firewalls allow through traffic on the standard HTTP port 80. When IIS is running on a machine, it reserves port 80 for its use. The only way to host a .NET Remoting object on port 80 on the same machine is by also using IIS, because an error will occur if another process attempts to listen on the same port.

Load balancing can be applied to stateless single-call server-activated objects hosted in IIS using standard Web techniques such as network load balancing, or by using Microsoft Application Center 2000.

The messages being passed between client and server objects can be secured by configuring IIS to require use of the SSL for a virtual directory and then specifying `https` as the protocol in the URL used by the client. Also, NTLM (now known as Windows Integrated Authentication) can be used to control access and to pass user authentication information from the client to the server object.

Finally, as you've seen from walking through the setup of both a Windows Service and IIS as object hosts, IIS is certainly relatively easy to use for hosting.

Versioning

So far in this chapter we've looked at how to configure and deploy a static, unchanging remoted application, but now it's time to introduce a bit of the real world. In the real world, applications change. Bugs are fixed, enhancements are made, and exciting new bugs are introduced. In a single-host environment, it can get messy, but in a client-server system, version management can be positively hideous. How can we ensure that by making a change at the server end to support application A, we don't wreck application B, which just happens to use the same remote object? Worse still, what if we can't upgrade all of our clients at once, and half our population is staying with an old version of the client (which needs an old version of the server)? How can we run several versions side by side?

Fortunately, all these questions have been answered in .NET Remoting, and this last section of the chapter discusses how you can manage different versions successfully.

Assigning a Version Number

Assemblies have a version number associated with them that takes this form:

```
<major version>.<minor version>.<build number>.<revision>
```

So for example 1.5.1234.2 is major version 1, minor version 5, build 1234, and revision 2. The .NET runtime distinguishes between assemblies that have different versions, to the extent that they are considered completely separate entities so there's no possibility of confusion. If a client requires remote object A, version 1.5.1234.2, and all it can find is version 1.5.1234.3, then it might as well be looking for remote object B.

The version number is held as an assembly attribute: `<AssemblyVersion>`. By default, this is set in the file `AssemblyInfo.vb` (which is generated automatically by Visual Studio) as follows:

```
<Assembly: AssemblyVersion("1.0.*")>
```

So if you want to set the version number to 1.5.1234.2, you would simply change this to:

```
<Assembly: AssemblyVersion("1.5.1234.2")>
```

However, that's not the whole story. The problem is that in a regular assembly, this information is as good as ignored, and the version number that is visible to the outside world is 0.0.0.0. Which means, of course, that all versions end up with the same version number, and no version control takes place.

For a version to be assigned to an assembly, the assembly must also be assigned a *strong name* so that it's securely and uniquely identified. You can generate a strong name key file by using the sn.exe utility located in the \bin directory of the .NET Framework SDK. To create the strong name file for our assembly, run sn.exe:

```
>sn /k exchangeobjects.snk
```

Place the resulting exchangeobjects.snk file in the top level of the ExchangeObjects project. You can then sign the assembly with this strong name and add the version number by adding the following code to the project:

```
<Assembly:AssemblyKeyFile("exchangeobjects.snk")>
<Assembly.AssemblyVersion("1.5.1234.2")>
```

Incidentally, an assembly must also be assigned a strong name before it can be written to the Global Assembly Cache, although it does not need to be cached for versioning to function.

Determining the Version to Use

For server-activated objects, the server also determines which version to activate. Where there are multiple versions of the assembly containing an object, the latest assembly is used by default. However, you can specify that a specific version be used inside the configuration file:

```
<?xml version="1.0" encoding="utf-8" ?>
<configuration>
  <system.runtime.remoting>
    <application>
      <service>
        <wellknown
          mode = "Singleton"
          type = "ExchangeObjects.Exchange,ExchangeObjects,
            version=1.5.1234.2"
          objectUri = "exchangeuri.soap"
        />
      </service>
    </application>
  </system.runtime.remoting>
</configuration>
```

On the other hand, with client-activated objects, the version cannot be configured and the version that the client was built against is always used. This information is included in the activation message passed from the client to the server when the proxy is created. Consequently, if there are two clients built with different versions of a remote assembly, both versions are activated by the server, one for each client.

Other Versioning Issues

That's about it for versioning. Aside from the mildly tedious business of creating that strong name, everything is handled for you. However, we should address a couple of other issues that might occur in more unusual circumstances.

Soapsuds and Versioning

If you're using Soapsuds to build a proxy, remember that it won't generate any version information. Instead, you need to run it using the -gc option to just generate the code, for example:

```
>Soapsuds -url:http://localhost:10000/Exchangeuri.soap?WSDL -gc
```

Then, you build the proxy from that, together with an assembly information file containing the version that you're interested in, like this:

```
Imports System.Reflection
<Assembly:AssemblyKeyFile("exchangeobjects.snk")>
<Assembly.AssemblyVersion("1.5.1234.2")>
```

MBV and Versioning

By default, version information is passed when you marshal an object by value. When the receiver deserializes the object, it attempts to create an object with the correct version. If this fails, it ignores the version information and tries again. This is not entirely unreasonable because versioning is less of an issue in this case. After all, you're just dealing with a serialized object, and the actual implementation details are not so important.

Two attributes of the `<formatter>` element used in configuration files can change this behavior. First, the sender of the object can elect to switch off versioning altogether by setting the attribute `includeVersions` to `"false"`. The default value for this attribute is `"true"`. Secondly, the receiver of the object can elect to enforce strict versioning by setting the attribute `strictBinding` to `"true"`. In this case, if the incoming object cannot be deserialized to the correct version, an exception is thrown. The default value for this attribute is `"false"`. If the sender has set `includeVersions` to `"false"`, the latest version is used in this case.

Summary

In this chapter we explored some of the deployment and configuration options available through the .NET Remoting Framework.

We started the chapter with a discussion of using XML configuration files. Remoting configuration via files makes your applications more flexible and adaptable than if you use programmatic configuration. There are several types of remoting configuration files, and you saw how to modify application configuration settings using the `application.config` file and the Configuration Tool.

We explored the use of metadata by remote applications. The remoting client needs to have access to the metadata of the remote object to be able to create a proxy object. Although one way to provide this metadata is to deploy the full implementation of the remote object class on the server, there are scenarios in which it's preferable to deploy an interface (implemented by the remote object class) on the client, rather than the full implementation. You also saw how it's possible to create a proxy assembly on the client using the Soapsuds tool.

Although most of the remote applications we've created in the book have used a console application to host the server object, you'll probably want to use a more robust application to host remote objects in the real world. Two other hosting options covered in this chapter were through IIS and through a Windows Service.

Finally, we rounded off the chapter with a discussion of versioning issues you should be aware of.

In the next chapter, we'll dive into the world of asynchronous remoting.

CHAPTER 5

Asynchronous Remoting

As much as we would like it to be otherwise, not everything in life happens immediately. Often we have to sit down and wait for all sorts of things, and that's precisely what all the remoting examples we have looked at so far do. This is because they are *synchronous*. As you saw in Chapter 1, a synchronous interaction occurs when the client sends a message to a server, and then waits for the response before continuing. This is fine if you're doing something that completes reasonably quickly, but if it doesn't complete quickly, you don't want to hold up the main client thread of execution waiting for it to do so. You might not even want to wait for a response at all, in fact. You need an *asynchronous* model, so that the client doesn't wait for the response.

That's not all. In some scenarios, you want to make an initial request, and then receive a stream of response events at irregular intervals in the future. Typical examples of this type of application are teleconferencing and anything that handles streams of real-time data. It would be grossly inefficient to have the client continually polling to find out if there were any new events, so you need to define *event handlers*, which get invoked whenever something interesting happens, leaving the main thread of execution to get on with something else.

Both of these patterns are available in standard single application domain .NET (although the first is less well-known than the second), but they acquire special significance in the remoting world, simply because the overheads involved in synchronous processing are so much magnified when each call has to cross application domain boundaries.

In this chapter, we'll look at asynchronous remoting with and without using event handlers.

Simple Asynchronous Remoting

The asynchronous .NET programming model is one of .NET's best-kept secrets, and hasn't been widely covered in detail anywhere. So before we launch into a demonstration of asynchronous remoting, let's take a good look at asynchronous .NET.

The idea behind the asynchronous model is deceptively simple. The paramount principle is that the *client* should decide whether to make the invocation synchronous or asynchronous, and that the server should have no knowledge of this. So the implementation of the called method is always synchronous; it's just how its completion is handled by the client that changes. The big advantage of this approach is that the implementation at the server is unaffected by the decision of whether to go for a synchronous or asynchronous implementation at the client.

Implementing a Slow Synchronous Process

Let's build a simple example. We'll construct an object that will calculate the given power of a given value. However, we'll do this the hard way, by multiplying the value by itself over and over again the specified number of times. With an eye on the way we'll develop this, we'll separate the interface from the base class. Create a solution and add two projects to it. The first is a class library called `Power`, and the second is a console application called `PowerClient`.

Implementing the Power Class Library

Here's the complete code of `Power`:

```
Public Interface IPower

  Function AnyPower(ByVal value As Double, ByVal power As Integer) _
    As Double

End Interface
```

Implementing the Client Code

In `PowerClient`, we have the main module and the actual class that implements `IPower`. Here's the implementation class:

```
Class MyPower
  Implements IPower

  Public Function AnyPower(ByVal value As Double, _
    ByVal power As Integer) As Double _
    Implements Power.IPower.AnyPower

    Dim dblResult As Double
    Dim intIter As Integer

    dblResult = 1.0

    For intIter = 1 To power
      dblResult = dblResult * value
    Next

    Return dblResult

  End Function
End Class
```

As stated before, it isn't supposed to be quick!

In our main module, all we're going to do is get the value and the required power from the user and invoke the `AnyPower()` method, timing it as we do so. We'll also need to add a reference to `Power` in the `PowerClient` project, and set the startup method to `PowerClient.Main()`. Here's how it goes:

```vb
Imports Power
Imports System

Module PowerClient

  Sub Main()

    Dim strInput As String
    Dim dblValue As Double
    Dim intPower As Integer
    Dim startTime As DateTime
    Dim endTime As DateTime
    Dim dblResult As Double
    Dim diffTime As TimeSpan

    Dim objPower As New MyPower()

    While True
      Console.Write("Enter value: ")
      strInput = Console.ReadLine()

      If strInput.Length = 0 Then
        Console.Write("Please enter a value: ")
        strInput = Console.ReadLine()

        If strInput.Length = 0 Then
          Exit While
        End If
      End If

      dblValue = CDbl(strInput)

      Console.Write("Enter power: ")
      strInput = Console.ReadLine

      If strInput.Length = 0 Then
        Console.Write("Please enter a power: ")
        strInput = Console.ReadLine()

        If strInput.Length = 0 Then
          Exit While
        End If
      End If

      intPower = CInt(strInput)
```

```
        startTime = DateTime.UtcNow
        dblResult = objPower.AnyPower(dblValue, intPower)
        endTime = DateTime.UtcNow

        diffTime = endTime.Subtract(startTime)

        Console.WriteLine("Result is <{0}>, in {1} seconds", _
            objPower.AnyPower(dblValue, intPower), diffTime.Seconds)

    End While

  End Sub

End Module
```

Note If you're using Visual Studio .NET to compile your application, you must add a reference to the Power project from the PowerClient project. If you are compiling these from a command line, you must compile the Power assembly first and then reference the DLL while compiling PowerClient.

Running the Example

Let's try it out and see what happens:

```
>PowerClient
Enter value: 3
Enter power: 3
Result is <27>, in 0 seconds
Enter value: 1.0000000001
Enter power: 1000000000
Result is <1.10517092721414>, in 24 seconds
Enter value:
```

That's 24 seconds of wasted time as far as the executing thread is concerned (especially if the power calculation is actually happening on another machine, but we'll come to that in a minute). It's also 24 seconds of the client sitting and waiting for something to happen without being able to do anything else. So what can we do?

Implementing a Slow Asynchronous Process

Remember the fundamental principle: *no changes to the server*? We need to adjust the way in which we are calling the AnyPower() method by wrapping the method in a delegate. A *delegate* is effectively a pointer to an instance of an object that retains knowledge of the original object's method signature. When we declare a function with the keyword Delegate, the compiler generates an object for us with a standard set of methods, two of which—Invoke() and BeginInvoke()—are adapted to the signature of the function itself. We won't be looking at all the methods here; in fact, we'll be concentrating on just two: BeginInvoke() and EndInvoke().

BeginInvoke()has precisely the same arguments as the original function, plus an optional reference to an asynchronous callback function and a state object. So if our original function has the signature

```
Public Function AnyPower(ByVal value As Double, _
  ByVal power As Integer) As Double
```

then the BeginInvoke() function of our delegate has the following signature:

```
Public Function BeginInvoke(ByVal value As Double, _
  ByVal power As Integer, _
  ByVal DelegateCallback As System.AsyncCallback, _
  ByVal DelegateAsyncState As Object) As System.IAsyncResult
```

Instead of calling AnyPower() directly on the original object to invoke the method synchronously, we call BeginInvoke() on our delegate to start an asynchronous invocation on a new thread. The callback function is then triggered when the asynchronous operation eventually completes. The state object can be used to keep track of a particular asynchronous invocation.

Figure 5-1 shows how this all fits together.

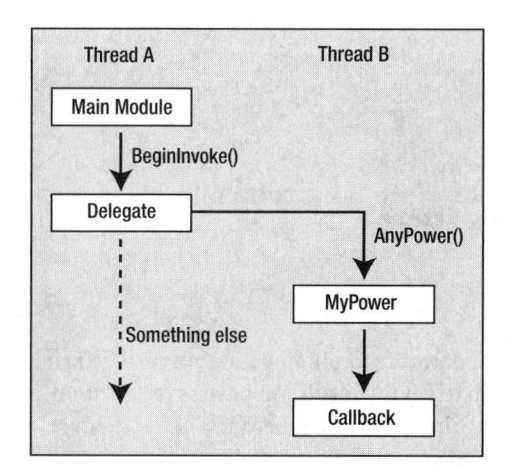

Figure 5-1. *Using the* BeginInvoke() *delegate to start an asynchronous invokation on a new thread*

The next example shows this process in action.

Modifying the Client Code

Let's make a few small changes to the example. The first thing we need to do is declare the delegate function. Here's what that declaration looks like:

```
Module PowerClient
  Delegate Function PowerDelegate(ByVal value As Double, _
    ByVal power As Integer) As Double
```

Notice that it has *exactly* the same signature as the `AnyPower()` method in the `IPower` interface. Here's how we instantiate it:

```
Sub Main()

    Dim strInput As String
    Dim dblValue As Double
    Dim intPower As Integer
    Dim dblResult As Double

    Dim objPower As New MyPower()
    Dim objDelegate As New PowerDelegate( _
            AddressOf objPower.AnyPower)
    Dim result As IAsyncResult
```

So our new delegate object, which already knows about the method signature of `AnyPower()`, is now given the address of the `AnyPower()` method in the `MyPower` object that we have just instantiated. In other words, it's got everything it needs to know to make `AnyPower()` go.

All we need to do now is replace the existing invocation of `objPower.AnyPower()` with a call on the delegate:

```
    Console.Write("Enter power: ")
    strInput = Console.ReadLine
    ...
    intPower = CInt(strInput)

    result = objDelegate.BeginInvoke(dblValue, intPower, _
        Nothing, Nothing)

    startTime = DateTime.UtcNow
```

The asynchronous invocation is off and running on a new thread obtained automatically from the thread pool. This leaves the question of what to do to get the result. We have several options, and we'll start with the simplest. If we place this code directly after the `BeginInvoke` statement, our code simply blocks until the asynchronous method completes:

```
    dblResult = objDelegate.EndInvoke(result)

    Console.WriteLine("Result is <{0}>", dblResult)
```

The net effect is the same as if we had invoked the method directly, although technically speaking, it has actually been run in a different thread.

The next alternative is to poll every now and then to see if the method has completed. This would involve adding code similar to the following:

```
    While Not result.IsCompleted
        ' Do something
    End While

    dblResult = objDelegate.EndInvoke(result)

    Console.WriteLine("Result is <{0}>", dblResult)
```

Another way of achieving the same kind of result would be to code the response handling as follows:

```
While Not result.AsyncWaitHandle.WaitOne(1000, True)
  ' Do something
End While
dblResult = objDelegate.EndInvoke(result)

Console.WriteLine("Result is <{0}>", dblResult)
```

These pieces of code can be executed in another thread or in the same scope. Handling asynchronous results will be more thoroughly covered in the threading chapters in this book. For now, note that the only difference with this approach is that a timeout is used to check for completion, rather than a continuous loop. This is more elegant, in that something can be done while the asynchronous operation is in progress. This might be as simple as outputting some sort of `Working ...` message to the user to indicate that the whole system hasn't seized up.

Using an Asynchronous Callback

The final option is to use an *asynchronous callback*. We've actually already encountered the mechanism for specifying a callback: it's all done by delegates again. A callback is simply a function with the following standard signature:

```
Private Sub MyCallback(ByVal result As IAsyncResult)
```

The way we pass this into our asynchronous invocation is via a delegate for this method signature. Here's how we instantiate this delegate object:

```
Sub Main()

  Dim strInput As String
  Dim dblValue As Double
  Dim intPower As Integer

  Dim objPower As New MyPower()
  Dim objDelegate As New PowerDelegate(AddressOf objPower.AnyPower)
  Dim objCallback As New AsyncCallback(AddressOf MyCallback)
  Dim result As IAsyncResult
```

The only difference between the delegate `AsyncCallback` and `PowerDelegate` is that the framework has already defined `AsyncCallback` for us. Note that we've also removed the declarations for `startTime`, `endTime`, `dblResult`, and `diffTime`.

This is what our call to `BeginInvoke()` now looks like:

```
    Console.Write("Enter power: ")
    strInput = Console.ReadLine
    ...
    intPower = CInt(strInput)

    result = objDelegate.BeginInvoke(dblValue, intPower, _
      objCallback, Nothing)
  End While
```

All that remains is to provide the callback itself. Before we do this, we need to import another namespace, which should provide a clue as to where this is all heading:

```
Imports Power
Imports System.Runtime.Remoting.Messaging
```

Here's the callback, which needs to be added to the `PowerClient` module:

```
Private Sub MyCallback(ByVal result As IAsyncResult)
  Dim objResult As AsyncResult = CType(result, AsyncResult)
  Dim objDelegate As PowerDelegate = _
    CType(objResult.AsyncDelegate, PowerDelegate)

  Dim dblResult As Double
  dblResult = objDelegate.EndInvoke(result)

  Console.WriteLine("Result is <{0}>", dblResult)
End Sub
```

All that casting is getting hold of a reference to the underlying `AsyncResult` object. After that, we can extract a reference to the original delegate to `MyPower.AnyPower()`. Then we can call `EndInvoke()` in the same way as we did before. Because the asynchronous callback has been invoked, we can be sure that this will return immediately.

Running the Example

Because each asynchronous invocation runs in a different client thread, you can now see some interesting effects:

```
>PowerClient
Enter value: 1.0000000001
Enter power: 1000000000
Enter value: 2
Enter power: 2
Enter value: Result is <4>
Result is <1.10517092721414>
```

As you can see, the second calculation of 2 to the power 2 actually overtook the first one. This is because the second calculation was a little simpler than the first one and took considerably less processing time. Because it was running on a different thread from the first calculation, there was no reason for it to wait until the first one was complete. Obviously in real life, we'd attach some kind of marker to each invocation to determine which one was which when it completed, probably by passing in a reference to a state object in the call to `BeginInvoke()`. Such a state object can be any object we like, and we can get hold of a reference to it inside the callback from the `AsyncState` property in the `AsyncResult` object.

As an aside, it's worth noting that if we were developing an object to be used asynchronously on a regular basis, it would be helpful to the client to provide some wrapper methods for the delegate invocation process to avoid imposing the hassle of creating delegates every time. This is the kind of thing that we might end up doing:

```vb
Delegate Function PowerDelegate(ByVal value As Double, _
   ByVal power As Integer) As Double
Dim mDelegate As PowerDelegate
Dim mResult As IAsyncResult

Public Function BeginAnyPower(ByVal value As Double, _
    ByVal power As Integer, _
    ByVal callback As AsyncCallback, ByVal state As Object) _
    As IAsyncResult

   mDelegate = New PowerDelegate(AddressOf Me.AnyPower)
   mResult = mDelegate.BeginInvoke(value, power, callback, state)

   Return mResult

End Function

Public Function EndAnyPower(ByVal result As IAsyncResult) As Double

   Dim objResult As AsyncResult = CType(result, AsyncResult)
   Dim objDelegate As PowerDelegate = _
      CType(objResult.AsyncDelegate, PowerDelegate)

   Return objDelegate.EndInvoke(result)

End Function
```

So our `Power` object now has two alternative methods to evaluate a power: the synchronous `AnyPower()` method and the asynchronous `BeginAnyPower()` method. If a client wants to request a power asynchronously, it uses `BeginAnyPower()`, obtaining the result with the `EndAnyPower()` method.

In fact, this is precisely what standard classes like `System.Net.Sockets.Socket` do; for an example of this in practice, refer to the custom channel implementation in Chapter 3. However, this isn't a useful technique for remoting, because the wrapper methods have to be implemented on the client side by necessity, so we won't be actually implementing any of this in our example.

Implementing a Slow Asynchronous Remote Process

It's time to add some remoting to all this. Actually, it's not so much a question of adding remoting, it's a question of dividing up the existing code. Create a new solution and copy over our `Power` class library. We need another console application, `PowerServer`.

Implementing the Server Code

Here's the main module of `PowerServer`:

CHAPTER 5 ■ ASYNCHRONOUS REMOTING

```
Imports System.Runtime.Remoting
Imports System.Runtime.Remoting.Channels
Imports System.Runtime.Remoting.Channels.Tcp
Imports System.Threading

Imports Power

Module PowerServer

  Sub Main()

    Dim channel As TcpChannel

    Console.WriteLine("Server started")

    channel = New TcpChannel(8086)
    ChannelServices.RegisterChannel(channel)

    RemotingConfiguration.RegisterWellKnownServiceType( _
      GetType(MyPower), "MyPower.rem", _
        WellKnownObjectMode.SingleCall)

    Console.ReadLine()

  End Sub

End Module
```

■**Note** You will have to add a reference to the `System.Runtime.Remoting.dll` assembly before compiling this application.

This should all look familiar to you. Our server begins by creating a TCP/IP channel listening on port 8086. It then registers our `MyPower` object as a single call object in the usual manner. The class `MyPower` is moved to `PowerServer` wholesale from the previous solution, except for one small change, which is required for remoting:

```
Class MyPower
  Inherits MarshalByRefObject
  Implements IPower
```

We also need a console message to keep tabs on what's going on the server:

```
Console.WriteLine("{0} ^ {1} = {2}", value, power, dblResult)
```

```
Return dblResult
```

Modifying the Client Code

The client will look familiar as well. This is based very heavily on the `PowerClient` class in the previous solution, with a few minor changes. The first two are that we need a string to hold the URL, and we also need to refer to the `Power` object by its interface, as we no longer have direct access to `MyPower` (because that's only available on the server):

```
Sub Main()

    Dim strurl As String
    Dim objPower As IPower
    Dim strInput As String
    Dim dblValue As Double
    Dim intPower As Integer
```

Next, we move the creation of the object into the `While` loop, and change it into a remote activation:

```
    While True

        Console.Write("Enter value: ")
        strInput = Console.ReadLine()

        If strInput.Length = 0 Then
            Exit While
        End If

        dblValue = CDbl(strInput)

        Console.Write("Enter power: ")
        strInput = Console.ReadLine

        intPower = CInt(strInput)

        strurl = "tcp://localhost:8086/MyPower.rem"
        objPower = CType(Activator.GetObject(GetType(IPower), strurl), _
            IPower)

        Dim objDelegate As New PowerDelegate( _
            AddressOf objPower.AnyPower)
        Dim objCallback As New AsyncCallback(AddressOf MyCallback)

        result = objDelegate.BeginInvoke(dblValue, intPower, _
            objCallback, Nothing)
```

Apart from that, no more changes need to be made.

Running the Example

Let's see what happens on the server when we run it:

```
>PowerServer
Server started
1.0000000001 ^ 1000000000 = 1.10517092721414
3 ^ 3 = 27
```

Here's the client:

```
>PowerClient
Enter value: 1.0000000001
Enter power: 1000000000
Result is <0>
Enter value: 3
Enter power: 3
Result is <0>
Enter value: Result is <1.10517092721414>
Result is <27>
```

You should note several things here. First, as soon as we enter the first calculation to perform at the client, the client asks what we want calculated next. So by using asynchronous remoting, we have accessed a remote object but also managed to make sure that our client is capable of handling several tasks at once.

However, you'll also note that, although the second calculation can be performed much more quickly than the first, we don't receive the result from the second calculation until just after we receive the result of the first. This means that, unlike the client, the server can only handle one request at a time. To get around this problem, we have to use a different approach by using *events*.

Using Events with Asynchronous Remote Processes

The next type of remote application to consider seems just as straightforward, although it isn't. This application is the kind where a client issues a single request to a server, and receives one or more asynchronous responses in the future. This is very much a session-oriented pattern, and consequently involves the use of persistent singleton objects that generate periodic events.

As introduced through the previous example, a problem with these types of applications is that the task running on the remote object could potentially last a long time, and therefore could block the use of the remote object for any other process. Therefore, we need to introduce multiple threads on the remote application.

The first example we'll look at is a timer class, which simply allows a server to request an event to be raised every second.

After looking at all the issues involved with that, we'll demonstrate the classic example of this kind of application, a teleconference, where several clients can talk to each other via a central server. Each time a client contributes to the conference, it is relayed to all the other participants via an event.

Generating Events in a Single Application Domain

We'll follow the same path as the previous example, and start by presenting the single application domain version of our timer application. After that, we'll attempt to remote it.

Create a new solution and add two projects to it: a class library called TickTock and a console application called TickClient.

Implementing the TickTock Class Library

TickTock contains the interface ITickTock, which looks like this:

```
Public Interface ITickTock

  Sub Tick()
  Event Tock(ByVal sender As Object, ByVal args As EventArgs)

End Interface
```

The idea is that the method Tick sets off the clock, and the event Tock is called every second. Notice the signature of the Tock event: this is a standard signature used by almost every event in the .NET infrastructure. The advantage of using a standard signature is that we can use the same delegate events for all of them.

Implementing the Client Code

Our TickClient project holds the main module and our implementation of ITickTock. Here's the main module. Notice that our instance of ITickTock is declared as WithEvents. This is so we can catch the events coming back from the called object. This sort of thing should be very familiar to VB6 users.

```
Imports System
Imports System.Threading
Imports TickTock

Module TickClient

  Dim WithEvents _TickTock As ITickTock

  Public Sub Main()

    Dim newThread As New Thread(AddressOf Start)
    newThread.Start()

    Console.ReadLine()
    newThread.Abort()

  End Sub
```

Inside the new thread, we create an instance of our implementation of ITickTock and start it ticking:

```
Public Sub Start()
  _TickTock = New MyTickTock()
  _TickTock.Tick()
End Sub
```

We end the module with the event handler that gets called with every tick:

```
Public Sub _TickTock_Tock(ByVal sender As Object, _
  ByVal args As System.EventArgs) Handles _TickTock.Tock
  Console.WriteLine("Tick at {0}", DateTime.UtcNow)
End Sub
End Module
```

Finally, here's our implementation of ITickTock:

```
Class MyTickTock
  Implements ITickTock

  Public Sub Tick() Implements TickTock.ITickTock.Tick

    While True
      Thread.CurrentThread.Sleep(1000)
      RaiseEvent Tock(Me, Nothing)
    End While

  End Sub

  Public Event Tock(ByVal sender As Object, _
    ByVal args As System.EventArgs) _
    Implements TickTock.ITickTock.Tock
End Class
```

So our implementation of the method Tick() simply loops around raising an event every second.

Running the Example

This is what we see if we run it:

```
>TickClient
Tick at 16/06/2002 14:06:14
Tick at 16/06/2002 14:06:15
Tick at 16/06/2002 14:06:16
Tick at 16/06/2002 14:06:17
Tick at 16/06/2002 14:06:18
```

. . . and so on (until we press Enter).

Passing Events Between Remote Applications

That was not particularly tricky, but let's consider what needs to happen before we can remote this. The central problem is that we need somehow to set things up so that the server can call back to the original client object as if it were a client rather than a server. This is definitely a nontrivial thing to do, which is why a lot of applications tend to go for implementations where a pair of object references are exchanged: The first object reference is used for client invocations on the server, and the second is used for server invocations on the client. However, we'll go the more complicated route, make a copy of our previous solution, and see what we need to do to make it work in a remote environment.

You might imagine that all you had to do was move the implementation of ITickTock into the server, add in the usual remoting stuff into the client, and invoke the object in the usual manner. Let's see what happens if you do this.

Implementing the Server Code

First, we add a new console application project, called TickServer, which contains the main server module. We also move the implementation of ITickTock from the client into it too:

```
Imports System.Runtime.Remoting
Imports System.Runtime.Remoting.Channels
Imports System.Runtime.Remoting.Channels.Tcp
Imports System.Threading
Imports TickTock
Module TickServer

   Sub Main()

      Dim channel As TcpChannel

      Console.WriteLine("Server started")

      channel = New TcpChannel(8086)
      ChannelServices.RegisterChannel(channel)

      RemotingConfiguration.RegisterWellKnownServiceType( _
        GetType(MyTickTock), "MyTickTock.rem", _
        WellKnownObjectMode.Singleton)

      Console.ReadLine()

   End Sub

End Module

Class MyTickTock
   Implements ITickTock
```

```vb
Public Sub Tick() Implements TickTock.ITickTock.Tick

  While True
    Thread.CurrentThread.Sleep(1000)
    RaiseEvent Tock(Me, Nothing)
  End While

End Sub

Public Event Tock(ByVal sender As Object, _
  ByVal args As System.EventArgs) _
  Implements TickTock.ITickTock.Tock
End Class
```

We note in passing that the well-known object is declared as a singleton, rather than as a single-call object like those that we have been dealing with until now.

Modifying the Client Code

Here's what the client looks like now:

```vb
Imports TickTock
Imports System.Threading

Module TickClient

  Dim WithEvents _TickTock As ITickTock
  Sub Main()

    Dim newThread As New Thread(AddressOf Start)
    newThread.Start()

    Console.ReadLine()
    newThread.Abort()

  End Sub

  Public Sub Start()
    Dim strurl As String
    strurl = "tcp://localhost:8086/MyTickTock.rem"

    _TickTock = CType(Activator.GetObject( _
        GetType(ITickTock), _
        strurl), ITickTock)
    _TickTock.Tick()
  End Sub
```

```
    Public Sub _TickTock_Tock(ByVal sender As Object, _
      ByVal args As System.EventArgs) _
      Handles _TickTock.Tock
      Console.WriteLine("Tick at {0}", DateTime.UtcNow)
    End Sub

End Module
```

Running the Example

This sort of thing should be second nature to you by now, but let's see what happens when we run the server and try to connect the client to it:

```
>TickClient

Unhandled Exception: System.IO.FileNotFoundException: File or assembly nameTickClient,➥
or one of its dependencies, was not found.
File name: "TickClient"

Server stack trace:
   at System.Reflection.Assembly.nLoad(AssemblyName fileName, String
codeBase, Boolean isStringized, Evidence assemblySecurity, Boolean
throwOnFileNotFound, Assembly locationHint, StackCrawlMark& stackMark)
   at System.Reflection.Assembly.InternalLoad(AssemblyName assemblyRef,
Boolean stringized, Evidence assemblySecurity, StackCrawlMark& stackMark)

...
```

What's gone wrong? Basically, this is a problem with the current version of the .NET Framework, in that the server can't find its way back to the calling client to invoke the event, because it has no knowledge of the structure of the client object. It's all described in article Q312114 in the Microsoft Knowledge Base, if you're interested in investigating it further (you can find it at http://support.microsoft.com/default.aspx?scid=kb;EN-US;q312114). For our purposes, all we need to do is implement a workaround, and the following is what Microsoft recommends.

Using Remotely Delegatable Objects

First, we need to define a new abstract class, called RemotelyDelegatableObject, and put it into the TickTock class library so that it's known to both client and server. This is what it looks like:

```
Public MustInherit Class RemotelyDelegatableObject
  Inherits MarshalByRefObject

  Sub ExternalCallback(ByVal sender As Object, _
      ByVal args As EventArgs)
    InternalCallback(sender, args)
  End Sub

  Protected MustOverride Sub InternalCallback( _
      ByVal sender As Object, ByVal args As EventArgs)
End Class
```

The key is in the phrase "remotely delegatable." If we derive a class from this on the client side, and put all the active client-side code into it, we are then in a position to associate the external callback in this class with a delegate on the server side with the same signature. Because the server knows the structure of the remotely delegatable class, it is then in a position to make a callback to the client (as shown in Figure 5-2).

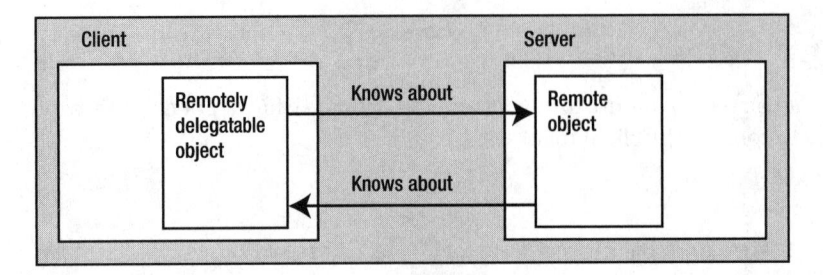

Figure 5-2. *Using classes with the same signature allows the server-side class to make a callback to the client.*

It's probably best to show this in practice.

Implementing the TockTick Class Library

Let's create a new class library project, called TockTick, and move most of the client code into it:

```
Imports System
Imports System.Threading
Imports TickTock

Public Class TockTick
  Inherits RemotelyDelegatableObject

  Dim WithEvents _TickTock As ITickTock

  Public Sub Run()

    Dim newThread As New Thread(AddressOf Start)
    newThread.Start()

    Console.ReadLine()
    newThread.Abort()

  End Sub

  Public Sub Start()
    Dim strurl As String
    strurl = "tcp://localhost:8086/MyTickTock.rem"
```

```vbnet
    _TickTock = CType(Activator.GetObject(GetType(ITickTock), _
      strurl), ITickTock)
    _TickTock.Tick()
  End Sub

  Public Sub _TickTock_Tock(ByVal sender As Object, _
    ByVal args As System.EventArgs) _
    Handles _TickTock.Tock
    Console.WriteLine("Tick at {0}", DateTime.UtcNow)
  End Sub

  Protected Overrides Sub InternalCallback(ByVal sender As Object, _
    ByVal args As System.EventArgs)
    Console.WriteLine("Tick at {0}", DateTime.UtcNow)
  End Sub
End Class
```

Modifying the Client Code

We'll be making a few more changes to `TockTick`, but before we do so, here's what's left of the client:

```vbnet
Imports TockTick

Module TickClient

  Sub Main()

    Dim tock As New TockTick.TockTick()
    tock.Run()

  End Sub

End Module
```

Modifying the TockTick Class Library

Now let's go back to that `TockTick` class. One problem we have is that we're now intending that the callback comes in via the `InternalCallback()` method, rather than the `_TickTock_Tock` event handler. However, our main problem is that we're still expecting to call back to `TockTick` without knowing the class's signature. The key to unlocking both problems is to get rid of the static event handling, and link in our new event handler dynamically using a delegate for the event handler that the server is going to call. So we can dispose of the `_TickTock_Tock` event handler, remove the `WithEvents` keyword from the declaration of `_TickTock`, and use `AddHandler` to make the dynamic association:

```vb
        _TickTock = _
            CType(Activator.GetObject(GetType(ITickTock), _
                        strurl), ITickTock)
        AddHandler _TickTock.TheDelegate, _
                        AddressOf ExternalCallback_TickTock.Tick()
```

Unfortunately, it's not that simple. Our delegate in the `TickTock` implementation will have a signature something like this:

```vb
Public Delegate Sub TockDelegate(ByVal sender as Object, _
    ByVal args as EventArgs)
```

The instance of the delegate will look like this:

```vb
Public Event TheDelegate as TockDelegate
```

Sadly, we can't just add this to our interface, because it's an instance of something, and requires space in memory; so it has to go in the class definition. All of which means that to access this from both client and server, we must share the class definition of `TickTock`, and not just the interface definition `ITickTock`. (You might think that you could get around this by deriving `MyTickTock` from a shell `TickTock` class, but that won't work either, because you can't access an event delegate from a derived class.)

This is all a little tiresome, because it will make the ultimate deployment slightly messier. However, there's no real alternative short of exchanging class references of some sort between client and server, so let's forge ahead. Let's delete our `ITickTock` interface, and implement our `TickTock` class directly.

Here's what our revised `TickTock` class library looks like:

```vb
Imports System.Threading

Public Delegate Sub TockDelegate(ByVal sender As Object, _
    ByVal args As EventArgs)

Public Class TickTock
    Inherits MarshalByRefObject

    Public Event TheDelegate As TockDelegate

    Sub Tick()
        While True
            Thread.CurrentThread.Sleep(1000)
            RaiseEvent TheDelegate(Me, Nothing)
        End While
    End Sub

End Class

Public MustInherit Class RemotelyDelegatableObject
    Inherits MarshalByRefObject
```

```vbnet
  Sub ExternalCallback(ByVal sender As Object, _
    ByVal args As EventArgs)
    InternalCallback(sender, args)
  End Sub

  Protected MustOverride Sub InternalCallback(ByVal sender _
    As Object, ByVal args As EventArgs)

End Class
```

The main change from the original implementation is that the event is now raised on the delegate passed in with the object. As you'll see, this is now going to be tied into the ExternalCallback() method in the calling client object. Here's what TockTick looks like now:

```vbnet
Imports System
Imports System.Threading
Imports TickTock

Public Class TockTick
  Inherits RemotelyDelegatableObject
  Dim _TickTock As TickTock.TickTock

  Public Sub Run()

    Dim newThread As New Thread(AddressOf Start)
    newThread.Start()

    Console.ReadLine()
    AddHandler _TickTock.TheDelegate, _
          AddressOf ExternalCallback
    newThread.Abort()

  End Sub

  Public Sub Start()
    Dim strurl As String
    strurl = "tcp://localhost:8086/MyTickTock.rem"

    _TickTock = CType(Activator.GetObject( _
      GetType(TickTock.TickTock), strurl), _
      TickTock.TickTock)
    AddHandler _TickTock.TheDelegate, _
          AddressOf ExternalCallback_TickTock.Tick()
  End Sub

  Protected Overrides Sub InternalCallback(ByVal sender As Object, _
    ByVal args As System.EventArgs)
    Console.WriteLine("Tick at {0}", DateTime.UtcNow)
  End Sub
End Class
```

The main difference here is that we're now referring to the class `TickTock` rather than the interface `ITickTock`, and that we've now made the event handling dynamic using `AddHandler`.

Modifying the Server Code

The code for the client main module itself is unchanged, so it only remains to show the code for the server:

```
Imports System.Runtime.Remoting
Imports System.Runtime.Remoting.Channels
Imports System.Runtime.Remoting.Channels.Tcp
Imports System.Threading
Imports TickTock

Module TickServer

    Sub Main()

        Dim channel As TcpChannel
        Console.WriteLine("Server started")

        channel = New TcpChannel(8086)
        ChannelServices.RegisterChannel(channel)

        RemotingConfiguration.RegisterWellKnownServiceType( _
            GetType(TickTock.TickTock), _
            "MyTickTock.rem", WellKnownObjectMode.Singleton)

        Console.ReadLine()

    End Sub

End Module
```

Running the Example

So let's try running this version:

```
>TickClient
Unhandled Exception: System.Runtime.Remoting.RemotingException: This remoting proxy has
no channel sink which means either the server has no registered server channels that are
listening, or this application has no suitable client channel to talk to the server.

Server stack trace:    at
System.Runtime.Remoting.Proxies.RemotingProxy.InternalInvoke(IMethodCall
Message reqMcmMsg, Boolean useDispatchMessage, Int32 callType)
   at System.Runtime.Remoting.Proxies.RemotingProxy.Invoke(IMessage
reqMsg)
...
```

This is a little surprising because you might be thinking that we already have a TCP/IP channel in place. However, that's used for client-initiated interactions. If our server is to talk back to the client, we also need the client to register a channel. It's a simple change to the client's main module:

```
Imports System.Runtime.Remoting
Imports System.Runtime.Remoting.Channels
Imports System.Runtime.Remoting.Channels.Tcp
Imports TockTick

Module TickClient

    Sub Main()

        Dim channel As TcpChannel
        channel = New TcpChannel(8088)
        ChannelServices.RegisterChannel(channel)
        Dim tock As New TockTick.TockTick()
        tock.Run()

    End Sub

End Module
```

Now if we run the server and then the client, we should see exactly what we saw in our original single application domain version.

So events *can* be remoted, even if the process is a little more convoluted than we perhaps imagined.

Multiuser Asynchronous Remote Applications

We're now going to conclude this section by implementing a simple teleconference application, which will demonstrate how we can put together a true multiuser remote application. This time around, we'll take the various techniques, launch straight into the implementation itself, and see what we need to do that's different.

Implementing the Conference Class Library

Start by creating a new solution. Add a new class library, called Conference, which contains several classes, including RemotelyDelegatableObject and Conference, as shown here:

```
Imports System.Runtime.Remoting.Messaging

Public Delegate Sub OutputDelegate(ByVal sender As Object, _
  ByVal args As EventArgs)

<Serializable()> Public Class MyEventArgs
    Inherits EventArgs

    Private _contribution As String
```

```vb
    Public Sub New(ByVal contribution As String)
      _contribution = contribution
    End Sub

    Public ReadOnly Property Contribution()
      Get
        Return _contribution
      End Get
    End Property

End Class
Public Class Conference
  Inherits MarshalByRefObject

  Public Event TheDelegate As OutputDelegate

  Sub Input(ByVal contribution As String)

    Console.WriteLine("Input received: <{0}>", contribution)

    Dim args As New MyEventArgs(contribution)
    RaiseEvent TheDelegate(Me, args)

  End Sub
End Class

Public MustInherit Class RemotelyDelegatableObject
  Inherits MarshalByRefObject

  Sub ExternalCallback(ByVal sender As Object, _
    ByVal args As EventArgs)
    InternalCallback(sender, args)
  End Sub

  Protected MustOverride Sub InternalCallback(ByVal sender _
    As Object, ByVal args As EventArgs)
End Class
```

This is very similar to what we were doing with TickTock. The only difference is the addition of a class derived from EventArgs in the System namespace. We'll use this for passing the inputs from the various conference attendees back to each other.

The actual Conference class structure is very simple, and has a single input method, called Input(), which takes in the contributions from each attendee (we have to be very careful not to refer to the attendees as *delegates* here, of course...).

Implementing the ConfAttendee Class Library

Add another class library called ConfAttendee, containing the class ConfAttendee, which looks like this (remember, this is the equivalent of the TockTick class in the previous example):

```vb
Imports Conference

Public Class ConfAttendee
  Inherits RemotelyDelegatableObject

  Public Sub Run()
    Dim strURL As String
    Dim myConference As Conference.Conference
    Dim contribution As String

    Dim name As String
    Dim nickName As String

    strURL = "tcp://localhost:8086/MyConference.rem"
    myConference = CType(Activator.GetObject( _
      GetType(Conference.Conference), _
      strURL), Conference.Conference)
    AddHandler myConference.TheDelegate, AddressOf ExternalCallback

    While True
      Console.Write("Input? ")
      contribution = Console.ReadLine()
      If contribution.Length = 0 Then
        Exit While
      End If

      myConference.Input(contribution)

    End While

    RemoveHandler myConference.TheDelegate, _
          AddressOf ExternalCallback
  End Sub

  Protected Overrides Sub InternalCallback(ByVal sender As Object, _
    ByVal args As System.EventArgs)

    Dim myArgs As MyEventArgs
    myArgs = CType(args, MyEventArgs)

    Console.WriteLine("Input received: <{0}>", myArgs.Contribution)

  End Sub
End Class
```

Again, this is very similar in style to what we were doing in the previous example. We're in a loop, constantly waiting for input from the attendee, while interrupting this from time to time with the contributions from the other ones. Next we need to add a couple of console applications for our client and server.

Implementing the Client Code

Here's the client, ConfClient:

```vb
Imports System.Runtime.Remoting
Imports System.Runtime.Remoting.Channels
Imports System.Runtime.Remoting.Channels.Tcp

Module ConfClient
  Sub Main()

    Dim commands As String
    Dim port As Integer

    commands = Microsoft.VisualBasic.Command

    If commands.Length = 0 Then
      port = 8088
    Else
      port = CInt(commands)
    End If

    Dim channel As TcpChannel
    channel = New TcpChannel(port)
    ChannelServices.RegisterChannel(channel)

    Dim attendee As New ConfAttendee.ConfAttendee()
    attendee.Run()

  End Sub

End Module
```

The only point of note here is that each client needs to have a unique channel, so if we're testing on the same machine, the ports must be configurable. We could clearly do this via configuration, but for convenience we'll do it via the command line.

Implementing the Server Code

Finally, here's the server, ConfServer:

```vb
Imports System.Runtime.Remoting
Imports System.Runtime.Remoting.Channels
Imports System.Runtime.Remoting.Channels.Tcp
Imports Conference

Module ConfServer
```

```
Sub Main()

    Dim channel As TcpChannel

    Console.WriteLine("Server started")

    channel = New TcpChannel(8086)
    ChannelServices.RegisterChannel(channel)
    RemotingConfiguration.RegisterWellKnownServiceType( _
       GetType(Conference.Conference), "MyConference.rem", _
       WellKnownObjectMode.Singleton)
    Console.ReadLine()
End Sub

End Module
```

This is nearly identical to what we had last time.

Running the Example

Now, let's put it all together and run a couple of clients against a server. Here's what we see on the server:

```
>ConfServer
Server started
Input received: <Good evening>
Input received: <Good evening to you, too>
Input received: <This seems to work>
Input received: <So it does>
```

Here's the first client:

```
>ConfClient
Input? Good evening
Input received: <Good evening>
Input? Input received: <Good evening to you, too>
This seems to work
Input received: <This seems to work>
Input? Input received: <So it does>
```

Here's the second one:

```
>ConfClient 8087
Input? Input received: <Good evening>
Good evening to you, too
Input received: <Good evening to you, too>
Input? Input received: <This seems to work>
So it does
Input received: <So it does>
Input?
```

Notice something odd? The server has no idea (at least at application level) how many clients it has attached. It simply raises a single event, and all the attached clients receive the invocation. This makes this kind of teleconferencing application very simple to implement.

However, you might notice one slight inelegance of this scheme. All the clients receive their own contributions back along with everyone else's. Worse than that, the various contributions carry no indication of their origin. Of course, we could pass this sort of information explicitly at the `Input()` method call. However, there's a slightly more subtle way of doing this, by using the call context, which we'll explore now.

Using Call Contexts with Asynchronous Remoting

If we want to pass around information about a client without cluttering up our method calls with loads of additional arguments, Chapter 1 noted that we can use the *call context*. The call context is a repository for any information that we want to pass around in remote calls, and it's very straightforward to use.

Using Call Contexts in the Teleconference Application

In our teleconference example, we'll use a context object to pass around each attendee's name and nickname. To do this, we need to create, get, and set the context in the application.

Creating a Context Object

First, we need to create a new class of object that we can insert into the call context. This class must satisfy only two criteria: it must be *serializable* and it must implement the interface `IlogicalThreadAffinative` in the namespace `System.Runtime.Remoting.Messaging`. We'll call our class `ConfAttendeeID`, and insert it into the class library that contains `Conference`. First, we need to import the relevant namespace:

```
Imports System.Runtime.Remoting.Messaging
```

Now here's our new class:

```
<Serializable()> Public Class ConfAttendeeID
  Implements ILogicalThreadAffinative

  Private _name As String
  Private _nickName As String

  Public Sub New(ByVal name As String, ByVal nickName As String)
    _name = name
    _nickName = nickName
  End Sub

  Public ReadOnly Property Name() As String
    Get
      Return _name
    End Get
  End Property
```

```
    Public ReadOnly Property NickName() As String
      Get
        Return _nickName
      End Get
    End Property
End Class
```

As you can see, this is a simple class, providing access to a name and nickname pair. Importantly, it satisfies our twin criteria for being a suitable context object, by being serializable and implementing the interface IlogicalThreadAffinative. Note, incidentally, that implementing this interface doesn't actually require us to implement any methods or properties. It's enough simply to implement the interface itself.

Setting the Call Context

At the client end, we need to make some changes to our ConfAttendee class. We start by importing the same namespace as for the context object:

```
Imports System.Runtime.Remoting.Messaging
Imports Conference

Public Class ConfAttendee
```

Next, we need to change the input sequence so that we get a name and nickname from the user, and then create a context object containing these:

```
AddHandler myConference.TheDelegate, AddressOf ExternalCallback

Console.Write("Name? ")
name = Console.ReadLine()

Console.Write("Nickname? ")
nickName = Console.ReadLine()

Dim id As New ConfAttendeeID(name, nickName)
```

After that, all we need to do is insert this into the call context, identified with the string "ID":

```
CallContext.SetData("ID", id)
```

The effect is that this information will be passed around with each remote invocation, which is why our ID object had to be serializable. Note that we could actually insert several objects into the call context, each identified by a different string.

Getting the Call Context

Let's see what we need to do on the server. Here's what the Input() method in the Conference object looks like now:

```vb
Sub Input(ByVal contribution As String)

    Dim id As ConfAttendeeID
    id = CType(CallContext.GetData("ID"), ConfAttendeeID)

    Console.WriteLine("Input received from {0} (""{1}""): <{2}>", _
        id.Name, id.NickName, contribution)

    Dim args As New MyEventArgs(contribution)
    RaiseEvent TheDelegate(Me, args)

End Sub
```

So extracting the information from the context is as simple as inserting it; the only difference being that we have to make the appropriate cast to get the correct object type.

We're not quite there yet, however, because we haven't got the identifier information back to the calling client. Actually, it's amazingly simple, because the context travels back to the client as well when we raise the event. So here's all we need to do to our `ConfAttendee` callback:

```vb
Protected Overrides Sub InternalCallback(ByVal sender As Object, _
    ByVal args As System.EventArgs)

    Dim myArgs As MyEventArgs
    myArgs = CType(args, MyEventArgs)

    Dim id As ConfAttendeeID
    id = CType(CallContext.GetData("ID"), ConfAttendeeID)

    Console.WriteLine("Input received from {0} (""{1}""): <{2}>", _
        id.Name, id.NickName, myArgs.Contribution)

End Sub
```

Running the Example

Let's try it out and see what happens with a couple of clients. First, here's what we see at the server:

```
>ConfServer
Server started
Input received from Jon ("Beardie"): <Hello everyone>
Input received from Not Jon ("Smoothie"): <Hello to you, too>
```

Here's the first client:

```
>ConfClient
Name? Jon
Nickname? Beardie
Input? Hello everyone
Input received from Jon ("Beardie"): <Hello everyone>
```

Finally, here's our second client:

```
>ConfClient 8000
Name? Not Jon
Nickname? Smoothie
Input? Input received from Jon ("Beardie"): <Hello everyone>
Hello to you, too
```

So the call context is a useful and straightforward way of passing around client-related information for asynchronous implementations, although as we know, it is used during synchronous processes too.

Summary

In this chapter, we've looked at two main types of asynchronous .NET applications, and how they can be successfully remoted.

We first looked at simple remote asynchronous method calls using delegates and asynchronous callbacks. In this case, a client sends a request to a server; while it waits for the request to be served, the client is still available to handle other processes.

Then we turned our attention to situations where the client might expect multiple responses for the server over time. We saw that we could handle this situation by using events, although we noted that remoting an event-oriented .NET application is not as straightforward as we might have hoped; we had to create a remotely delegatable object on the client, which the server will recognize.

Finally, we looked at how the call context is useful for passing client information around between remote objects running asynchronous processes.

CHAPTER 6

Debugging and Error Handling

In distributed applications in general, and .NET Remoting in particular, errors can occur at many different places in the application. This presents several challenges. First, you must identify which errors are possible at each tier in the application. You must then decide how to detect (and hopefully preempt) these errors at the most appropriate place in the application. Finally, you must devise an appropriate, consistent, and robust strategy for dealing with errors when they arise at runtime, and for reporting these errors to the user.

Error handling is an important part of industrial-strength software development, but it can be difficult to get enthusiastic about it. To liven the debate, we'll look at a real remoting application that has no error handling whatsoever, and investigate the problems that can arise. Step-by-step, we'll add error-handling code to address each of the shortcomings in the application.

As you know, error handling in VB .NET is based on the concept of *exceptions*. Throughout the chapter, it's important to bear in mind that exceptions can be informational events, rather than error conditions. For example, you can use exceptions to help you decide how to configure a remoting application. A client application might try to connect to a variety of different remote hosts. If a particular host is unavailable, an exception will occur; the client application can use this as a signal to try a different remote host.

As the chapter evolves, you'll see how to use exceptions to control the flow between the remote object and the client; the real challenge is trying to divide the error-handling code appropriately between the client and server tiers in the application. To achieve uniformity in the way you handle errors in the application, it's often also beneficial to define custom exception classes to represent application-specific errors. As you'll see, you must address several technical issues when defining custom exception classes in a remoting application.

To close the chapter, you'll see how to log error information to persistent storage, such as a flat file, a central database, or the Windows event log. It's important to log errors in a remoting application to combat the inherent complexity of executing a distributed application.

To start, let's examine the common exceptions that can arise in a remoting application.

Common Exceptions in Remoting Applications

As you've probably already noticed, a lot of things can go wrong in a remoting application. Exceptions can occur at just about any stage, from the moment the client application creates a proxy object representing a remote object, to the moment the client application tries to invoke methods on that object. Here's a brief summary of some of the common errors you can expect as the client and server applications communicate with each other:

- The client application invokes a remote method, but the server application isn't currently running.
- The client application specifies an invalid URL for a well-known remoting object. For example, the protocol, machine name, port number, or object URI might be incorrect.
- The client application tries to pass an MBV (marshal by value) object into a remote method, but the object is not serializable.
- A remote method tries to return an MBV object, but the returned object is not serializable.
- A remote method decides to throw its own exceptions. For example, the remote method might throw an exception if it receives invalid parameters from the client application.

Some of these exceptions are due to runtime conditions, such as server unavailability or losing a network connection. Other exceptions indicate design problems, such as failing to mark objects as serializable when necessary; these latter exceptions should be anticipated in the design where possible, and code should be written in such a way as to prevent these exceptions from happening.

Illustrating Common Remoting Exceptions

In this section of the chapter, we'll write a useful utility application to illustrate when these exceptions occur, and show the error messages you can expect to see in each case. We'll also show how to throw your own exceptions in a remoting object, and discuss exactly what happens when you do this.

Defining a Remotable Object

To illustrate these error conditions, we'll write a remoting object named `DemoError`. The class has four simple methods to highlight different issues. Create a project named `MyRemoteNamespace` and add a file named `DemoError` to it. We'll look at the full code for this class first, and then we'll discuss the details:

```
Imports System

Namespace MyRemoteNamespace

  Public Class DemoError
    Inherits MarshalByRefObject

    ' Method1 executes successfully
    Public Sub Method1()
      Console.WriteLine("Method1 called")
    End Sub

    ' Method2 takes an unserializable parameter
    Public Sub Method2(ByVal param1 As MyUnserializable)
      Console.WriteLine("Method2 called")
    End Sub
```

```vb
    ' Method3 returns an unserializable result
    Public Function Method3() As MyUnserializable
      Console.WriteLine("Method3 called")
      Return New MyUnserializable(42)
    End Function

    ' Method4 throws an exception if it receives an invalid parameter
    Public Sub Method4(ByVal param1 As MySerializable)
      Console.WriteLine("Method4 called")
      If param1 Is Nothing Then
        Throw New ArgumentNullException( _
                          "param1", _
                          "You must specify a real object")
      ElseIf param1.Data < 0 Or param1.Data > 100
        Throw New ArgumentOutOfRangeException( _
                          "param1", _
                          "Data value must be between 0 and 100")
      End If
      Console.WriteLine("Method4 accepted parameter's value, {0}", _
                    param1.Data)
    End Sub

  End Class

End Namespace
```

Here's the source code for the `MyUnserializable` and `MySerializable` classes. Notice that `MyUnserializable` isn't tagged with the `<Serializable>` attribute, whereas `MySerializable` is. These classes should be located in the same file as the `DemoError` class:

```vb
Public Class MyUnserializable

  Private mData As Integer

  Public Sub New(ByVal data As Integer)
    mData = data
  End Sub

  Public ReadOnly Property Data() As Integer
    Get
      Return mData
    End Get
  End Property

End Class

<Serializable()> _
Public Class MySerializable
```

```vbnet
    Private mData As Integer

    Public Sub New(ByVal data As Integer)
        mData = data
    End Sub

    Public ReadOnly Property Data() As Integer
        Get
            Return mData
        End Get
    End Property

End Class
```

Let's now dissect each of the methods in the `DemoError` class:

- `Method1()` is entirely uncontroversial. Nothing should go wrong in this method.

- `Method2()` takes a single parameter of type `MyUnserializable`. As you'll see shortly (and as its name suggests), `MyUnserializable` is an unserializable class. You can expect an error when we call `Method2()` from the client application—the .NET Remoting infrastructure will be unable to marshal `MyUnserializable` objects into this method.

- `Method3()` returns a `MyUnserializable` object. You can expect an exception when we call `Method3()` from the client application; the .NET Remoting infrastructure will be unable to marshal the `MyUnserializable` object returned by the method.

- `Method4()` takes a single parameter of type `MySerializable`. As you'll see in a moment, this is a serializable class, so there should be no problem using this class with remote methods.

Using Predefined .NET Exception Classes

Notice that `Method4()` performs some tests on its parameter. If the parameter is `Nothing`, we throw an `ArgumentNullException` to indicate this is not acceptable. Likewise, if the parameter's value is invalid (whatever that might mean in the context of this method), we throw an `ArgumentOutOfRangeException`. Both of these exception types are defined in the `System` namespace in the .NET Framework class library.

We encourage you to use `ArgumentNullException` and `ArgumentOutOfRangeException` for validating parameters in your own methods, whether they are remote methods or plain-vanilla local methods. This will make your methods consistent with existing methods in .NET. There is also an exception class named `InvalidEnumArgumentException`, which you can use to indicate that an invalid enumeration value has been passed to a method or property setter.

We should point out one other issue about exceptions thrown by a remote method: When a remote method throws an exception, the .NET Remoting infrastructure automatically marshals the exception object by value, from the server application to the client application. The exception object is serialized at the server machine, and then deserialized when it arrives at the client machine.

This implies exception classes must be annotated with the `<Serializable>` attribute, to support serialization. Luckily for us, all the predefined exception classes in the .NET Framework class library do indeed have this attribute. Later in the chapter, when we define our own exception classes, we must remember to decorate these classes with `<Serializable>`.

Defining the Host Application

Let's write a simple server application, `DemoErrorServer`, to host the remoting object. The server program registers a TCP channel on port 6001, and registers the `DemoError` class as a single-call remoting service type. We could have chosen different configuration options here, such as using an HTTP channel, a different port number, or a different activation mode; feel free to experiment.

Notice that the `RegisterWellKnownServiceType()` method call is enclosed in a `Try...Catch` block to handle any exceptions that might arise when we register the remoting object:

```vb
Imports System
Imports System.Runtime.Remoting
Imports System.Runtime.Remoting.Channels
Imports System.Runtime.Remoting.Channels.Tcp
Imports MyRemoteNamespace

Public Class DemoErrorServer

  Public Shared Sub Main()

    Dim aChannel As New TcpChannel(6001)
    ChannelServices.RegisterChannel(aChannel)

    Try
      RemotingConfiguration.RegisterWellKnownServiceType( _
              GetType(DemoError), _
              "DemoErrorTcp.rem", _
              WellKnownObjectMode.SingleCall)

      Console.WriteLine("DemoErrorServer running. " & _
                        "Press Enter to quit.")
      Console.ReadLine()
    Catch ex As Exception
      Console.WriteLine("DemoErrorServer error: " & ex.Message)
    End Try

  End Sub

End Class
```

Defining the Client Application

Now let's write a client application, `DemoErrorClient`, to connect to a remote `DemoError` object and invoke its methods. The application begins by asking the user for the URL of a well-known remote object. If an exception occurs at this early stage, we display the exception's type and an information message, and the application terminates immediately. Otherwise, the application enters a loop to allow the user to choose which method to invoke on the remote object. This enables us to test various error conditions quickly and easily in our application.

```vb
Imports System
Imports Microsoft.VisualBasic
Imports MyRemoteNamespace

Public Class DemoErrorClient

  Public Shared Sub Main()

    Console.Write("Please enter URL of well-known object: ")
    Dim url As String = Console.ReadLine()

    ' Create proxy for remote DemoError object
    Dim aRemoteObject As DemoError
    Try
      aRemoteObject = CType( _
              Activator.GetObject(GetType(DemoError), url), _
              DemoError)
    Catch ex As Exception
      Console.WriteLine("Exception creating proxy object.")
      Console.WriteLine("Type:    {0}", ex.GetType().ToString())
      Console.WriteLine("Message: {0}", ex.Message)
      Exit Sub
    End Try

    ' Display a menu, to tell the user what options are available
    Console.WriteLine(vbCrLf & "Choose a remote method to call:")
    Console.WriteLine("1  Method1, executes successfully")
    Console.WriteLine("2  Method2, takes an unserializable parameter")
    Console.WriteLine("3  Method3, returns an unserializable result")
    Console.WriteLine("4a Method4, pass Nothing parameter")
    Console.WriteLine("4b Method4, pass out-of-range parameter")
    Console.WriteLine("4c Method4, pass valid parameter")
    Console.WriteLine("<type anything else to quit>")

    Do While True
      Try
        Console.Write(vbCrLf & "==> ")
        Dim choice As String = Console.ReadLine()
        Select choice
          Case "1"
            aRemoteObject.Method1()
            Console.WriteLine("Method1 returned successfully")
          Case "2"
            aRemoteObject.Method2(new MyUnserializable(42))
            Console.WriteLine("Method2 returned successfully")
          Case "3"
            Dim data As MyUnserializable = aRemoteObject.Method3()
            Console.WriteLine("Method3 returned successfully")
```

```vb
          Case "4a"
            aRemoteObject.Method4(Nothing)
            Console.WriteLine("Method4 returned successfully")
          Case "4b"
            aRemoteObject.Method4(new MySerializable(180))
            Console.WriteLine("Method4 returned successfully")
          Case "4c"
            aRemoteObject.Method4(new MySerializable(42))
            Console.WriteLine("Method4 returned successfully")
          Case Else
            Exit Do
        End Select
      Catch ex As Exception
        Console.WriteLine("Exception: {0}", ex.GetType().ToString())
        Console.WriteLine("Message: {0}", ex.Message)
      End Try
    Loop

  End Sub

End Class
```

Finally, compile the code in `DemoError.vb`, `DemoErrorServer.vb`, and `DemoErrorClient.vb`.

Testing the Remoting Application

Now that we've written the remote object, including the server and the client, we can investigate how errors occur in our remoting application. We'll explore six specific scenarios, and show screenshots to illustrate the error messages we get in each case.

Scenario 1: Server Application Isn't Currently Running

If the server application isn't currently running, the client application will receive an exception when it tries to invoke a remote method. This happens because the client application cannot open a connection with the server application. The exception occurs each time we try to call a remote method, not just when we create the proxy object initially.

The exception will either be a `SocketException` or a `WebException`, depending on whether we're using a TCP or HTTP channel. Our client application is using a TCP channel, so we get the following error message:

```
>DemoErrorClient
Please enter URL of well-known object: tcp://localhost:6001/DemoErrorTcp.rem

Choose a remote method to call:
1  Method1, executes successfully
2  Method2, takes an unserializable parameter
3  Method3, returns an unserializable result
4a Method4, pass Nothing parameter
4b Method4, pass out-of-range parameter
4c Method4, pass valid parameter
<type anything else to quit>
```

```
==> 1
Exception: System.Net.Sockets.SocketException
Message: No connection could be made because the target machine actively refused it
```

Scenario 2: Client Application Specifies an Invalid Protocol

Assuming the server application is running, several potential errors might arise. For example, if the client application specifies an invalid protocol (something other than TCP or HTTP), the client application will receive a `RemotingException`. The error message indicates the client application cannot create a channel for this protocol; only TCP and HTTP channels are supported:

```
>DemoErrorClient
Please enter URL of well-known object: ftp://localhost:6001/DemoErrorTcp.rem
Exception creating proxy object.
Type:    System.Runtime.Remoting.RemotingException
Message: Cannot create channel sink to connect to URL
ftp://localhost:6001/DemoErrorTcp.rem. An appropriate channel has probably
not been registered.
```

Scenario 3: Client Application Specifies an Invalid Host Name

If the client application specifies an invalid host machine name (that is, an unrecognized server machine name), the client application will receive a `SocketException` or a `WebException` when it calls a remote method. The exception message indicates that the host name cannot be resolved:

```
>DemoErrorClient
Please enter URL of well-known object:
tcp://AnInvalidMachineName:6001/DemoErrorTcp.rem

Choose a remote method to call:
1  Method1, executes successfully
2  Method2, takes an unserializable parameter
3  Method3, returns an unserializable result
4a Method4, pass Nothing parameter
4b Method4, pass out-of-range parameter
4c Method4, pass valid parameter
<type anything else to quit>

==> 1
Exception: System.Net.Sockets.SocketException
Message: The parameter is incorrect
```

Scenario 4: Client Application Specifies an Invalid Port

If the client application specifies an invalid port on the host machine, the client application will receive a `SocketException` (if we are using a TCP channel) or a `WebException` (if we are using an HTTP channel) when it calls a remote method. The exception message indicates a connection cannot be opened on this port, because there is no server application listening on this port:

```
>DemoErrorClient
Please enter URL of well-known object: tcp://localhost:1234/DemoErrorTcp.rem

Choose a remote method to call:
1  Method1, executes successfully
2  Method2, takes an unserializable parameter
3  Method3, returns an unserializable result
4a Method4, pass Nothing parameter
4b Method4, pass out-of-range parameter
4c Method4, pass valid parameter
<type anything else to quit>

==> 1
Exception: System.Net.Sockets.SocketException
Message: No connection could be made because the target machine actively refused it
```

Scenario 5: Client Application Specifies an Invalid Object URI

If the client application specifies an invalid object URI for the remote object, a RemotingException will occur when it tries to invoke a remote method. This happens regardless of whether we are using a TCP channel or an HTTP channel. The fact that we get a RemotingException, rather than a lower-level SocketException or WebException, usually indicates we've specified incorrect configuration information in the client or server application. The following console listing shows the RemotingException:

```
>DemoErrorClient
Please enter URL of well-known object: tcp://localhost:6001/AnInvalidURL.rem

Choose a remote method to call:
1  Method1, executes successfully
2  Method2, takes an unserializable parameter
3  Method3, returns an unserializable result
4a Method4, pass Nothing parameter
4b Method4, pass out-of-range parameter
4c Method4, pass valid parameter
<type anything else to quit>

==> 1
Exception: System.Runtime.Remoting.RemotingException
Message: Object </AnInvalidURL.rem> has been disconnected or does not exist at the
server.
```

Scenario 6: Other Miscellaneous Error Conditions

Let's assume for a moment the client application manages to connect to a remoting object. This doesn't necessarily mean we're home free; a host of other errors can occur when we invoke methods on the remoting object. The following shows what happens when the user selects each of the menu options in our client application, to exercise all the methods in the DemoError remoting object:

```
>DemoErrorClient
Please enter URL of well-known object: tcp://localhost:6001/DemoErrorTcp.rem
Choose a remote method to call:
1   Method1, executes successfully
2   Method2, takes an unserializable parameter
3   Method3, returns an unserializable result
4a  Method4, pass Nothing parameter
4b  Method4, pass out-of-range parameter
4c  Method4, pass valid parameter
<type anything else to quit>

==> 1
Method1 returned successfully

==> 2
Exception: System.Runtime.Serialization.SerializationException
Message: The type MyUnserializable in Assembly DemoError,
Version=1.0.569.30244, Culture=neutral, PublicKeyToken=null is not marked as
serializable.

==> 3
Exception: System.Runtime.Serialization.SerializationException
Message: The type MyUnserializable in Assembly DemoError,
Version=1.0.569.30244, Culture=neutral, PublicKeyToken=null is not marked as
serializable.

==> 4a
Exception: System.ArgumentNullException
Message: You must specify a real object
Parameter name: param1

==> 4b
Exception: System.ArgumentOutOfRangeException
Message: Data value must be between 0 and 100
Parameter name: param1

==> 4c
Method4 returned successfully
```

Here's what we see on the server:

```
>DemoErrorServer
DemoErrorServer running. Press Enter to quit.
Method1 called
Method3 called
Method4 called
```

```
Method4 called
Method4 called
Method4 accepted parameter's value, 42
```

Note the following points here:

* `Method1()` completes successfully as expected, without any exceptions.

- When `Method2() is called`, we receive a `SerializationException` because we cannot pass a `MyUnserializable` object into remote methods. Notice that the server does not print `Method2 called`, because the serializer throws an exception as soon as the method is invoked with an unserializable object.

- When `Method3() is called`, we receive another `SerializationException` because the remote method cannot return a `MyUnserializable` object. Again, notice that the server does print `Method3 called` in this case, because the exception occurs when the serializer tries to serialize the return object.

- When `Method4() is called` with a `Nothing` parameter, we receive an `ArgumentNullException`. `Method4` throws this exception to indicate that `Nothing` is not an acceptable parameter.

- When `Method4()` is called with an out-of-range parameter, we receive an `ArgumentOutOfRangeException`. `Method4()` throws this exception to indicate the parameter's data value should be between 0 and 100.

- When we call `Method4()` with a valid parameter, no exceptions occur. The `MySerializable` object was serialized by the client, passed to the server, and deserialized on the server without any problems.

Diagnosing and Preventing Errors in Remoting Applications

Now that we've identified some of the common exceptions that can occur in the .NET Remoting infrastructure, we'll focus on how to diagnose and act upon these exceptions in our remoting applications.

It's important to keep a broad perspective on the benefits of throwing exceptions. Although there are times when you have no control of an exception being thrown, the fact that the exception is totally unpreventable by the client may be welcomed. For example, the client can't control if a remote server is down, but by being thrown an appropriate exception, you know the exact cause of the problem, and the client application might be able to log on to another server. In this scenario, the exception gives you the opportunity to change your course of action, rather than representing an insidious coding error in the application.

To provide a context for our discussions, we'll now introduce a remoting application that allows users to create bank accounts, deposit and withdraw money, and so on. Rather unimaginatively, the remoting object is called `Bank`, and provides services to create and manage bank accounts. The client application comprises a Windows Form to allow users to access these services remotely from their desktops. The form appears as shown in Figure 6-1.

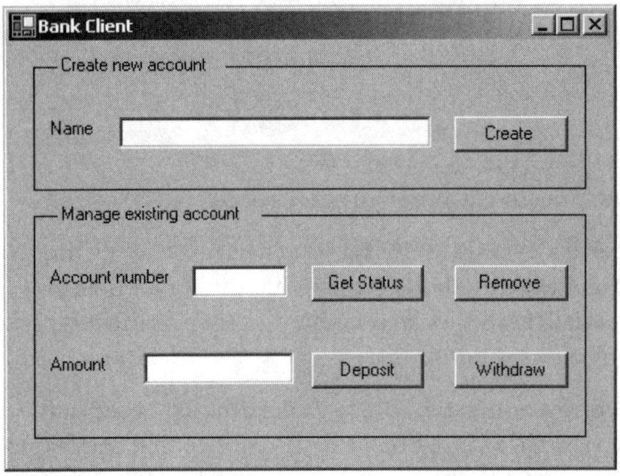

Figure 6-1. *Illustration of the Bank client form*

To create a new account, the user enters his name and then clicks the Create button. As you'll see shortly, this causes the client application to connect to the remote Bank object, and invoke an appropriate remote method to create a new bank account. The Bank object holds all the bank account information remotely, at the server machine.

After the user has created an account, he can click other buttons on the form to get status information about the account, deposit money into the account, withdraw money from the account, or remove (close) the account. In each case, the client application invokes an appropriate remote method on the Bank object, to perform the required task.

Implementing the Bank Application

The initial version of the bank application has no error checking whatsoever. Never write software like this yourself! We'll spend a few pages describing this simplistic implementation, and then pick out numerous opportunities for error checking and error handling. This will make the application much more resilient, reliable, and robust.

Defining the Bank Class Library

We'll begin by looking at a simplified implementation of the remoting object, Bank. The Bank object will hold a collection of bank accounts, so we'll need an Account class too. Place both of these classes in a class library project called Bank.

First, here are the Imports statements we need for the Bank and Account classes:

```
Imports System                              ' General .NET types
Imports System.Collections                  ' SortedList class
Imports System.IO                           ' File class, etc.
Imports System.Threading                    ' Mutex class
Imports System.Runtime.Serialization        ' <Serializable> attribute
Imports Microsoft.VisualBasic               ' vbCrLf constant
Imports System.Runtime.Serialization.Formatters.Soap   ' SoapFormatter
```

> **Note** You need to add a reference to the assembly, System.Runtime.Serialization.Formatters.Soap.dll.

Now let's look at the Account class. We've tried to keep this class as simple as possible to avoid unnecessary complications. There is one remoting-related issue to observe: the Account class is serializable to allow Account objects to be marshaled by value between the client application and the Bank object at the server:

```
Namespace MyRemoteNamespace

  <Serializable()> _
  Public Class Account

    Private mName As String         ' Name of account holder
    Private mNumber As Integer      ' Bank account number
    Private mBalance As Double      ' Current balance in
                                    ' this account

    Public Sub New(ByVal name As String, _
                   ByVal number As Integer, _
                   ByVal balance As Double)
      mName = name
      mNumber = number
      mBalance = balance
    End Sub

    Public Sub Deposit(ByVal amount As Double)
      mBalance += amount
    End Sub

    Public Sub Withdraw(ByVal amount As Double)
      mBalance -= amount
    End Sub

    Public ReadOnly Property Balance() As Double
      Get
        Return mBalance
      End Get
    End Property

    Public ReadOnly Property Number() As Integer
      Get
        Return mNumber
      End Get
    End Property
```

```vb
    Public Overrides Function ToString() As String
      Return String.Format( _
              "Account Number: {0}, Name: {1}, Balance: {2:C}", _
              mNumber, mName, mBalance)
    End Function

  End Class

End Namespace
```

The `Bank` class is more interesting, so we'll introduce it in several bite-size portions. First, `Bank` requires two fields: `mAccounts` is a list of all the accounts currently in existence, and `mNextAccountNumber` is the account number to use for the next account to be created:

```vb
Namespace MyRemoteNamespace

  Public Class Bank
    Inherits MarshalByRefObject

    Private mAccounts As SortedList
    Private mNextAccountNumber As Integer = 0

    ' Plus other members...

  End Class

End Namespace
```

Now let's look at the `Bank` constructor. The constructor deserializes a previously created file named `Accounts.dat`. This file contains a serialized list of `Account` objects, and is created by the `Bank`'s `Finalize()` method (coming up shortly) when the `Bank` object is garbage collected. Storing account data in a flat file is clearly a simplification; in a real-world scenario, we would probably store this data in a relational database, and use ADO.NET to retrieve and update data in the database.

In this simple example, we assume a hard-coded file name `Accounts.dat` for the bank account data. To make the application more generic, we could specify the file name as a parameter to the `Bank` constructor.

We also need to lock the file `Accounts.dat` while we're reading it. The last parameter to the `File.Open()` method specifies `FileShare.Read()` as the file share mode to restrict other processes to read-only access to the file while we're using it. It's important to consider concurrency issues in remoting objects, just in case several client applications invoke the same functionality simultaneously.

We'll use a `SoapFormatter` for serialization and deserialization purposes, rather than using a `BinaryFormatter`. `SoapFormatter` is less efficient than `BinaryFormatter`, but it's easier to see what's happening if we get any problems. When we're happy the application is working correctly, we can rewrite the serialization and deserialization code to use a `BinaryFormatter` instead.

```
Public Sub New()
  If File.Exists("Accounts.dat") Then
    Dim stream As FileStream = File.Open("Accounts.dat", _
                                        FileMode.Open, _
                                        FileAccess.Read, _
                                        FileShare.Read)
    Dim formatter As New SoapFormatter()
    mAccounts = CType( _
                  formatter.Deserialize(stream), SortedList)
              stream.Close()
    If mAccounts.Count <> 0 Then
      mNextAccountNumber = 1 + _
            CInt(mAccounts.GetKey(mAccounts.Count - 1))
    End If
  Else
    mAccounts = new SortedList()
    mNextAccountNumber = 0
  End If
End Sub
```

Next, let's see the `Finalize()` method. The .NET Common Language Runtime (CLR) will call this method when the `Bank` object is garbage collected at the server machine. The `Finalize()` method is responsible for tidying up the `Bank` object before it departs the scene; specifically, the `Finalize()` method should serialize the current list of accounts to `Accounts.dat`:

```
Protected Overrides Sub Finalize()
  Dim stream As FileStream = File.Create("Accounts.dat")
  Dim formatter As New SoapFormatter()
  formatter.Serialize(stream, mAccounts)
  stream.Close()
End Sub
```

The `Bank` class also needs some methods to create accounts, remove accounts, query account status, and deposit and withdraw money. The `Bank` object keeps a `SortedList` of all these accounts, and uses the account numbers as keys into this list. Therefore, if we know the account number for an existing account, we can find the corresponding `Account` object in the `SortedList`.

We need to be careful how we write these account-management methods to prevent multiple threads from accessing `Bank` fields simultaneously. For example, it would be disastrous if one thread at the server was in the middle of depositing money into an account, while another thread intervened and deleted the account. To prevent such concurrency problems, the .NET Framework class library provides several classes to control access to shared resources. The `Mutex` class is particularly helpful. Whenever we want to access a shared resource, such as the list of `Account` objects, we call the `Mutex`'s `WaitOne()` method to wait for the resource to become available. If the resource is currently in use by a different thread, our thread blocks until the resource becomes available again. When that happens, our thread is awoken and given exclusive access to the resource. When we have finished using the resource, we must call the `Mutex`'s `ReleaseMutex()` method to release the resource so that it may be used by another thread.

The following code shows how to create new accounts, query the status of existing accounts, remove accounts, and deposit and withdraw money. The `CreateAccount()` method acts as a factory for creating `Account` objects. This is an example of how design patterns can be used effectively in VB .NET.

Also notice that we've created a class-level `Mutex` object in the `Bank` class, which is used in each method to ensure thread-safe access to the `mAccounts` and `mNextAccountNumber` fields in `Bank`.

```
Private mMutex As New Mutex()

Public Function CreateAccount(ByVal name As String) As Account
    Dim acc As New Account(name, mNextAccountNumber, 0)
    mMutex.WaitOne()
    mAccounts.Add(mNextAccountNumber, acc)
    mNextAccountNumber += 1
    mMutex.ReleaseMutex()
    Return acc
End Function

Public Function GetAccountDetails(ByVal number As Integer) As Account
    mMutex.WaitOne()
    Dim acc As Account = CType(mAccounts(number), Account)
    mMutex.ReleaseMutex()
    Return acc
End Function

Public Sub RemoveAccount(ByVal number As Integer)
    mMutex.WaitOne()
    mAccounts.Remove(number)
    mMutex.ReleaseMutex()
End Sub

Public Function DepositInAccount(ByVal number As Integer, _
                                  ByVal amount As Double) As Double
    mMutex.WaitOne()
    Dim acc As Account = CType(mAccounts(number), Account)
    acc.Deposit(amount)
    Dim newBalance As Double = acc.Balance
    mMutex.ReleaseMutex()
    Return newBalance
End Function

Public Function WithdrawFromAccount(ByVal number As Integer, _
                                     ByVal amount As Double) As Double
    mMutex.WaitOne()
    Dim acc As Account = CType(mAccounts(number), Account)
    acc.Withdraw(amount)
    Dim newBalance As Double = acc.Balance
    mMutex.ReleaseMutex()
    Return newBalance
End Function
```

Defining the Host for the Bank Remotable Object

Let's write a simple server application to host the Bank remoting object. The server program registers a TCP channel on port 6000, and registers the Bank class as a singleton remoting service type.

It's important we use the singleton activation mode for Bank, because of the way we've implemented the account storage mechanism. All client applications must talk to the same Bank object, to ensure the Bank object holds a list of all the accounts created by every user. If we had adopted a different account storage mechanism, such as a central database, we could have used any remoting activation mode; the Bank object would no longer hold the account data in memory, so it wouldn't matter if client applications connected to different instances of Bank.

Here is the source code for the server application; place it in a console application project called BankServer:

```
Imports System
Imports System.Runtime.Remoting
Imports System.Runtime.Remoting.Channels
Imports System.Runtime.Remoting.Channels.Tcp

Public Class BankServer

  Public Shared Sub Main()

    Dim aChannel As New TcpChannel(6000)
    ChannelServices.RegisterChannel(aChannel)

    Try
      RemotingConfiguration.RegisterWellKnownServiceType( _
                GetType(MyRemoteNamespace.Bank), _
                "Bank.rem", _
                WellKnownObjectMode.Singleton)

      Console.WriteLine("InitialBankServer running. " & _
                        "Press Enter to quit.")
      Console.ReadLine()

    Catch ex As Exception
      Console.WriteLine("InitialBankServer error: " & ex.Message)
    End Try

  End Sub

End Class
```

Compile this server application, and start it running in a console window.

Defining the BankClient Application

The client application is a Windows Form. The form has five buttons:

- btnCreateAccount (the Create button)
- btnGetStatus (the Get Status button)
- btnRemoveAccount (the Remove button)
- btnDeposit (the Deposit button)
- btnWithdraw (the Withdraw button)

There are also three text boxes:

- txtName (the box labeled "Name")
- txtAccountNumber (the box labeled "Account Number")
- txtAmount (the box labeled "Amount")

These controls allow the user to create new accounts, get the status of an existing account, remove an account, and deposit and withdraw money. All these tasks are actually carried out by the remote Bank object; all we do in the client application is connect to the Bank object and invoke the appropriate remote method.

We'll examine the event handlers for each button in the client application, starting with the Create button. In this method, we connect to the remote Bank object, and call its CreateAccount() method to create a new Account object. CreateAccount() returns the new Account object to the client application, and we display the initial account details in a message box on the screen. We've deliberately ignored the possibility of errors for the time being.

Place the client application in a project called BankClient:

```
Private Sub btnCreateAccount_Click( _
              ByVal sender As System.Object, _
              ByVal e As System.EventArgs) _
              Handles btnCreateAccount.Click

    Dim theBank As Bank = CType( _
        Activator.GetObject(GetType(Bank), _
        "tcp://localhost:6000/Bank.rem"), Bank)

    Dim newAccount As Account = _
        theBank.CreateAccount(txtName.Text.ToString())
    MessageBox.Show(newAccount.ToString(), "New Account Details")

End Sub
```

Next, let's look at the event handler method for the Get Status button. This method reads the account number entered by the user, and calls GetAccountDetails() on the remote Bank object. This method returns the requested Account object, and we display its details in a message box. You can probably imagine at least half a dozen things that can go wrong in this sequence of events; we'll ignore these potential errors until later in the chapter.

```vb
Private Sub btnGetStatus_Click(ByVal sender As System.Object, _
                            ByVal e As System.EventArgs) _
                Handles btnGetStatus.Click

    Dim theBank As Bank = CType( _
          Activator.GetObject(GetType(Bank), _
                            "tcp://localhost:6000/Bank.rem"), _
          Bank)

    Dim number As Integer = _
      Integer.Parse(txtAccountNumber.Text.ToString())
    Dim acc As Account = theBank.GetAccountDetails(number)
    MessageBox.Show(acc.ToString(), "Account Details")

End Sub
```

The event handler for the Remove button is similar. The primary difference is that it calls RemoveAccount() on the remote Bank object to remove the specified account from the Bank's account list.

```vb
Private Sub btnRemoveAccount_Click(ByVal sender As System.Object, _
                    ByVal e As System.EventArgs) _
                Handles btnRemove.Click
    Dim theBank As Bank = CType( _
                    Activator.GetObject(GetType(Bank), _
                  "tcp://localhost:6000/Bank.rem"), Bank)

    Dim number As Integer = _
      Integer.Parse(txtAccountNumber.Text.ToString())
    theBank.RemoveAccount(number)
    MessageBox.Show("Account number " & number, "Removed Account")

End Sub
```

The last two methods we'll look at in the client application are the event handlers for the Deposit and Withdraw buttons. These methods read the account number and the amount entered by the user, and call DepositInAccount() and WithdrawFromAccount(), respectively, on the remote Bank object.

```vb
Private Sub btnDeposit_Click(ByVal sender As System.Object, _
                    ByVal e As System.EventArgs) _
                Handles btnDeposit.Click
    Dim theBank As Bank = CType( _
          Activator.GetObject(GetType(Bank), _
          "tcp://localhost:6000/Bank.rem"), Bank)
```

```vb
    Dim num As Integer = _
      Integer.Parse(txtAccountNumber.Text.ToString())
    Dim amount As Double = _
      Double.Parse(txtAmount.Text.ToString())

    Dim newBalance As Double = theBank.DepositInAccount(num, amount)
    MessageBox.Show( _
      String.Format("New balance: {0:C}", newBalance), _
      String.Format("Deposited {0:C} into account {1}", amount, num))

End Sub

Private Sub btnWithdraw_Click(ByVal sender As System.Object, _
                ByVal e As System.EventArgs) _
                Handles btnWithdraw.Click

    Dim theBank As Bank = CType( _
          Activator.GetObject(GetType(Bank), _
          "tcp://localhost:6000/Bank.rem"), Bank)

    Dim num As Integer = _
      Integer.Parse(txtAccountNumber.Text.ToString())
    Dim amount As Double = _
      Double.Parse(txtAmount.Text.ToString())
    Dim newBalance As Double = _
            theBank.WithdrawFromAccount(num, amount)
    MessageBox.Show( _
      String.Format("New balance: {0:C}", newBalance), _
      String.Format("Withdrawn {0:C} from account {1}", amount, num))

End Sub
```

Compile and run the client application in a console window.

Testing the Bank Application

If you've followed all these steps, you'll soon find that the application isn't very resilient. Here are some simple ways to break the application:

- Try running the client application before starting the server application. The client application will fail whenever you try to click any of the buttons on the form. The exception message shown in Figure 6-2 is extremely user hostile. The typical user will have no idea what this means, nor will they know whether the application is now in a stable or unstable state.

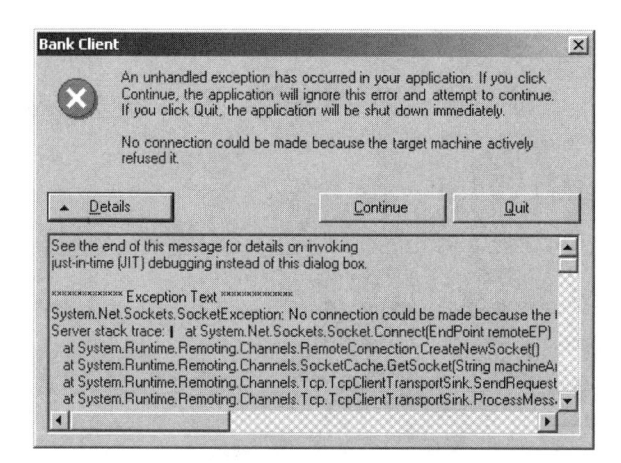

Figure 6-2. *The default exception message is extremely unfriendly to the user.*

- Start the server application. Then, in the client application, click the Create button without entering a user's name. The application creates an account without an owner's name as shown in Figure 6-3. This is undesirable; the application should insist on an owner's name. The application could also perform additional checks such as testing for duplicate names, to make sure we don't create the same account twice.

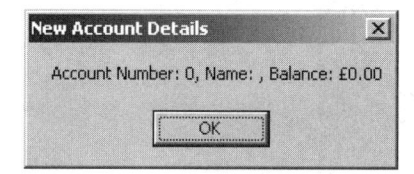

Figure 6-3. *Creating an account without an owner's name using the Create button*

- Click Get Status, Remove, Deposit, or Withdraw without entering an account number. An "unhandled exception" dialog box appears (see Figure 6-4), indicating an exception occurred when the client application tried to convert the (empty) account number string into an integer. A similar problem occurs if you click Deposit or Withdraw without entering an amount, or if you type nonnumeric text into the text box.

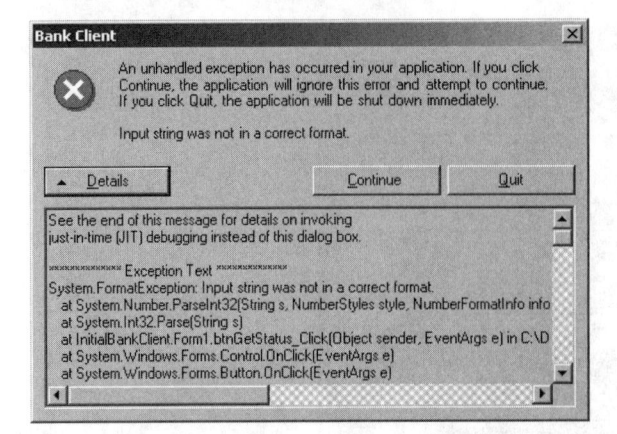

Figure 6-4. *An unhandled exception occurs when the client tries to convert the empty account number string.*

- Enter an invalid account number such as -12345, and click Get Status, Remove, Deposit, or Withdraw. An "unhandled exception" dialog box appears (as shown in Figure 6-5), indicating a null object reference. This problem arises because the remote Bank object is unable to find an Account object with the specified account number, and just returns Nothing instead.

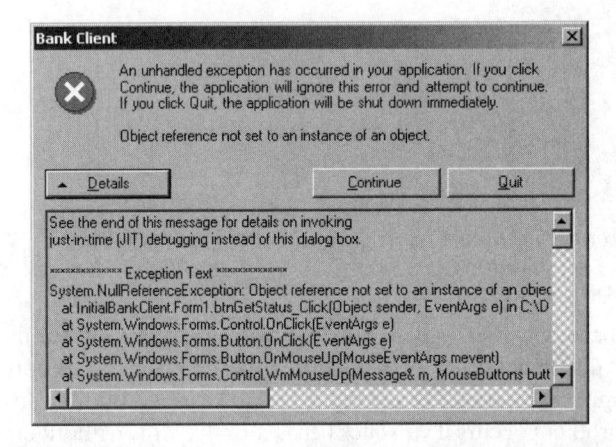

Figure 6-5. *The unhandled exception thrown when an invalid account number is entered*

Enabling Remote Debugging

You can use the VS .NET debugger to debug remoting objects. This can help identify where problems arise in the remoting object. For example, suppose you have a client application that makes calls to a remoting object, and an error occurs when you call a remote method. The administrator of the server machine can configure the server machine so that it lets you debug the remoting object from the client machine, to see what happened.

VS .NET provides two ways to perform remote debugging:

- **Using DCOM and the Machine Debug Manager (MDM) tool** (`mdm.exe`): This is the preferred way to perform remote debugging, so we'll concentrate on this approach here.

- **Using TCP/IP**: This approach is only supported for native C/C++ applications, so it's irrelevant to the discussions in this book.

To achieve remote debugging using DCOM, we must install the MDM tool on the server machine. The easiest way to do this is to install a full copy of VS .NET onto the server. An alternative (and more minimalist) approach is to run the VS .NET setup on the server machine, and select `Remote Components Setup` in the setup wizard.

MDM runs as a service on the server machine to facilitate debugging sessions with client machines. This is feasible in a development scenario, but is not recommended in a production environment. To check if MDM is currently running on the server, select `Start ➤ Programs ➤ Administrative Tools ➤ Services`. The `Services` dialog box displays the status of the MDM service as shown in Figure 6-6.

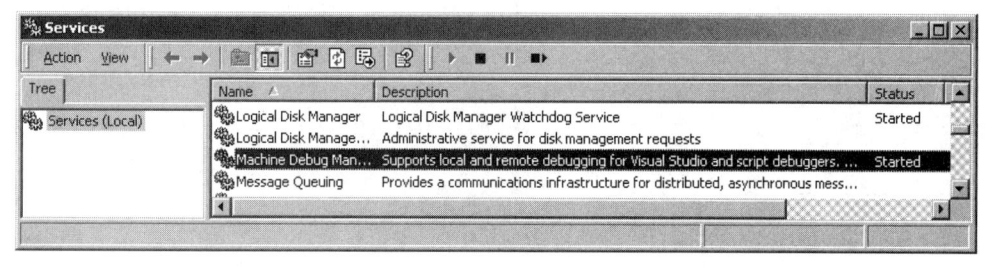

Figure 6-6. *Checking that the MDM service is running*

To debug a remoting object, you must add yourself to the Debugger Users group on the server machine. This is a security measure, to prevent just anyone from debugging applications on the server. In Windows 2000 and Windows XP, you can configure the Debugger Users group by selecting `Start ➤ Programs ➤ Administrative Tools ➤ Computer Management`. The `Computer Management` dialog box appears. Expand the `System Tools` folder, then expand the `Local Users and Groups` folder, and then select `Groups`. Notice one of the groups is named `Debugger Users` as shown in Figure 6-7.

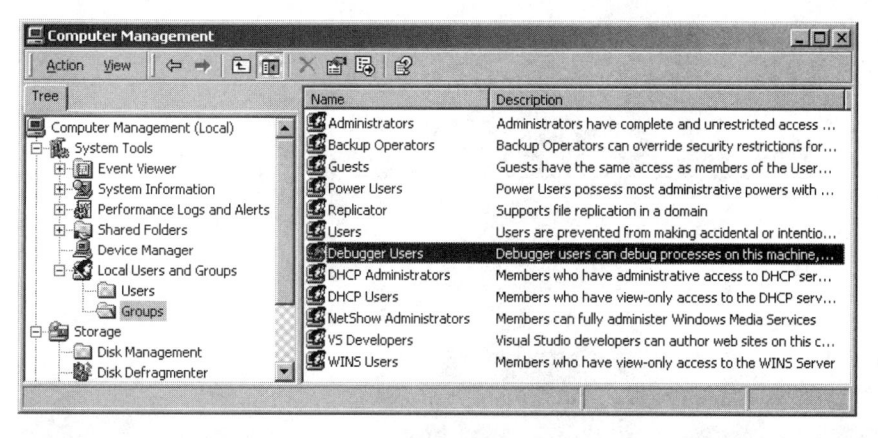

Figure 6-7. *The Debugger Users group shown in the Computer Management dialog box*

Right-click `Debugger Users` and select `Properties` from the shortcut menu. The `Debugger Users Properties` dialog box appears (see Figure 6-8), showing a list of users who are currently in this group (and are therefore allowed to debug applications that execute on this machine).

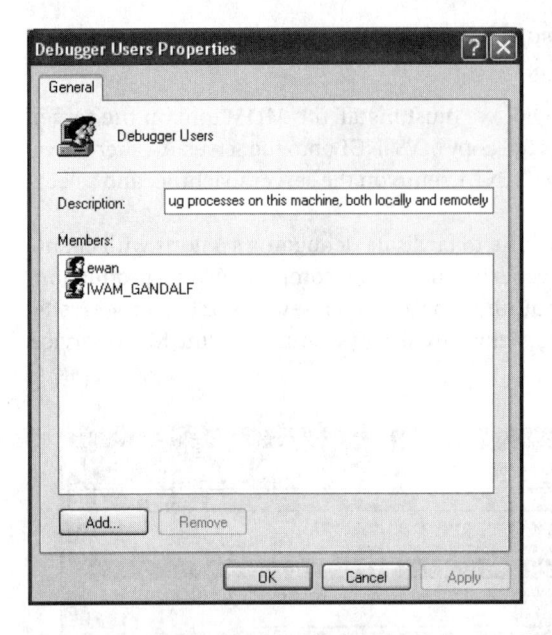

Figure 6-8. *The Properties window for Debugger Users*

To add a new user to this group, click the `Add` button and select an entry from the list of users and groups as shown in Figure 6-9. *Do not* select `Everyone`, as this would enable any user to debug applications executing on the server.

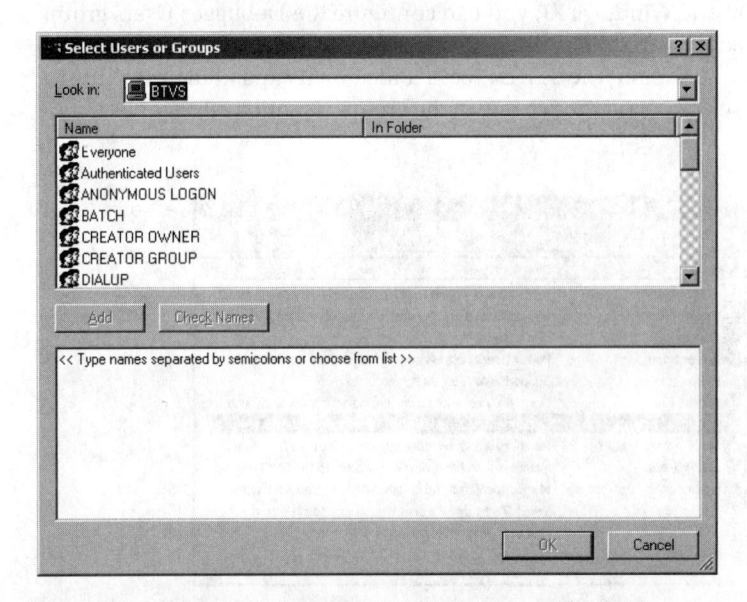

Figure 6-9. *Adding a new user or group to Debugger Users*

After you've added yourself to the Debugger Users group, you can proceed to debug remoting objects. For example, you can create a VS .NET solution for a client application that makes calls into a remoting object. You can then set a break point in the client application, just before the point where you call a remote method. When you run the client application in Debug mode, you can single-step into the source code for the remoting object; under the covers, DCOM and the MDM cooperate to allow you to debug the remoting object using the VS .NET debugger on the client machine.

Sometimes, errors occur when you least expect them. At times like these, it's handy to use the VS .NET Just-In-Time debugger to examine the source code at the point of failure. The debugger starts up and attaches itself to the errant process to allow you to examine its status. To achieve JIT debugging for remote code, you must perform some preliminary administrative tasks, as follows:

1. At the server machine, open a .NET Framework command prompt window, and move to the folder \Program Files\Common Files\Microsoft Shared\VS7Debug.

2. Type the following command:

   >mdm.exe /remotecfg

3. The Remote Just-In-Time Debugging Configuration dialog box appears (see Figure 6-10), showing the list of machines to contact if an exception occurs.

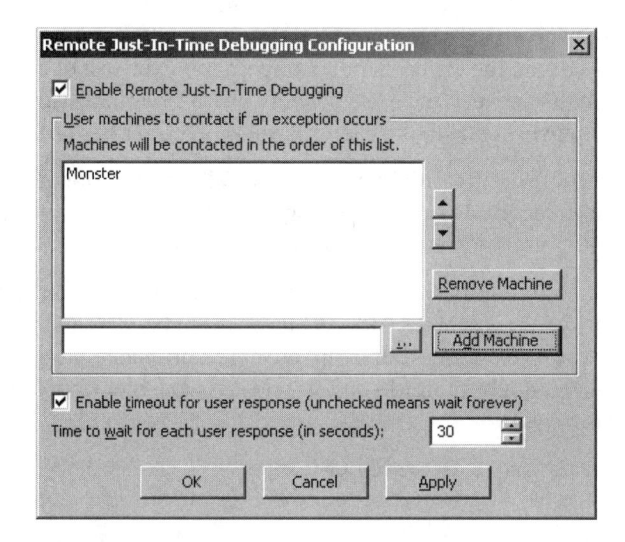

Figure 6-10. *The Remote Just-In-Time Debugging Configuration window*

4. To add another machine to this list, click the ellipsis (. . .) button and choose the appropriate machine. For example, you can add the machine that will host the client application, which will allow you to debug the remoting object from the client machine.

Dealing with Errors in the Client

Let's get back to the banking application we introduced earlier. Currently, the client application performs no error checking. It takes the user's input in good faith, and blindly tries to invoke remote methods even if the user enters something completely invalid. A better approach is to validate the data at the client first to avoid wasted round-trips to the server. This can help improve the performance of the client application (and therefore the responsiveness to the user), because errors are trapped locally rather than waiting for the remote object to signal an error. It also helps to reduce network load, and to alleviate some of the processing burden at the server machine.

The only downside with client-side error checking is that if you have several client applications that use the same remote class, you might need to duplicate the error-handling code in each client application. As with most programming tasks, you must choose an appropriate design based on your specific requirements.

Here are some specific recommendations to help deal with errors in the client application:

- If possible, validate parameter values before passing them into remote methods. It's much more efficient to trap invalid parameters at the client, rather than passing them across a remoting boundary for the remote object to validate.

- It's not always appropriate (or possible) to perform all validation tests at the client. Some validation tests might still be best performed by the remote object to centralize the business rules in one place. For example, the Bank remote object might validate all deposit and withdrawal requests to make sure the amount of money is allowable.

  Additionally, some validation tests simply cannot be performed in the client application. For example, a validation test might require access to server-side information that is only available to the remote object.

  The recommendation is to design accordingly. If you have multiple clients, only deploy logic to the clients if you are certain the logic will not change; deploy the rest of the logic at the server. Weigh the tradeoffs between the extra network hit of server-side validation, compared to the task of redeploying code to the clients if the validation rules change.

- Be prepared to catch any exceptions that might occur when calling a remote method. Actually, this is a general truism in all .NET programming. Write a Try...Catch block to envelop any method calls or operations that might cause an exception.

Let's take these recommendations and see how they affect the code in the bank client application. For example, here's an enhanced version of the Deposit button event handler method, to trap invalid user input and to catch any exceptions that might arise. For simplicity, we've only defined a single Catch block here; you might prefer to define several Catch blocks to handle specific exception types in different ways.

```
Private Sub btnDeposit_Click(ByVal sender As System.Object, _
                ByVal e As System.EventArgs) _
                Handles btnDeposit.Click

    Try
        Dim theBank As Bank = CType( _
            Activator.GetObject(GetType(Bank), _
                    "tcp://localhost:6000/Bank.rem"), _
                    Bank)

        If txtAccountNumber.Text = "" Then
            MessageBox.Show( _
                    "You must enter an account number.", _
                    "Deposit, error", _
```

```vb
                    MessageBoxButtons.OK, _
                    MessageBoxIcon.Warning)
    ElseIf txtAmount.Text = "" Then
      MessageBox.Show("You must enter an amount.", _
                    "Deposit, error", _
                    MessageBoxButtons.OK, _
                    MessageBoxIcon.Warning)
    Else
      Dim number As Integer = _
              Integer.Parse(txtAccountNumber.Text)
      Dim amount As Double = Double.Parse(txtAmount.Text)

      Dim newBalance As Double
      newBalance = _
              theBank.DepositInAccount(number, amount)
      MessageBox.Show( _
                String.Format( _
                      "New balance: {0:C}", newBalance), _
                String.Format( _
                      "Deposited {0:C} into account {1}", _
                      amount, number))
    End If
  Catch ex As Exception
    MessageBox.Show(ex.Message, _
                    "Deposit, exception occurred", _
                    MessageBoxButtons.OK, _
                    MessageBoxIcon.Error)
  End Try

End Sub
```

We can make similar changes to each of the methods in the bank client application to ensure invalid data entry is trapped locally and exceptions are handled safely. Using the `Message` property of an exception gives you a great opportunity to provide useful information to a client; for example, you can even suggest alternative courses of action to the user, such as logging on to a different server.

Dealing with Errors in the Remote Object

You can use a variety of techniques to detect error conditions at the server and to trace execution flow through the remoting object. You can actually use these techniques in any .NET application, but they are particularly useful in remoting applications where the complexity of interactions between multiple tiers can complicate matters, and where debugging isn't always practicable. For example, it's usually infeasible to debug remote code that resides on a production server machine.

Displaying Debug and Trace Messages

The .NET Framework has a namespace called `System.Diagnostics`, which contains useful classes named `Debug` and `Trace`. These classes provide utility methods to display diagnostic messages on the screen or to a log file. The Debug class only emits messages when you compile the application in Debug mode by using the /d:DEBUG=True compiler switch. The Trace class always emits messages as long as you use the /d:TRACE=True compiler switch.

To see these messages, you must register *debug listeners* or *trace listeners*. For example, the following statements cause debug messages to be written to a file named BankDebugLog.txt, and trace messages to be written to BankTraceLog.txt. We've placed these statements in a Shared constructor for the Bank class, so the statements are executed as soon as the class loader loads the Bank class into the runtime:

```
Imports System.Diagnostics    ' Contains the Debug and Trace classes
...
Public Class Bank
  Inherits MarshalByRefObject

  Shared Sub New()
    Debug.Listeners.Add( _
          New TextWriterTraceListener("BankDebugLog.txt"))
    Debug.AutoFlush = True        ' Flush log after every write
    Debug.IndentSize = 2          ' 2 spaces per indent

    Trace.Listeners.Add( _
          New TextWriterTraceListener("BankTraceLog.txt"))
    Trace.AutoFlush = True        ' Flush log after every write
    Trace.IndentSize = 2          ' 2 spaces per indent
  End Sub

  ' Plus other members in the Bank class...

End Class
```

Note that the Debug and Trace classes share the same Listeners collection. This has two important consequences:

- If we call a Debug output method (and we've used the /d:DEBUG=True compiler switch), the message will be sent to any listeners registered via Debug.Listeners.Add() or Trace.Listeners.Add().

- If we call a Trace output method (and we've used the /d:TRACE=True compiler switch), the message will be sent to any listeners registered via Debug.Listeners.Add() or Trace.Listeners.Add().

Let's look at some of the methods in the Debug and Trace classes. First, both classes have a WriteLine() method to display a simple text message. The Debug.WriteLine() method is useful for displaying diagnostic information about an application during development. These messages can provide helpful information about the current state of the objects to help locate potential errors in the code:

```
Debug.WriteLine("There are currently " & _
mAccounts.Count & "accounts")
```

The `Trace.WriteLine()` method has a different purpose—to help trace the execution path through the code. For example, you can embed `Trace.WriteLine()` statements at the start of every method to show which methods have been called:

```
Trace.WriteLine("Bank DepositInAccount called, " & _
        DateTime.Now)
```

The `Debug` and `Trace` classes also have an `Assert()` method to check if some condition is true (presumably a condition required to be true if the application is to function properly). If the condition isn't true, the specified error message is displayed in a message box. You can use `Assert()` at the beginning of every method to test the required preconditions are true before the method does its thing. For example, the `DepositInAccount()` method can test that the `mAccounts` object correctly refers to a `SortedList` object:

```
Public Function DepositInAccount(ByVal number As Integer, _
                    ByVal amount As Double) As Double

  Debug.Assert(Not (mAccounts Is Nothing), _
          "Precondition assertion error in DepositInAccount.", _
          "mAccounts is 'Nothing'.")

  Debug.Assert(TypeOf mAccounts Is SortedList, _
          "Precondition assertion error in DepositInAccount.", _
          "mAccounts is not a SortedList.")

  ' Plus other code, as before...

End Function
```

It's also possible to use `Assert()` at the end of a method to test that the postconditions are still true after the method has done its work. For example, you can test to see that the method hasn't caused any damage to any of our objects.

These techniques can considerably simplify the task of error detection and error prevention. However, if you litter the code with too many `Debug` and `Trace` method calls, it can become difficult to pick out the actual business logic among all the diagnostic aids. To clarify the methods, it's often useful to separate the diagnostic code into a dedicated method. You can annotate the method with the `<Conditional>` attribute (from the `System.Diagnostics` namespace), so the method is only compiled if the specified symbol is defined.

Here's a useful diagnostic method for the `Bank` class. The method displays all the accounts in the `mAccounts` list to help test whether the `Bank` class is correctly creating and removing accounts, and depositing and withdrawing money. This method is only compiled if the `DEBUG` symbol is defined; otherwise, the compiler ignores this method (and all calls to this method):

```
<Conditional("DEBUG")> _
Public Sub DumpStatus(ByVal message As String)

  Debug.WriteLine("-------------------------------------------------")
  Debug.WriteLine(message)
  Debug.WriteLine("-------------------------------------------------")
```

```vbnet
    Debug.Indent()        ' Indent the debug messages
                          ' by one tab-stop

    Dim index As Integer
    For index = 0 To mAccounts.Count - 1
      Dim acc As Account = CType( _
               mAccounts.GetByIndex(index), Account)
      Debug.WriteLine(acc)
    Next

    Debug.Unindent()      ' Unindent the debug messages
                          ' by one tab-stop
    Debug.WriteLine(vbCrLf)
End Sub
```

> **Note** You can use a `TraceSwitch` variable to control the trace and debug messages displayed by the application. The `TraceSwitch` class has properties named `TraceError`, `TraceWarning`, `TraceInfo`, and `TraceVerbose`, which enable you to test the level of a `TraceSwitch` variable. You can test the `TraceSwitch` variable against these levels to decide which error messages to display in the application.

Detecting Errors at Runtime

The `Debug` and `Trace` classes help verify the correctness of code, but they do not help handle runtime error conditions such as database exceptions, file I/O errors, invalid parameters to a method, and so on.

To handle these situations, you must write explicit tests in the remote object, and throw exceptions (or return error codes) if you detect problems you can't deal with. You can either throw standard .NET exceptions, such as `ArgumentOutOfRangeException`, or define your own application-specific exception classes to contain additional contextual information about the error. We'll adopt the former approach initially, and then see how to define custom exception classes later in the chapter.

The following code fragment shows how to test for error conditions in the `Bank.DepositInAccount()` method. We need to ensure the client application has provided a recognized account number, and the amount to deposit is acceptable. In this example, we've defined a class constant named `mMaxDeposit` to limit the amount of money the user can deposit in one go. You might reasonably argue that the client application could perform this test, but we prefer to centralize this business logic in the `Bank` remote object instead:

```vbnet
Public Function DepositInAccount(ByVal number As Integer, _
                       ByVal amount As Double) As Double

  If Not (mAccounts.Contains(number)) Then
    Throw New ArgumentOutOfRangeException( _
          "number", "Account number not recognized.")
```

```vb
    ElseIf amount < 0 Or amount > mMaxDeposit Then
      Throw New ArgumentOutOfRangeException( _
             "amount", "Invalid deposit amount.")
    End If

    ' Plus other code, as before...

End Function
```

Improving the Bank Application

In the last few pages, you've seen a variety of techniques for dealing with errors in remoting objects. Let's bring all these recommendations together, and see how the Bank class looks now:

```vb
Imports System.Diagnostics
...

Public Class Bank
  Inherits MarshalByRefObject

  ' Constants, used in error checking
  Private Const mMaxDeposit As Double = 10000
  Private Const mMaxWithdrawal As Double = 200
    ' Shared constructor, to initialize debug log and trace log
  Shared Sub New()
    Debug.Listeners.Add( _
           New TextWriterTraceListener("BankDebugLog.txt"))
    Debug.AutoFlush = True
    Debug.IndentSize = 2

    Trace.Listeners.Add( _
           New TextWriterTraceListener("BankTraceLog.txt"))
    Trace.AutoFlush = True
    Trace.IndentSize = 2
  End Sub


  ' Deposit money into the specified account
  Public Function DepositInAccount( _
         ByVal number As Integer, _
         ByVal amount As Double) As Double

    Trace.WriteLine( _
           "Bank DepositInAccount called, " & DateTime.Now)

    Debug.Assert( Not (mAccounts Is Nothing), _
             "Precondition assertion error in DepositInAccount.", _
             "mAccounts is 'Nothing'.")
```

```vb
    Debug.Assert(TypeOf mAccounts Is SortedList, _
            "Precondition assertion error in DepositInAccount.", _
            "mAccounts is not a SortedList.")

    If Not (mAccounts.Contains(number)) Then
        Throw New ArgumentOutOfRangeException( _
                "number", "Account number not recognized.")
    ElseIf amount < 0 Or amount > mMaxDeposit Then
        Throw New ArgumentOutOfRangeException( _
                "amount", "Invalid deposit amount.")
    End If
    mMutex.WaitOne()
    Dim acc As Account = _
            CType(mAccounts(number), Account)
    acc.Deposit(amount)
    Dim newBalance As Double = acc.Balance

    Me.DumpStatus( _
        String.Format("After depositing {0:C} into account {1}", _
                    amount, number))
    mMutex.ReleaseMutex()

    Return newBalance

End Function

' Conditionally-compiled method, to display current bank status
<Conditional("DEBUG")> _
Public Sub DumpStatus(ByVal message As String)
    Debug.WriteLine("----------------------------------------------")
    Debug.WriteLine(message)
    Debug.WriteLine("----------------------------------------------")
    Debug.Indent()

    Dim index As Integer
    For index = 0 To mAccounts.Count - 1
        Dim acc As Account = _
            CType(mAccounts.GetByIndex(index), Account)
        Debug.WriteLine(acc)
    Next
```

```
        Debug.Unindent()
        Debug.WriteLine(vbCrLf)
    End Sub

    ' Plus other members ...

End Class
```

Defining Custom Exception Classes for Remote Objects

The .NET Framework uses exceptions as the standard way of indicating error conditions in an application. You can also define your own exception classes to indicate application-specific errors. Any time you detect an anomalous situation, you can create an instance of the exception class and provide contextual information about the current state of your application. You can also perform additional tasks when an exception occurs; for example, you can log all exceptions to a persistent storage device to capture exception information for posterity. You'll see how to do that later in the chapter.

In the next few pages, we'll define an exception class named BankException (for consistency, all exception classes should have a name that ends with "Exception") that should be placed in the Bank project. BankException will illustrate several important rules for defining exception classes in a remoting application. We'll also modify some of the methods in our Bank class, so that they throw BankExceptions if they detect a problem. We could even extend this concept and provide a family of exception classes that inherits from BankException to represent all the different kinds of problems that can arise.

Note If you define a custom exception class in a remoting application, you must ensure the client application has sufficient metadata to enable it to catch custom exceptions. You can achieve this by deploying the custom exception class to the client, or by deploying an interface that fully describes the methods and properties in the custom exception class.

Defining Exception Classes in the Exception Inheritance Hierarchy

All exception classes should inherit from System.Exception. To be more precise, all the predefined exception classes in the .NET Framework class library inherit from System.SystemException. If you want to define your own exception classes, they should inherit from System.ApplicationException. This allows client code to specify System.ApplicationException in a Catch block, as a simple way of catching any kind of application-specific error. Figure 6-11 shows how BankException will fit into this inheritance hierarchy.

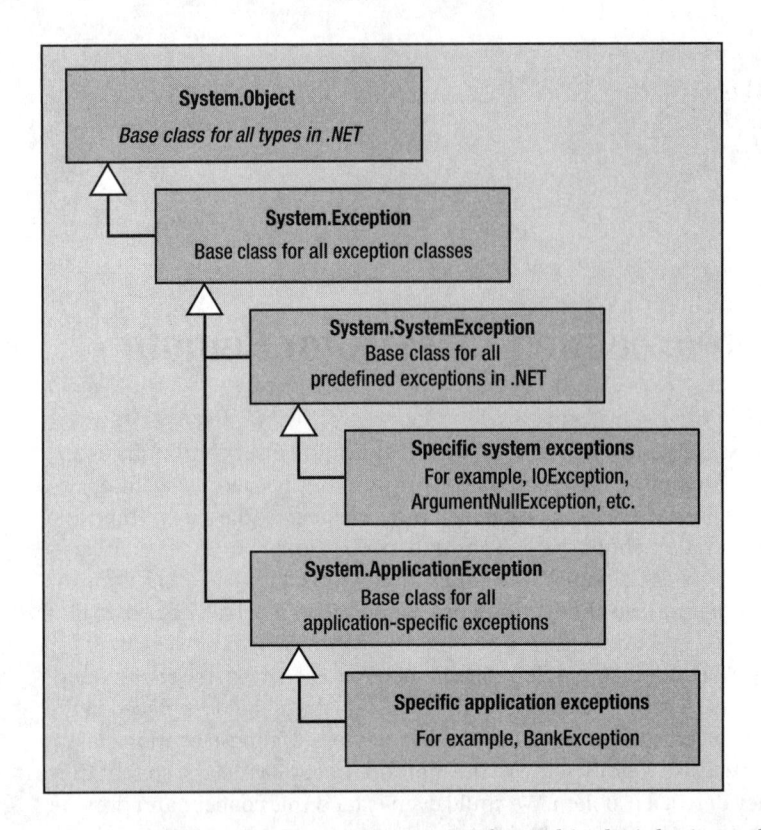

Figure 6-11. *Showing where* `BankException` *fits within the inheritance hierarchy*

Exceptions and Serialization

When a remoting object throws an exception, the exception object is marshaled by value to the client application. The exception object is serialized prior to transmission at the server machine, and deserialized again when it arrives at the client machine. To support this mechanism in the `BankException` class, we must annotate `BankException` with the `Serializable` attribute as follows:

```
Imports System.SerializableAttribute ' For <Serializable> attribute

<Serializable()> _
Public Class BankException
  Inherits ApplicationException

  ' Extra fields, constructors, methods, etc.

End Class
```

If the exception class defines any fields, we must write some extra code to serialize and deserialize these fields so that they can be marshaled and unmarshaled across remoting boundaries. The following code shows how to do this:

```vb
<Serializable()> _
Public Class BankException
  Inherits ApplicationException

  ' Instance fields, to hold extra information
  ' about this exception
  Private mTimestamp As DateTime
  Private mMachineName As String

  ' Custom serialization method
  Public Overrides Sub GetObjectData( _
                         ByVal info As SerializationInfo, _
                         ByVal context As StreamingContext)

    ' Call superclass GetObjectData method first,
    ' to serialize the fields in the superclass
    MyBase.GetObjectData(info, context)

    ' Now serialize the BankException's extra fields
    info.AddValue("Timestamp", mTimestamp)
    info.AddValue("MachineName", mMachineName)

  End Sub

  ' Deserialization constructor, to deserialize a BankException
  ' when received at the client
  Public Sub New(ByVal info As SerializationInfo, _
                 ByVal context As StreamingContext)
    ' Call superclass constructor first, to deserialize the fields
    ' in the superclass
    MyBase.New(info, context)

    ' Now deserialize the BankException's extra fields
    mTimestamp = info.GetDateTime("Timestamp")
    mMachineName = info.GetString("MachineName")

  End Sub

End Class
```

Let's briefly pick out some of the important points here.

- The `BankException` class has two fields named `mTimestamp` and `mMachineName` to hold additional information about the exception. The timestamp information could become a critical synchronization feature if cross-machine objects are engaged in a mutually dependent transaction, and might use timestamps as some sort of sanity check on the integrity of each request. If the two sources aren't time synchronized, this check could fail. The timestamp information in the `BankException` object would diagnose this problem.

- The `GetObjectData()` method serializes these fields, along with any predefined fields in our superclass. The .NET Remoting infrastructure calls `GetObjectData()` automatically to serialize `BankException` objects during marshaling at the server machine.

  The `GetObjectData()` method is actually defined in the `ISerializable` interface. Classes that require custom serialization must implement this interface, and provide a suitable implementation for `GetObjectData()`. This task is made easier when we write exception classes, because the base class for all exceptions (`System.Exception`) already implements `ISerializable`. Therefore, if we need custom serialization in the exception class, all we have to do is override the `GetObjectData()` method; there is no need to explicitly use the syntax `Implements ISerializable` in the class definition.

- The `New()` method is a special deserialization constructor to deserialize the fields in `BankException` and its superclass. The .NET Remoting infrastructure calls this constructor automatically to reconstitute `BankException` objects during unmarshaling at the client machine.

Defining Constructors

The next step is to define constructors for the `BankException` class. We suggest you define three overloaded constructors, as follows:

```
' Constructor #1: no parameters
Public Sub New()
  Me.New("", Nothing)        ' Call the 'main' constructor (#3)
End Sub


' Constructor #2: takes a single param (a string message)
Public Sub New(ByVal message As String)
  Me.New(message, Nothing)   ' Call the 'main' constructor (#3)
End Sub


' Constructor #3: takes two params (a string and an inner exception)
Public Sub New(ByVal message As String, _
               ByVal innerException As Exception)
  ' Do all the initialization work in this constructor (see later)...
End Sub
```

Each of these constructors has a different role to play:

- The first constructor doesn't take any parameters, and allows BankExceptions to be thrown without specifying an error message (if we really want to do this):

Throw New BankException()

- The second constructor takes a String parameter, specifying the error message for this exception. We can use this constructor whenever we want to throw a new exception in the Bank class. For example, the DepositInAccount() method can throw a BankException if the account number is unrecognized or the deposit amount is out of range:

```
Public Function DepositInAccount(ByVal number As Integer, _
                                 ByVal amount As Double) As Double

   If Not (mAccounts.Contains(number)) Then
     Throw New BankException( _
         String.Format( _
                  "Account number {0} not recognized.", number) )
   ElseIf amount < 0 Or amount > mMaxDeposit Then
     Throw New BankException( _
         String.Format("Invalid deposit amount: {0:C}", amount) )
   End If

   ' Plus other code, as before...

End Function
```

We can add similar functionality to check for a withdrawal amount that is greater than nMaxWithdrawal in the WithdrawFromAccount() method too.

- The third constructor in the BankException class takes two parameters: a String and an "inner exception" object. We can use this constructor to create a BankException that wraps low-level exceptions in the remoting application. The idea is that the Bank class catches low-level exceptions (such as file I/O exceptions), and wraps them up in higher-level BankException objects. The BankException object provides business-related information about the error, and the inner exception provides the technical details about what actually went wrong.

This technique is particularly useful in remoting applications because low-level server-related error messages can be bundled together with more meaningful business-related error messages that make more sense to the client application.

To illustrate how inner exceptions work, let's consider the Finalize() method in the Bank class. As you might recall, this method stores bank accounts to the file Accounts.dat. If an exception occurs, we can catch the exception, wrap it up in a BankException, and rethrow the BankException instead. The client application receives a BankException, and can use its InnerException property to get at the technical exception information in the inner exception.

So, here's the revised code for the Finalize() method:

```vb
Protected Overrides Sub Finalize()

  Dim stream As FileStream = Nothing
  Try
    stream = File.Create("Accounts.dat")
    Dim formatter As New SoapFormatter()
    formatter.Serialize(stream, mAccounts)
  Catch ex As Exception
    Throw New BankException( _
               "Bank finalization exception.", ex)
  Finally
    If Not stream Is Nothing Then
      stream.Close()
    End If
  End Try

End Sub
```

Note that the `stream.Close()` statement in the `Finally` block might throw an exception. This would replace any exception that might have occurred earlier in the method. The following code shows how to deal with this possibility in the `Finally` block:

```vb
Finally
  If Not stream Is Nothing Then
    Try
      stream.Close()
    Catch ex As Exception
      Throw New BankException( _
                 "Bank finalization exception.", ex)
    End Try
  End If
End Try
```

Now that we've described each of the three constructors in the `BankException` class, let's see how to write them. In fact, only the third constructor does any real work; the other two constructors simply call this constructor to avoid code duplication.

Here's the code for the third constructor. Notice how we call the superclass constructor first to initialize the fields in our superclass. Then we initialize `mTimestamp` with the current date and time at the server machine. We also initialize `mMachineName` with the name of the server machine; the .NET `Environment` class has a variety of useful properties and methods for finding out information about the current execution environment of the application:

```vb
' Constructor #3: takes two params (a string and an inner exception)
Public Sub New(ByVal message As String, _
               ByVal innerException As Exception)

  MyBase.New(message, innerException)
```

```
    mTimestamp = DateTime.Now
    mMachineName = Environment.MachineName
End Sub
```

Defining Informational Properties and Methods

To conclude the implementation of the `BankException` class, we can define some properties and methods to expose the error information contained in a `BankException` object. We need to expose the following information:

- The string message in the `BankException` object, which provides high-level information about what went wrong. The `Message` property in the `Exception` class already exposes this message, so we don't need to do anything extra in the class.

- The inner exception associated with this `BankException` object (if there is an inner exception). The `InnerException` property in the `Exception` class already exposes this inner exception, so once again we don't need to do anything extra in our class.

- The values of the `mTimestamp` and `mMachineName` fields in this `BankException` object. We defined these fields, so we must provide our own methods or properties to expose them.

The easiest way to expose all this information in an easy-to-use bundle is by overriding the `Message` property in our `BankException` class, as shown next. In this code, we return all the three pieces of information listed previously.

```
Public Overrides ReadOnly Property Message() As String

  Get
    ' Use superclass Message property, to get the message string
    Dim Result As String = MyBase.Message

    ' Append timestamp and machine name
    Result &= vbCrLf & "Timestamp: " & mTimestamp
    Result &= vbCrLf & "Machine name: " & mMachineName

    'Append inner exception (if there is one)
    If Not (InnerException Is Nothing) Then
      Result &= vbCrLf & "Inner exception: " & InnerException.Message
    End If

    ' Return all this information
    Return Result
  End Get

End Property
```

When the client application receives a `BankException`, it can use the `Message` property as follows to obtain comprehensive information about the message, the time it occurred on the server machine, and the name of that server machine. The technical error information held in the inner exception is also available.

```
' Sample code in the client application
Try
  theBank.DepositInAccount(number, amount)
Catch ex As BankException
  MessageBox.Show(ex.Message, "Caught a BankException")
End Catch
```

Logging Error Information at the Server

In a distributed application, one of the challenges is to keep track of any errors that occur as the remoting object executes at the server machine. It's important to log this information in a consistent way to help diagnose problems quickly and accurately.

You've seen how to use the `Debug` and `Trace` classes to display error or status messages on the console (or write them to a file). In this section of the chapter, you'll see some more persistent ways to log errors in a remoting application. Specifically, you'll see how to log errors to a flat file, a database, or the Windows event log. This task is made easier because we've defined a custom `BankException` class to represent all exceptions emanating from the remote object. We can extend the `BankException` constructor so that it logs every exception as it occurs.

Logging Errors to a File

The easiest way to log error information is to write a simple text message to a log file every time an exception occurs in the remoting object. The following code shows how to achieve this; we've modified the third `BankException` constructor to write error information to a file named `BankException.log` on the server machine:

```
<Serializable()> _
Public Class BankException
  Inherits ApplicationException

  ' Constructor, for a BankException that wraps
  ' an inner exception
  Public Sub New(ByVal message As String, _
             ByVal innerException As Exception)

    ' Call superclass constructor first
    MyBase.New(message, innerException)

    ' Then set the exception-related fields in our class
    mTimestamp = DateTime.Now
    mMachineName = Environment.MachineName
    Dim logMessage As String = _
       message & " [" & mTimestamp & "] [" & _
       mMachineName & "]"

    Dim writer As StreamWriter
    Try
```

```
        ' Write message to log file
        writer = New StreamWriter("BankException.log", True)
        writer.WriteLine(logMessage)
      Catch ex As Exception
        ' If we get a logging exception, display
        ' Trace message instead
        Trace.Write("Couldn't log error: " & _
                            logMessage)
      Finally
        ' Close the StreamWriter
        If Not writer Is Nothing Then
          writer.Close()
        End If
      End Try
    End Sub
    ' Plus other members, as before...
End Class
```

In this code listing, the `BankException` constructor uses a `StreamWriter` object to append text to the log file `BankException.log` on the server. The `True` parameter to the `StreamWriter` constructor indicates we're appending to the log file to preserve the existing error messages already written to the log file. If the file doesn't exist, it will be created the first time we try to open it.

If we're really unlucky, we might get a file I/O exception as we try to log the error information to the file! For example, an `UnauthorizedAccessException` will occur if file access is denied; an `IOException` will occur if the file name, path, or drive letter is incorrect; and so on. If any of these exceptions occur, we catch the exception and display a trace message instead; at least this will alert us to the fact that there's a problem in the application.

Figure 6-12 provides an example of the sort of error messages we can expect to see in the log file. These error messages occur if the user tries to deposit money into an unrecognized account, or tries to deposit or withdraw too much money from a recognized account. In this example, the name of the server machine is BTVS.

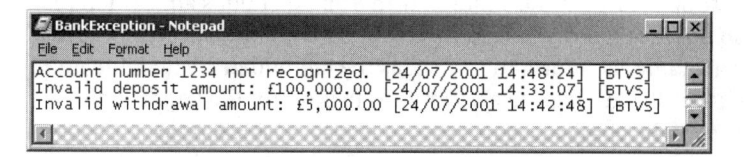

Figure 6-12. *Example of the error messages provided in the log files*

Using a file for error logging is a fairly simplistic approach, so there are some limitations. First, we must ensure the file is locked while we're updating it to prevent concurrent access by different processes. Second, we need to provide some utility tools to allow administrators to view and manage the contents of the file; it's unreasonable to expect a human reader to sift through a log file containing thousands of entries trying to spot a particular error message. Third, the developer should be notified if certain errors occur, rather than having to manually look at the log file.

Logging Errors to a Database

To overcome some of the difficulties we just mentioned, we can log errors to a database rather than to a simple file. This is a more centralized and scalable approach, which is a necessity in some scenarios such as Web farms; for example, we can use the same database to hold error information for many remoting objects potentially running on different computers. Another advantage is that databases hold information in a structured format, which is easier to query and analyze than free-format text in a flat file. Of course, we also have the added benefit of off-the-shelf database query tools, administration tools, and reporting tools, such as Query Analyzer and Enterprise Manager in the Microsoft SQL Server database product.

To illustrate how to log error messages to a database, we'll create a new database in SQL Server, and add a simple table to house the error messages. (If you use a different database product, such as Oracle or Sybase, you should use the equivalent tools supplied with that product.) Then we'll write some ADO.NET code in the `BankException` constructor to log error messages to this error table.

To create a new database in SQL Server, follow these steps (if you use a different database product, use the appropriate database management tool to create the new database):

1. From the Windows `Start` menu, select `Programs` ➤ `Microsoft SQL Server` ➤ `Query Analyzer`. A `Connect to SQL Server` dialog box appears. Enter the appropriate connection information, and click `OK`.

2. In the Query Pane in Query Analyzer, type the following SQL statement. This statement creates a new database named `MyDatabase`:

   CREATE DATABASE MyDatabase

3. Click the green triangle on the toolbar to execute this SQL statement. A message should appear in the Results Pane, indicating that the database was created successfully.

4. Take a look in the Object Browser to see the new database (if the Object Browser isn't visible, select the menu item `Tools` ➤ `Object Browser` ➤ `Show/Hide`). In the Object Browser, right-click the computer name and select `Refresh` from the shortcut menu. There should be an entry for `MyDatabase`.

For this example, we'll adopt a fairly simple strategy, where all exceptions are written to a single `Errors` table. It's also possible to log much more elaborate and sophisticated information. For example, we can log additional information such as the method name and line number where an exception occurred. We may also use exceptions to monitor the application, by logging how long it takes users of the application to perform mission-critical tasks. If the user complains that things are "too slow," we have an audit record of performance from which we can verify the claim.

To create the simple `Errors` table for this example, follow these steps:

1. In the Query Pane in Query Analyzer, type the following SQL statement. This statement creates a new table named `Errors` in the `MyDatabase` database:

```
Use MyDatabase
CREATE TABLE Errors
(
  ErrorID int IDENTITY (1, 1) NOT NULL,
                                      /* Primary key column   */
  Message nvarchar(50) NOT NULL,
                                      /* Error message        */
  Timestamp datetime NOT NULL,
                                      /* Date and time of error */
  MachineName nvarchar(50) NOT NULL
                                      /* Name of host machine  */
)
```

2. Click the green triangle on the toolbar to execute this SQL statement. A message should appear in the Results Pane, indicating that the command completed successfully.

3. In the Object Browser, click the + sign next to MyDatabase to expand this entry. Also expand User Tables, then dbo.Errors, and then Columns. The new Errors table should appear in the Object Browser as shown in Figure 6-13.

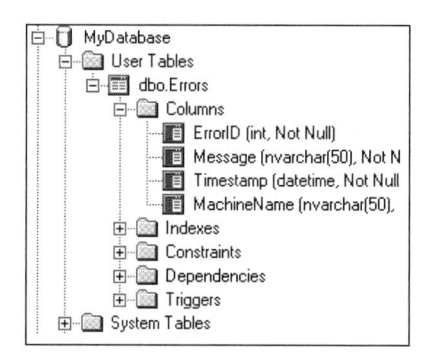

Figure 6-13. *Viewing the Errors table in the Object Browser*

Now that we've created the Errors table in MyDatabase, we're ready to add some database code to the BankException constructor. We'll use the ADO.NET classes defined in the System.Data.SqlClient namespace to access SQL Server 7.0 (and above) databases. The following Imports statement will make life easier for us:

```
Imports System.Data.SqlClient
```

We'll also need to reference the assembly System.Data.dll when we build the remoting object. We'll show how to do this later.

> **Note** To access an earlier version of SQL Server, or a different database such as Oracle or Sybase, import the namespace `System.Data.OleDb` instead. Also, in the next code samples, use the `OleDbConnection` and `OleDbCommand` classes, rather than `SqlConnection` and `SqlCommand`.

The following code shows how to enhance the `BankException` constructor, so that it logs every exception object as it is created. This approach has the benefit of simplicity, but it assumes the bank application creates a separate `BankException` object every time it wants to throw an exception. This is not the only way to work with exceptions. For example, the bank application could precreate a single exception object, and use the same object every time it throws an exception. In this case, an alternative approach should be used for logging; for example, the code that throws the exception should manually log the exception, rather than relying on the exception object to perform the logging itself.

Back to the Bank example. The `BankException` constructor begins by creating a `SqlConnection` object and specifying a connection string for `MyDatabase` on the `local` machine. Note that `integrated security=true` means we want to use integrated (Windows) authentication, rather than relying on SQL Server authentication.

```
<Serializable()> _
Public Class BankException
  Inherits ApplicationException

  ' Constructor, for a BankException that wraps
  ' an inner exception
  Public Sub New(ByVal message As String, _
                 ByVal innerException As Exception)

    ' Call superclass constructor first
    MyBase.New(message, innerException)

    ' Then set the exception-related fields in our class
    mTimestamp = DateTime.Now
    mMachineName = Environment.MachineName

    Dim cnBank As SqlConnection
    Try
      ' Specify the database connection string
      cnBank = New SqlConnection("data source=(local); " & _
        "initial catalog=MyDatabase; integrated security=true")
```

Next, we create and execute a `SqlCommand` object to insert a new row into the `Errors` table. The new row will contain information about the current `BankException`:

```
      ' Set up a SQL command, to insert a row into the Errors table
      Dim cmdInsertError As New SqlCommand( _
        "INSERT INTO Errors " & _
        "(Message, Timestamp, MachineName) VALUES (" & _
        "'" & @message          & "', " & _
```

```
            "'" & @time    & "', "   & _
            "'" & @machine  &  "')", cnBank)
      cmdInsertError.Parameters.Add("@message", _
                     message)
      cmdInsertError.Parameters.Add("@time", _
                     mTimestamp)
      cmdInsertError.Parameters.Add("@machine", _
                     mMachineName)

      ' Open the database connection, and execute
      ' execute the command
      cnBank.Open()
      cmdInsertError.ExecuteNonQuery()

    Catch ex As Exception
      Trace.Write("Couldn't log error: " & _
            message & " [" & mTimestamp & "] [" & _
            mMachineName & "]")
    Finally
      If Not cnBank Is Nothing Then
        cnBank.Close()
      End If
    End Try
  End Sub

  ' Plus other members, as before...

End Class
```

Figure 6-14 shows the sort of error messages we can expect to see in the Errors table in MyDatabase. The information is readily available in Query Analyzer; right-click the dbo.Errors table in the Object Browser, and select Open from the shortcut menu.

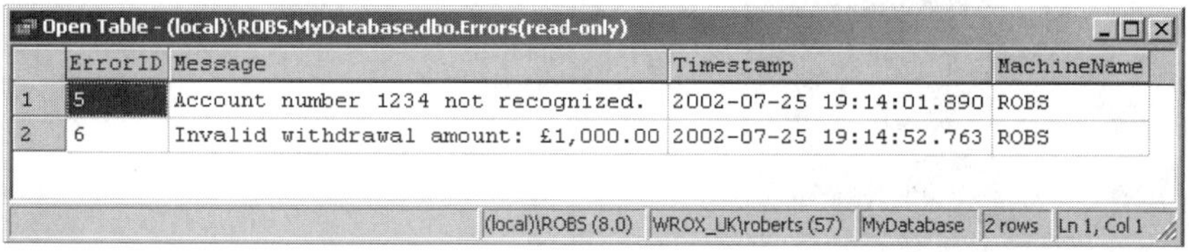

Open Table - (local)\ROBS.MyDatabase.dbo.Errors(read-only)

	ErrorID	Message	Timestamp	MachineName
1	5	Account number 1234 not recognized.	2002-07-25 19:14:01.890	ROBS
2	6	Invalid withdrawal amount: £1,000.00	2002-07-25 19:14:52.763	ROBS

(local)\ROBS (8.0) | WROX_UK\roberts (57) | MyDatabase | 2 rows | Ln 1, Col 1

Figure 6-14. *Example of the errors recorded within the* Errors *table*

Logging Errors to the Windows Event Log

Windows NT, Windows 2000, and Windows XP include a set of event logs to hold error messages, warnings, and informational messages for a single computer. There are predefined event logs for operating system messages, security messages, and application messages.

You can view these event logs using the Event Viewer utility in Windows. From the Windows `Start` menu, select `Programs` ➤ `Administrative Tools` ➤ `Event Viewer`. The left-hand pane of the Event Viewer window displays the event logs on the local computer. When you click one of these entries, the right-hand pane shows the messages in this event log. For example, Figure 6-15 shows some of the messages in a typical `System Log`; it's also possible to view event logs on remote machines.

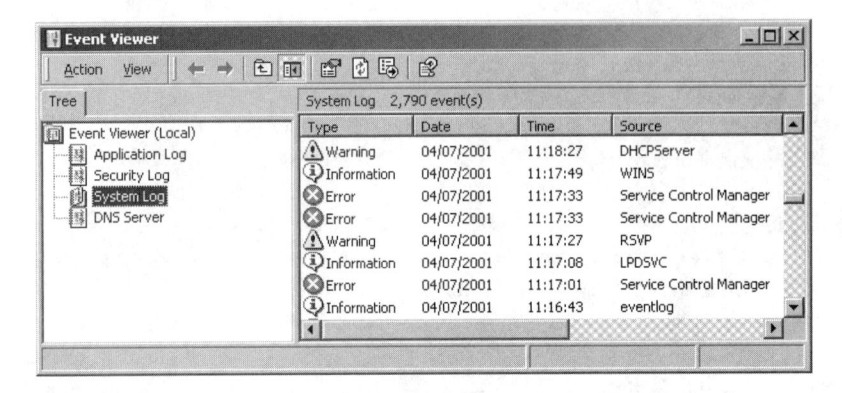

Figure 6-15. *Example of messages within a typical system log*

You can also use Event Viewer to manage the event logs. For example, if you right-click the `System Log` entry and select `Properties` from the shortcut menu, the dialog box shown in Figure 6-16 appears.

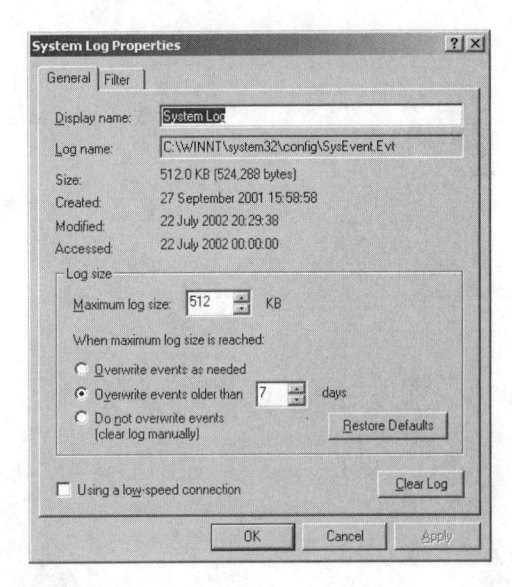

Figure 6-16. *The System Log Properties window within the Event Viewer*

This dialog box allows you to control the maximum log size, the lifetime of events in the event log, and so on. You can also define filters to specify precisely what kinds of events you're interested in. All these features are extremely useful as you build remoting applications; they make it much easier for you to detect problems and act upon them. Note that you require administrator permissions to specify some of these settings.

To help you in your endeavors, the .NET Framework provides the EventLog class in the System.Diagnostics namespace. This class allows you to create your own event log, write messages to the event log, and query the event log easily in your .NET applications.

Let's modify the BankException class so that it logs all BankExceptions to the event log. To be more specific, we'll create a separate event log just for BankExceptions. This will isolate our log messages from all other applications' log messages, so we can spot our messages more readily. For added excitement, we could even define some additional behavior to send notification to mobile devices when exceptions occur in mission-critical sections or classes of our application. We'll leave this as an exercise for the reader.

Here's the revised code for the BankException class. We'll pick out the salient points after the code listing:

```
<Serializable()> _
Public Class BankException
  Inherits ApplicationException

  ' Shared field, to enable exceptions to be logged to event log
  Private Shared mEventLog As EventLog

  ' Shared constructor, to create event log if it
  ' doesn't exist yet
  Shared Sub New()
    If Not EventLog.SourceExists("BankSource") Then
      EventLog.CreateEventSource("BankSource", "BankLog")
    End If
    mEventLog = New EventLog("BankLog")
    mEventLog.Source = "BankSource"
  End Sub

  ' Constructor, for a BankException that wraps
  ' an inner exception
  Public Sub New(ByVal message As String, _
              ByVal innerException As Exception)

    ' Call superclass constructor first
    MyBase.New(message, innerException)

    ' Then set the exception-related fields in our class
    mTimestamp = DateTime.Now
    mMachineName = Environment.MachineName

    Dim logMessage As String = _
              message & " [" & mTimestamp & "] [" & _
              mMachineName & "]"
```

```
    Try
        ' Write the error message to the event log
        mEventLog.WriteEntry(logMessage, EventLogEntryType.Error)
    Catch ex As Exception
        Trace.Write("Couldn't log error: " & logMessage)
    End Try

End Sub

' Plus other members, as before...
End Class
```

Note the following points in this code:

- The `BankException` class has a `Shared` field named `mEventLog`. We'll use this object every time we want to write a message to the event log.

- The `BankException` class has a `Shared` constructor to create the `BankLog` event log if it doesn't yet exist in Windows.

  We then create an `EventLog` instance and assign it to the `mEventLog` field. The `EventLog` constructor takes two parameters here: the name of the Windows event log to which we want to write our messages and the name of the event source. Each application can use a different event source name to allow administrators to differentiate events from different applications in the Event Viewer.

- The instance constructor in `BankException` calls the `WriteEntry()` method on the `mEventLog` object to write information about the current exception to the "BankLog" event log. The `EventLogEntryType` enumeration parameter allows us to specify whether this is an error message, a warning, an informational message, or a success or failure audit message.

Figure 6-17 shows an example of the sort of message we can expect to see in the "BankLog" event log.

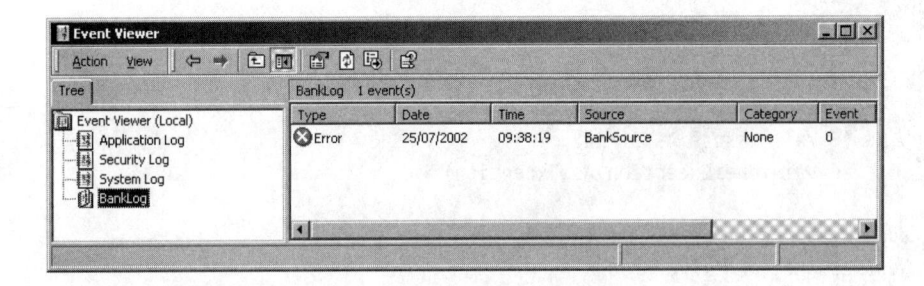

Figure 6-17. *Example message from the BankLog event*

To get more information about a specific event, right-click the event and select `Properties` from the shortcut menu. For example, Figure 6-18 shows the details for the first event shown earlier.

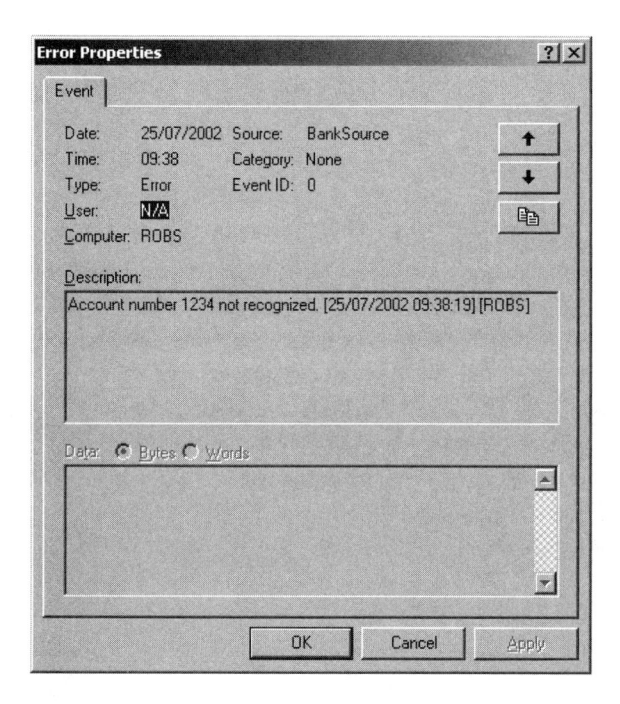

Figure 6-18. *The Properties window for the* `BankLog` *event*

Summary

Debugging and error handling is a thankless task at the best of times, but when you develop remoting applications, you have many more hurdles to overcome. There seems to be an almost endless list of things that can go wrong, such as server unavailability, incorrect configuration at the client or server, user error, or application-specific exceptions.

In this chapter, we've presented several techniques to help you through the mire. First, you've seen the common exceptions that can typically occur in .NET remoting applications. You've also seen how to perform error checking at the client application and in the remoting object, to detect anomalous situations at runtime. In addition, you've seen how to use debug and trace messages to help you understand whether the application is behaving as expected.

At the end of the chapter, we defined custom exception classes to represent application-specific errors in the remoting object. We used the custom exception class as a natural placeholder for centralized error handling in the remoting object, such as logging all exceptions to a flat file, a database, or the Windows event log.

In the next chapter, we'll consider some best practices that, if followed, should make your remoting applications as efficient, maintainable, and reusable as they can be.

CHAPTER 7

Flexible Programming

This section of the book is, as the title says, about the .NET Reflection API. But rather than concentrate on describing what reflection is, we'll spend most of our time looking at what it's actually for. So, this book is as much about dynamic programming as it is about reflection.

By dynamic programming, we mean developing applications that are flexible, dynamic, and extensible; programs whose behavior can be modified after they are written, after they are installed, and even while they are running.

You'll see how to make applications less tightly coupled, and more modular. We'll look at how you can build flexible base classes that bestow powerful functionality on classes derived from them. You'll see how to use attributes to make information about your programs available to other pieces of code. We'll examine .NET's component model, a system for enabling diverse objects to be treated as interchangeable blocks, which is the basis of all .NET user interface technologies.

In this chapter, we'll look at some theoretical issues that place the Reflection API into context. We'll define reflection, look into some other key terms that you'll encounter in the book, and see why reflection is needed.

Reflection Defined

Reflection is easily described in terms of what it enables you to do, and how it does it. Explaining why you might want to use reflection is a little more difficult. Before we attempt the latter, let's take a shot at the first two. First, what is reflection for?

Reflection is a mechanism for examining, manipulating, and creating objects dynamically at runtime. Reflection enables you to examine an object, determine its type, discover information about that type, find out what members the type has, and manipulate or modify those members. You can also use reflection to examine assemblies, find what types they define, and create new instances of those types.

That's exactly what you do anyway when you're programming, except that when you write code that calls a method, creates an object, or modifies a property, you can only take into account information that you know about at the time you're writing the code. Reflection allows you to take into account information that isn't available at compile-time, which is only available at runtime. You can only compile method calls to methods that have already been written and refer to types that exist at the time we're coding. Reflection allows you to access any method of any type, even if it hasn't been written yet.

So, second, how does it work? Reflection accesses metadata stored in .NET assemblies to discover information about the original code. This means that to provide information about an object's type, methods, properties, and so on, reflection relies on information about the object's code, which was encoded into the assembly by the .NET compiler. This metadata (data about data) can also be used to discover a great deal about the assembly, the types it defines, and the resources it requires.

So, with the easy questions out of the way, on to the big one: What can we use reflection for?

What Is Reflection For?

Many objects you use in your programs represent real-world entities external to your program—a purchase order, an invoice, a bill of sale. Others represent constructs you create within your program to help order these real-world entities—a hashtable, a database connection pool, a focus manager. Reflection is an interesting API because its objects represent the actual entities that make up the application itself—a type, a method, an assembly.

Reflection is .NET's way of letting your code look at itself, and examine and manipulate objects not as windows, purchase orders, hashtables, but as instances of a .NET type defined in a .NET assembly. Because *every* object you encounter in your code is an instance of a .NET type, this means you can write code that can process *any* object.

To give an example, it's interesting to note that there are more than 140 types in the .NET class library that define a property called Name. In almost all cases, this returns a String, representing the name of the entity it represents. You've probably coded a few classes with a property like this. In the course of profiling or debugging an application, it might become necessary to track exactly which objects are being created, so you might code a method to output a diagnostic message. It might be nice to include the name of the object, when available, to ease debugging. In VB .NET, by default you are allowed to write code like this:

```
Public Sub ShowDiagnostic(o As Object)
  Console.WriteLine(o.Name)
End Sub
```

This takes advantage of VB .NET's late binding facility (and should be familiar coding style to VB6 programmers). We'll look at late binding in a moment. For now, consider it as meaning that you can call any property or method on an instance of type Object, because .NET will work out whether the underlying object has the method or property and access it if it can. Of course, if there is no such method or property, the binding will fail, and an error will occur.

However, if you turn Option Strict on, the code won't compile. This is because System.Object doesn't define a Name property, and there's no guarantee that there will be a property of that name on the object o. Accessing this property on an object that doesn't have a Name causes an error, and because no error trapping is in place, it breaks the program. To prevent this very likely runtime error, VB .NET catches the error at compile-time.

Option Strict disables VB .NET's syntactic late binding facility. It's recommended best practice that you turn Option Strict on in all your code, because for every instance where the call to an undefined property is deliberate, there are a hundred instances where you could just mistype the name of the called method; Option Strict lets the compiler help you catch them. This line would compile with Option Strict off:

```
Public Sub ShowDiagnostic(o As Object)
  Console.WriteLine(o.ToStrin())
End Sub
```

Reflection, however, lets you explicitly write code that says, "Does this object's type define a Name property that returns a String? If so, display it, if not, don't." This will work whether Option Strict is turned on or off. It makes the questions that we're asking explicit, and suggests that an object not having a Name property is a normal, expected possibility, not an error condition. So, reflection provides a clean, logical way to write code that performs late binding, even under Option Strict.

Late binding of this sort allows you to develop coding *protocols*. A protocol is a set of rules that defines the behavior of a set of types. A type that obeys all the rules is said to follow the protocol. For example, having a property called Name that returns a String is a protocol—one which 140 or so .NET classes follow. .NET provides a means for codifying a protocol of this sort into an interface, but it doesn't always allow the required flexibility. For example, imagine .NET has an interface INamed like this:

```
Public Interface INamed
    Public Property Name As String
End Interface
```

If all the classes that define a Name property implemented this interface, that would allow you to write typesafe code to manipulate all of .NET's named objects. This is true, but at the expense of forcing all the classes that implement the interface to make their Name property readable *and writable*. Many of the .NET name properties are, not surprisingly, read-only. So, you couldn't use an interface to impose a uniform type convention on those names. In this situation, you must rely on defining a protocol, which you can only use through late binding.

.NET uses protocols. If a type has a Shared Main() method with one of a fixed set of signatures, it can be used as an entry point. Any type that defines a method called GetEnumerator() that returns an object of a type with a method called MoveNext() that returns a Boolean, and defines a method called Current() that returns an object of the original type, is regarded by .NET as following the collection protocol. Instances of such classes can be iterated by a For Each statement. You can determine whether an object follows the entry point or collection protocol by using reflection, and you can call the methods using late binding—preferably through reflection.

These protocols are interesting, because again, they can't be defined by an interface. An entry-point defines a shared method that a type must have. Interfaces can't define shared methods. While a collection protocol defines a method signature in terms of the characteristics of the type it should return and its initial type, an interface can only define a method signature with a fixed return type. Reflection provides the only way of binding to such methods.

Reflection also allows you to bind to methods in other ways that VB .NET's syntactic late binding doesn't allow, as you'll see a little later on.

Reflection's late binding, unlike VB .NET's syntactic late binding, is not only used to select a method or property, but it also can be used to select an assembly or type as well.

Here's a simple example we've all encountered. An application is built to be modular, with extension modules sold separately, possibly by completely independent vendors. It might be a drawing package, with visual effects provided by extension modules; it might be an IDE, with different language compilers supplied separately; or it could be a mail server, with filter or protocol modules available as configurable plug-ins. Whatever the program's particular requirements, the problems are how to get a core application to recognize and interoperate with code that it was not compiled against, containing classes whose names it doesn't know, and how to seamlessly integrate it.

Reflection provides the mechanism for doing this, and we'll look at how you can make such systems in Chapter 10. The basis for the solution is to have all the modules provide a class that implements a particular interface, and then to use reflection to load the assembly containing the module and seek out that class. After finding the class, you can use reflection to create an instance, and then use it just like any object that implements the interface.

Other examples of reflection in action are provided by .NET itself. The dynamic Web technology ASP.NET, for example, is just a .NET program running alongside your Web server. When the server receives a request for a Web page ending in .aspx, it passes the request on to the ASP.NET program. ASP.NET identifies the file or files containing the code that makes up a page, and if it hasn't done so before, compiles them into a .NET assembly, containing one or more .NET classes that contain the code that makes up the logic required to deliver the requested page. The mechanism that ASP.NET then uses to create an instance of the correct class to service a particular request relies in part on reflection. The ASP.NET page classes inherit from a .NET base class called Page that contains functionality that uses reflection to create all the controls that make up the page, hook up event handlers, and set up the necessary initial properties on all the items that make up the page. Every ASP.NET page you write is a new class, but the ASP.NET runtime uses reflection to ensure that you don't have to duplicate a lot of tedious boilerplate code in every page. In this case, reflection provides mechanisms for code reuse far beyond the basic system of class inheritance.

We will look at the component system that ASP.NET uses in Chapter 12, and we will examine how to build reflective base classes later as well. However, let's look at some of the underlying theory about reflection:

- **Type Terminology**: Review some of the key terminology relating to types in .NET. Reflection, as a .NET API, uses the .NET terminology for a lot of things, rather than the VB .NET terms.

- **Binding:** How calls to methods are resolved in .NET. You'll see how VB .NET provides a partially dynamic binding system, and how reflection makes it truly dynamic.

- **Metadata:** Metadata is data compiled into .NET assemblies that describes the code in the assembly. You'll see that metadata is a prerequisite of reflection, and how .NET provides an extensible framework for metadata.

Type Terminology

In dealing with reflection, you'll be dealing with types, and the words used to describe those types and their members are important. Here are the most important ones:

- **Type**: A type is a combination of a data structure and some code. There are two kinds of type: reference types and value types. Classes, arrays, and delegates are all reference types. Structures, primitives, and enumerations are all value types.

- **Instance**: Whereas an object type is the blueprint for an object, an instance is a created type. Much like the blueprint for a house is the definition of what a house will look like, an implemented floor plan at a mailing address is an instance of a house. An instance of a class is an object.

- **Type Member**: A type member is anything that is defined inside a type. Methods, fields, properties, events, and nested classes are all type members. Type members can be shared (known in .NET as a whole as static) members or instance members.

- **Method**: A named block of code. In VB .NET, this is a Sub or a Function.
- **Field**: A container for data. Also called a member variable. Depending on whether it is shared or not, it may also be called a shared variable, or instance variable.
- **Signature**: The combination of a method's name and parameter list. Every method in a type has a unique signature.

When we say something is *typesafe*, we mean it guarantees that no operations are attempted on an instance that are not permitted for an instance of that type. This guarantee is enforced at compile-time by the compiler, if Option Strict is turned on. If code is not typesafe, then the compiler can't guarantee this, and you must check to be sure you haven't made any logic errors. If you have, then a runtime error may result.

Binding

We've talked briefly about late binding, but it's important, for understanding when exactly you need to use reflection, to consider it a little more formally. *Binding* is the process in which a reference to a piece of code in your program is resolved to an actual program routine in memory. It's a fundamental part of the way programming languages operate, and in .NET, the way binding works enables such important object-oriented (OO) concepts as interfaces, polymorphism, and, of course, reflection.

Early (Static) Binding

In a basic procedural programming language, resolving a procedure call is not a complicated process. In such a language, you can define procedures, and then call them from other points in your code. So, if you have the following code (in an imaginary procedural language with VB .NET-like syntax):

```
Sub Foo()
  MsgBox("Foo called")
End Sub
```

And you have a call elsewhere in your code that looks like this:

```
Foo()
```

It should be obvious that when execution reaches this line, the code in the Foo() subroutine will be executed. The fact that this will happen is rigidly dictated by the code—no code elsewhere will interfere in the link between the call to Foo() and the code in the Foo() procedure being executed. This call is *statically bound* because it is fixed and unchanging.

If the preceding code were in a compiled language, then the compiler can do a lot of work to check that the procedure call is valid and optimize the resulting code. If you misspelled the name of the procedure or provided the wrong number of arguments, the compiler would tell you that the call would definitely not work. The compiler also knows exactly where in memory the Foo() function will be loaded, and can compile the call to Foo() as a direct jump to that piece of memory. In fact, when the called function is short—as it is here—the compiler can just compile the code in the function inline where it's called, optimizing the code by eliminating an unnecessary jump.

Runtime Binding

Many procedural programming languages offer a second method for calling functions via function pointers. This might (in our fictional language again) allow you to write code something like this:

```
PointerToProc = AddressOf Foo
PointerToProc()
```

Now things are a bit less static. At the point where the procedure is called—the `PointerToProc()` instruction—the exact code that is executed next is determined not by the instruction itself, but by the value previously assigned to `PointerToProc`. If the line setting the value of `PointerToProc` was inside, for example, a conditional construction such as an `If` block, the code that is executed by the call instruction will depend on the state of the program at the time that the `If` block was executed. In this situation, the call to the procedure is *runtime bound*; which piece of code will be executed next is not fixed when the instruction is written, but will only be determined at runtime, depending on which instructions have been executed previously and the state of the program.

You should note that the compiler can't make the assumptions it could make before with an early bound call. It knows where the procedure `Foo` is in memory, so it can put this value into the variable `PointerToProc`, but it can't optimize the call to the procedure. The call will take a little longer at runtime, but the program can do many things that weren't possible in the completely static system.

Object-Orientation

As you know, however, .NET is not a procedural programming environment, and VB .NET is not a procedural programming language—we have to think in terms of objects and methods, not procedures.

Object-orientation makes binding more complicated, because instead of procedures, you have methods, and methods are defined in types (usually classes). When you define a type and give it a method, that method can be called on any object that is an instance of that type. So, say you have the following type definition (this is now proper VB .NET code, and the reason we've declared this method `Overridable` will become clear shortly):

```
Public Class Thing
  Public Overridable Sub Foo()
    MsgBox("Foo called on a Thing instance")
  End Sub
End Class
```

Then, you can write code like the following:

```
Dim myThing As Thing
myThing = New Thing()
myThing.Foo()
```

As before, we're interested in how that call to `Foo()` is dispatched. The class definition containing a method declaration is really not all that different from the code that declared a procedure in our procedural language. Just like such a procedure, it will be loaded into memory at runtime and sit at a particular location in memory. The challenge for the runtime engine is to work out that our call to myThing.Foo() needs to be translated into a jump to this point in memory. In the case shown here, it's not that complicated; the variable myThing contains an object of type Thing, so when the myThing.Foo() line is reached, it can be determined that the call is to the Foo() method on the Thing class. So far, it looks just like early binding, but that's not the case.

Because VB .NET is compiled, you should consider what the compiler will make of this. Obviously, the compiler is aware of the declared type of the myThing variable. So it would appear that the compiler can translate the call to Foo() as a jump to the Foo() method defined in the Thing class, just like it could in the early bound example. However, consider the following case:

```
Public Class SpecialThing
    Inherits Thing
  Public Overrides Sub Foo()
    MsgBox("Foo called on a SpecialThing instance")
  End Sub
End Class
```

We write another class that extends Thing. Instead of creating an instance of the Thing type in our other code, we create an instance of this new subclass:

```
Dim myThing As Thing
myThing = New SpecialThing()
myThing.Foo()
```

Now, recall that the compiler believes that the type of the myThing variable is Thing; however, this doesn't preclude instances of subclasses of Thing being in that variable, as in this example. So the compiler can't assume that the call to myThing.Foo() needs to be sent to the Foo() subroutine in the Thing class. The actual type of the object in the variable will not be determined until runtime because it depends on the code that has executed previously. The declared type of a variable is referred to as its *compile-time type*, and the type of an object actually stored in a variable is referred to as its *runtime type*. The choice of which method is executed will be made at runtime, just like it was in the case of function pointers. So calls to instance methods on .NET objects are normally runtime bound. We say "normally" here because there are circumstances when the compiler can determine what the runtime type of a variable must be. This could be the case if the variable is of a type that is declared NotInheritable, for example. This is only true of instance methods, because Shared methods (which aren't inherited) are always statically (early) bound. In fact, .NET's name for what VB .NET calls Shared type members is static, reflecting the fact that calls to them are statically bound.

So, whenever you make a statically bound call, you are setting in stone in the code what will happen when the line you're writing is executed. The state of the program at the time the line is executed will not affect which code is executed next. A runtime bound call does not fix which code will execute alone; it depends on previous code putting the application in a particular state to specify exactly which code will be executed.

Late Binding

As well as the compile-time checked early binding and runtime binding you've just seen, .NET allows late binding—both through VB .NET syntax with Option Strict off and through reflection. The important question is when do you need to use late binding because runtime binding isn't adequate.

Let's consider the following problem: we have a variable of type Object that might contain a String or an Integer. If it contains a String, we want to display it on screen. If it contains an integer, we want to format it as a quantity of money, and display it on screen.

Here's one way we might attempt to code it:

```
Public Class Handler

  Public Overloads Sub Handle(ByVal s As String)
    Console.WriteLine(s)
  End Sub

  Public Overloads Sub Handle(ByVal i As Integer)
    Console.WriteLine(System.String.Format("{0:c}", i))
  End Sub

End Class

Module MainModule

  Public Sub Main()
    Dim a As New Handler()
    Dim o As Object
    o = "Hello"
    a.Handle(o)

    o = 1
    a.Handle(o)
  End Sub

End Module
```

With Option Strict off, this works just fine; however, if you turn on Option Strict, it doesn't compile, complaining that there's no overload of Handle() that takes an Object. We can add one, like this, and in fact it will reveal something interesting about how runtime and even late binding can sometimes be unpredictable:

```
Option Strict On

Public Class Handler

  Public Overloads Sub Handle(ByVal o As Object)
    Console.WriteLine("Can't Handle Object types")
  End Sub

  Public Overloads Sub Handle(ByVal s As String)
    Console.WriteLine(s)
  End Sub
```

```vb
    Public Overloads Sub Handle(ByVal i As Integer)
        Console.WriteLine(System.String.Format("{0:c}", i))
    End Sub

End Class

Module MainModule
    Public Sub Main()
        Dim a As New Handler()
        Dim o As Object
        o = "Hello"
        a.Handle(o)
        o = 1
        a.Handle(o)
    End Sub

End Module
```

So, if we call Handles() with an instance of String or Integer that's stored in a variable of type Object, will the runtime or compile-time type of the variable be used to decide which overload to execute? The call to Handle() is runtime bound, so the compiler does not decide which class's definition of the method to use at compile-time, in case a contains an instance of a subclass of Handler. So, you might expect the overload resolution to be based on the runtime type of the object in o. That would be String or Integer, so the Handle() variation for the appropriate type should be executed. However, as you'll see if you run this code, the result is that the Object variation is executed.

What actually happens is that .NET regards overloaded methods as completely different—as different as they would be if they had different names—so resolution of which variant of the method should be called happens at compile-time, in exactly the same way as method names are resolved at compile-time. The compiler uses the information it has available—the compile-time type of the o variable—to select which method will be called. At runtime, the decision is made about which class to look in for that method, but the overload resolution has already been solved, so the runtime type of the o variable is not queried.

What's particularly interesting is that if we turn Option Strict off on this code, the behavior isn't changed—the Object variant is always called. Supporting the default case, when someone passes in an object of an unsupported type, it means that even VB .NET's late binding doesn't pass the object to the overload matching the runtime type of the variable.

In other words, we've just found a limit of the late binding provided by VB .NET. If you want to select a method that can accept a particular kind of object based on its runtime type, overloading doesn't provide a good mechanism for it, because overload resolution uses the compile-time type. In fact, no syntactic mechanism exists to reliably accept an object based on its runtime type. What you need is controllable late binding. Reflection provides this capability to take complete control at runtime of what code is executed.

Through the Reflection API, you can examine objects to determine their runtime type, look for methods that have a particular signature, and invoke those methods completely dynamically. Remember, however, the compiler will not be able to help you by checking that the types you're using are correct, and the language will not provide the convenient syntax for calling such methods. You'll have to write more complex code, which might introduce errors. To give you an idea of what we're talking about, the following invocation would replace the preceding statically overloaded method call with a dynamic call to the most appropriate overload given the runtime type of the instance in the o variable:

```
a.GetType() _
    .GetMethod("OverloadedMethod", New Type() {o.GetType()}) _
    .Invoke(a, New Object() {o})
```

We'll look at exactly what all this means in the next few chapters. All this coding overhead for a simple method call is, naturally, not the sort of thing you want to do every day, and we're certainly not advocating you use this technique to call all overloaded instance methods. There's a performance cost for all Reflective API calls, and this code is more error-prone than the compile-time type-checked code you're used to writing. However, in those situations where the default binding behavior doesn't execute the code you want, you have no choice but to use reflection to get the job done. Even VB .NET's late binding doesn't solve all our problems.

Metadata

For a late bound system to work, certain information needs to be available at runtime, which in many languages wouldn't normally be retained after compilation. As you saw in the static bound examples, a compiler can replace a call to a static procedure or method with a jump directly to the location in memory where the method is located. There's no need, for example, for it to create a lookup table of procedure names, and compile each call as a lookup in this table. The actual name given to the procedure is irrelevant at runtime, and is typically discarded, just like variable names, original line numbers, and so on. The only reason for retaining this information might be for debugging, so that the programmer can be told which subroutine a crash occurred in. Similar arguments apply to the late bound examples, in which names—only meaningful to the programmer, not the computer—are generally discarded. This isn't the case in .NET.

To allow late binding of methods, you need to access them by name at runtime. .NET stores the names of all methods as part of the metadata of every type, so it's possible to look up methods by name at runtime.

Similarly, in a statically bound language where the compiler has been able to check that the arguments for every procedure call are all the correct type, there is no need to retain at runtime the information about how many arguments, of what type, are required to call the function. Every statically bound call has already been checked out and will be correct; no calls are going to be constructed on-the-fly, so there is no need to perform a check at runtime.

In a late bound system, however, you need this information so that you can correctly formulate method calls at runtime. So .NET also includes all the information about a method's signature in the compiled assembly.

All this additional data stored in the assembly is called *metadata*. Metadata is data about the code in an assembly.

The Reflection API provides full functionality for examining the metadata in an assembly, associated with a type or type member. .NET also provides a mechanism for adding your own custom metadata to your code through *attributes*, which can also be examined through reflection.

Accessing .NET Metadata

Reflection makes available all the metadata stored in an assembly. .NET assemblies can tell you about all the following things:

- The version of the assembly
- The modules contained in the assembly
- External assemblies referenced
- Classes, interfaces, and value types contained in the modules
- Class members: methods, properties, events, fields, constructors, and enumerations
- Other resources used by the assembly (such as image files)

There are, essentially, two "ways in" to the metadata used by the reflection system. Both routes lead to exactly the same set of data. You can essentially go in from the top or the bottom:

- From the bottom, you can start by obtaining metadata about the type of a particular object, and then discover the assembly that contains it.
- From the top, you can start with a reference to an assembly, obtain assembly metadata, and discover what types it contains.

It helps to visualize the metadata in a hierarchical fashion as shown in Figure 7-1.

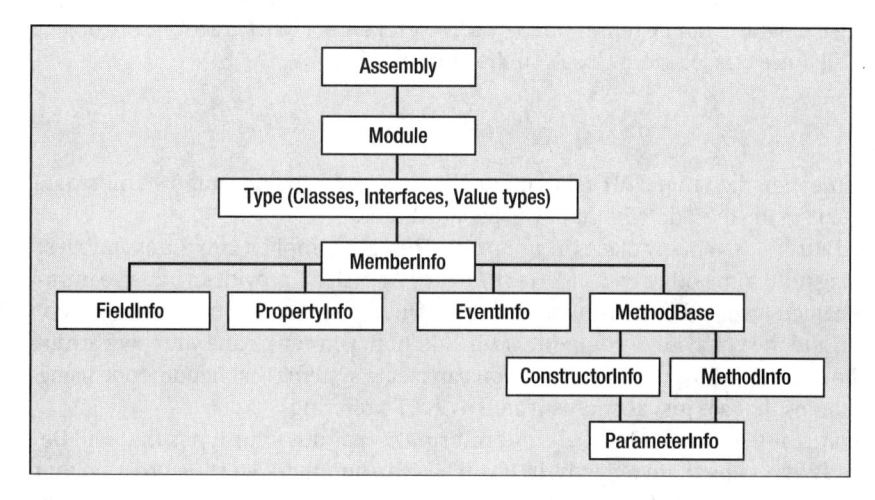

Figure 7-1. *The metadata heirarchy*

At the top of the hierarchy is the information about the assembly. The assembly metadata contains information about the assembly version, about other assemblies that it accesses, about other resources such as images, and so on.

At the next level of the hierarchy is information on modules. A module (in the sense used by .NET, rather than VB .NET) represents a DLL or EXE file, and it's possible to have more than one module in a single assembly. Modules contain a collection of types that represent classes, interfaces, or value types. Further down the metadata hierarchy, each type has a collection of members, such as methods, constructors, properties, fields, and events.

Assembly, module, type, and member metadata are all retrievable using classes from the System.Reflection namespace.

Assemblies, modules, and types are represented in reflection by instances of the System.Reflection.Assembly, System.Reflection.Module, and System.Type classes, respectively.

The System.Reflection.MemberInfo class is the base class for classes that contain class member metadata. Subclasses provide specific interfaces for accessing metadata relating to a particular kind of member. For example, to retrieve information about a field, you obtain a System.Reflection.FieldInfo object. Similarly, we have the following subclasses:

- System.Reflection.MethodInfo
- System.Reflection.PropertyInfo
- System.Reflection.ConstructorInfo
- System.Reflection.EventInfo

The MethodInfo and ConstructorInfo classes have some common characteristics and are not directly derived from the MemberInfo class, but from a base class derived from MemberInfo called System.Reflection.MethodBase. The MethodInfo and ConstructorInfo classes can be further drilled down to one more level of the metadata hierarchy to retrieve information about its parameters, each of which can be represented by a System.Reflection.ParameterInfo object.

We'll look at all these classes more closely in the next chapter.

Attributes

In addition to all the metadata that .NET relies on to function, you can add your own metadata to any of these items in the metadata hierarchy using attributes.

You can place attributes in many places in your code. They are compiled into the assemblies, and sit there waiting until some other code asks to see if they exist. .NET provides a massive number of attributes, which are used to control mechanisms such as serialization, remoting, Web Services, ASP.NET, and the behavior of components. In addition, you can define your own attributes. These are the same as .NET's attributes, and you can create systems that handle code using your custom attributes that are just as sophisticated as .NET's offerings.

You can use attributes to provide labels and information about your types that will be visible to other code accessing them reflectively. If you have an automated testing program that checks all your code and meets the functional specification after you run a build, you could use an attribute to label and name a test method to be called on each type. A generic test harness could use this information to locate all the unit tests and execute them, regardless of the precise methods provided on each class.

We'll look at attributes in more depth in Chapter 11.

Reflection in .NET

In the remoting section of this book in Chapters 2 through 5, we broke down the kinds of tasks you can accomplish with reflection into the following sections.

Examining Objects

First, we looked at what reflection can tell you about an object at runtime. We used reflection to show the names of an object's members, and the values of its fields. We examined the object's inheritance hierarchy, and determined if it could be safely cast to another type.

Manipulating Objects

We then looked at how you can change an object's state and calling methods reflectively. You saw how a base class can provide services to its subclasses, and examined when to use reflection and when not to. We particularly compared reflective access to delegates to determine which is appropriate and when.

Creating Objects

We looked at how reflection can load assemblies and create new objects. We implemented some of the classic creational Design Patterns, and you saw how reflection can effectively decouple an application's requirements from the module providing the service.

Summary

Reflection is a powerful late-binding mechanism that allows you to examine, modify, and create objects at runtime. This means you can use information not available at compile-time to decide how your program should behave, including adding code later on in the form of extension modules.

We examined how .NET performs binding:

- Early (static) bound calls are fixed; if the call is executed, it will always lead to the same code being executed, regardless of the state of the program.

- Late bound calls are dynamic; they take account of the runtime type of objects.

- Polymorphism in .NET is handled through late binding of methods. Overloading, however, does not always use late binding.

- Reflection can be used to perform late binding using information ignored by static and runtime bound calls. You can use it to access overloaded methods based on the runtime type of parameters, and to access methods defined by complex protocols that can't be declared in an interface.

- Reflection can also bind types and assemblies dynamically.

Reflection relies on metadata being present at runtime to allow its dynamic binding. .NET provides a lot of metadata, and allows programmers to add metadata in the form of attributes. They can even define their own custom attributes.

We examined the reasons reflection exists, and some cases where its use is necessary.

CHAPTER 8

Examining Assemblies, Objects, and Types

In the previous chapter, we discussed the advantages of dynamic object binding, and you learned that reflection is a mechanism you can use to perform dynamic binding from your programs. You saw how dynamic binding relies on metadata stored in assemblies, and then considered an overview of .NET's Reflection API. We discussed how the classes associated with it can be used to discover, examine, and manipulate the contents of an assembly, by accessing its metadata.

In this chapter, we'll start playing with some reflection classes by using them in our programs. We'll concentrate on the passive use of reflection in this chapter: examining the types of objects; searching through assemblies for classes, interfaces, and their members; and retrieving their metadata. We'll leave more active uses of reflection—invoking methods, manipulating properties, and instantiating objects via reflection—until later chapters.

The chapter begins by considering what metadata is available to the reflection system by looking at what exactly assemblies contain. You'll see why you would want to examine and retrieve assembly-level metadata, and how to do this using the classes of the Reflection API. We'll look at two classes that are particularly important to reflection: `System.Reflection.Assembly`, which contains information about an assembly, and `System.Type`, which contains information about the type (the class) of an object. You'll then see how to retrieve the type of an object as well as the metadata associated with its members. Finally, we'll take a close look at the `info` classes used as containers for class member metadata.

Examining Assembly Metadata

Assemblies are the basic units of deployment; they contain a collection of types and resources. They can be considered as the building blocks of any .NET application. They are reusable, versionable, self-describing, and stored as an EXE or a DLL file.

Assemblies also contain the infrastructure information that the CLR requires to understand the contents of the assembly and to enforce dependency and security rules defined by the application.

CHAPTER 8 ■ EXAMINING ASSEMBLIES, OBJECTS, AND TYPES

The contents of an assembly can be broadly classified into:

- The assembly manifest
- Type metadata (to store information about the members)
- Microsoft Intermediate Language (MSIL)
- A set of resources

These contents can be grouped into a single file as shown in Figure 8-1.

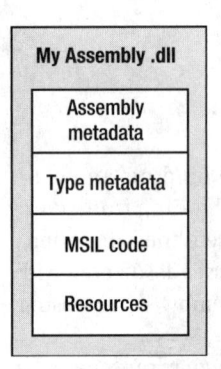

My Assembly .dll
- Assembly metadata
- Type metadata
- MSIL code
- Resources

Figure 8-1. *Ilustration of the contents of an assembly DLL file*

Alternatively, it can be in more than one file resulting in a *multifile assembly* as shown in Figure 8-2.

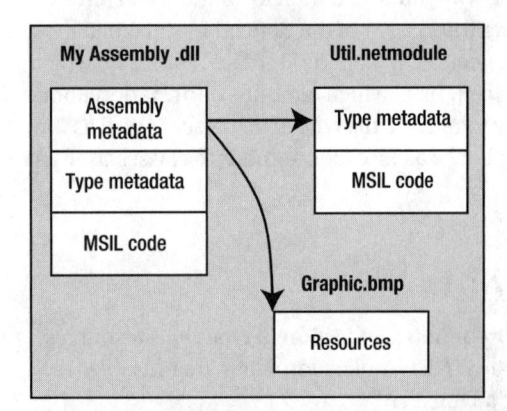

My Assembly .dll
- Assembly metadata
- Type metadata
- MSIL code

Util.netmodule
- Type metadata
- MSIL code

Graphic.bmp
- Resources

Figure 8-2. *The same assembly information can be spread over several files forming a multifile assembly.*

A multifile assembly is desirable when you want to combine modules written in different languages, or when you want to separate out code that is rarely used into separate modules, so that loading and executing modules is faster.

Multifile assemblies are linked to their components using the information in the assembly's *manifest*, which contains the assembly metadata—a collection of data that describes how the elements in the assembly relate to each other. An assembly manifest contains all the metadata needed to specify the assembly's version requirements and security identity, and to define the scope of the assembly and resolve references to resources and classes.

The assembly manifest can be stored in either a portable executable (PE) file (an EXE or DLL) with MSIL code or in a standalone PE file that contains only assembly manifest information. The metadata can be analyzed to retrieve the assembly name, version number, culture, and strong name information, which when combined together, forms the assembly's identity. We'll look at assembly naming and loading in detail in Chapter 10.

An assembly is represented in the Reflection class library by an object of type `System.Reflection.Assembly`. Let's look now at that class.

The Assembly Class

The `System.Reflection.Assembly` class provides access to all the metadata stored in the assembly's manifest. You can't obtain an `Assembly` object just by calling a constructor—you have to get one through one of the following mechanisms:

- Through a call to one of the `Assembly` class's shared `Get...()` methods:
  - `GetAssembly(t As Type)`
  - `GetCallingAssembly()`
  - `GetEntryAssembly()`
  - `GetExecutingAssembly()`

  These return an `Assembly` object representing an already-loaded assembly. We'll look at them in detail in a moment.

- Through a call to one of the `Assembly` class's shared `Load...()` methods:
  - `Load(...)`
  - `LoadWithPartialName(...)`
  - `LoadFrom(...)`

  These methods are all overloaded. They load a specified assembly into memory, and return an `Assembly` object representing the loaded assembly. We'll look at these methods in Chapter 10.

- By querying the `Assembly` property of a `Type` object, to obtain an `assembly` object representing the assembly that defines that type. This returns exactly the same value as calling `Assembly.GetAssembly()` with the same type object.

- `AppDomain.GetAssemblies()` returns the assemblies loaded in a particular application domain. `AppDomain` also provides a number of events and other methods related to assembly loading.

The `Get...Assembly()` methods deserve a little more explanation, because they are the simplest ways to get at an assembly that's already loaded into the .NET runtime.

- `Assembly.GetAssembly(t As Type)` returns the assembly in which the specified type is declared. As stated previously, this is functionally equivalent to calling `t.GetAssembly()`.
- `Assembly.GetExecutingAssembly()` returns the assembly containing the currently executing code.
- `Assembly.GetCallingAssembly()` returns the assembly containing the method that called the currently executing method. This can be the same as the executing assembly, if the method was called by another method in the same assembly.
- `Assembly.GetEntryAssembly()` returns the assembly that contains the entry point for the current `AppDomain`. This will be the assembly containing the main form or `Main()` method of the application.

As you can see, you can find the current assembly, the assembly from which the currently executing code was called, or the assembly that was originally the entry point for the application in which your code is being run.

Note More detailed analysis of the current call stack (the list of methods which were called in order for execution to reach the current point in the program) can be performed using `System.Diagnostics.StackTrace`. This class enables you to locate objects representing all the executing methods, from which, you can work your way up through the reflection object model to locate the assemblies that contain them. This same process can be used to examine the assemblies that caused an exception to be thrown, because a `StackTrace` object can be obtained from an exception's `StackTrace` property.

After obtaining an `Assembly` object, you have access to a number of methods and properties that give you information from the assembly's metadata. The key properties are listed in Table 8-1.

Table 8-1. *Key Properties of the* Assembly *Object*

Property	Type	Description
CodeBase	String	Full path of the assembly file, including the name of the assembly file.
EntryPoint	System.Reflection.MethodInfo	Gets an instance of MethodInfo that represents the method that would be called if this assembly was executed, or Nothing if the assembly is a DLL.
EscapedCodeBase	String	The CodeBase expressed as a clean URL, using standard URL escape characters for those that aren't valid in a URL (such as %20 for a space character).
Evidence	System.Security.Policy.Evidence	Evidence is used by the .NET security system to decide what permissions to grant to the code in an assembly. Objects of any type that are recognized by a security policy represent evidence. Common forms of evidence include signatures and location of origin of code, but can potentially be anything.

Property	Type	Description
FullName	String	The full screen name of the assembly, including version, culture, and strong name information.
GlobalAssemblyCache	Boolean	A value indicating whether the assembly was loaded from the GAC (Global Assembly Cache) or not.
Location	String	Location of the file containing the assembly manifest. Differs from CodeBase in that the CodeBase is always the location of a physical assembly, whereas a dynamically created assembly, which has no physical source file or manifest, has a blank Location and a CodeBase that is the same as the assembly that created it.

Assembly also provides the methods listed in Table 8-2.

Table 8-2. Assembly *Methods*

Method	Description
CreateInstance()	Used to create an instance of a type defined in the assembly. You'll see this in use in Chapter 10.
GetCustomAttributes()	Gets any custom attributes defined on this assembly.
GetExportedTypes()	Returns an array of Type objects representing all the exported types in the assembly; exported types are types visible to COM applications.
GetFile()	Obtains a FileStream for a file referenced from the assembly manifest.
GetFiles()	Returns an array of FileStream objects connected to the files from the assembly manifest.
GetLoadedModules()	Returns an array of objects representing the modules in the assembly.
GetManifestResourceInfo()	Returns information about a specified resource.
GetManifestResourceNames()	Returns an array of strings representing the names of all the assembly's resources.
GetManifestResourceStream()	Returns a Stream for reading the specified resource.
GetModule()	Returns an object representing the specified module.
GetModules()	Gets all the modules that are part of this assembly. The first module in the returned array contains the assembly's manifest.
GetName()	Returns an AssemblyName object containing the assembly's name, version, culture, and public key information.
GetReferencedAssemblies()	Returns an array of AssemblyName objects for all the assemblies referenced.

(continues)

Table 8-2. Assembly *Methods (continued)*

Method	Description
GetSatelliteAssembly()	A satellite assembly contains a set of resources for a specific culture. This method returns the satellite assembly for the specified culture.
GetType()	Returns a Type object for the type defined in the assembly with the specified name. Note that this overloads the GetType() no-arg method defined by System.Object, which returns the Type object representing the type of the object on which it's called.
GetTypes()	Returns an array of Type objects for all the types defined in the assembly.
IsDefined()	Returns a Boolean value indicating whether the assembly is decorated with an attribute of the specified type.
LoadModule()	Loads a specified module into the assembly.

Let's write a program that examines an assembly and retrieves the assembly metadata:

```
Imports System.Reflection
Module MainModule
  Sub Main()

    'Loads the assembly file
    Dim myAssembly As System.Reflection.Assembly = _
        System.Reflection.Assembly.GetExecutingAssembly()

    'Display the CodeBase
    Console.WriteLine("Code Base = {0}", myAssembly.CodeBase())
    Console.WriteLine()
    'Display the EntryPoint
    Console.WriteLine("Entry Point = {0}", _
                       myAssembly.EntryPoint.Name)
    Console.WriteLine()
    'Display the FullName
    Console.WriteLine("Full Name = {0}", myAssembly.FullName)
    Console.WriteLine()

    'Get the AssemblyName object of the assembly
    Dim asmName As AssemblyName = myAssembly.GetName
    'Display the simple name
    Console.WriteLine("Simple Name = {0}", AsmName.Name)
    Console.WriteLine()

    'Display the version information
    Dim asmVer As System.Version = asmName.Version
    Console.WriteLine("Major Version = {0}", AsmVer.Major)
    Console.WriteLine("Minor Version = {0}", AsmVer.Minor)
```

```vbnet
        Console.WriteLine("Build Version = {0}", AsmVer.Build)
        Console.WriteLine("Revision Version = {0}", AsmVer.Revision)
        Console.WriteLine()

        'Get an array of AssemblyName objects that represent the
        'assemblies referenced by this assembly
        Dim refAsmbs As AssemblyName() = _
            myAssembly.GetReferencedAssemblies
        Dim refAsmb As AssemblyName

        'Display the simple name of each referenced assembly
        System.Console.Write("Referenced Assemblies: ")
        For Each refAsmb In refAsmbs
          System.Console.Write("{0}, ", refAsmb.Name)
        Next
        Console.WriteLine()
        Console.WriteLine()

        'Get an array of Module objects that are contained in this
        'assembly
        Dim myModules As System.Reflection.Module() = _
            myAssembly.GetModules
        Dim myModule As System.Reflection.Module

        'Display the name of each module
        System.Console.Write("Modules Contained: ")
        For Each myModule In myModules
          System.Console.Write("{0}, ", myModule.Name)
        Next
        Console.WriteLine()
        Console.ReadLine()
    End Sub
End Module
```

If you look at the output from the program, you can see that the program examines the assembly associated with the program (we called the application AssemblyMeta):

```
Code Base = file:///C:/Documents and Settings/andrewpTEST/
My Documents/Visual Studio Projects/AssemblyMeta/bin/AssemblyMeta.exe

Entry Point = Main

Full Name = AssemblyMeta, Version=1.0.960.24866, Culture=neutral,
PublicKeyToken=null
```

```
Simple Name = AssemblyMeta

Major Version = 1
Minor Version = 0
Build Version = 960
Revision Version = 24866

Referenced Assemblies: mscorlib, Microsoft.VisualBasic, System,
System.Data, System.Xml,

Modules Contained: AssemblyMeta.exe,
```

Examining Type Metadata

The `System.Type` class is the gateway to all the reflection operations that you can perform. `Type` is an abstract class that can be used to represent any type declaration:

- classes
- interfaces
- arrays
- value types
- enumerations
- pointers

Retrieving Types

Now that you know the kind of information that you can retrieve from a `Type` object, let's consider how you can obtain a `Type` object in the first place.

The GetType() Method and Operator

All classes inherit the `GetType()` method from `System.Object`. Therefore, if we call this method on *any* object, it will return a `Type` for that object:

```
Dim myType As System.Type = myObj.GetType()
```

If we want to get a `Type` object for a class we haven't instantiated, we can use a `Shared` overload of `GetType()` from the `Type` class:

```
Dim doubleType As System.Type = Type.GetType("System.Double")
```

As you can see, the `Type.GetType()` method requires that we pass the fully qualified name of a class along with the namespace as a `String`. This technique is generally used to get the type of a class that is contained in an external assembly.

You should note that, by default, any version of `GetType()` where we supply the name of the class as a parameter will perform a case-sensitive search for the type in question.

VB .NET also has an operator called GetType, which returns the type. This GetType operator is equivalent to the typeof operator in C#. It takes the defined classname (with namespaces if required) and returns the Type object; it is not necessary to instantiate the class in this case:

```
Dim doubleType As System.Type = GetType(System.Double)
```

The GetInterfaces() Method

The Type.GetInterfaces() can be used to obtain an array of Type objects representing the types of all the interfaces implemented or inherited by the object we're interested in:

```
Dim myInterfaces As System.Type = myObj.GetInterfaces()
```

Module Methods

The System.Reflection.Module class (which represents a module for the purposes of reflection) contains several methods you can use to retrieve type information.

First, if we want to retrieve the Type object of one of the classes contained in this module, we can use the Module.GetType() method. We need to pass a string containing the fully qualified name of the class:

```
Dim classType As System.Type = myModule.GetType("ClassName")
```

Because a module can contain more than one class definition, we may want to retrieve an array of Type objects representing all the types defined in the module. To do this, call the Module.GetTypes() method. It is even possible to return an array of Type objects from a module that has been filtered according to some criteria, using the FindTypes() method (for more information about this method, refer to the MSDN documentation).

Let's look at the members of the Type class.

Type Class Members

The members of Type can be used to retrieve information about a particular class, such as the constructors, methods, fields, properties, and events of a class, and even the module and the assembly in which the class is deployed. Table 8-3 shows some selected properties of the Type class.

Table 8-3. *Select* Type *Class Properties*

Property	Type	Description
Name	String	Gets the name of the class. Note that only the simple name is returned, not the fully qualified name. For example, for the System.Reflection.Assembly class, the Name property would be Assembly.
FullName	String	Gets the fully qualified name of the class, including the namespace of the class.
Assembly	System.Reflection.Assembly	Retrieves the assembly in which the class is declared.
AssemblyQualifiedName	String	Gets the fully qualified name of the class (including the name of the assembly from which the class was loaded).

(continues)

Table 8-3. *Select* Type *Class Properties (continued)*

Property	Type	Description
Attributes	TypeAttributes	Gets an instance of a TypeAttributes enumeration object representing the attribute set of the class. Using TypeAttributes, you can find out whether the class is an interface or is an abstract class; whether the class is public or not; and whether the class is serializable, among other information.
IsClass	Boolean	Indicates whether the type is a class (not a value type or interface).
BaseType	System.Type	Gets the Type of the class from which the class directly inherits.
Module	System.Reflection.Module	Gets an instance of the Module (DLL or EXE) in which the class is defined.

Table 8-4 lists some methods of the Type class.

Table 8-4. Type *Class Methods*

Method	Description
IsSubclassOf()	Returns a Boolean specifying whether the class derives from the class specified as an argument to the method.
IsInstanceOfType()	Returns a Boolean indicating whether the specified object (passed as a parameter to the method) is an instance of the current class.
GetMember()	Gets the specified member of the Type object as a MemberInfo object. The member is specified via a String.
GetMembers()	Gets the members of the Type object as an array of MemberInfo objects.
GetField()	Gets the specified field of the Type object as a FieldInfo object. The field is specified via a String.
GetFields()	Gets the fields of the Type object as an array of FieldInfo objects.
GetProperty()	Gets the specified property of the Type object as a PropertyInfo object. The property is specified via a String.
GetProperties()	Gets the properties of the Type object as an array of PropertyInfo objects.
GetMethod()	Gets the specified method of the Type object as a MethodInfo object. The property is specified via a String.
GetMethods()	Gets the methods of the Type object as an array of MethodInfo objects.
GetConstructor()	Gets the specified constructor of the Type object as a ConstructorInfo object. The property is specified via a String.
GetConstructors()	Gets the constructors of the Type object as an array of ConstructorInfo objects.
GetEvent()	Gets the specified public event of the Type object as an EventInfo object. The property is specified via a String.
GetEvents()	Gets the public events of the Type object as an array of EventInfo objects.

Let's create a simple console program that illustrates how to access type metadata:

```
Module Module1
  Sub Main()
    Dim t As Type = GetType(System.Object)
    Console.WriteLine("Type Name : {0}", t.Name)
    Console.WriteLine("Full Name : {0}", t.FullName)
    Console.WriteLine("Namespace : {0}", t.Namespace)
    Console.WriteLine("Assembly Name : {0}", _
                      t.Assembly.GetName.Name)
    Console.WriteLine("Module Name : {0}", t.Module.Name)
    Console.WriteLine("Assembly Qualified Name : {0}", _
                      t.AssemblyQualifiedName)
    Console.WriteLine("IsAbstract : {0}", t.IsAbstract)
    Console.WriteLine("IsArray : {0}", t.IsArray)
    Console.WriteLine("IsClass : {0}", t.IsClass)
    Console.WriteLine("IsCOMObject : {0}", t.IsCOMObject)
    Console.WriteLine("IsEnum : {0}", t.IsEnum)
    Console.WriteLine("IsInterface : {0}", t.IsInterface)
    Console.WriteLine("IsNotPublic : {0}", t.IsNotPublic)
    Console.WriteLine("IsPointer : {0}", t.IsPointer)
    Console.WriteLine("IsPrimitive : {0}", t.IsPrimitive)
    Console.WriteLine("IsPublic : {0}", t.IsPublic)
    Console.WriteLine("IsSealed : {0}", t.IsSealed)
    Console.WriteLine("IsSerializable : {0}", t.IsSerializable)
    Console.WriteLine("IsSpecialName : {0}", t.IsSpecialName)
    Console.WriteLine("IsValueType : {0}", t.IsValueType)
    Console.ReadLine()
  End Sub
End Module
```

As you can see from the output from the program, it examines the metadata for the System.Object type:

```
Type Name : Object
Full Name : System.Object
Namespace : System
Assembly Name : mscorlib
Module Name : mscorlib.dll
Assembly Qualified Name : System.Object, mscorlib, Version=1.0.3300.0,
Culture=neutral, PublicKeyToken=b77a5c561934e089
IsAbstract : False
IsArray : False
IsClass : True
IsCOMObject : False
IsEnum : False
IsInterface : False
IsNotPublic : False
IsPointer : False
IsPrimitive : False
IsPublic : True
```

```
IsSealed : False
IsSerializable : True
IsSpecialName : False
IsValueType : False
```

Examining Class Member Metadata

In the previous section we retrieved information about classes using reflection. Now let's see how to access information about class members: fields, properties, methods, and events, as well as value types such as enumerations.

To examine class member metadata, you'll need to retrieve one or more of the following `info` objects:

- `System.Reflection.MemberInfo`: Base class for all member `info` classes.
- `System.Reflection.FieldInfo`: Represents metadata about a field.
- `System.Reflection.PropertyInfo`: Represents metadata about a property.
- `System.Reflection.MethodInfo`: Represents metadata about a method.
- `System.Reflection.ConstructorInfo`: Represents metadata about a constructor.
- `System.Reflection.EventInfo`: Represents metadata about an event.
- `System.Reflection.ParameterInfo`: Represents parameter metadata.

You should note that whereas `FieldInfo`, `PropertyInfo`, and `EventInfo` all derive directly from `MemberInfo`, `MethodInfo` and `ConstructorInfo` derive from another subclass of `MemberInfo` called `MethodBase`. `ParameterInfo` derives directly from `System.Object`.

One last thing worth noting before we dive into the `info` classes is that the `System.Type` class is itself a direct subclass of `MemberInfo`.

Figure 8-3 shows the class hierarchy we've just discussed in an easy-to-digest graphical form.

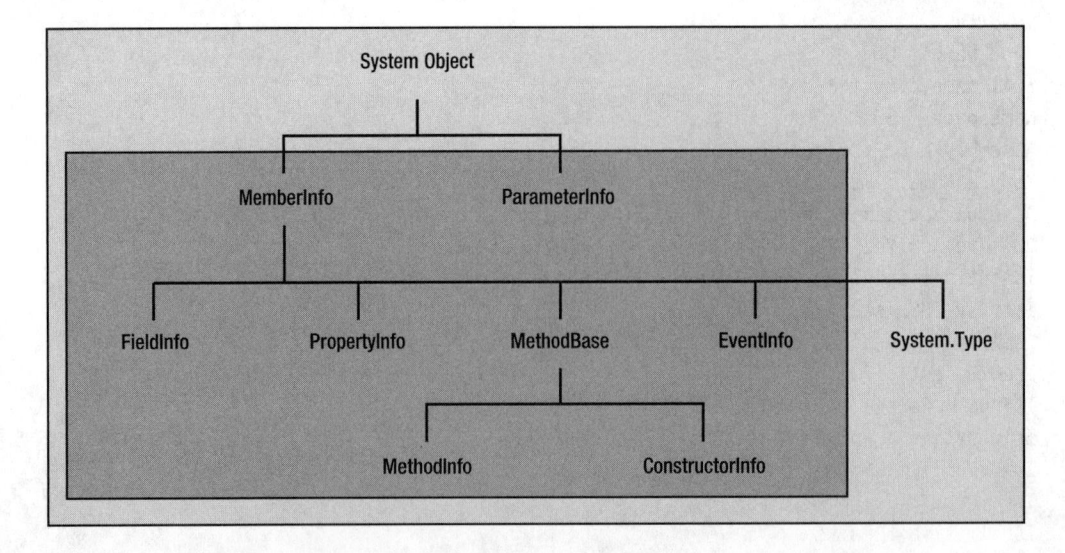

Figure 8-3. *Class hierarchy within* `System.Object`

The classes within the darker shaded box in the figure are within the `System.Reflection` namespace.

The `MemberInfo` Class

The `MemberInfo` class is an abstract base class, which provides an interface that is common to every member type. It contains some public properties that are inherited by all `info` classes as shown in Table 8-5.

Table 8-5. *The `MemberInfo` Public Properties*

Property	Type	Description
Name	String	Gets the name of the member
MemberType	System.Reflection.MemberTypes	Gets the member type (field, method, and so on)
DeclaringType	System.Type	Returns the Type of the class that declares this member
ReflectedType	System.Type	Returns the Type of the object that was used to obtain this `MemberInfo` instance

The `System.Reflection.MemberTypes` enumeration can take the following values:

- Field
- Property
- Method
- Constructor
- Event
- NestedType (specifies a nested type, that extends `MethodInfo`)
- TypeInfo (specifies that the member is a type)
- Custom (specifies a custom member type)
- All (specifies all member types)

The `MemberInfo` class can be retrieved from a `Type` object using either `GetMember()` or `GetMembers()`. The `GetMember()` method takes the name of the member as a parameter and returns a `MemberInfo` object. The `GetMembers()` method returns an array of `MemberInfo` objects. By default, if you do not provide any parameters to these methods, they retrieve only the public members.

The `BindingFlags` Enumeration

Both the `GetMember()` and the `GetMembers()` methods (and many other methods that you'll encounter as you use reflection) have overloaded versions that take a `System.Reflection.BindingFlags` enumeration value as a parameter. This enumeration specifies flags that control binding and the way in which the search for members and types is conducted by reflection. It is often used to filter and retrieve only those members that are of interest to the application. Table 8-6 lists the most commonly used `BindingFlag` flag values.

Table 8-6. *Commonly Used* BindingFlag *Values*

Enumeration Value	Description
CreateInstance	Specifies that an instance of the specified type should be created
DeclaredOnly	Specifies that inherited members should be ignored
Default	Specifies no binding flag
GetField	Specifies that the value of the specified field should be returned
GetProperty	Specifies that the value of the specified property should be returned
InvokeMethod	Specifies that a particular method (not a constructor) is to be invoked
Public / NonPublic	Specifies that only public/nonpublic members are to be returned
SetField	Specifies that the value of the specified field should be set
SetProperty	Specifies that the value of the specified property should be set
Static / Instance	Specifies that only shared/instance members are to be returned

BindingTypes is an enumeration type that allows a bitwise combination of its member values, so we can specify more than one of the previously listed conditions at once.

Let's have a few snippets of code to illustrate the use of GetMembers() and BindingFlags. If you want to retrieve only those members of a Type object myType that are static and public, you can use the following syntax:

```
myType.GetMembers(Reflection.BindingFlags.Static _
                  Or Reflection.BindingFlags.Public)
```

Alternatively, if you want to retrieve only those members that are nonpublic and nonstatic, you can use:

```
myType.GetMembers(Reflection.BindingFlags.NonPublic _
                  Or Reflection.BindingFlags.Instance)
```

Note that you must specify either BindingFlags.Instance or BindingFlags.Static, and either BindingFlags.Public or BindingFlags.NonPublic to get a return.

In both cases, the return you get is an array of MemberInfo objects that fulfill the conditions of the member search.

The following program retrieves the members of a class (called Employee) and displays their names and types:

```
Imports System.Reflection
Module Module1

  Sub Main()
    Dim typ As System.Type = GetType(Employee)
    Dim membs As MemberInfo() = _
        typ.GetMembers(BindingFlags.Public Or _
        BindingFlags.NonPublic Or _
        BindingFlags.Static Or _
        BindingFlags.Instance Or _
        BindingFlags.DeclaredOnly)
    Dim memb As MemberInfo
    Console.WriteLine("MEMBER NAME".PadRight(20) + "MEMBER TYPE")
```

```vbnet
    Console.WriteLine()
    For Each memb In membs
      Dim nameStr As String = (memb.Name).PadRight(20)
      Console.WriteLine("{0}" + "{1}", nameStr, memb.MemberType)
    Next
    Console.ReadLine()
  End Sub

  Public Class Employee
    Private EmpName As String
    Private DoB As Date

    Public Function GetAge() As Integer
    End Function

    Private Sub ComputeOvertime()
    End Sub

    Private Property DateOfBirth() As Date
      Get
        Return DoB
      End Get
      Set(ByVal Value As Date)
        DoB = Value

      End Set
    End Property

    Public Property Name() As String
      Get
        Return EmpName
      End Get
      Set(ByVal Value As String)
        EmpName = Value
      End Set
    End Property
  End Class
End Module
```

Here's what we expect to see from the program:

MEMBER NAME	MEMBER TYPE
EmpName	Field
DoB	Field
GetAge	Method
ComputeOvertime	Method
get_DateOfBirth	Method
set_DateOfBirth	Method

get_Name	Method
set_Name	Method
.ctor	Constructor
DateOfBirth	Property
Name	Property

The `FieldInfo` Class

This class provides access to field metadata. Tables 8-7 and 8-8 list some of its most important properties and methods (remember that because `FieldInfo` inherits from `MemberInfo`, it inherits its members too).

Table 8-7. `FieldInfo` *Class Properties*

Property	Type	Description
Name	String	Gets the name of this field
IsPrivate	Boolean	Gets a value indicating whether the field is private
IsPublic	Boolean	Gets a value indicating whether the field is public
IsStatic	Boolean	Gets a value indicating whether the field is static
IsAssembly	Boolean	Returns a value indicating whether this field has Assembly level visibility (it can be accessed only from members inside the same assembly)
IsFamily	Boolean	Returns a value indicating whether this field has Family level visibility (it can be accessed only from members in the same class or from subclasses of that class)
IsFamilyAndAssembly	Boolean	Returns a value indicating whether this field has both Family and Assembly level visibility
IsFamilyOrAssembly	Boolean	Returns a value indicating whether this field has either Family or Assembly level visibility
IsInitOnly	Boolean	Gets a value showing whether the field can only be set in the body of the constructor
IsLiteral	Boolean	Gets a value showing whether the value is written at compile-time and cannot be changed
IsNotSerialized	Boolean	Gets a value indicating whether this field has the NotSerializedAttribute

Table 8-8. `FieldInfo` *Class Methods*

Method	Description
FieldType()	Returns a Type object that corresponds to the type of the field.
GetValue()	Retrieves the value of the field. It takes an Object as a parameter, which should be an instance of the class in which it is declared or must be an instance of a class that inherits the field. It returns an Object type, which contains the appropriate subclass.
SetValue()	Used to assign a new value to the field. You need to pass two Object parameters to the method: an instance of the class in which the field is declared (or an instance of a class that inherits the field), and the new value of the field.

You should note that as long as code in the assembly is trusted, there is no problem with retrieving or modifying the values of private fields using GetValue() and SetValue().

FieldInfo can be retrieved from any Type object using one of the two methods GetField() and GetFields(). The GetFields() method returns an array of FieldInfo objects each corresponding to one field inside the class. The GetField() method returns one FieldInfo object corresponding to the name of the field that is passed as a String parameter. Both methods can also take the BindingFlags enumeration, although if no BindingFlags enumeration values are passed to the methods, they will retrieve only the public fields.

For example, if you want to retrieve only private and instance fields from a Type object myType, use the following syntax:

myType.GetFields(BindingFlags.NonPublic Or BindingFlags.Instance)

In the following program, the FieldInfo class is used to retrieve metadata about the field NaN of the System.Double class:

```
Imports System.Reflection
Module Module1
  Sub Main()
    Dim t As Type = GetType(System.Double)
    Dim myFieldInfo As FieldInfo = t.GetField("NaN")
    Console.WriteLine("FIELD NAME: {0}", myFieldInfo.Name)
    Console.WriteLine()
    Console.WriteLine("Member type: {0}", _
                      myFieldInfo.MemberType.ToString)
    Console.WriteLine("Class declared in: {0}", _
                      myFieldInfo.DeclaringType.Name)
    Console.WriteLine("Field Type: {0}", _
                      myFieldInfo.FieldType.Name)
    Dim x As Double = 5.0
    Console.WriteLine("Field Value: {0}", myFieldInfo.GetValue(x))
    Console.WriteLine("Has Assembly Level Visibility: {0}", _
                      myFieldInfo.IsAssembly)
    Console.WriteLine("Has Family Level Visibility: {0}", _
                      myFieldInfo.IsFamily)
    Console.WriteLine("Has FamilyAndAssembly Level Visibility: {0}", _
                      myFieldInfo.IsFamilyAndAssembly)
    Console.WriteLine("Has FamilyOrAssembly Level Visibility: {0}", _
                      myFieldInfo.IsFamilyOrAssembly)
    Console.WriteLine("IsInitOnly: {0}", myFieldInfo.IsInitOnly)
    Console.WriteLine("IsLiteral: {0}", myFieldInfo.IsLiteral)
    Console.WriteLine("IsNotSerialized: {0}", _
                       myFieldInfo.IsNotSerialized)
    Console.WriteLine("IsPrivate: {0}", myFieldInfo.IsPrivate)
    Console.WriteLine("IsPublic: {0}", myFieldInfo.IsPublic)
    Console.WriteLine("IsStatic: {0}", myFieldInfo.IsStatic)
    Console.ReadLine()
  End Sub
End Module
```

Here's what you'll see when the program is run:

```
FIELD NAME: NaN
Member type: Field
Class declared in: Double
Field Type: Double
Field Value: NaN
Has Assembly Level Visibility: False
Has Family Level Visibility: False
Has FamilyAndAssembly Level Visibility: False
Has FamilyOrAssembly Level Visibility: False
IsInitOnly: False
IsLiteral: True
IsNotSerialized: False
IsPrivate: False
IsPublic: True
IsStatic: True
```

The PropertyInfo Class

The PropertyInfo class provides access to property metadata. Table 8-9 provides the relevant properties of the class

Table 8-9. PropertyInfo *Class Properties*

Property	Type	Description
Name	String	Returns the name of the property as a String
PropertyType	System.Type	Returns a Type object that represents the type of the property field
CanRead	Boolean	Returns a Boolean stating if the property can be read
CanWrite	Boolean	Returns a Boolean stating if the property can be written to

Table 8-10 lists the relevant methods of the PropertyInfo class.

Table 8-10. *PropertyInfo Class Methods*

Method	Description
GetValue()	Retrieves the value of the property as an Object (takes the same arguments as FieldInfo.GetValue())
SetValue()	Assigns a new value to the property (requires the same arguments as FieldInfo.SetValue())
GetGetMethod()	Returns a MethodInfo object that contains information about the Get accessor of the property
GetSetMethod()	Returns a MethodInfo object that contains information about the Set accessor of the property

Similar to how we retrieved field metadata for a class in the previous section, it is possible to retrieve `PropertyInfo` objects for a class using the `Type.GetProperties()` or the `Type.GetProperty()` methods. The `GetProperty()` method is used to retrieve information about a single property of the class, so you need to supply the name of the property as the `String` argument to the method. The `GetProperties()` method returns all the public properties of the class if you do not pass any `BindingFlags` parameters.

Let's write a program that loads an external assembly file (System.dll) and scans through all the members of the assembly to find nonabstract classes. It then delves into those nonabstract classes and retrieves only those properties that are static and nonpublic. We then examine each of them and display only those properties whose values can be read but cannot be modified:

```
Imports System.Reflection
Module Module1
  Sub Main()
    Dim strAsmbName As String = _
      String.Format("{0}\\Microsoft.NET\\Framework\\v1.0.3705\\System.dll", _
        Environment.GetEnvironmentVariable("windir"))
    Dim objAssembly As System.Reflection.Assembly = _
      System.Reflection.Assembly.LoadFrom(strAsmbName)

    Dim typs As System.Type() = objAssembly.GetTypes
    Dim typ As System.Type
    Dim i As Integer = 0
    Console.WriteLine("PROPERTY NAME".PadRight(35) + _
                      "PROPERTY TYPE")
    Console.WriteLine()
    For Each typ In typs
      If typ.IsClass And Not typ.IsAbstract Then
        Dim props As PropertyInfo() = _
            typ.GetProperties(BindingFlags.NonPublic Or _
            BindingFlags.Static)
        Dim prop As PropertyInfo
        For Each prop In props
          If prop.CanRead And Not prop.CanWrite Then
            i += 1
            Dim strName As String = (prop.Name).PadRight(35)
            Console.WriteLine("{0}" + "{1}", strName, _
                prop.PropertyType.Name)
          End If
        Next
      End If
    Next
    Console.WriteLine()
    Console.WriteLine("Total Properties Displayed = {0}", i)
    Console.ReadLine()
  End Sub
End Module
```

> **Note** In the preceding program, the `System.dll` assembly file is loaded from the directory where the .NET Framework is installed on a specific system (C:\WINNT\Microsoft.NET\Framework\v1.1.4322\System.dll). You may have to change the path in code to point to the correct location of the file in your system.

Here's what you'll see if you run the program:

PROPERTY NAME	PROPERTY TYPE
Empty	RegexPrefix
IntrinsicTypeConverters	Hashtable
UiPermission	Boolean
UserInteractive	Boolean
SwitchSettings	Dictionary
AssertUIEnabled	Boolean
LogFileName	String
AutoFlush	Boolean
IndentSize	Int32
PerfomanceCountersFileMappingSize	Int32
HashCodeProvider	IHashCodeProvider
Comparer	IComparer
UserInteractive	Boolean
LocalHost	IPHostEntry
ConfigTable	Hashtable
ModuleList	ArrayList
SetConfigurationSystemInProgress	Boolean
MsCorLibDirectory	String
MachineConfigurationFilePath	String
AppConfigPath	Uri
ComputerName	String
DllPath	String
IniFilePath	String
SymbolFilePath	String
FileView	FileMapping
CurrentEnvironment	Int32
Total Properties Displayed = 26	

The `MethodBase` Class

`MethodBase` is an abstract class, which is inherited from the `MemberInfo` class. It provides information about methods and constructors. The `MethodInfo` and `ConstructorInfo` classes are inherited from the `MethodBase` class.

The `MethodBase` class declares certain methods and properties that are inherited in the `ConstructorInfo` and `MethodInfo` classes as shown in Table 8-11.

Table 8-11. `MethodBase` *Class Properties*

Property	Type	Description
`IsConstructor`	Boolean	Gets a value indicating whether the method is a constructor.
`IsAbstract`	Boolean	Returns a value indicating whether the method must be overridden.
`IsPrivate`	Boolean	Gets a value indicating whether this member is private.
`IsPublic`	Boolean	Gets a value indicating whether this is a public method.
`IsStatic`	Boolean	Gets a value indicating whether the method is shared.
`IsVirtual`	Boolean	Gets a value indicating whether the method is overridable.
`IsFamily`	Boolean	This property is True if the method is accessible only by the members of the class and its derived classes.
`IsFamilyAndAssembly`	Boolean	This property is True if the method is accessible only by the members of the class and its derived classes that are in the same assembly.
`IsFamilyOrAssembly`	Boolean	This property is True if the method is accessible only by the members of the class and its derived classes, and also if it can be accessed by other classes in the same assembly.
`IsFinal`	Boolean	This property is True if the method is Final, which means that this method cannot be overridden.

The methods are described in Table 8-12.

Table 8-12. `MethodBase` *Class Methods*

Method	Description
`GetParameters()`	When overridden in a subclass, returns the parameters of the specified method or constructor as `ParameterInfo` objects.
`Invoke()`	Invokes the method or constructor. You need to pass this method an array containing the parameters for the method/constructor you want to invoke. If you want to invoke a method, you need to pass the instance that created that method as well.

The `MethodInfo` Class

The `MethodInfo` class is used to access the method metadata. Because it is a subclass of `MethodBase`, it inherits the properties of that class, although it also adds a few other properties and methods of its own, including the `ReturnType` property. This property retrieves the return type of the method as a `Type` object.

The `MethodInfo` class can be obtained by invoking the `GetMethod()` or `GetMethods()` methods on a `Type` object.

Just as in the case of `GetProperty()` and the `GetProperties()` methods, the `GetMethod()` and the `GetMethods()` methods of the `Type` class are used depending on whether you want to examine a particular method whose name is known in advance (and you supply as a `String` argument), or whether you want to examine all the methods in a class that match a particular criteria using the `BindingFlags` parameters.

The following program illustrates how to access the method metadata discussed previously, for a method called `ComputeOvertime()` of the `Employee` class:

```vb
Imports System.Reflection
Module Module1

  Sub Main()
    Dim typ As System.Type = GetType(Employee)
    Dim myMethod As MethodInfo = typ.GetMethod("ComputeOvertime", _
        BindingFlags.NonPublic Or BindingFlags.Instance _
        Or BindingFlags.Static Or BindingFlags.Public)
    Console.WriteLine("Member Type: {0}", myMethod.MemberType)
    Console.WriteLine("Method Name: {0}", myMethod.Name)
    Console.WriteLine("Method declared in Class : {0}", _
        myMethod.DeclaringType.Name)
    Console.WriteLine("IsAbstract : {0}", myMethod.IsAbstract)
    Console.WriteLine( _
      "Can be called from other classes in the same assembly: {0}", _
      myMethod.IsAssembly)
    Console.WriteLine("IsConstructor: {0}", myMethod.IsConstructor)
    Console.WriteLine("IsFinal: {0}", myMethod.IsFinal)
    Console.WriteLine("IsPrivate: {0}", myMethod.IsPrivate)
    Console.WriteLine("IsPublic: {0}", myMethod.IsPublic)
    Console.WriteLine("IsStatic: {0}", myMethod.IsStatic)
    Console.WriteLine("IsVirtual: {0}", myMethod.IsVirtual)
    Console.WriteLine("Return type: {0}", myMethod.ReturnType.Name)
    Console.ReadLine()
  End Sub
  Public Class Employee
    Private Shared Function ComputeOvertime() As Double
    End Function
  End Class

End Module
```

When the program is run, here's what is displayed in the console:

```
Member Type: Method
Method Name: ComputeOvertime
Method declared in Class : Employee
IsAbstract : False
Can be called from other classes in the same assembly: False
IsConstructor: False
IsFinal: False
IsPrivate: True
IsPublic: False
IsStatic: True
IsVirtual: False
Return type: Double
```

The ConstructorInfo Class

The `ConstructorInfo` class provides access to constructor metadata. The members of the `ConstructorInfo` class are similar to the members of the `MethodInfo` class because both classes are derived from the `MethodBase` class.

A `ConstructorInfo` object can be retrieved by invoking the `GetConstructors()` or `GetConstructor()` methods on the `Type` object associated with a class, in the same way as you use `GetMethod()` and `GetMethods()` to retrieve `MethodInfo` objects.

Let's write a program that will retrieve all the constructors of our `Employee` class:

```
Imports System.Reflection
Module Module1

  Sub Main()
    Dim typ As System.Type = GetType(Employee)
    Dim myMethod As ConstructorInfo = typ.GetConstructors()(0)

    Console.WriteLine("Member Type: {0}", myMethod.MemberType)
    Console.WriteLine("Constructor Name: {0}", _
        myMethod.ConstructorName)
    Console.WriteLine("Constructor declared in Class : {0}", _
        myMethod.DeclaringType.Name)
    Console.WriteLine("IsAbstract : {0}", myMethod.IsAbstract)
    Console.WriteLine( _
      "Can be called from other classes in the same assembly: {0}", _
      myMethod.IsAssembly)
    Console.WriteLine("IsConstructor: {0}", _
        myMethod.IsConstructor)
    Console.WriteLine("IsFinal: {0}", myMethod.IsFinal)
    Console.WriteLine("IsPrivate: {0}", myMethod.IsPrivate)
    Console.WriteLine("IsPublic: {0}", myMethod.IsPublic)
    Console.WriteLine("IsStatic: {0}", myMethod.IsStatic)
    Console.WriteLine("IsVirtual: {0}", myMethod.IsVirtual)
    Console.ReadLine()
  End Sub
  Public Class Employee
    Private Shared Function ComputeOvertime() As Double
    End Function
  End Class
End Module
```

Here's what you'll see when the program is executed. Because we haven't defined a constructor for the `Employee` class explicitly, the constructor metadata retrieved is for the default constructor (.ctor):

```
Member Type: Constructor
Constructor Name: .ctor
Constructor declared in Class : Employee
IsAbstract : False
Can be called from other classes in the same assembly: False
IsConstructor: True
IsFinal: False
IsPrivate: False
IsPublic: True
IsStatic: False
IsVirtual: False
```

The `EventInfo` Class

The `EventInfo` class is used to access event metadata. Table 8-13 shows the properties it declares.

Table 8-13. `EventInfo` *Class Properties*

Property	Type	Description
IsMulticast	Boolean	Returns True if the event is part of a multicast delegate
EventHandlerType	System.Type	Returns the Type of the event handler delegate associated with this event

Table 8-14 shows the `EventInfo` methods.

Table 8-14. `EventInfo` *Class Methods*

Method	Description
GetAddMethod()	Returns the method used to add an event handler delegate to the event source as a `MethodInfo` object
GetRaiseMethod()	Returns the method that is called when the event is raised as a `MethodInfo` object
GetRemoveMethod()	Returns the method used to remove an event handler delegate from the event source as a `MethodInfo` object
AddEventHandler()	Adds an event handler to an event source (you need to supply two arguments for this: an `Object` representing the event source, and a delegate encapsulating the event handler)
RemoveEventHandler()	Removes an event handler from an event source (requires the same arguments as `AddEventHandler()`)

The `EventInfo` class can be obtained by invoking the `GetEvent()` or `GetEvents()` methods on the `Type` object of a class. Similar to other info classes, you can specify the event you're interested in as a `String` and pass it to `GetEvent()`, or you can retrieve an array of `EventInfo` objects from `GetEvents()`.

In the following program, we retrieve metadata about the events in our `Employee` class:

```
Imports System.Reflection
Module Module1
```

```
    Sub Main()
        Dim x As Employee = New Employee()
        Dim typ As System.Type = x.GetType
        Dim myEvent As EventInfo = typ.GetEvent("AnEvent")
        Console.WriteLine("Event Name: {0}", myEvent.Name)
        Console.WriteLine("Declared in Class: {0}", _
            myEvent.DeclaringType.Name)
        Console.WriteLine("GetAddMethod: {0}", myEvent.GetAddMethod.Name)
        Console.WriteLine("GetRemoveMethod: {0}", _
            myEvent.GetRemoveMethod.Name)
        Console.WriteLine("IsMulticast: {0}", myEvent.IsMulticast)
        Console.WriteLine("Member Type: {0}", myEvent.MemberType.ToString)
        Console.ReadLine()
    End Sub
End Module
Public Class Employee
    Public Event AnEvent(ByVal EventNumber As Integer)
End Class
```

As you can see the from the output, the program states that there is just one event, called AnEvent, defined in the Employee class:

```
Event Name: AnEvent
Declared in Class: Employee
GetAddMethod: add_AnEvent
GetRemoveMethod: remove_AnEvent
IsMulticast: True
Member Type: Event
```

The ParameterInfo Class

The ParameterInfo class allows access to event metadata. As mentioned earlier, it is not derived from MemberInfo, but directly from System.Object.

Table 8-15 shows the properties for the ParameterInfo class.

Table 8-15. ParameterInfo *Class Properties*

Property	Type	Description
Attributes	System.Reflection.ParameterAttributes	Gets the attributes for this parameter as a ParameterAttributes enumeration
DefaultValue	Boolean	Gets a value indicating the default value of the parameter
IsRetval	Boolean	Gets a value indicating whether this is a Retval parameter
IsIn	Boolean	True, if this is used as an input parameter
IsOut	Boolean	True, if this is used as an output parameter

(continues)

Table 8-15. *ParameterInfo Class Properties (continued)*

Property	Type	Description
Position	Integer	Returns the position of the parameter in the signature of the method, as an Integer
IsOptional	Boolean	Returns True if this parameter is an optional parameter
ParameterType	System.Type	Returns the type of the parameter such as String, Integer, Object, Employee, and so on

You can retrieve information about parameters of a method or a constructor by invoking the GetParameters() method on ConstructorInfo or MethodInfo objects. The GetParameters() method does not require any parameters and returns an array of ParameterInfo objects.

Let's write a program that illustrates the use of ParameterInfo. This program retrieves the parameter metadata for the method ComputeOvertime() of the class Employee:

```
Imports System.Reflection
Module Module1

  Sub Main()
    Dim typ As System.Type = GetType(Employee)
    Dim myMethod As MethodInfo = typ.GetMethod("ComputeOvertime", _
        BindingFlags.Static Or BindingFlags.Public)
    Dim myParameters As ParameterInfo() = myMethod.GetParameters
    Dim myParameter As ParameterInfo
    Console.WriteLine("Function Name : {0}", myMethod.Name)
    Console.WriteLine("Number of Parameters : {0}", _
        myParameters.Length)
    Console.WriteLine()
    Dim i As Integer = 0
    For Each myParameter In myParameters
      i += 1
      Console.WriteLine("Parameter{0}", i)
      Console.WriteLine("Parameter Name: {0}", myParameter.Name())
      Console.WriteLine("Parameter Type: {0}", _
          myParameter.ParameterType.Name)
      Console.WriteLine("Function Name: {0}", myParameter.Member.Name)
      Console.WriteLine("Parameter Position: {0}", _
          myParameter.Position)
      Console.WriteLine("Is Input Parameter: {0}", myParameter.IsIn)
      Console.WriteLine("Is Parameter Optional: {0}", _
          myParameter.IsOptional)
      Console.WriteLine("Is Output Parameter: {0}", myParameter.IsOut)
      Console.WriteLine("Is Return Value Parameter: {0}", _
          myParameter.IsRetval)
      Console.WriteLine()
```

```
    Next
    Console.ReadLine()
  End Sub
  Public Class Employee
    Public Shared Function ComputeOvertime( _
        ByVal EmployeeNo As String, ByVal FromDate As Date, _
        ByVal ToDate As Date) As Double

    End Function
  End Class
End Module
```

Here's what you'll see when the program is run. As you can see, the program reports that the ComputeOvertime() method has three parameters:

```
Function Name : ComputeOvertime
Number of Parameters : 3

Parameter1
Parameter Name: EmployeeNo
Parameter Type: String
Function Name: ComputeOvertime
Parameter Position: 0
Is Input Parameter: False
Is Parameter Optional: False
Is Output Parameter: False
Is Return Value Parameter: False

Parameter2
Parameter Name: FromDate
Parameter Type: DateTime
Function Name: ComputeOvertime
Parameter Position: 1
Is Input Parameter: False
Is Parameter Optional: False
Is Output Parameter: False
Is Return Value Parameter: False

Parameter3
Parameter Name: ToDate
Parameter Type: DateTime
Function Name: ComputeOvertime
Parameter Position: 2
Is Input Parameter: False
Is Parameter Optional: False
Is Output Parameter: False
Is Return Value Parameter: False
```

Summary

This chapter covered why you would want to examine assembly metadata, and then showed you how to do so using the classes of the Reflection API.

We took a close look at the `System.Type` class, often considered the gateway to most of the activities you'll want to do using reflection. You saw that the `Type` class represents a type, and contains data such as the name of the type, the attributes associated with it, the assembly that it is located in, and so on. We also noted that you could retrieve the `Type` associated with any object by calling the `GetType()` method.

We then discussed how to dive a little deeper and examine the metadata associated with the members of a particular type. You saw that each kind of member—fields, properties, methods, constructors, and events—has an `info` class associated with it:

- `FieldInfo`
- `PropertyInfo`
- `MethodInfo`
- `ConstructorInfo`
- `EventInfo`

You can call the properties and methods of these classes to retrieve metadata about the class members they are associated with. Method parameters also have an `info` class associated with them—`ParameterInfo`.

To retrieve these `info` classes, you need to call the `Get` methods associated with the class member we're interested in—such as `GetProperty()` or `GetMethod()`—on the object that contains the member. You also can control the metadata returned by these methods using the `BindingFlags` enumeration.

This chapter focused on the passive use of reflection. We examined the contents of assemblies using reflection, but we didn't attempt to call any members or modify any class data. In the next chapter, we will look at using reflection in this more active way.

CHAPTER 9

Using Objects

In the previous chapter, we started looking at how to use the Reflection API in VB .NET code, specifically to retrieve the metadata from an assembly. This was a passive use of reflection because we didn't actually create or use any objects from the assembly. In this chapter, you'll see how you can use reflection in a more active way to do the following:

- Dynamically invoke and access instantiated objects
- Dynamically modify object fields
- Dynamically modify object properties

After you see how to do this in the example code, we'll consider situations that are best tackled using other approaches (such as using delegates).

However, let's first take a step back and consider why you would want to use reflection to dynamically invoke or manipulate methods, fields, and properties.

Why Invoke Members Using Reflection?

Many applications use reflection in a far more active way than simply browsing through the metadata of a class or assembly. For example, the Visual Studio .NET IDE (Integrated Development Environment) comes equipped with programming tools such as Intellisense, a Class browser, a Property viewer, a Debugger, or even the ToolBox, which all use reflection to do many things that wouldn't otherwise be possible. On the surface, these tools might seem plain and simple, but underneath, they're busy discovering types, analyzing types, instantiating objects, and accessing and invoking methods dynamically.

Let's consider a situation when you might want to invoke members reflectively. Say you had several Windows user interface (UI) forms, and each had a host of controls: text boxes, list boxes, radio controls, and so on. Because you are dealing with user input, you also want to implement some kind of mechanism to check that these controls have been filled in or selected correctly by the user before your application uses the data from the UI.

Now, you could create user input-checking routines for each form. However, a simpler approach is to create an input-checking method for each type of control that might be used on the form. You could then create a generic routine that would be invoked for any form that uses reflection to discover the types of controls on the form, and dynamically invoke the correct input-checking method. This technique is not only simpler, but it also enhances the extensibility of the system because you could easily add new forms to your application without needing to create a specific routine to handle input checking. If the form contained a control you haven't dealt with before, you just create a new input-checking routine for that control, which can be reused in other new forms.

A different scenario where invoking dynamic methods could be useful might arise if you used existing COM servers in your application. Briefly, COM servers cannot be directly instantiated because they have no manifest information. You need to have a wrapper class (also known as an Interop Assembly) that allows you to be able to use your COM logic, but even then, your application has to be aware of this at compile-time (early binding), because you need the component's type library to create the wrapper class. Suppose this type library is inaccessible. The only way to invoke the component's methods is to use reflection to find and invoke the methods dynamically.

There really are endless possibilities and situations where you might consider dynamic invocation through reflection. We'll move on through the chapter and see how to use these capabilities and implement them in real-world situations.

Invoking Members Dynamically

Previously you've seen how the `info` classes (`MethodInfo`, `PropertyInfo`, and so on) can be used for determining and retrieving metadata associated with an object. However, these classes can do even more. These classes from the Reflection API allow you to dynamically invoke members of an object, such as invoking methods, retrieving or modifying properties, or fields. We'll take a close look at the `Type.InvokeMember()` method, which can do this too.

Invoking Class Members Using the `Info` Classes

We've instantiated a type and located the correct method; next, we want to invoke and access object members (methods, properties, or fields) at runtime. There are mainly two different ways to perform dynamic invocation. The first is through the `info` classes from the `System.Reflection` namespace, and the other is the `Type` class itself.

Before we carry on, you should be aware of the fact that you may stumble upon code in the following sections and throughout the chapter (and during your own development times) that invokes and modifies private members of an object. If you've come from a strict object-oriented (OO) world programming background (C++ anyone?) where trespassing was not allowed, this can be quite a shock. Accessing private fields, properties, or methods directly was not allowed; manipulating them via public accessor methods or properties was encouraged (because it provided a way to check that the user was modifying the data correctly).

Although .NET generally also encourages this style of OO coding, in reflection it also gives developers the ability to "break the rules." Let's not interpret this incorrectly, however. Breaking the rules of encapsulation is one of those features that Microsoft has made possible with reflection, but it should almost never be used. Accessing private methods by using reflection is possible, but how can you be sure of your results? The original publisher of the component would not have designed the method to be called by consumers and calling it out of the context might produce adverse effects.

Invoking Methods Using `MethodInfo`

We've come across the `MethodInfo` class before. This class is fascinating because not only does it provide you with *all* metadata related to a single method, but it also provides you with the

Invoke() method that can be used for all your dynamic method invocations. Needless to say, to invoke a method using the Invoke() method, you'll need a valid MethodInfo instance pointing to an existing method or you'll see some nasty runtime errors you *don't* want to see.

The MethodInfo.Invoke() method has several overloaded forms, although the most common takes two arguments:

Invoke(obj As Object, parameters() As Object) As Object

The first parameter is the instance of the object that the method belongs to. However, if the method you want to invoke has an access type of Shared, you should ignore it by passing a null reference (Nothing in VB .NET) to it. The second parameter is a list of parameters to be passed to the invoking method. The parameters passed should be the same order and type as the parameters of the method being invoked. However, if the method takes no parameters, the second argument should be passed a null reference (Nothing) so that it's ignored. After the method is invoked, the returned value is of type Object that must be cast to the correct type before use. For instance, if you have a method called Multiply() in a class called MathClass, which takes two Integers as parameters and returns an Integer after multiplying the two, you would invoke it the following way:

```
Dim objMathClass As New MathClass()
Dim params As Object() = {4, 5}
Dim method As MethodInfo = _
    objMathClass.GetType().GetMethod("Multiply")
Dim result As Integer

result = CInt(method.Invoke(objMathClass, params))
```

Note that the Multiply() method has to be declared Public for this to work, or your program will fail at runtime. This is because we didn't specify any binding flags, so GetMethod() used default bindings and searched for public members of the type only. Because GetMethod() returned a null reference, Invoke() will fail. To set binding flags manually, you can use an overload of the GetMethod() method that accepts a combination of binding flags for searching for the correct method.

Consider the following code snippet for the same code shown previously, with the assumption that this time, Multiply() has been declared with shared access:

```
Dim objMathClass As New MathClass()
Dim params As Object() = {4, 5}
Dim method As MethodInfo = GetType(MathClass).GetMethod( _
        "Multiply", BindingFlags.NonPublic Or _
        BindingFlags.Static)
Dim result As Integer
result = CInt(method.Invoke(Nothing, params))
```

Notice how we explicitly requested GetMethod() to look for a Non-Public (Private) member, which is also declared with a Static (shared) access type. We then invoked our method, passing a null reference as the first argument, as we're invoking a shared function and it doesn't require an instance of the type.

Using MethodInfo is one way of invoking methods dynamically. We'll see other ways as we move on through the chapter.

Invoking Properties Using `PropertyInfo`

Properties in a type can be defined with modifiers such as private, public, and shared. They are one way of letting you modify the state of internal type members in a safe, secure manner. This section teaches you how to invoke properties using reflection. We will also look at a real-world situation later in the chapter.

There are two methods of the `PropertyInfo` class that are useful for manipulating property values:

- `GetValue()`: Gets the value of the underlying property.
- `SetValue()`: Sets the underlying property to a new value.

Following is one of the two overloaded `SetValue()` methods with its signature:

`SetValue(obj as Object, NewValue as Object, index() as Object)`

You'll most likely find yourself modifying a property's value with the method shown. Similar to what you saw using the `Invoke()` method of `MethodInfo`, the first parameter of the `SetValue()` method accepts the instance whose property value is to be set. The second parameter takes the new value to be set for the property, and the third parameter takes an indexer for indexed properties. Nonindexed properties should have this third parameter set to a null reference (`Nothing`).

Likewise, the `GetValue()` method is used for retrieving a property's value. Its signature is shown here:

`GetValue(obj as Object, index() as Object) as Object`

The first parameter is the instance of the object you're trying to invoke, while the second parameter is an indexer representing indexed properties. Again, this should be set to `Nothing` if not applicable.

Let's look at a trivial example that uses the `PropertyInfo` class to invoke properties in a class. The following shows a simple class that implements a single private property, `Name`. We use an instance of this class in our `Main()` subroutine to get a valid `PropertyInfo` object and then use it to invoke the single private property it encapsulates:

```
Imports System
Imports System.Reflection

Public Class Human
  Private strName As String
  Private Property Name() As String
    Get
      Return strName
    End Get
    Set(ByVal Value As String)
        strName = Value
    End Set
  End Property
End Class
```

Next, our main program begins by first instantiating the Human class and then grabbing hold of a valid PropertyInfo associated with the private property Name. Notice how we specifically tell the GetProperty() method of the Type class that the property we're searching for is an instance property (a property that can only be accessed through an instance of the type) and that its access type is nonpublic:

```
Public Class PropExample
  Public Shared Sub Main()
    Dim NewHuman As New Human()
    Dim prop As PropertyInfo

    prop = NewHuman.GetType.GetProperty("Name", _
                                  BindingFlags.Instance Or _
                                  BindingFlags.NonPublic)
```

We then declare a parameter of type String and initialize it with a value. Note that we could have used an Object type here as well because that would cast correctly into the target type, which is a String in this case. But it is recommended that you use the same as that of the target type. The parameter is then passed to the SetValue() method for the property to be invoked and modified:

```
    Dim param As String = "Fahad"
    prop.SetValue(NewHuman, param, Nothing)
```

We finish by displaying the value of the Name property of our object by invoking the GetValue() method. The method returns an Object type that we explicitly cast into a String:

```
    Console.WriteLine(prop.GetValue(NewHuman, Nothing).ToString)
  End Sub
End Class
```

Invoking Fields Using FieldInfo

Like PropertyInfo, the FieldInfo class also contains GetValue() and SetValue() methods that you can use to manipulate field values. They have similar signatures to the PropertyInfo methods, although there are no indexer-related parameters:

```
GetValue(obj As Object) as Object
SetValue(obj As Object, value as Object)
```

The GetValue() method takes a single argument, the instance of the type you're invoking.

Note Before we continue, recall the previous warnings about using reflection to bypass code or access private members out of their intended scope. Accessing a private member directly instead of modifying it through the accessor may bypass input validation and cause your application to behave undesirably.

Consider this code snippet:

```
Dim objFoo As New Foo()
Dim field As FieldInfo = objFoo.GetType.GetField("PrivateField", _
                                    BindingFlags.NonPublic Or _
                                    BindingFlags.Instance)
Console.WriteLine(field.GetValue(objFoo).ToString)
...
field.SetValue(objFoo, "New value")
```

We instantiate a type and get a private field by calling the `GetField()` method. We specify what field we're looking for, `PrivateField` in this case, and tell it that our field is a private instance member. We then call the `GetValue()` method of `FieldInfo` to get the value of the field and display it on the console. The last line of code sets our private field to a new value by passing it the instance of the object we're invoking and the new value.

Invoking Class Members Using `InvokeMember()`

The `Type` class exposes a powerful and flexible method in the Reflection API, namely the `InvokeMember()` method. This method allows you to invoke a reflected member of the supplied type (fields, properties, and methods). This is because all dynamic invocations you've seen so far using `MethodInfo`, `PropertyInfo`, or `FieldInfo`, can be performed using the `InvokeMember()` method. This is made possible by switching between the binding flags passed to the method during invocation.

If that's the case, you must be wondering why we bothered discussing the `info` classes for this purpose when we could have just relied on `InvokeMember()`. Well, that's where the downside of `InvokeMember()` comes in. You can definitely make all sorts of dynamic calls to any member of a type via `InvokeMember()`, but if you want to play around with and examine metadata and then invoke members dynamically, it may be easier to use the `info` classes. However, because we're mainly concerned with dynamic invocation of members at the moment, let's find out more about this useful method and learn how to use it. In the next section, you'll see how this can be implemented in a more real-word fashion.

The `InvokeMember()` method comes with a total of three overloads. Most likely, you'll find yourself using just one of its overloaded methods:

```
InvokeMember(name As String, invokeAttr As BindingFlags, _
            binder As Binder, target As Object, params() as Object)
```

This overload accepts five parameters. The first parameter describes the member to be invoked. This can be a property name, a method name or a field name. The second parameter is a single or a combination of different binding flags that tells the method how to search for the desired member and also tells the method what to treat the member as. For example, a `BindingFlags.InvokeMethod` flag tells the method that the first parameter supplied is the name of the method to be invoked.

The third parameter accepts a `Binder` object. A `Binder` object can be explicitly created to be used for binding to specific fields or methods from a list of overloads, and can also be used for specific type conversions of supplied arguments. If you pass `Nothing` (a null reference) to this parameter, the method automatically uses the `DefaultBinder` available. `DefaultBinder` takes care of type conversions of supplied arguments for you (conversions from source type to target types).

The fourth parameter takes the instance of the type whose member we're invoking. This should be supplied as Nothing if dealing with shared members of a type. The last parameter accepts an array of parameters to be passed to the invoked member. This can be used when dealing with properties or methods. When invoking fields, this parameter should be supplied as Nothing.

Invoking Methods Using InvokeMember()

Let's look at a code excerpt that uses the InvokeMember() method of the Type class to invoke a method of a type. The following code uses the type System.Math and invokes its shared method Max(). This method has 11 overloads and accepts different combinations of arguments. You'll see how the InvokeMember() method finds and matches the correct one depending on the type of arguments passed to it. For demonstration purposes, we'll pass two integers to the method:

```
Dim MathType As Type = GetType(System.Math)
Dim params As Object() = {5, 8}
Dim result As Integer

result = CInt(MathType.InvokeMember("Max", BindingFlags.Public Or _
                                    BindingFlags.InvokeMethod Or _
                                    BindingFlags.Static, Nothing, _
                                    Nothing, params))
Console.WriteLine(result)
```

As you can see, we invoked the method by explicitly adding the BindingFlags.InvokeMethod flag to tell InvokeMember that the first parameter passed is the name of a method we want to invoke. We passed Nothing as an object instance, which tells InvokeMember() that the given method has a shared access and does not need an instance. The last parameter we passed was declared as an array of Objects, holding values of two integers. You should be aware that unlike MethodInfo.Invoke(), InvokeMember() has greater flexibility especially when it comes to sending arguments over to the method to be invoked. This method takes care of all implicit type conversions from the source type to the target type, and does an implicit search on overloaded methods by matching the number and type of parameters of the target method with the ones supplied. The returned result is cast to an Integer and displayed on the console.

Notice how simple and subtle this was. All you have to care about is that you supply the correct binding flags during invocation. If the BindingFlags.InvokeMethod flag was omitted or replaced with some other flag, this wouldn't have worked.

The main advantage of using InvokeMember() is its flexibility. If we had tried using similar code with a MethodInfo object, the code would have failed miserably giving us an AmbiguousMatchException because it wouldn't be able to tell which overloaded method to call. For that, we would have to explicitly declare a Binder object and use its SelectMethod() method to search for an appropriate overloaded method and invoke it. On the contrary, this was all taken care of by the InvokeMember() method. It looked at the number of arguments we supplied, examined the argument types, matched the correct method from the list of overloads, and invoked the method.

`InvokeMember()` Method Invocation Example

Near the start of the chapter, we discussed some very tempting features of dynamic method invocation and suggested its use in a number of situations and scenarios. Now let's see how these features can accent your applications to become more flexible, and easy to extend and implement. We're going to precede this section by modeling a real-world situation, where reflection could prove to be a solution.

We'll use a variation on the user input-checking scenario we discussed at the start of the chapter. Briefly, we'll have a Scuba Diving registration form to be filled in by applicants. The application involves a Windows Form that includes a number of different controls. After the applicant decides to submit the information on the form to be filed and reviewed, we need to check whether all the compulsory items on the form were completed before the form was dismissed. Because we need to establish some code that accepts different controls at runtime to check whether the control's not empty, reflection is the best choice (among other alternatives we'll discuss later in the chapter) for deciding which method should be invoked for the type of control that's passed. Therefore we will code up a bunch of input-checking methods that take different control types as parameters, select the appropriate one using reflection at runtime, and invoke it.

This approach has several other advantages. You could later extend your code by introducing new or more controls and you won't have to make changes to the control-checking mechanism. You could also think of compiling these methods into a separate assembly and invoke them with any application you develop. (You'll learn more about this in the next chapter.)

To begin, create a new Windows application using Visual Studio .NET. Call it `MethodInvocation` and open the Design View of the form. Using the toolbox, drag controls onto your form so that it looks similar to the one shown in Figure 9-1.

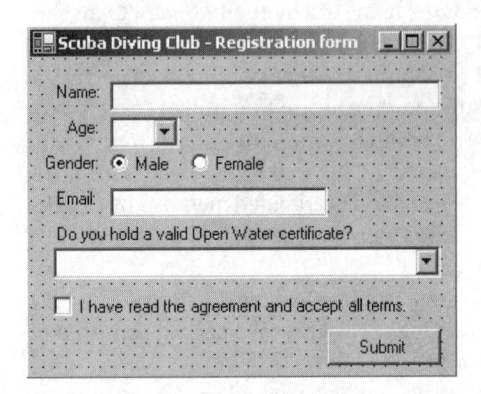

Figure 9-1. *The design view of the* `MethodInvocation` *form*

Table 9-1 lists the controls used by the application, along with their names.

Table 9-1. *Controls Used in the Scuba Diving Application Form*

Control Type	Name	Initial Text value
Label	Label1	"Name:"
Label	Label2	"Age:"
Label	Label3	"Gender:"

Control Type	Name	Initial Text value
Label	Label4	"Email:"
Label	Label5	"Do you hold a valid Open Water certificate?"
TextBox	txtName	Empty
ComboBox	comboAge	Filled with values ranging from 15 to 60
RadioButton	radMale	"Male"
RadioButton	radFemale	"Female"
TextBox	txtEmail	Empty
ComboBox	comboQuestion	Filled with three optional answers
Button	btnSubmit	"Submit"
CheckBox	checkAgreement	"I have read the agreement and accept all terms."

After you're done adding controls onto your form, open up the form code and make sure you include the `System.Reflection` namespace into your project:

```
Imports System
Imports System.Reflection
```

Next, add a single field called `ErrorInForm` to the form class. We'll later make use of this variable to count the numbers of controls that have been left empty at the time the user submits the form:

```
Public Class Form1
  Inherits System.Windows.Forms.Form
  Private ErrorInForm As Integer = 0
```

Double-click on the form to create the `Form1_Load()` method. Because this method is called at the time the application loads, we're going to use it for initializing our controls, namely the two `ComboBox` controls: `comboAge` and `comboQuestion`. We make sure the controls are initialized with values so that our user may choose the correct one at the time of registration.

```
Private Sub Form1_Load(ByVal sender As System.Object, ByVal e As _
    System.EventArgs) Handles MyBase.Load
  Dim i As Integer
  For i = 15 To 60
    comboAge.Items.Add(i)
  Next
  comboQuestion.Items.Add( _
                  "Yes, I currently hold a valid certificate")
  comboQuestion.Items.Add("No, I don't have one at the moment")
  comboQuestion.Items.Add( _
                  "I hold a temporary allowance certificate")
End Sub
```

Here is the part where we implement our dynamic methods. Copy the following list of methods into your form class:

```vb
'Handle all TextBoxes
Private Sub ValidateField(ByVal control As TextBox)
  If control.Text.Trim.Equals("") Then
    ErrorInForm += 1
    control.BackColor = Color.Yellow()
  Else
    control.BackColor = Color.White()
  End If
End Sub

'Handle all ComboBoxes
Private Sub ValidateField(ByVal control As ComboBox)
  If control.Text.Trim.Equals("") Then
    ErrorInForm += 1
    control.BackColor = Color.Yellow()
  Else
    control.BackColor = Color.White()
  End If
End Sub

'Handle all CheckBoxes
Private Sub ValidateField(ByVal control As CheckBox)
  If Not control.Checked Then
    ErrorInForm += 1
  End If
End Sub

'Other unhandled controls
Private Sub ValidateField(ByVal control As Label)
End Sub

Private Sub ValidateField(ByVal control As Button)
End Sub

Private Sub ValidateField(ByVal control As RadioButton)
End Sub
End Class
```

As you can see, these methods all have the same base name: ValidateField. However, each one of these accepts different controls as parameters and then handles each control separately. For the method shown next, the method takes in a control of type TextBox and checks whether its Text property is empty. If it is, we increment the error counter (ErrorInForm variable) and highlight the background color of the control. Similarly, in the case of a ComboBox, we check whether its Text property is empty, and in the case of a CheckBox, we make sure it's checked. The rest of the methods (for Label, Button, and RadioButton controls) are left untouched as we're not interested in validating their controls. Note that we could add any number of methods to this list to handle other controls. For instance, a ListBox control would require different validation checks, so a method can be implemented to handle that separately too. As you'll see next, using these methods, you can use reflection to dynamically identify the type of the control and invoke the appropriate one. The method that's invoked can handle the rest.

Next we have a set of handlers for different control types. All we need to do is invoke the correct one at runtime. We do this in the btnSubmit_Click() event. To implement this, simply switch to Design mode again and double-click on the Submit button. This should place your cursor back in the code again, in the method btnSubmit_Click. Copy the highlighted text, compile your project, and run it.

```
Private Sub btnSubmit_Click(ByVal sender As System.Object, _
    ByVal e As System.EventArgs) Handles btnSubmit.Click
  Try
    Dim FormControl As Control
    For Each FormControl In Me.Controls
      Me.GetType().InvokeMember("ValidateField", _
                               BindingFlags.Instance Or _
                               BindingFlags.InvokeMethod Or _
                               BindingFlags.NonPublic, Nothing, _
                               Me, New Object() {FormControl})
    Next

    If ErrorInForm = 0 Then
        MsgBox("Application has been processed. Thank you.", , _
            "Scuba Registration")
    Else
      MsgBox( _
          "There was at least one error in processing the form." & _
          " Please check again.", , "Scuba Registration")
      ErrorInForm = 0
    End If

  Catch ex As Exception
    'Catch exception here
  End Try
End Sub
```

In this method, we're performing a very simple task. For each of the child controls present on the form, we instruct the InvokeMember() method to invoke the correct ValidateField() method, depending on the type of control that was passed as an argument. Via reflection, InvokeMember() matches all available ValidateField methods for the correct type, selects the correct one, and invokes it in a dynamic fashion.

The preceding code produces the following output (see Figure 9-2) if we forget to fill in the Age and Email fields before clicking Submit.

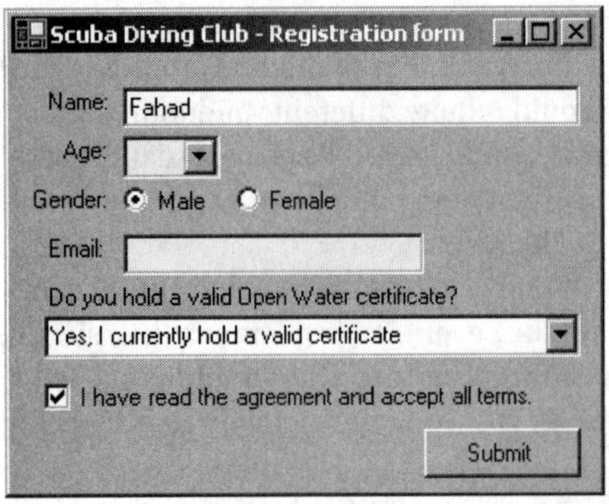

Figure 9-2. *How the* MethodInvocation *form looks when running*

You can tell from the approach, that reflection can most certainly help you overcome a lot of problems. On top of that, in scenarios where you're dealing with an external source, such as a database or an XML file, you can use this approach to handle incoming streams of data dynamically, and invoke correct handlers (or events) on the type of data you receive.

Manipulating Property Values Using InvokeMember()

InvokeMember goes beyond just dynamic method invocation. You can access and modify property values of an object by tweaking the binding flags passed to it during invocation. Because there isn't much difference between a call made to modify a property and a call made to invoke a method, let's hit some code straight away.

The following code invokes two properties of an object. The first one is a Private Shared property and we try to get its value by using the Bindings.GetProperty flag:

```
Dim FooType As Type = GetType(Foo)
Dim result As String

result = CStr(FooType.InvokeMember("PrivateShared", _
                                   BindingFlags.NonPublic Or _
                                   BindingFlags.Static Or _
                                   BindingFlags.GetProperty, _
                                   Nothing, Nothing, Nothing))
```

The second one is a Public Instance property and we try to set a new value to it by using the Bindings.SetProperty flag:

```
Dim objFoo As New Foo()
Dim params As Object() = {"New Value"}
FooType.InvokeMember("PublicInstance", BindingFlags.Public Or _
                                      BindingFlags.Instance Or _
                                      BindingFlags.SetProperty, _
                                      Nothing, objFoo, params)
```

The same rule applies to invoking properties via InvokeMember() as it did for invoking methods; if there are a number of properties with the same base name but different signatures, InvokeMember() implicitly matches the correct property and invokes it.

It's worth mentioning here that properties in the .NET Framework are regarded as methods. For instance, if you examine all public methods of an instance of a TextBox control, you are provided with all available public methods such as Copy(), Cut(), and the methods that have a prefix of get_ and set_. These methods are actually public properties of the instance. For example, the Text property of the TextBox control would be shown as two methods: get_Text() and set_Text(). Because these properties are exposed as methods, you can invoke them using a MethodInfo object or by using the InvokeMember() of the Type class by supplying the BindingFlags.InvokeMethod flag. The following line of code displays the power of using InvokeMember(). It shows the Text property of an instance of a TextBox control being invoked and treated as a method:

```
TextBoxType.InvokeMember("get_Text", BindingFlags.Public Or _
                                     BindingFlags.Instance Or _
                                     BindingFlags.InvokeMethod, _
                         Nothing, txtBox1, Nothing)
```

InvokeMember() Property Value Modification Example

Many IDEs come with integrated property pages that allow you to set initial values and configure object properties at design time. These property pages are interesting because they accommodate any type of object or component and expose their internal properties to be viewed and modified. For example, while developing Windows applications, you probably fill your form with a number of controls. Each time you click on a different control, the property viewer refreshes its contents and exposes all available properties of that object type. Behind the scenes, this nifty little tool is actually using reflection to reflect all properties; every time a property is modified, it invokes the property of that particular instance and passes the new argument to it.

To get the idea across, we'll make our own property page that will reflect the loaded type's properties and allow you to modify them. However, because this book is really not about making controls and making a full-fledged property page would cross chapter boundaries, we'll implement a very basic type of property page using a TreeView, a TextBox, and a Button control.

For this example, let's implement a test class that we'll use with the property page, but you can later use the idea to extend the application and use it for loading types at runtime.

Create a new Windows application, and call it ReflectProperties. Create a form that looks similar to the one shown in Figure 9-3.

Figure 9-3. *The design view of the ReflectProperties form.*

Table 9-2 lists the controls used by this application, along with their names and values.

Table 9-2. *Controls for the Property Page*

Control Type	Name	Initial Text value
Label	Label1	"Property Value:"
Label	Label2	"Type:"
TreeView	TreeView1	Empty
TextBox	TextBox1	Empty
Button	btnModify	"Modify"

Add the `System.Reflection` namespace to your form code:

```
Imports System
Imports System.Reflection
```

Before we look at the code in the main public class, let's create a small test class for our purpose. We'll instantiate and use this class for demonstrating property invocation in objects.

```
Public Class Test
  ' Set Default private values
  Private MyName As String = "Fahad"
  Private MyAge As String = "22"
  Private MyCountry As String = "Pakistan"

  Public Property Name() As String
    Get
      Return Me.MyName
    End Get
    Set(ByVal Value As String)
      Me.MyName = Value
    End Set
  End Property

  Public Property Age() As String
    Get
      Return Me.MyAge
    End Get
    Set(ByVal Value As String)
      Me.MyAge = Value
    End Set
  End Property

  Public Property Country() As String
    Get
      Return Me.MyCountry
    End Get
    Set(ByVal Value As String)
```

```
      Me.MyCountry = Value
    End Set
  End Property
End Class
```

The Test class has three public properties and three private variables corresponding to them. The private variables, all String variables, have been initialized with default values. Now we move on to implementing the main public class.

To use the instance of the Test class, we declare a Shared object as a class variable, MyObj, shown next. Also, we add a string to our class, SelectedNode, with class scope. This is because every time the user selects a new property, the TreeView1_AfterSelect event will be launched. We need to make sure to save the name of the current selected property so that we can use this information while invoking the property:

```
Public Class Form1
    Inherits System.Windows.Forms.Form

    Public Shared MyObj As Object
    Private SelectedNode As String
```

Next, to use our sample class, we need to instantiate it in the Form1_Load() event, because that's the first method called when the form is loaded. The Form1_Load() method is used for instantiating the shared object—MyObj—that we earlier declared as a class variable; it can be added to the form class by double-clicking on the form.

```
Private Sub Form1_Load(ByVal sender As System.Object, ByVal e As _
                                      System.EventArgs) Handles MyBase.Load
    MyObj = New Test()

    ReflectProperties(MyObj.GetType)
End Sub
```

Notice that we also make a call to the ReflectProperties() method in Form1_Load(). This method is shown next. Note that ReflectProperties() is passed the type of the object we're using, which it uses for reflecting all public properties of the type onto the TreeView control.

```
Private Sub ReflectProperties(ByVal MyType As Type)
    Dim properties As PropertyInfo() = MyType.GetProperties()
    Dim prop As PropertyInfo

    TreeView1.BeginUpdate()

    ' Fill tree with property names
    For Each prop In properties
      TreeView1.Nodes.Add(New TreeNode(prop.Name))
    Next

    TreeView1.EndUpdate()

  End Sub
```

Every time the user selects a node on the TreeView control, the TreeView1_AfterSelect() event is launched. We need to make sure every time this happens, we get the chosen node (corresponding to a property) and reflect its value in the TextBox control. In this method, we save the name of the node in the string class variable we declared earlier, and use the GetProperty() method of the Type class to return a PropertyInfo object for the underlying property. Near the end of the method, we use the GetValue() method of PropertyInfo to display the returned value of the property in the Textbox control on the form.

```
' Show value of property when property is selected
Private Sub TreeView1_AfterSelect(ByVal sender As System.Object, _
    ByVal e As System.Windows.Forms.TreeViewEventArgs) _
    Handles TreeView1.AfterSelect

    SelectedNode = e.Node.Text

    Dim PropInfo As PropertyInfo = _
        MyObj.GetType.GetProperty(SelectedNode)

    TextBox1.Text = PropInfo.GetValue(MyObj, Nothing)
End Sub
```

The following code deals with the modification part of the Property Page. We'll be implementing this in the Click event handler of the Modify button, which we can generate automatically in VS .NET by double-clicking on the button.

Here, we simply call the InvokeMember() method of Type and pass BindingFlags.SetProperty as one of the binding flags. Note that the new value to be set to the property is taken from the Textbox control on our form and is passed as a variable of type Object.

```
Private Sub btnModify_Click(ByVal sender As System.Object, _
        ByVal e As  System.EventArgs) Handles btnModify.Click
    ' Get new value from TextBox
    Dim NewValue As Object() = {TextBox1.Text}

    ' Set new value to the property
    MyObj.GetType.InvokeMember(SelectedNode, _
                            BindingFlags.SetProperty Or _
                            BindingFlags.Instance Or _
                            BindingFlags.Public, _
                            Nothing, MyObj, NewValue, Nothing)

    TreeView1.Refresh()
End Sub
```

If you run the application, you will see the Property Page in Figure 9-4.

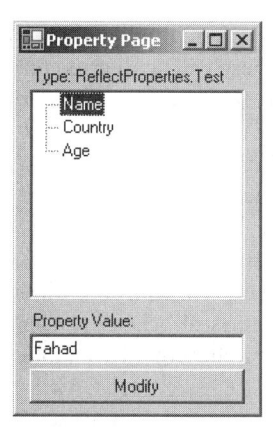

Figure 9-4. *How the* `ReflectProperties` *form looks when running*

You should be able to click on any properties in the tree to view a property value, and you can modify it by entering the new value in the text box and clicking the Modify button.

Manipulating Field Values Using `InvokeMember()`

We'll once again look at a trivial code snippet that shows `InvokeMember()` invoking fields in a loaded type. To do this, we'll concentrate only on the binding flags and make sure we include the `BindingFlags.GetField` flag to the list of flags to retrieve the value of the specified field, or `BindingFlags.SetField`, to set the value of the specified field. The code for setting a value of a private, shared field is shown here:

```
Dim FooType As Type = GetType(Foo)
Dim params As Object() = {"New Value"}

FooType.InvokeMember("PublicInstance", BindingFlags.NonPublic Or _
                                      BindingFlags.Static Or _
                                      BindingFlags.SetField, _
                                      Nothing, Nothing, params)
```

The `InvokeMember()` method of the `Type` class is undoubtedly superior to other available invocation methods when it comes to pure dynamic invocation. It is highly flexible, powerful, and does the job in a simple manner. You should try using this method over other invocation methods (exposed by the `info` classes) as much as possible, unless of course you need to deal with the metadata, in which case you'll be bound to use other available classes such as `MethodInfo`, `PropertyInfo`, or `FieldInfo`.

`InvokeMember()` Field Value Modification Example

In this section, we'll build a runnable example that shows how fields can be directly invoked in certain cases. The application models a terminal program at a car retailer. There are a number of forms with different questions the customer has to answer before placing an order for a car.

However, we're concerned with only the final form of the questionnaire, where the customer is asked to select a car model along with a number of optional features (these will be referred to as fields in the implementation) that come along with it. For example, let's say the customer selects the 1999 model. That model had two optional features (fields): the car could be a convertible and could have a built-in refrigerator. The customer can select either one, or both of them, and choose to submit the application to be lodged. The selection the customer makes is saved via reflection by dynamically modifying the fields.

What's so dynamic about the application we're about to see is that the main program will have no clue as to what type of model the user will decide to select at runtime. In fact, at runtime the program will load a list of available car models (defined by different classes). When the user makes a selection, the program dynamically selects the correct class, searches for all available fields (optional features for that model) at runtime, and then populates a `CheckedListBox` with all available fields found. Similarly, when the user makes a modification to any field, the modification is saved via dynamic invocation and the form is processed.

The advantage of this approach is that this system is completely independent of the car models available, because it loads all available models at runtime and invokes the appropriate one using reflection, so the system can be extended by all means. New car models can be introduced to the list without making any changes to your code.

Let's now look at the code and see how it's done.

Create a new Windows application and name your project `InvokingFields`. Add controls to your form so that it looks like the form shown in Figure 9-5.

Figure 9-5. *The* `InvokingFields` *form in design view*

Table 9-3 lists the controls used by this application, along with their names and values.

Table 9-3. *Controls Used in the Car Retailer Terminal Application*

Control Type	Name	Initial Text Value
Label	Label1	"Select a Model:"
Label	Label2	"Please Select Optional Specifications:"
ComboBox	ComboBox1	Empty
CheckedListBox	CheckedListBox1	Empty
Button	btnModifyOptions	"Modify Options & Buy Car"

Start by adding the `System.Reflection` namespace to your form code:

```
Imports System
Imports System.Reflection
```

Next add the following `Cars` class that contains a list of nested classes that represent car models. Each class holds definitions of some `Shared` fields (optional features of the model). Note that fields can be added or subtracted from the classes without changing the code that invokes these classes.

```
Public Class Cars

  'Previous models come here

  Public Class Model_1999
    'Optional or Customizable items
    Public Shared Refrigerator As Boolean
    Public Shared Convertible As Boolean = True

  End Class

  Public Class Model_2000
    'Optional or Customizable items
    Public Shared Automatic_Windows As Boolean

  End Class

  Public Class Model_2001
    'Optional or Customizable items
    Public Shared Dvd_Player As Boolean
  End Class

End Class
```

These classes are nested in the main `Cars` class for demonstration purposes. You'll see how you can use reflection to get a list of nested classes from within a parent class in the `Form1_Load()` method next. Also, because the code was intended to be dynamic and choosing an external source to load a list of car models didn't seem like a very good idea, this approach should allow you to think in broader terms and show you how powerful reflection can be.

Now, entering the form class, add the following line to declare a field, `SelectedType` of type Type. This variable will hold the type of the car model the user selects at runtime:

```
Public Class Form1
    Inherits System.Windows.Forms.Form

    Public SelectedType As Type
```

Next, create the `Form1_Load()` method by double-clicking the form. In this method, we perform the basic tasks of loading available car model types and filling the `ComboBox` control with them. Here we introduce you to a new method of the `Type` class, the `GetNestedTypes()`

method. This method accepts a combination of binding flags, searches for types nested within the supplied type, and returns an array of types found (this is empty if no types are found). We can also use the GetNestedType() method to search for a single type. In the following code, we retrieve all nested types inside Cars and display their names in the ComboBox control. Initially, the Button control is disabled (we don't want the user clicking it right away without selecting a model—in other words, we haven't implemented any checks).

```
Private Sub Form1_Load(ByVal sender As System.Object, _
    ByVal e As System.EventArgs) Handles MyBase.Load

  Dim MyType As Type = GetType(Cars)

  'Get the Nested classes with the Access-Specifier as public.
  Dim NestedClasses As Type() = _
      MyType.GetNestedTypes(BindingFlags.Public Or _
                            BindingFlags.Instance)
  Dim NestedClass As Type

  For Each NestedClass In NestedClasses
    ComboBox1.Items.Add(NestedClass.Name)
  Next

  Button1.Enabled = False
End Sub
```

Every time the user selects a different car model from the drop-down combo box, the ComboBox1_SelectedIndexChanged event is launched, and the user is shown the fields (features) associated with that type. For that reason, we'll perform all our basic "reflect fields" routines in the ComboBox1_SelectedIndexChanged() method:

```
Private Sub ComboBox1_SelectedIndexChanged( _
    ByVal sender As System.Object, ByVal e As System.EventArgs) _
    Handles ComboBox1.SelectedIndexChanged

  Dim SelectedModel As String = _
      "InvokingFields.Cars+" & ComboBox1.SelectedItem

  SelectedType = Type.GetType(SelectedModel)

  Dim fields As FieldInfo() = SelectedType.GetFields()
  Dim i As Integer

  CheckedListBox1.Items.Clear()
  For i = 0 To fields.Length - 1
    CheckedListBox1.Items.Add(fields(i).Name)
    If fields(i).GetValue(Nothing) = True Then
      CheckedListBox1.SetItemChecked(i, True)
    End If
```

```
        Next

        Button1.Enabled = True
End Sub
```

The important work is being done inside the `For` loop here. We obtain an array of `FieldInfo` objects from the `GetFields()` method and, for each field discovered, it is added to the `CheckedListBox` control's items list. At the same time, we perform a single check to determine whether the current field's value is `True`. If it is, we check the corresponding field name in the `CheckedListBox` control.

For the rest of the method, you're probably familiar with most of the code, except for the following lines:

```
Dim SelectedModel As String = _
    "InvokingFields.Cars+" & ComboBox1.SelectedItem
SelectedType = Type.GetType(SelectedModel)
```

What we're doing here is actually very straightforward. The `SelectedItem` property of the `ComboBox` returns the item that the user selected from the drop-down list. For instance, if the user selected `Model_1999` from the drop-down list, that's just what `ComboBox1.SelectedItem` will return. However, we have to obtain a valid `Type` of the selected item so that we can invoke its fields. To do that, we use the `Type.GetType()` method, which accepts a string describing the complete path of the class we're trying to discover. In our case, `InvokingFields` is the namespace and `Cars` is the class that contains other nested classes, so the access path to `Cars` from our namespace is `InvokingFields.Cars`. The + sign, however, is used for accessing nested classes from within a parent class. Therefore, the complete path supplied to the `Type.GetType()` method turns out to be of the format

InvokingFields.Cars+Model_XXXX

where XXXX is the model number.

After the fields have been retrieved and reflected, the user can pick whichever feature he wants for the model of the car he's buying. Upon clicking the Modify button, we go through a series of statements in the `Button1_Click()` event handler to make sure all modifications are reflected back to the fields. In our code, we run through a loop for all items present in the `CheckedListBox` control and retrieve each item one by one. Each item in the list represents a single field, so we use its name and its current value to invoke the corresponding field using the `InvokeMember()` method. Notice how we use the `BindingFlags.SetField` flag to tell `InvokeMember()` that we're interested in setting a new value for a field that has a `Public` and `Shared` access in the underlying type:

```
Private Sub btnModifyOptions_Click(ByVal sender As System.Object, _
    ByVal e As System.EventArgs) Handles btnModifyOptions.Click

    Dim i As Integer
    Dim FieldName As String
    Dim Field As FieldInfo

    For i = 0 To CheckedListBox1.Items.Count() - 1
      FieldName = CheckedListBox1.Items.Item(i)
      Dim Value As Object() = {CheckedListBox1.GetItemChecked(i)}
```

```
            SelectedType.InvokeMember(FieldName, BindingFlags.Public Or _
                                                BindingFlags.Static Or _
                                                BindingFlags.SetField, _
                                                Nothing, Nothing, Value)
    Next
    MsgBox("Thank you. Your car order has been processed.")
End Sub
```

After the button is clicked, the application ends with an approval message.

When you run the application and select a model, you should see the dialog box shown in Figure 9-6.

Figure 9-6. *How the* InvokingFields *form looks when running*

You will notice that the number of options, and the options themselves, change depending upon the model you select. If you then select your options and click the button, you will see an acknowledgement message.

In spite of our strong inclination toward using reflection in almost "all" messy situations, let's now switch places and see how reflection can sometimes *not* be the best option.

Reflective Invocation at a Price

Over the course of the chapter, we've seen reflection do some useful things, including dynamically searching and invoking members at runtime. However, there are some fairly clumsy aspects about reflection that sometimes are not very inviting when you look more closely at it. Talking about dynamic invocation of methods specifically, at times you may find (the hard way) that all the pain of writing lengthier code and spending hours trying to implement the "perfect" reflective solution didn't quite pay off in the end, especially when you discover several reasons why this might happen:

- Dynamic invocation features of reflection are not type-safe.

- Sometimes, there are better alternatives to using reflection (we'll talk about this shortly).

When we say reflection is not type-safe, we simply mean that the compiler will let you get away with most of the things (trying to access methods that don't exist, trying to modify a field with an invalid cast, and so on) it will usually complain about at compile-time, so what initially should have been a compile-time error will become a runtime error instead. However, in many ways that's just something we have to live with: the whole point about dynamic binding is that the type isn't known until runtime, so we can't check types at compile-time.

Other than that, if you're creating a small-scale application, using reflection can be overkill—and adding unnecessary complexity to your code in this way may result in code that has more bugs, is slower, more difficult to maintain, and less extensible.

Indeed, .NET offers you a type-safe alternative to reflective method invocation: using delegates. The next section discusses how delegates can be used for creating type-safe abstractions.

Reflection or Delegates?

Delegates are completely type-safe, secure, managed objects that are used for invoking methods of other objects in a late-binding fashion (sound familiar?). Sure, you can do this using `MethodInfo.Invoke()` or `Type.InvokeMember()`, but you can't be absolutely sure the call will point to a valid method at runtime, and you won't find out until it gives a runtime error—completely nontype-safe and risky. On the other hand, we have delegates provide the same functionality and results (also considerably faster in most cases).

A delegate does just what its literal meaning suggests; it hands control over to the appropriate method when called. At the point of instantiating a delegate, it is passed a reference to the object to use and the address of the method (of the loaded object) that is called indirectly when a call is made to the delegate. At the time of declaration, the compiler does a lot of background work for you and creates a class for the delegate you declare. Every delegate exposes the `Invoke()` method, similar to what you saw using reflection, which is used for passing parameters to the correct method (static or instance method). However, a delegate is interesting because it does not treat static methods differently than it would treat instance methods. In contrast with reflection, if you remember, we had to tweak the binding flags around a bit to tell the method what type of call it was.

To see how using a delegate to invoke a method programmatically differs from using reflection, consider the following console application. This example shows the workings of a delegate, trying to dynamically invoke the correct method at runtime.

```
Imports System

' Declare a delegate
Public Delegate Function Invoker(ByVal x As Integer, _
    ByVal y As Integer) As Integer

Module Module1

    ' A Test class
    Private Class MyMath

        ' A shared method
        Public Shared Function Pow(ByVal x As Integer, _
                                   ByVal y As Integer) As Integer
            Return x ^ y
        End Function
```

```
        ' An instance method
        Public Function Multiply(ByVal x As Integer, _
                                 ByVal y As Integer) As Integer
            Return x * y
        End Function
    End Class

    Sub Main()
        Try
            Dim result As Object
            Dim x As Integer = 2
            Dim y As Integer = 3
            Dim objMath As New MyMath()

            ' Call instance method "Multiply"
            Dim MyDelegate As New Invoker(AddressOf objMath.Multiply)
            result = MyDelegate.Invoke(2, 3)
            Console.WriteLine("The product of {0} and {1} is: {2}", _
                              x, y, result)

            ' Call shared method "Pow"
            Dim MyDelegate2 As New Invoker(AddressOf MyMath.Pow)
            result = MyDelegate2.Invoke(x, y) ' Same as MyMath.Pow(args)
            Console.WriteLine("{0} to the power of {1} is: {2}", _
                              x, y, result)
        Catch e As Exception
            MsgBox(e.Message, , "Exception Caught")
        End Try
        Console.ReadLine()
    End Sub
End Module
```

The example produces the following output.

```
The product of 2 and 3 is: 6
2 to the power of 3 is: 8
```

As you can see, using a delegate to invoke methods is extremely simple. All we had to do was create an instance of our publicly defined delegate, as shown next, and pass it the address of the function to be called:

```
Public Delegate Function Invoker(ByVal x As Integer, _
                                 ByVal y As Integer) As Integer
```

The rest is taken care of by the runtime. Note that if you had passed an incorrect address of a method that did not exist, it would have given you a compile-time error rather than giving you a runtime error as it would have when using reflection. Also note that we didn't have to set any binding flags, worry about the wrong method being called, or anything else. In fact, you can see how a delegate doesn't even distinguish between calls made to static or instance methods:

```
Dim MyDelegate As New Invoker(AddressOf objMath.Multiply)
```

This is the same as the next snippet, with the only difference being the method invoked:

```
Dim MyDelegate2 As New Invoker(AddressOf MyMath.Pow)
```

It's interesting to consider how we might attempt to mimic the Invoke() method of the delegate class using reflection. Using reflection, you must indirectly invoke the correct method depending on the number and type of parameters passed. The Invoker class, implemented next, has equivalent functionality to a delegate class but uses reflection instead:

```
Imports System
Imports System.Reflection

Public Class Invoker

  ' Private variables to store received arguments from the constructor
  Private myType As Type
  Private myObject As Object
  Private myMethod As String

  ' In case of a static method invocation
  ' Constructor takes a type and a method name
  Public Sub New(ByVal TargetType As Type, _
                 ByVal TargetMethod As String)
    myType = TargetType
    myMethod = TargetMethod
  End Sub

  ' In case of an instance method invocation
  ' Constructor takes an object and a method name
  Public Sub New(ByVal TargetObject As Object, _
                 ByVal TargetMethod As String)
    myObject = TargetObject
    myType = TargetObject.GetType()
    myMethod = TargetMethod
  End Sub

  ' Mimicking the Invoke method of a delegate
  Public Function Invoke(ByVal args As Object()) As Object

    If Not myType Is Nothing AndAlso Not myMethod = Nothing Then
      Dim myBindingFlags As Long
      myBindingFlags = _
          BindingFlags.InvokeMethod Or BindingFlags.Public
```

```vb
            If myObject Is Nothing Then
                myBindingFlags = myBindingFlags Or BindingFlags.Static
            Else
                myBindingFlags = myBindingFlags Or BindingFlags.Instance
            End If
            ' invoking the appropriate method
            Return myType.InvokeMember(myMethod, myBindingFlags, Nothing, _
                                      myObject, args)
        Else
            Throw New Exception("Incorrect parameter passed")
        End If

    End Function

End Class

Module Module1

    ' A Test class
    Private Class MyMath

        'A shared method
        Public Shared Function Pow(ByVal x As Integer, _
                                   ByVal y As Integer) As Integer
            Return x ^ y
        End Function

        'An instance method
        Public Function Multiply(ByVal x As Integer, _
                                 ByVal y As Integer) As Integer
            Return x * y
        End Function

    End Class

    Sub Main()
        Try
            Dim result As Object
            Dim args As Object() = {2, 3}
            Dim objMath As New MyMath()

            Dim MyDelegate As New Invoker(objMath, "Multiply")
            result = MyDelegate.Invoke(args)
            Console.WriteLine("The product of {0} and {1} is: {2}", _
                              args(0), args(1), result)
```

```
        ' Call shared method "Pow"
        Dim objDelegate1 As New Invoker(GetType(MyMath), "Pow")
        result = objDelegate1.Invoke(args) ' Same as MyMath.Pow(args)
        Console.WriteLine("{0} to the power of {1} is: {2}", _
                          args(0), args(1), result)
      Catch e As Exception
        MsgBox(e.Message, , "Exception Caught")
      End Try
      Console.ReadLine()
    End Sub

End Module
```

As you can see, if delegates weren't there, this is how you would implement one of your own. The Invoker class acts more or less like a delegate, using Invoke() to call the appropriate method after programmatically setting BindingFlags to decide which method to call. You've certainly seen how to dynamically invoke methods using reflection, but what's of more interest is the way we invoked it. Have a look at the code from the main subroutine:

```
Dim MyDelegate As New Invoker(objMath, "Multiply")
result = MyDelegate.Invoke(args)
```

We instantiated a new Invoker object and passed its constructor a reference to the object to use along with a method name. We then called the Invoke() method of our "delegate" and passed a number of arguments. This call indirectly invoked the Multiply() method of the Math object we created. The call made to the Invoke() method is similar to the following code:

```
result = objMath.Multiply(args)
```

Or reflectively and more accurately:

```
result = myType.InvokeMember(Multiply, myBindingFlags, _
                             Nothing, objMath, args)
```

However, because our copy (Invoker) of the real delegate is still not type-safe and was much harder to implement, considering the size and scope of the problem at hand, you can see the advantages of using delegates.

It is important to note here that in spite of delegates having an advantage over reflection, they still are limited in their use. For example, a single delegate can cast only a single method signature at one time, meaning that if the method Pow() in our example took both parameters as Double rather than Integer, we would have been forced to declare another delegate specifically for that method. However, we do have the option of using *multicast* delegates. In this case, you define a list of methods to be invoked by the delegate and they're all invoked at a single go, one by one. However, sometimes you really don't want that. Delegates also cannot be used as flexibly as we used reflection for modifying private members of an object.

As a conclusion, there really isn't a hard and fast rule for which technique to use. For that, you'll have to judge your application, and perceive if you'll ever need something as powerful as reflection to add ultimate extendibility to your applications. However, in general, it is recommended that for situations such as the one you just saw, you should avoid reflection and consider alternatives such as delegates.

Summary

In this chapter we discussed how to use reflection in an active way to control class members. We considered the following topics:

- Reasons you should consider using dynamic invocation techniques on types and their members
- How to dynamically invoke methods, properties, and fields using `Type.InvokeMember()`
- How to dynamically invoke methods using `MethodInfo.Invoke()`
- How to dynamically modify fields and properties using the `GetValue()` and `SetValue()` methods of the `FieldInfo` and `PropertyInfo` classes
- Why using dynamic invocation via reflection is not always the best choice, and when you should use delegates instead

In the next chapter, we'll consider how to create objects using reflection.

CHAPTER 10

Creating Objects

A powerful tool for .NET developers is dynamic assembly loading. This allows new code to be added to an application after compile-time so that a new assembly can be plugged into an application on-the-fly. As with other dynamic programming techniques, there are pitfalls that can trap a programmer; however, with a thorough understanding of the technology, dynamic programming can lead to incredibly flexible and supportable applications.

This chapter describes how to dynamically load an assembly in .NET. It covers some of the method calls that dynamically load the assemblies, as well as dynamic object creation, and then briefly describes how .NET loads types under the hood. The next section discusses the abstract factory pattern, which is a useful programming technique that helps you take advantage of dynamically loaded objects and helps create extremely flexible applications. The final section discusses how the combination of dynamically loaded objects and the abstract factory patterns can be used to design extremely flexible and manageable architectures, including a potential business need for a flexible application, and how it can be implemented in .NET.

Dynamic Assembly Loading

Applications often require a minor extension of functionality to be added after the release of an application. Usually this entails rewriting some segments of code to accommodate the changes, but significant retesting must be done to ensure that the previous functionality is intact. Consider an example of a Web site that caters specifically to handheld devices with wireless connectivity. Unlike desktop browsers, the specifications for the HTML supported by such browsers are changing rapidly because there are more platforms to support and capabilities are rapidly evolving as the devices become more powerful. A Web site that caters to these users needs to add support for the latest browsers, without affecting the other users. The capability to add a component that dynamically loads the software for each browser type could allow a Web site to greatly reduce the amount of retesting that needs to be done when a new browser type is added.

The reflection library allows the programmer to dynamically load assemblies by specifying an assembly name and version information. Because the .NET Framework checks the version of the assembly loaded, the old problems associated with "DLL Hell" (the source of many COM woes, where the incorrect version of a DLL is loaded by an application) are virtually eliminated. Binding an assembly to another assembly can happen either statically at designtime or dynamically at runtime. The static references are stored in the assembly's metadata when the assembly is built, whereas the dynamic references are created on-the-fly using a method such as `System.Reflection.Assembly.Load()`, as you'll see later.

Creating Assembly References

Assemblies can be loaded either by fully referencing the assembly name, version, cultural environment, and public key token, or by partially referencing the assembly by omitting any of the attributes, except the name, which is required. Fully referencing an assembly is the best way to create a reference, because this guarantees the caller that the expected assembly will be loaded, eliminating potential DLL Hell situations. Statically referenced assemblies are always fully referenced—the compiler includes all the assembly reference information in the referencing assembly's metadata.

Regardless of how an assembly reference is specified (dynamically or statically; fully or partially), the next step is for .NET to turn the assembly reference information into the location of a particular .NET assembly file—usually a DLL. So how does .NET find the DLL from the provided reference information?

Application Configuration Files and Binding

First, the runtime examines the application configuration files to determine whether they specify a DLL containing a particular named assembly. They can also help resolve full names from partial references, and give information about which version should be used. Assembly binding behavior can be configured at three levels based on these files:

- **Application Configuration File**: The standard .NET application configuration file.
- **Publisher Policy File**: These files can indicate that a new assembly should be loaded in place of an old one. Useful to redirect previous assemblies to the latest version.
- **Machine Configuration File**: Settings that apply to the entire computer.

The second step is to check whether the assembly has been bound to beforehand; if so, the previously loaded version is used. Because the assembly name and other attributes match, you are guaranteed that this is the identical version that you are looking for, so there's no reason to reload the assembly. The Global Assembly Cache (GAC) is searched next, and if the assembly is found there, the runtime uses that assembly. If the assembly is not found in the GAC, the runtime *probes* for the assembly. Probing consists of searching the application path for a DLL containing the required assembly. The framework searches for a folder under the application root named the same as the assembly to be loaded. It also uses the culture to determine whether the assembly's DLL is located in a folder with the same name as the culture.

The paths searched are as follows:

- `[application base] / [assembly name] / [assembly name].dll`
- `[application base] / [culture] / [assembly name].dll`
- `[application base] / [culture] / [assembly name] / [assembly name].dll`

Defining an `AssemblyName`

To load a fully referenced assembly dynamically, you need to create an `AssemblyName` object to specify which assembly to load. Four main parameters identify an assembly:

- Name
- Version
- Culture
- Strong name or signature

```
' Create and populate the AssemblyName object
Dim assemblyName As New System.Reflection.AssemblyName()
assemblyName.Name = "TestAssembly"
```

You can specify a partial query without the version, culture, or strong name, however, you are not guaranteed that the assembly will be unique, and the first assembly found matching those parameters is returned. It is best practice to include every parameter to guarantee the assembly loaded is the one you intended to load.

The version parameter is an object of type `Version` that contains the major and minor version numbers, an optional build number, and an optional revision number. If the runtime finds an assembly with a higher build number, but the major and minor versions match, it will load that assembly.

- **Major**: Assemblies with the same name but different major versions are not interchangeable, so backward compatibility cannot be assumed.
- **Minor**: The new version offers a significant enhancement, but backward compatibility is maintained.
- **Build**: The number of the build of the same set of source code. Code could be rebuilt to optimize for a new processor, OS, or compiler feature. The code is compatible and the feature set should remain the same. If the code is a work in progress, the major and minor versions will remain the same, and the build number will be incremented for each build.
- **Revision**: A revision is meant to be interchangeable with the previous version, except with a possible hot patch for a bug or security hole, so the runtime will load an assembly with a higher revision number (but not a lower one).

```
assemblyName.Version = New Version("1.0.3300.0")
```

The `Culture` parameter specifies a `CultureInfo` class that determines the cultural environment this code is intended to be run in. For example, the culture string en indicates English. You can provide different versions of an assembly designed to be used in different cultures, perhaps to provide different language support. A word processor might load its grammar checking, hyphenation, and spelling modules from an assembly, using the culture to specify the language required.

```
assemblyName.CultureInfo = New System.Globalization.CultureInfo("en")
```

The `StrongName` is a cryptographically sound signature of the compiled contents of an assembly. Strong naming relies on public key cryptography (PKC).

In PKC, a public-private key pair is created. The public key can be used to decrypt data encrypted with the private key, and the private key can be used to decrypt data encrypted with the public key. The public key is given to everyone who might need to communicate with the person who owns the key, and the owner keeps the private key secret. To digitally sign some data, the owner of the key takes a hash of the data using a cryptographic hashing algorithm such as SHA or MD5. The owner then encrypts the hash (sometimes called a digest) using the private key to create a digital signature. The owner can then distribute the original data, accompanied by the signature. Someone in possession of the public key, having received the data, can verify that it is the data that was originally signed by performing the same hashing process on the data, generating the same hash that the owner of the key created. The receiver then decrypts the signature using the owner's public key, and if the result is the same as the hash, the signature is valid and the data is the same as the data the owner/originator signed.

A strong name, then, is a digital signature derived from the entire compiled contents of the assembly. Because it is signed using a particular developer's private key, the strong name generated for a particular assembly can't be duplicated by anyone else, meaning you can't pass off a different assembly under the same strong name (even if you have the original developer's private key).

Partially Referencing Assemblies

If some of the reference information is unavailable, an assembly can be loaded with only partial reference information. The simple name of the assembly is required, but the assembly can be loaded without the version, culture, or signature. Using a partial reference can be helpful in situations where you simply want to grab the latest version of the assembly, because the assembly with the highest version number will be loaded if the version is omitted. Partial references must be used carefully, because you are not guaranteed that the version of the assembly you are calling is compatible with the client. Creating a partial reference without the version information is not recommended, because it will load assemblies with major revision changes, which do not guarantee backward compatibility.

If the runtime loads an assembly with partial reference information, it will first search the application configuration file. The application configuration file may include the full reference. If so, the runtime proceeds with the full reference from the application configuration. This method can be useful in defining the version of the assembly to use without recompiling the assembly, but should not be used on assemblies that are shared among several applications. Because the runtime searches the configuration file at the application level and not the assembly level, every application configuration file needs the fully updated assembly reference.

If the configuration file does not include the full reference, the runtime searches the application directory and then the GAC. If the version is not specified in the reference, the runtime attempts to load the version with the highest version that matches the other criteria.

Methods Used for Dynamic Assembly Loading

To dynamically load an assembly into an application, one of the following methods must be used:

- System.Reflection.Assembly.Load()
- System.Reflection.Assembly.LoadFrom()
- System.Reflection.Assembly.LoadWithPartialName()

The System.Reflection.Assembly.Load() function can be used to either load a fully referenced assembly or partially referenced assembly. It takes a single AssemblyName object as a parameter, which the runtime uses to determine which assembly to load. The LoadWithPartialName() method differs from the Load() method in that it takes a string argument and skips the application configuration file lookup. The LoadFrom() method takes in a string argument that determines the path for the DLL file that holds the assembly.

```
' Load the assembly from the reflection library
 oAssembly = System.Reflection.Assembly.Load(oAssemblyName)

' Load the assembly from the reflection library
' with a partial reference
partial = "TestAssembly,version=1.0.0.1001"
oAssembly = System.Reflection.Assembly.LoadWithPartialName(partial)
```

Instantiating Classes Dynamically

After the assembly is loaded, you can create an instance of a class inside the assembly using the CreateInstance() method of the Assembly class. The CreateInstance() method has three overloaded implementations:

- CreateInstance(typeName As String) As Object

- CreateInstance(typeName As String, ignoreCase as Boolean) as Object

- CreateInstance(typeName As String, ignoreCase as Boolean, bindingAttr as BindingFlags, binder as Binder, args as Object(), culture as CultureInfo, and activationAttributes as Object()) As Object

In the simplest case, the CreateInstance() method has one argument, which accepts a string that identifies the type to be loaded. The classname is case sensitive, unless the second parameter is set to True.

The third method gives the developer the most control over the creation of the instance of the class. The reflection library uses the binding flags to determine which methods to search through to find the object's constructor. The binding flags enumeration is used in many methods in the refection library, but only the following two flags are relevant and can be combined by using an OR in the argument:

- **BindingFlags.Public:** Search only public methods. This includes both instance and shared methods.

- **BindingFlags.Instance:** Search instance methods in any scope. An instance method requires an instance of the object to be created, whereas static methods declared with the Shared keyword do not require the class to be instantiated.

The binder argument is an object that the BindingFlags and args arguments use to determine the constructor. Passing NULL in this field results in the default binder being used.

The args argument is an object array that contains the arguments to pass into the constructor. The reflection runtime searches through all the constructors and calls the one appropriate for that list of objects.

The CultureInfo object determines the cultural environment that governs the coercion of types on the argument array. This occurs when a type is converted to another in the argument that may require some cultural information. For example, if a string object is passed into a date parameter, the conversion of "7/9/02" will differ depending on the cultural context, because some cultures define that date as July 9th, while others define it as September 7th. Setting this value to Nothing will default to the current thread's culture.

CHAPTER 10 ■ CREATING OBJECTS

The `activationAttributes` argument is an array of objects that contain some activation attributes. The `UrlAttribute` object is an example of a parameter to the `CreateInstance()` method, which determines where activation will take place.

```
' Load the assembly from the reflection library with a
' partial reference
partial = "DynamicAssembly"
oAssembly = System.Reflection.Assembly.LoadWithPartialName(partial)

' Load the assembly with a full reference,
' but using the LoadWithPartialName
partial = "DynamicAssembly, Version=1.0.950.28158, _
          Culture=neutral, PublicKeyToken=null"
oAssembly = System.Reflection.Assembly.LoadWithPartialName(partial)
```

The following is a trivial example that demonstrates how to load the assembly dynamically and create an instance of the class. First in a class library, the example creates a simple class with two constructors: a default constructor that takes in no arguments, and another constructor that takes in a long argument. It stores the argument in a private variable. We also create a method that returns that number.

```
Public Class CDynamicLoadedClass
   Sub New()
      m_lNumber = -1
   End Sub
   Sub New(ByVal lDefault As Long)
      m_lNumber = lDefault
   End Sub
   Public Function GetNumber() As Long
      Return m_lNumber
   End Function

   Private m_lNumber As Long
End Class
```

Now, we'll create a simple Windows form application that has a single command button on it. In the command button routine, we'll place the code to dynamically load the object.

```
Private Sub Button1_Click(ByVal sender As System.Object, _
    ByVal e As System.EventArgs) Handles Button1.Click
Dim oAssemblyName As System.Reflection.AssemblyName
Dim oAssembly As System.Reflection.Assembly
Dim oClass As DynamicAssembly.CDynamicLoadedClass
Dim args(0) As Object

   ' Use the AssemblyName object
   oAssemblyName = New System.Reflection.AssemblyName()
   oAssemblyName.Name = "DynamicAssembly"
   oAssemblyName.Version = New Version("1.0.950.28158")
   oAssembly = System.Reflection.Assembly.Load(oAssemblyName)
```

```
' Since you are not passing in an args array,
' use the default constructor
oClass = _
    oAssembly.CreateInstance("DynamicAssembly.CDynamicLoadedClass")
MsgBox(oClass.GetNumber())
oClass = Nothing

' Set up the args array.
' We will pass in 1 object with a datatype of Long
args(0) = CLng(5)
oClass = _
oAssembly.CreateInstance(         _
            "DynamicAssembly.CDynamicLoadedClass", _
            True, Nothing, Nothing, args, Nothing, Nothing)
MsgBox(oClass.GetNumber())
End Sub
```

The result of this simple program is two message boxes. The first displays a value of -1 and the second displays a value of 5. This demonstrates which constructor was used in instantiating the object.

Abstract Factory Pattern

Dynamic assembly loading is a powerful tool provided by .NET, but to fully utilize it, a structure must be created that organizes the logic to decide which assembly to load and which object to instantiate without affecting the calling assembly. The technique of centralizing object instantiation is not unique to .NET. Object-oriented (OO) developers in languages such as C++ and Java use a construct called the *abstract factory pattern*. This technique, like many common OO architectures, derives from SmallTalk, and the *Design Patterns* book (Addison Wesley, 1994). The authors of that book identified the abstract factory pattern as a way to provide a centralized location for the selection of a class to dynamically load.

The abstract factory pattern allows a programmer to obtain an object matching a particular interface, but only choosing which specific class to instantiate at runtime. One of several possible classes could be instantiated, but whichever is returned, the calling code can treat the object the same because it implements a particular interface. The specific type of the returned object might be completely unknown to the calling code.

■**Tip** The word abstract, in the context of the abstract factory pattern, refers to the fact that it is based upon an abstract class. *Abstract classes*, in OO parlance, are classes that declare only a partial implementation—they leave some of their methods with signatures, but no method body. They cannot be instantiated, but they can be subclassed, and the subclasses must provide a complete implementation for the class, filling in the missing methods. A class that inherits from an abstract class and completes the implementation is called a *concrete class*. In VB .NET, you can create an abstract class by marking it with the MustInherit keyword.

Figure 10-1 shows what an abstract factory tries to do.

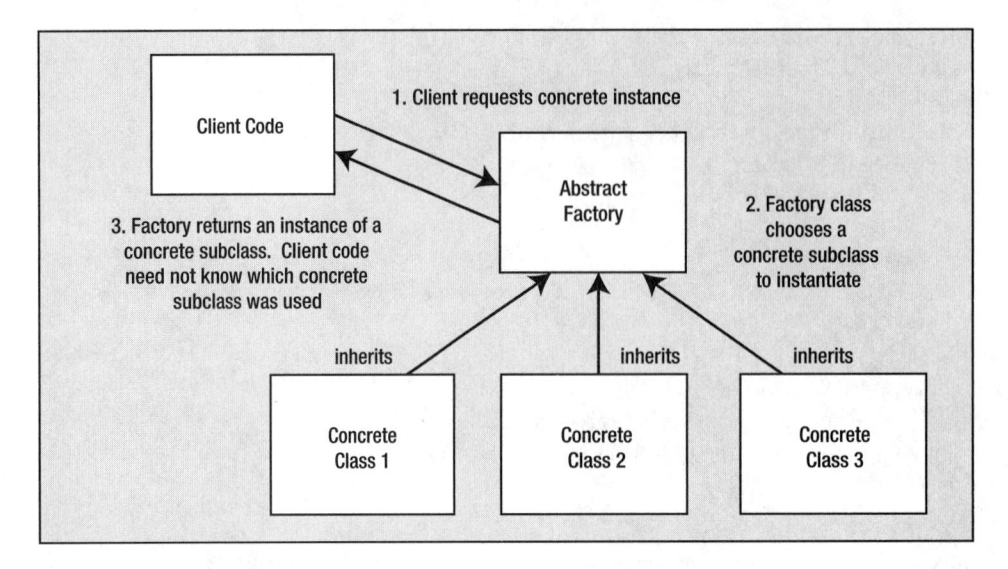

Figure 10-1. *Illustration of an abstract factory pattern*

The implementation of the abstract factory pattern consists of implementing an abstract class and some concrete classes that extend it. The client code, however, only has to know about the abstract factory class, and doesn't need to know about the concrete classes. This is because of polymorphism; an instance of any of the concrete classes can be referred from a variable whose type is that of the abstract factory class. So, although the abstract class itself can never be instantiated, instances of the subclasses can be treated, for all intents and purposes, as if they are instances of the abstract type. The client makes method calls on the concrete class through the interface provided by the abstract class.

Note As a general rule and best practice, interfaces and abstract classes should be put in their own assembly. Concrete classes or implementation classes should be placed in an assembly separate from the abstract class or interface. This allows other implementers or subclasses to easily reference your interface or abstract class.

Advantages of Using the Abstract Factory Pattern with Dynamic Assembly Loading

All this information about reflection, inheritance, and abstract factory patterns may seem interesting, but how is this practical? Almost all the examples in the chapter could be programmed without dynamic object creation, with a much simpler solution. Well, the power of dynamic assembly loading and object creation is its flexibility. The developer can design an architecture that can easily be expanded and extended without redevelopment, and in some cases, can be added on-the-fly without recompiling the original source code. Imagine adding a module that handles a new set of electronic invoices with new business rules and data transformations to the existing data import program, without disturbing any of the original source code and without taking the system down. Although flexible software is more complex and includes a slight increase in overhead that might hinder performance, the benefits of flexibility often outweigh the increased complexity and overhead. This is especially true in VB .NET, now that it is fully object oriented and can utilize inheritance.

A Simple Abstract Factory Pattern in VB .NET

An abstract class in .NET is identified by the `MustInherit` keyword. This means that the class cannot be created through a `New` keyword, but subclasses can inherit from the abstract class. The subclasses must implement methods declared in the abstract class to provide the underlying functionality. The abstract class supplies the interface that the clients communicate with, but also it can supply a set of generic methods and utility functions the concrete classes inherit.

In addition, the abstract class must provide a method that the client code calls when it wants the factory to create a new instance for it. This can be implemented as a `Shared` method. This method can take arguments, which it can use to decide which concrete class to return, or it can use information found elsewhere without taking arguments to make the decision. In either case, it returns an instance of one of the concrete classes, so its return type is the abstract factory's type.

Following is a trivial example that shows how you could use an abstract factory pattern to display a greeting. The client of the factory has no knowledge of the `NightGreeter`, `MorningGreeter`, or the other concrete classes, but rather uses the `Greeter`'s `GetGreeter()` method to decide which concrete class is appropriate for the situation.

```
Public MustInherit Class Greeter
  Public Shared Function GetGreeter() As Greeter
    Dim now As DateTime = DateTime.Now
    Dim hour As Integer = now.Hour
    Dim currentGreeter As Greeter
    Select Case hour
      Case 0 To 6
        currentGreeter = New NightGreeter()
      Case 7 To 12
        currentGreeter = New MorningGreeter()
      Case 13 To 17
        currentGreeter = New AfternoonGreeter()
      Case Else
        currentGreeter = New EveningGreeter()
    End Select

    Return currentGreeter
  End Function
  Public MustOverride Function Greet() As String

End Class

Public Class MorningGreeter
  Inherits Greeter
  Public Overrides Function Greet() As String
    Return "Good morning"
  End Function
End Class
```

```
Public Class AfternoonGreeter
  Inherits Greeter
  Public Overrides Function Greet() As String
    Return "Good afternoon"
  End Function
End Class

Public Class EveningGreeter
  Inherits Greeter
  Public Overrides Function Greet() As String
    Return "Good evening"
  End Function
End Class

Public Class NightGreeter
  Inherits Greeter
  Public Overrides Function Greet() As String
    Return "What are you doing running this code at this hour?"
  End Function
End Class
```

Here's a trivial command-line client:

```
Public Module MainModule
  Public Sub Main()
    Dim g As Greeter = Greeter.GetGreeter()
    Console.WriteLine(g.Greet())
  End Sub
End Module
```

The output now depends on the time of day. Notice how this pattern breaks up responsibility for different parts of the system neatly into logically distinct units. The logic of which greeting to deliver is all in the `GetGreeting()` method; the logic for each greeting is parceled up in a different class; the client code doesn't worry about how each different class implements the `Greet()` method, it just calls it. This is OO encapsulation at its best.

So far so good, but we're not actually using reflection here. However, because the `GetGreeting()` method neatly encapsulates all the logic that decides which object to create, it is easy to insert reflective code here without affecting the implementation of the concrete classes or the client code at all. Using reflective object loading, you can make the decision about which class to instantiate far more dynamic. For example, the application could read a configuration file to determine which class to use at any particular hour, using reflection to load the appropriate class. Simply by adding a new class to the application and altering the configuration file, you could add new greetings. On Christmas Day, you could change the configuration file completely so that no matter what time the program is run, an instance of `ChristmasGreeting` is returned.

A more realistic business situation for the abstract factory pattern is a data pipeline architecture. Data pipeline architectures push data through a series of processors that perform some operations on the data, such as transformations, database modifications, and email notifications.

A common application of a data pipeline is an Enterprise Resource Planning (ERP) integration Web service that a company exposes to communicate with vendors or customers. An ERP is an enterprise application that processes a wide range of business functions such as customer databases, accounting, and human resources. Typically, each node in a pipeline needs to discover another node to forward data onto after it has finished processing it. An abstract factory system allows nodes to request other nodes by name, not worrying about the underlying type of the node which is returned, but still able to interact at a high level.

We'll look now at a real application of a dynamic assembly loading abstract factory, in a similar business workflow situation.

Implementing the Abstract Factory Pattern with Dynamic Assembly Loading in VB .NET

Let's examine a situation where you might apply these techniques. A manufacturing company's accounting department wants to create an EDI (Electronic Data Interchange) invoicing and billing system. EDI systems are electronic connections to send information between the two companies electronically. To keep material costs low, the purchasing department wants as little barrier to switching suppliers as possible. Unfortunately, different vendors all use different systems for communication: email, FTP file drop, or more recently, XML Web services. XML helps simplify some of the issues, but each vendor still needs individualized business rules applied to their incoming data.

The billing department also has similar concerns. To satisfy their customers, the sales team used numerous rebates and discounts as incentives. The billing system has to be flexible enough to accommodate any customer demands on the contract terms. The software development team has found it impossible to create a data model to store all the possible contract terms in the database, because so many different contact terms are possible.

We can implement this EDI system using a data pipeline that accommodates the various departments' needs for flexibility, yet keeps the system manageable. The pipeline has two stages, as shown in Figure 10-2:

- **Initial Transformation**: Data is received via email, FTP, Web service, and so on in either a flat file or XML. It is then converted from the native format to an XML document. The transformation logic will be specific to each vendor's file format.

- **Database load**: Loads the information into the ERP system after applying any special customer-specific logic.

The pipeline uses a factory to load the assembly and component that processes the data as it flows through the pipeline. The factory class uses an XML file to store the assembly and class data, which allows new vendors to be added to the pipeline on-the-fly by coding up a new vendor-specific assembly, and editing the XML file. When an object is requested by the client, the factory queries the XML document and obtains the assembly identification data. The data is passed into the `Assembly.Load()` method to load the assembly, and the `CreateInstance()` method is called on the assembly object. The factory method is shared, which means that an instance of the class does not have to exist to call the method. The first time the shared method is called, the static constructor is run, which loads the XML document.

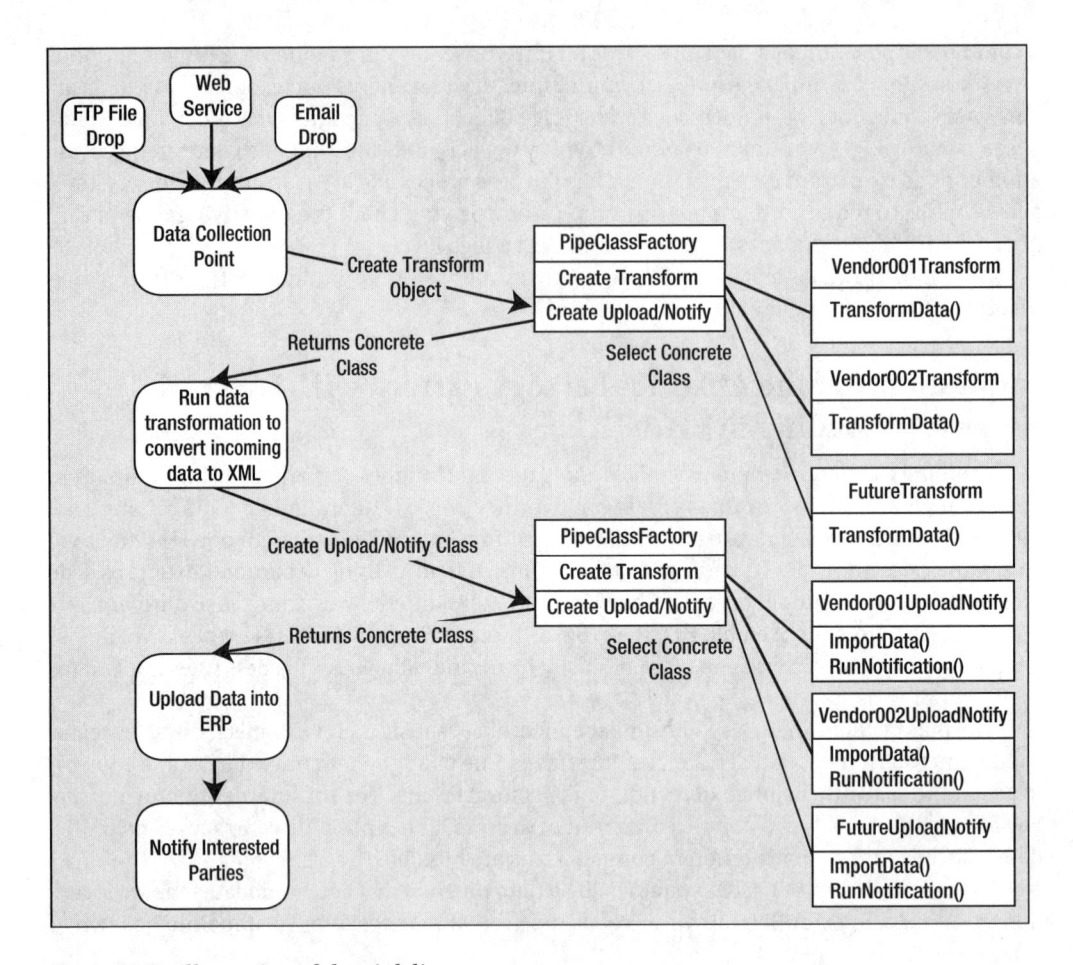

Figure 10-2. *Illustration of the pipleline*

Let's look at the configuration document for the application first:

```xml
<?xml version="1.0" encoding="utf-8" ?>
<Pipeline>
  <vendor id="001">
    <assembly name="PipelineExample1" version="1.0">
      <class type="Transform"
        name="PipelineExample1.Vendor001Transform"/>
      <class type="UploadNotify"
        name="PipelineExample1.Vendor001UploadNotify"/>
    </assembly>
  </vendor>
  <vendor id="002">
    <assembly name="PipelineExample1" version="1.0">
      <class type="Transform"
        name="PipelineExample1.Vendor002Transform"/>
```

```
      <class type="UploadNotify"
        name="PipelineExample1.Vendor002UploadNotify"/>
    </assembly>
  </vendor>
</Pipeline>
```

As you can see, the file specifies the name of a transformation and upload/notification class for each vendor. The factory uses this to select the appropriate DLL to load and the appropriate class to use.

Here is the code for the factory class. It starts with the shared constructor, which loads the XML configuration file. It looks in the base directory for the current application domain, which means the configuration file must be in the directory containing the executable application that is currently running.

```
Public Class PipeLineClassFactory
  Private Shared _xmlDoc As Xml.XmlDocument

  Shared Sub New()
    _xmlDoc = New Xml.XmlDocument()
    ' NOTE- Hardcoding the filename is NOT recommended, but for
    ' the purposes of this example it will suffice.
    _xmlDoc.Load(AppDomain.CurrentDomain.BaseDirectory & _
                "/pipelineconfig.xml")
  End Sub
```

The first of the factory methods creates a vendor-specific Transform object, from the vendor ID passed in:

```
Public Shared Function CreateTransform(ByVal vendorID As Long) _
                                    As Transformation
  Dim xmlAssembly As Xml.XmlElement
  Dim xmlClass As Xml.XmlElement
  Dim name As String
  Dim version As String
  Dim className As String
  Dim args(0) As Object
  Dim assemblyName As System.Reflection.AssemblyName
  Dim loadedAssembly As System.Reflection.Assembly
  Dim ret As Transformation
  ' Load the data from the preloaded configuration XML Document
  xmlAssembly = _xmlDoc.SelectSingleNode("/Pipeline/vendor[@id=" _
     & CStr(vendorID) & "]/assembly")
  xmlClass = _
     xmlAssembly.SelectSingleNode("class[@type='Transform']")

  ' Pull out the assembly information from the Configuration
  ' File. This example uses a partial reference to load the assembly
  ' a full reference would include the culture and public key token
  name = xmlAssembly.GetAttribute("name")
```

```vb
        version = xmlAssembly.GetAttribute("version")
        className = xmlClass.GetAttribute("name")

        ' Create and populate the AssemblyName object
        assemblyName = New System.Reflection.AssemblyName()
        assemblyName.Name = name
        assemblyName.Version = New Version(version)

        ' Load the assembly from the reflection library
        loadedAssembly = System.Reflection.Assembly.Load(assemblyName)
        ' The contructor takes no parameters
        args = Nothing
        ' Create the instance of the class specified in the configuration
        ' file.
        ret = loadedAssembly.CreateInstance(className, True, _
                    Reflection.BindingFlags.Public Or _
                    Reflection.BindingFlags.Instance, _
                    Nothing, args, Nothing, Nothing)
        Return ret
    End Function
```

The next function is the factory that creates the vendor-specific upload and notification object, which is mostly the same, but requires an argument for the constructor:

```vb
    Public Shared Function CreateUploadNotify(ByVal vendorID As Long, _
                ByVal xmlInvoice As Xml.XmlDocument) As UploadNotify
        Dim xmlAssembly As Xml.XmlElement
        Dim xmlClass As Xml.XmlElement
        Dim name As String
        Dim version As String
        Dim className As String
        Dim args(0) As Object

        Dim assemblyName As System.Reflection.AssemblyName
        Dim loadedAssembly As System.Reflection.Assembly
        Dim ret As UploadNotify

        xmlAssembly = _xmlDoc.SelectSingleNode("/Pipeline/vendor[@id=" _
                & CStr(vendorID) & "]/assembly")
        xmlClass = _
            xmlAssembly.SelectSingleNode("class[@type='UploadNotify']")
        name = xmlAssembly.GetAttribute("name")
        version = xmlAssembly.GetAttribute("version")
        className = xmlClass.GetAttribute("name")

        assemblyName = New System.Reflection.AssemblyName()
        assemblyName.Name = name
        assemblyName.Version = New Version(version)
```

```
        loadedAssembly = System.Reflection.Assembly.Load(assemblyName)

        ' The XmlInvoice parameter is the argument to the constructor
        args(0) = xmlInvoice
        ret = loadedAssembly.CreateInstance(className, True, _
                    Reflection.BindingFlags.Public And _
                    Reflection.BindingFlags.Instance, _
                    Nothing, args, Nothing, Nothing)
        Return ret

    End Function
End Class
```

The abstract classes in the data pipeline define the interface that the pipeline uses to pass the data along the pipeline. They also provide a default implementation that the subclass can override when the vendor requires special treatment. Lastly, the abstract base classes provide a set of utility functions that the subclasses can use to reuse code in common situations.

The first class handles transformation of data into the appropriate internal format. Here's an example of the XML format that the system requires:

```
<?xml version="1.0" encoding="utf-8" ?>
<Invoice VendorID="001" ProductName="WidgetComponent1"
        ProductID="212" Price=".02" Quantity="12500">
</Invoice>
```

Additional vendor-specific data is allowed if the vendor wants to supply it, in the form of additional XML attributes.

The base data transformation class caters to the case in which the vendor sends invoices in the desired XML format, and they therefore require no transformation. The data is simply loaded into an XML document and returned to the caller. Some vendors may send the file in a comma-delimited format, which needs to be parsed and loaded into an XML document before the method completes. You might also want to include some utility functions to help import some commonly used file formats.

```
Public MustInherit Class Transformation
    Public Overridable Function TransformData(ByVal data As String) _
                    As Xml.XmlDocument
        ' The default behavior is that the data provider
        ' sends the data in an XML format that
        ' conforms to the rules of the internal XML schema
        Dim xmlDoc As Xml.XmlDocument

        xmlDoc = New Xml.XmlDocument()
        ' You will want to provide error handling to
        ' ensure data loaded correctly.
        xmlDoc.LoadXml(data)

        Return xmlDoc
    End Function
End Class
```

The upload and notify class constructor uses reflection to look at the implementing subclass's public properties. For each property, it checks the XML document for a value to assign. If there is a match between the public property's name and a field in the XML file, the field is populated with the value. Properties are provided on the abstract class for the three compulsory fields that must be provided for an invoice, but this mechanism allows the code to process data from other vendors that provide additional information. Once again, extensibility is the goal.

```
Public MustInherit Class UploadNotify
  Public Sub New(ByVal xmlDoc As Xml.XmlDocument)
    Dim myType As Type
    Dim myPropertyInfos As PropertyInfo()
    Dim myPropertyInfo As PropertyInfo
    Dim xmlElt As Xml.XmlElement
    Dim i As Integer

    myType = Me.GetType()
    myPropertyInfos = myType.GetProperties()

    For Each myPropertyInfo In myPropertyInfos
      xmlElt = xmlDoc.SelectSingleNode("/Invoice[@" & _
          myPropertyInfo.Name & "]")
      myPropertyInfo.SetValue(Me, _
          CStr(xmlElt.GetAttribute(CStr(myPropertyInfo.Name))), _
          Nothing)
    Next
  End Sub
```

The two public methods that are called on an upload/notification class are next. First, the notification method:

```
Public Overridable Sub RunNotification()
  ' The base case in no notification, do nothing
End Sub
```

Here are some utility functions—the implementation is left out and we just post a message to the screen:

```
Protected Sub SendEmail(ByVal name As String, _
                       ByVal emailAddr As String, _
                       ByVal subject As String, _
                       ByVal body As String)
  MsgBox(String.Format("Sending mail '{0}' to {1} ({2})", _
                       subject, name, emailAddr))
End Sub
Protected Sub SendFax(ByVal name As String, _
                     ByVal faxNbr As String, _
                     ByVal subject As String, _
                     ByVal body As String)
```

```
    MsgBox(String.Format("Sending fax '{0}' to {1} ({2})", _
                        subject, name, faxNbr))
End Sub
```

The other key public method is called to import the data into the ERP system. The `ImportData()` method of the `UploadNotify` class creates the connection to the ERP system and loads the data. The implementation of this varies greatly from one system to another, so the specific implementation of this functionality is omitted in this example. One possible way to import the data is to pass a SQL statement to the database and insert the data directly. This may not be possible in a real system, as many ERPs lock the database down so modifications must be made through ERP's import API, but it suffices to show what we're doing here.

We provide a default implementation here, but expect that vendor-specific logic might be required, so allow this implementation to be overridden. We call one method that generates an appropriate SQL statement, and another that executes it against our ERP database:

```
Public Overridable Sub ImportData()
    ' The base case is to just create the SQL insert statement
    ' dynamically and run the query in the DB.
    Dim sql As String
    sql = GenerateSQL()
    ExecuteSQL(sql)
End Sub
```

The SQL generation logic again uses reflection to examine the properties exposed by the current implementing class, and builds a SQL statement using them:

```
Friend Function GenerateSQL()
    Dim sql As String
    Dim myType As Type
    Dim myPropertyInfos As PropertyInfo()
    Dim myPropertyInfo As PropertyInfo
    Dim xmlElt As Xml.XmlElement
    Dim i As Integer
    myType = Me.GetType()
    myPropertyInfos = myType.GetProperties()
    sql = "INSERT INTO AcctPayable ("
    For Each myPropertyInfo In myPropertyInfos
        sql = sql & myPropertyInfo.Name & ", "
    Next
    sql = sql.Substring(0, sql.Length - 2) ' Remove trailing comma
                                            ' and space
    sql = sql & ") VALUES ("

    For Each myPropertyInfo In myPropertyInfos
        sql = sql & "'" & myPropertyInfo.GetValue(Me, Nothing) & "', "
    Next
```

```
    sql = sql.Substring(0, sql.Length - 2) ' Remove trailing comma
                                           ' and space
    sql = sql & ")"

    Return sql
End Function
```

The next sub would execute the generated SQL query, but in our demonstration, it just shows it to the user using a message box:

```
Friend Sub ExecuteSQL(ByVal sql As String)
    MsgBox("Executing SQL Statement " & sql)
End Sub
```

Finally, we have the three properties that are required for every invoice:

```
Private _productID As String
Private _price As String
Private _quantity As String

' Required Field Names
Public Property ProductID() As String
    Get
        Return _productID
    End Get
    Set(ByVal Value As String)
        _productID = Value
    End Set
End Property

Public Property Price() As String
    Get
        Return _price
    End Get
    Set(ByVal Value As String)
        _price = Value
    End Set
End Property

Public Property Quantity() As String
    Get
        Return _quantity
    End Get
    Set(ByVal Value As String)
        _quantity = Value
    End Set
End Property
End Class
```

Now we need to implement the actual vendor-specific classes. Suppose this is Vendor 001's first EDI project, and the vendor is willing to send its data in the desired XML format. This means that no transformation is required. The concrete `Transform` class created for Vendor 001 will not override the `Transform()` method and will default to the implementation provided by the abstract class.

```
Public Class Vendor001Transform
  ' Vendor 001 agreed to use XYZ's internal layout, so no
  ' initial transformation must be done
  Inherits Transformation
End Class
```

However, on the notification side, Vendor 001 provides an additional shipping date field in the XML file it passes to the EDI Web service. The loading dock's manager might use this shipping field to help plan his workload because he will know roughly when shipments are due to arrive. The notification section of the pipeline needs to send an email out to him when the data is received. This is done by overriding the `RunNotification()` method of the `UploadNotify` class, and by adding a `ShipDate` public property to the subclass. Remember, the constructor in the base class must be called using the `MyBase.New()` function, which will automatically set the new property from the data in the XML.

```
Public Class Vendor001UploadNotify
  Inherits UploadNotify

  Private _shipDate As String

  Public Sub New(ByVal xmlDoc As System.Xml.XmlDocument)
    MyBase.New(xmlDoc)
  End Sub

  Public Property ShipDate() As String
    Get
      Return _shipDate
    End Get
    Set(ByVal Value As String)
      _shipDate = Value
    End Set
  End Property
  ' Once again, the hard-coded email address is not recommended,
  ' but simply demonstrates what data could be sent.
  Public Overrides Sub RunNotification()
    Me.SendEmail("Loading Docks Manager", _
                "ldmgr@CompanyXYZ.com", _
                "Shipment from Vender 001", _
                "Shipping date: " & _shipDate)
  End Sub
End Class
```

Now, suppose Vendor 002 has been using EDI for some time and is unwilling to rewrite their existing EDI system to accommodate XML. Instead, their data is sent via a flat file to an FTP server. A process then watches for files being uploaded, and loads them into the pipeline server. The data within the flat file is comma delimited, with one row per line. The data must be parsed and loaded into an XML document before it can be passed onto the next stage in the pipeline system. By overriding the `TransformData()` method of the `Transform` class, the class can perform this data transformation without having to change the architecture and data flow through the rest of the system.

Here is an example of the Vendor 002 invoice format:

```
"Product","Price","Quantity","Ship-Date"
"WidgetComponent2","0.02","456","06/13/2002"
```

We need to turn this data into an XML file matching the format specified before—an `<invoice>` element—with the data stored as attributes:

```vb
' Vendor 002 uses a flat comma-delimited file format for all EDI.
Public Class Vendor002Transform
  Inherits Transformation

  Public Overrides Function TransformData(ByVal data As String) _
              As Xml.XmlDocument
    ' Parse the data sent in via the CSV
    Dim xmlDoc As Xml.XmlDocument
    Dim invoice As Xml.XmlElement

    xmlDoc = New Xml.XmlDocument()
    xmlDoc.LoadXml("<Invoice/>")

    invoice = xmlDoc.DocumentElement

    Dim lines As String()
    Dim line As String
    Dim fields As String()
    Dim field As String
    Dim header As Boolean
    data = data.Replace("""", "") ' remove quotes
    lines = data.Split(vbCrLf) ' split into lines
    header = True
    For Each line In lines
      If header Then
        header = False ' omit the first line
      Else
        fields = line.Split(",") ' split on commas
        invoice.SetAttribute("VendorID", "002")
        invoice.SetAttribute("ProductID", _
              ConvertProductNameToID(fields(0).Trim()))
        invoice.SetAttribute("Price", fields(1))
        invoice.SetAttribute("Quantity", fields(2))
        invoice.SetAttribute("EstimatedArrivalDate", fields(3))
```

```
        End If
      Next
      Return xmlDoc
  End Function

  Private Function ConvertProductNameToID( _
          ByVal productName As String) As String
    Select Case productName
      Case "WidgetComponent1"
        Return "212"
      Case "WidgetComponent2"
        Return "213"
    End Select
  End Function
End Class
```

Unlike Vendor 001, however, no notifications are required, so we accept the default behavior. We must implement a constructor, so the XML document passed in is correctly stored and uploaded into the ERP system by the base class:

```
Public Class Vendor002UploadNotify
  Inherits UploadNotify
  Public Sub New(ByVal xmlDoc As Xml.XmlDocument)
    MyBase.New(xmlDoc)
  End Sub
End Class
```

Coding a client application isn't too difficult. For a quick demonstration, we can build a fast Windows program. Drag a text box, a couple of buttons, and a list box onto a form. The text box should be multiline enabled. Change the caption on Button1 to `Process Vendor File`, and on Button2 to `Browse...`. Add the two strings `001` and `002` to the list box. With a pair of labels added, the form should look like Figure 10-3.

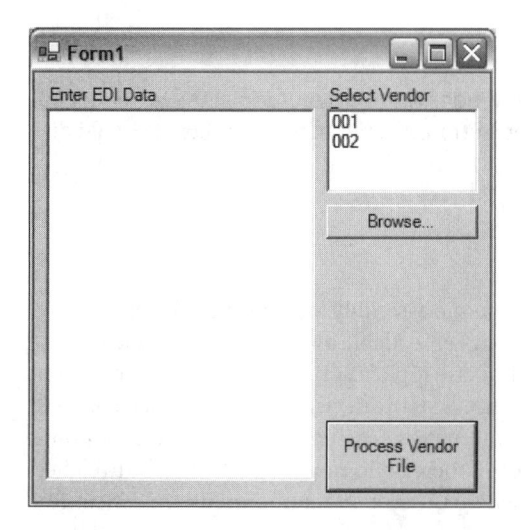

Figure 10-3. *Illustration of the form layout*

Add an `OpenFileDialog` component to the form as well, and switch to code view. We just need to handle clicks on the two buttons. First, the `Browse` button, which we'll use to let the user load a vendor's EDI file into the text box (you can type it in, but a file-based import is useful):

```
Private Sub Button2_Click(ByVal sender As System.Object, _
            ByVal e As System.EventArgs) Handles Button2.Click
  Dim result As DialogResult
  Dim fileReader As System.IO.StreamReader
  result = OpenFileDialog1.ShowDialog()
  If result = DialogResult.OK Then
    fileReader = _
        New System.IO.StreamReader(OpenFileDialog1.FileName)
    TextBox1.Text = fileReader.ReadToEnd
    fileReader.Close()
  End If
End Sub
```

Next, the `Process Vendor File` button, which uses the pipeline system to import the data:

```
Private Sub Button1_Click(ByVal sender As System.Object, _
            ByVal e As System.EventArgs) Handles Button1.Click
  Dim transformer As PipeLineExample1.Transformation
  Dim uploadNotifier As PipeLineExample1.UploadNotify
  Dim xmlDoc As Xml.XmlDocument
  transformer = _
        PipeLineExample1.PipeLineClassFactory.CreateTransform( _
                  ListBox1.SelectedItem)
  xmlDoc = transformer.TransformData(TextBox1.Text)
  uploadNotifier = _
      PipeLineExample1.PipeLineClassFactory.CreateUploadNotify( _
                  ListBox1.SelectedItem, xmlDoc)
  uploadNotifier.ImportData()
  uploadNotifier.RunNotification()
End Sub
```

Now, enter either an XML-formatted file from Vendor 001, or a comma-delimited Vendor 002 file, select the vendor ID from the list, and click the button. A series of message boxes should display showing that processing is progressing.

Summary

By joining the abstract factory pattern concept, dynamic assembly loading, and object creation in VB .NET, a developer can create a highly flexible and extendable application. Dynamic assembly loading allows new assemblies to be loaded into an application, even after the application has been compiled. The abstract factory pattern centralizes the decision logic for which concrete instance of an object should be created given the parameters sent into the factory class. Although these structures add some complexity to the code, this increase in complexity is often outweighed by the flexibility gained, especially in situations where the system requirements are constantly changing.

CHAPTER 11

Attributes

You've seen how reflection allows you to examine objects, determine their type, and access metadata that the compiler places in the compiled type, which tells you the names of its members, the signatures of its methods, and so on. You can discover a great deal about the object, and how to interact with it. This might not be all you want to know about a type, however, especially when you're manipulating it reflectively. You might have a routine that can take any object, and create a dialog box with text boxes that allows you to manipulate its properties; however, some properties might not be suitable for manipulation in this way. How can the programmer of a class let this dialog box code know that a particular property should be ignored? You need to add additional metadata to the type, which the dialog box generator can examine to determine whether or not to add an entry for each property. .NET provides a mechanism for you to add such custom metadata through the system of attributes.

The concept of metadata harkens back to artificial intelligence research in the 1960s and 1970s, when it was first recognized that computers needed to have data about data in order to manipulate it. We've come a long way since then; the .NET Framework relies fundamentally on metadata to load and run applications in the Common Language Runtime (CLR).

Attributes provide a standard and extensible way for .NET programmers to insert additional metadata into their assemblies. This metadata can be inspected by the CLR to determine how to load and run a .NET application, by classes in the .NET Framework to determine how to manipulate objects, and by your own code. There are also attributes that are understood by compilers and that modify the way the code is compiled. Effectively, attributes provide an escape mechanism from the syntax of your chosen programming language, enabling you to provide active information about the assemblies, types, fields, methods, and so on in your code to any other piece of code that is interested in them.

Attributes pave the way for an entirely new style of programming, often referred to as *aspect-oriented programming*. Developers can use attributes to declaratively annotate their assemblies, type definitions, methods, properties, and fields with additional aspects of behavior. For example, you can use attributes to indicate whether transactions are required on a type, whether a method can be invoked as a Web Service method, and whether a particular field is serializable. You can also use attributes to gain direct access to the Windows API, to mark methods as obsolete or conditionally compiled, to control the XML serialization format for objects, and much more.

When you use attributes in your code, the compiler injects *attribute objects* into the compiled MSIL code. These attribute objects inform the code that encounters instances of your types to provide the requested service, without requiring you to write any additional procedural code. For example, if you use an attribute to indicate that a data type requires transactions, and pass an object of this type to a library that provides transaction support for objects that request it, this library will provide the transactional logic on your behalf; you do not need to write any procedural code to create or manage transactions.

So, what exactly is an attribute? An *attribute* is a specialized class that inherits from `System.Attribute` and allows the programmer to attach extra meaning to the code. As we move through this chapter, we'll look at a variety of examples that illustrate how to use existing attribute classes defined in the .NET Framework class library. You'll also see how to define new attribute classes of your own, and discuss why this might be a useful thing to do.

As well as being able to define and use attributes, you can also use reflection to access the attributes defined on an assembly, a type, a method, or a field. For example, you can use reflection to ascertain the version number and title of an assembly, establish whether a type is serializable, determine whether a type is visible to COM clients, and so on. Reflection allows you to write very smart code to interrogate the full capabilities of the coding elements in your application.

Here's a roadmap for the chapter:

- First, we'll introduce the essential syntax for using attributes in VB .NET. You'll see how to annotate a class definition with attributes to inform the world that the class should support a particular feature. As a concrete example, you'll see how to use `SerializableAttribute` to indicate that a class is serializable.

- You'll also see how to use attributes on specific fields within a class. For example, you'll see how to use `NonSerializedAttribute` to exclude specific fields from serialization in a serializable class.

- After we've tackled the syntactic issues, we'll take a detailed look at a variety of existing attribute classes in the .NET Framework class library. For example, you'll see how to use the `ConditionalAttribute` attribute class to define conditionally compiled methods. This enables you to define additional context for your code; for instance, you can clearly differentiate between debug code and release code in an application. This technique can be particularly helpful when you develop large-scale applications, because you don't have to comment out your diagnostic code; you can simply annotate diagnostic code with `ConditionalAttribute`.

- Another important use of attribute classes is to define metadata for an entire assembly. For example, you can define the assembly's name, version, public key token, and culture information. These assembly attributes allow you to create strongly named assemblies, which in turn enables you to insert the assemblies into the global assembly cache. We'll investigate all these issues during the chapter.

- The final section of the chapter discusses the rules for defining new attribute classes, and shows how to use reflection to retrieve the custom attributes defined on a target.

Before we delve into the details, let's take some time out to explore the syntax for defining and using attribute classes.

Understanding Attributes

The best way to understand attributes is to look at some of the existing attribute classes in the .NET Framework class library. Table 11-1 introduces some of the most commonly used attribute classes in .NET.

Table 11-1. *Common .NET Attribute Classes*

Attribute Class Name	Description
System.SerializableAttribute	Marks a type (such as a class or structure) as being serializable. This means the fields in the type can be serialized to SOAP or binary format, to allow instances of this type to be passed across .NET remoting boundaries. If you do not require a type to be serializable, omit this attribute when you define the type; the default behavior is nonserializable.
System.NonSerializedAttribute	When you serialize an instance of a serializable type, all the fields in the instance will be serialized by default. There are some occasions where you might not want to serialize particular fields. For example, there is no point serializing fields that are specific to the original context of execution, such as a thread ID or a window handle obtained from a Win32 API call. To indicate that a specific field in a serializable type should not be serialized, annotate the field with NonSerializedAttribute.
System.Web.Services.WebServiceAttribute	This attribute provides additional information about a Web Service class, such as the XML namespace for the Web Service. By default, VS .NET generates the XML namespace "http://tempuri.org/" for Web service classes.
System.Web.Services.WebMethodAttribute	This attribute indicates that a method in a Web Service class is a Web Service method.
	If you do not annotate a method with this attribute, the method will not be exposed as a Web Service method.
System.Reflection.AssemblyVersionAttribute	This attribute defines a version number for an assembly. This enables applications to bind to a specific version of an assembly. By default, VS .NET generates the version number 1.0.* for each assembly. The * is a wildcard character, which allows the compiler to choose an appropriate build number and revision for the assembly.
System.Diagnostics.ConditionalAttribute	This attribute indicates to the compiler that the method should only be compiled if a particular preprocessor identifier has been defined. Methods that are not annotated with this attribute are always compiled unconditionally.

Notice that all the standard attribute classes in the .NET Framework end with Attribute. This is only a convention, but it's a very strong convention. We'll follow this convention when we define our own custom attribute classes later in this chapter.

Also, each attribute class can be used in conjunction with a particular type (or group of types). For example:

- SerializableAttribute can be applied to classes, structures, enums, and delegates. SerializableAttribute cannot be applied to other kinds of coding elements, such as interfaces, methods, constructors, or fields.

- NonSerializedAttribute can only be applied to fields.

- WebServiceAttribute can only be applied to classes.

- WebMethodAttribute can only be applied to methods.

- AssemblyVersionAttribute can only be applied to assemblies.

- ConditionalAttribute can only be applied to methods.

You should also have spotted that each attribute class is used for a specific purpose. For example:

- `SerializableAttribute` and `NonSerializedAttribute` are used by the CLR to control serialization and deserialization of objects.
- `WebServiceAttribute` and `WebMethodAttribute` are used by ASP.NET to facilitate Web Services.
- `AssemblyVersionAttribute` is used by the CLR to identify which version of an assembly should be loaded.
- `ConditionalAttribute` is used by the compiler to decide whether a method should be compiled or ignored.

Later in the chapter, when we write our own custom attributes, you'll see how to use attributes for your own purposes. It's important to realize, however, that the power of an attribute doesn't come from applying it, but from the code that looks to see if it's there, and changes its behavior accordingly. In other words, coding attributes alone isn't worthwhile without also coding a method that looks for them and varies its actions accordingly.

Obviously, many of the methods developed by the Microsoft developers who created the .NET framework classes use attributes.

Syntax for Using Attributes

To illustrate the syntax for using attributes, we'll look at a simple VB .NET application that defines a serializable class named `Account`. The application will create an `Account` object and serialize it to an XML document in the Simple Object Access Protocol (SOAP) format.

Note SOAP is an XML-based protocol for invoking methods across the Internet, and for passing simple and structured data as parameters and return values for these methods. SOAP is defined by the World Wide Web Consortium (W3C). The latest version of SOAP, version 1.2, is currently still at the Working Draft stage at the time of writing; for a very readable introduction, see `http://www.w3c.org/TR/soap12-part0/`.

Our sample application also shows how to deserialize SOAP data held in an XML document to reconstitute the `Account` object in memory. You can download the source code for this example from `ch05\SerializationDemo.vb` in the Downloads section of the Apress Web site for this book.

To kick off, the application requires three `Imports` statements as follows:

```
Imports System
Imports System.IO
Imports System.Runtime.Serialization.Formatters.Soap
```

These three namespaces provide the following functionality:

- The System namespace contains the SerializableAttribute and NonSerializedAttribute classes, which we'll use to specify the serialization capabilities of our Account class.
- The System.IO namespace contains the standard file I/O classes in .NET.
- The System.Runtime.Serialization.Formatters.Soap namespace contains the SoapFormatter class, which we'll use to perform the serialization and deserialization of our Account object.

Now let's define the Account class as a serializable class. Here is the code for the class, with the serialization aspects highlighted:

```
<SerializableAttribute()> _
Public Class Account

  ' These fields will be serialized
  Private mName As String
  Private mBalance As Double

  ' This (rather contrived) field will not be serialized
  <NonSerializedAttribute()> _
  Private mMachineName As String

  ' Constructor
  Public Sub New(ByVal Name As String)
    mName = Name
    mBalance = 0.0
  End Sub

  ' Deposit funds
  Public Sub Deposit(ByVal Amount As Double)
    mBalance += Amount
  End Sub

  ' Withdraw funds
  Public Sub Withdraw(ByVal Amount As Double)
    mBalance -= Amount
  End Sub

  ' Property to get the machine name (lazy initialization)
  Public ReadOnly Property MachineName() As String
    Get
      If mMachineName Is Nothing Then
        mMachineName = Environment.MachineName
      End If
      Return mMachineName
    End Get
  End Property
```

```
    ' Return object's state as a string
    Public Overrides Function ToString() As String
        Return mName & ", $" & mBalance & ", machine name " & MachineName
    End Function
End Class
```

Note the following points in the `Account` class:

- The `Account` class is annotated with the `<SerializableAttribute()>` attribute, which means `Account` is a serializable class. The angled brackets `<>` are VB .NET syntax for an attribute block.

Note Visual C# and Managed Extensions for C++ use square brackets rather than angled brackets for attribute blocks. For example, the syntax for using `SerializableAttribute` in these languages is `[SerializableAttribute]`.

- An attribute block can contain any number of attributes separated by commas. In the preceding `Account` example, we've just defined a single attribute, `SerializableAttribute`. In the following example, we use a pair of attributes to indicate the class is both serializable and transactional:

```
Imports System                          ' For SerializableAttribute class
Imports System.EnterpriseServices       ' For TransactionAttribute class

<SerializableAttribute(),TransactionAttribute()> _
Public Class MyAwesomeClass
    ' Members ...
End Class
```

- The empty parentheses () after an attribute declaration indicate that the attribute doesn't require any initialization arguments. Later in the chapter, you'll see examples of attributes that do require initialization arguments in the parentheses.

- The `mMachineName` field in our `Account` class is annotated with `<NonSerializedAttribute()>`, which means `mMachineName` should be ignored when `Account` objects are serialized and deserialized. The purpose of the `mMachineName` field is to hold the name of the local computer; this field is initialized the first time it is requested in the `MachineName` property procedure. There is no point in serializing this field, because chances are the object will be deserialized on a different computer. For example, if you pass an `Account` object to a remoting application, the object will be serialized on your computer and then deserialized on the server computer (which has a different name).

- The `Account` class has additional methods, a constructor, and a `MachineName` property procedure, to provide simple bank account functionality.

> **Note** When using attributes, VB .NET allows you to omit the `Attribute` part at the end of attribute names. For example, you can specify `<Serializable()>` rather than `<SerializableAttribute()>`. The class is still named `SerializableAttribute`, it's just that when you use the attribute, the compiler allows you to use the abbreviated name, `Serializable`. When using attributes, it's common practice to use the abbreviated syntax rather than the full attribute name, so we'll adopt this approach from now on in this chapter.

Let's continue with our sample application, located in `SerializationDemo.vb`. The following code shows how to serialize an `Account` object to SOAP format using a `SoapFormatter` object; the serialized data is written to an XML file named `AccountData.xml`. The example also shows how to deserialize the data from this XML file to recreate an `Account` object in memory:

```
Public Class TestSerialization

  Public Shared Sub Main()
    MySerialize("AccountData.xml")
    MyDeserialize("AccountData.xml")
  End Sub

  Public Shared Sub MySerialize(ByVal FileName As String)
      ' Create an Account object, and perform some transactions
      Dim acc1 As New Account("Jayne")
      acc1.Deposit(3000)
      acc1.Withdraw(1000)
      Console.WriteLine("Object state: {0}", acc1)
       ' Use a SoapFormatter to serialize the Account object
      Dim stream As FileStream = File.Create(FileName)
      Dim formatter As New SoapFormatter()
      Console.Write("Serializing object... ")
      formatter.Serialize(stream, acc1)
      stream.Close()
      Console.WriteLine("done.")
  End Sub

  Private Shared Sub MyDeserialize(ByVal FileName As String)
       ' Use a SoapFormatter to deserialize data
      Dim stream As FileStream = File.OpenRead(FileName)
      Dim formatter As New SoapFormatter()
      Console.Write("Deserializing object... ")
      Dim acc1 As Account = CType(formatter.Deserialize(stream), _
                          Account)
      stream.Close()
       Console.WriteLine("done.")
      Console.WriteLine("Object state: {0}", acc1)
    End Sub
End Class
```

> **Note** The .NET Framework also allows you to serialize objects in binary format using the `BinaryFormatter` class rather than `SoapFormatter`. Binary serialization is more memory-efficient than SOAP serialization, which can be an important issue if you want to pass objects to remote methods across a network. However, note that binary serialization only works if the recipient application is written in .NET, because binary serialization uses a proprietary format that is only recognized by .NET applications. To use binary serialization, import the namespace `System.Runtime.Serialization.Formatters.Binary`, and replace all occurrences of `SoapFormatter` in the code with `BinaryFormatter`.

To examine the metadata for the application, navigate a command-prompt window to the directory containing the compiled code, and type the following command to run the MSIL Disassembler. The `/adv` switch runs the MSIL Disassembler in advanced mode, which offers a great deal of additional information about the compiled code:

> `ildasm /adv SerializationDemo.exe`

The MSIL Disassembler window displays the information in Figure 11-1 for the Account class.

Figure 11-1. *The MSIL Disassembler window displaying information from the* account *class*

Notice the following points in the MSIL Disassembler window:

- The `Account` class is qualified as `serializable` because we annotated this class with `<SerializableAttribute()>` in our code.

- The `mMachineName` field is qualified as `notserialized` because we annotated this field with `<NonSerializedAttribute()>` in our code.

To obtain more detailed metadata, select the menu command View ➤ MetaInfo ➤ Show! in the MSIL Disassembler window. Another window appears displaying the information shown in Figure 11-2. The relevant parts are highlighted.

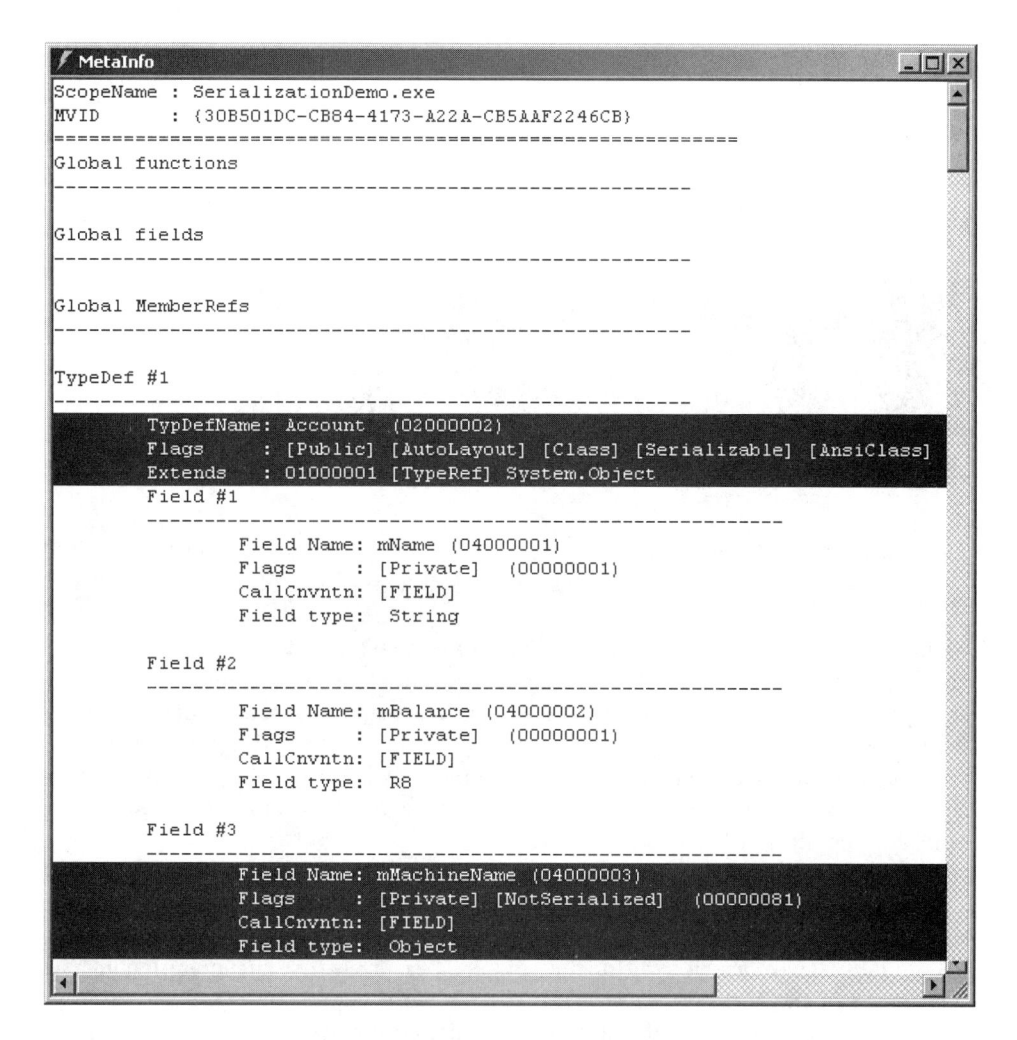

```
  MetaInfo                                                          _ □ ×
ScopeName : SerializationDemo.exe
MVID      : {30B501DC-CB84-4173-A22A-CB5AAF2246CB}
=============================================================
Global functions
-------------------------------------------------------------

Global fields
-------------------------------------------------------------

Global MemberRefs
-------------------------------------------------------------

TypeDef #1
-------------------------------------------------------------
        TypDefName: Account    (02000002)
        Flags     : [Public] [AutoLayout] [Class] [Serializable] [AnsiClass]
        Extends   : 01000001 [TypeRef] System.Object
        Field #1
        -------------------------------------------------
                Field Name: mName  (04000001)
                Flags     : [Private]    (00000001)
                CallCnvntn: [FIELD]
                Field type: String

        Field #2
        -------------------------------------------------
                Field Name: mBalance (04000002)
                Flags     : [Private]    (00000001)
                CallCnvntn: [FIELD]
                Field type: R8

        Field #3
        -------------------------------------------------
                Field Name: mMachineName (04000003)
                Flags     : [Private] [NotSerialized]   (00000081)
                CallCnvntn: [FIELD]
                Field type: Object
```

Figure 11-2. *Detailed metadata accessed through the MSIL Dissassembler window*

Notice the following points:

- The metadata for the Account class includes the [Serializable] flag to indicate to the CLR that this is a serializable class. Later in this section, we'll show how to use reflection to interrogate an object for its attributes.

- The metadata for the mMachineName field includes the [NotSerialized] flag to indicate to the CLR that this field should not be serialized or deserialized.

It's worth noting here that the serialization capabilities of our type are listed under the heading of Flags, along with such information as the accessibility modifier (Private or Public). These are all regarded as "standard attributes" in .NET, and obviously we apply many of them using language keywords. Where the language doesn't provide a keyword (note VB .NET's lack of a Serializable keyword) .NET provides an attribute, which the compiler interprets, inserting the appropriate flags into the IL metadata.

Custom attributes such as those we write, many of which are also defined in the .NET class libraries, are included in the metadata but inside a slightly different flag.

To run the application, type the following command:

> **SerializationDemo.exe**

The application displays the messages on the console as shown in Figure 11-3.

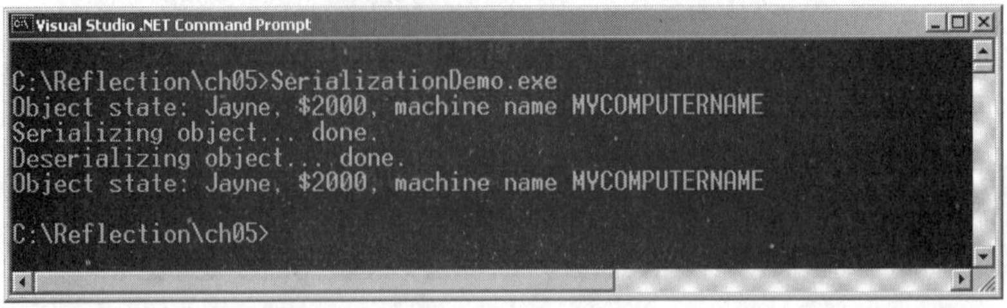

Figure 11-3. *Messages displayed when running* SerializationDemo.exe *on the console*

The first two messages on the console indicate the initial state of the object, before it is serialized to the XML document. The final two messages indicate the state of the object that is deserialized from the XML document. Note that the machine name information isn't serialized or deserialized; when we display the MachineName property using the deserialized object, the machine name is recalculated on the current machine. Our sample application serializes and deserializes the data on the same machine, so we happen to see the same machine name (MYCOMPUTERNAME) before and after serialization.

To prove that the machine name information isn't serialized, open AccountData.xml in Internet Explorer. AccountData.xml is a SOAP document. SOAP documents begin with a <SOAP-ENV:Envelope> root element, and have a <SOAP-ENV:Body> element containing the actual information. We won't discuss the SOAP-related content of the document here, because we're more interested in .NET attributes than SOAP nuances.

Notice the following points inside the <SOAP-ENV:Body> element:

- The <a1:Account> element contains the serialized data for our Account object. a1 is a namespace prefix for the following namespace URL, which specifies details for the assembly that contains the Account class. We'll see how to use .NET attributes to specify an assembly's name, version, culture, and public key token later in this chapter. The CLR uses this information during deserialization to identify the assembly in which the Account class is defined. This enables the runtime to load the required assembly into memory to gain access to the Account class definition:

    ```
    "http://schemas.microsoft.com/clr/assem/SerializationDemo%2C%20
    Version%3D0.0.0.0%2C%20Culture%3Dneutral%2C%20PublicKeyToken
    %3Dnull"
    ```

- The <Account> element has an id="ref-1" XML attribute. When you serialize a reference-type object, such as an instance of the Account class, the serialization mechanism generates a unique ID number for the object. Each time you perform serialization, every serialized object has a unique ID within the serialized document. This enables you to serialize objects that contain reference to other objects; the serialization mechanism uses the object's ID numbers to remember which objects refer to which other objects.

- The <Account> element has child elements named <mName> and <mBalance>, which contain the values of the serializable fields in the Account object. Notice that <mName> has a reference number, because the mName field is a reference type (String); however, <mBalance> does not have a reference number because the mBalance field is a value type (double).

- The serialized document does not have an element named <mMachineName> because we annotated the mMachineName field with the <NonSerializedAttribute()> .NET attribute.

Testing a Data Type for Standard Attributes

As we've just shown in the previous section, the <Serializable()> attribute marks a type as serializable. When you try to serialize an object in the application, the CLR inspects the metadata for the object's type to see if the type is serializable. If you try to serialize an unserializable type, the runtime will detect this error condition and throw a System.Runtime.Serialization.SerializationException.

Serializability is, as we said, one of .NET's standard attributes, and as such, you can discover if an object is serializable using a special mechanism that tells all the standard attributes defined for a type. The .NET Framework defines an enumeration type named System.Reflection.TypeAttributes, which you can use to determine the standard attributes that were compiled into the type. TypeAttributes yields an integer value, and uses combinations of bits to indicate various pieces of information about a data type. Table 11-2 describes some of the 29 enumeration values defined in TypeAttributes ; for a comprehensive list, see TypeAttributes enumeration in VS .NET Help.

Table 11-2. *Enumeration Values in* TypeAttributes

TypeAttributes Enumeration	Description
Abstract	Indicates the type is an abstract class, which means you cannot create instances of this class type
Class	Indicates the type is a class, rather than an interface
Interface	Indicates the type is an interface
Serializable	Indicates the type is serializable

■**Note** It's also possible to define custom attribute classes, as you'll see later in this chapter. You can use reflection to test for the presence of custom attributes, including predefined custom attributes (such as WebServiceAttribute) and custom attributes that you've written. To test for custom attributes, call the GetCustomAttribute() or GetCustomAttributes() methods defined in the System.Attribute class and the System.Reflection.MemberInfo class. We'll show how to do this later in the chapter

The following example shows how to test for standard .NET attributes on a data type. We'll show the code listing first, and then discuss the important issues afterward. You can download the source code for this example from ch05\ ExamineStandardAttributes.vb in the Downloads section of the Apress Web site (http://www.apress.com).

```vb
Imports System                    ' For SerializableAttribute class
Imports System.Reflection         ' For TypeAttributes enumeration
Imports System.IO                 ' For file I/O classes
Imports System.Runtime.Serialization.Formatters.Soap    ' SoapFormatter

' ----------------------------------------------------------------------
' This is a serializable class
' ----------------------------------------------------------------------
<Serializable()> _
Public Class MySerializableClass

  Private mData As Integer        ' Some sample data

  Public Sub New(ByVal Data As Integer)
    mData = Data
  End Sub

  Public Overrides Function ToString() As String
    Return "mData is " & mData
  End Function

End Class

' ----------------------------------------------------------------------
' This is not a serializable class
' ----------------------------------------------------------------------
Public Class MyUnserializableClass

  Private mOtherData As String  ' Some sample data

  Public Sub New(ByVal OtherData As String)
    mOtherData = OtherData
  End Sub

  Public Overrides Function ToString() As String
    Return "mOtherData is " & mOtherData
  End Function

End Class
```

```vbnet
' --------------------------------------------------------------
' This is the main class in the application
' --------------------------------------------------------------
Public Class MyMainClass

   Public Shared Sub Main()

      MySerialize( New MySerializableClass(42),         "File1.xml" )
      MySerialize( New MySerializableClass(97),         "File2.xml" )
      MySerialize( New MyUnserializableClass("Hello"), "File3.xml" )
      MySerialize( New MyUnserializableClass("World"), "File4.xml" )

   End Sub

   Public Shared Sub MySerialize(ByVal theObject As Object, _
                                 ByVal FileName As String)

      ' Get the Type object for the object
      Dim theType As Type = theObject.GetType()

      ' Get the standard attributes defined on this type
      Dim attributes As TypeAttributes = theType.Attributes

      ' Test if this type has the Serializable attribute
      If (attributes And TypeAttributes.Serializable) <> 0 Then

         Console.Write("{0} is a serializable type. ", theType.FullName)

         Dim stream As FileStream = File.Create(FileName)
         Dim formatter As New SoapFormatter()
         formatter.Serialize(stream, theObject)
         stream.Close()
         Console.WriteLine("Serialized object: {0}", theObject)

      Else
         Console.WriteLine("{0} is NOT a serializable type", _
                           theType.FullName)
      End If
   End Sub
End Class
```

Notice the following points in this sample application:

- The application defines two classes: MySerializableClass is a serializable class, but MyUnserializableClass is not.

- In the Main() method in the application, we create some instances of each class, and pass these instances into the MySerialize() method.

- The `MySerialize()` method is declared with an argument type of `Object`, which means it is able to accept any kind of object as an argument. Inside the method, we get the `Type` object associated with this object's type as follows:

  ```
  Dim theType As Type = theObject.GetType()
  ```

- The `Type` class has an `Attributes` property, which allows you to get a list of all the attributes defined for the type. The CLR inspects the type's metadata, and returns a `TypeAttributes` enumeration value that lists the attributes for the type:

  ```
  Dim attributes As TypeAttributes = theType.Attributes
  ```

- We test the attribute list to see if it includes the `<Serializable()>` attribute. `TypeAttributes` uses bit fields to represent allowable combinations of attributes, so we use a bitwise `And` to test if the `TypeAttributes.Serializable` bits are set:

  ```
  If (attributes And TypeAttributes.Serializable) <> 0 Then
  ```

Note `TypeAttributes` is an enumeration value, not a collection. The only way to use a `TypeAttributes` value is to test for explicit attributes, as we've done in the example. It is not possible to iterate through all the attributes that are defined on a type.

- If the `TypeAttributes.Serializable` bits are set, this indicates that the data type is serializable. In this case, we serialize the object to SOAP format as in the earlier example in this chapter. We also use the `FullName` property on the `Type` object to display the full type name (namespace plus classname) of the object:

  ```
  Console.Write("{0} is a serializable type. ", theType.FullName)

  Dim stream As FileStream = File.Create(FileName)
  Dim formatter As New SoapFormatter()
  formatter.Serialize(stream, theObject)
  stream.Close()
  Console.WriteLine("Serialized object: {0}", theObject)
  ```

- If the `TypeAttributes.Serializable` bits are not set, this indicates the data type is not serializable. If we tried to serialize this object, we would get a `SerializationException`. To avoid this outcome, we display an error message on the console instead:

  ```
  Console.WriteLine("{0} is NOT a serializable type", _
                    theType.FullName)
  ```

  When run, the application displays the messages on the console as shown in Figure 11-4.

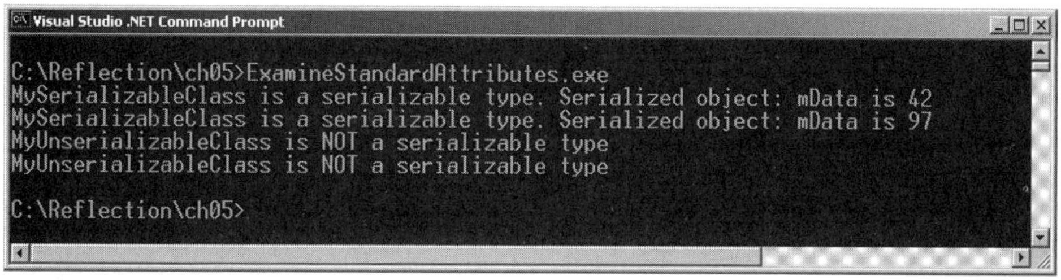

Figure 11-4. ExamineStandardAttributes.exe *displaying output on the console*

The first two messages on the console indicate the first two objects are serializable. The final two messages indicate the third and fourth objects are not serializable.

This example has shown how to use the `TypeAttributes` enumeration to test whether a data type has the `<Serializable()>` attribute. It is also possible to test for other standard .NET attributes, as illustrated in the following code snippet. This is not an exhaustive example; for a complete list of standard attributes that you can test, see `TypeAttributes Enumeration` in VS .NET Help.

```
' Is this type an interface?
If (attributes And TypeAttributes.Interface) = _
                TypeAttributes.Interface Then
  Console.WriteLine("{0} is an interface type", theType.FullName)
End If


' Is this type a public type?
If (attributes And TypeAttributes.Public) = _
                TypeAttributes.Public Then
  Console.WriteLine("{0} is a public type", theType.FullName)
End If


' Is this type an auto-layout type?
If (attributes And TypeAttributes.AutoLayout) = _
                TypeAttributes.AutoLayout Then
  Console.WriteLine("{0} is an auto-layout type", theType.FullName)
End If
```

Using Predefined .NET Attributes

In this section, we'll take a detailed look at several predefined attributes in the .NET class library. We'll present a variety of examples that will help you understand attribute syntax, and give you an appreciation of the wide range of tasks you can achieve using attributes. Here is a list of the examples in this section:

- We'll begin by explaining the essential syntax for attribute classes. We'll describe how to determine whether an attribute is applicable for classes, methods, fields, or some other kind of coding element. We'll also describe how to find out whether an attribute requires any mandatory or optional arguments, and show how to provide these arguments.

- After we've described the syntactic issues, we'll show how to use the <Conditional()> attribute to mark a method as conditionally compiled, depending on whether a preprocessor identifier has been defined.

- The final example shows how to define attributes for an entire assembly. We'll show how to specify assembly information such as a title, description, copyright information, and so on.

Understanding Attribute Class Definitions

To use attributes effectively, it's essential that you understand the basic syntax of attribute class definitions. You also need to know whether (and how) to pass arguments into an attribute when you use it.

Understanding Attribute Class Syntax

As mentioned earlier in the chapter, attribute classes inherit from System.Attribute, and all the predefined attribute classes in .NET end with the word Attribute. There are two additional restrictions for attribute classes:

- Attribute classes must not be declared as MustInherit. In other words, an attribute class must be a concrete class, not an abstract class.

- Attribute classes must be preceded by an <AttributeUsage()> attribute, which indicates whether the attribute applies to a class, a method, a field, or some other coding element.

We can also use <AttributeUsage()> to specify two additional characteristics for an attribute:

- We can define whether the attribute can be used multiple times on the same coding element. For example, later in the chapter we'll define an attribute class named AuthorAttribute, which we'll use to identify the author of a class. We'll allow AuthorAttribute to be used multiple times on the same class, because some classes have multiple authors.

- We can also define whether the attribute can be inherited by subclasses. For example, we'll indicate that AuthorAttribute is not inherited by subclasses, because the author of the subclass might be different from the author of the original class.

To illustrate these rules, let's take a closer look at the <Serializable()> attribute we used earlier in the chapter. As you'll recall, you can use the <Serializable()> attribute to indicate that a class (or structure, enumerated type, or delegate) is serializable. Figure 11-5 shows the VS .NET Help screen for the <Serializable()> attribute; to obtain this help screen, type **SerializableAttribute class, about** SerializableAttribute class in the VS .NET Help Index field.

```
SerializableAttribute Class
▶ ☑ ▼ .NET Framework Class Library
SerializableAttribute Class [Visual Basic]
Indicates that a class can be serialized. This class cannot be inherited.
For a list of all members of this type, see SerializableAttribute Members.
System.Object
   System.Attribute
      System.SerializableAttribute

      <AttributeUsage(AttributeTargets.Class Or AttributeTargets.Struct _
         Or AttributeTargets.Enum Or AttributeTargets.Delegate)>
      NotInheritable Public Class SerializableAttribute
         Inherits Attribute
```

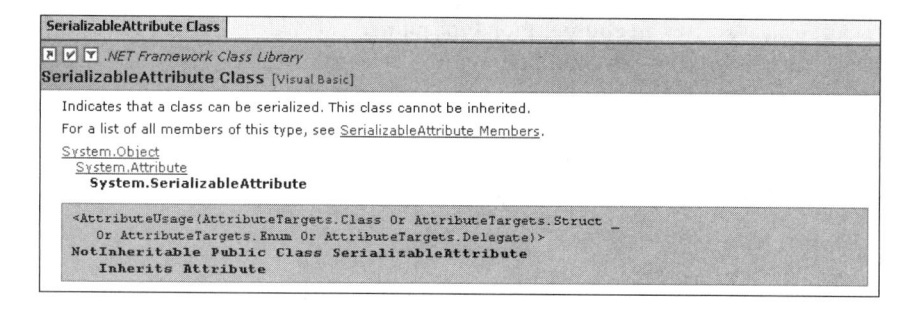

Figure 11-5. *Visual Studio .NET 2003 help screen for the* Serializable() *attribute*

Notice the following points in Figure 11-5:

- The class SerializableAttribute is defined in the System namespace. Later in the chapter, you'll see many examples of attributes that are defined in different namespaces. In this respect, attribute classes are just like normal classes; they are defined in whichever namespace makes the most sense.

- SerializableAttribute inherits from System.Attribute. All attribute classes inherit from System.Attribute.

- SerializableAttribute is not declared as MustInherit, which means it is a concrete class. However, notice that SerializableAttribute is declared as NotInheritable, which means it is a sealed class; we cannot derive new subclasses from SerializableAttribute. This is a particular facet of the SerializableAttribute class; there is no intrinsic .NET requirement for attribute classes to be declared as NotInheritable.

Note The fact that SerializableAttribute is NotInheritable indicates that this attribute class has not been designed for extension through inheritance. The designers and authors of SerializableAttribute at Microsoft have decided that this class is already complete, and there are no situations where a specialized subclass might be necessary.

- The SerializableAttribute class definition is preceded by an <AttributeUsage()> attribute, which specifies where and how the <Serializable()> attribute can be used. The <AttributeUsage()> attribute for <Serializable()> is defined as follows:

    <AttributeUsage(AttributeTargets.Class Or AttributeTargets.Struct _
        Or AttributeTargets.Enum Or AttributeTargets.Delegate)>

    - This indicates that the <Serializable()> attribute can be applied to class types, structures types, enumeration types, and delegate types. In other words, it is possible to serialize class objects, structure objects, enumeration objects, and delegate objects.

- `<AttributeUsage()>` uses an enumeration type named `AttributeTargets` to specify the allowable targets for an attribute. For example, `AttributeTargets.Class` indicates an attribute can be applied to class definitions, `AttributeTargets.Struct` indicates an attribute can be applied to structure definitions, and so on. Table 11-3 shows a complete list of `AttributeTargets` values; these can be bitwise-Or'd together, as shown in the preceding example, to specify multiple target types.

Table 11-3. *Values of* `AttributeTargets`

AttributeTargets Enumeration	Description and example
AttributeTargets.All	The attribute in question can be applied to any coding element. An example of an attribute with this usage is `<CLSCompliant()>`, which indicates a coding element complies with the rules defined in the .NET common language specification.
AttributeTargets.Assembly	The attribute in question can be applied to an assembly. An example of an attribute with this usage is `<AssemblyVersion()>`, which specifies the version number for an assembly.
AttributeTargets.Class	The attribute in question can be applied to a class. An example of an attribute with this usage is `<WebService()>`, which specifies information about Web Service classes.
AttributeTargets.Constructor	The attribute in question can be applied to a constructor. An example of an attribute with this usage is `<FileIOPermission()>`. We can annotate constructors with this attribute, to indicate that the code in the constructor uses declarative security checks when accessing files in the file system. You can also use `<FileIOPermission()>` on assemblies, classes, structures, and methods.
AttributeTargets.Delegate	The attribute in question can be applied to a delegate. An example of an attribute with this usage is `<ComVisible()>`, which specifies whether a .NET delegate should be made visible to COM when you export a .NET component to COM clients. You can also use `<ComVisible()>` to specify COM visibility for .NET assemblies, classes, structures, enums, fields, methods, properties, and interfaces.
AttributeTargets.Enum	The attribute in question can be applied to an enumeration. An example of an attribute with this usage is `<Obsolete()>`, which specifies that an enumeration is obsolete. You can also use `<Obsolete()>` to mark classes, structures, interfaces, constructors, methods, properties, fields, events, and delegates as obsolete.
AttributeTargets.Event	The attribute in question can be applied to an event. An example of an attribute with this usage is `<DispId()>`, which specifies the COM DispId of an event. You can also use `<DispId()>` to specify the COM DispId of methods, properties, and fields.
AttributeTargets.Field	The attribute in question can be applied to a field. An example of an attribute with this usage is `<NonSerialized()>`, which indicates that a particular field in a serializable class should not be serialized.

AttributeTargets Enumeration	Description and example
AttributeTargets.Interface	The attribute in question can be applied to an interface. An example of an attribute with this usage is `<InterfaceType()>`, which we can use when exporting a .NET interface to COM. The attribute indicates whether the interface should be exposed as a dual interface, an IDispatch-based interface, or an IUnknown-based interface.
AttributeTargets.Method	The attribute in question can be applied to a method. An example of an attribute with this usage is `<WebMethod()>`, which indicates that a method is a Web Service method.
AttributeTargets.Module	The attribute in question can be applied to a module (that is, a DLL or EXE file that comprises a multifile assembly). An example of an attribute with this usage is `<Debuggable()>`, which indicates that a module supports just-in-time debugging. You can also use `<Debuggable()>` on assemblies.
AttributeTargets.Parameter	The attribute in question can be applied to a parameter. An example of an attribute with this usage is `<ParamArray()>`, which specifies that a method allows a variable number of parameters to be passed in. The parameters will be delivered to the method as an array.
AttributeTargets.Property	The attribute in question can be applied to a property. An example of an attribute with this usage is `<IndexerName()>`, which specifies the name of the indexer method in a class, for the benefit of programming languages that do not directly provide special syntax for indexers.
AttributeTargets.ReturnValue	The attribute in question can be applied to a return value from a method or property. An example of an attribute with this usage is `<XmlElement()>`. This attribute can be used (among other reasons) to specify the allowable types of elements in an array when a method returns an array of objects. This information is required by the XML serializer, so that it knows what data types to expect in the returned array.
AttributeTargets.Struct	The attribute in question can be applied to a structure. An example of an attribute with this usage is `<StructLayout()>`, which specifies a particular layout for fields in a structure. This is important when you pass structures to unmanaged APIs, because the unmanaged API usually expects a particular layout for fields in the structure. You can also use `<StructLayout()>` on classes.

Passing Arguments into Attributes

Another important characteristic of attributes is whether they require any arguments. The `<Serializable()>` attribute is a fairly simple example, because it doesn't require any arguments at all; when we use `<Serializable()>` to mark a class as serializable, we don't need to pass any extra information in the attribute's parentheses:

```
<Serializable()> _    ' No need to pass any arguments between the ()
Public Class Account
  ' Members...
End Class
```

However, many attributes do require arguments to provide supporting information for the attribute. There are two kinds of arguments for attributes:

- **Positional arguments**: These arguments are mandatory, and must be supplied in a specific order at the beginning of the attribute's argument list. Positional arguments are passed into the attribute's constructor to perform essential initialization for the attribute. To find out what positional arguments are required for an attribute, consult the documentation for the attribute's constructor(s).

    - The following example illustrates positional arguments. The example shows how to use `<DllImport()>` to expose the `MessageBeep()` Win32 API to a .NET application. The `DllImportAttribute` constructor takes a single `String` parameter, which indicates the name of the DLL that contains the Win32 API. The `MessageBeep()` API resides in `User32.dll`, so we specify the parameter `"User32.dll"` in the `<DllImport()>` attribute:

        ```
        <DllImport("User32.dll")> _
        Public Shared Function MessageBeep(type As Integer) As Boolean
            ' Leave function empty: this is just a wrapper for the Win32 API
        End Function
        ```

- **Named arguments**: These arguments are optional, and can be supplied in any order after the positional arguments in the attribute's argument list. Named arguments correspond to the names of fields or properties in the attribute class. You must use := syntax to assign a value to a named argument.

    - The following example illustrates named arguments. The example shows how to use `<DllImport()>` to expose the `MessageBox()` Win32 API to .NET. The `DllImportAttribute` class has properties named `CharSet` and `EntryPoint` (among others), which allow us to provide supplemental information about the API we want to expose:

        ```
        <DllImport("User32.dll", _
                   CharSet := CharSet.Unicode, _
                   EntryPoint := "MessageBoxW")> _
        Public Shared Function MessageBox(hWnd As IntPtr, _
                                          text As String, _
                                          caption As String, _
                                          type As Integer) As Integer
            ' Leave function empty: this is just a wrapper for the Win32 API
        End Function
        ```

Note For more information about the `<DllImport()>` attribute and the `MessageBox()` Win32 API, see VS .NET Help.

To further illustrate the rules for positional and named arguments in an attribute, we'll consider the `TransactionAttribute` class defined in the `System.EnterpriseServices` namespace. `TransactionAttribute` can be used to specify automatic transactional support for a .NET class, and to write .NET code that integrates easily with COM+ transactions and database transactions.

The `TransactionAttribute` class has two constructors, with the following signatures:

```
' No-arg constructor for the TransactionAttribute class,
' which sets the automatic transaction type to "required".
Public Sub New()

' One-arg constructor for the TransactionAttribute class, which allows
' us to choose the level of automatic transaction support we need.
Public Sub New(ByVal Val As TransactionOption)
```

The following code snippet shows how to use the first constructor in a `<Transaction()>` attribute. The compiler calls the `TransactionAttribute` no-argument constructor, which sets the transaction type to "required" for `MyClass1`:

```
<Transaction()> _
Public Class MyClass1
  ' Members...
End Class
```

The next code snippet shows how to use the parameterized constructor in a `<Transaction()>` attribute. The compiler calls the second `TransactionAttribute` constructor listed previously, and passes `TransactionOption.RequiresNew` as a parameter. This sets the transaction type to "requires new" for `MyClass2`, which means the runtime is obliged to create a new transaction whenever a `MyClass2` object is created:

```
<Transaction(TransactionOption.RequiresNew)> _
Public Class MyClass2
  ' Members...
End Class
```

In addition to the constructors defined in the `TransactionAttribute` class, there are also two public get/set properties as follows:

```
' Get or set the transaction isolation level
Public Property Isolation As TransactionIsolationLevel
  Get
    ' Get the isolation level defined by this TransactionAttribute
  End Get
  Set(ByVal Value As TransactionIsolationLevel)
    ' Set the isolation level for this TransactionAttribute
  End Set
End Property

' Get or set the transaction timeout value
Public Property Timeout As Integer
  Get
    ' Get the timeout defined by this TransactionAttribute
  End Get
  Set(ByVal Value As Integer)
    ' Set the timeout for this TransactionAttribute
  End Set
End Property
```

We can use these properties to provide optional additional initialization when we use the `<Transaction()>` attribute.

The following example shows how to use these properties in conjunction with the no-argument constructor for `TransactionAttribute`. In this example, we indicate that `MyClass3` has the "repeatable read" isolation level, which means that data in a database is locked during a SQL query operation. The transaction timeout is set to 10 seconds, which means each transactional operation must complete in this time span:

```
<Transaction(Isolation := TransactionIsolationLevel.RepeatableRead, _
            Timeout := 10)> _
Public Class MyClass3
  ' Members...
End Class
```

The order of property assignments is insignificant, providing the property assignments come after any constructor arguments. The following example shows how to combine constructor arguments and optional property assignments in an attribute declaration. The constructor argument comes first, followed by the property assignments; note that constructor arguments do not have a name as such, so we do not use the syntax name := value for constructor arguments:

```
<Transaction(TransactionOption.RequiresNew,   _
            Isolation := TransactionIsolationLevel.RepeatableRead, _
            Timeout := 10)> _
Public Class MyClass4
  ' Members...
End Class
```

Now that we've described the meaning of the syntax in attribute class definitions, and you've seen how to pass mandatory and optional arguments into attribute declarations, let's embark on a series of examples that will give you a flavor of the diverse use of attributes in .NET. After we've done that, we'll see how to define and use new custom attribute classes of our own.

Using Attributes to Control the Compiler

In this example, you'll see how to use the `<Conditional()>` attribute to mark a method as conditionally compiled. Calls to the method will only be compiled if a specified preprocessor identifier is defined; if the identifier is not defined, the VB .NET compiler will ignore calls to the method in the code. By using the `<Conditional()>` attribute, you don't need to comment out the diagnostic code for a release version of the application. Thus attributes enable you to give "context" to the code; which is very convenient and a major boost to developer efficiency, particularly when you have a very large and complex application that may span many versions and had a multitude of developers working on it.

The following application shows a typical use of the `<Conditional()>` attribute, to display diagnostic information about the current state of an object. You can download the source code for this example from ch05\ ConditionalCompilation.vb in the Downloads section of the Apress Web site (http://www.apress.com).

In this example, we define an `Account` class that represents a simple bank account; the class keeps track of the current balance, and uses an `ArrayList` to record every deposit and withdrawal. The `Deposit()` and `Withdraw()` methods call a diagnostic method named `MyDumpStatus()` to display the current state of the `Account` object before performing deposit or withdrawal operations.

This information will help verify that the `Account` object is in a valid state before the operation takes place. The `MyDumpStatus()` method is annotated with the `<Conditional("Debug")>` attribute, which means method invocations will only be compiled if the `Debug` preprocessor identifier is defined:

```vb
Imports System                          ' For Console and String classes
Imports System.Collections              ' For ArrayList class
Imports System.Diagnostics  ' For Conditional attribute
Public Class Account

  ' Fields
  Private mName As String
  Private mBalance As Double
  Private mActivity As ArrayList

  ' Constructor
  Public Sub New(ByVal Name As String)
    mName = Name
    mBalance = 0.0
    mActivity = new ArrayList()
  End Sub

  ' Deposit funds
  Public Sub Deposit(ByVal Amount As Double)
    MyDumpStatus( String.Format("About to deposit {0:C}", Amount) )
    mBalance += Amount
    mActivity.Add(Amount)
  End Sub

  ' Withdraw funds
  Public Sub Withdraw(ByVal Amount As Double)
    MyDumpStatus( String.Format("About to withdraw {0:C}", Amount) )
    mBalance -= Amount
    mActivity.Add(-Amount)
  End Sub

  ' Return object's state as a string
  Public Overrides Function ToString() As String
    Return String.Format("{0}, {1:C}", mName, mBalance)
  End Function

  ' Calls to this method will only be compiled if "Debug" is defined
  <Conditional("Debug")> _
  Public Sub MyDumpStatus(ByVal Message As String)

    Console.WriteLine("-----------------------------------------")
    Console.WriteLine("MyDump STATUS: {0}", Message)
    Console.WriteLine("-----------------------------------------")
```

```vbnet
      Console.WriteLine("Name {0}, balance {1:C}", mName, mBalance)
      Dim index As Integer
      For index = 0 To mActivity.Count - 1
        Console.WriteLine(" ({0})   {1:C}", index, mActivity(index))
      Next
      Console.WriteLine()

    End Sub

End Class
' This is the main class in the application, to test the Account class
Public Class MainClass
  Public Shared Sub Main()
    Dim acc1 As New Account("Joseph")
    acc1.Deposit(1000)
    acc1.Deposit(5000)
    acc1.Withdraw(2000)
    acc1.Deposit(3000)
    Console.WriteLine("FINAL STATUS: {0}", acc1)
  End Sub
End Class
```

To take control of the preprocessor symbols, we'll use the command-line compiler. Let's see what happens if we compile the application as follows, without defining the Debug preprocessor symbol:

> `vbc ConditionalCompilation.vb`

To run the application, type the following command:

> `ConditionalCompilation.exe`

The application displays the message on the console shown in Figure 11-6.

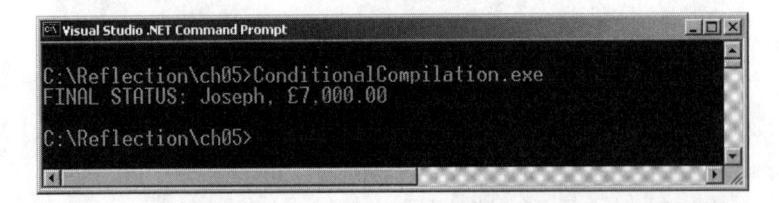

```
C:\Reflection\ch05>ConditionalCompilation.exe
FINAL STATUS: Joseph, £7,000.00

C:\Reflection\ch05>
```

Figure 11-6. ConditionalCompilation.exe *running on the console*

As you can see, there is no diagnostic information here. Let's look at the MSIL for the application to see what's happening. Type the following command to run the MSIL Disassembler:

> `ildasm.exe ConditionalCompilation.exe`

When the MSIL Disassembler window appears, double-click the MyDumpStatus() method of the Account class. The MSIL code for this method is displayed as follows:

```
.method public instance void  MyDumpStatus(string Message) cil managed
{
  .custom instance void
    [mscorlib]System.Diagnostics.ConditionalAttribute::.ctor(string) =
                ( 01 00 05 44 65 62 75 67 00 00 )    // ...Debug..
  // Additional implementation code for MyDumpStatus() not shown...
}
```

The first MSIL statement inside the method is a call to the constructor for the ConditionalAttribute class, passing the string "Debug" as an argument. This indicates the method is conditionally compiled, depending on whether the Debug preprocessor identifier is defined. You'll see how to define this preprocessor identifier shortly.

Close this window, and return to the main MSIL Disassembler window. Now double-click the Deposit() method, to see the MSIL code for this method:

```
.method public instance void  Deposit(float64 Amount) cil managed
{
  // Code size       33 (0x21)
  .maxstack  8
  IL_0000:  ldarg.0
  IL_0001:  ldarg.0
  IL_0002:  ldfld      float64 Account::mBalance
  IL_0007:  ldarg.1
  IL_0008:  add
  IL_0009:  stfld      float64 Account::mBalance
  IL_000e:  ldarg.0
  IL_000f:  ldfld      class [mscorlib]System.Collections.ArrayList
                       Account::mActivity
  IL_0014:  ldarg.1
  IL_0015:  box        [mscorlib]System.Double
  IL_001a:  callvirt   instance int32 [mscorlib]
                       System.Collections.ArrayList::Add(object)
  IL_001f:  pop
  IL_0020:  ret
} // end of method Account::Deposit
```

Notice that the Deposit() method does not contain any instructions to call the MyDumpStatus() method, because the Debug preprocessor identifier isn't defined.

To display diagnostic information, we must recompile our application with the Debug preprocessor identifier defined as follows:

```
> vbc  -d:Debug=1 ConditionalCompilation.vb
```

When we run the application, it now displays diagnostic information on the console as shown in Figure 11-7.

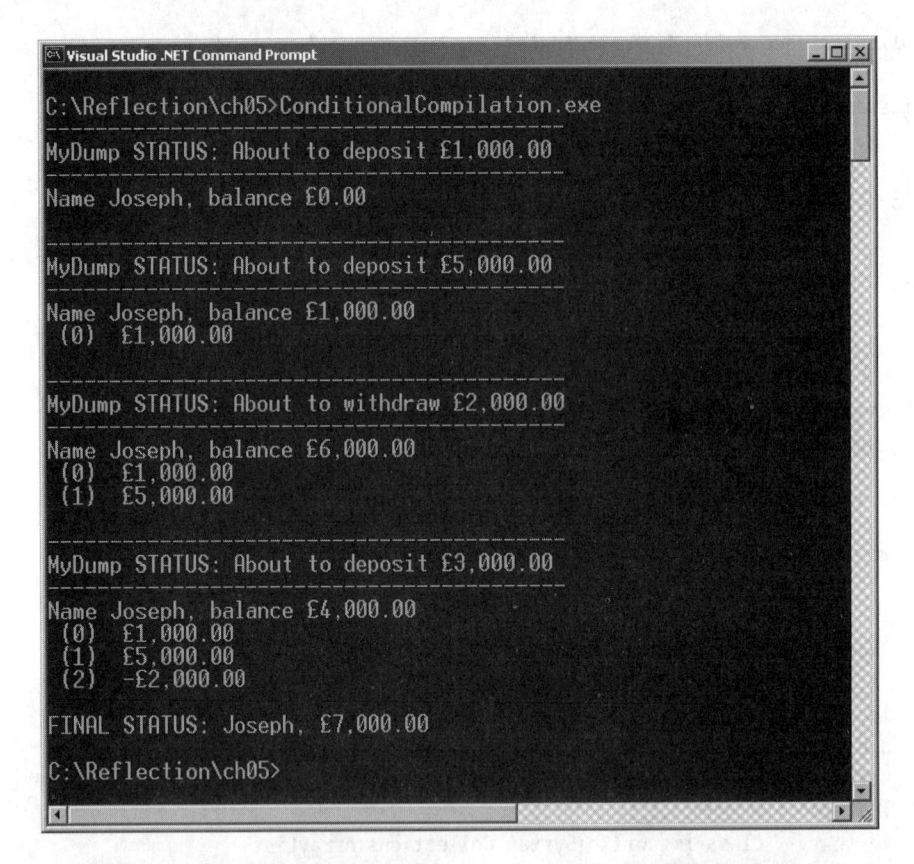

Figure 11-7. ConditionalCompilation.exe *displaying diagnostic information on the console*

Here is the revised MSIL for the Deposit() method, now that the Debug preprocessor identifier has been defined. Notice that the statements numbered IL_0001 through IL_0011 call the MyDumpStatus() method with an appropriately formatted diagnostic message:

```
.method public instance void  Deposit(float64 Amount) cil managed
{
  // Code size       55 (0x37)
  .maxstack  8
  IL_0000:  ldarg.0
  IL_0001:  ldstr       "About to deposit {0:C}"
  IL_0006:  ldarg.1
  IL_0007:  box         [mscorlib]System.Double
  IL_000c:  call        string [mscorlib]System.String::Format(string,
                                                               object)
  IL_0011:  callvirt    instance void Account::MyDumpStatus(string)
  IL_0016:  ldarg.0
  IL_0017:  ldarg.0
  IL_0018:  ldfld       float64 Account::mBalance
  IL_001d:  ldarg.1
```

```
    IL_001e:    add
    IL_001f:    stfld       float64 Account::mBalance
    IL_0024:    ldarg.0
    IL_0025:    ldfld       class [mscorlib]System.Collections.ArrayList
                            Account::mActivity
    IL_002a:    ldarg.1
    IL_002b:    box         [mscorlib]System.Double
    IL_0030:    callvirt    instance int32 [mscorlib]
                            System.Collections.ArrayList::Add(object)
    IL_0035:    pop
    IL_0036:    ret
} // end of method Account::Deposit
```

One final point: the MSIL code for the `MyDumpStatus()` method is the same as before. The `<Conditional()>` attribute determines whether the compiler should compile calls to the method; the method itself is always compiled into the same MSIL.

Defining and Using Assembly Attributes

When we create a VB .NET project in VS .NET, the project automatically contains a file named `AssemblyInfo.vb`. This file contains global attributes such as `<AssemblyTitle()>` and `<AssemblyDescription()>`, which provide metadata for the assembly as a whole.

Global attributes must be defined directly after any `Imports` statements, and outside of any namespace or type definitions. The reason for this latter restriction is because assemblies can comprise multiple namespaces; in order for global attributes to apply across all these namespaces, the attributes must be defined outside of any namespace definition.

The general syntax for declaring assembly attributes is as follows. `Assembly` is a VB .NET keyword, and indicates that the attribute applies to the entire assembly:

`<Assembly: AttributeDeclaration>`

It is also possible to declare global attributes for a specific module in an assembly. The general syntax for declaring module attributes is as follows. `Module` is a VB .NET keyword, and indicates (in this context) that the attribute applies just to the current .NET module:

`<Module: AttributeDeclaration>`

To illustrate how to define and use assembly attributes, we have provided a sample VB .NET project named `AssemblyAttributeDemo.sln`, which you can find in the Downloads section of the Apress Web site under `ch11\AssemblyAttributeDemo`.

The `AssemblyInfo.vb` source file contains a variety of assembly attributes, as follows. These attributes are self-explanatory, but we've included some comments:

```
Imports System.Reflection                ' For Assembly attributes
Imports System.Runtime.InteropServices   ' For GuidAttribute

' User-friendly title for this assembly
<Assembly: AssemblyTitle("Greetings assembly")>

' Additional descriptive text for this assembly
<Assembly: AssemblyDescription("This assembly displays a time-sensitive greeting")>
```

```
' Name of the company that developed the assembly
<Assembly: AssemblyCompany("My Cool Company Ltd")>

' Product name
<Assembly: AssemblyProduct("My Cool Product")>

' Copyright information
<Assembly: AssemblyCopyright("(c) Copyright My Cool Company, 2002")>

' Trademark information
<Assembly: AssemblyTrademark("TM My Cool Company Ltd")>

' This assembly is CLS-compliant
<Assembly: CLSCompliant(True)>

'The following GUID is for the ID of the typelib if this project
' is exposed to COM (this GUID was generated by Visual Studio .NET)
<Assembly: Guid("DABB3C50-F150-4743-977A-C670902EC183")>

' Version information for an assembly consists of four values:
'     Major Version : Minor Version : Build Number : Revision
<Assembly: AssemblyVersion("1.0.*")>
```

In a moment, we'll build the application and see how to view the assembly's metadata. Before we do that, we'll introduce a new technique for inspecting custom attributes programmatically. Here is the high-level code in the `MainClass.vb` source file:

```
Imports System                 ' For miscellaneous classes
Imports System.Reflection      ' For Attribute class

Public Class MainClass

  ' This is the entry point of the application
  Public Shared Sub Main()
    DisplayGreeting()
    DisplayAssemblyTitle()
    DisplayAssemblyDescription()
  End Sub

  Public Shared Sub DisplayGreeting()
    ' See below...
  End Sub

  Public Shared Sub DisplayAssemblyTitle()
    ' See below...
  End Sub
```

```vb
  Public Shared Sub DisplayAssemblyDescription()
    ' See below...
  End Sub
End Class
```

The DisplayGreeting() method isn't directly relevant to the reflection code, but it adds a little more personality to the application's startup:

```vb
Public Shared Sub DisplayGreeting()
  Dim currentHour As Integer = DateTime.Now.Hour
  If currentHour < 12 Then
    Console.WriteLine("Good morning!")
  ElseIf currentHour < 18 Then
    Console.WriteLine("Good afternoon!")
  Else
    Console.WriteLine("Good evening!")
  End If
End Sub
```

The DisplayAssemblyTitle() method shown next illustrates how to test for custom attributes programmatically. Study the code first, and then read the explanations that follow.

```vb
Public Shared Sub DisplayAssemblyTitle()

  ' Get the custom attribute, AssemblyTitleAttribute
  Dim attr As Attribute
  attr = Attribute.GetCustomAttribute( _
                    [Assembly].GetCallingAssembly(), _
                    GetType(AssemblyTitleAttribute), _
                    False)

  ' Convert attr to actual data type, AssemblyTitleAttribute
  Dim ta As AssemblyTitleAttribute
  ta = CType(attr, AssemblyTitleAttribute)

  ' Display the AssemblyTitleAttribute's Title property
  If Not (ta Is Nothing) Then
    Console.WriteLine("AssemblyTitle attribute: {0}", ta.Title)
  Else
    Console.WriteLine("AssemblyTitle attribute not found")
  End If

End Sub
```

Note the following points in the DisplayAssemblyTitle() method shown previously:

- The `Attribute.GetCustomAttribute()` method allows you to retrieve a specific attribute on a particular coding element (such as an assembly, a class, a method, and so on). `Attribute` is a standard .NET class that enables you to perform attribute-related programming tasks in your code.

- In this example, we use the `GetCustomAttribute()` method to get the `<AssemblyTitle()>` attribute for the current assembly. Note that `Assembly` is both a classname and a keyword in VB .NET, so we must use the escape syntax `[Assembly]` to indicate we're using the `Assembly` classname rather than the `Assembly` keyword:

```
Dim attr As Attribute
attr = Attribute.GetCustomAttribute( _
                 [Assembly].GetCallingAssembly(), _
                 GetType(AssemblyTitleAttribute), _
                 False)
```

- The `GetCustomAttribute()` method can be used to retrieve any kind of custom attribute, and consequently the method has a declared return type of `Attribute`. We therefore use `CType` to convert the retrieved attribute into the correct data type, namely `AssemblyTitleAttribute`.

```
Dim ta As AssemblyTitleAttribute
ta = CType(attr, AssemblyTitleAttribute)
```

- The `AssemblyTitleAttribute` has a `Title` property, which indicates the title of the assembly. We display this information on the console window as follows (the `If` test guards against the possibility that our assembly doesn't have an `AssemblyTitleAttribute`):

```
If Not (ta Is Nothing) Then
   Console.WriteLine("AssemblyTitle attribute: {0}", ta.Title)
Else
   Console.WriteLine("AssemblyTitle attribute not found")
End If
```

Now let's see how to implement the `DisplayAssemblyDescription()` method, to display the `<AssemblyDescription()>` custom attribute. This method is essentially the same as `DisplayAssemblyTitle`, except that it retrieves `AssemblyDescriptionAttribute` rather than `AssemblyTitleAttribute`. The only other difference is that `AssemblyDescriptionAttribute` has a `Description` property, whereas `AssemblyTitleAttribute` has a `Title` property:

```
Public Shared Sub DisplayAssemblyDescription()

   ' Get the custom attribute, AssemblyDescriptionAttribute
   Dim attr As Attribute
   attr = Attribute.GetCustomAttribute( _
                    [Assembly].GetCallingAssembly(), _
                    GetType(AssemblyDescriptionAttribute), _
                    False)

   ' Convert attr to actual data type, AssemblyDescriptionAttribute
   Dim da As AssemblyDescriptionAttribute
   da = CType(attr, AssemblyDescriptionAttribute)
```

```
' Display the AssemblyDescriptionAttribute's Description property
If Not (da Is Nothing) Then
  Console.WriteLine("AssemblyDescription: {0}", da.Description)
Else
  Console.WriteLine("AssemblyDescription attribute not found")
End If
End Sub
```

When we build and run the application, it displays the following information on the console (as shown in Figure 11-8). Notice the assembly title and assembly description are displayed as expected.

Figure 11-8. *Running* AssemblyAttributeDemo.exe

It's also possible to view the assembly metadata using Windows Explorer. Navigate to the folder that contains the assembly file AssemblyAttributeDemo.exe, and view the properties for the file. The Properties window appears as shown in Figure 11-9; notice that the assembly's description corresponds to the <AssemblyTitle()> attribute we specified earlier:

Figure 11-9. *Properties of the* AssemblyAttributeDemo.exe *file*

To obtain more detailed information, click the Version tab at the top of the Properties window. This allows you to inspect any aspect of assembly metadata, simply by selecting one of the entries in the Item Name list box on the left-hand side of the window as shown in Figure 11-10.

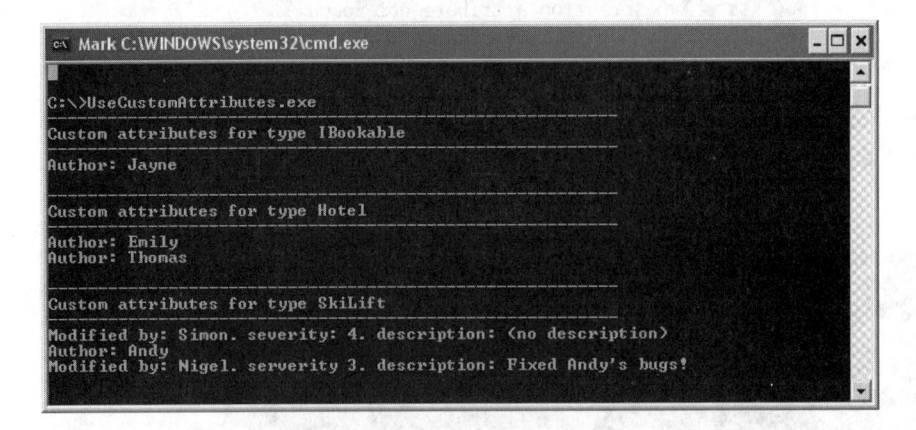

Figure 11-10. *The* Version *tab within the Properties window*

Defining New Custom Attributes

In this section, you'll see how to define new custom attribute classes, and how to use these attributes on a variety of coding elements such as classes and methods. We'll also recap how to access custom attributes on a coding element, by using the Attribute.GetCustomAttribute() method.

Defining a custom attribute class isn't that much different from defining a normal class. Here's a reminder of the distinguishing features of attribute classes:

- Attribute classes must be preceded by an <AttributeUsage()> attribute to specify the applicability of the attribute class. The <AttributeUsage()> attribute can specify three pieces of information:

  - The allowable kinds of target for the attribute, such as a class, a structure, a field, and so on. This information is mandatory.

  - Whether the attribute can be applied multiple times on the same code element. Specify AllowMultiple:=True or AllowMultiple:=False; the default is False.

  - Whether the attribute is inherited by subclasses. Specify Inherited:=True or Inherited:=False; the default is True.

- Attribute classes must inherit (directly or indirectly) from System.Attribute.

- Attribute classes cannot be declared as MustInherit.

- By convention, attribute classes should end with the word Attribute.

- Attribute classes should define constructor(s) to receive mandatory initialization parameters. Developers are forced to supply these parameters in the order they appear in the constructor(s) . If you want to allow the developer a bit more flexibility, you can define a variety of constructors each taking different combinations of arguments; the developer can choose which constructor to specify when using the attribute.

- Attribute classes may define get/set properties to receive optional initialization parameters. Developers can supply these parameters in any order, after the constructor parameters.

There are strict limitations on the parameters that a programmer using your attributes will be able to pass in to your attribute. The only expressions that are valid in an attribute declaration are called constant expressions; that is, they must be able to be wholly evaluated at compile-time. The result of such an expression must belong to one of the following types:

- Byte
- Short
- Integer
- Long
- Char
- Single
- Double
- Decimal
- Boolean
- String
- Any enumeration type
- The null type

The coder using your attribute will be able to specify expressions involving literals, references to constants defined in other types, and specific enumeration values, but won't be able to call methods or VB .NET functions, or access reference types.

The following example illustrates these rules for defining attribute classes. You can download the source code for this example from ch05\MyCustomAttributes.vb in the Downloads section of the Apress Web site (http://www.apress.com).

We'll begin with the Imports statements:

```
Imports System            ' For miscellaneous classes
Imports System.Reflection ' For Attribute class
```

Next, let's define a custom attribute class named `AuthorAttribute`. This attribute will contain information about the author of a class, structure, or interface. Multiple `<Author()>` attributes are allowed on the same target, but `<Author()>` attributes are not inherited by subclasses. Furthermore, when a programmer uses an `<Author()>` attribute on their class, structure, or interface, they must specify the author's name as a parameter to the `<Author()>` attribute.

```
<AttributeUsage(AttributeTargets.Class Or _
                AttributeTargets.Struct Or _
                AttributeTargets.Interface, _
                AllowMultiple := True, _
                Inherited := False)> _
Public Class AuthorAttribute
  Inherits Attribute

  Private mAuthor As String
  Public Sub New(ByVal Author As String)
    mAuthor = Author
  End Sub

  Public ReadOnly Property Author As String
    Get
      Return mAuthor
    End Get
  End Property

  Public Overrides Function ToString() As String
    Return "Author: " & mAuthor
  End Function

End Class
```

Now let's define another custom attribute class named `ModifiedAttribute`. This attribute will contain information about when a class, structure, or interface was modified by a programmer. This is the sort of information you typically find in a version-control system. Multiple `<Modified()>` attributes are allowed on the same target, but `<Modified()>` attributes are not inherited by subclasses. When a programmer uses a `<Modified()>` attribute on their class, structure, or interface, they must provide their name and a severity number (for example, 1=severe bug, 2=important bug, and so on). Optionally, the programmer can also provide a textual description of the modification made to the class, structure, or interface:

```
<AttributeUsage(AttributeTargets.Class Or _
                AttributeTargets.Struct Or _
                AttributeTargets.Interface, _
                AllowMultiple := True, _
                Inherited := False)> _
Public Class ModifiedAttribute
  Inherits Attribute
```

```vb
    Private mWho As String
    Private mSeverity As Integer
    Private mDescription As String

    Public Sub New(ByVal Who As String, ByVal Severity As Integer)
      mWho = Who
      mSeverity = Severity
    End Sub

    Public ReadOnly Property Who As String
      Get
        Return mWho
      End Get
    End Property
    Public ReadOnly Property Severity As Integer
      Get
        Return mSeverity
      End Get
    End Property

    Public Property Description As String
      Get
        If mDescription Is Nothing Then
          Return "(no description)"
        Else
          Return mDescription
        End If
      End Get
      Set
        mDescription = Value
      End Set
    End Property

    Public Overrides Function ToString() As String
      Return "Modified by: "   & Who & _
           ", severity: "    & Severity & _
           ", description: " & Description
    End Function

End Class
```

Now let's see how to use the custom attributes, `<Author()>` and `<Modified()>`, in our classes, structures, and interfaces. The following example shows how to use these attributes. You can download the source code for this example from ch05\UseCustomAttributes.vb in the Downloads section of the Apress Web site (http://www.apress.com).

As before, we'll begin with the Imports statements:

```vb
Imports System                ' For miscellaneous classes
Imports System.Reflection     ' For Attribute class
```

The following interface shows how to define a single `<Author()>` attribute:

```vbnet
<Author("Jayne")> _
Public Interface IBookable

  ' Members...

End Interface
```

The following class shows how to define multiple `<Author()>` attributes on the same target:

```vbnet
<Author("Thomas"), _
 Author("Emily")> _
Public Class Hotel
  Implements IBookable

  ' Members...

End Class
```

The following class shows how to define multiple `<Author()>` and `<Modified()>` attributes on the same target. Notice that the first `<Modified()>` attribute provides an optional Description, but the second `<Modified()>` attribute does not provide a Description:

```vbnet
<Author("Andy"), _
 Modified("Nigel", 3, Description:="Fixed Andy's bugs!"), _
 Modified("Simon", 4)> _
Public Structure SkiLift

    Private mCapacityPerHour As Integer

End Structure
```

We can use reflection to retrieve the set of custom attributes on a particular coding element. The following code shows what we need to do. In this example, the MyDisplayAttributes() method receives a MemberInfo parameter containing reflection information for a coding element. We call MyDisplayAttributes() three times, passing in Type objects representing the IBookable, Hotel, and SkiLift types (note that Type is derived from MemberInfo, so there is no problem passing Type parameters into the MyDisplayAttributes() method).

MemberInfo has a GetCustomAttributes() method, which returns an array of custom attributes defined on the coding element (the False parameter in the GetCustomAttributes() method means we aren't interested in any custom attributes defined in our superclass). In this example, we simply use a loop to display the information contained in each custom attribute:

```vbnet
Public Class MainClass

  Public Shared Sub Main()
    MyDisplayAttributes( GetType(IBookable) )
    MyDisplayAttributes( GetType(Hotel) )
    MyDisplayAttributes( GetType(SkiLift) )
  End Sub
```

```vbnet
    Public Shared Sub MyDisplayAttributes(ByVal info As MemberInfo)

      Console.WriteLine("-------------------------------------------")
      Console.WriteLine("Custom attributes for type {0}", info)
      Console.WriteLine("-------------------------------------------")

      Dim attribs As Object() = info.GetCustomAttributes(False)
      Dim i As Integer
      For i = 0 To attribs.Length - 1
        Console.WriteLine("{0}", attribs(i))
      Next i
      Console.WriteLine()

    End Sub
End Class
```

The application displays the following information on the console as shown in Figure 11-11. If you run this application yourself, you may find the attributes are displayed in a different order; the ordering of attributes retrieved by `GetCustomAttributes()` is not guaranteed:

```
C:\>UseCustomAttributes.exe
Custom attributes for type IBookable
Author: Jayne

Custom attributes for type Hotel
Author: Emily
Author: Thomas

Custom attributes for type SkiLift
Modified by: Simon. severity: 4. description: (no description)
Author: Andy
Modified by: Nigel. severity: 3. description: Fixed Andy's bugs!
```

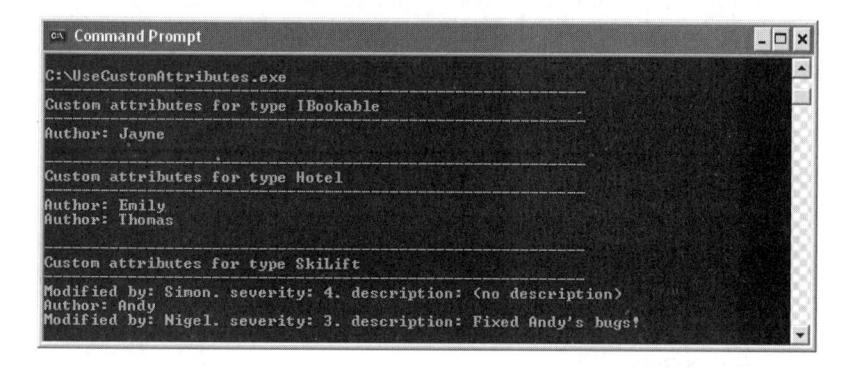

Figure 11-11. *Use* `CustomAttributes.exe` *running on the console*

This example shows how to define custom attributes with a combination of mandatory and optional parameters, and how to use these custom attributes when we define new data types. The example also shows how to use reflection to retrieve the custom attributes programmatically.

This opens the door to an entirely new style of programming in .NET. Here are some examples of the kinds of tasks we can achieve using custom attributes:

- Define a visual appearance for fields and properties defined in a class. Create an attribute class that specifies the font name, color, and other visual features for each field and property.

- Map classes and structures to tables in a relational database. Create an attribute class that specifies the name of the database that contains data, which can be used to initialize instances of the class or structure. Map fields and properties to columns in a database table. Create an attribute class that identifies the name of the appropriate column for a specific field of property.

These are just a few suggestions for using custom attributes. We're sure you can think of many more.

The attributes we've explored here only spring into action when they are examined reflectively by other code. However, there is a class in the .NET framework, System.ContextBoundObject, part of the .NET remoting infrastructure, which automatically activates any attributes that extend System.Runtime.Remoting.Contexts.ContextAttribute associated with it. It is possible, using this class as a base for our own classes, to create attributes that are activated whenever the class is instantiated, or its methods are called. Unfortunately, much of the required functionality to do so is undocumented in the current release of .NET, because it is only really used internally by .NET itself. As a quick demonstration of what's seemingly possible with context-bound attributes, we can put together a simple method-call logging framework.

Take a look at the following code—most of which is just boilerplate for a context-bound attribute:

```
Imports System
Imports System.Runtime.Remoting.Contexts
Imports System.Runtime.Remoting.Messaging
Imports System.Runtime.Remoting.Activation

Public Class LoggedAttribute
  Inherits ContextAttribute
  Implements IContributeObjectSink, IMessageSink

  Private _nextSink As IMessageSink
  Private _target As MarshalByRefObject

  Public Sub New()
    MyBase.New("Logging Service")
  End Sub

  Public Overrides Sub GetPropertiesForNewContext _
                    (ByVal ccm As IConstructionCallMessage)
    ccm.ContextProperties.Add(Me)
  End Sub

  Public Function GetObjectSink(ByVal target As MarshalByRefObject, _
                ByVal nextSink As IMessageSink) As IMessageSink _
        Implements IContributeObjectSink.GetObjectSink
    _target = target
    _nextSink = nextSink
```

```
    Return Me
End Function

Public ReadOnly Property NextSink() As IMessageSink _
      Implements IMessageSink.NextSink
  Get
    Return _nextSink
  End Get
End Property

Public ReadOnly Property Target() As MarshalByRefObject
  Get
    Return _target
  End Get
End Property
```

After the basic lifecycle methods are out of the way, we can get on with handling messages inbound to the object to which we're attached. We have to handle synchronous and asynchronous messages. In both cases, we pass the object representing the inbound message to another procedure for handling:

```
Public Function SyncProcessMessage(ByVal msg As IMessage) _
          As IMessage Implements IMessageSink.SyncProcessMessage
  HandleCall(msg)
  Return _nextSink.SyncProcessMessage(msg)
End Function

Public Function AsyncProcessMessage(ByVal msg As IMessage, _
              ByVal replySink As IMessageSink) As IMessageCtrl _
          Implements IMessageSink.AsyncProcessMessage
  HandleCall(msg)
  Return _nextSink.AsyncProcessMessage(msg, replySink)
End Function
```

Now, we extract the name of the called method, and display a message box:

```
Private Sub HandleCall(ByVal msg As IMessage)
  Dim name As String = msg.Properties("__MethodName")
  If Not name Is Nothing Then
    MsgBox(String.Format("Intercepted a call to {0}", name))
  End If
End Sub
End Class
```

Now, when we apply an attribute like this to a ContextBoundObject, all calls to methods on that object will trigger a message box.

Here is such a context-bound type:

```
<Logged()> Public Class LoggedObject
  Inherits ContextBoundObject
```

```
    Public Sub TestMethod()

    End Sub
End Class
```

It contains a Sub that does nothing. Now, we can make a simple Windows application that instantiates a LoggedObject, and calls the TestMethod when we click a button. Drag a button onto a standard WinForm, and edit the code as follows:

```
Public Class Form1
    Inherits System.Windows.Forms.Form

    Private _obj As New LoggedObject()

' Windows Form Designer generated code

    Private Sub Button1_Click(ByVal sender As System.Object, _
               ByVal e As System.EventArgs) Handles Button1.Click
      _obj.TestMethod()
    End Sub
End Class
```

Now, when we click the button, the message box appears telling us it intercepted the call to a method on our logged class. This opens up a potentially powerful ability to attach functionality onto classes simply by decorating them with attributes, but it also creates a large overhead in object management through its reliance on the remoting model. In the absence of detailed Microsoft documentation, it is difficult to discover the real side effects of this technique.

Summary

Attributes play a vital role in a wide range of scenarios in .NET. As you've seen in the chapter, attribute classes inherit from System.Attribute, and are decorated with an <AttributeUsage()> attribute to define the applicability of the attribute class.

You can use reflection techniques to determine the standard and custom attributes defined on a particular target: to get the list of standard attributes defined on a type, use the Attributes property; to get the list of custom attributes defined on a type, use the GetCustomAttributes() method.

You've seen many uses of attributes in the chapter; here's a quick reminder of some of the attribute classes you've encountered:

- <Serializable()> indicates that a class, structure, enumeration, or delegate is serializable. <NonSerialized()> indicates a field should not be serialized.

- <Conditional()> indicates that a method is conditionally compiled. This attribute is commonly used to control how diagnostic information is displayed in a .NET application.

- <AssemblyTitle()>, <AssemblyDescription()>, <AssemblyCompany()>, <AssemblyProduct()>, <AssemblyCopyright()>, <AssemblyTrademark()>, and <AssemblyGuid()> provide metadata for an entire assembly.

This is not a comprehensive list of attribute classes available in .NET. For a complete list, take a look at `Attribute class,` about `Attribute class` in VS .NET Help, and click on the hyperlink for `Derived classes`.

If none of these attribute classes meet your needs, you can of course define new custom attribute classes of your own. Choose a classname that ends with `Attribute`, and inherit from `System.Attribute`. Remember to provide an `<AttributeUsage()>` attribute to specify the applicability of your attribute class, and define suitable constructors and get/set properties to initialize attribute instances accordingly.

We also looked at some of the possibilities offered by the poorly documented context-bound attributes. The examples covered in this chapter should give you a good idea of what's possible using attributes in .NET.

The next chapter will look at how reflection and attributes empower a part of the .NET Framework that defines and uses more attributes than any other—the component model.

CHAPTER 12

The .NET Component Model

This is the final chapter dealing with .NET reflection in the book, and it gives you the opportunity to see how attributes, metadata, and reflection are used within the .NET Framework.

In this chapter, we'll investigate the various classes, interfaces, and other data types defined in the System.ComponentModel namespace. The .NET component model provides an extremely rich programming model for creating and using component classes. We'll explain exactly what *component class* means shortly. The aim of the chapter is to show how you can use reflection and attribute-based techniques to write programs that are generic and can handle any kind of component. The chapter provides an effective case study in writing code that makes use of attribute-laden objects, and offers some insight into the way the developers at Microsoft have employed attributes within .NET.

This chapter is divided into two halves:

- The first half of the chapter introduces the important interfaces, classes, and attributes in the System.ComponentModel namespace. You'll see how to use reflection to interrogate a type about its runtime capabilities, such as obtaining a list of its properties and events. This enables you to write your code in a very flexible and extensible manner. Rather than constraining your applications to deal with specific types containing predefined properties and events, you can write generic code that determines these capabilities dynamically at runtime.

  You'll also see how to determine whether a type can be converted to other data types by using a converter class. This is an essential ingredient if you want to use types generically in your application; you must be able to interrogate types to determine whether their data can be converted to or from other types. For example, the Visual Designer in VS .NET needs to convert components' property values to and from string format to display and edit these values in the Properties window.

- The second part of the chapter shows you how to create new component classes to take advantage of the rich set of attributes and other metadata capabilities defined in the System.ComponentModel namespace. We'll define a new component class, decorate it with attributes, and then add it to the ToolBox in VS .NET. Then we'll show how to drag and drop component objects onto a new application, and see how the Component Designer in VS .NET deals with these component objects. This will illustrate the power of attributed programming, and the use of reflection to determine a component's capabilities at runtime.

Let's begin with a tour of the .NET component model, to gain an understanding of the classes, interfaces, and attributes that are available.

Investigating the .NET Component Model

As its name suggests, the .NET component model is geared for creating and using components. Therefore, a logical place to start is by defining a component. We'll also describe the differences between components, controls, and classes.

The component model defines a standard programming model for creating and using any kind of component in a .NET application. Attributes and reflection play a pivotal role in this programming model.

Components, Controls, and Classes

In traditional programming terminology, a component is a black box of compiled code, which hides its functionality behind a well-defined interface. COM components were always accessed through COM interfaces, regardless of the underlying programming technology. In .NET, almost any object is a component by this definition. A .NET component goes beyond the basics any object offers by providing:

- Simplified discovery of its capabilities via reflection

- Designtime support, allowing it to be configured by an IDE such as VS .NET

- A container architecture that enables components to discover and interact with one another

The strict definition of a component in .NET is that it's a class that implements the System.ComponentModel.IComponent interface and provides an accessible no-argument constructor. The IComponent interface defines a standard mechanism for placing component objects into a container. All component classes in the .NET Framework class library implement IComponent.

The System.ComponentModel.IContainer interface specifies the requirements for container classes to ensure that all container classes provide a consistent mechanism for adding and removing components.

What does all this mean in practical terms? Components and containers allow you to write code in a generic fashion; you can write component classes that implement the IComponent interface, and then insert component objects into any container. Conversely, you can write container classes that implement the IContainer interface, and then add any kind of component object.

The IComponent and IContainer interfaces also make it possible for visual designers such as VS .NET to work with component objects. As we'll show later, it's easy to add a component class to the VS .NET ToolBox, and then drag and drop component objects onto the Visual Designer.

It is important to realize that the term *containment* means logical containment rather than visual containment. Later in the chapter, we'll underline this assertion by defining a nonvisual component class named Employee; we'll also define a corresponding nonvisual container class named EmployeeContainer to contain Employee component objects. This example will illustrate the use of containers and components as a way of organizing groups of objects in a collection to satisfy a one-to-many relationship in an object-oriented (OO) design.

You can also define components that can reside in Windows Forms or ASP.NET Web pages. These kinds of components are generally referred to as *controls*. Controls can be nonvisual, in which case they are really just specialized components, or visual, in which case they provide a UI element. There are two ways to create a new control class, depending on whether you want to add the control to Windows Forms or ASP.NET Web pages:

- To create a new Windows Forms control, define a class that inherits from System.Windows.Forms.Control. This class provides basic UI capabilities for Windows Forms controls. System.Windows.Forms.Control inherits from Component, which provides a basic implementation of the IComponent interface.

- To create a nonvisual ASP.NET Web control, define a class that inherits from System.Web.UI.Control. This class implements the IComponent interface directly. To create a visual ASP.NET Web control, define a class that inherits from System.Web.UI.WebControls.WebControl.

Figure 12-1 shows a UML (Unified Modeling Language) diagram illustrating the relationship between the classes and interfaces introduced in this section. For more information about control classes in Windows Forms and ASP.NET Web pages, see System.Windows.Forms.Control or System.Web.UI.Control, respectively, in VS .NET Help.

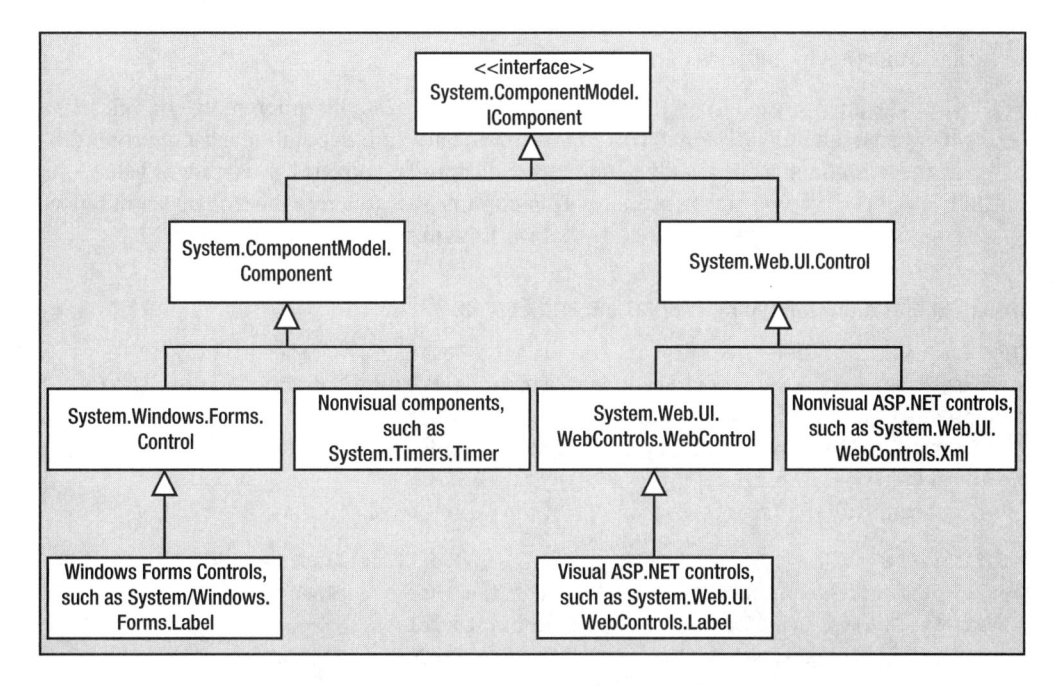

Figure 12-1. *UML diagram of the classes and interfaces used in this section of the book*

Using Reflection with the Component Model

The System.ComponentModel namespace provides a great deal of support for reflection to enable the Visual Designer to interrogate the capabilities of components at designtime. You can also use these reflection capabilities in your own programs at runtime to find out anything you want to know about types and objects in your programs. You can also use reflection to modify property values, and even add new properties and events dynamically.

To illustrate how to use reflection with the component model, we'll present two sample applications:

- The first sample application will show how to use `System.ComponentModel.TypeDescriptor` to obtain general metadata for a component data type, such as the attributes defined on the type, and the default property and the default event for the type. The default property is the property that is initially highlighted in the Properties window when you select a component in the Visual Designer. The default event is the event that gets handled if you double-click a component in the Visual Designer; for example, the default event for `Button` is the `Click` event.

  We'll also show how to retrieve further information about the properties and events on a specified type. Property information is represented by the `PropertyDescriptor` class; event information is represented by the `EventDescriptor` class.

- The second sample application will show how to use reflection to dynamically modify properties at runtime. The application will allow you to select any property you like on a component, and change the property value on-the-fly. This illustrates the ability to deal with components in an entirely generic way, and reinforces the importance of attributes and reflection in this style of programming.

  This task might sound like a trivial undertaking, but in fact it's much more complicated than you might imagine. First, you'll need to use reflection to obtain the list of properties on the component. Then you'll need to use reflection to convert the user's new value into the correct data type for the property. This example will illustrate the true power of reflection to write extremely generic code that works with any type of component.

Obtaining Metadata for Types, Properties, and Events

The `TypeDescriptor`, `EventDescriptor`, and `PropertyDescriptor` classes in the `System.ComponentModel` namespace provide you with a great deal of metadata information. The following console application shows how to use these classes to find metadata for any data type in any assembly. You can download this sample application from the Downloads section on the Apress Web site (http://www.apress.com).

Let's begin with the `Imports` statements for the sample application:

```
Imports System                        ' For miscellaneous .NET types
Imports System.Reflection             ' For the Assembly class
Imports System.ComponentModel   ' For the descriptor classes
Imports System.Collections            ' For the IEnumerator interface
```

The application begins by displaying a message on the console to ask the user for the name of the assembly to load into the runtime. The application also asks the user for the name of a data type in the assembly, and gets a `Type` object for the requested type. The application then displays a menu on the console, offering the user a chance to display various aspects of metadata for the specified data type:

```
Public Class MainClass
  ' Helper variable
  Private Shared nl As String = System.Environment.NewLine
  Public Shared Sub Main()
    Try
```

```vb
      ' Ask the user for an assembly name
      Console.Write("Please enter the assembly name: ")
      Dim assemblyName As String = Console.ReadLine()

      ' Load the requested assembly into the runtime
      Dim theAssembly As [Assembly] = _
        [Assembly].LoadWithPartialName(assemblyName)
      Console.WriteLine("Loaded " & theAssembly.FullName & nl)

      ' Ask the user for a type name
      Console.Write("Please enter a fully-qualified type name: ")
      Dim typeName As String = Console.ReadLine()
      ' Get the Type object for this type
      Dim theType As Type = theAssembly.GetType(typeName, True, True)
      Console.WriteLine("Found the type " & theType.FullName & nl)

      ' Display a menu of options to the user
      Dim response As String
      Do
        Console.WriteLine("MAIN MENU, choose an option: ")
        Console.WriteLine("-----------------------------------------")
        Console.WriteLine("   t  Display general type information")
        Console.WriteLine("   e  Display all events for this type")
        Console.WriteLine("   p  Display all properties for this type")
        Console.WriteLine("   q  Quit")
        Console.WriteLine()
        Console.Write("> ")
        response = Console.ReadLine()

        ' Call appropriate method to display the requested information
        If response = "t" Then
          MyDisplayTypeInfo(theType)
        ElseIf response = "e" Then
          MyDisplayEventsInfo(theType)
        ElseIf response = "p" Then
          MyDisplayPropertiesInfo(theType)
        End If
      Loop Until response = "q"
    Catch Ex As Exception
      Console.WriteLine("Exception: " & Ex.Message & nl)
    End Try
  End Sub
  ' The methods MyDisplayTypeInfo(), MyDisplayEventsInfo(), and
  ' MyDisplayPropertiesInfo() are discussed below...
End Class
```

The following code shows the implementation of the `MyDisplayTypeInfo()` method to display general metadata for the specified type. We use the `TypeDescriptor` class (defined in the `System.ComponentModel` namespace) to obtain this metadata:

1. Call `TypeDescriptor.GetDefaultEvent()` to get information about the default event for the specified data type. The event information is returned in an `EventDescriptor` object, which contains information such as the name of the event.

Note The default event for a component is defined by the `<DefaultEvent()>` attribute on the component class definition. When we call `TypeDescriptor.GetDefaultEvent()`, the method returns the event specified by this attribute. You'll see how to use `<DefaultEvent()>` in the second part of the chapter, when we define a new component class.

---

2. Call `TypeDescriptor.GetDefaultProperty()` to get information about the default property for the specified data type. The property information is returned in a `PropertyDescriptor` object, which contains information such as the name of the property.

Note The default property for a component is defined by the `<DefaultProperty()>` attribute on the component class definition. You'll see how to use `<DefaultProperty()>` in the second part of the chapter.

---

3. Call `TypeDescriptor.GetAttributes()` to get the collection of attributes defined on the specified data type. Iterate through this collection, and display the name of each attribute on the console:

```
Public Shared Sub MyDisplayTypeInfo(ByVal theType As Type)
  Console.WriteLine("{0}Type information for type {1}", _
                    nl, theType.FullName)
  Console.WriteLine("-----------------------------------------------")

  ' Display name of default event (if there is one) for this type
  Dim defaultEvent As EventDescriptor
  defaultEvent = TypeDescriptor.GetDefaultEvent(theType)
  If defaultEvent Is Nothing Then
    Console.WriteLine("Default event:    none")
  Else
    Console.WriteLine("Default event:    {0}", defaultEvent.Name)
  End If

  ' Display name of default property (if there is one) for this type
  Dim defaultProperty As PropertyDescriptor
  defaultProperty = TypeDescriptor.GetDefaultProperty(theType)
  If defaultProperty Is Nothing Then
    Console.WriteLine("Default property: none")
  Else
    Console.WriteLine("Default property: {0}", defaultProperty.Name)
  End If
```

```vbnet
    ' Display the names of all the attributes defined on this type
    Console.WriteLine("Attributes:")
    Dim attribs As AttributeCollection
    attribs = TypeDescriptor.GetAttributes(theType)
    Dim iter As IEnumerator = attribs.GetEnumerator()
    While iter.MoveNext
      Console.WriteLine("  {0}", iter.Current)
    End While
    Console.WriteLine()
  End Sub
```

The following code shows the implementation of the `MyDisplayEventsInfo()` method. The method calls `TypeDescriptor.GetEvents()` to get the collection of events defined in the specified type. We iterate through this collection, and display detailed information for each event. The `EventDescriptor` class provides complete information about the event, including the name of the event, the delegate type of the event, a textual description of the event, the category of the event when displayed in the Properties window, whether the event is available only at designtime, and whether the event is multicast (multiple listeners supported) or single-cast (only one listener supported):

```vbnet
Public Shared Sub MyDisplayEventsInfo(ByVal theType As Type)

  Console.WriteLine(nl & "Event information")
  Console.WriteLine("----------------------------------------------")

  ' Get descriptive information for all events defined in this type
  Dim eventDescriptors As EventDescriptorCollection
  eventDescriptors = TypeDescriptor.GetEvents(theType)

  ' Iterate through the events, and display info for each event
  Dim iter As IEnumerator = eventDescriptors.GetEnumerator()
  While iter.MoveNext

    Dim cur As EventDescriptor
    cur = CType(iter.Current, EventDescriptor)

    Console.WriteLine("Event Name:            {0}", cur.Name)
    Console.WriteLine("Event Type:            {0}", cur.EventType)
    Console.WriteLine("Event Description:     {0}", cur.Description)
    Console.WriteLine("Event Category:        {0}", cur.Category)
    Console.WriteLine("Event DesignTimeOnly:  {0}", cur.DesignTimeOnly)
    Console.WriteLine("Event IsBrowsable:     {0}", cur.IsBrowsable)
    Console.WriteLine("Event IsMulticast:     {0}", cur.IsMulticast)
    Console.WriteLine()

  End While

End Sub
```

To complete the sample application, the following code shows the implementation of `MyDisplayPropertiesInfo()`. This method is similar to `MyDisplayEventsInfo()` shown earlier; this time, we call `TypeDescriptor.GetProperties()` to get the collection of properties defined in the specified type, and iterate through the collection to display information for each property:

```
Public Shared Sub MyDisplayPropertiesInfo(ByVal theType As Type)

  Console.WriteLine("{0}Property information", nl)
  Console.WriteLine("-----------------------------------------------")

  ' Get descriptive information for all properties in this type
  Dim propDescriptors As PropertyDescriptorCollection
  propDescriptors = TypeDescriptor.GetProperties(theType)
  ' Iterate through the properties, and display info for each property
  Dim iter As IEnumerator = propDescriptors.GetEnumerator()
  While iter.MoveNext

    Dim cur As PropertyDescriptor
    cur = CType(iter.Current, PropertyDescriptor)

    Console.WriteLine("Property Name:          {0}", cur.Name)
    Console.WriteLine("Property Type:          {0}", cur.PropertyType)
    Console.WriteLine("Property Description:   {0}", cur.Description)
    Console.WriteLine("property Category:      {0}", cur.Category)
    Console.WriteLine("Property DesignTimeOnly:{0}", _
                                            cur.DesignTimeOnly)
    Console.WriteLine("Property IsBrowsable:   {0}", cur.IsBrowsable)
    Console.WriteLine("Property IsReadOnly:    {0}", cur.IsReadOnly)
    Console.WriteLine()
  End While
End Sub
```

When we build and run the application, it asks for an assembly name and a type name (see Figure 12-2). We've specified the `System` assembly and the `System.Timers.Timer` component type, because it has a reasonably small number of events and properties. Feel free to choose a different assembly name and type name if you run this application yourself.

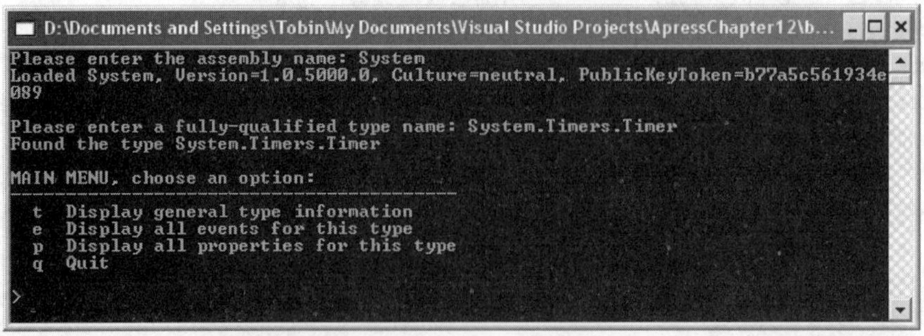

Figure 12-2. *The Timer application running on the console*

When we choose the t option, the application displays the general type information for the Timer type as shown in Figure 12-3. The default event is Elapsed, and the default property is Interval. There is a sizable list of attributes on the Timer class, and this is a hint of things to come. As you'll see later in the chapter, attributes play a major role in defining the designtime and runtime capabilities of components. To corroborate this assertion, notice that most of the attributes displayed are located in the System.ComponentModel namespace.

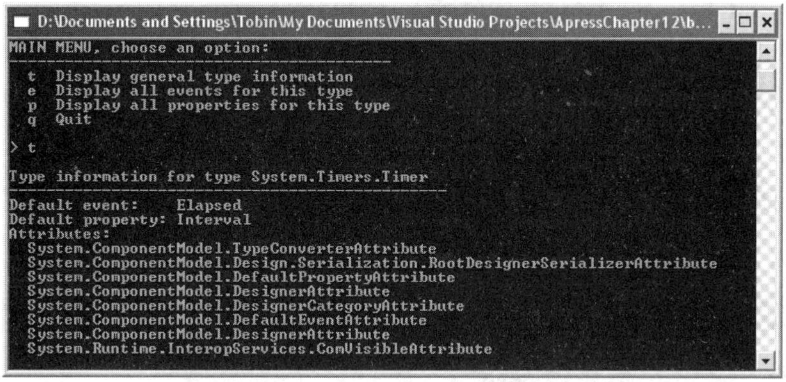

Figure 12-3. *List of attributes for the* Timer *type*

When we choose the e option, our application displays the information about the events in the Timer type as shown in Figure 12-4. The Name, Description, IsBrowsable, and Category information for each event is primarily intended for designtime consumption by the Visual Designer (IsBrowsable indicates whether the event is viewable in the Visual Designer, and Category is used to group related events together in the Visual Designer). In contrast, the Type and IsMulticast information actually affects how the events behave at runtime. As this example illustrates, components must provide a suitable combination of designtime and runtime metadata to support the Visual Designer and the CLR, respectively.

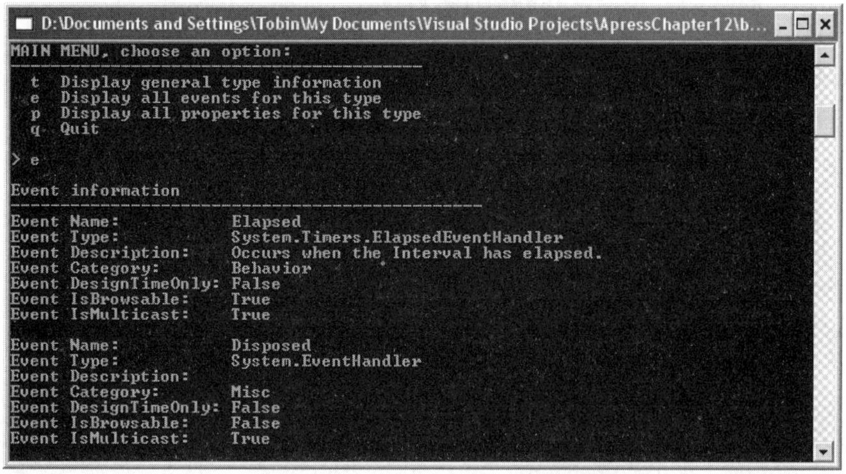

Figure 12-4. *The events for the* Timer *type*

To conclude this example, let's see what happens when we choose the p option in our application. The information is displayed for the properties in the Timer type (see Figure 12-5); we've only listed the first few properties here.

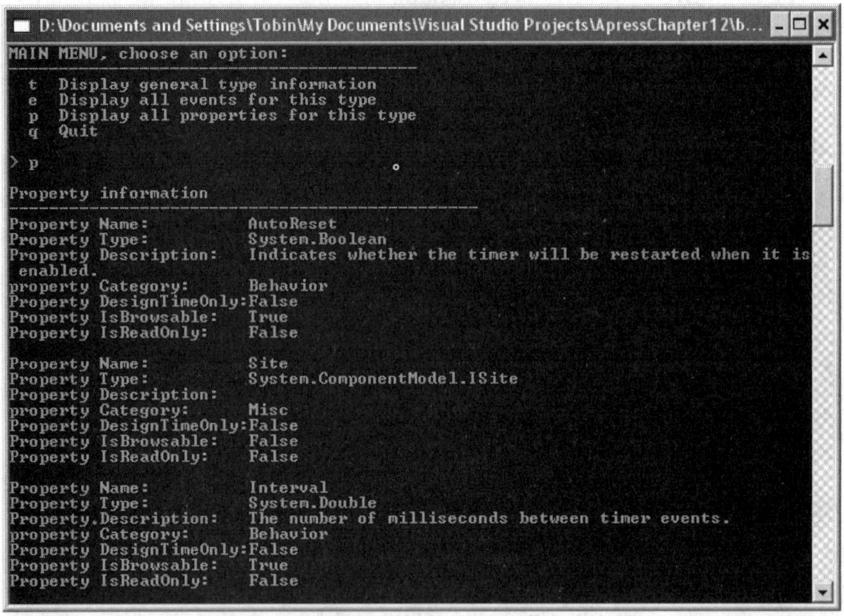

Figure 12-5. *The properties for the* Timer *type*

Let's briefly summarize what you've seen in this example. The System.ComponentModel namespace contains the descriptor classes TypeDescriptor, EventDescriptor, and PropertyDescriptor to provide full and detailed metadata for data types, events, and properties. This metadata is defined using a wide range of attributes, most of which are also defined in the System.ComponentModel namespace. You'll see how to use these attributes later in the chapter.

Using Metadata to Write Generic Code

The previous example showed how to query the metadata in types, events, and properties. It's also possible to use this metadata to change the state of objects at runtime. The metadata provides all the information you need to manipulate any kind of component; you can write generic code that can happily deal with any members on any type of component. Rather than being restricted to using hard-coded property and event names, you can use reflection to determine these features dynamically. This means you can write applications that are flexible enough to deal with component types that didn't even exist when you first wrote your code; your applications are resilient enough to detect the types and capabilities of these new components at runtime.

One of the exciting possibilities with this style of programming is the ability to write pluggable software. This software can dynamically load any kind of component, can be based on locale or user details, and can interact with these components via reflection.

This sounds almost too good to be true, and, as is usually the case, it's more difficult to write generic code than it is to write code for a specific component, event, or property. You have to work a bit harder to discover the information that you need to achieve your task. Furthermore, using reflection can cause inefficiencies at runtime due to the extra effort the application has to expend to access the required metadata. However, the overall effect is worth the effort, as you'll see in the following application.

The sample application for this section of the chapter appears in Figure 12-6. You can download this Windows Forms application from the Downloads section of the Apress Web site (http://www.apress.com).

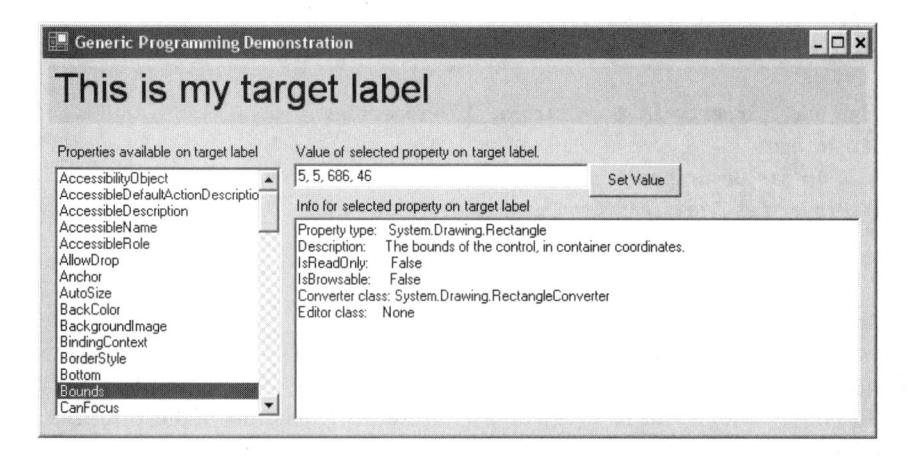

Figure 12-6. *Illustration of the sample application downloadable from* http://www.apress.com

The application allows the user to dynamically change any property on the upper label component on the form. Table 12-1 lists the components in the form.

Table 12-1. *Form Components*

Component type	Component name
System.Windows.Forms.Label	lblTarget
System.Windows.Forms.ListBox	lstProperties
System.Windows.Forms.TextBox	txtNewValue
System.Windows.Forms.Button	btnSetValue
System.Windows.Forms.RichTextBox	txtInfo

The main VB source file in the application has the following Imports statements:

```
Imports System                      ' For general .NET types
Imports System.Windows.Forms        ' For general Windows Forms types
Imports System.Drawing.Design       ' For the UIEditor class (see later)
Imports System.ComponentModel       ' For the .NET Component Model types
```

This is how the application works:

- When the form loads, the application uses reflection to get the list of available properties for the label component, lblTarget. These properties are displayed in the list box on the left side of the form, lstProperties. The following code shows these tasks:

```
Private Sub Form1_Load(ByVal sender As System.Object, _
                      ByVal e As System.EventArgs) _
                      Handles MyBase.Load

    ' Get descriptive information for all the properties on lblTarget
    Dim propDescriptors As PropertyDescriptorCollection
    propDescriptors = TypeDescriptor.GetProperties(Me.lblTarget)

    ' Display each property in the ListBox, lstProperties
    Dim I As Integer
    For I = 0 To propDescriptors.Count - 1
        Me.lstProperties.Items.Add(propDescriptors(I).Name)
    Next

End Sub
```

- The following code shows what happens when the user selects a property in the list box. The application uses reflection to get further information for the selected property, and displays this information in the large text area in the lower-right corner of the form. The property information includes

    - The data type of the property. For example, the data type of the Bounds property is displayed as System.Drawing.Rectangle in Figure 12-6, shown previously.

    - A textual description of the property. Components provide this information for the benefit of the Visual Designer.

    - A flag that indicates whether the property is read-only. For example, Figure 12-6 showed that the Bounds property is not read-only.

    - A flag that indicates whether the property is browsable at designtime. For example, Figure 12-6 showed that the Bounds property is not browsable at designtime. In other words, the Bounds property will not be displayed in the Properties window in the Visual Designer; the Bounds property is only usable at runtime.

    - The name of a converter class associated with the data type of this property. For example, Figure 12-6 showed that the converter class for the Bounds property is System.Drawing.RectangleConverter. This converter class converts Rectangle objects to strings and vice versa to allow the value to be edited as a string in the Properties window in VS .NET. The .NET Framework class library provides a suite of converter classes, all inherited from System.ComponentModel.TypeConverter, whose purpose is to convert values to and from other data types.

- The name of an editor class associated with the data type of this property. Editor classes are provided by the .NET Framework to help the user edit nontrivial data types such as Font, DateTime, and Color. To get the editor for the selected property's type, we call the TypeDescriptor.GetEditor() method. This method requires two parameters: the data type of the property and the base data type for the editor. UITypeEditor is the base class for all the editor classes in .NET; all editor classes inherit from UITypeEditor. If you take another look at Figure 12-6, you'll notice that there is no editor class associated with the Bounds property; this means Rectangle values must be edited directly in string format (for example, 16, 16, 752, 40) .

- The application also gets the current value of the selected property, and uses the appropriate converter class (such as System.Drawing.RectangleConverter) to convert this value into a string. Later in the chapter, you'll see how the Visual Designer ascertains which converter class to use for each property. The string value of the property is displayed in the small text field in the middle of the form.

```
' Helper variable
Private nl As String = Environment.NewLine

' Remember property information for the currently selected property
Private mSelectedProp As PropertyDescriptor

' Remember the TypeConverter for the currently selected property
Private mConverter As TypeConverter

Private Sub lstProperties_SelectedIndexChanged( _
                                        ByVal sender As Object, _
                                        ByVal e As System.EventArgs) _
                    Handles lstProperties.SelectedIndexChanged

    ' Get the selected property in the lstProperties Listbox
    Dim selectedPropName As String = Me.lstProperties.SelectedItem

    ' Get the PropertyDescriptor for the selected property
    Dim propDescriptors As PropertyDescriptorCollection
    propDescriptors = TypeDescriptor.GetProperties(Me.lblTarget)
    Me.mSelectedProp = propDescriptors.Find(selectedPropName, False)

    ' Use the PropertyDescriptor to display simple info for the property
    Me.txtInfo.Clear()
    Me.txtInfo.AppendText("Property type:   {0} {1} ", _
                        Me.mSelectedProp.PropertyType.ToString(), nl)
    Me.txtInfo.AppendText("Description:     {0} {1} ", _
                        Me.mSelectedProp.Description, nl)
    Me.txtInfo.AppendText("IsReadOnly:      {0} {1} ", _
                        Me.mSelectedProp.IsReadOnly, nl)
    Me.txtInfo.AppendText("IsBrowsable:     {0} {1} ", _
                        Me.mSelectedProp.IsBrowsable, nl)
```

```vbnet
' Can this property be modified in string format?
' Assume it can't, for now...
Dim canModifyFlag As Boolean = False

' Display info about the property's type-converter class
Me.mConverter = Me.mSelectedProp.Converter
If Me.mConverter Is Nothing Then
  Me.txtInfo.AppendText("Converter class: None{0}", nl)
ElseIf Me.mConverter.CanConvertFrom(GetType(String)) = False Then
  Me.txtInfo.AppendText("Converter class: {0} {1} ", _
                        "Cannot convert from string value", nl)
Else
  Me.txtInfo.AppendText("Converter class: {0} {1} ", _
                        Me.mConverter.GetType().ToString() , nl)
  If Not Me.mSelectedProp.IsReadOnly Then
    canModifyFlag = True
  End If
End If


' Enable or disable editing of the property's value
Me.txtNewValue.Enabled = canModifyFlag
Me.btnSetValue.Enabled = canModifyFlag

' Display current value of property (if expressable as a string)
If (Me.mConverter Is Nothing) Or _
   (Me.mConverter.CanConvertTo(GetType(String))) = False Then
  Me.txtNewValue.Text = ""
Else
  Dim objValue As Object
  objValue = Me.mSelectedProp.GetValue(Me.lblTarget)
  Dim strValue As String
  strValue = Me.mConverter.ConvertTo(objValue, GetType(String))
  Me.txtNewValue.Text = strValue
End If


' Display info about the property's editor class
Dim editor As Object
editor = TypeDescriptor.GetEditor(Me.mSelectedProp.PropertyType, _
                        GetType(UITypeEditor))
If editor Is Nothing Then
  Me.txtInfo.AppendText("Editor class:    None{0}", nl)
Else
  Me.txtInfo.AppendText("Editor class:    {0}{1} ", _
                        editor.GetType().ToString(), nl)
End If

End Sub
```

- The application allows the user to type in a new value for the property. When the user clicks the Set Value button, the application gets the string value entered by the user, and converts it into the appropriate data type for the property. To achieve this conversion, the application uses the appropriate conversion class for the property in question.

```
Private Sub btnSetValue_Click(ByVal sender As System.Object, _
                ByVal e As System.EventArgs) _
                Handles btnSetValue.Click
   Try
     ' Get the property value entered in the TextBox, txtNewValue
     Dim strValue As String = Me.txtNewValue.Text

     ' Use the PropertyDescriptor for the selected property,
     ' to convert the string into the correct type for the property
     Dim objValue As Object = Me.mConverter.ConvertFrom(strValue)

     ' Set the property on the Label, lblTarget
     Me.mSelectedProp.SetValue(Me.lblTarget, objValue)

   Catch Ex As Exception
     MessageBox.Show(Ex.Message, _
                "Exception occurred", _
                MessageBoxButtons.OK, _
                MessageBoxIcon.Error)
   End Try

End Sub
```

Let's build and run the application to see what we can do. When the application form appears, make some changes to the properties of the target label. Here are some suggestions, but feel free to experiment with your own property changes:

- **BackColor:** DarkBlue
- **Font:** Tahoma, 20pt
- **ForeColor:** 255, 122, 78
- **Height:** 32
- **Left:** 50
- **RightToLeft:** Yes
- **Text:** This is my new label text
- **Width:** 500

If you make the changes we've suggested, the target label will appear as shown in Figure 12-7 on the form.

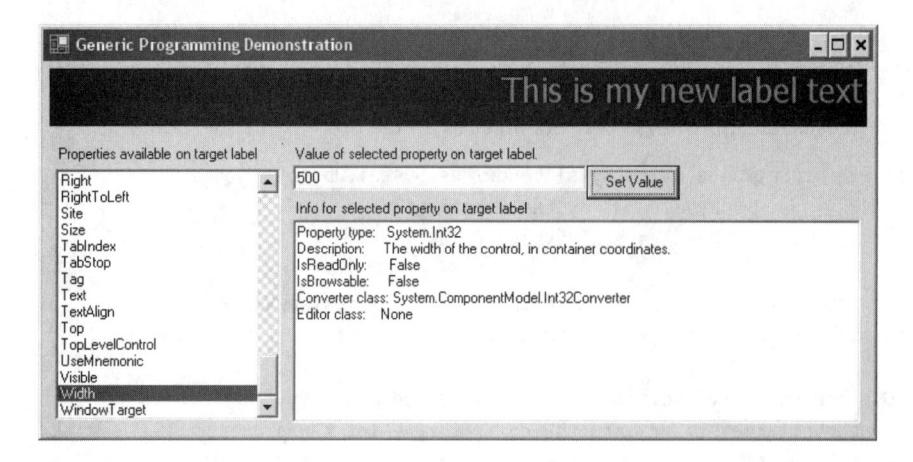

Figure 12-7. *Changes to the target label*

Creating New Components

Now that you've seen how to use reflection to access metadata for predefined .NET components, let's consider how to write new components of your own. This will consolidate your understanding of how components work, and provide a deeper insight into the role of attributes and other data types defined in the `System.ComponentModel` namespace.

After you've written components, developers can use them just like they use standard components defined in the .NET Framework class library. For example, developers will be able to add your components to the ToolBox in VS .NET, and drag and drop component objects onto the Visual Designer. This helps developers build applications quickly and (relatively) effortlessly by plugging together prefabricated components and using their functionality as required.

We'll tackle the following tasks in this section of the chapter:

- We'll begin by defining a simple component class named `Employee`. Along the way, we'll present various guidelines for defining "good" component classes.

- After we've written our embryonic version of the `Employee` component class, we'll show how to store components in a container. The `System.ComponentModel` namespace has an interface named `IContainer`, which defines the basic requirements for container classes. To simplify application development, there is also a standard class named `Container`, which provides a base implementation of `IContainer`. You'll see how to use `Container` to hold `Employee` component instances. You'll also see how to write a custom container class by implementing `IContainer` directly, which is a useful approach if we need more functionality than is provided by the standard `Container` class.

- It's also possible to host components in Windows Forms and ASP.NET Web pages by adding our component class to the ToolBox in VS .NET. This will allow application developers to drag and drop `Employee` component objects onto the Visual Designer, in the same way as they can drag and drop predefined components such as `System.Windows.Forms.Timer` and `System.Data.SqlClient.SqlConnection`. We'll look at the code that gets generated when we add component objects to an application.

- Our next task will be to add properties and events to our `Employee` component class. We'll annotate these properties and events with attributes to enable VS .NET to display these members properly at designtime. For example, we'll use the `<Description()>` attribute to define a textual description for each property in `Employee`. We'll also use the `<Category()>` attribute to group related properties into categories.

- You'll also see how these attributes affect the code that gets generated when we add `Employee` component objects to a host application.

- To close the chapter, we'll show how to write converter classes for an `Address` class and a `TelephoneNumber` class. The converter classes will enable `Address` and `TelephoneNumber` objects to be converted to strings, and vice versa. You'll see how the Visual Designer uses these converter classes to allow the user to modify complex properties in the Properties window at designtime.

By the end of this section, we'll have built a fully functional component class that exhibits many of the characteristics found in standard .NET component classes. If you want to skip ahead, you can download a complete and working version of this component class from the Downloads section of the Apress Web site (http://www.apress.com). You can also download a sample application that uses this component.

Defining a Component Class

As described at the beginning of the chapter, a component class is simply a class that implements the `IComponent` interface. There is another technical constraint we haven't mentioned yet: component classes must either provide a no-argument constructor, or a constructor that takes a single parameter of type `IContainer`.

The easiest way to implement the `IComponent` interface is to inherit it directly or indirectly from one of the following:

- `System.ComponentModel.Component`: This class provides a base implementation of the `IComponent` interface, suitable for marshal by reference (MBR) components. If we pass an instance of any MBR class into a method on a remote server, the CLR passes an object reference rather than a copy of the object.

- `System.ComponentModel.MarshalByValueComponent`: As its name suggests, this class provides a base implementation of `IComponent` suitable for marshal by value (MBV) components. If we pass an instance of an MBV component into a method on a remote server, the CLR passes a copy of the object rather than an object reference. MBV types are typically used to represent data-laden objects that are passed back and forth between the client and server in a .NET Remoting application.

- `System.Web.UI.Control`: This class defines the methods, properties, and events that are common for all ASP.NET server controls. Note that the equivalent base class for Windows Forms controls, `System.Windows.Forms.Control`, extends `Component` rather than implementing `IComponent` directly.

- `System.Web.HttpApplication`: This class will be of interest to you if you are familiar with ASP.NET and Web applications. The `HttpApplication` class defines the methods, properties, and events that are common for all ASP.NET application objects defined in a `Global.asax` file in a Web application. Application objects provide information and services that are shared and accessed by all users of a Web application, rather than for a specific session (session-specific state is maintained in an `HttpSessionState` object).

When we write a component class, the first step is to choose an appropriate access modifier for the component class. The choices are the same as for a normal class:

- If we want the component to be available to all client applications, we must define the accessibility of the component class as `Public`:

  ```
  ' This component can be accessed anywhere
  Public Class Employee
    Inherits System.ComponentModel.Component
    ' Members ...
  End Class
  ```

- If we want the component to be available only to other code in the same assembly, we can declare the accessibility as `Friend`. This is the default accessibility if we do not specify any accessibility specifiers:

  ```
  ' This component can only be accessed by code in the same assembly
  Friend Class Employee
    Inherits System.ComponentModel.Component
    ' Members ...
  End Class
  ```

- If we want the component to be available only to a specific class, we can define the component class as a nested class as shown next (nested classes are often referred to as inner classes in other OO programming languages). We can use the `Private`, `Protected`, `Friend`, or `Protected Friend` accessibility modifiers to control the accessibility of the nested component:

  ```
  Public Class MyOuterClass

    ' This component can only be accessed by MyOuterClass, because we've
    ' used the Private access modifier. Alternatively, we can specify:
    '    Protected (accessible by derived classes)
    '    Friend (accessible by classes in the same assembly)
    '    Protected Friend (combination of Protected and Friend access)
    Private Class Employee
      Inherits System.ComponentModel.Component
      ' Members ...
    End Class
  End Class
  ```

Another important issue is to specify a meaningful namespace and assembly information for our component. This is especially important if we intend our component to be used widely by other developers, to avoid name clashes with any other components these developers might be using. If we want to allow developers to drag and drop instances of our component onto their applications from the VS .NET ToolBox, we need to provide as much useful information as possible about our component.

To define a component class, we can either type all the source code into a text editor such as Notepad, or we can use VS .NET to help generate some of the boilerplate code. We'll take the latter approach, but we'll also show all the generated code to prove there's nothing magical happening under the covers.

To create a template component class in VS .NET, follow these steps:

1. Create a new project containing a VB .NET class library. Choose a meaningful name for the project, such as MyComponent.

2. VS .NET generates a mostly empty class file named Class1.vb. Right-click on this file name in Solution Explorer, and select Delete from the shortcut menu. We won't be using this file.

3. In Solution Explorer, right-click the project name (MyComponent in this example) and select Add ➤ Add New Item from the shortcut menu. The Add New Item dialog box appears; click Component Class from the Templates list, and enter a suitable name for the component class (see Figure 12-8). For this example, enter the file name **Employee.vb**, and then click Open.

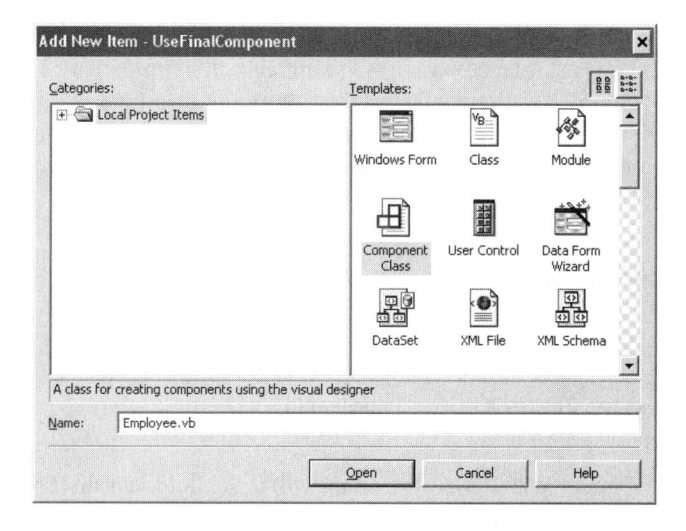

Figure 12-8. *Creating a template component class*

The Component Designer in VS .NET generates starter source code in Employee.vb to define a simple component class. Let's dissect this code, and investigate the component-related features.

First, the new class inherits from System.ComponentModel.Component as expected:

```
Imports System
Imports System.ComponentModel

Public Class Employee
  Inherits System.ComponentModel.Component
  ' Members...
End Class
```

If we want an MBV component rather than an MBR component, all we have to do is change the superclass from Component to MarshalByValueComponent as follows:

```
' This is a marshal-by-value component class
Public Class Employee
  Inherits System.ComponentModel.MarshalByValueComponent
  ' Members...
End Class
```

The `Employee` component class contains two constructors generated by the Component Designer. These constructors are in the `Component Designer generated code` region in the `Employee` class. The first constructor takes an `IContainer` parameter, which represents the logical container of the component. The constructor calls the no-arg constructor (discussed next), and then adds the current component (`me`) to the container:

```
Public Sub New(Container As System.ComponentModel.IContainer)
  ' Call the no-arg constructor (see below)
  MyClass.New()
  'Required for Windows.Forms Class Composition Designer support
  Container.Add(me)
End Sub
```

The second constructor is shown next. This constructor calls the base-class constructor, and then calls a helper method named `InitializeComponent()` to initialize this component. The code in `InitializeComponent()` is generated automatically by the Component Designer, so we must not edit the code in `InitializeComponent()` directly. Instead, if we have any additional initialization to perform for our component, we should add code at the end of the constructor as indicated by the final comment:

```
Public Sub New()
  ' Call the base-class constructor
  MyBase.New()
  'This call is required by the Component Designer.
  InitializeComponent()
  'Add any initialization after the InitializeComponent() call
End Sub
```

The `InitializeComponent()` method is shown next, along with the definition of an `IContainer` field named `components`. The `InitializeComponent()` method creates a new `Container` object and assigns it to the `components` field as follows:

```
'Required by the Component Designer
Private components As System.ComponentModel.IContainer

'NOTE: The following procedure is required by the Component Designer
'It can be modified using the Component Designer.
'Do not modify it using the code editor.
<System.Diagnostics.DebuggerStepThrough()>_
Private Sub InitializeComponent()
  components = New System.ComponentModel.Container()
End Sub
```

This arrangement allows our component to act as a container for other components. For example, if we viewed our component in Design view, we could add other components to it from the ToolBox or Server Explorer, such as timer components, MSMQ components, database connection components, and so on.

Our component class has a `Dispose()` method as shown next, to dispose of the additional components owned by our component. This `Dispose()` method overrides `Dispose()` in the base class, `Component`. The `Component` class implements `IDisposable`, which means all components exhibit disposable behavior. This means we can call `Dispose()` on any component object to deterministically dispose of its subcomponents.

```
Protected Overloads Overrides Sub Dispose(ByVal disposing As Boolean)

  If disposing Then
    If Not (components Is Nothing) Then
      components.Dispose()
    End If
  End If
  MyBase.Dispose(disposing)
End Sub
```

Our project also has an AssemblyInfo.vb source file, which contains a set of assembly attributes to define metadata for our assembly. Let's define some (reasonably) meaningful assembly attributes, as follows.

```
Imports System.Reflection
Imports System.Runtime.InteropServices

' General Information about an assembly is controlled through the
' following set of attributes. Change these attribute values to modify
' the information associated with an assembly.

' Review the values of the assembly attributes
<Assembly: AssemblyTitle("My assembly")>
<Assembly: AssemblyDescription("This assembly contains my component")>
<Assembly: AssemblyCompany("My Company")>
<Assembly: AssemblyProduct("")>
<Assembly: AssemblyCopyright("")>
<Assembly: AssemblyTrademark("")>
<Assembly: CLSCompliant(True)>

' The following GUID is for the ID of the typelib if this project
' is exposed to COM
<Assembly: Guid("837D85C8-C217-4FB6-A1E3-D3DCDF8E1C25")>

' Version information for an assembly consists of four values:
'
'       Major Version
'       Minor Version
'       Build Number
'       Revision
'
' You can specify all the values or you can default the Build and
' Revision Numbers by using the '*' syntax:

<Assembly: AssemblyVersion("1.0.0.0")>
```

If you are following these steps on your own computer, build the component in VS .NET to produce an assembly named MyComponent.dll. Later in the chapter, you'll see how to add this component to the ToolBox in VS .NET, and drag and drop component instances into a sample application.

Storing Components in a Container

As described earlier in the chapter, the primary difference between component classes (that is, classes that implement IComponent) and other classes is that components possess the capability to be logically stored in containers. The System.ComponentModel namespace defines a standard class named Container, which implements IContainer and provides methods to add, remove, and retrieve components in a container. In many cases, the Container class is sufficient and there is no need to write our own custom class to implement IContainer directly.

Before we dive into the technicalities, let's recall the motivation for developing and using components and containers. Components are written to provide chunks of functionality that you can leverage later in your project (and other developers can leverage in their projects); components provide a very effective way of building reusable software. Furthermore, because VB .NET is a .NET-compliant language, you can even reuse your components in other .NET-compliant languages such as Visual C# and Managed Extensions for C++. For example, you can write a container object that can hold components written in any .NET language.

Using the Standard Container Class to Host Components

To show how to use the standard Container class to hold components, we've provided a sample application in the Downloads section of the Apress Web site (http://www.apress.com). The application uses an enhanced version of the Employee class that holds some employee data, and provides an Equals() method to compare Employee objects to see if they hold the same employee data. This source code is located in the file Employee.vb:

```
Imports System
Imports System.ComponentModel

Public Class Employee
  Inherits System.ComponentModel.Component

  ' Some simple data for this employee
  Private mFullName As String

  ' Constructor, to initialize the data for this employee
  Public Sub New(ByVal FullName As String)
    mFullName = FullName
  End Sub

  ' Property to get the employee's full name
  Public ReadOnly Property FullName() As String
    Get
      Return mFullName
    End Get
  End Property

  ' Override Equals(), to compare two Employee objects for equality
  Public Overloads Function Equals(ByVal other As Object) As Boolean
    Dim otherEmp As Employee = CType(other, Employee)
```

```
      If mFullName = otherEmp.mFullName Then
        Return True
      Else
        Return False
      End If
    End Function

#Region " Component Designer generated code "
    ' Same as before...
#End Region

End Class
```

The Main() method for this sample application is located in a file named MainClass.vb. The full source code for the method is shown next.

The Main method begins by creating an instance of the standard Container class, and then creates four Employee component objects. To insert a component into a container, we call the Add() method on the container object. Add() takes two arguments: the component we want to insert and a site name that uniquely identifies each component in this container. We'll discuss the role of site names in container classes shortly, when we discuss how to write your own custom container classes. In this example, we use an employee's ID number as the unique site name for each employee. Notice the last call to Add() will fail deliberately, because the site name "003" is already in use.

The Container class also has a Remove() method, which allows us to remove a component from a container. By default, Remove() compares object references to locate the object to remove; when we write our own custom container class shortly, you'll see how to compare object values by calling the Equals() method on Employee objects.

If we want to access the components in a container, we use the Components property as shown at the bottom of the Main() method. The Components property returns a ComponentCollection object, and we use an enumerator object to iterate through the components in this collection:

```
Imports System
Imports System.Collections
Imports System.ComponentModel

Public Class MainClass

  Public Shared Sub Main()

    ' Create a standard Container instance
    Dim firm As New Container()

    ' Create some components
    Dim emp1 As New Employee("Roger Smith")
    Dim emp2 As New Employee("Emily Jones")
    Dim emp3 As New Employee("Tommy Evans")
    Dim emp4 As New Employee("Hazel Ellis")
```

```
    Try
        ' Add components to the container. The last statement will fail
        ' deliberately, because the site name "003" is already in use.
        firm.Add(emp1, "001")
        firm.Add(emp2, "002")
        firm.Add(emp3, "003")
        firm.Add(emp4, "003")
    Catch e As SystemException
        Console.WriteLine("Exception: " + e.Message)
    End Try
    ' Remove an employee
    firm.Remove(emp1)
    ' Get a collection of all the components in the container
    Dim allEmps As ComponentCollection = firm.Components

    ' Loop through the component collection, and display each employee
    Dim iter As IEnumerator = allEmps.GetEnumerator()
    While (iter.MoveNext())
        Dim emp As Employee = CType(iter.Current, Employee)
        Console.WriteLine("Employee name: " + emp.FullName)
    End While
  End Sub
End Class
```

When we build and run the application, it displays the messages on the console as shown in Figure 12-9. These messages confirm that the first three `Employee` components were successfully inserted into the container, but the fourth `Employee` component failed due to a duplicate site name. The console messages also confirm that the employee "Roger Smith" was successfully removed from the container.

Figure 12-9. `MySimpleContainer` *application generating output on the console*

Defining a Custom Container Class to Host Components

On occasion, it may be necessary to write a custom container class that provides more specialized business logic than the predefined `Container` class. For example, you might want to write a container class that logs all insertions and removals to a Windows log file, or creates a backup copy of all removed objects in a database.

Whatever the motivation, there are two distinct steps when defining a custom container class:

- Define a class that implements the `ISite` interface to associate a component object and a container object.

- Define a class that implements the `IContainer` interface to manage the insertion, removal, and retrieval of components.

We've provided a sample application in the Downloads section of the Apress Web site called `MyComplexContainer` to illustrate these tasks.

Let's begin with the `ISite` interface. The `ISite` interface specifies the following members to associate a component with a container. `ISite` also allows us to get or set a site name for each component in the container, and to query whether we're currently in Design mode:

```
' This is the standard ISite interface in the .NET class library
Public Interface ISite
  Inherits IServiceProvider

  ' Property to get the component for this site
  Public ReadOnly Property Component() As IComponent

  ' Property to get the container for this site
  Public ReadOnly Property Container() As IContainer

  ' Property to indicate whether we're in design mode
  Public ReadOnly Property DesignMode() As Boolean

  ' Property to get/set the name of this site
  Public Property Name() As String

  ' Get the service for this site (inherited from IServiceProvider)
  Public Function GetService(ByVal serviceType As Type) As Object

End Interface
```

The following code shows how to implement the `ISite` interface to associate `Employee` components with their container. This is a fairly generic implementation, and should suffice for most occasions where you need to implement the `ISite` interface. This code is available in the file `EmployeeSite.vb`.

Notice that all references to component objects are expressed using the interface type `IComponent`, rather than a specific component class such as `EmployeeComponent`. We have to use generic interface types to comply with method signatures in the `ISite` interface. Similarly, all references to container objects are expressed using the interface type `IContainer`, rather than a specific container class such as `EmployeeContainer`. Despite this loss of strong type information at compile-time, we can still discover everything we need about the component and container classes at runtime by using reflection, as you saw earlier in the chapter:

```
Imports System
Imports System.ComponentModel

Class EmployeeSite
  Implements ISite
```

```vb
' A site object associates a container with a component
Private mTheContainer As IContainer
Private mTheComponent As IComponent

' A site object uses a unique site name for each component in a
' container. Because we're in the EmployeeSite class, we'll use the
' employee's ID as the site name.
Private mEmpID As String

' Constructor, to associate a container with a component
Public Sub New(ByVal TheContainer As IContainer, _
               ByVal TheComponent As IComponent)
  mTheContainer = TheContainer
  mTheComponent = TheComponent
  mEmpID = Nothing
End Sub

' Property to get the component for this site
Public ReadOnly Property Component() As IComponent _
                            Implements ISite.Component
  Get
    Return mTheComponent
  End Get
End Property

' Property to get the container for this site
Public ReadOnly Property Container() As IContainer _
                            Implements ISite.Container
  Get
    Return mTheContainer
  End Get
End Property

' Property to indicate whether we're in design mode
' (always return False in this example - we're never in design mode)
Public ReadOnly Property DesignMode() As Boolean _
                            Implements ISite.DesignMode
  Get
    Return False
  End Get
End Property

' Property to get/set the name of this site
Public Property Name() As String Implements ISite.Name
  Get
    Return mEmpID
  End Get
```

```
      Set(ByVal Value As String)
         mEmpID = Value
      End Set
   End Property
   ' Function to get the service for this site
   ' (inherited from IServiceProvider)
   Public Function GetService(ByVal serviceType As Type) As Object _
                             Implements ISite.GetService
      Return Nothing
   End Function

End Class
```

Now let's turn our attention to the `IContainer` interface. The `IContainer` interface specifies the following methods and properties to insert, remove, and retrieve components in a container. Also, because `IContainer` inherits from the `IDisposable` interface, `IContainer` has a `Dispose()` method to perform deterministic destruction of the container:

```
' This is the standard IContainer interface in the .NET class library

Public Interface IContainer
   Inherits IDisposable

   ' Add a component (without specifying a Site name)
   Public Sub Add(ByVal aComponent As IComponent)

   ' Add a component (specifying a Site name)
   Public Sub Add(ByVal aComponent As IComponent, _
                  ByVal SiteName As String)

   ' Remove the specified component from the container
   Public Sub Remove(ByVal emp As IComponent)

   ' Return all the components, wrapped up in a ComponentCollection
   Public ReadOnly Property Components() As ComponentCollection

   ' Dispose all components in container (inherited from IDisposable)
   Public Sub Dispose()

End Interface
```

The following sections of code show how to implement the `IContainer` interface to contain `Employee` components. This implementation is also fairly generic, and should provide a good starting point if you need to implement the `IContainer` interface yourself some day. This code is available in the file `EmployeeContainer.vb`.

We've decided to use an `ArrayList` to store the `Employee` components, because it's easy to insert and remove items in an `ArrayList`:

```
Imports System
Imports System.ComponentModel
Imports System.Collections
```

```
Class EmployeeContainer
  Implements IContainer

  ' Hold a collection of Employee objects
  Private mEmployees As New ArrayList()
  ' Plus other members (see below...)
End Class
```

Here are the two overloaded Add() methods for our container class:

- The first Add() method adds the specified component to the ArrayList. No site name is specified for the new component, so we don't create an EmployeeSite object for this component. Without an EmployeeSite object, the component has no way of accessing its container object, should it need to do so:

```
Public Sub Add(ByVal emp As IComponent) Implements IContainer.Add
    mEmployees.Add(emp)
End Sub
```

- The second Add() method receives a site name for the new component. We test that the site name isn't already in use by an existing component in the container, and then insert the new component into the ArrayList. We also create a new Site object to remember the container object, the component object, and the component's site name:

```
Public Sub Add(ByVal emp As IComponent, ByVal empID As String) _
                    Implements IContainer.Add

  ' Loop through components, to see if the site name is already in use
  Dim i As Integer
  For i = 0 To mEmployees.Count - 1
    Dim cur As IComponent = CType(mEmployees(i), IComponent)
    If (Not cur.Site Is Nothing) And (cur.Site.Name = empID) Then
      Throw New SystemException("Employee ID {0} {1}", empID, _
                          " already exists in container")
    End If
  Next

  ' Site name is OK, so add the component to the container
  mEmployees.Add(emp)

  ' Create a Site object to associate the container and the component
  Dim theSite As EmployeeSite = New EmployeeSite(Me, emp)
  theSite.Name = empID
  emp.Site = theSite

End Sub
```

Now let's see the Remove() method. Remove() receives a component as a parameter, and loops through all the components in the ArrayList searching for a match. The equality test is performed by calling the Equals() method defined in Employee to compare the value of Employee objects rather than comparing object references (as was the case with the standard Container class earlier). If a matching Employee object is found, it is removed from the ArrayList:

```
Public Sub Remove(ByVal emp As IComponent) _
                        Implements IContainer.Remove

  Dim i As Integer
  Dim cur As Employee = CType(emp, Employee)

  ' Find a matching component in the container, and then remove it
  For i = 0 To mEmployees.Count - 1
    If cur.Equals(mEmployees(i)) Then
      mEmployees.RemoveAt(i)
      Exit For
    End If
  Next
End Sub
```

Moving swiftly on, the EmployeeContainer class also has a Components property as shown next. This property returns a ComponentCollection object containing all the components held in the ArrayList:

```
Public ReadOnly Property Components() As ComponentCollection _
                        Implements IContainer.Components

  Get
    Dim componentArray(mEmployees.Count - 1) As IComponent
    mEmployees.CopyTo(componentArray)
    Return New ComponentCollection(componentArray)
  End Get

End Property
```

Finally, here is the code for the Dispose() method. This method disposes of each component, and then empties the ArrayList:

```
Public Sub Dispose() Implements IContainer.Dispose

  Dim i As Integer
  For i = 0 To mEmployees.Count - 1
    Dim cur As IComponent = mEmployees(i)
    cur.Dispose()
  Next

  mEmployees.Clear()

End Sub
```

To test the custom container class, we can use the same `Main()` method as before. The only difference is that we create an `EmployeeContainer` object, rather than a standard `Container` object:

```
Dim firm As New EmployeeContainer()
```

When we build and run the application, it displays the same messages as before (see Figure 12-10). However, our application offers much more flexibility than before; we can enhance the `EmployeeSite` and `EmployeeContainer` classes to perform additional business processing as needed.

Figure 12-10. *Output of the* `MyComplexContainer` *application*

Using Components in VS .NET

In the previous section, you saw how to use the `Container` class to manage collections of components. You also saw how to write a custom container class to take greater control over how components are stored, retrieved, and removed.

In this section, we'll change tack slightly and see how to add components to an application using VS .NET. You'll see how to add components to the ToolBox, and then drag and drop component objects onto a new application. We'll also look at the source code that gets generated by the Component Designer to create the component object in our application.

Adding a Component to the ToolBox in VS .NET

To add a component to the ToolBox in VS .NET, follow these steps:

1. Launch VS .NET, and open the ToolBox if it is not already visible.

2. Select one of the tabs on the ToolBox, to choose where to add the new component. The choice of available tabs depends on the type of project that is currently open in VS .NET. If in doubt, we suggest you select the `General` tab.

3. Right-click on your chosen tab in the ToolBox, and select `Customize Toolbox` from the shortcut menu.

4. The `Customize Toolbox` dialog box appears. Click the `.NET Framework Components` tab on the top of this dialog box to display a list of .NET components. Click `Browse`, and navigate to the `MyComponent.dll` assembly file we created earlier. The dialog box displays information about the `Employee` component in this assembly as shown in Figure 12-11.

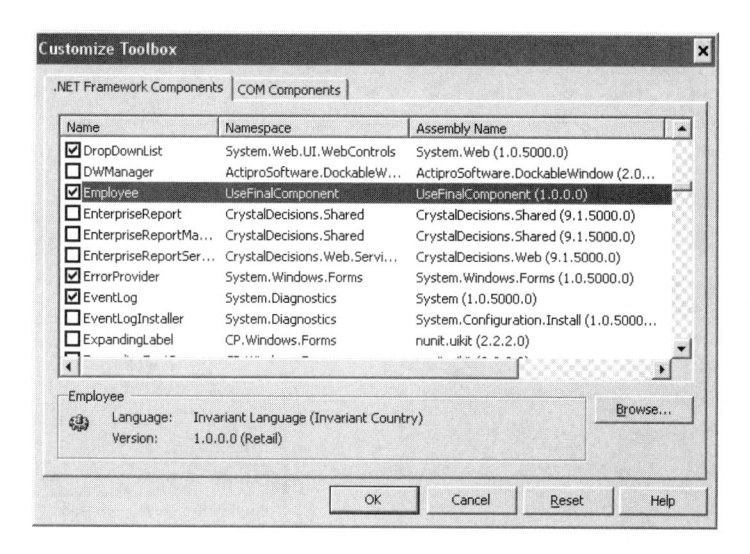

Figure 12-11. *Information about the* Employee *component within* MyComponent.dll

5. Click OK to add this Employee component to the ToolBox.
6. Verify that the Employee component now appears in the ToolBox.

Adding Component Objects to an Application

Now that we've added the Employee component to the ToolBox in VS .NET, we can drag and drop Employee component objects onto our applications. Follow these steps:

1. In VS .NET, create a new VB .NET Windows application (for example).

2. Select the Form component in Visual Designer. Change its (Name) property to something more meaningful, such as TestEmployeeForm. Also change its Text property to Test Employee Form. Finally, rename the source file Form1.vb to TestEmployeeForm.vb.

3. Drag-and-drop an Employee component object onto the Visual Designer for the form. This causes the Component Designer to add code to our application to create an Employee component object. The new component is displayed in the component tray in the Visual Designer. The properties for the Employee component object are shown in the Properties window (see Figure 12-12).

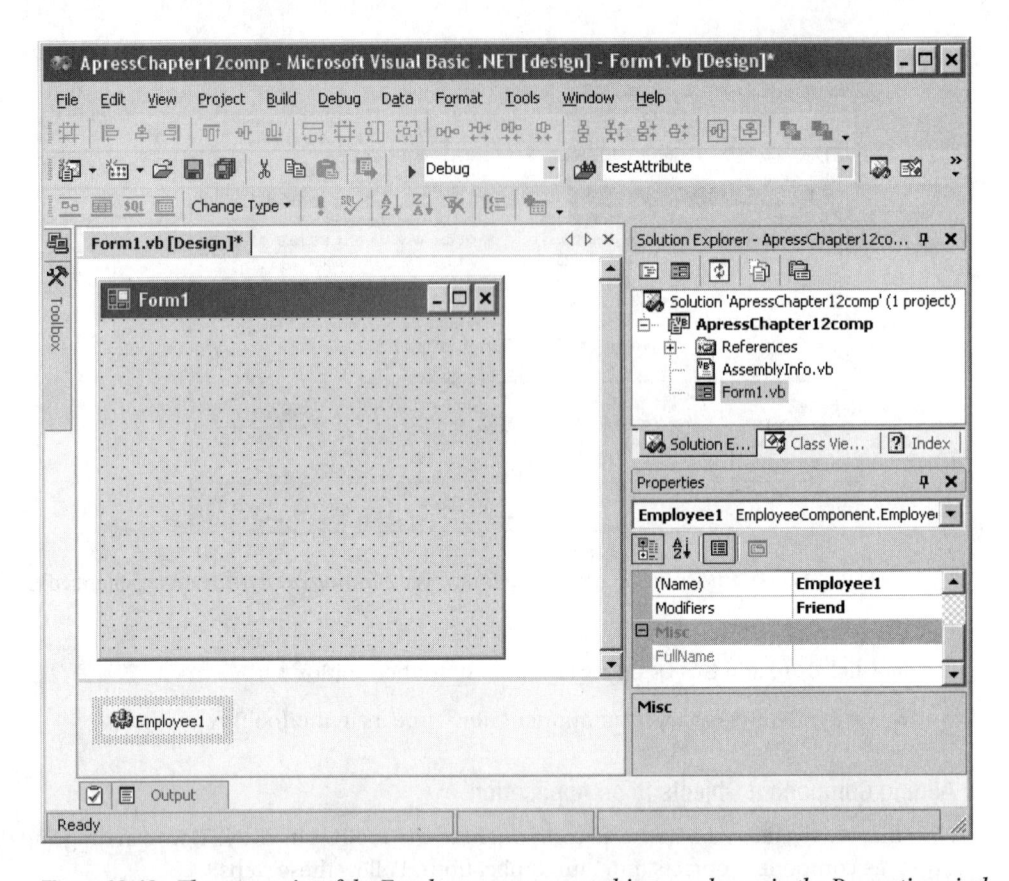

Figure 12-12. *The properties of the Employee component object are shown in the Properties window.*

4. View the source code file for `TestEmployeeForm.vb`. The following code has been generated to create an `Employee` component object and associate it with a `Container` object. VS .NET only creates the `Container` object if we add one or more components to the form.

Note As you may recall from our earlier discussion about the `Employee` class, the `Employee` constructor invokes the `Add()` method on the `Container` object to add the component object to the container.

```
Friend WithEvents Employee1 As MyComponent.Employee

<System.Diagnostics.DebuggerStepThrough()> _
Private Sub InitializeComponent()

  Me.components = New System.ComponentModel.Container()
  Me.Employee1 = New MyComponent.Employee(Me.components)
```

```
    '
    ' TestEmployeeForm
    '
    Me.AutoScaleBaseSize = New System.Drawing.Size(5, 13)
    Me.ClientSize = New System.Drawing.Size(292, 273)
    Me.Name = "TestEmployeeForm"
    Me.Text = "Test Employee Form"

End Sub
```

The next section shows how to define properties in a component class, and describes how to use attributes to make these properties accessible at designtime to the Visual Designer.

Defining Properties and Events for a Component

When we add properties and events to a component, we should annotate these members with attributes to enable VS .NET to display the members correctly at designtime. The following list describes the attributes we'll use in our example. All these attribute classes are defined in the `System.ComponentModel` namespace. See VS .NET Help for a complete list of attribute classes in this namespace.

- **<Browsable()>**: Indicates that a property or event is browsable at designtime; in other words, the property or event appears in the Properties window. By default, properties and events are browsable. Therefore, the only time you need to use this attribute is to prevent a member from being browsable: in this case, specify `<Browsable(False)>`.

- **<Category()>**: Indicates that a property or event belongs to a particular category. Items in the same category are grouped together in the Properties window. If we don't specify a category, the property or event will be added to a category named `Misc` by default.

- **<DefaultEvent()>**: This attribute is used on a class or structure definition to indicate the default event in the class.

- **<DefaultProperty()>**: This attribute is used on a class or structure definition to indicate the default property in the class.

- **<DefaultValue()>**: Indicates the default value for a property. If the property currently has this value, it is shown unbolded in the Properties window. If the property has a different value, it is displayed in bold. Note that if we don't specify a default value, the Properties window will always show the property in bold.

- **<Description()>**: Provides a designtime textual description of the property.

- **<ParenthesizePropertyName()>**: Indicates that the property name should be displayed in parentheses. For example, the standard UI controls in .NET display the `Name` property in parentheses: (Name).

- **<ReadOnlyAttribute()>**: Indicates that the property is read-only at designtime. If we omit this attribute, and the property has `get` and `set` property procedures, the property is deemed to be not read-only.

  Note that if the property doesn't have a `set` property procedure, the property will be deemed to be read-only regardless of whether we specify this attribute.

- `<RefreshProperties()>`: This attribute tells the Visual Designer how to refresh the display of other properties in the Properties window, if the user changes the value of this property. For example, `<RefreshProperties(RefreshProperties.All)>` indicates that all the properties are to be refreshed. This is useful if there are other properties that depend on the value of this property.

- `<TypeConverter()>`: This attribute is used on a class or structure definition to indicate the name of the type converter class to use for data conversions on this type.

Now that we've discussed which attributes we need, let's add some events and properties to the `Employee` component class. We'll begin by defining the default event and default property in the `Employee` class (we'll introduce the `SalaryChanged` event and the `FullName` property shortly):

```
<DefaultEvent("SalaryChanged"), _
 DefaultProperty("FullName")> _
Public Class Employee
    Inherits System.ComponentModel.Component

    ' Members...

End Class
```

Next, let's define some fields in the `Employee` class to hold employee information. These fields use a combination of simple types (such as `String`) and more interesting types (such as `DateTime`, `Color`, and an array of `String`s). Also, we've initialized some of these fields for added excitement:

```
' Personal details
Private mFullName As String = "Name Unknown"
Private mDob As DateTime = DateTime.Today


' Employment details
Private mSalary As Double = 0.0
Private mSkills As String()
Private mCarColor As Color
```

We can define properties to expose the aforementioned fields at designtime and at runtime. We'll introduce each property separately to highlight the interesting attributes on each property:

- The `FullName` property has a `<DefaultValue("Name Unknown")>` attribute to match the initial value of the `mFullName` field:

    ```
    <Category("Personal details"), _
     Description("The employee's fullname"), _
     DefaultValue("Name Unknown")> _
    Public Property FullName() As String
      Get
        Return mFullName
      End Get
    ```

```
    Set(ByVal Value As String)
      mFullName = Value
    End Set
End Property
```

- The `DateOfBirth` property, shown next, has a `<RefreshProperties(RefreshProperties.All)>` attribute. Whenever the user changes this property in the Properties window, all the other properties will be refreshed too. You'll see why this is important when we introduce an Age property in a moment.

```
<Category("Personal details"), _
 Description("The employee's date of birth"), _
 RefreshProperties(RefreshProperties.All)> _
Public Property DateOfBirth() As DateTime
  Get
    Return mDob
  End Get
  Set(ByVal Value As DateTime)
    mDob = Value
  End Set
End Property
```

- The .NET class library defines an editor class named `DateTimeEditor` in the `System.ComponentModel.Design` namespace to allow `DateTime` values to be edited graphically in the Properties window. There is no need to use the `<Editor()>` attribute when we define `DateTime` properties (unless we want to specify a different editor class to edit this property). The `DateTimeEditor` appears as shown in Figure 12-13.

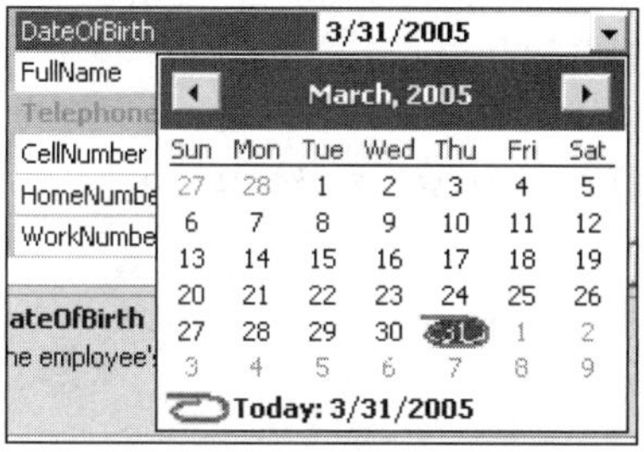

Figure 12-13. *The* `DataTimeEditor` *from the .NET class library*

- The Age property displays the employee's current age. This is a read-only value, and is calculated by subtracting the employee's date of birth from the current date. Therefore, the Age property has to be refreshed if the `DateOfBirth` property changes. This explains why we annotated the `DateOfBirth` property with `<RefreshProperties(RefreshProperties.All)>`.

```vb
<Category("Personal details"), _
 Description("The employee's age (calculated from Date Of Birth)"), _
 ReadOnlyAttribute(True), _
 ParenthesizePropertyName(True)> _
Public ReadOnly Property Age() As Integer
  Get
    Dim years As Integer = Date.Today.Year - mDob.Year
    If Date.Today.DayOfYear < mDob.DayOfYear Then
      years -= 1
    End If
    Return years
  End Get
End Property
```

- The Salary property is entirely innocuous...

```vb
<Category("Employment details"), _
 Description("The employee's total annual salary"), _
 DefaultValue(0.0)> _
Public Property Salary() As Double
  Get
    Return mSalary
  End Get
  Set(ByVal Value As Double)
    mSalary = Value
  End Set
End Property
```

- The Skills property gets and sets an array of strings, representing the employee's skill set. There is no problem using array types with properties.

```vb
<Category("Employment details"), _
 Description("An array of strings, containing employee's skills")> _
Public Property Skills() As String()
  Get
    Return mSkills
  End Get
  Set(ByVal Value As String())
    mSkills = Value
  End Set
End Property
```

- The .NET class library defines an editor class named ArrayEditor in the System.ComponentModel.Design namespace to allow arrays to be edited graphically in the Properties window. The ArrayEditor is shown in Figure 12-14.

Figure 12-14. *The* `ArrayEditor` *from the .NET class library*

- The `CarColor` property gets and sets a `Color` value.

```
<Category("Employment details"), _
 Description("The color of the employee's company car")> _
Public Property CarColor() As Color
  Get
    Return mCarColor
  End Get
  Set(ByVal Value As Color)
    mCarColor = Value
  End Set
End Property
```

- The .NET class library defines an editor class named `ColorEditor` in the `System.Drawing.Design` namespace to allow `Color` values to be edited graphically via a palette in the Properties window. The `ColorEditor` is shown in Figure 12-15 (if we don't set the color, the editor displays the color as white by default).

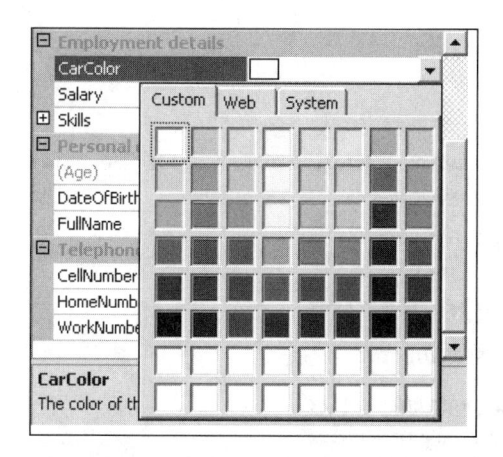

Figure 12-15. *The* `ColorEditor` *from the .NET class library*

Next we need to define some events in the Employee class, to indicate when an employee's salary changes, and when the employee becomes a higher-rate taxpayer (due to a healthy pay raise) or a lower-rate taxpayer (due to cuts in operating costs in the company).

The first step is to define an EmployeeEventArgs class, to provide information about the event. All the events raised in the Employee class will use EmployeeEventArgs as part of the event signature. The EmployeeEventArgs class is shown next; this source code is available in EmployeeEventArgs.vb in the Downloads section of the Apress Web site:

```
Imports System

Public Class EmployeeEventArgs
  Inherits EventArgs

  ' Private fields
  Private mEmployeeName As String
  Private mEmployeeSalary As Double

  ' Constructor, to initialize private fields
  Public Sub New(ByVal EmployeeName As String, _
                 ByVal EmployeeSalary As Double)
    mEmployeeName = EmployeeName
    mEmployeeSalary = EmployeeSalary
  End Sub
  ' Properties, to get the values held in the private fields
  Public ReadOnly Property EmployeeName() As String
    Get
      Return mEmployeeName
    End Get
  End Property

  Public ReadOnly Property EmployeeSalary() As Double
    Get
      Return mEmployeeSalary
    End Get
  End Property

End Class
```

We can now define a delegate in Employee.vb to specify the signature for all events raised in the Employee class:

```
Public Delegate Sub EmployeeEventHandler( _
                 ByVal Source As Employee, _
                 ByVal e As EmployeeEventArgs)
```

The Employee class will raise three events, as follows:

```
Public Event SalaryChanged      As EmployeeEventHandler
Public Event HigherRateTaxPayer As EmployeeEventHandler
Public Event LowerRateTaxPayer  As EmployeeEventHandler
```

Let's write some methods to raise these events when the employee's salary changes. We've specified $100,000 as an arbitrary threshold for tax payment; if the employee earns this amount or more, the employee pays a higher rate of tax. Of course, this is an entirely unrealistic taxation model; taxes in the real world are much more complicated.

```vb
Private Shared mTaxThreshold As Double = 100000.0

Public Sub PayRaise(ByVal Amount As Double)

  Dim OriginalSalary As Double = mSalary
  mSalary += Amount

  RaiseEvent SalaryChanged(Me, _
                   New EmployeeEventArgs(mFullName, mSalary))

  If (mSalary >= mTaxThreshold) And _
      Not (OriginalSalary >= mTaxThreshold) Then
    RaiseEvent HigherRateTaxPayer(Me, _
                   New EmployeeEventArgs(mFullName, mSalary))
  End If

End Sub

Public Sub PayCut(ByVal Amount As Double)
  Dim OriginalSalary As Double = mSalary
  mSalary -= Amount
  RaiseEvent SalaryChanged(Me, _
                   New EmployeeEventArgs(mFullName, mSalary))
  If (mSalary < mTaxThreshold) And _
      Not (OriginalSalary < mTaxThreshold) Then
      RaiseEvent LowerRateTaxPayer(Me, _
                   New EmployeeEventArgs(mFullName, mSalary))
  End If
End Sub
```

Defining Converter Classes for Components

To complete the implementation of our Employee component, we'll add fields and properties to represent the employee's telephone number and home address. We'll write two new classes named TelephoneNumber and Address to encapsulate these details. We'll also write two converter classes named TelephoneNumberConverter and AddressConverter, to allow TelephoneNumber properties and Address properties to be displayable and editable in the Properties window.

Defining the TelephoneNumber Class

Let's begin with the TelephoneNumber class. For the sake of simplicity, our example assumes US-formatted numbers such as (123) 456-7890; in an industrial-strength application, we would probably need to cater for the wider world too! We might also want to perform some intelligent error checking, such as testing the area code to make sure it's valid.

This source code is available in TelephoneNumber.vb in the Downloads section on the Apress Web site. The `<TypeConverter(GetType(TelephoneNumberConverter))>` attribute at the start of the TelephoneNumber class definition associates the TelephoneNumberConverter converter class with TelephoneNumber:

```
Imports System
Imports System.ComponentModel

<TypeConverter(GetType(TelephoneNumberConverter))> _
Public Class TelephoneNumber

  Private mAreaCode As String
  Private mLocalNumber As String

  Public Sub New(ByVal AreaCode As String, _
                 ByVal LocalNumber As String)
    mAreaCode = AreaCode
    mLocalNumber = LocalNumber
  End Sub

  Public Property AreaCode() As String
    Get
      Return mAreaCode
    End Get
    Set(ByVal Value As String)
      mAreaCode = Value
    End Set
  End Property

  Public Property LocalNumber() As String
    Get
      Return mLocalNumber
    End Get
    Set(ByVal Value As String)
      mLocalNumber = Value
    End Set
  End Property

End Class
```

Defining the TelephoneNumberConverter Class

The TelephoneNumberConverter class illustrates the general rules for defining converter classes. You can download this source code from TelephoneNumberConverter.vb. Converter classes are technical, so we'll take this a step at a time:

As ever, we begin with a clutch of Imports statements:

```vb
Imports System                              ' For misc .NET types
Imports System.ComponentModel               ' For misc ComponentModel types
Imports System.Globalization                ' For ICultureInfo
Imports System.ComponentModel.Design.Serialization
                                            ' For InstanceDescriptor
Imports System.Text.RegularExpressions      ' For Regex, to parse telnums
Imports System.Reflection                   ' For ConstructorInfo
```

Here is the definition of the `TelephoneNumberConverter` class. All converter classes inherit from `System.ComponentModel.TypeConverter`:

```vb
Public Class TelephoneNumberConverter
  Inherits TypeConverter
  ' Members ...
End Class
```

The first method we're going to implement is `CanConvertFrom()`. This method indicates whether the `TelephoneNumber` object can be created from some other data type. For example, the Visual Designer calls this method to establish whether `TelephoneNumber` objects can be created from a string value.

It's up to us to choose what data types we're prepared to convert from. The way we've implemented the method indicates we're definitely prepared to convert from a string. For any other data type, we pass the question back up to our base class.

```vb
Public Overloads Overrides Function CanConvertFrom( _
              ByVal context As ITypeDescriptorContext, _
              ByVal sourceType As Type) As Boolean

  If sourceType Is GetType(String) Then
    Return True
  Else
    Return MyBase.CanConvertFrom(context, sourceType)
  End If

End Function
```

The next method on our to-do list is `ConvertFrom()`. This method receives a parameter of some compatible data type (as established by a prior call to `CanConvertFrom()`). The method must use the supplied value to create and return a `TelephoneNumber` with a corresponding value.

The way we've implemented this method, we expect a string in the format (123) 456-7890; the parentheses, space character, and dash are optional. We use a Regular Expression to extract the area code and local number from this string, and then create and return a `TelephoneNumber` object with these values.

```vb
Public Overloads Overrides Function ConvertFrom( _
              ByVal context As ITypeDescriptorContext, _
              ByVal culture As CultureInfo, _
              ByVal value As Object) As Object
```

```vbnet
    If TypeOf value Is String Then

        Dim m As Match = Regex.Match( _
            CStr(value), _
            "\(?(?<area>\d{1,3})\)?\s?(?<local1>\d{3})-?(?<local2>\d{4})")

        Return New TelephoneNumber(m.Groups("area").Value, _
                                   m.Groups("local1").Value & "-" & _
                                   m.Groups("local2").Value)

    Else

        ' If the value-to-be-converted is not a String, pass the
        ' conversion request up to our base class
        Return MyBase.ConvertFrom(context, culture, value)

    End If

End Function
```

The previous two methods dealt with the task of converting from some other data type into a `TelphoneNumber`. We must also write two methods to deal with conversions in the opposite direction, where we need to convert a `TelphoneNumber` object to some other type.

Let's see the `CanConvertTo()` method first. This method indicates that `TelephoneNumber` objects can be converted into a string value or an `InstanceDescriptor` object. We'll describe `InstanceDescriptor` in a moment.

```vbnet
Public Overloads Overrides Function CanConvertTo( _
                ByVal context As ITypeDescriptorContext, _
                ByVal destinationType As Type) As Boolean

    If (destinationType Is GetType(String)) Or _
       (destinationType Is GetType(InstanceDescriptor)) Then

        Return True

    Else

        ' If the destinationType is not String or InstanceDescriptor,
        ' pass the conversion request up to our base class
        Return MyBase.CanConvertFrom(context, destinationType)

    End If

End Function
```

The `ConvertTo()` method performs these conversions from a `TelephoneNumber` object into a string value or an `InstanceDescriptor` object. The string conversion is quite simple; the conversion yields a string in the format "(123) 456-7890".

The InstanceDescriptor conversion is much more complicated. An InstanceDescriptor object is like a playback object; it contains information about how to create TelephoneNumber objects in source code. We must tell the InstanceDescriptor which constructor to call, and what parameter values to use in that constructor.

The Visual Designer uses the information in the InstanceDescriptor object to generate source code in the InitializeComponents method in the host application. This source code creates a TelephoneNumber object and initializes it with the values we specified in the Properties window.

```
Public Overloads Overrides Function ConvertTo( _
                ByVal context As ITypeDescriptorContext, _
                ByVal culture As CultureInfo, _
                ByVal value As Object, _
                ByVal destinationType As Type) As Object

  If destinationType Is GetType(String) Then

    Dim tn As TelephoneNumber = CType(value, TelephoneNumber)
    If tn Is Nothing Then
      Return ""
    Else
      Return String.Format("({0}) {1}", tn.AreaCode, tn.LocalNumber)
    End If

  ElseIf destinationType Is GetType(InstanceDescriptor) Then

    Dim ci As ConstructorInfo
    ci = GetType(TelephoneNumber).GetConstructor( _
                New Type() {GetType(String), GetType(String)})

    Dim tn As TelephoneNumber = CType(value, TelephoneNumber)

    Return New InstanceDescriptor( _
                ci, New Object() {tn.AreaCode, tn.LocalNumber})
  Else

    Return MyBase.ConvertTo(context, culture, value, destinationType)

  End If

End Function
```

That concludes the implementation of the TelephoneNumberConverter and TelephoneNumber classes. We are now ready to add some TelephoneNumber fields and properties to the Employee class. We'll add three TelephoneNumber fields to hold the employee's work number, cell phone number, and home number. In a real application, we might also allow the employee to have additional numbers such as a fax number, a pager number, and so on:

```vb
<DefaultEvent("SalaryChanged"), _
 DefaultProperty("FullName")> _
Public Class Employee
  Inherits System.ComponentModel.Component

  ' Telephone numbers
  Private mHomeNumber As TelephoneNumber
  Private mWorkNumber As TelephoneNumber
  Private mCellNumber As TelephoneNumber

  <Category("Telephone numbers"), _
   Description("The employee's work telephone number")> _
  Public Property WorkNumber() As TelephoneNumber
    Get
      Return mWorkNumber
    End Get
    Set(ByVal Value As TelephoneNumber)
      mWorkNumber = Value
    End Set
  End Property

  <Category("Telephone numbers"), _
   Description("The employee's cell (mobile) telephone number")> _
  Public Property CellNumber() As TelephoneNumber
    Get
      Return mCellNumber
    End Get
    Set(ByVal Value As TelephoneNumber)
      mCellNumber = Value
    End Set
  End Property

  <Category("Telephone numbers"), _
   Description("The employee's home telephone number")> _
  Public Property HomeNumber() As TelephoneNumber
    Get
      Return mHomeNumber
    End Get
    Set(ByVal Value As TelephoneNumber)
      mHomeNumber = Value
    End Set
  End Property

  ' Plus other members, as before

End Class
```

Figure 12-16 shows how these `TelephoneNumber` properties will appear in the Properties window.

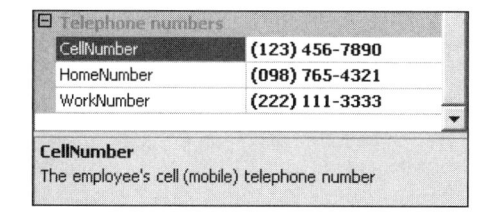

Figure 12-16. *How the telephone numbers will appear within the Properties window*

Defining the Address Class

We can now turn our attention to the Address class. This source code is available in the Address.vb folder in the Downloads section of the Apress Web site.

Let's view the Address class first, and then pick out a couple of important features. For the sake of simplicity, our Address class just holds the employee's street name, city, and country; in an industrial-strength application, we would probably need to store additional information such as the state (or area) and ZIP code (or postal code):

```
Imports System
Imports System.ComponentModel

<TypeConverter(GetType(AddressConverter))> _
Public Class Address

  Private mStreet As String
  Private mCity As String
  Private mCountry As String

  Public Sub New(ByVal Street As String, _
                 ByVal City As String, _
                 ByVal Country As String)
    mStreet = Street
    mCity = City
    mCountry = Country
  End Sub

  <RefreshProperties(RefreshProperties.All)> _
  Public Property Street() As String
    Get
      Return mStreet
    End Get
    Set(ByVal Value As String)
      mStreet = Value
    End Set
  End Property
  <RefreshProperties(RefreshProperties.All)> _
  Public Property City() As String
```

```
      Get
        Return mCity
      End Get
      Set(ByVal Value As String)
        mCity = Value
      End Set
    End Property

    <RefreshProperties(RefreshProperties.All)> _
    Public Property Country() As String
      Get
        Return mCountry
      End Get
      Set(ByVal Value As String)
        mCountry = Value
      End Set
    End Property

End Class
```

Notice the `<TypeConverter(GetType(AddressConverter))>` attribute at the start of the Address class definition to associate the AddressConverter converter class with Address. You'll see the AddressConverter class shortly.

Also notice that each of the properties in the Address class is prefixed with a `<RefreshProperties (RefreshProperties.All)>` attribute. We've done this to make the Street, City, or Country properties editable individually in the Properties window, as shown in Figure 12-17.

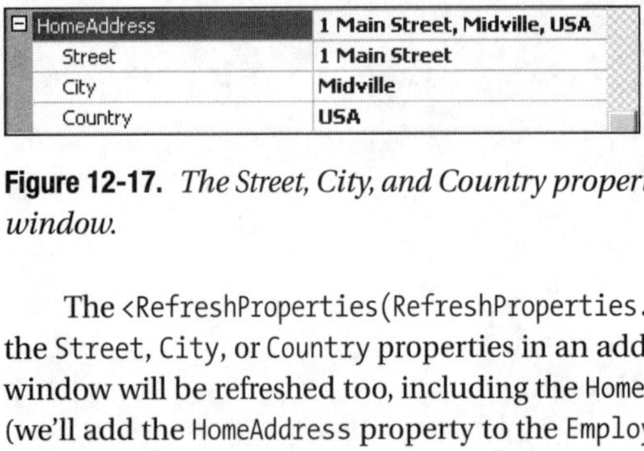

HomeAddress	1 Main Street, Midville, USA
Street	1 Main Street
City	Midville
Country	USA

Figure 12-17. *The Street, City, and Country properties can be edited individually in the Properties window.*

The `<RefreshProperties(RefreshProperties.All)>` attribute ensures that if the user changes the Street, City, or Country properties in an address, all the other properties in the Properties window will be refreshed too, including the HomeAddress property in the Employee component (we'll add the HomeAddress property to the Employee class shortly).

Defining the AddressConverter Class

The AddressConverter class is available in AddressConverter.vb in the Downloads section of the Apress Web site. The class is similar in scope and intent to the TelephoneNumberConverter class you saw earlier. Here's the outline for the class:

```vbnet
Imports System                                ' For misc .NET types
Imports System.ComponentModel                 ' For misc ComponentModel types
Imports System.Globalization                  ' For ICultureInfo
Imports System.ComponentModel.Design.Serialization
                                              ' For InstanceDescriptor
Imports System.Reflection                     ' For ConstructorInfo

Public Class AddressConverter
   Inherits TypeConverter
  ' Conversion class methods and properties (discussed below...)
End Class
```

The class requires a `CanConvertFrom()` method, to allow conversions from string values into `Address` objects. The class also requires a `ConvertFrom()` method to perform conversions from string values into `Address` objects. The string is expected to be formatted as streetname, cityname, countryname.

```vbnet
Public Overloads Overrides Function CanConvertFrom( _
               ByVal context As ITypeDescriptorContext, _
               ByVal sourceType As Type) As Boolean

   If sourceType Is GetType(String) Then
     Return True
   Else
     Return MyBase.CanConvertFrom(context, sourceType)
   End If
End Function

Public Overloads Overrides Function ConvertFrom( _
               ByVal context As ITypeDescriptorContext, _
               ByVal culture As CultureInfo, _
               ByVal value As Object) As Object
   If TypeOf value Is String Then
     Dim str As String = CStr(value)
     Dim strings As String() = str.Split(New Char() {","c})
     Return New Address(strings(0), strings(1), strings(2))
   Else
     Return MyBase.ConvertFrom(context, culture, value)
   End If
End Function
```

The `CanConvertTo()` method, shown next, allows `Address` objects to be converted into string values and `InstanceDescriptor` objects. The `ConvertTo()` method performs conversions from an `Address` object into a string or an `InstanceDescriptor` object, as appropriate. Notice that the `ConvertTo()` method performs some rudimentary error checking and formatting for string values.

```vbnet
Public Overloads Overrides Function CanConvertTo( _
               ByVal context As ITypeDescriptorContext, _
               ByVal destinationType As Type) As Boolean
```

```vb
    If (destinationType Is GetType(String)) Or _
       (destinationType Is GetType(InstanceDescriptor)) Then
      Return True
    Else
      Return MyBase.CanConvertFrom(context, destinationType)
    End If

End Function

Public Overloads Overrides Function ConvertTo( _
                ByVal context As ITypeDescriptorContext, _
                ByVal culture As CultureInfo, _
                ByVal value As Object, _
                ByVal destinationType As Type) As Object

  If destinationType Is GetType(String) Then

    Dim addr As Address = CType(value, Address)
    Dim street, city, country As String
    If (addr.Street Is Nothing) Or (addr.Street = "") Then
      street = "<street>"
    Else
      street = addr.Street
    End If
    If (addr.City Is Nothing) Or (addr.City = "") Then
      city = "<city>"
    Else
      city = addr.City
    End If
    If (addr.Country Is Nothing) Or (addr.Country = "") Then
      country = "<country>"
    Else
      country = addr.Country
    End If

    Return street & ", " & city & ", " & country

  ElseIf destinationType Is GetType(InstanceDescriptor) Then

    Dim ci As ConstructorInfo
    ci = GetType(Address).GetConstructor( _
      New Type(){GetType(String), GetType(String), GetType(String)})

    Dim addr As Address = CType(value, Address)
    Return New InstanceDescriptor( _
      ci, New Object() {addr.Street, addr.City, addr.Country})
```

```
    Else

        Return MyBase.ConvertTo(context, culture, value, destinationType)
    End If
End Function
```

Finally, the AddressConverter class requires two additional methods:

- GetPropertiesSupported() indicates that Address objects have internal properties of their own, and that these properties should be displayed separately when an Address property is displayed in the Properties window.

    ```
    Public Overloads Overrides Function GetPropertiesSupported( _
                    ByVal context As ITypeDescriptorContext) As Boolean
        Return True
    End Function
    ```

- GetProperties() returns a PropertyDescriptionCollection, containing information about all the internal properties inside Address. The Visual Designer queries the underlying class for these properties. Notice we've used the Sort() method to ensure these internal properties are displayed in the order Street, City, and Country.

    ```
    Public Overloads Overrides Function GetProperties( _
                    ByVal context As ITypeDescriptorContext, _
                    ByVal value As Object, _
                    ByVal attributes() As Attribute) _
                              As PropertyDescriptorCollection

        Dim properties As PropertyDescriptorCollection
        properties = TypeDescriptor.GetProperties(GetType(Address))
        properties = properties.Sort( _
                        New String() {"Street", "City", "Country"})
        Return properties

    End Function

    End Class
    ```

That concludes the implementation of the AddressConverter and Address classes. We're now ready to add some Address fields and properties to the Employee class:

```
<DefaultEvent("SalaryChanged"), _
 DefaultProperty("FullName")> _
Public Class Employee
  Inherits System.ComponentModel.Component

  Private mHomeAddress As New Address( _
                            "<street>", "<city>", "<country>")

  <Category("Personal details"), _
   Description("The employee's home address")> _
  Public Property HomeAddress() As Address
```

```
      Get
         Return mHomeAddress
      End Get
      Set(ByVal Value As Address)
         mHomeAddress = Value
      End Set
   End Property

   ' Plus other members, as before
End Class
```

Testing the Final Employee Component Class

A final implementation of the `Employee` component class is available in the Downloads section of the Apress Web site. We've also provided a sample test application.

The test application appears as follows in VS .NET. The application has a single `Employee` component object, whose properties are displayed in the Properties window (as shown in Figure 12-18). These properties exhibit the appearance and capabilities we've worked hard to define during the chapter.

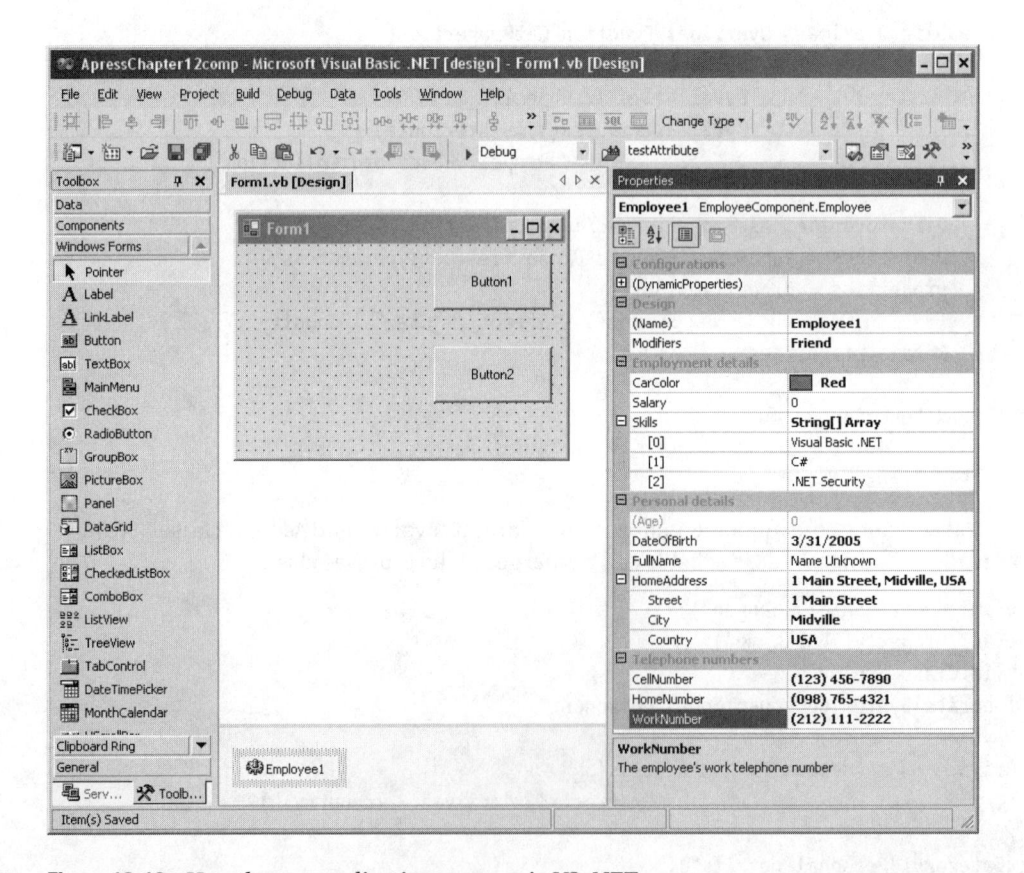

Figure 12-18. *How the test application appears in VS .NET*

Here is a partial listing of some of the code generated by the Visual Designer to achieve the property settings we specify in the Properties window. This code resides in MainForm.vb:

```
Public Class MainForm
  Inherits System.Windows.Forms.Form

  Friend WithEvents Employee1 As MyFinalComponent.Employee

  <System.Diagnostics.DebuggerStepThrough()> _
  Private Sub InitializeComponent()

    Me.Employee1 = _
      New MyFinalComponent.Employee(Me.components)

    Me.Employee1.CarColor = System.Drawing.Color.Red

    Me.Employee1.CellNumber = _
      New MyFinalComponent.TelephoneNumber("123", "456-7890")

    Me.Employee1.DateOfBirth = _
      New Date(1964, 7, 2, 0, 0, 0, 0)

    Me.Employee1.HomeAddress = _
      New MyFinalComponent.Address("1 Main Street", _
                                   "Midville", _
                                   "USA")
    Me.Employee1.HomeNumber = _
      New MyFinalComponent.TelephoneNumber("098", "765-4321")
    Me.Employee1.Skills = _
      New String() {"Visual Basic .NET", _
                    "Object Oriented Analysis and Design", _
                    "Playing Football"}
    Me.Employee1.WorkNumber = _
      New MyFinalComponent.TelephoneNumber("212", "111-2222")
    ' Plus other code

  End Sub
  ' Plus other members
End Class
```

The test application also exercises the events on the Employee component object. Every time the user clicks one of the buttons on the form, the salary is changed and a SalaryChanged event is raised. If the employee's salary goes above $100,000, a HigherRateTaxPayer event is raised. If the employee's salary slips back below $100,000, a LowerRateTaxPayer event is raised. Here are the event handler methods for these events, along with the message boxes displayed for each event:

Here is the event handler method for the SalaryChanged event, along with the message box that gets displayed when this event is handled (see Figure 12-19).

```vb
Private Sub Employee1_SalaryChanged( _
                ByVal Source As MyFinalComponent.Employee, _
                ByVal e As MyFinalComponent.EmployeeEventArgs) _
                    Handles Employee1.SalaryChanged

    MessageBox.Show("New salary " & e.EmployeeSalary, _
                "Salary changed for " & e.EmployeeName)

End Sub
```

Figure 12-19. *The message box displayed by the* SalaryChanged *event handler*

Here is the event handler method for the HigherRateTaxPayer event, together with the associated message box for this event (see Figure 12-20).

```vb
Private Sub Employee1_HigherRateTaxPayer( _
                ByVal Source As MyFinalComponent.Employee, _
                ByVal e As MyFinalComponent.EmployeeEventArgs) _
                    Handles Employee1.HigherRateTaxPayer

    MessageBox.Show("New salary " & e.EmployeeSalary, _
        e.EmployeeName & " has just become a higher-rate tax payer")

End Sub
```

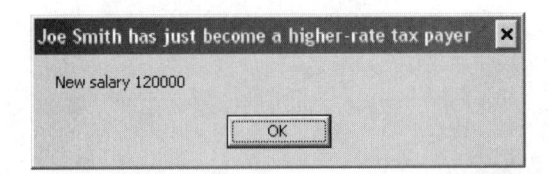

Figure 12-20. *The associated message box for the event handler*

```
Private Sub Employee1_LowerRateTaxPayer( _
                ByVal Source As MyFinalComponent.Employee, _
                ByVal e As MyFinalComponent.EmployeeEventArgs) _
                    Handles Employee1.LowerRateTaxPayer

  MessageBox.Show("New salary " & e.EmployeeSalary, _
    e.EmployeeName & " has just become a lower-rate tax payer")

End Sub
```

Summary

In this chapter, we've seen how to use the classes, interfaces, and attributes defined in the `System.ComponentModel` namespace. This namespace defines the following key interfaces, which allow you to create and use components in a consistent manner:

- The `IComponent` interface specifies the methods and properties required in component classes. A component class is any class that implements `IComponent`.

- The `IContainer` interface specifies the methods and properties required in container classes. A container class is any class that implements `IContainer`.

- The `ISite` interface specifies the glue between components and containers. Site objects facilitate communication between component objects and container objects.

The `System.ComponentModel` namespace also defines a veritable gamut of attribute classes, type converter classes, and descriptor classes. Here's a brief reminder of the roles of these classes:

- Attribute classes enable you to specify metadata on components, properties, events, and other member types. Numerous attributes allow you to provide designtime information for consumption by the Visual Designer.

- Type converter classes provide a standard infrastructure for querying the conversion capabilities to and from different types, and for performing these conversions. Type converter classes are used extensively by the Visual Designer to display property and event information in the Properties window, and to generate source code to persist these settings.

- Descriptor classes open the gateway to a tremendously powerful and versatile style of generic programming. You can use descriptor classes to obtain full information about any type, and any of the members defined in these types

CHAPTER 13

Defining Threads

Threading refers to an application's capability to handle executing more than one instruction set at a time. In most programming languages, an application starts with a special function. For Visual Basic .NET this might be the Main() subroutine. Each instruction, or piece of software code, is executed in sequence. The second instruction won't begin until the first instruction has completed. You could think of this as a line at an amusement park where no one can cut!

Another concept, *free threading*, is completely new for many Visual Basic developers; I'll define this term and further explain the support provided in Visual Basic .NET. I'll briefly compare this free-threading model to Visual Basic 6.0's apartment threading model. I won't dwell on the differences too much, but recognizing what sets these models apart will help you understand why free-threading was one of the most requested and most anticipated features in Visual Basic .NET. This chapter's concepts are essential to your understanding of the remainder of this book, as you will

- Learn the definition of a thread
- Compare various multitasking and threading models
- Understand where threads exist and how they are allocated processor time
- See how threads are controlled and managed using interrupts and priorities
- Realize the importance of application domains

Threading Defined

By understanding threading concepts and how threads are structured in .NET, you'll be better able to decide how to implement these features in your applications. To define threading, let's break it down into a number of sections. These sections will cover the following:

- Different types of multitasking
- Processes
- Threads
- Primary threads
- Secondary threads

Multitasking

As you probably know, *multitasking* refers to an operating system's capability to run more than one application at a time. For instance, while this chapter is being written, Microsoft Outlook is open as well as two Microsoft Word documents. Additionally, the system tray shows even more applications running in the background. When clicking back and forth between applications, it appears that all of them are executing at the same time. The word "application" is a little vague here, however; what I'm really referring to are *processes*. You'll learn about processes later in this chapter.

Classically speaking, multitasking actually exists in two different flavors. These days Windows uses only one style in threading, which is discussed at length in this book. However, I'll also show you the previous type of multitasking so you can understand the differences and advantages of the current method.

In earlier versions of Windows, and in some other operating systems, a program was allowed to execute until it cooperated by releasing the processor to the other applications that were running. Because it's up to the application to cooperate with all other running programs, this type of multitasking is called *cooperative multitasking*. The downside to this type of multitasking is that if one program does not release execution, the other applications will be locked up. Actually, the running application hangs and the other applications are waiting in line, much like a line at a bank. A teller takes one customer at a time. The customer more than likely will not move from the teller window until all his transactions are complete. Once finished, the teller can take the next person in line. It doesn't really matter how much time each person is going to spend at the window. Even if one person only wants to deposit a check, she must wait until the person in front of her—who has five transactions—has finished.

You shouldn't encounter this problem with current versions of Windows (2000 and XP). The current method of multitasking used by the operating system is very different. An application is now allowed to execute for a short period before it is involuntarily interrupted by the operating system and another application is allowed to execute. This interrupted style of multitasking is called *preemptive multitasking*. Preemption is defined as interrupting an application to allow another application to execute. It's important to note that an application might not have finished its task, but the operating system allows another application to have its time on the processor. The earlier bank teller example doesn't fit here. In the real world, this would be like the bank teller pausing one customer in the middle of his transaction to allow another customer to start working on her business. This doesn't mean that the next customer would finish her transaction either. The teller could continue to interrupt one customer after another—eventually resuming with the first customer. This is similar to how the human brain deals with social interaction and various other tasks.

Although preemption solves the problem of the processor becoming locked, it also has its own share of problems. As you know, some applications share resources such as database connections and files. What happens if two applications are accessing the same resource at the same time? One program might change the data, become interrupted, and then allow the other program to again change the data. Now two applications have changed the same data. Both applications assumed that they had exclusive access to the data. Let's look at the simple scenario illustrated in Figure 13-1.

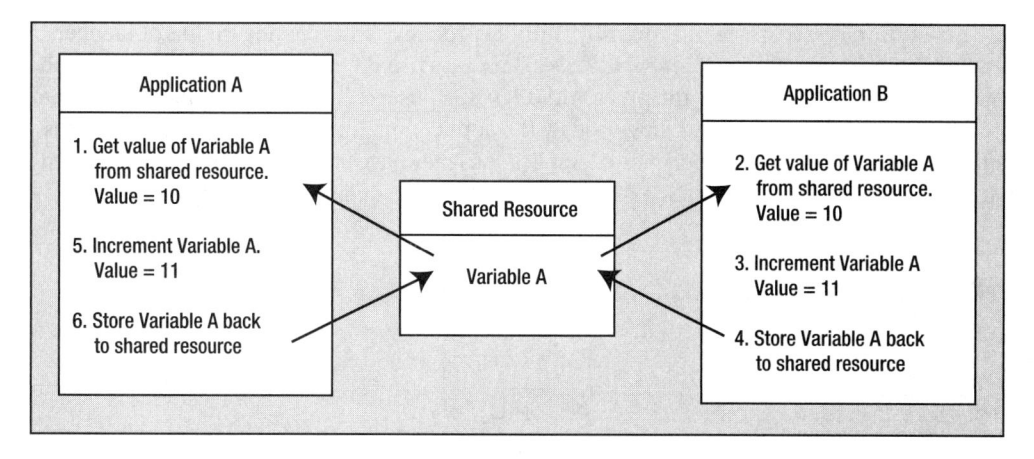

Figure 13-1. *Example of how errors can occur when two applications share a resource.*

In step 1, Application A obtains an integer value from a data store and places it in memory. That integer variable is set to 10. Application A is then preempted and forced to wait on Application B. Step 2 begins and Application B then obtains that same integer value of 10. In step 3, Application B increments the value to 11. The variable is then stored to memory by Application B in step 4. In step 5, Application A increments this value as well. However, because they both obtained a reference to this value at 10, this value will still be 11 after Application A completes its increment routine. The desired result was for the value to be set to 12. Both applications had no idea that another application was accessing this resource, and now the value they were both attempting to increment is incorrect. What would happen if this scenario actually involved two ticket agencies booking the same plane tickets?

One other problem associated with preemption is the cost of context switching. Growing up, children love to pull one toy after another out of their closet. This accumulation of toys strewn about the room obviously causes a mess. Parents often solve this problem by instructing their children to put one toy away before playing with another. Although this solves one problem, the child quickly realizes that it can be time consuming putting everything away before getting a new toy out. The same goes for context switching. There is a time cost associated with switching from one thread to the next in a preemptive manner.

The problems associated with preemptive multitasking are solved by synchronization, which is covered later in Chapter 15.

Processes

When an application is launched, memory, and any other resource for that application, is allocated. This physical separation of memory and resources is called a *process*. Of course, the application can launch more than one process. It's important to note that the words "application" and "process" are not synonymous. The memory allocated to the process is isolated from that of other processes and is allowed access by only that process.

In Windows, you can see the currently running processes by accessing the Task Manager. The Task Manager has three tabs: Applications, Processes, and Performance. The Processes tab shows the name of the process, the process id (PID), CPU usage, the processor time used by the process so far, and the memory being used by the application. Applications and the processes appear on separate tabs, for a good reason. Applications may have one or more processes involved. Each process has its own separation of data, execution code, and system resources.

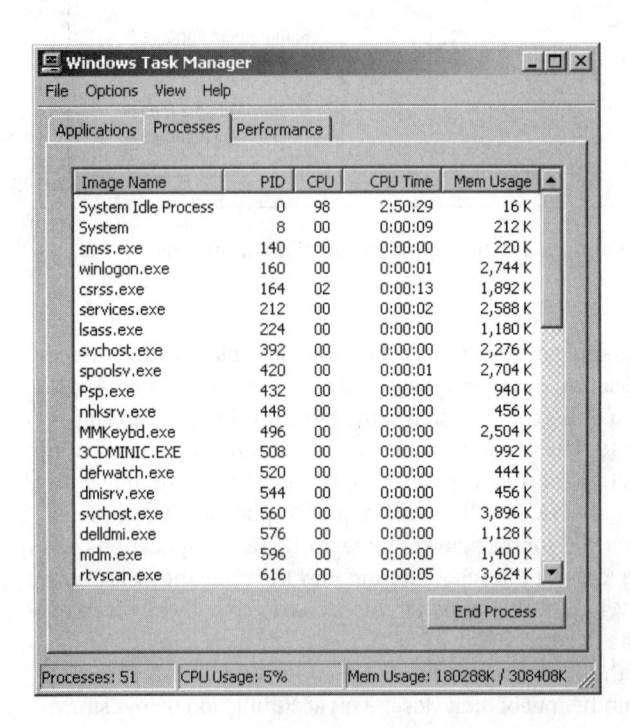

Threads

You'll also notice that the Task Manager has summary information about process CPU use. This is because the process also has an execution sequence that is used by the computer's processor. This execution sequence is known as a *thread*. The registers in use on the CPU define this thread, the stack used by the thread, and a container that keeps track of the thread's current state. The container is known as *Thread Local Storage (TLS)*. The concepts of registers and stacks should be familiar if you're used to dealing with low-level issues such as memory allocation; however, all you need to know here is that a stack in the .NET Framework is an area of memory that can be used for fast access and either stores value types, or pointers to objects, method arguments, and other data that is local to each method call.

Single-Threaded Processes

As noted previously, each process has at least one of these sequential execution orders, or threads. Creating a process includes starting the process running at a point in the instructions. This initial thread is known as the *primary* or *main thread*. The thread's actual execution sequence is determined by what you code in your application's functions and subroutines. For instance, in a simple Visual Basic 6.0 application, the primary thread is defined in your application's property dialog box, where you choose a form, or Sub Main(), as your startup object.

Now that you have an idea of what a process is and know that it has at least one thread, let's look at a visual model of this relationship in Figure 13-2.

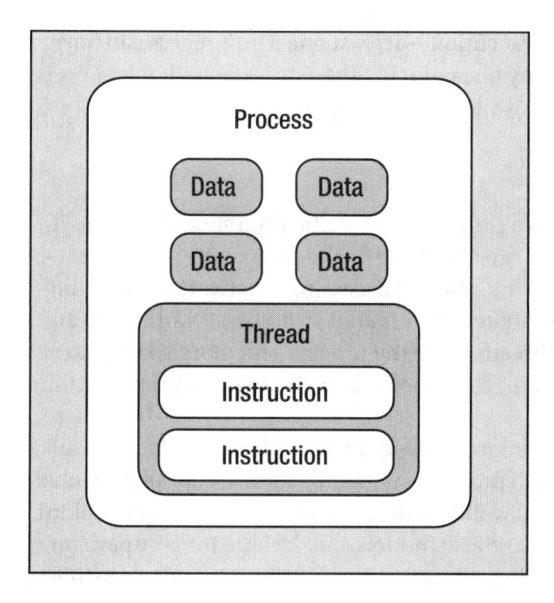

Figure 13-2. *The single-thread process model*

You'll notice that the thread is in the same isolation as the data. This demonstrates that the thread can access the data you declare in this process. The thread executes on the processor and uses the data within the process, as required. This all seems simple; you have a physically separated process that is isolated so no other process can modify the data. As far as this process knows, it is the only process running on the system. You don't need to know the details of other processes and their associated threads to make this process work.

■**Tip** To be more precise, the thread is really a pointer into the instruction stream portion of a process. The thread does not actually contain the instructions, but rather it indicates the current and future possible paths through the instructions determined by data and branching decisions.

Time Slices

Earlier you read that in multitasking, the operating system grants each application a period to execute before interrupting that application and allowing another one to execute. This is not entirely accurate. The processor actually grants time to the process. The period that the process can execute is known as a *time slice* or a *quantum*. The period of this time slice is also unknown to the programmer and unpredictable to anything besides the operating system. Programmers should not consider this time slice as a constant in their applications. Each operating system and each processor can have a different time allocated.

Nevertheless, I mentioned a potential problem with concurrency earlier, and we should consider how that would come into play if each process were physically isolated. This is where the challenge starts, and is the focus of the remainder of this book.

A process must have at least one thread of execution—at least one. Our process can have more than one task that it needs to be doing at any one point in time. For instance, it might need to access a SQL Server database over a network, while also drawing the user interface (UI).

Multithreaded Processes

As you probably already know, you can split up a process to share the time slice allotted to it. This happens by spawning additional threads of execution within the process. You might spawn an additional thread to do some background work, such as accessing a network or querying a database. Because these secondary threads are usually created to do some work, they are commonly known as *worker threads*. Worker threads share the process's memory space that is isolated from all the other processes on the system. The concept of spawning new threads within the same process is known as *free threading*.

The concept of free threading is very different from the apartment-threading model used in Visual Basic 6.0. With apartment threading, each process was granted its own copy of the global data needed to execute. Each thread was spawned within its own process, so that threads couldn't share data in the process's memory. Let's look at these models side by side for comparison. Figure 13-3 demonstrates the apartment-threading concept, whereas Figure 13-4 demonstrates the free-threading concept.

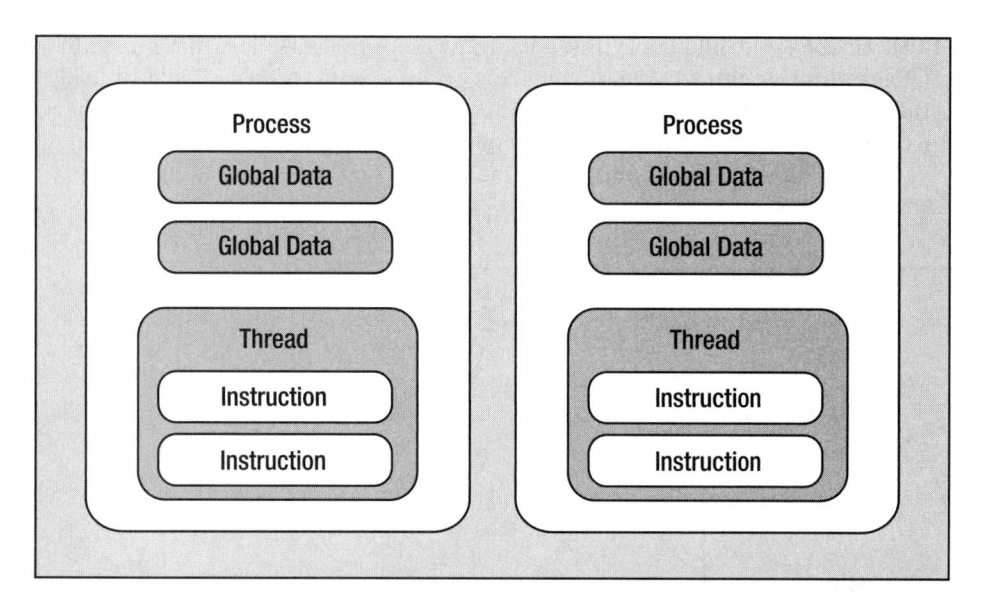

Figure 13-3. *The apartment-threading concept*

As you can see, each time you want to do some background work, it happens in its own process. This thread is therefore running *out-of-process*. This model is vastly different from the free-threading model shown in Figure 13-4.

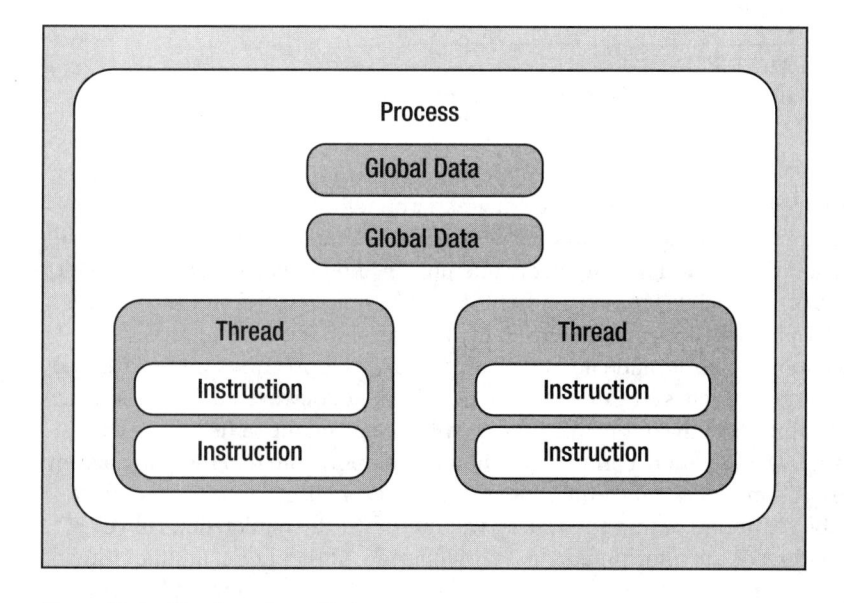

Figure 13-4. *The free-threading concept*

The CPU can execute an additional thread using the same process's data. This is a significant advantage over single-threaded apartments. You get the benefits of an additional thread as well as the ability to share the same data. Note, however, that only one thread is executing on the processor at a time. Each thread within that process is then granted a portion of that execution time to do its work. Let's go one more time to a diagram (see Figure 13-5) to help illustrate how this works.

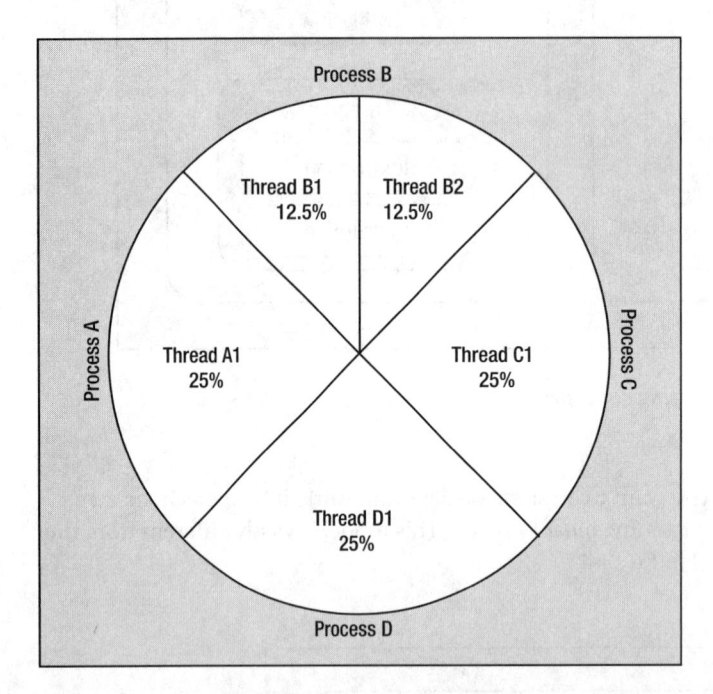

Figure 13-5. *Additional threads executed using the same process's data*

For the sake of this book, the examples and diagrams assume a single processor. However, multithreading your applications provides an even greater benefit if the computer has more than one processor. The operating system now has two places to send execution of the thread. In the earlier bank example, this would be similar to opening up another line with another teller. The operating system is responsible for assigning which threads are executed on which processor. However, the .NET platform does provide the ability to control which CPU a process uses if the programmer so chooses. This is made possible with the ProcessorAffinity property of the Process class in the System.Diagnostics namespace. Bear in mind, however, that this is set at the process level so all threads in that particular process will execute on the same processor.

Scheduling threads is vastly more complicated than was demonstrated in the last diagram, but for our purposes, this model is sufficient for now. Because each thread is taking its turn to execute, you might be reminded of that frustrating wait in line at the bank teller. However, remember that these threads are interrupted after a brief period. At that point, another thread, perhaps one in the same process, or perhaps a thread in another process, is granted execution. Before moving on, let's look at the Task Manager again.

Launch Task Manager and return to the Processes tab. Go to the View ➤ Select Columns menu. You'll see a list of columns that you can display in the Task Manager. For now, just focus on the Thread Count option. Select this check box and click OK. You should see something similar to the following image.

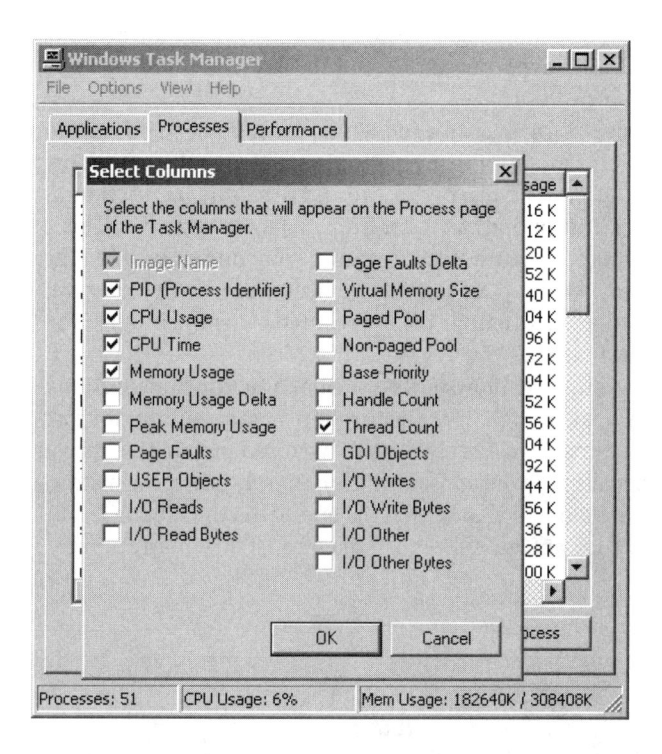

You'll notice that several of your processes have more than one thread. This reinforces the idea that your program may have many threads for just one process.

How Interrupts and TLS Works

When one thread runs out of time in its allocated time slice, it doesn't just stop and wait its turn again. Each processor can only handle one task at a time, so the current thread has to get out of the way. However, before it jumps out of line again, it has to store the state information that will allow its execution again. If you remember, this is a function of Thread Local Storage (TLS). The TLS for this thread, as stated previously, contains the registers, stack pointers, scheduling information, address spaces in memory, and information about other resources in use. One of the registers stored in the TLS is a program counter, which tells the thread which instruction to execute next.

Interrupts

Remember that processes don't necessarily need to know about other processes on the same computer. If that were the case, how would the thread know that it's supposed to give way to another process? This scheduling decision nightmare is handled by the operating system for the most part. Windows itself (which after all is just another program running on the processor) has a main thread, known as the system thread, which is responsible for scheduling all other threads. Windows knows when it needs to make a decision about thread scheduling by using *interrupts*.

An interrupt is a mechanism that causes the normally sequential execution of CPU instructions to branch elsewhere in the computer memory without the knowledge of the execution program. Windows determines how long a thread has to execute and places an instruction in the current thread's execution sequence. This period can differ from system to system and even from thread to thread on the same system. Because this interrupt is obviously placed in the instruction set, it's known as a software interrupt. This should not be confused with hardware interrupts, which occur outside the specific instructions being executed. After the interrupt is placed, Windows then allows the thread to execute.

When the thread comes to the interrupt, Windows uses a special function known as an interrupt handler to store the thread's state in the TLS. The current program counter for that thread, which was stored before the interrupt was received, is then stored in that TLS. As you might remember, this program counter is simply the address of the currently executing instruction. After the thread's execution has timed out, it is moved to the end of the thread queue for its given priority to wait its turn again. Look at Figure 13-6 for a diagram of this interruption process.

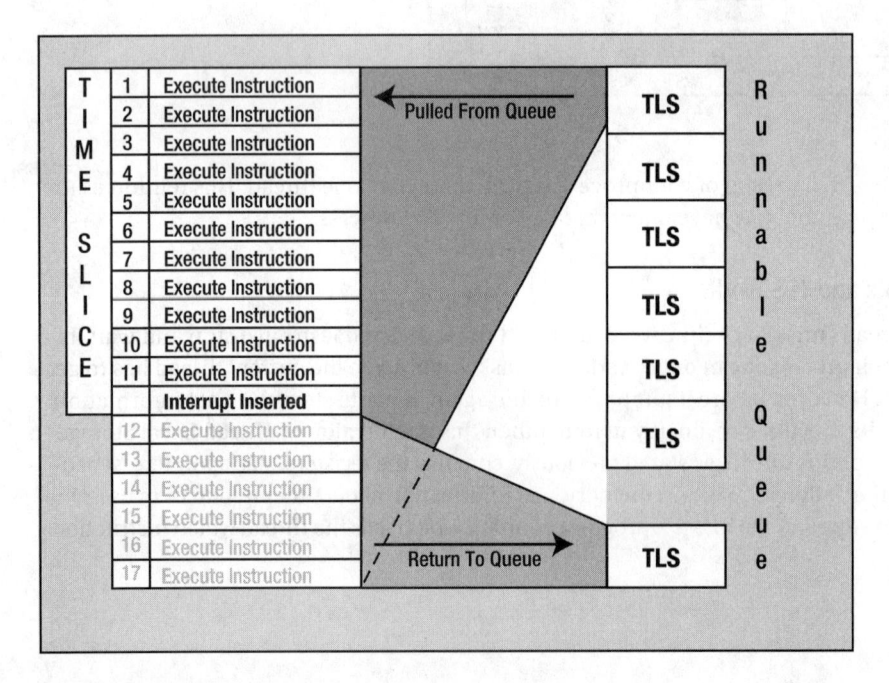

Figure 13-6. *The interrupt process*

> **Tip** The TLS is not actually saved to the queue; it's stored in the memory of the process that contains the thread. A pointer to that memory is what is actually saved to the queue.

This is, of course, fine if the thread isn't done yet or if the thread needs to continue executing. However, what happens if the thread decides that it doesn't need to use all its execution time? The process of context switching is slightly different initially, but the results are the same. A thread might decide that it needs to wait on a resource before it can execute again. Therefore, it can yield its execution time to another thread. This is the responsibility of the programmer as well as the operating system. The programmer signals the thread to yield. The thread then clears any interrupts that Windows might have already placed in its stack. A software interrupt is then simulated. The thread is stored in TLS and moved to the end of the queue just as before. The only thing to remember is that Windows might have already placed an interrupt on the thread's stack. This must be cleared before the thread is packed up; otherwise, when the thread is executed again, it might be interrupted prematurely. Of course, the details of this are abstracted from you. Programmers do not have to worry about clearing these interrupts themselves.

Thread Sleep and Clock Interrupts

As stated previously, the programs may have yielded execution to another thread so it can wait on some outside resource. However, the resources may not be available the next time the thread is brought back to execute. In fact, it may not be available the next 10 or 20 times a thread is executed. The programmer might want to take this thread out of the execution queue for a long period so that the processor doesn't waste time switching from one thread to another just to realize it has to yield execution again. When a thread voluntarily takes itself out of the execution queue for a period, it is said to *sleep*. When a thread is put to sleep, it's packed up into TLS again, but this time, the TLS is not placed at the end of the running queue; instead, it's placed on a separate sleep queue.

For threads on a sleep queue to run again, they are marked with a different kind of interrupt called a *clock interrupt*. When a thread is put into the sleep queue, a clock interrupt is scheduled for the time when this thread should be awakened. When a clock interrupt occurs that matches the time for a thread on the sleep queue, it's moved back to the runnable queue where it will be scheduled for execution again, as illustrated in Figure 13-7.

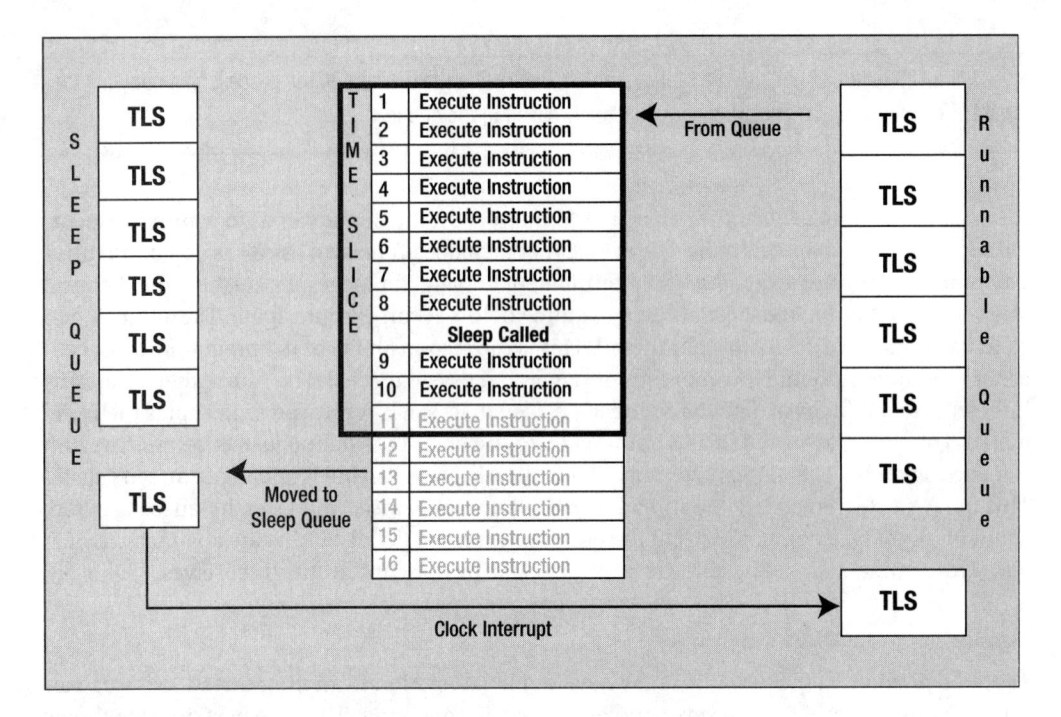

Figure 13-7. *Clock interrupt is moved back to the runnable queue.*

Thread Abort

You've seen a thread interrupted, and you've seen a thread sleep. However, like all good things in life, threads must end. Threads can be stopped explicitly as a request during the execution of another thread. When a thread is ended in this way, it is called an *abort*. Aborting a thread manually can cause some serious undesirable side effects. Threads also stop when they come to the end of their execution sequence. In any case, when a thread is ended, the TLS for that thread is deallocated. The data in the process used by that thread does not go away, however, unless the process also ends. This is important because the process can have more than one thread accessing that data. Threads cannot be aborted from within themselves; a thread abort must be called from another thread.

Thread Priorities

You've seen how a thread can be interrupted so that another thread can execute. You've also seen how a thread can yield its execution time by either yielding that execution once, or by putting itself to sleep. You've also seen that thread just end. The last thing to consider about the basics of threading is how threads prioritize themselves. Using the analogy of daily life, you understand that some tasks take priority over other tasks. For instance, although I have a grueling deadline to meet with this book, I also need to eat. Eating may take priority over writing this book because of the need to eat to live. In addition, if I stay up too late working on this book, sleep deprivation may elevate the body's priority to sleep. Additional tasks may be given to me, but those tasks wouldn't be given a higher priority over sleep. Someone can emphasize that a task is important, but it's ultimately up to the task recipient to determine what is of extremely high importance, and what can wait.

This same idea relates to the threading concept. Some threads just need to have a higher priority. Just as eating and sleeping are high priorities because they allow us to function, system tasks have higher priorities because the computer needs them to function. Windows prioritizes threads on a scale of 0 to 31, with larger numbers meaning higher priorities. A priority of 0 can only be set by the system and means that the thread is idle. Windows system users can set priorities between 1 and 15. The administrator must set priorities that are higher than 15 (how an administrator does this is discussed later). Threads running in priority between 16 and 31 are considered to be running in real-time. The priority is so high for these threads that they preempt threads in lower priorities. This preemption has the effect of making their execution more immediate. The types of items that might need to run in real-time are processes such as device drivers, file systems, and input devices. Imagine what would happen if your keyboard and mouse input were not high priorities to the system. The default priority for user-level threads is 8. One last thing to remember is that threads inherit the priority of the processes in which they reside. This is diagrammed for your reference in Figure 13-8. We'll also use this diagram to break these numbers down even further.

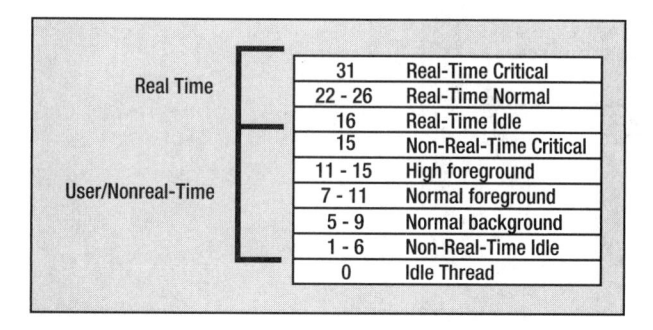

Real Time	31	Real-Time Critical
	22 - 26	Real-Time Normal
	16	Real-Time Idle
User/Nonreal-Time	15	Non-Real-Time Critical
	11 - 15	High foreground
	7 - 11	Normal foreground
	5 - 9	Normal background
	1 - 6	Non-Real-Time Idle
	0	Idle Thread

Figure 13-8. *Threads and priorities*

In some operating systems, such as Windows, as long as threads of a higher priority exist, threads in lower priority are not scheduled for execution. The processor schedules all threads at the highest priority first. Each thread of that same priority level takes turns executing in a round-robin fashion. After all threads in the highest priority have completed, then the threads in the next highest level are scheduled for execution. If a thread of a higher priority is available again, all threads in a lower priority are preempted and use of the processor is given to the higher priority thread.

Administrating Priorities

Based on what you've learned about priorities, it may be desirable to set certain process priorities higher so that any threads spawned from those processes will have a higher likelihood of being scheduled for execution. Windows provides several ways to set priorities of tasks administratively and programmatically. Right now, you'll learn how to set priorities administratively. This can be done with tools such as the Task Manager (which you've already seen), and two other tools called pview and pviewer. You can also view the current priorities using the Window's Performance Monitor. I won't cover all these tools right now; instead, let's briefly look at how to set the general priority of processes. Earlier in the chapter when processes were introduced, you saw how to use the Task Manager to view all the processes currently running on the system. You can use that very same window to elevate the priority of a particular process.

To change a process's priority, first open an instance of an application such as Microsoft Excel. Now launch the Task Manager and go to the `Processes` tab. Look at an instance of Excel running as a process. Right-click `EXCEL.EXE` in the list and choose `Set Priority` from the menu. As you can see, you can change the priority class as desired wish. It wouldn't make much sense to set the priority of Excel high, but the point is you can if you want to. Every process has a priority and the operating system isn't going to tell you what priorities you should and should not have. However, it will warn you that you might be about to do something with undesirable consequences, but the choice is still left up to you.

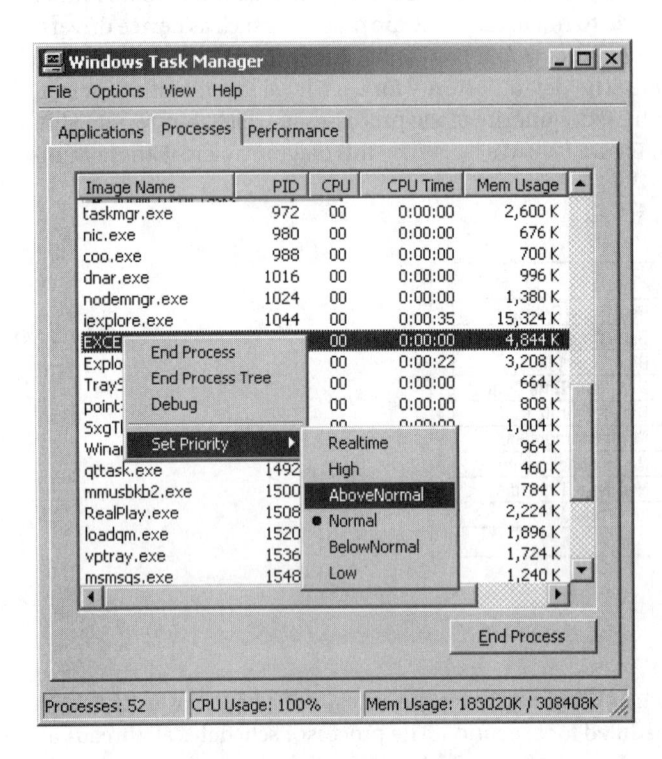

In the previous screenshot, you can see that one of the priorities has a mark next to it. This mark represents the current priority of the process. It should be noted that when you set a priority for one process, you are setting it for that one instance only. This means that all other currently running instances of that same application retain their default process levels. Additionally, any future instances of the process that are launched also retain their default process levels.

Thread Support in Visual Basic .NET

As mentioned earlier, the idea of free threading is a very new concept to the Visual Basic developer. Many developers have found ways to manipulate the API to attempt spawning new threads, but this often can result in undesirable consequences. The other option that Visual Basic developers had in the past was to create an out-of-process component that would spawn a new thread—but within a new process and therefore with its own set of data. However, when Microsoft adapted Visual Basic to fit the .NET Framework, it came up with a major set of upgrades, including the ability to free thread an application. The next section explains how that support is provided and how threading is done as opposed to what threading is. You'll also learn about some of the additional support provided to help further separate processes.

By the end of this section, you will understand

- What the System.AppDomain class is and what it can do for you
- How the .NET runtime monitors threads

System.AppDomain

As explained earlier in this chapter, processes are the physical isolation of the memory and resources needed to maintain themselves, and each process has at least one thread. When designing the .NET Framework, Microsoft added one more layer of isolation called an *application domain* or *AppDomain*. This application domain is not a physical isolation like a process is; instead, it's a further logical isolation within the process. Major advantages come from the fact that more than one application domain can exist within a single process. In general, it's impossible for standard processes to access each other's data without using a proxy. Using a proxy causes much overhead and coding can be complex. However, with the introduction of the application domain concept, you can now launch several applications within the same process. The same isolation provided by a process is also available with the application domain. Threads can execute across application domains without the overhead associated with interprocess communication. Another benefit of these additional in-process boundaries is that they provide type checking of the data they contain.

■Note AppDomains and communication between two AppDomains was covered more thoroughly in the Remoting section of this book (Chapters 1 through 3). Refer to those chapters for more detailed information on this topic.

Microsoft encapsulated all the functionality for these application domains into a class called System.AppDomain. Microsoft .NET namespaces have a very tight relationship with these application domains. Any time that a namespace is loaded in an application, it's loaded into an AppDomain. Unless otherwise specified, the namespace is loaded into the calling code's AppDomain. Application domains also have a direct relationship with threads; they can hold one or many threads, just like a process. However, the difference is that an application domain can be created within the process and without a new thread. This relationship could be modeled as shown in Figure 13-9.

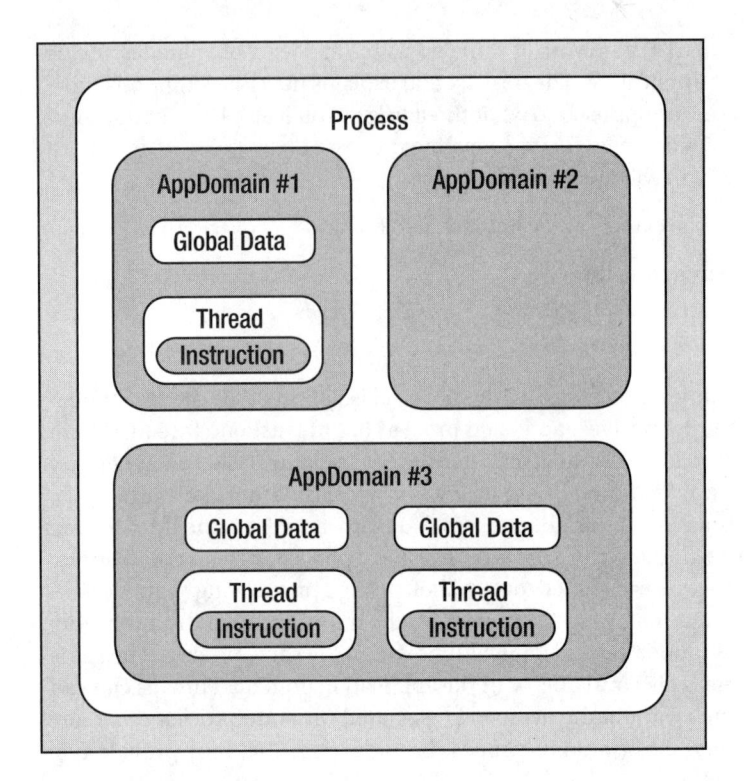

Figure 13-9. *Modelling the application domains within the process.*

Tip In .NET, the `AppDomain` and `Thread` classes cannot be inherited for security reasons.

Each application contains one or more `AppDomain`s. Each `AppDomain` can create and execute multiple threads. In Figure 13-10, the two OS processes Y and Z are running in machine X. The OS process X has four running `AppDomain`s: A, B, C, and D. The OS process Y has two `AppDomain`s: A and B.

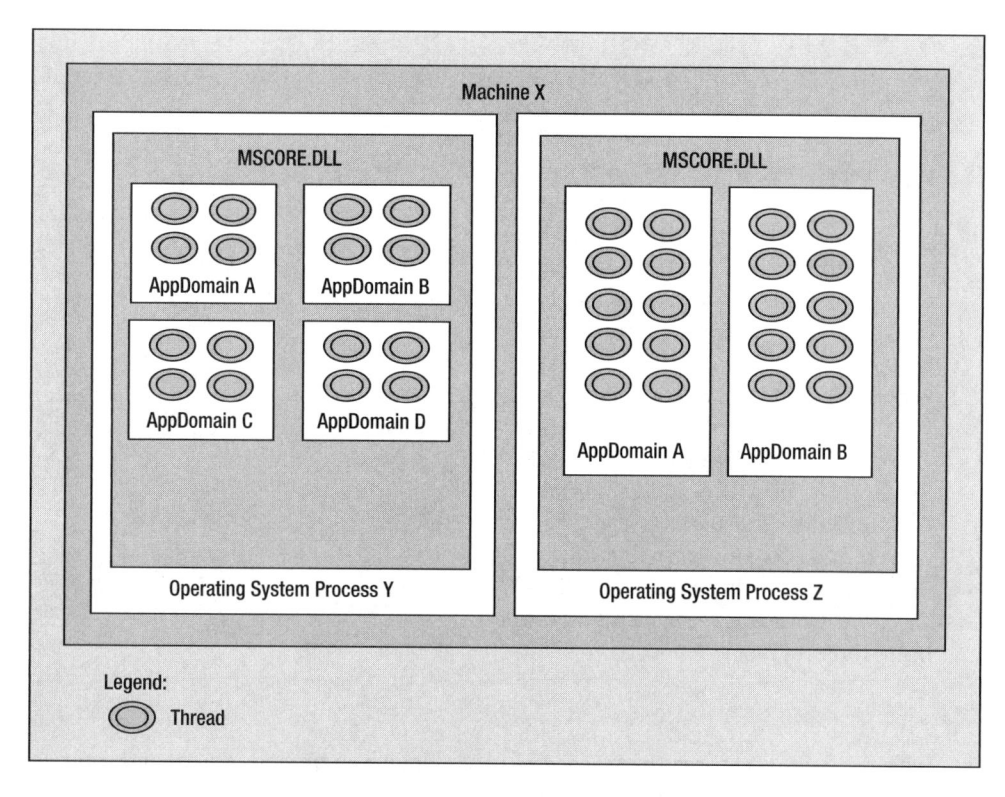

Figure 13-10. *Multiple threads in an* AppDomain

Setting AppDomain Data

You've heard the theory and seen the models; it's time to get your hands on some real code. The following example uses the AppDomain to set data, retrieve data, and identify the thread that the AppDomain is executing. Open Notepad and enter the following code into it:

```
Imports System

Public Class MyAppDomain
    Public Const DataName As String = "MyData"
    Public Shared Sub Main()
        Dim Domain As AppDomain
        Dim CurDomain As AppDomain
        Dim DataMessage As String
        Dim DataValue As String = "DataValue"
```

```vb
            DataMessage = "Getting Data From " + _
                        " '{0}': '{1}' " + _
                        "running on thread id: {2}"
        Domain = AppDomain.CreateDomain("DataDomain")
        Console.WriteLine("Created new " + _
                        "AppDomain: {0}", _
                        Domain.FriendlyName)
        Console.WriteLine("Setting data on: {0}", _
                        Domain.FriendlyName)
        Domain.SetData(DataName, DataValue)
        CurDomain = AppDomain.CurrentDomain
        Console.WriteLine(DataMessage, _
                    CurDomain.FriendlyName, _
                    CurDomain.GetData(DataName), _
                    Domain.GetCurrentThreadId)
        Console.WriteLine(DataMessage, _
                    Domain.FriendlyName, _
                    Domain.GetData(DataName), _
                    Domain.GetCurrentThreadId)
        Console.ReadLine()
    End Sub
End Class
```

Save the file as C:\handbook\threading\myappdomain.vb. Open a command prompt and compile the application using the following command line:

`C:\handbook\threading>vbc.exe myappdomain.vb`

Now execute the new application by typing the following command:

C:\handbook\threading>myappdomain.exe

Your output should look something like this (with the exception of the thread id's, which will almost certainly be different each time this application is run):

```
Created new AppDomain: DataDomain
Setting data on: DataDomain
Getting Data From  'myAppDomain.exe': '' running on thread id: 1476
Getting Data From  'DataDomain': 'DataValue' running on thread id: 1476
```

This is straightforward for the experienced VB.NET developer. However, let's look at the code and determine exactly what is happening here. The first line

`Imports System`

simply allows you to access the AppDomain objects without having to reference the fully qualified class names every time.

Let's look at the Sub Main() routine:

```vb
Public Shared Sub Main()
    Dim Domain As AppDomain
    Dim CurDomain As AppDomain
    Dim DataMessage As String
    Dim DataValue As String = "DataValue"

    DataMessage = "Getting Data From " + _
                " '{0}': '{1}' " + _
                "running on thread id: {2}"

    Domain = AppDomain.CreateDomain("DataDomain")
    Console.WriteLine("Created new " + _
                    "AppDomain: {0}", _
                    Domain.FriendlyName)

    Console.WriteLine("Setting data on: {0}", _
                    Domain.FriendlyName)
    Domain.SetData(DataName, DataValue)
    CurDomain = AppDomain.CurrentDomain
    Console.WriteLine(DataMessage, _
            CurDomain.FriendlyName, _
            CurDomain.GetData(DataName), _
            Domain.GetCurrentThreadId)

    Console.WriteLine(DataMessage, _
            Domain.FriendlyName, _
            Domain.GetData(DataName), _
            Domain.GetCurrentThreadId)
    Console.ReadLine()
End Sub
```

The code starts by dimensioning a few variables. It then creates the string that will be used to format the output to the console. Next, the following code sets the Domain variable with a new instance of an AppDomain:

```vb
Domain = AppDomain.CreateDomain("DataDomain")
```

Notice that AppDomains are created with a static factory method called CreateDomain. This is done so that the current AppDomain doesn't "own" the new instance of the AppDomain. When the CreateDomain method is called, a name is passed in that we want to use to refer to this AppDomain again. You'll notice in the next two lines, as data is output to the console, that you can again reference this value by using the AppDomain's instance member, FriendlyName. After outputting data to the console, the SetData method is called of our AppDomain instance:

```vb
Domain.SetData(DataName, DataValue)
```

This method sets data that is specific for the AppDomain instance that the data is set on. Other AppDomains can reference this data, but only when referencing the AppDomain instance the data was set with as demonstrated with the remainder of the code. The next line provides a reference to the currently executing AppDomain by requesting the static CurrentDomain member of the AppDomain class:

```
CurDomain = AppDomain.CurrentDomain
```

The code then tries to reference the data made available with the SetData method on the CurDomain instance:

```
Console.WriteLine(DataMessage, _
        CurDomain.FriendlyName, _
        CurDomain.GetData(DataName), _
        Domain.GetCurrentThreadId)
```

If you'll notice, this method fails to retrieve any data and an empty string is output to the console. This is because we didn't set the data on our CurrentDomain instance. Instead, we set the data on our new AppDomain instance. The next line attempts to retrieve the data from that instance, and succeeds!

```
Console.WriteLine(DataMessage, _
        Domain.FriendlyName, _
        Domain.GetData(DataName), _
        Domain.GetCurrentThreadId)
```

One last thing to notice, is that you can obtain the currently executing ThreadID with a simple call to the GetCurrentThreadId property of the AppDomain object. This will be useful when debugging code with multiple running threads. In the example, take note that both calls have executed on the same ThreadID.

Executing Code Within a Specified AppDomain

So far, you've seen how to successfully set and get data on a new AppDomain; however, this technique is not very useful and definitely is not great for application performance. This technique is only good if you want to pass data to code that is executing in the context of a new application domain. You can actually make your current thread execute inside a different AppDomain without much effort. Let's go ahead and demonstrate a simple example of this technique. Open your favorite text editor again and place the following code inside. Save the file as C:\handbook\threading\ThreadThroughAppDomains.vb.

```
Imports System

Public Class ThreadThroughAppDomains
  Public Shared Sub Main()
    Dim DomainA As AppDomain
    Dim DomainB As AppDomain
    DomainA = AppDomain.CreateDomain("MyDomainA")
    DomainB = AppDomain.CreateDomain("MyDomainB")
    Dim StringA = "DomainA Value"
    Dim StringB = "DomainB Value"
    DomainA.SetData("DomainKey", StringA)
    DomainB.SetData("DomainKey", StringB)
    CommonCallBack()
    DomainA.DoCallBack(AddressOf CommonCallBack)
    DomainB.DoCallBack(AddressOf CommonCallBack)
    Console.ReadLine()
  End Sub
```

```
    Shared Sub CommonCallBack()
      Dim Domain As AppDomain
      Domain = AppDomain.CurrentDomain
      Console.WriteLine("The Value '{0}' " + _
          "was found in '{1}' " + _
          "running on thread id: {2}", _
        Domain.GetData("DomainKey"), _
        Domain.FriendlyName, _
        Domain.GetCurrentThreadId )
    End Sub
End Class
```

The output of this compiled class should look similar to this:

```
The Value '' was found in 'ThreadThroughAppDomains.exe' running on thread id: 1372
The Value 'DomainA Value' was found in 'MyDomainA' running on thread id: 1372
The Value 'DomainB Value' was found in 'MyDomainB' running on thread id: 1372
```

You'll notice this example has created two application domains. To do this, you call the shared method CreateDomain():

```
Dim DomainA As AppDomain
Dim DomainB As AppDomain
DomainA = AppDomain.CreateDomain("MyDomainA")
DomainB = AppDomain.CreateDomain("MyDomainB")
```

Next you call the SetData() method again. I won't redisplay the code here because I explained its use in the last example. However, you do need to know how to get the code to execute in a given AppDomain. This is done using the DoCallBack() method. This method takes a CrossAppDomainDelegate as its parameter. In this instance, using the AddressOf operator along with the method that you want to execute will work in the same way:

```
CommonCallBack()
DomainA.DoCallBack(AddressOf CommonCallBack)
DomainB.DoCallBack(AddressOf CommonCallBack)
```

Here, CommonCallBack() is called first to execute the CommonCallBack() method within the context of the main AppDomain. Take note from the output that the FriendlyName property of the main AppDomain is the executable's name.

Next let's look at the CommonCallBack() method:

```
Shared Sub CommonCallBack()
  Dim Domain As AppDomain
  Domain = AppDomain.CurrentDomain

  Console.WriteLine( _
     "The Value '{0}' was found in '{1}' " + _
     "running on thread id: {2}", _
     Domain.GetData("DomainKey"), _
     Domain.FriendlyName, _
     Domain.GetCurrentThreadId )
End Sub
```

This method is rather generic, so it will work no matter what AppDomain instance it runs in. This code uses the CurrentDomain property you learned about in the previous example. This property obtains a reference to the domain that is executing the code. The FriendlyName property is then used again to identify the AppDomain we're using.

Finally, the GetCurrentThreadId() method is called. When you look at the output, you can see that you get the same ThreadID no matter what AppDomain you're executing in. This is important to note because this not only means that an AppDomain can have zero or many threads, but also that a thread can execute across different domains.

AppDomains and .NET Remoting

The code demonstrated in the previous section might sound sort of cool, but it doesn't really explain why you would want your thread to wander into new AppDomains. There are actually many reasons dealing mostly with the idea of isolating code execution. One thing to note is the way the .NET runtime loads assemblies into AppDomains. After an assembly is loaded into an AppDomain, it cannot be unloaded from the AppDomain. The only way to release that assembly reference is to destroy the AppDomain instance. This is useful if you want to load an assembly dynamically to execute some operation, and then release the resources that assembly is taking up by destroying the new AppDomain. This new isolation level provides flexibility for assembly loading and unloading as well as a sandbox to handle failing operations. The concept of communication between AppDomains is called *Remoting* in the .NET world. This concept is covered in detail in the .NET Remoting section of this book (Chapters 1 through 3). For now, however, you've learned the relevance of AppDomains to threading within the .NET Framework.

Thread Management and the .NET Runtime

The .NET Framework provides more capabilities than just free-threaded processes and logical application domains. In fact, the framework supplies an object representation of processor threads. These object representations are instances of the System.Threading.Thread class. The next chapter covers this class in depth. However, before getting to that level of detail, you must understand how *unmanaged threads* work in relation to *managed* threads. That is to say, how unmanaged threads created outside of the .NET world relate to instances of the managed Thread class that represents threads running inside the .NET CLR.

The .NET runtime monitors all threads that are created by .NET code. It also monitors all unmanaged threads, which can execute managed code. You may be familiar with the technology Microsoft has made available to non-.NET code called a COM-callable wrapper. This wrapper allows non-.NET applications to call .NET code as though it were a COM object. Because COM-callable wrappers can expose managed code, it's possible for unmanaged threads to wander into the .NET runtime.

When unmanaged code executes in a managed thread, the runtime checks the TLS for the existence of a managed Thread object. If a managed thread is found, the runtime uses that thread. If a managed thread isn't found, the runtime creates one and uses it. It's very simple, but is necessary to note. You still want to get an object representation of the thread no matter where it came from. If the runtime didn't manage and create the threads for these types of inbound calls, you wouldn't be able to identify the thread, or even control it, within the managed environment.

The last important note to make about thread management is that once an unmanaged call returns to unmanaged code, the thread is no longer monitored by the runtime.

Summary

This chapter outlined a wide range of important threading topics. The chapters began with the basics of multitasking and how it is accomplished by using threads and then moved on to discuss the differences between multitasking and free threading. Next, it considered processes and how they isolate data from other applications, before looking at the function of threads in an operating system such as Windows. You now know that Windows interrupts threads to grant execution time to other threads for a brief period called a time slice or a quantum and what implications this has for program execution as a whole. You've learned the function of thread priorities and the different levels of these priorities, and also that threads will inherit their parent process's priority by default.

This chapter also described how the .NET runtime monitors threads created in the .NET environment and additionally any unmanaged threads that execute managed code. You learned about the support for threading in the .NET Framework and how the `System.AppDomain` class provides an additional layer of logical data isolation on top of the physical process data isolation. The chapter has looked at how threads can cross easily from one `AppDomain` to another. Finally, you learned how an `AppDomain` doesn't necessarily have its own thread as all processes do.

CHAPTER 14

Threading in .NET

In Chapter 13, you learned *what* threading is. The chapter covered a lot of common ground that you might be familiar with already. Knowing the *what* portion of threading is important. In this chapter, you will see *how* to implement some basic threading; however, it's equally important, if not more important, to understand *when* to use threading.

In this chapter, you will

- Understand the System.Threading namespace
- Consider the design issues involved with threads
- Identify the resources threads use
- Recognize good opportunities for threading
- Learn what mistakes to avoid when using threads

System.Threading **Namespace**

Threads in the managed code are represented by a System.Threading.Thread class instance. This section discusses the System.Threading namespace and its contents in depth. Some of the more prominent classes available in the System.Threading namespace are listed in Table 14-1.

Table 14-1. *The* System.Threading *Namespace*

Class	Description
AutoResetEvent	This class, which cannot be inherited, notifies one or more waiting threads that an event has occurred.
Interlocked	This class protects against errors by providing atomic operations for variables that are shared by multiple threads.
ManualResetEvent	This class cannot be inherited and occurs when notifying one or more waiting threads that an event has occurred.
Monitor	This class provides a mechanism that synchronizes access to objects.
Mutex	A synchronization primitive that grants exclusive access to a shared resource to only one thread. It can also be used for interprocess synchronization.
ReaderWriterLock	This class defines the lock that implements single-writer and multiple reader semantics.
RegisteredWaitHandle	This class, which cannot be inherited, represents a handle that has been registered when calling the RegisterWaitForSingleObject() method.
SynchronizationLockException	This exception is thrown when a synchronized method is invoked from an unsynchronized block of code.
Thread	This class creates and controls a thread, sets its priority, and gets its status.
ThreadAbortException	This class, which cannot be inherited, is the exception that is thrown when a call is made to the Abort() method.
ThreadExceptionEventArgs	This class provides data for the ThreadException event.
ThreadInterruptedException	This exception is thrown when a thread is interrupted while it is in a waiting state.
ThreadPool	This class provides a pool of threads that can be used to post work items, process asynchronous I/O, wait on behalf of other threads, and process timers.
ThreadStateException	This is the exception that is thrown when a Thread is in an invalid ThreadState for the method call.
Timeout	This class, which cannot be inherited, contains a constant that is used to specify an infinite amount of time.
Timer	This class, which cannot be inherited, provides a mechanism for executing methods at specified intervals.
WaitHandle	This class encapsulates operating system-specific objects that wait for exclusive access to shared resources.

All these classes wont' be used in this section, but it's useful to understand what this namespace makes available to you.

Thread Class

The Thread class represents processor threads. This class allows you to do everything from manage a thread's priority to reading its status.

Let's start by looking at Table 14-2, which lists this class's Public methods.

Table 14-2. *The* Public *Methods of the* Thread *Class*

Public Method Name	Description
Abort()	To begin the process of terminating the thread, this overloaded method raises a ThreadAbortException in the thread on which it is invoked. Calling this method usually terminates the thread.
AllocateDataSlot()	This Shared method allocates an unnamed data slot on all the threads.
AllocateNamedDataSlot()	This Shared method allocates a named data slot on all threads.
Equals()	This overloaded method determines whether two object instances are equal.
FreeNamedDataSlot()	This Shared method frees a previously allocated named data slot.
GetData()	This Shared method retrieves the value from the specified slot on the current thread, within the current thread's current domain.
GetDomain()	This Shared method returns the current domain in which the current thread is running.
GetDomainID()	This Shared method returns a unique application domain identifier.
GetHashCode()	This method serves as a hash function for a particular type, suitable for use in hashing algorithms and data structures like a hash table.
GetNamedDataSlot()	This Shared method looks up a named data slot.
GetType()	This method gets the Type of the current instance.
Interrupt()	This method interrupts a thread that is in the WaitSleepJoin thread state.
Join()	This overloaded method blocks the calling thread until a thread terminates.
ResetAbort()	This Shared method cancels an Abort() requested for the current thread.
Resume()	This method resumes a thread that has been suspended.
SetData()	This Shared method sets the data in the specified slot on the currently running thread for that thread's current domain.
Sleep()	This Shared and overloaded method blocks the current thread for the specified number of milliseconds.
SpinWait()	This Shared method causes a thread to wait the number of times defined by the iterations parameter.
Start()	This method causes the operating system to change the state of the current instance to ThreadState.Running.
Suspend()	This method either suspends the thread, or if the thread is already suspended, has no effect.
ToString()	This method returns a String that represents the current object.

Now let's look at Table 14-3, which contains the Thread class's Public properties.

Table 14-3. *The* Public *Properties of the* Thread *Class*

Public Property Name	Description
ApartmentState	Sets or gets the apartment state of this thread.
CurrentContext	This Shared property gets the current context in which the thread is executing.
CurrentCulture	Sets or gets the culture for the current thread.
CurrentPrincipal	This Shared property sets or gets the thread's current principal. It is used for role-based security.
CurrentThread	This Shared property gets the currently running thread.
CurrentUICulture	Used at runtime, this property sets or gets the current culture used by the Resource Manager to look up culture-specific resources.
IsAlive	Gets a value that indicates the execution status of the current thread.
IsBackground	Sets or gets a value that indicates whether a thread is a background thread.
IsThreadPoolThread	Gets a value indicating whether a thread is part of a thread pool.
Name	Sets or gets the name of the thread.
Priority	Sets or gets a value that indicates the scheduling priority of a thread.
ThreadState	Gets a value that contains the states of the current thread.

Seeing these class members does you little good until you can at least create a thread or a reference to one. So, it's time to get your feet wet with a simple VB .NET Threading example.

Creating a Thread

This simple example isn't a good example of *why* you should use a new thread, but it strips off all the complexities that will be covered later. Create a new console application with a file called simple_thread.vb and place the following code in it:

```
Imports System
Imports System.Threading

Public Class SimpleThread
    Public Shared Sub SimpleMethod()
        Dim I As Integer = 5
        Dim X As Integer = 10
        Dim iResult As Integer = I * X
        Console.WriteLine("This code calculated the value {0}" & _
                    " from thread ID: {1}", iResult, _
                    AppDomain.GetCurrentThreadId().ToString())
    End Sub

    Public Shared Sub Main()
        Call SimpleMethod()
        Dim t As New Thread(AddressOf SimpleMethod)
        t.Start()
```

```
        Console.ReadLine()
    End Sub
End Class
```

Now save, compile, and execute the file. Your output should look something like this:

```
This code calculated the value 50 from thread id: 1400
This code calculated the value 50 from thread id: 1040
```

Let's walk through this simple example to make sure you understand what is happening here. As stated previously, the threading functionality is encapsulated in the `System.Threading` namespace. As such, this namespace must first be imported into the project. After the namespace is imported, you want to create a method that can be executed on the main (primary) thread and one on the new worker thread. The example used `SimpleMethod()`:

```
Public Shared Sub SimpleMethod()
    Dim I as Integer = 5
    Dim X as Integer = 10
    Dim iResult as Integer = I * X
    Console.WriteLine( _
        "This code calculated the value {0}" & _
        " from thread ID: {1}", iResult, _
        AppDomain.GetCurrentThreadId())
End Sub
```

We are using the `AppDomain` class that was introduced in Chapter 13 to determine what thread we are running on.

The program's entry point is the `Main()` method. The first thing you do inside this method is execute the `SimpleMethod()` subroutine. The next part is important. Your first look at creating a thread may seem a bit confusing:

```
Dim t As New Thread(AddressOf SimpleMethod)
```

This declares a variable called t as a new `Thread`. The `Thread` class constructor takes a method name as its sole parameter. In front of that method name, you use the `AddressOf` operator. This parameter is actually a `ThreadStart` delegate, which is a member of the `System.Threading` namespace as well. One last thing to notice is that the method name is not accompanied by parentheses; it simply takes the method's name prefixed with an `AddressOf` operator.

Alternatively, you could have used the following code:

```
Dim ts As New ThreadStart(AddressOf SimpleMethod)
Dim t As New Thread(ts)
```

This seems superfluous at first glance, but you can find a good use for this method in the future.

The next line calls the `Start()` method of the `Thread` object. This is followed by `Console.ReadLine()` so the program will wait on your key input before exiting the main thread:

```
t.Start()
Console.ReadLine()
```

So now you've created a thread that doesn't really do anything. The fact that different thread IDs are displayed doesn't really do much as far as describing what is happening. To get a real feeling for what is going on, you'll create another program that simulates a long process executing in the background while another process executes in the foreground. Create a new console application and place this code in a new file called do_something_thread.vb:

```vbnet
Imports System
Imports System.Threading

Public Class DoSomethingThread

    Shared Sub WorkerMethod()
        Dim i As Integer
        For i = 1 To 1000
            Console.WriteLine("Worker Thread: {0}", i)
        Next
    End Sub

    Shared Sub Main()
        Dim ts As New ThreadStart(AddressOf WorkerMethod)
        Dim t As New Thread(ts)
        t.Start()

        Dim i As Integer
        For i = 1 To 1000
            Console.WriteLine("Primary Thread: {0}", i)
        Next

        Console.ReadLine()
    End Sub
End Class
```

Your output may be somewhat different every time. The thread execution will be switched at different points in the loop every time, but your concatenated results will look something like this:

```
Primary Thread: 1
Primary Thread: 2
Primary Thread: 3
...
Worker Thread: 743
Worker Thread: 744
Worker Thread: 745
...
Primary Thread: 1000
```

This code demonstrates that the execution of one thread is interrupted to allow the other thread to execute. To get a better understanding of what is happening, try debugging the source code. Place a conditional break point in the worker thread that will halt execution when the loop has reached a certain count. I'll discuss debugging threads in depth later in this book, but feel free to play around with this code until you understand what is happening.

ThreadStart and Execution Branching

Think back to the ThreadStart delegate. Remember that you can use a ThreadStart instance as the Thread constructor's parameter. Wondering why you might want to use these objects instead of just passing in the function name with an AddressOf operator?

Let's examine a quick example in a real-world threading scenario. Suppose you want to perform some background routine when a user launches an application. Depending on who is launching the application, you want to perform different routines. For instance, let's say when an administrator logs in to an application, you want to run a background process that gathers report data and formats it. That background process will alert the administrator when the report is available. You probably wouldn't want to perform the same reporting function for an ordinary user as you would for an administrator. This is where ThreadStart is useful.

Let's look at some example code. This isn't the exact scenario described in the preceding paragraph, but the example will show you how you can branch based on a certain criteria defined in a ThreadStart. Create a new console application and place the following code in a file called ThreadStartBranching.vb:

```vb
Imports System
Imports System.Threading

Public Class ThreadStartBranching
  Shared ts As ThreadStart
  Shared Sub AdminMethod()
    Console.WriteLine( _
    "(ThreadId {0}) Admin Executing", _
    AppDomain.GetCurrentThreadId())
  End Sub

  Shared Sub UserMethod()
    Console.WriteLine( _
      "(ThreadId {0}) User Executing", _
      AppDomain.GetCurrentThreadId())
  End Sub

  Shared Sub AuthenticateUser()
    ' Replace with your own authentication
    ' mechanism
    Console.Write("(ThreadId {0}) Login: ", _
      AppDomain.GetCurrentThreadId())
    If (Console.ReadLine().ToLower() = "admin") Then
      ts = New ThreadStart(AddressOf AdminMethod)
    Else
      ts = New ThreadStart(AddressOf UserMethod)
    End If
  End Sub
```

```vb
    Shared Sub Main()
      AuthenticateUser()
      Dim t As New Thread(ts)
      t.Start()
      Dim i As Integer
      For i = 1 To 20
        Console.WriteLine("Main continues executing")
      Next

      Console.ReadLine()
    End Sub
End Class
```

Compile the code file and execute it. When prompted, type **admin** for the login and press Enter.

The output from the code might look something like this:

```
(ThreadId 2200) Login: admin
Main continues executing
Main continues executing
...
Main continues executing
Main continues executing
(ThreadId 3920) Admin Executing
Main continues executing
Main continues executing
```

Now let's look at this example in some detail. The first part of the class declares a `ThreadStart` delegate as `Shared` that you can use globally in your class:

```vb
Shared ts As ThreadStart
```

Next the code created two methods: `AdminMethod()` and `UserMethod()`. Theoretically, these methods would execute a long series of instructions that would be completely different for the two different user types. In this example, we just want to identify that they have run so we write them out to the console:

```vb
Shared Sub AdminMethod()
  Console.WriteLine( _
    "(ThreadId {0}) Admin Executing", _
    AppDomain.GetCurrentThreadId())
End Sub
Shared Sub UserMethod()
  Console.WriteLine( _
    "(ThreadId {0}) User Executing", _
    AppDomain.GetCurrentThreadId())
End Sub
```

Moving on, you'll find the `AuthenticateUser()` method. Of course, this method is far from secure, but you could replace this method with your own secure authentication mechanism.

```vb
Shared Sub AuthenticateUser()
  ' Replace with your own authentication
  ' mechanism
  Console.Write("(ThreadId {0}) Login: ", _
    AppDomain.GetCurrentThreadId())
  If (Console.ReadLine().ToLower() = "admin") Then
    ts = New ThreadStart(AddressOf AdminMethod)
  Else
    ts = New ThreadStart(AddressOf UserMethod)
  End If
End Sub
```

This method not only authenticates the user, but it also sets the appropriate `ThreadStart` delegate that will be used by the main method.

Lastly, the `Main` subroutine is where the methods are called to authenticate the user and execute the thread:

```vb
Shared Sub Main()
  AuthenticateUser()
  Dim t As New Thread(ts)
  t.Start()
  Dim i As Integer
  For i = 1 To 20
    Console.WriteLine("Main continues executing")
  Next

  Console.ReadLine()
End Sub
```

`AuthenticateUser()` is first called to check the user's credentials. As stated earlier, this method sets the method that is executed in the thread. The code then creates a new `Thread` and calls `Start`. The `Start()` method immediately returns and allows main to continue executing while also sharing the processor with the worker thread. Try executing this application again, but this time, type **user** for the login. The example application, of course, executes the method for the appropriate user level. The authentication method determines what process will run in the background, and the `Main` subroutine actually starts the worker thread's execution.

Thread Properties and Methods

As you saw in the beginning of this chapter, the `Thread` class has many properties and methods. I promised that controlling thread execution was made much simpler with the `System.Threading` namespace. So far, all you've done is create threads and start them.

Now, let's look at two more members of the `Thread` class: the `Sleep()` method and the `IsAlive` property. Chapter 13 said that a thread can go to sleep for a time until it is clock-interrupted. Putting a thread to sleep is as simple as calling an instance member's `Sleep()` method. You can also determine a thread's state. The following example uses the `IsAlive` property to determine whether a thread has completed its executions and the `Sleep()` method to pause the execution of a thread. Look at the following code, `threadstate.vb`, where we will make use of both of these members:

```vb
Imports System
Imports System.Threading

Public Class ThreadState
  Shared Sub WorkerFunction()
    Dim i As Integer
    Dim ThreadState As String
    For i = 1 To 500000
      If i Mod 50000 = 0 Then
        ThreadState = _
          Thread.CurrentThread.ThreadState
        Console.WriteLine("Worker: {0}", ThreadState)
      End If
    Next
    Console.WriteLine("Worker Function Complete")
  End Sub

  Shared Sub Main()
    Dim ThreadState As String
    Dim t As New Thread(AddressOf WorkerFunction)
    t.Start()
    While t.IsAlive
      Console.WriteLine( _
        "Still waiting. I'm going back to sleep.")
      Thread.CurrentThread.Sleep(10)
    End While

    ThreadState = t.ThreadState.ToString()
    Console.WriteLine( _
      "He's finally done! Thread state is: {0}", _
      ThreadState)
    Console.ReadLine()
  End Sub
End Class
```

Your output should look similar to the following (try experimenting with the values in the For loop and passed to the sleep() method to see different results):

```
Still waiting. I'm going back to sleep.
Worker: Running
Worker: Running
Worker: Running
Still waiting. I'm going back to sleep.
Worker: Running
Worker: Running
Worker: Running
Worker: Running
```

```
Still waiting. I'm going back to sleep.
Worker: Running
Worker: Running
Worker: Running
Worker Function Complete
He's finally done! Thread state is: Stopped
```

Let's look at the Main() method where you've used the new concepts. First, you created a thread and passed it the method to execute as a delegate:

```
Dim t As New Thread(AddressOf WorkerFunction)
t.Start()
```

This was nothing new. As usual, the Main() method continues to execute alongside the new thread as the processor switches between them. The IsAlive property of our newly created thread checks to see whether the thread is still executing. The code continues to test this variable. While the thread is alive, the code continues to sleep for 200 milliseconds, wake up the thread, and test whether the other thread is still alive:

```
While t.IsAlive
    Console.WriteLine( _
       "Still waiting. I'm going back to sleep.")
    Thread.CurrentThread.Sleep(10)
End While
```

Next, let's look at the ThreadState property that has been used twice in the code. The ThreadState property is actually a property that returns an enumerated type. The enumeration tells you the exact state the thread is in. You can either test this property with an If statement as in the last example or use the ToString() method on the property and write out its state in text form:

```
Console.WriteLine( _
   "He's finally done! Thread state is: {0}",
   t.ThreadState)
```

The rest of this code is standard and doesn't need to be reviewed. Take away from this example just a few concepts. First you tell one thread to sleep for a specified period so that you can yield execution to your other threads. We do that with the Thread object's Sleep() method—passing in the length of time in milliseconds that you want the thread to sleep. In addition, you can test the threads to see whether they have finished executing by using the IsAlive property. Lastly, you can use the ThreadState property of your thread instances to determine their exact thread state.

Thread Priorities

The thread priority determines the relative priority of the threads between one another. The ThreadPriority enumeration defines the possible values for setting a thread's priority. The available values are

```
Highest
AboveNormal
Normal
BelowNormal
Lowest
```

When a thread is created by the runtime and has not been assigned any priority, it initially has the Normal priority. However, this can be changed using the ThreadPriority enumeration. Before seeing an example for the thread priority, let's see what a thread priority looks like. The following simple threading example just displays the name, state, and the priority information about the current thread, threadpriority.vb:

```
Imports System
Imports System.Threading

Public Class ThreadPriority
  Public Shared worker As Thread

  Shared Sub Main()
    Console.WriteLine("Entering Sub Main()")
    worker = New Thread(AddressOf FindPriority)
    'Let's give a name to the thread
    worker.Name = "FindPriority() Thread"
    worker.Start()
    Console.WriteLine("Exiting Sub Main()")
    Console.ReadLine()
  End Sub

  Shared Public Sub FindPriority()
    Console.WriteLine("Name: {0}", _
      worker.Name())
    Console.WriteLine("State: {0}", _
      worker.ThreadState )
    Console.WriteLine("Priority: {0}", _
      worker.Priority )
  End Sub

End Class
```

A simple method called FindPriority() displays the name, state, and priority information of the current thread, which produces output like the following:

```
Entering the Sub Main()
Exiting the Sub Main()
Name: FindPriority() Thread
State: Running
Priority: Normal
```

We know the worker thread is running with a Normal priority, so let's add another thread with a higher priority. Create the following file and save it as threadpriority2.vb:

```vb
Imports System
Imports System.Threading

Public Class ThreadPriority
  Public Shared worker As Thread
  Public Shared worker2 As Thread

  Shared Sub Main()
    Console.WriteLine("Entering Sub Main()")
    worker = New Thread(AddressOf FindPriority)
    worker2 = New Thread(AddressOf FindPriority2)
    'Let's give a name to the thread
    worker.Name = "FindPriority() Thread"
    worker2.Name = "FindPriority2() Thread"
    ' Give the new thread object the highest priority
    worker2.Priority = _
      Threading.ThreadPriority.Highest
    worker.Start()
    worker2.Start()
    Console.WriteLine("Exiting Sub Main()")
      Console.ReadLine()
  End Sub

  Shared Public Sub FindPriority()
    Console.WriteLine("Name: {0}", _
      worker.Name())
    Console.WriteLine("State: {0}", _
      worker.ThreadState)
    Console.WriteLine("Priority: {0}", _
      worker.Priority)
  End Sub

  Shared Public Sub FindPriority2()
    Console.WriteLine("Name (2): {0}", _
      worker.Name())
    Console.WriteLine("State (2): {0}", _
      worker.ThreadState)
    Console.WriteLine("Priority (2): {0}", _
      worker.Priority)
  End Sub
End Class
```

The output from `thread_priority2.vb` will be something like the following:

```
Entering Sub Main()
Name(2): FindPriority2() Thread
State(2): Running
Priority(2): Highest
Exiting Sub Main()
Name: FindPriority() Thread
State: Running
Priority: Normal
```

Threads are scheduled for execution based on the priority set using the `Priority` property. Every operating system executes thread priorities differently and the operating system can change the priority of the thread.

> **Note** The application is unable to restrict the operating system from changing the priority of the thread that was assigned by the developer because the OS is the master of all threads and knows when and how to schedule them. For example, the OS could change the priority of the thread dynamically due to several factors, including system events such as user input that has higher priority or lack of memory that will trigger the garbage collection process.

Timers and Callbacks

So far, you've seen some simple examples of threading. We haven't covered the issue of synchronization at all, although we'll cover that in much greater detail in the next chapter. As threads run out of sequence from the rest of the application code, you can't be certain that actions affecting a particular shared resource occurring in one thread will be completed before code in another thread accesses that same shared resource. You can deal with these issues in various ways, but here we'll cover the use of timers. Using a timer, you can specify that a method is executed at a specific regular interval, and this method could check that the required actions have been completed before continuing. This simple model can apply to a variety of situations.

Timers are made up of two objects, a `TimerCallback` and a `Timer`. The `TimerCallback` defines the action to be performed at a specified interval, whereas the `Timer` object is the counting mechanism. The `TimerCallback` associates a specific method with the timer. The `Timer`'s constructor (which is overloaded) requires four arguments. The first is the `TimerCallback` specified earlier. The second is an object that can be used to transmit state across to the method specified. The latter two arguments are the period after which to start counting, and the period in which it will fire the `TimerCallback` method call. They can be entered as integers or longs, but as you'll see in the following code, you can also use the `System.TimeSpan` object to specify the intervals in ticks, milliseconds, seconds, minutes, hours, or days.

The easiest way to show how this works is by demonstration, so consider the following application, `thread_timer.vb`, that fires two threads. The second thread will not perform its operations until the first has completed its operations.

```vbnet
Imports System
Imports System.Threading
Imports System.Text

Public Class TimerExample
  Private Shared message As String
  Private Shared tmr As Timer
  Private Shared complete As Boolean
```

This code declares `tmr` as shared. It will be set in the `Main()` method:

```vbnet
Public Shared Sub Main()
  Dim t As New Thread(AddressOf GenerateText)
  t.Start()
  Dim tmrCallBack As New TimerCallback ( _
    AddressOf GetText)
  tmr = New Timer(tmrCallBack, Nothing, _
    TimeSpan.Zero, TimeSpan.FromSeconds(2))
```

Here we fire up a new thread that will execute on the `GenerateText()` method, which iterates through a `For` loop to generate a string and store it in the class wide `message` field:

```vbnet
  Do
     If (complete) Then Exit Do
  Loop
  Console.WriteLine("Exiting Main...")
  Console.ReadLine()
End Sub
```

This loop just freezes the `Main()` loop until the `complete` field is `True`. In a GUI, different methods could be used because the `Application.Run()` method puts the application in a perpetual loop anyway:

```vbnet
Public Shared Sub GenerateText()
  Dim i As Integer
  Dim sb As StringBuilder = New StringBuilder()

  For i = 1 To 200
    sb.AppendFormat("This is Line {0}{1}", _
       i, Environment.NewLine)
  Next
  message = sb.ToString()
End Sub
```

The previous code snippet is the first method, which uses a `StringBuilder` object to generate 200 lines and then stores them in the `message` field:

```vbnet
Public Shared Sub GetText(ByVal state As Object)
  If message Is Nothing Then Exit Sub
  Console.WriteLine("Message is :")
  Console.WriteLine(message)
```

```
    tmr.Dispose()
    complete = True
  End Sub
End Class
```

The timer fires the last method used in this class every two seconds. If message hasn't been set yet, it exits; otherwise, it outputs a message and then disposes of the timer. This stops the timer from continuing to count. This should be performed as soon as the timer is no longer necessary.

The output from thread_timer.vb is as follows:

```
Message is :
This is Line 1
This is Line 2
...
This is Line 199
This is Line 200
Exiting Main...
```

Spinning Threads with Threads

You've seen in code how to spawn a thread from the Sub Main(). In a similar way, you can also spawn multiple threads within a thread. For example, say you have a Car class that has a Public method called StartTheEngine(). The StartTheEngine() method calls another three Private methods called CheckTheBattery(), CheckForFuel(), and CheckTheEngine(). Because each of these tasks, checking the battery, fuel, and engine, can happen simultaneously, you can run each of these methods in a different thread. Here is how the Car class is implemented in thread_spinning.vb:

```
Imports System
Imports System.Threading

Class Car
  Public Sub StartTheEngine()
    Console.WriteLine("Starting the engine!")
    'Declare three new threads
    Dim batt As Thread = New Thread( _
      AddressOf CheckTheBattery)
    Dim fuel As Thread = New Thread( _
      AddressOf CheckForFuel)
    Dim eng As Thread = New Thread( _
      AddressOf CheckTheEngine)
    batt.Start()
    fuel.Start()
    eng.Start()
    Dim i As Integer
    For i = 1 To 100000000
```

```vb
      Next
      Console.WriteLine("Engine is ready!")
    End Sub

    Private Sub CheckTheBattery()
      Console.WriteLine("Checking the Battery!")
      Dim i As Integer
      For i = 1 To 100000
        '
      Next

      Console.WriteLine( _
        "Finished checking the Battery!")
    End Sub

    Private Sub CheckForFuel()
      Console.WriteLine("Checking for Fuel!")
      Dim i As Integer
      For i = 1 To 100000
        '
      Next
      Console.WriteLine("Fuel is available!")
    End Sub

    Private Sub CheckTheEngine()
      Console.WriteLine("Checking the engine!")
      Dim i As Integer
      For i = 1 To 100000
        '
      Next
      Console.WriteLine( _
        "Finished checking the engine!")
    End Sub
End Class
```

In the `StartTheEngine()` method, we create three threads and then start each of them one by one:

```vb
Module CarStarter
  Sub Main()
    Console.WriteLine("Entering Sub Main!")
    Dim j As Integer
    Dim myCar As New Car()
    Dim worker As Thread = New Thread( _
      AddressOf myCar.StartTheEngine)
    worker.Start()
    For j = 1 To 10000000
      '
```

```
    Next
    Console.WriteLine("Exiting Sub Main!")
      Console.ReadLine()
  End Sub
End Module
```

In the Sub Main() method, we simply create one more thread and execute the StartTheEngine() method in that thread, as illustrated in Figure 14-1.

```
+-------------------------------------------+
|                AppDomain                  |
|  +-------------------------------------+  |
|  |         Main Thread (Sub Main)      |  |
|  |  +-------------------------------+  |  |
|  |  |  Car Thread (Car.StartTheEngine) | |  |
|  |  |  +-------------------------+  |  |  |
|  |  |  |  CheckTheBattery Thread |  |  |  |
|  |  |  +-------------------------+  |  |  |
|  |  |  +-------------------------+  |  |  |
|  |  |  |  CheckForFuel Thread    |  |  |  |
|  |  |  +-------------------------+  |  |  |
|  |  |  +-------------------------+  |  |  |
|  |  |  |  CheckTheEngine Thread  |  |  |  |
|  |  |  +-------------------------+  |  |  |
|  |  +-------------------------------+  |  |
|  +-------------------------------------+  |
+-------------------------------------------+
```

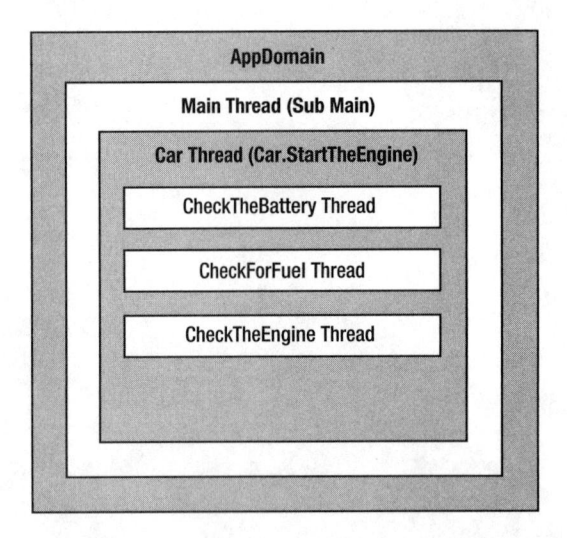

Figure 14-1. *Creating a thread and executing the* StartTheEngine() *method*

The output should look something like the following:

```
Entering Sub Main!
Exiting Sub Main!
Starting the engine!
Checking the Battery!
Checking for Fuel!
Checking the engine!
Finished checking the Battery!
Fuel is available!
Finished checking the engine!
Engine is ready!
```

As you can see, each of these methods works in its own thread and executes in its own time-sliced slot.

Spinning Threads with Threads with Threads

You can split the Car class into separate classes and you can build two more methods in a new Engine class called check1() and check2(). The Engine class will then execute the check1() and check2() methods in its own thread as shown in Figure 14-2.

```
┌─────────────────────────────────────────────┐
│                  AppDomain                  │
│  ┌───────────────────────────────────────┐  │
│  │         Main Thread (Sub Main)        │  │
│  │  ┌─────────────────────────────────┐  │  │
│  │  │   Car Thread (Car.StartTheEngine)│  │  │
│  │  │  ┌───────────────────────────┐  │  │  │
│  │  │  │  CheckTheBattery Thread   │  │  │  │
│  │  │  └───────────────────────────┘  │  │  │
│  │  │  ┌───────────────────────────┐  │  │  │
│  │  │  │   CheckForFuel Thread     │  │  │  │
│  │  │  └───────────────────────────┘  │  │  │
│  │  │  ┌───────────────────────────┐  │  │  │
│  │  │  │Engine Thread (CheckTheEngine)│  │  │
│  │  │  │ ┌──────────┐ ┌──────────┐ │  │  │  │
│  │  │  │ │Check1 Thrd│ │Check2 Thrd│ │  │  │  │
│  │  │  │ └──────────┘ └──────────┘ │  │  │  │
│  │  │  └───────────────────────────┘  │  │  │
│  │  └─────────────────────────────────┘  │  │
│  └───────────────────────────────────────┘  │
└─────────────────────────────────────────────┘
```

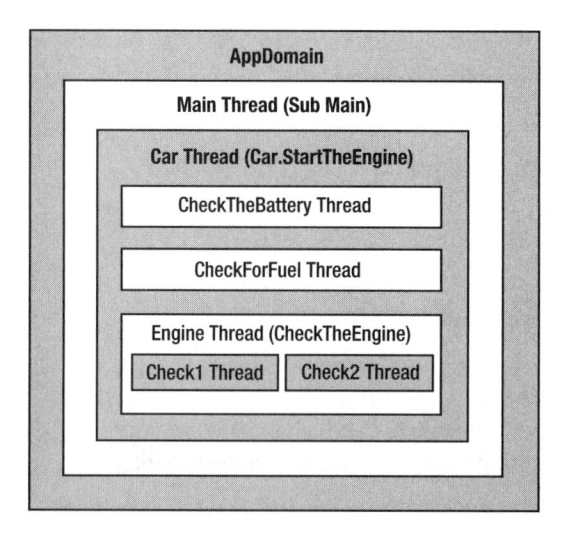

Figure 14-2. *The Engine class executes the* check1() *and* check2() *methods in its own thread.*

Now, let's remove the CheckTheEngine() method from the Car class and create one more class called Engine (see thread_spinning2.vb):

```
Class Engine
  Public Sub CheckTheEngine()
    Dim chck1 As Thread = New Thread( _
      AddressOf Check1)
    Dim chck2 As Thread = New Thread( _
      AddressOf Check2)
    check1.Start()
    check2.Start()
    Console.WriteLine("Checking the engine!")
    Dim count As Integer
    For count = 1 To 10000
      '
    Next
    Console.WriteLine( _
      "Finished checking the engine!")
  End Sub
```

```vb
    Private Sub Check1()
      Console.WriteLine("Starting the engine check!!")
      Dim i As Integer
      For i = 1 To 10000
        '
      Next
      Console.WriteLine("Finished engine check1!")
    End Sub

    Private Sub Check2()
      Console.WriteLine("Starting the engine check2!")
      Dim i As Integer
      For i = 1 To 10000
        '
      Next
      Console.WriteLine("Finished engine check2!")
    End Sub
End Class
```

The `Engine` class has the `Public` method `CheckTheEngine()`, which creates two more threads and calls the `check1()` and `check2()` methods. Here is how the results may look:

```
Entering Sub Main!
Exiting Sub Main!
Starting the engine!
Checking the Battery!
Checking for Fuel!
Checking the engine!
Starting the engine check!!
Starting the engine check2!
Finished checking the Battery!
Fuel is available!
Engine is ready!
Finished engine check1!
Finished checking the engine!
Finished engine check2!
```

As you can see, spawning threads with threads is easy. However, this method has disadvantages as well. The code degrades in performance, for instance.

Performance Considerations

The more threads you create, the more work the system has to do to maintain the thread contexts and CPU instructions. The Processes tab of the Windows Task Manager tells you how many processes and threads are currently running. The Task Manager does not currently display the number of `AppDomains` in each process.

If you want to know how many threads are running inside the CLR, then you have to use the Windows Performance Monitor tool and add a couple of CLR-specific performance categories. The CLR exposes a performance category called .NET CLR LocksAndThreads that you can use to get more information about the CLR-managed threads. Let's run the Performance Monitor and add the counter shown in the following table from the .NET CLR LocksAndThreads category.

Performance Counter	Description
# of current logical threads	Displays the number of current managed threads in the application and includes both the running and stopped threads.
# of current physical threads	Displays the number of OS threads created and owned by CLR. This counter cannot map one to one with managed threads.
# of total recognized threads	Displays the number of current recognized threads by the CLR.
Current Queue Length	Displays the number of threads that are waiting to acquire locks in the managed application.
Total # of Contentions	Displays the number of failures when the managed applications try to acquire locks.

The following illustration shows the values for the thread_spinning2 application.

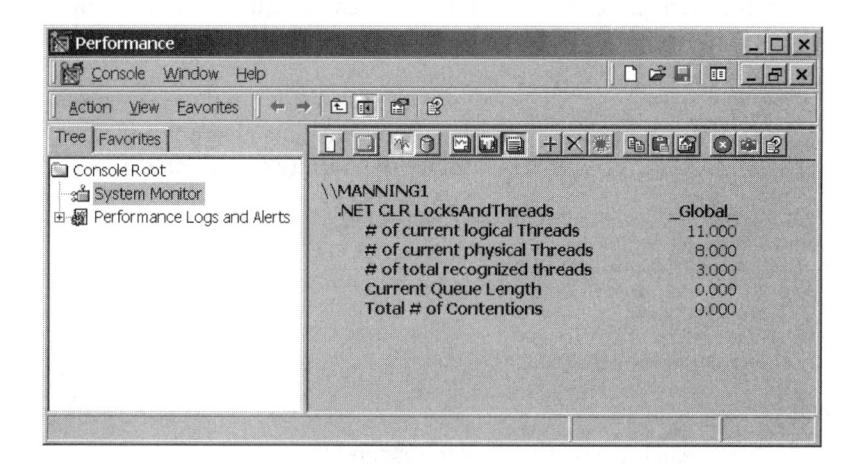

The following is a comprehensive overview of the .NET CLR LocksAndThreads performance counter information:

- The counter # of current local Threads specifies that 11 managed threads are created and owned by the CLR.

> **Tip** Because we've added the counter instance "_Global_", we see all the threads created by the CLR.

- The counter # of current physical Threads specifies that eight OS threads are created and owned by the CLR.
- The counter # of total recognized Threads specifies that three OS threads are recognized by the CLR and they're created by the Thread object.
- The counter Total # of Contentions specifies that the runtime did not fail when it tried to acquirer managed locks. Managed lock fails are bad for the execution of code.

Life Cycle of Threads

When a thread is scheduled for execution, it can go through several states, including unstarted, alive, sleeping, and so on. The Thread class contains methods that allow you to start, stop, resume, abort, suspend, and join (wait for) a thread. You can find the current state of the thread using its ThreadState property, which is one of the values specified in the ThreadState enumeration:

- Aborted: The thread is in the Stopped state.
- AbortRequested: The Abort() method has been called, but the thread has not yet received the System.Threading.ThreadAbortexception that will try to terminate it.
- Background: The thread is being executed in the background.
- Running: The thread has started and is not blocked.
- Stopped: The thread has stopped.
- StopRequested: The thread is being requested to stop.
- Suspended: The thread has been suspended.
- SuspendRequested: The thread is being requested to suspend.
- Unstarted: The Start() method has not yet been called on the thread.
- WaitSleepJoin: The thread has been blocked by a call to Wait(), Sleep(), or Join().

Figure 14-3 shows the life cycle of a thread.

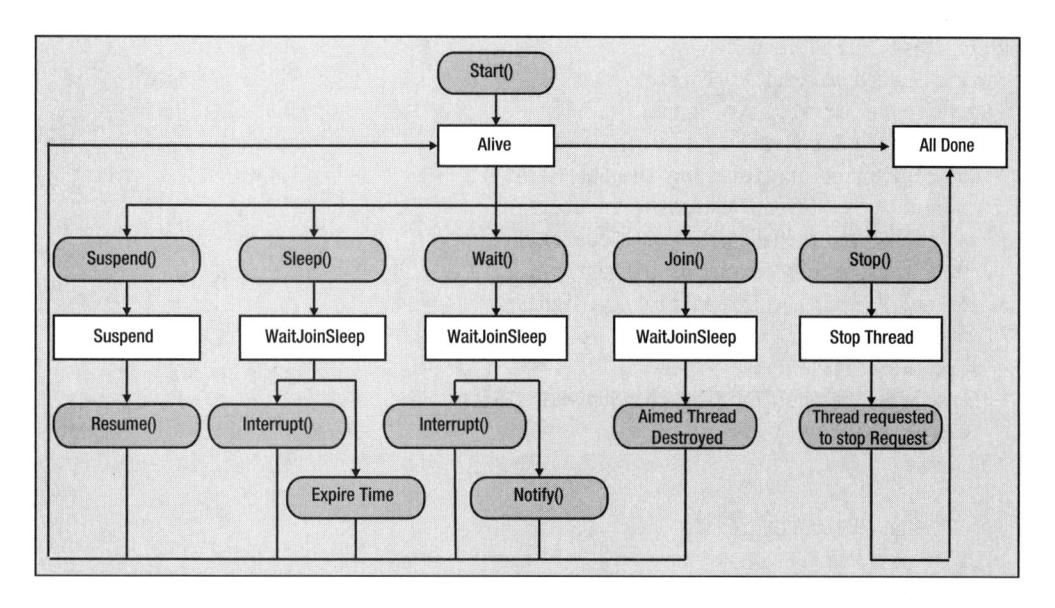

Figure 14-3. *A thread lifecycle*

Next, we'll explore the life cycle of threads.

Putting a Thread to Sleep

When you create a new thread, you have to call the Start() method of the Thread object to schedule that thread. At this time, the CLR allocates a time slice to the address of the method passed to the constructor of the Thread object. After the thread is in the Running state, it can go back to either the Sleep or Abort states when the OS is processing the other threads. You can use the Sleep() method of the Thread class to put a thread to sleep. The Sleep() method is really useful if you are waiting for a resource and want to occasionally check its availability. For example, let's say your application cannot proceed due to unavailability of a resource that it is trying to access. You might want your application to try to access the resource again after a few milliseconds, in which case the Sleep() method is a good way to put the thread to sleep for a specified time before the application tries to access the resource again.

The Sleep() method has two overloads. The first overload takes an integer as the parameter that will suspend the thread for the number of milliseconds specified. For example, if you pass 100 to the parameter, the thread will be suspended for 100 milliseconds. This places the thread into the WaitSleepJoin state. For example in thread_sleep.vb:

```
Imports System
Imports System.Threading
```

```vbnet
Public Class ThreadSleep
  Public Shared worker1 As Thread
  Public Shared worker2 As Thread
  Public Shared Sub Main()
    Console.WriteLine("Entering the Sub Main!")
    Worker1 = New Thread(AddressOf Counter1)
    worker2 = New Thread(AddressOf Counter2)
    'Make the worker2 object as highest priority
    worker2.Priority = ThreadPriority.Highest
    worker1.Start()
    worker2.Start()
    Console.WriteLine("Exiting the Sub Main!")
    Console.ReadLine()
  End Sub

  Public Shared Sub Counter1()
    Dim i As Integer
    Console.WriteLine("Entering Counter")
    For i = 1 To 50
      Console.Write(i & " ")
      If i = 10 Then worker1.Sleep(1000)
    Next

    Console.WriteLine()
    Console.WriteLine("Exiting Counter")
  End Sub

  Public Shared Sub Counter2()
    Dim i As Integer
    Console.WriteLine("Entering Counter2")
    For i = 51 To 100
      Console.Write("{0} ", i)
      If i = 70 Then worker1.Sleep(5000)
    Next
    Console.WriteLine()
    Console.WriteLine("Exiting Counter2")
  End Sub
End Class
```

The Counter1() method counts from 1 to 50; when it reaches 10, the method sleeps for 1,000 milliseconds. The Counter2() method counts from 51 to 100; when it reaches 70, it sleeps for 5,000 milliseconds. Here is how the output might look:

```
Entering the Sub Main!
Entering Counter2
51 52 53 54 55 56 57 58 59 60 61 62 63 64 65 66 67 68 69 70 Exiting the Sub Main!
```

```
Entering Counter
1 2 3 4 5 6 7 8 9 10 11 12 13 14 15 16 17 18 19 20 21 22 23 24 25 26 27 28 29 30
31 32 33 34 35 36 37 38 39 40 41 42 43 44 45 46 47 48 49 50
Exiting Counter
71 72 73 74 75 76 77 78 79 80 81 82 83 84 85 86 87 88 89 90 91 92 93 94 95 96 97
 98 99 100
Exiting Counter2
```

The second overload takes a `TimeSpan` as parameter and, based on the `TimeSpan` value, the current thread will be suspended. The `TimeSpan` is a structure defined in the `System` namespace. The `TimeSpan` structure has a few useful properties that return the time interval based on clock ticking. You can use `Public` methods such as `FromSeconds()` and `FromMinutes()` to specify the sleep duration. For example, consider thread_sleep3.vb:

```
  Public Shared Sub Counter1()
    ...
    For i = 1 To 50
      Console.Write(i & " ")
      If i = 10 Then
        worker1.Sleep( _
          System.TimeSpan.FromSeconds(1))
    Next
    ...
  End Sub

  Public Shared Sub Counter2()
    ...
    For i = 51 To 100
      Console.Write(i & " ")
If i = 70 Then
  worker1.Sleep( _
    System.TimeSpan.FromMinutes(0.1))
    Next
    ...
  End Sub
```

The output is similar to that of thread_sleep2.

Interrupting a Thread

When a thread is put to sleep, the thread goes to the `WaitSleepJoin` state. If the thread is in the sleeping state, the only way to wake the thread is by using the `Interrupt()` method. The `Interrupt()` method places the thread back in the scheduling queue. For example, here's thread_interrupt.vb:

```
Imports System
Imports System.Threading
```

```vb
Public Class Interrupt
  Public Shared sleeper As Thread
  Public Shared worker As Thread
  Public Shared Sub Main()
    Console.WriteLine("Entering the Sub Main!")
    sleeper = New Thread(AddressOf SleepingThread)
    worker = New Thread(AddressOf AwakeTheThread)
    sleeper.Start()
    worker.Start()
    Console.WriteLine("Exiting the Sub Main!")
     Console.ReadLine()
  End Sub

  Public Shared Sub SleepingThread()
    Dim i As Integer
    For i = 1 To 50
      Console.Write(i & " ")
      If i = 10 Or i = 20 Or i = 30 Then
        Console.WriteLine("Going to sleep at: " & i)
        sleeper.Sleep(20)
      End If
    Next
  End Sub

  Public Shared Sub AwakeTheThread()
    Dim i As Integer
    For i = 51 To 100
      Console.Write("{0} ", i)
      If sleeper.ThreadState = _
        System.Threading.ThreadState.WaitSleepJoin _
        Then
          Console.WriteLine( _
            "Interrupting the sleeping thread")
          sleeper.Interrupt()
      End If
    Next
    sleeper.Abort()
  End Sub
End Class
```

In the preceding example, the first thread (sleeper) is put to sleep when the counter reaches 10, 20, and 30. The second thread (worker) checks whether the first thread is asleep. If so, it interrupts the first thread and places it back in the scheduler. The Interrupt() method is the best way to bring the sleeping thread back to life. You can use this functionality if the resource is now available and you want the thread to become alive. The output will look similar to the following:

```
Entering the Sub Main!
Exiting the Sub Main!
51 52 53 54 55 56 57 58 59 60 61 62 63 64 65 66 67 68
69 70 71 72 73 74 75 76 77 78 79 80 81 82 83 84 85 86
87 88 89 90 91 92 93 94 95 96 97 98 99 100 1 2 3 4 5
6 7 8 9 10
Going to sleep at: 10
11 12 13 14 15 16 17
18 19 20
Going to sleep at: 20
21 22 23 24 25 26 27 28 29 30
Going to sleep at: 30
31 32 33 34 35 36 37 38 39 40 41 42 43 44 45 46 47 48
49 50
```

Pausing and Resuming Threads

The Suspend() and Resume() methods of the Thread class can be used to suspend and resume the thread. The Suspend() method suspends the current thread indefinitely until another thread wakes it up. When you call the Suspend() method, the thread is placed in the SuspendRequested or Suspended state.

Now let's create an example of this by creating a new VB .NET application that generates prime numbers in a new thread. This application will also have options to pause and resume the prime number generation thread. To make this happen, we need to create a new VB .NET WinForms project called PrimeNumbers and build a UI like this in Form1.

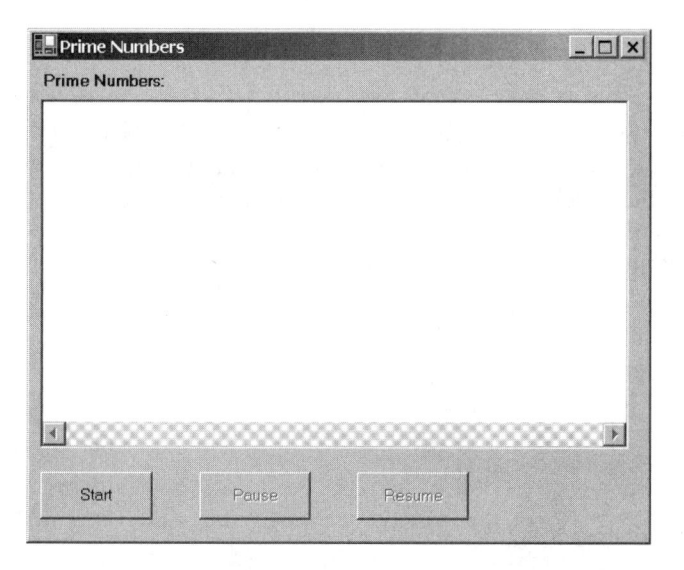

The UI contains a list box and three command buttons. The list box is used to display the prime numbers; the three command buttons are used to start, pause, and resume the thread. Initially, the Pause and Resume buttons are paused because they can't be used until the thread is started. Let's see what the code looks like. We've declared a class level `Thread` object that is going to generate prime numbers.

```
Imports System
Imports System.Threading

Public Class Form1
   Inherits System.Windows.Forms.Form
   'Class level thread object
   Dim objWorkerThread As Thread
```

Double-click on the Start button and add the following code:

```
Private Sub BtnStart_Click( _
    ByVal sender As System.Object, _
    ByVal e As System.EventArgs) _
    Handles BtnStart.Click

   'Let's create a new thread
   objWorkerThread = New Thread( _
      AddressOf GeneratePrimeNumbers)
   'Let's give a name for the thread
   objWorkerThread.Name = "Prime Numbers Example"
   'Enable the Pause Button
   BtnPause.Enabled = True
   'Disable the Start button
   BtnStart.Enabled = False
   'Let's start the thread
   objWorkerThread.Start()
End Sub
```

The Start button creates a new `Thread` object with the address of the `GeneratePrimeNumbers()` method and assigns the name "Prime Number Example" to the thread. The Start button then enables the Pause button, disables the Start button, and starts the prime number generating thread using the `Start` method of the `Thread` class.

Double-click on the Pause button and add the following code:

```
Private Sub BtnPause_Click( _
    ByVal sender As System.Object, _
    ByVal e As System.EventArgs) _
    Handles BtnPause.Click
   Try
      'If current state of thread is Running, then
      ' pause the Thread
      If ((objWorkerThread.ThreadState And _
         ThreadState.Running) Or _
         (objWorkerThread.ThreadState And _
```

```
            ThreadState.WaitSleepJoin)) Then
                'Pause the Thread
                objWorkerThread.Suspend()
                'Disable the Pause button
                btnPause.Enabled = False
                'Enable the resume button
                btnResume.Enabled = True
            End If
        Catch Ex As ThreadStateException
            MessageBox.Show(Ex.ToString, _
                "Exception", MessageBoxButtons.OK, _
                MessageBoxIcon.Error, _
                MessageBoxDefaultButton.Button1)
        End Try
    End Sub
```

The Pause button checks whether the thread is in the Running state. If it is in the Running state, it pauses the thread by calling the Suspend method of the Thread object. The Pause button then enables the Resume button and disables the Pause button. Because the Suspend method can raise the ThreadStateException exception, we're wrapping the code within a Try...Catch block.

Double-click on the Resume button and add the following code:

```
Private Sub BtnResume_Click( _
    ByVal sender As System.Object, _
    ByVal e As System.EventArgs) _
    Handles BtnResume.Click
    'Check the thread state first
    If ((objWorkerThread.ThreadState And _
        ThreadState.Suspended) Or _
        (objWorkerThread.ThreadState And _
        ThreadState.SuspendRequested)) Then
      Try
        'Resume the thread
        objWorkerThread.Resume()
        'Disable the resume button
        BtnResume.Enabled = False
        'Enable the Pause button
        BtnPause.Enabled = True
      Catch Ex As ThreadStateException
        MessageBox.Show(Ex.ToString, "Exception", _
          MessageBoxButtons.OK, MessageBoxIcon.Error, _
          MessageBoxDefaultButton.Button1)
      End Try
    End If
End Sub
```

The Resume button checks whether the state of the thread is Suspended or SuspendRequested before resuming the thread. If the state of the thread is either Suspended or SuspendRequested, the Resume button resumes the thread, disables the Resume button, and enables the Pause button.

Now that the business logic is ready, let's see the code that generates the prime numbers. Because the main aim is to use multithreading and not prime number generation, I'm not going to delve deep into the code. The GeneratePrimeNumbers() method generates the first 255 prime numbers starting from 3. When the method finds a prime number, it adds the new prime number to an array as well as to the list box. The first prime number, 2, is automatically added to the list box. Finally, the method enables the Start button and disables the Pause button.

```vb
Public Sub GeneratePrimeNumbers()
  Dim lngCounter As Long
  Dim lngNumber As Long
  Dim lngDevideCounter As Long
  Dim bolIsPrime As Boolean
  Dim lngUpper As Long
  Dim PrimeArray(255) As Long

  'Init
  lngNumber = 3
  lngCounter = 2
  lngUpper = 1

  'We know that the first prime is 2. Therefore,
  'let's add it to the list and start from 3
  PrimeArray(1) = 2
  lstPrime.Items.Add(2)

  Do While lngCounter <= 255
    'Find the array index that contains
    'the known prime smaller than the
    'root of the number.
    Do While PrimeArray(lngUpper + 1) < _
      Math.Sqrt(lngNumber) And Not _
      PrimeArray(lngUpper + 1) = 0
      lngUpper += 1
    Loop
    bolIsPrime = True
    'Try dividing this number by any
    'already found prime which is smaller
    'than the root of this number.
    For lngDevideCounter = 1 To lngUpper
      If lngNumber Mod _
        PrimeArray(lngDevideCounter) = 0 Then
        'This is not a prime number
        bolIsPrime = False
        Exit For
      End If
```

```
    Next lngDevideCounter
    'If this is a prime number then display it
    If bolIsPrime Then
        'We found a new prime.
        PrimeArray(lngCounter) = lngNumber
        lngCounter += 1

        lstPrime.Items.Add(lngNumber)
        'Let's put the thread to sleep for 100
        'milliseconds. This will simulate the
        'time lag and we'll get time to pause
        'and resume the thread
        objWorkerThread.Sleep(60)
    End If

    'Increment number by two
    lngNumber += 2
  Loop

  'Once the thread has finished execution, enable the
  'Start button and disable the Pause button
  BtnStart.Enabled = True
  BtnPause.Enabled = False
End Sub
```

Everything is ready now, so let's run the code and see how the application looks.

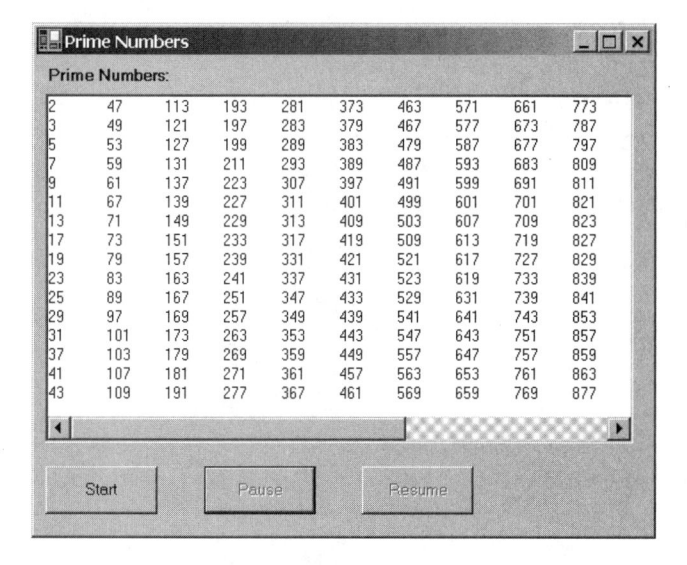

Well everything looks good now and the code is working fine, except for a huge flaw in the code. When the `GeneratePrimeNumbers()` method finds a prime number, it adds the prime number back to the list box control. It may not look like a problem for you if this code is running in synchronize execution manner where both the prime number generation code and the UI are running on the same thread. But in our example, the UI is running in a different thread from the `GeneratePrimeNumbers()` method. Therefore, when you go between threads to write data, this could cause some unexpected behaviors in the application.

The best way to address this problem is to use the delegates. In simple words, *delegates* are smart function pointers that provide a starting point to a function. You can use the delegate to inform the UI thread to update the list box control. In this way, you're not crossing the threading boundaries and the application stability is not compromised.

To implement this operation, add one more public delegate called `UpdateData` next to the `objWorkerThread` thread declaration:

```
Public Class Form1
  Inherits System.Windows.Forms.Form

  'Class level thread object
  Dim objWorkerThread As Thread

  Public Delegate Sub UpdateData( _
    ByVal RtnVal As String)
```

Let's modify the `GeneratePrimeNumbers()` method a little bit to call the delegate from it. In the following code, we added a new string array with the initial value as 2 because the first prime number is 2. Then we declared a new object of the type `UpdateData` delegate and passed the address of the `UpdateUI` method. Finally, we used the `Me.Invoke` method with the delegate object and the string array to inform the UI to update itself. The same occurs when the prime number is found.

Note Form1 is represented as `Me` in this context.

```
Public Sub GeneratePrimeNumbers()
  Dim lngCounter As Long
  Dim lngNumber As Long
  Dim lngDevideCounter As Long
  Dim bolIsPrime As Boolean
  Dim lngUpper As Long
  Dim PrimeArray(255) As Long
  Dim Args() As String = {"2"}
  Dim UIDel As New UpdateData(AddressOf UpdateUI)
  ...
```

```
'We know that the first prime is 2. Therefore,
'let's add it to the list and start from 3
PrimeArray(1) = 2
If Me.InvokeRequired Then  Me.Invoke(UIDel, Args)
...
'If this is a prime number then display it
If bolIsPrime Then
  'Guess we found a new prime.
  PrimeArray(lngCounter) = lngNumber
  'Increase prime found count.
  lngCounter += 1
  Args(0) = lngNumber
  Me.Invoke(UIDel, Args)
  'Let's put the thread to sleep for 100
  'milliseconds. This will simulate the time lag
  'and we'll get time to pause and resume the
  'thread
    objWorkerThread.Sleep(60)
End If
...
```

The `UpdateUI` method simply accepts the value needs to be added to the list box in its parameter and adds the value to the list box. Because the `UpdateUI` method runs in the UI thread, there are no cross boundary thread updates and the stability of our application is not compromised:

```
Sub UpdateUI(ByVal strResult As String)
  lstPrime.Items.Add(strResult)
End Sub
```

Destroying Threads

The `Abort()` method can be used to destroy the current thread. The `Abort()` method is useful if you want to terminate the thread for any reason. For example, if the operation the thread is executing is taking too much time, you might want to destroy the thread. When this method is called against a thread, the `ThreadAbortException` exception is raised. So, it's always a good idea to watch for this exception in the code.

Again, we'll see an example of this by creating a new project called Destroying. Copy the code from the previous prime number generation code into the new `Form1.vb class`. Add the Stop button to the UI like this:

Prime Numbers

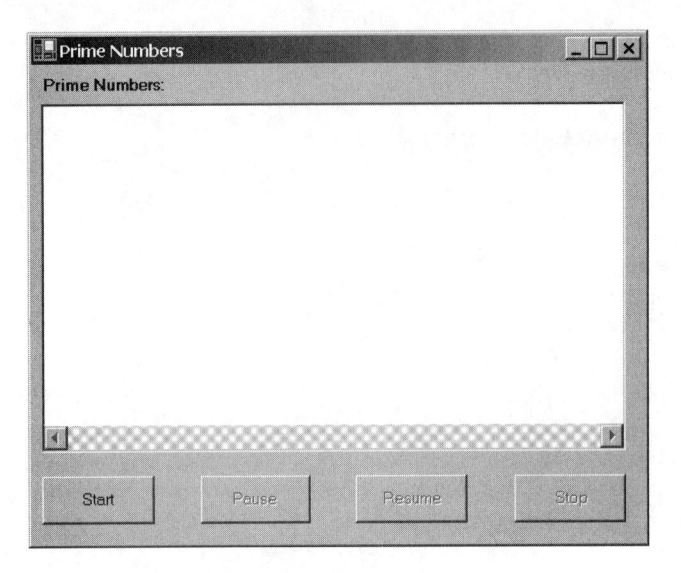

[Screenshot of "Prime Numbers" window with an empty list box labeled "Prime Numbers:" and four buttons: Start, Pause (disabled), Resume (disabled), Stop (disabled).]

Add the following code into the Stop button:

```vb
Private Sub BtnStop_Click( _
  ByVal sender As System.Object, _
  ByVal e As System.EventArgs) Handles BtnStop.Click
  Try
    'Enable the Start button and disable all others
    BtnStop.Enabled = False
    BtnPause.Enabled = False
    BtnResume.Enabled = False
    BtnStart.Enabled = True
    'Destroy the thread
    objWorkerThread.Abort()
  Catch Ex As ThreadAbortException
    MessageBox.Show(Ex.ToString, "Exception", _
      MessageBoxButtons.OK, MessageBoxIcon.Error, _
      MessageBoxDefaultButton.Button1)
  End Try
End Sub
```

This example is similar to the previous example. The only difference is that we're using the Abort() method to destroy the thread when the user clicks on the Stop button. We're then enabling the Start button and disabling all other buttons as shown here:

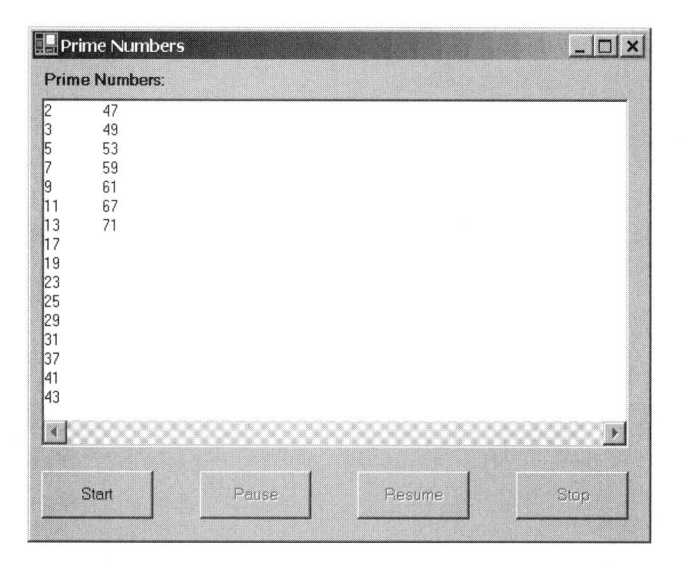

Joining Threads

The `Join()` method blocks the thread until the current thread is terminated. When you call the `Join()` method against another instance of a thread, the current thread is placed in the `WaitSleepJoin` state. This method is very useful when one thread is dependant upon another thread. In logical terms, calling the `Join()` method tells the CLR that you are joining your call to the end of the other thread's execution. Technically, however, your thread is simply yielding its execution time to the other thread until it has completed. After the other thread completes, the thread regains an execution time slice. Let's look at the following example named thread_joining.vb:

```
Imports System
Imports System.Threading
Imports System.DirectoryServices

Public Class JoiningThreads
    Public Shared TCreateUser As Thread
    Public Shared TGrantPermissions As Thread
    Private Shared AD As DirectoryEntry
    Private Shared NewUser As DirectoryEntry

    Shared Sub CreateUser()
      ' Get the Machine to Add to
      AD = New DirectoryEntry( _
        String.Format("WinNT://{0},computer", _
        Environment.MachineName))
      ' Add the account
```

```vb
            NewUser = AD.Children.Add("TestUser4", "user")
            ' Set the password
            NewUser.Invoke("SetPassword", _
              New Object() {"TestUserPassword"})
            ' Set the Description
            NewUser.Invoke("Put", New Object() _
                {"Description", "Threading Example"})
            NewUser.CommitChanges()
            Thread.Sleep(200)
            Console.WriteLine("- User Account Created - ")
        End Sub

        Shared Sub GrantPermissions()
            ' Join to the TCreateUser instance
            ' We can't grant permissions to a
            ' user until he has been created!
            Console.WriteLine( _
               "- Joining CreateUser Thread - ")
            TCreateUser.Join()
            Console.WriteLine( _
               "Resuming GrantPermissions Thread")
            Dim grp As DirectoryEntry
            grp = AD.Children.Find("Guests", "group")
            If grp.Name <> "" Then
              grp.Invoke("Add", New Object() _
                  {NewUser.Path.ToString()})
            End If

            Console.WriteLine("- Group Account Set - ")
        End Sub

    Public Shared Sub Main()
        TCreateUser = New Thread(AddressOf CreateUser)
        TGrantPermissions = New Thread( _
          AddressOf GrantPermissions)
        TCreateUser.Start()
        TGrantPermissions.Start()
        Console.ReadLine()
    End Sub
End Class
```

Caution Note that you need to add a reference to System.DirectoryServices.dll for this sample.

In this simple example, the aim is to create a user and then grant the new user permissions. You obviously don't want to try to grant permissions until the user is created, so the `CreateUser()` method creates a user and the `GrantPermissions()` method puts the user into a group. Without the `TCreateUser.Join()` line in the `GrantPermissions()` method, the second method could try to assign the user to a group before the user is created. By calling the `TCreateUser.Join()` method within the `GrantPermissions()` method, the execution of the `GrantPermissions()` method is paused until the execution of the `TCreateUser` thread has completed.

The `Join()` method is overloaded; it can accept either an integer or a `TimeSpan` as a single parameter and returns a Boolean. The effect of calling one of the overloaded versions of this method is that the thread is blocked until either the other thread completes or the time period elapses, whichever occurs first. The return value will be `True` if the thread has completed and `False` if it has not. This is useful if you only want to wait for a thread for so long before giving up. For instance, if the user wasn't created within 5 seconds, you might want to give up and log an error to the Event Log. By checking the return value of the `Join()` method, you can determine whether the return was a result of the other thread completing or a timeout being reached.

Why Not Thread Everything?

As you've seen threading is very beneficial because you can have several processes running at once, and several threads running within those processes. So, why don't we just use new threads for all functions? Wouldn't that just make everything run fast? Not really. As a matter of fact, this section shows that quite the opposite can happen if you overuse threading.

Multithreaded applications require resources. Threads require memory to store the thread local storage container. As you can imagine, the number of threads used is limited by the amount of memory available. Memory is fairly inexpensive these days, so many people have large amounts of memory. However, you should not assume that this is always true. If you are running your application on an unknown hardware configuration, you cannot assume that your application will have enough memory. Additionally, you cannot assume that your process will be the only one spawning threads and consuming system resources. Just because a machine has a lot of memory, doesn't mean it's all for your application.

You'll also discover that each thread also incurs additional processor overhead. Creating too many threads in your applications limits the amount of time that your thread has to execute. Therefore, your processor could potentially spend more time switching between threads as opposed to actually executing the instructions that the threads contain. If your application is creating more threads, your application will gain more execution time than all the other processes with fewer threads.

To make this concept easier to understand, take the parallel example you'll find at your local grocery store. Two cashiers are scanning groceries for their customers. However, there is only one bagger who takes turns switching between the two cashiers. He is rather efficient at jumping back and forth between the two registers and bagging the groceries because they don't pile up any faster than it takes him to bag the groceries. However, if two more cashiers open up lanes, he will spend more time jumping back and forth between the registers than he spends actually bagging groceries. Eventually, the store will need to get another bagger. In the case of threading, think of the cashiers as applications—or threads—and the bagger as a processor. The processor has to switch between threads. As the "threads" increase, the grocery store has to add another "processor" to be sure that the customers get the attention they need.

The phrase "too many threads" is a rather generic term—and rightly so. What constitutes "too many" on one system could be fine on another. Because hardware configurations largely dictate the amount of threads available on a system, "too many" is an unquantifiable variable without specific configuration details and a lot of testing.

These reasons prompt Microsoft to recommend that you use as few threads as possible in your applications to limit the amount of resources required by the operating system.

Threading Opportunities

So, now you might be wondering why you would thread at all if it could potentially have a negative impact on our application. The idea is that there is a time and a place for threading. Learning which circumstances represent good opportunities to spawn a new thread is the key to making good design decisions. There are two distinct opportunities to consider spawning a new thread. In this section, we'll discuss those opportunities.

Background Processes

The first opportunity to spawn a new thread occurs when your application needs to run a large process in the background while still keeping its UI active and usable. We've all experienced an application that just didn't seem to respond because we told it to query data or process a large piece of information. Take, for example, the case of professional graphics packages that are required to render graphics into a specific file format. In early versions of some products, asking the application to render a large graphic would result in the application becoming unresponsive until the render process had finished. This problem presents an ideal time to set a background thread to do your computer-intensive processing while leaving your UI to run on the main application thread.

Let's look at an example of a background process that needs to spawn a new thread. This example demonstrates searching for files (see illustration). When the search routine finds a file matching the pattern specified, it adds a new item to the list box.

The following code demonstrates that this function needs its own thread:

```vb
Imports System.Threading
Imports System.IO

Public Class Form1
  Inherits System.Windows.Forms.Form
  Dim searchTerm as String
  Dim totalFiles As Int32
  Private Sub Button1_Click( _
    ByVal sender as System.Object, _
    ByVal e as System.EventArgs) _
    Handles Button1.Click
      Search()
  End Sub

  Public Sub Search()
     searchTerm = TextBox1.Text
     ListBox1.Items.Clear()
     totalFiles = 0
     SearchDirectory(Environment.SystemDirectory)
     MsgBox(totalFiles.ToString)
  End Sub

  Public Sub SearchDirectory(ByVal Path as String)
    ' Search the directory
    Dim di as New DirectoryInfo(Path)
    Dim f() as FileInfo = di.GetFiles(searchTerm)
    Dim myFile as FileInfo
    For Each myFile in f
      ListBox1.Items.Add(myFile.FullName)
    Next
    ' Search its subdirectories
    Dim d() as DirectoryInfo = di.GetDirectories()
    Dim myDir as DirectoryInfo
    For Each myDir in d
      SearchDirectory(myDir.FullName)
    Next
  End Sub
End Class
```

Compile this example and run it. Type a search term in the search text box, such as *.*, click the Single Thread Search button, and observe the problem. As you'll see, the example searches for files and tries to update the UI every time a file is found with the search criteria. However, because both the UI and the search code are running on the same thread, you don't see the updates until the search code has completely finished processing. Additionally, you cannot resize the form while the search is processing. The UI might even stop responding altogether as show in the following screenshot.

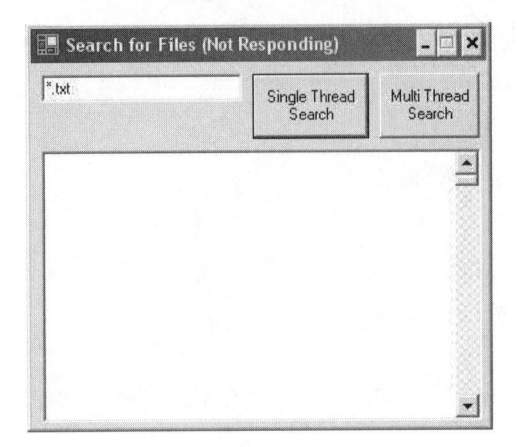

This long piece of code is actually a simple demonstration. Most of the code listing is used to create and set up the form layout. Let's see if we can correct this problem with a simple change. In the Button2_Click routine, add the following code to call the Search() function with the use of a new thread:

```
Private Sub Button2_Click( _
   ByVal sender As System.Object, _
   ByVal e As System.EventArgs) _
   Handles Button2.Click
      Dim t As New Thread(AddressOf Search)
      t.Start()
End Sub
```

Now recompile and run the program again. This time, type in the same search term and click the Multi Thread Search button. You can see quite a difference. This time the results are displayed immediately because Windows is now switching execution back and forth between the UI and the search thread. The processor is now given a time slice to update the interface to reflect the changes in the list box. You'll also notice that you can now resize the form while it is searching.

One last thing to notice with this change is that the search thread can access the data in the main thread. Data such as the searchTerm variable and the list box can be accessed from within the search thread. This is one more demonstration of the fact that the global data of our process is available to all threads within the same process.

Other background processes might cause the interface to be unresponsive. For example, you might want to do some intense processing, such as searching, sorting, formatting, parsing, and filtering a large amount of records in a database. This would be another opportunity to consider using a new thread. You might also want to spawn a new thread if you want to run a routine that is constantly logging information. The UI won't necessarily be unresponsive in this instance, but it might appear slow or sluggish if this type of routine isn't on its own thread.

Accessing External Resources

The second circumstance in which you might want to consider spawning a new thread occurs when you are accessing resources that are not local to your system. This might be a database process or a network file share somewhere on your network. In such cases, network performance could adversely affect your application's performance.

Consider the following example, in which We're going to connect to a database. Let's assume that network performance is poor and may cause this application to be slow. Let's also assume that company policy dictates that no applications can be installed on the database server:

```vb
Imports System.Threading
Imports System.IO
Imports System.Data
Imports System.Data.SqlClient

Public Class Form1
  Inherits System.Windows.Forms.Form

  Public Sub Button1_Click( _
    ByVal sender as System.Object, _
    ByVal e as System.EventArgs) _
    Handles Button1.Click
      QueryData()
  End Sub

  Public Sub QueryData()
    Dim objReader as SqlDataReader
    Dim objConn as SqlConnection
    Dim objCommand as SqlCommand
    Dim intEmployeeID as Int32
    Dim strFirstName as String
    Dim strTitle as String
    Dim intReportsTo as Int32
    Dim item as String

    objConn = new SqlConnection( _
      "server=RemoteServer; UID=RemoteUser;" & _
      " PWD=Password;database=northwind")
    objCommand = new SqlCommand( _
      "SELECT EmployeeID, FirstName, " & _
      "Title, ReportsTo FROM Employees", objConn)
    objConn.Open()
    objReader = objCommand.ExecuteReader( _
      CommandBehavior.CloseConnection)

    Do While (objReader.Read())
      intEmployeeID = objReader.GetInt32(0)
```

```
          strFirstName = objReader.GetString(1)
          strTitle = objReader.GetString(2)
          If (objReader.IsDBNull(3)) Then
             intReportsTo = 0
          Else
             intReportsTo = objReader.GetInt32(3)
          End If

          item = string.Format( _
             "{0} {1} {2} {3}", intEmployeeID, _
             strFirstName, strTitle, intReportsTo )
          ListBox1.Items.Add(item)
      Loop
      objReader.Close()
      objConn.Close()
   End Sub
End Class
```

As you can see in this example, all we are doing is querying a remote database. The data returned will not be excessive, but you'll notice that the UI freezes while it takes time to get the data and update the list box. You can correct this by simply spawning a new thread and executing your database code within that thread. Add a second button and use the following code:

```
   Public Sub Button2_Click( _
     ByVal sender as System.Object, _
     ByVal e as System.EventArgs) _
     Handles Button1.Click
        Dim t as New Thread(AddressOf QueryData)
        t.Start()
   End Sub
```

Now when you run the code, you get a result similar to the last example. You can resize the form while the query runs. The interface is responsive throughout the entire query process.

Of course, this doesn't necessarily mean you should spawn a new thread every time you connect to a database. However, analyze your options to find out if you can move the database or the application so they reside on the same server. Also, make sure that this component isn't going to be continuously called from various client applications. Doing so would spawn additional threads for every call and consume more resources than you intended. There are ways to reuse objects and their threads without using a new thread every time your object is called. These issues will be covered in the chapters on thread synchronization and thread pooling.

Threading Traps

You've now seen the two main situations in which it can be a good idea to use threading in your applications. However, sometimes spawning a new thread is a bad idea. Obviously, this isn't going to be a complete listing of inappropriate times to create new threads, but it will give you an idea of what constitutes a bad threading decision. We'll look at two main areas: the first is an instance where execution order is extremely important, and the second is a common coding mistake—creating new threads in a loop.

Execution Order Revisited

Recall the example, do_something_thread.vb, from earlier in the chapter where we created some code demonstrating the fact that execution randomly jumped from one thread to the other. It looked like one thread would execute and show 10 lines in the console, and then the next thread would show 15 and then return back to the original thread to execute 8. A common mistake in deciding whether to use threads or not is to assume that you know exactly how much code is going to execute in the thread's given time slice.

The following example demonstrates this problem. It looks like the thread t1 will finish first because it starts first, but that's a big mistake. Create a console application called ExecutionOrder and set its startup object to Sub Main. Build and run this example a few times—you'll get differing results:

```vb
Imports System
Imports System.Threading

Public Class ExecutionOrder
  Shared t1 as Thread
  Shared t2 as Thread
  Public Shared Sub WriteFinished( _
    ByVal threadName as String)
    Select Case threadName
      Case "T1"
        Console.WriteLine()
        Console.WriteLine("T1 Finished")
      Case "T2"
        Console.WriteLine()
        Console.WriteLine("T2 Finished")
    End Select
  End Sub

  Public Shared Sub Main()
    t1 = New Thread(AddressOf Increment)
    t2 = New Thread(AddressOf Increment)
    t1.Name = "T1"
    t2.Name = "T2"
    t1.Start()
    t2.Start()
    Console.ReadLine()
  End Sub
  Public Shared Sub Increment()
    Dim I as Long
    For I = 1 to 1000000
      If I MOD 100000 = 0 Then
        Console.Write("({0})", _
          Thread.CurrentThread.Name)
      End If
    Next
```

```
      WriteFinished(Thread.CurrentThread.Name)
   End Sub
End Class
```

Sometimes t1 will finish, and then t2 will execute some more code and then finish. Sometimes t2 will finish completely and then t1 will execute to completion. The point is that you can't count on the threads completing in the order they were started. In Chapter 15, we'll discuss how you can synchronize threads to execute in a specified order. However, it's important to note that synchronization doesn't happen by default.

This isn't the only problem associated with execution order. Take the next piece of example code, ExecutionOrder2, where we show that data can be adversely affected by unsynchronized threads:

```
Imports System
Imports System.Threading

Public Class ExecutionOrder2
   Shared t1 As Thread
   Shared t2 As Thread
   Shared iIncr As Integer

   Public Shared Sub WriteFinished( _
      ByVal threadName As String)

      Select Case threadName
        Case "T1"
          Console.WriteLine()
          Console.WriteLine( _
             "T1 Finished: iIncr = {0}", iIncr)
        Case "T2"
          Console.WriteLine()
          Console.WriteLine( _
             "T2 Finished: iIncr = {0}", iIncr)
      End Select
   End Sub

   Public Shared Sub Main()
      iIncr = 0
      t1 = New Thread(AddressOf Increment)
      t2 = New Thread(AddressOf Increment)
      t1.Name = "T1"
      t2.Name = "T2"
      t1.Start()
      t2.Start()
      Console.Read()
   End Sub

   Public Shared Sub Increment()
      Dim I As Long
```

```
    For I = 1 To 1000000
      If I Mod 100000 = 0 Then
        Console.WriteLine("-{0}- {1}", _
          Thread.CurrentThread.Name, iIncr)
      End If
    Next
    iIncr += 1
    WriteFinished(Thread.CurrentThread.Name)
  End Sub
End Class
```

This class is very similar to `ExecutionOrder`. This time, however, we created a shared incrementing counter called `iIncr`. We tell the application to increment the variable before moving on to the `WriteFinished()` method. If you execute this application a few times, you'll notice that the value of the incrementing counter changes at different times. Keep in mind again that you'll learn how to synchronize these threads later, in Chapter 15. These two examples should caution you threads do not execute in the order that you want by default.

Threads in a Loop

One other common mistake made when someone discovers the joys of threading is their creation and use within a loop. The following code example demonstrates this mistake, which I've seen on at least two occasions recently in my interaction with programmers who are new to the threading concept. It's common for developers or system administrators to send notifications when an event occurs. The idea isn't bad, but its implementation using a thread in the loop can cause many problems.

Tip Please be aware that running this code might disable your system. Don't run it unless you don't mind rebooting your machine to reclaim the resources the program will waste.

```
Imports System
Imports System.Threading
Imports System.Web.Mail
Imports System.Collections

Public Class LoopingThreads
  Delegate Sub SendMail(ByVal oMessageTo as String)

  Private Class MyMail
    Public EmailTo as String
    Public EmailFrom as String
    Public EmailSubject as String
    Public EmailBody as String
    Public SendThisEmail as SendMail
```

```vbnet
    Public Sub Send()
       Dim oMail as New System.Web.Mail.MailMessage()
       oMail.To   = EmailTo
       oMail.From = EmailFrom
       oMail.Body = EmailBody
       oMail.Subject = EmailSubject
       oMail.BodyFormat = MailFormat.Text
       SmtpMail.Send(oMail)
       SendThisEmail(EmailTo)
    End Sub
  End Class

  Public Shared Function CreateEmail( _
     ByVal oSendEmail as SendMail, _
     ByVal EmailTo as String, _
     ByVal EmailFrom as String, _
     ByVal EmailBody as String, _
     ByVal EmailSubject as String) as Thread

      Dim oMail as New MyMail()
      oMail.EmailFrom = EmailFrom
      oMail.EmailBody = EmailBody
      oMail.EmailSubject = EmailSubject
      oMail.EmailTo = EmailTo
      oMail.SendThisEmail = oSendEmail

      Dim t as New Thread(AddressOf oMail.Send)
      Return t
   End Function
End Class

Class Mailer
   Public Shared Sub MailMethod( _
     ByVal oString as String)
       Console.WriteLine("Sending Email: " + oString)
   End Sub
End Class

Public Class DoMail
  Shared al as New ArrayList()

  Public Shared Sub Main()
    Dim I as Integer
    For I = 1 to 1000
      al.Add(i.ToString() + "@someplace.com")
    Next
    SendAllEmail()
  End Sub
```

```
    Public Shared Sub SendAllEmail()
      Dim I As Integer
      For I = 0 to al.Count - 1
        Dim t as thread = LoopingThreads.CreateEmail( _
          AddressOf Mailer.MailMethod, Al(i), _
          "johndoe@somewhere.com", _
          "Threading in a loop", "Mail Example")
        t.Start()
        t.Join(Timeout.Infinite)
      Next
    End Sub
End Class
```

Caution Note that you'll have to add a reference to `System.Web.dll` for this sample to work.

The code might be a little more complex than you thought because it also demonstrates how to use a delegate and a lengthy set of classes to call a thread with parameters. This is necessary **because threads can only create an entry on a subroutine that has no parameters.** As such, it's the programmer's duty to create proxy methods that create the parameters for another function and return a thread object (you'll see more of this in later chapters). The calling method can then use the reference to the returned Thread to start execution.

Let's concentrate on the SendAllEmail method. This is where you loop through the ArrayList and send your parameters to the proxy method. You start a new thread for each email you want to send:

```
Public Shared Sub SendAllEmail()
  Dim I As Integer
  For I = 0 to al.Count - 1
    Dim t as Thread = LoopingThreads.CreateEmail( _
      AddressOf Mailer.MailMethod, Al(i), _
      "johndoe@somewhere.com", _
      "Threading in a loop", "Mail Example")
    t.Start()
    t.Join(Timeout.Infinite)
  Next
End Sub
```

At first glance, this sounds like a good idea. Why not send email on another thread? It takes a long time to process sometimes doesn't it? This is true, but the problem is that we are now tying up the processor's execution time by switching between the threads. By the time this process is done, the time slice allocated to each thread is mainly spent unpacking and packing the thread local storage. Very little time is spent executing the instructions in the thread. The system may even lock up completely leaving poor John without any mail from us. It might make more sense to create a single thread and execute the SendAllEmail method on that thread. Additionally, you could use a thread pool with a fixed number of threads. In this instance, when one thread in the pool has completed, it spawns the next thread and sends another email.

One common programming practice is to place work into a queue to be processed by a service. For instance, a bank may place an XML-based file in a network directory to be picked up by a service running on another server. The service scans the directory for new files and processes them one at a time. If more than one file is placed in the directory at a time, the service processes them one by one. In a typical environment, new files are placed in this directory infrequently. Based on this information, at first glance, you might think this seems like a good time to start a new thread when a file is found. You're right, but think about what would happen if the service that processes these files was stopped. What happens if a network problem prevents the service from accessing the directory for a long period of time? The files would pile up in the directory. When the service finally started again, or was allowed access to the directory once again, each file would essentially spawn a new thread on the service. Anyone who has used this model can tell you that this situation can bring a server to its knees.

The file model is just one example. Another similar model may be to use Microsoft BizTalk Server or Microsoft Message Queue with a service that processes items in a queue. All these implementations have the same basic structure. The actual implementation isn't the important thing to note here; the point to walk away with is that if your work is being placed into a queue and you feel that multithreading is the answer; you might want to consider using thread pooling.

Summary

This chapter introduced the `System.Threading` namespace and examined the `Thread` class in detail. We also discussed some basic ideas to help you hone your decision-making skills when it comes to multithreading your applications. You must always keep in mind the fact that threads require resources. Before you consume those resources, analyze the effect their use will have on the system and how you can minimize that overhead. You should consider creating a thread if you are accessing outside resources such as a network share or remote databases. You should also consider spawning a new thread when you plan to execute a lengthy process such as printing, I/O operations, and background data processing.

Whatever your situation, keep the number of your threads to a minimum. You'll reduce the overhead on your processor, increase the amount of time that your time slice uses to process instructions within your thread, and reduce the amount of memory required by your application.

CHAPTER 15

Working with Threads

In the previous chapters, we discussed how threads play an important role in developing multiuser applications. We used threads to solve some significant problems such as giving multiple users or clients access to the same resource at the same time. We ignored one issue that now needs to be addressed: what would happen to the resource if one user changes the state of the resource at the same time another user wants to change the state of the same resource?

For example, Mr. and Mrs. Smith both decide to empty their joint checking account by withdrawing the balance of $1,000 from an ATM. Unfortunately, they forget to decide who will actually do the job. So, ironically, Mr. and Mrs. Smith both access the checking account from different ATMs at exactly the same time. If two people access the same account at the same time, and the application is not thread-safe, it's possible that both ATMs will detect that there is enough amount in the checking account and dispense $1,000 to each person. In effect, the two users are causing two threads to access the account database at the same time.

Note The .NET Framework provides specific mechanisms to deal with such problems. The phenomenon of allowing only one thread to access a resource at any point of time is called Synchronization. Synchronization is a feature available to developers for creating thread-safe access to critical resources.

Why Worry About Synchronization?

.NET developers need to keep synchronization in mind when designing a multithreaded application for these two main reasons:

- To avoid race conditions

- To ensure thread-safety

Because the .NET Framework has built-in support for threading, it's possible that any class you develop may eventually be used in a multithreaded application. Although you don't need to (and shouldn't) design every class to be thread-safe because thread-safety isn't free, you should at least *think* about thread-safety every time you design a .NET class. The costs of thread-safety and guidelines concerning when to make classes thread-safe are discussed later in this chapter. You don't need to worry about multithreaded access to local variables, method parameters, and return values, because these variables reside on the stack and are inherently thread-safe. Instance and class variables, however, will only be thread-safe if you design the class appropriately.

Before we examine the nuts and bolts of synchronization, let's consider in detail the earlier ATM example in which Mr. and Mrs. Smith are both trying to withdraw the last $1,000 from the same account at the same time. Figure 15-1 clarifies the ATM scenario. Such a condition, where two or more threads try to access the same resource to change its state at the same time and produce an undesirable effect, is called a *race condition*. To avoid the race condition, you need to make the Withdraw() method thread-safe so that only one thread can access the method at any point of time.

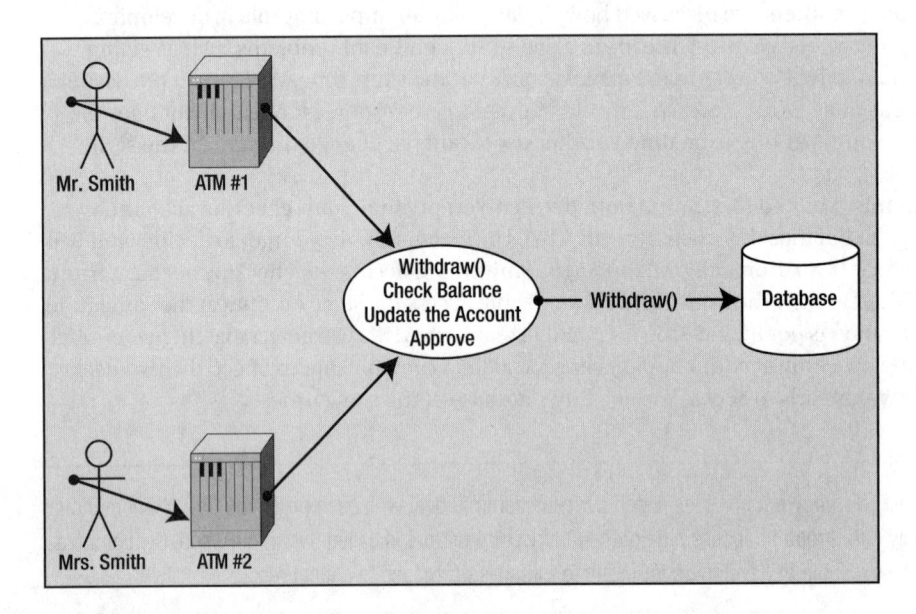

Figure 15-1. *Two threads accessing the same resource.*

There are at least three ways to make an object thread-safe:

- Synchronize critical sections within the code.

- Make the object immutable.

- Use a thread-safe wrapper.

Synchronize Critical Sections

To avoid undesirable effects caused by multiple threads updating a resource at the same time, you need to make the resource thread-safe by restricting the resource so that only one thread can update the resource at any point of time. The most straightforward way to make an object or an instance variable thread-safe is to identify and synchronize their critical sections. For example, in the preceding ATM scenario in which Mr. Smith and Mrs. Smith both try to access the same Withdraw() method at the same time, the Withdraw() method becomes the critical section and needs to be thread-safe. The easiest way to do this is to synchronize the method Withdraw() so that only one thread (either Mr. Smith or Mrs.) can enter it at any one time. A transaction that cannot be interrupted during its execution is called *atomic*. Making the Withdraw() method atomic ensures that no other thread can check the balance of the same account until the first thread has finished changing the state of the account (to empty in this case). The following code listing is a pseudo code representation of a nonthread-safe Account class:

```
Class Account
   Sub ApprovedOrNot Withdraw (Amount)
      1. Make sure that the user has enough cash
         (Check the Balance)
      2. Update the Account with the new balance
      3. Send approval to the ATM
   End Sub
End Class
```

This next listing represents a thread-safe pseudo code version of the Account class:

```
Class Account
   Sub ApprovedOrNot Withdraw (Amount)
      lock this section (access for only one thread)
         1. Check the Account Balance
         2. Update the Account with the new balance
         3. Send approval to the ATM
      End lock
   End Sub
End Class
```

In the first listing, two or more threads can enter the critical section at the same time, so both threads might check the balance at the same time, with both threads receiving the balance ($1,000) of the account. Due to this, the ATM might dispense the $1,000 amount to both users, causing the account to be overdrawn unexpectedly.

On the contrary, in the second listing, only one thread is allowed access to the critical section at any one time. So, when Mr. Smith's thread begins to execute the Withdraw() method, Mrs. Smith's thread is not allowed access to the critical section and has to wait until Mr. Smith's thread returns. As a result, Mr. Smith's thread checks the balance of the account, updates the account with the new balance, which is $0 in this case, and then returns the approval Boolean value (True in this case) to the ATM for dispensing the cash. Until the cash is dispensed, no other thread has access to the critical section of Mr. and Mrs. Smith's Account object. After Mr. Smith receives the cash, Mrs. Smith's thread enters the critical section of the Withdraw() method. Now, when the method checks for the account balance, the returned amount is $0, the method returns a Boolean value of False indicating insufficient balance and the ATM denies the withdrawal.

Making the Account Object Immutable

An alternative way to achieve thread-safety for an object is to make the object immutable. An *immutable object's* state can't be changed after the object has been created. This can be achieved by not allowing any thread to modify the state of the Account object after it is created. This approach separates the critical sections that read the instance variables from those that write to instance variables. The critical sections that only read the instance variables are left as-is; the critical sections that change the instance variables of the object are changed, so instead of changing the state of the current object, a new object that embodies the new state is created, and a reference to that new object is returned. In this approach, you don't need to lock the critical section because no methods (only the constructor) of an immutable object actually write to the object's instance variables; thus, an immutable object is by definition thread-safe.

Using a Thread-Safe Wrapper

Another approach to making an object thread-safe is to write a wrapper class over the object that will be thread-safe rather than making the object itself thread-safe. The object remains unchanged and the new wrapper class contains synchronized sections of thread-safe code. The following listing is a wrapper class over the Account object:

```
Class AccountWrapper
  Private _a As Account
  public Sub New (Account a)
    Me._a = a
  End Sub
  Public Sub Withdraw(Double amount) As Boolean
    SyncLock Me
      return this._a.Withdraw(amount)
    End SyncLock
  End Sub
End Class
```

The AccountWrapper class acts as a thread-safe wrapper of the Account class. The Account class is declared as a Private instance variable of the AccountWrapper class so that no other object or thread can access the Account variable. In this approach, the Account object does not have any thread-safe features, because the AccountWrapper class provides all the thread-safety. This approach is typically useful when you're dealing with a third-party library that has classes that are not designed for thread-safety. For example, assume that the bank already has an Account class that is used for developing software for the bank's mainframe system and, for the sake of consistency, the bank wants to use the same Account class for writing the ATM software. From the documentation of the Account class that the bank has provided, it's clear that the Account class is not thread-safe. Also, we are not given access to the Account source code for security reasons. In such a case, we would have to adopt the thread-safe wrapper approach. With this approach, we will develop the thread-safe AccountWrapper class as an extension to the Account class.

.NET Synchronization Support

The .NET Framework provides a few classes in the System.Threading and System.EnterpriseServices namespaces that allow the programmer to develop thread-safe code. The following table briefly describes some of the synchronization classes in the .NET Framework.

Class	Description
Monitor	Monitor objects are used to lock the critical sections of the code so that only one thread has access to the critical section at any point of time. Monitor objects help ensure the atomicity of critical code sections.
Mutex	Mutex objects are similar to Monitor objects with the exception that they grant exclusive access to a resource shared across processes to only one thread. The Mutex overloaded constructor can be used to specify Mutex ownership and name.
AutoResetEvent, ManualResetEvent	AutoResetEvent and ManualResetEvent are used to notify one or more waiting threads that an event has occurred. Both classes are NotInheritable.
Interlocked	The Interlocked class has methods CompareExchange(), Decrement(), Exchange(), and Increment() that provide a simple mechanism for synchronizing access to a variable that is shared by multiple threads.
SynchronizationAttribute	SynchronizationAttribute ensures that only one thread at a time can access an object. This synchronization process is automatic and does not need any kind of explicit locking of critical sections.

.NET Synchronization Strategies

The Common Language Infrastructure provides three strategies to synchronize access to instance and Shared methods and instance fields:

- Synchronized contexts

- Synchronized code regions

- Manual synchronization

Synchronized Contexts

A context is a set of properties or usage rules that is common to a collection of objects with related runtime execution. The context properties that can be added include policies regarding synchronization, thread affinity, and transactions. In this strategy, the SynchronizationAttribute class is used to enable simple, automatic synchronization for ContextBoundObject objects. Objects that reside in a context and are bound to the context rules are called *context-bound objects*. .NET automatically associates a synchronization lock with the object, locking it before every method call and unlocking it (to be used by other threads) when the method returns. This is a huge productivity gain because thread synchronization and concurrency management are among the most common development pitfalls. There is a lot more to this attribute than mere synchronization, including strategies for sharing the lock with other objects. The SynchronizationAttribute class is good for programmers who do not have experience dealing with synchronization manually because it covers the instance variables, instance methods, and instance fields of the class to which this attribute is applied. It does not, however, handle synchronization of Shared fields and methods. This class also does not help if you have to synchronize specific code blocks; synchronizing the entire object is the price you have to pay for ease of use.

Coming back to the Account example, we can make the Account class thread-safe using the SynchronizationAttribute. The following listing shows an example of synchronizing the Account class using the SynchronizationAttribute:

```
[SynchronizationAttribute] Public Class Account
  Inherits ContextBoundObject
  Sub ApprovedOrNot Withdraw (Amount)
    1. Check the Account Balance
    2. Update the Account with the new balance
    3. Send approval to the ATM
  End Sub
End Class
```

Synchronized Code Regions

The second synchronization strategy concerns synchronizing specific code regions. This section looks at the Monitor and ReaderWriterLock classes.

Monitors

Monitors are used to synchronize sections of code by acquiring a lock with the Monitor.Enter() method and then releasing the lock using the Monitor.Exit() method. The concept of a lock is normally used to explain the Monitor class. One thread gets a lock, while others wait until the lock is released. After the lock is acquired on a code region, you can use the following methods within the Monitor.Enter() and Monitor.Exit() block:

- Monitor.Wait(): Releases the lock on an object and blocks the current thread until it reacquires the lock.

- Monitor.Pulse(): Notifies a thread that is waiting in a queue that there has been a change in the object's state.

- Monitor.PulseAll(): Notifies all threads that are waiting in a queue that there has been a change in the object's state.

The Enter() and Exit() Methods

Note that the Monitor methods are Shared and can be called on the Monitor class itself rather than an instance of that class. In the .NET Framework, each object has a lock associated with it that can be obtained and released so that only one thread at any time can access the object's instance variables and methods. Similarly, each object in the .NET Framework also provides a mechanism that allows it to be in a waiting state. Just like the lock mechanism, the main reason for this mechanism is to aid communication between threads. Such mechanisms are necessary when one thread enters the critical section of an object, needs a certain condition to exist, and assumes that another thread will create that condition from the same critical section. The trick is that only one thread is allowed in any critical section at any point of time, and when the first thread enters the critical section, no other threads can enter. So, how will the second thread create a condition in the critical section when the first thread is already in it? This is achieved by the *Wait and Pulse* mechanism. The first thread enters the critical section and executes the Wait() method. The Wait() method releases the lock prior to waiting and the second thread is now allowed to enter the critical section, changes the required condition, and calls the Pulse() method to notify the waiting thread that the condition has been reached and it can now continue its execution. The first thread then reacquires the lock prior to returning from the Monitor.Wait() method and continues execution from the point where it called Monitor.Wait().

No two threads can ever enter the Enter() function simultaneously. It is analogous to an ATM machine where only one person is allowed to operate at any point of time and another person can get his chance only after the first person leaves. You can see that the names Enter and Exit have been chosen very aptly. Figure 15-2 illustrates the Monitor functionality:

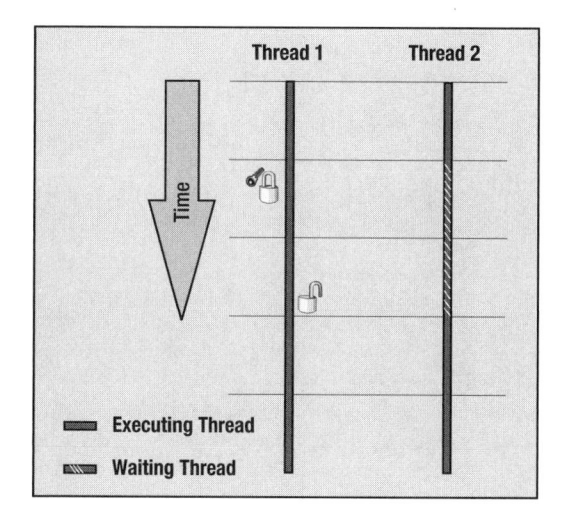

Figure 15-2. *Illustration of the monitor functionality*

Here is an example of how the Enter() and Exit() methods are implemented in MonitorEnterExit.vb.

```vb
Imports System
Imports System.Threading

Namespace MonitorEnterExit
  Public Class EnterExit
    Private result As Integer = 0
    Public Sub NonCriticalSection()
      Console.WriteLine( _
        String.Format("Entered Thread {0}", _
        AppDomain.GetCurrentThreadId()))
      Dim i As Integer
      For i = 1 To 5
        Console.WriteLine( _
          "Result = {0} ThreadID: {1}", _
          result, AppDomain.GetCurrentThreadId())
        result += 1
```

```vbnet
      Thread.Sleep(1000)
    Next i
    Console.WriteLine( _
      String.Format("Exiting Thread {0}", _
      AppDomain.GetCurrentThreadId()))
  End Sub

  Public Sub CriticalSection()
    Monitor.Enter(Me)
    Console.WriteLine( _
      String.Format("Entered Thread {0}", _
      AppDomain.GetCurrentThreadId()))
    Dim i As Integer
    For i = 1 To 5
      Console.WriteLine( _
        "Result = {0} ThreadID: {1}", _
        result, AppDomain.GetCurrentThreadId())
      result += 1
      Thread.Sleep(1000)
    Next i

    Console.WriteLine( _
      String.Format("Exiting Thread {0}", _
      AppDomain.GetCurrentThreadId()))
    Monitor.Exit(Me)
  End Sub

  Public Overloads Shared Sub Main( _
    ByVal args() As String)
      Dim e As New EnterExit

      If args.Length > 0 Then
        Dim nt1 As New Thread( _
          New ThreadStart( _
          AddressOf e.NonCriticalSection))
        nt1.Start()

        Dim nt2 As New Thread( _
          New ThreadStart( _
          AddressOf e.NonCriticalSection))
        nt2.Start()
      Else
        Dim ct1 As New Thread( _
          New ThreadStart( _
          AddressOf e.CriticalSection))
        ct1.Start()
```

```
        Dim ct2 As New Thread( _
            New ThreadStart( _
            AddressOf e.CriticalSection))
        ct2.Start()
      End If
      Console.ReadLine()
    End Sub
  End Class
End Namespace
```

When you run the application without providing an input parameter, you'll get the output from the `CriticalSection()` method as follows:

```
Entered Thread 280
Result = 0   ThreadID 280
Result = 1   ThreadID 280
Result = 2   ThreadID 280
Result = 3   ThreadID 280
Result = 4   ThreadID 280
Exiting Thread 280
Entered Thread 316
Result = 5   ThreadID 316
Result = 6   ThreadID 316
Result = 7   ThreadID 316
Result = 8   ThreadID 316
Result = 9   ThreadID 316
Exiting Thread 316
```

When you provide an input parameter, the corresponding output from the `NonCriticalSection()` method is as follows:

```
Entered Thread 280
Result = 0   ThreadID 280
Entered Thread 316
Result = 1   ThreadID 316
Result = 2   ThreadID 280
Result = 3   ThreadID 316
Result = 4   ThreadID 280
Result = 5   ThreadID 316
Result = 6   ThreadID 280
Result = 7   ThreadID 316
Result = 8   ThreadID 280
Result = 9   ThreadID 316
Exiting Thread 280
Exiting Thread 316
```

In the preceding example, class `EnterExit` is declared with a global variable `result` and two methods `NonCriticalSection()` and `CriticalSection()`. In the `NonCriticalMethod()` section, we don't specify any monitors to lock the section; whereas in the `CriticalSection()` method, we lock the critical section using a monitor. Both the methods modify the value of `result`.

The critical section is defined between the code block `Monitor.Enter(Me)` and `Monitor.Exit(Me)`. The `Me` parameter indicates that the lock should be held on the current object in the example. In the `Main()` method, we run the appropriate methods based on the arguments provided. If no argument is supplied, we use the `CriticalSection()` method and, if any argument is supplied, we use the `NonCriticalSection()` method. In both cases, we have two threads accessing the methods, started from the `Main()` section, at the same time and changing the variable `result`. Although they are declared sequentially, the `For` loop and the sleep time ensure that the threads will try to compete for resources.

Comparing the outputs of the critical and noncritical sections makes the concept of critical sections clear. If you observe the output from the `NonCriticalSection()` method, both the threads `nt1` and `nt2` are changing the variable result at the same time, thus resulting in a mixed output. This is because there are no locks in the method `NonCriticalSection()` and thus the method is not thread-safe. Multiple threads can access the method and in turn the global variable at the same time. On the contrary, if you observe the output from the `CriticalSection()` method, it's clear that until the `ct` thread exits the critical section (`Monitor.Enter()` and `Monitor.Exit()`) block, no other thread (`ct2` in this case) is allowed access to the critical section.

The Wait and Pulse Mechanism

The Wait and Pulse mechanism is used for interaction between threads. When a `Monitor.Wait()` is issued on an object, the thread that is accessing that object waits until it gets a signal to wake up. `Monitor.Pulse()` and `Monitor.PulseAll()` are used for signaling the waiting thread(s). The following listing is an example of how the `Wait()` and `Pulse()` methods work in `WaitAndPulse.vb`.

Note `Wait()` and `Pulse()` methods can be called only in the `Enter()` and `Exit()` code block.

```
Imports System
Imports System.Threading

Namespace WaitAndPulse
  Public Class WaitPulse1
    Private result As Integer = 0
    Private lockObject As Object

    Public Sub New(ByVal lock As Object)
      Me.lockObject = lock
    End Sub

    Public Sub CriticalSection()
      Monitor.Enter(Me.lockObject)
```

```vb
      'Enter the Critical Section
      Console.WriteLine( _
        "WaitPulse1: Entered Thread {0}", _
        AppDomain.GetCurrentThreadId)
      Dim i As Integer
      For i = 1 To 5
        Monitor.Wait(Me.lockObject)
        Console.WriteLine("WaitPulse1: WokeUp")
        Console.WriteLine( _
          "WaitPulse1: Result = {0} ThreadID {1}", _
          result, AppDomain.GetCurrentThreadId)
        result += 1
        Monitor.Pulse(Me.lockObject)
      Next i
      Console.WriteLine( _
        "WaitPulse1: Exiting Thread {0}", _
        AppDomain.GetCurrentThreadId)

      'Exit the Critical Section
      Monitor.Exit(Me.lockObject)
    End Sub
End Class

Public Class WaitPulse2
  Private result As Integer = 0
  Friend lockObject As Object

  Public Sub New(ByVal l As Object)
    Me.lockObject = l
  End Sub 'New

  Public Sub CriticalSection()
    Monitor.Enter(Me.lockObject)
    'Enter the Critical Section
    Console.WriteLine( _
      "WaitPulse2: Entered Thread {0}", _
      AppDomain.GetCurrentThreadId)
    Dim i As Integer
    For i = 1 To 5
      Monitor.Pulse(Me.lockObject)
      Console.WriteLine( _
        "WaitPulse2: Result = {0} ThreadID {1}", _
        result, AppDomain.GetCurrentThreadId)
      result += 1
      Monitor.Wait(Me.lockObject)
      Console.WriteLine("WaitPulse2: WokeUp")
    Next i
```

```vb
      'Wait for 10 seconds
      Console.WriteLine( _
        "WaitPulse2: Exiting Thread {0}", _
        AppDomain.GetCurrentThreadId)

      'Exit the Critical Section
      Monitor.Exit(Me.lockObject)
    End Sub
  End Class

  Public Class ClassForMain
    Public Shared Sub Main()
      Dim lock As New Object
      Dim e1 As New WaitPulse1(lock)
      Dim e2 As New WaitPulse2(lock)

      Dim t1 As New Thread( _
        New ThreadStart(AddressOf _
        e1.CriticalSection))
      t1.Start()

      Dim t2 As New Thread( _
        New ThreadStart(AddressOf _
        e2.CriticalSection))
      t2.Start()
      Console.ReadLine()
    End Sub
  End Class
End Namespace
```

The output from WaitAndPulse is

```
WaitPulse1: Entered Thread 280
WaitPulse2: Entered Thread 316
WaitPulse2: Result = 0   ThreadID 316
WaitPulse1: WokeUp
WaitPulse1: Result = 0   ThreadID 280
WaitPulse2: WokeUp
WaitPulse2: Result = 1   ThreadID 316
WaitPulse1: WokeUp
WaitPulse1: Result = 1   ThreadID 280
WaitPulse2: WokeUp
WaitPulse2: Result = 2   ThreadID 316
WaitPulse1: WokeUp
WaitPulse1: Result = 2   ThreadID 280
WaitPulse2: WokeUp
WaitPulse2: Result = 3   ThreadID 316
WaitPulse1: WokeUp
```

```
WaitPulse1: Result  = 3   ThreadID 280
WaitPulse2: WokeUp
WaitPulse2: Result  = 4   ThreadID 316
WaitPulse1: WokeUp
WaitPulse1: Result  = 4   ThreadID 280
WaitPulse1: Exiting Thread 280
WaitPulse2: WokeUp
WaitPulse2: Exiting Thread 316
```

In the Main() function, we create a LockMe object called lock. Next, we create two objects of type WaitPulse1 and WaitPulse2, and pass them as delegates, so that the threads can call the CriticalSection() method of both the objects. Note that the lockObject object in WaitPulse1 is the same as the lockObject object in WaitPulse2 because the object has been passed by reference to their respective constructors. After initializing the objects, we create two threads, t1 and t2, and pass them the two created objects, respectively. If WaitPulse1.CriticalSection() gets called first, the thread t1 enters the critical section of the method with a lock on the lockObject object and then executes Monitor.Wait() in the For loop. By executing Monitor.Wait(), t1 is waiting for a runtime notification (Monitor.Pulse()) from another thread to be woken up. Note that when the thread executes the Monitor.Wait() method, it releases the lock on the lockObject object temporarily, so that other threads can access it. After thread t1 goes into the waiting state, thread t2 is free to access the lockObject object. Even though the lockObject object is a separate object (WaitPulse1 and WaitPulse2), they both refer to the same object reference. Thread t2 acquires the lock on the lockObject object and enters the WaitPulse2.CriticalSection() method. As soon as it enters the For loop, it sends a runtime notification (Monitor.Pulse()) to the thread that is waiting on the lockObject object (t1 in this case) and goes off to the waiting state. As a result, t1 wakes up and acquires the lock on the lockObject object. Thread t1 then accesses the result variable and sends a runtime notification to the thread waiting on the lockObject object (thread t2 in this case). This cycle continues until the For loop ends. If you compare this description with the output of the program, the concept becomes clear. It's important to note that every Monitor.Enter() function should be accompanied by a Monitor.Exit() function or else the program will never quit.

Monitor.Enter() takes an object as a parameter. If the object parameter is null, a variable, or an object of a value type like an integer, an ArgumentNullException will be thrown.

The TryEnter() Method

The Monitor.TryEnter() method is similar to the Enter() method in that it tries to acquire an exclusive lock on an object; however, it does not block like the Enter() function. If the thread enters successfully, then the TryEnter() method returns True. Consider an example of this in MonitorTryEnter.vb:

```
Imports System
Imports System.Threading

Namespace MonitorTryEnter
    Public Class TryEnter
        Public Sub CriticalSection()
            Dim b As Boolean = Monitor.TryEnter(Me, 1000)
```

```vb
      Console.WriteLine( _
        "Thread {0} TryEnter Value {1}", _
        AppDomain.GetCurrentThreadId, b)

      Dim i As Integer
      For i = 1 To 3
        Thread.Sleep(1000)
        Console.WriteLine("{0} {1}", _
          i, AppDomain.GetCurrentThreadId)
      Next i

      Monitor.Exit(Me)
    End Sub 'CriticalSection

    Public Shared Sub Main()
      Dim a As New TryEnter
      Dim t1 As New Thread( _
        New ThreadStart( _
          AddressOf a.CriticalSection))
      Dim t2 As New Thread( _
        New ThreadStart( _
          AddressOf a.CriticalSection))
      t1.Start()
      t2.Start()
      Console.ReadLine()
    End Sub
  End Class
End Namespace
```

The output from `MonitorTryEnter` is

```
Thread 2 TryEnter Value True
Thread 3 TryEnter Value False
1 2
1 3
2 2
2 3
3 2
3 3
```

The SyncLock Statement

The `SyncLock` keyword can be used as an alternative to the `Monitor` methods. The following two blocks of code are equivalent:

```
Monitor.Enter(x)
  ...
Monitor.Exit(x)
```

```
SyncLock Me
   ...
End SyncLock
```

The following example, Locking.vb, uses the SyncLock keyword instead of the explicit Monitor methods:

```
Imports System
Imports System.Threading

Namespace Locking
  Public Class Locking
    Private result As Integer = 0

    Public Sub CriticalSection()
      SyncLock Me
        Console.WriteLine("Entered Thread {0}", _
          AppDomain.GetCurrentThreadId)
        Dim i As Integer
        For i = 1 To 5
          Console.WriteLine( _
            "Result = {0}  ThreadID {1}", _
            result, AppDomain.GetCurrentThreadId)
          result += 1
          Thread.Sleep(1000)
        Next i
        Console.WriteLine("Exiting Thread {0}", _
          AppDomain.GetCurrentThreadId)
      End SyncLock
    End Sub

    Public Overloads Shared Sub Main( _
      ByVal args() As [String])

      Dim e As New Locking
      Dim t1 As New Thread( New ThreadStart( _
        AddressOf e.CriticalSection))
      t1.Start()

      Dim t2 As New Thread( New ThreadStart( _
        AddressOf e.CriticalSection))
        t2.Start()
    End Sub
  End Class
End Namespace
```

The output from Locking.vb will be the same as for MonitorEnterExit (when a parameter has been supplied):

```
Entered Thread 2272
Result = 0   ThreadID 2272
Result = 1   ThreadID 2272
Result = 2   ThreadID 2272
Result = 3   ThreadID 2272
Result = 4   ThreadID 2272
Exiting Thread 2272
Entered Thread 3616
Result = 5   ThreadID 3616
Result = 6   ThreadID 3616
Result = 7   ThreadID 3616
Result = 8   ThreadID 3616
Result = 9   ThreadID 3616
Exiting Thread 3616
```

The ReaderWriterLock Class

ReaderWriterLock defines the lock that implements single-writer and multiple-reader semantics. The four main methods in the ReaderWriterLock class are

- AcquireReaderLock(): This overloaded method acquires reader lock, using either an integer or a TimeSpan for the timeout value.

- AcquireWriterLock(): This overloaded method acquires writer lock, using either an integer or a TimeSpan for the timeout value.

- ReleaseReaderLock(): This method releases the reader lock.

- ReleaseWriterLock(): This method releases the writer lock.

Note Using the ReaderWriterLock class, any number of threads can safely read data concurrently. Data is locked only when threads are updating. Reader threads can acquire a lock only if there are no writers holding the lock. Writer threads can acquire a lock only if there are no readers or writers holding the lock.

The following listing, ReadWriteLock.vb, shows the use of the ReaderWriterLock() lock:

```
Imports System
Imports System.Threading

Namespace ReadWriteLock
    Public Class ReadWrite
        Private rwl As ReaderWriterLock
        Private x As Integer
        Private y As Integer
```

```vbnet
    Public Sub New()
      rwl = New ReaderWriterLock()
    End Sub 'New

    Public Sub ReadInts(ByRef a As Integer, _
      ByRef b As Integer)
      rwl.AcquireReaderLock(Timeout.Infinite)
      Try
        a = Me.x
        b = Me.y
      Finally
        rwl.ReleaseReaderLock()
      End Try
    End Sub 'ReadInts

    Public Sub WriteInts(ByVal a As Integer, _
      ByVal b As Integer)
      rwl.AcquireWriterLock(Timeout.Infinite)
      Try
        Me.x = a
        Me.y = b
        Console.WriteLine( _
          "x = {0} y = {1} ThreadID = {2}", _
          Me.x, Me.y, AppDomain.GetCurrentThreadId)
      Finally
        rwl.ReleaseWriterLock()
      End Try
    End Sub
End Class

Public Class RWApp
  Private rw As New ReadWrite()

  Public Overloads Shared Sub Main( _
    ByVal args() As [String])
    Dim e As New RWApp()

    'Writer Threads
    Dim wt1 As New Thread( _
      New ThreadStart(AddressOf e.Write))
    wt1.Start()

    Dim wt2 As New Thread( _
      New ThreadStart(AddressOf e.Write))
    wt2.Start()
```

```vb
        'Reader Threads
        Dim rt1 As New Thread( _
          New ThreadStart(AddressOf e.Read))
        rt1.Start()

        Dim rt2 As New Thread( _
          New ThreadStart(AddressOf e.Read))
        rt2.Start()
        Console.ReadLine()
    End Sub

    Private Sub Write()
        Dim a As Integer = 10
        Dim b As Integer = 11
        Console.WriteLine("******** Write *********")

        Dim i As Integer
        For i = 0 To 4
          Me.rw.WriteInts(a, b)
          a += 1
          b += 1
            Thread.Sleep(1000)
        Next i
    End Sub

    Private Sub Read()
        Dim a As Integer = 10
        Dim b As Integer = 11

        Console.WriteLine("******** Read   *********")
        Dim i As Integer
        For i = 0 To 4
          Me.rw.ReadInts(a, b)
          Console.WriteLine( _
            "For i={0} a={1} b={2} ThreadID={3}", _
            i, a, b, AppDomain.GetCurrentThreadId)
          Thread.Sleep(1000)
        Next i
    End Sub
  End Class
End Namespace
```

An example, output from ReadWriteLock could be as follows:

```
******** Write *********
x = 10 y = 11 ThreadID = 2852
******** Write *********
x = 10 y = 11 ThreadID = 3532
******** Read  *********
For i = 0 a = 10 b = 11 ThreadID = 3364
******** Read  *********
For i = 0 a = 10 b = 11 ThreadID = 3112
x = 11 y = 12 ThreadID = 2852
x = 11 y = 12 ThreadID = 3532
For i = 1 a = 11 b = 12 ThreadID = 3364
For i = 1 a = 11 b = 12 ThreadID = 3112
x = 12 y = 13 ThreadID = 2852
x = 12 y = 13 ThreadID = 3532
For i = 2 a = 12 b = 13 ThreadID = 3364
For i = 2 a = 12 b = 13 ThreadID = 3112
x = 13 y = 14 ThreadID = 2852
x = 13 y = 14 ThreadID = 3532
For i = 3 a = 13 b = 14 ThreadID = 3364
For i = 3 a = 13 b = 14 ThreadID = 3112
x = 14 y = 15 ThreadID = 2852
x = 14 y = 15 ThreadID = 3532
For i = 4 a = 14 b = 15 ThreadID = 3364
For i = 4 a = 14 b = 15 ThreadID = 3112
```

In the preceding listing, threads wt1 and wt2 are writer threads that acquire writer locks in the WriteInts() method, and threads rt1 and rt2 are reader threads that acquire reader locks in the ReadInts() method. In the WriteInts() method, the instance variables x and y are changed to the new values a and b, respectively. When thread wt1 or wt2 acquires a writer lock by calling AcquireWriterLock(), no other thread (including the reader threads rt1 and rt2) is allowed access to the object until the thread releases the lock by calling the ReleaseWriterLock() method. This, behavior is similar to that of Monitors. In the ReadInts() method, threads rt1 and rt2 acquire reader locks by calling the AcquireReaderLock() method. In the ReadInts() method, both rt1 and rt2 can be given concurrent access to the instance variables x and y. Until the reader threads release the reader lock, none of the writer threads (wt1 and wt2) is given access to the object. Only reader threads can have concurrent access to the object after acquiring the reader lock.

Monitors might be "too safe" for threads that plan only to read the data rather than modify it. Monitors also have a performance hit associated with them, and for read-only access, this performance hit is not necessary. The ReaderWriterLock class offers an elegant solution that deals with read and write access to data by allowing any number of concurrent threads to read the data. It locks the data only when threads are updating the data. Reader threads can acquire the lock only if there are no writer threads holding the lock. Writer threads can acquire the lock only if there are no reader or writer threads holding the lock.

Manual Synchronization

The third synchronization strategy concerns manual techniques. The .NET Framework provides a classic suite of techniques that give the programmer the ability to create and manage multi-threaded applications using a low-level threading API (Application Programming Interface) similar to the WIN32 Threading API.

The following table shows some of the classes in the System.Threading namespace that can be used for manual synchronization.

Class	Description
AutoResetEvent	The AutoResetEvent class is used to make a thread wait until some event puts it in the signaled state by calling the Set() method. The AutoResetEvent is automatically reset to nonsignaled by the system after a single waiting thread has been released. If no threads are waiting, the event object's state remains signaled. The AutoResetEvent corresponds to a Win32 CreateEvent call, specifying False for the bManualReset argument.
ManualResetEvent	The ManualResetEvent class is also used to make a thread wait until some event puts it in the signaled state by calling the Set() method. The state of a ManualResetEvent object remains signaled until it is set explicitly to the nonsignaled state by the Reset() method. The ManualResetEvent corresponds to a Win32 CreateEvent call, specifying True for the bManualReset argument.
Mutex	Mutex lock provides cross-process as well as cross-thread synchronization. The state of the Mutex is signaled if no thread owns it. Mutex doesn't have all the Wait and Pulse mechanism functionality of the Monitor class, however, it does offer the creation of named mutexes (using the overloaded constructor) that can be used between processes. The benefit of using Mutex over Monitors is that Mutex can be used across processes, whereas Monitors cannot.
Interlocked	The Interlocked class provides methods for atomic, nonblocking integer updates that are shared between multiple threads. The threads of different processes can use this mechanism if the variable is in shared memory.

The ManualResetEvent Class

A ManualResetEvent object can possess only one of the two states, signaled (True) or nonsignaled (False). The ManualResetEvent class inherits from the WaitHandle class and occurs when notifying one or more waiting threads that an event has occurred. The following listing, NETThreadEvents.vb, shows the use of the ManualResetEvent class with a nonsignaled state. First we create an object called mansig and give it a value of False. As such, the function WaitOne() waits until the mansig turns into True or the time value expires. Because the time duration elapsed while waiting, and the value of mansig was not set to True, it stopped blocking and returned with a value of False:

```
Imports System
Imports System.Threading

Namespace NETThreadEvents

  Public Class NonSignaledManual

    Public Shared Sub Main()
      Dim mansig As ManualResetEvent
      mansig = New ManualResetEvent(False)
```

```
        Console.WriteLine("Before WaitOne ")
        Dim b As Boolean = mansig.WaitOne(1000, False)
        Console.WriteLine("After WaitOne {0}", b)
        Console.ReadLine()
      End Sub

  End Class

End Namespace
```

The output from NETThreadEvents with a value of False is

```
Before WaitOne
After WaitOne False
```

In NETThreadEvents, a ManualResetEvent object is created with a value of False. The Boolean value False set the initial state of the ManualResetEvent object to nonsignaled. Next we call the WaitOne() method of the base-class WaitHandle. The WaitOne() method takes two parameters. The first one is the number of milliseconds the thread should wait at the WaitOne() method; the thread therefore waits for 1 second before quitting. The second parameter is exitContext, which is set to True if you want to exit the synchronization domain for the context before the wait (if in a synchronized context), and reacquire it; otherwise it's False.

The program blocks for 1 second at the WaitOne() method and then quits because of the timeout. The state of the ManualResetEvent is still False, thus the Boolean b returned by WaitOne() is False. Now let's figure out what will happen if we set the state of ManualResetEvent to signaled (True):

```
Imports System
Imports System.Threading

Namespace NETThreadEvents
  Public Class NonSignaledManual
    Public Shared Sub Main()
      Dim mansig As ManualResetEvent
      mansig = New ManualResetEvent(True)
      Console.WriteLine("Before WaitOne ")
      Dim b As Boolean = mansig.WaitOne(1000, False)
      Console.WriteLine("After WaitOne {0}", b)
      Console.ReadLine()
    End Sub
  End Class
End Namespace
```

The output from NETThreadEvents with a value of True is

```
Before WaitOne
After WaitOne True
```

By changing initial state of the `ManualResetEvent` to signaled, the thread does not wait at the `WaitOne()` method even though we specified the timeout value of 1,000 milliseconds. When the `ManualResetEvent` was nonsignaled, the thread waited for the state to change to signaled, but it timed out after 1,000 milliseconds. The state is already signaled, so the thread has no reason to wait on the `WaitOne()` method. To change the state of the `ManualResetEvent` to nonsignaled, you call the `Reset()` method of `ManualResetEvent`; to change the state to signaled, you call the `Set()` method.

The following listing, `ManualReset.vb`, shows the usage of the `Reset()` method, and the next, `ManualSet.vb`, shows the usage of the `Set()` method:

```
Imports System
Imports System.Threading

Namespace ManualReset
  Class Reset
    <STAThread> Shared Sub Main()
      Dim manRE As ManualResetEvent
      manRE = New ManualResetEvent(True)
      Console.WriteLine("Before WaitOne ")
      Dim state As Boolean = _
        manRE.WaitOne(1000, True)
      Console.WriteLine( _
        "After first WaitOne {0}", state)

      'Change the state to signaled
      manRE.Reset()
      state = manRE.WaitOne(1000, True)
      Console.WriteLine( _
        "After second WaitOne {0}", state)
      Console.ReadLine()
    End Sub
  End Class
End Namespace
```

The output from `ManualReset` is

```
Before WaitOne
After first WaitOne True
After second WaitOne False
```

In `ManualReset`, we set the state of the `ManualResetEvent` object to signaled (`True`) in its constructor. As a result, the thread does not wait at the first `WaitOne()` method and returns `True`. Next, we `Reset` the state of the `ManualResetEvent` object to nonsignaled (`False`), so the thread has to wait for 5 seconds until it times out.

In `ManualSet.vb`, we use the `Set()` method:

```
Imports System
Imports System.Threading
```

```
Namespace ManualSet
  Class ManualSet
    <STAThread> Shared Sub Main()
      Dim manRE As ManualResetEvent
      manRE = New ManualResetEvent(False)
      Console.WriteLine("Before WaitOne ")
      Dim state As Boolean = _
        manRE.WaitOne(1000, True)
      Console.WriteLine( _
        "After first WaitOne {0}", state)

      'Change the state to signaled
      manRE.Set()
      state = manRE.WaitOne(1000, True)
      Console.WriteLine( _
        "After second WaitOne {0}", state)
      Console.ReadLine()
    End Sub
  End Class
End Namespace
```

The output from ManualSet is

```
Before WaitOne
After first WaitOne False
After second WaitOne True
```

In ManualSet, we set the initial state of the ManualResetEvent object to nonsignaled (False). As a result, the thread has to wait on the first WaitOne() method. We then set the state to signaled using the Set() method; the thread refuses to wait on the second WaitOne() method, and quits.

Just as the WaitOne() method waits for a single event object to become signaled, the WaitAll() function waits for all the event objects to become True or signaled, or it will stay there until the timeout occurs and the WaitAny() method waits for any of the event objects to become True or signaled.

The AutoResetEvent Class

The AutoResetEvent class is similar to the ManualResetEvent class because it waits for the timeout to take place or the event to be signaled and then notifies the waiting threads about the event. One important difference between ManualResetEvent and AutoResetEvent is that AutoResetEvent changes state at the WaitOne() method. The following listing shows the usage of AutoResetEvent class:

```
Imports System
Imports System.Threading

Namespace AutoReset
  Class AutoReset
    <STAThread> Shared Sub Main()
```

```vb
        Dim aRE As AutoResetEvent
        aRE = New AutoResetEvent(True)
        Console.WriteLine("Before first WaitOne ")
        Dim state As Boolean = aRE.WaitOne(1000, True)
        Console.WriteLine( _
          "After first WaitOne {0}", state)
        state = aRE.WaitOne(1000, True)
        Console.WriteLine( _
          "After second WaitOne {0}", state)
    End Sub
  End Class
End Namespace
```

The output from `AutoReset` is the same as that from the `ManualReset` example shown earlier:

```
Before first WaitOne
After first WaitOne True
After second WaitOne False
```

In `AutoReset`, the differences between the `AutoResetEvent` and `ManualResetEvent` are clear. The state of the event object changes from the signaled to nonsignaled at the first `WaitOne()` and then it again changes state from nonsignaled to signaled at the second `WaitOne()` method. As a result, the thread does not wait at the first `WaitOne()` method and has to wait at the second `WaitOne()` method until the time expires.

The Mutex Class

Like the `ManualResetEvent` and the `AutoResetEvent` classes, the `Mutex` class is also derived from the `WaitHandle` class. It is very similar to the `Monitor` class with the exception that it can be used for *interprocess* synchronization. Consider an example, NetMutex.vb:

```vb
Imports System
Imports System.Threading

Namespace NetThreading
  Class NetMutex
    Private Shared resourceMutex As Mutex
      <STAThread()> Public Shared Sub Main()
        resourceMutex = New Mutex(True, "NetThread")
        Dim nm As New NetMutex
        For i As Integer = 1 To 5
          Dim t As New Thread( _
            New ThreadStart(AddressOf nm.Run))
          t.Name = String.Format("Thread_{0}", i)
          t.Start()
        Next
        resourceMutex.ReleaseMutex()
        Console.ReadLine()
      End Sub
```

```vbnet
    Public Sub Run()
      Console.WriteLine("{0} is waiting...", _
        Thread.CurrentThread.Name)
        resourceMutex.WaitOne()

      Console.WriteLine( _
        "{0} is now working!", _
        Thread.CurrentThread.Name)
      Thread.Sleep(5000)

      Console.WriteLine( _
        "{0} is releasing resource.", _
        Thread.CurrentThread.Name)
      resourceMutex.ReleaseMutex()
    End Sub
  End Class
End Namespace
```

The output from NetMutex is

```
Thread_1 is waiting...
Thread_2 is waiting...
Thread_3 is waiting...
Thread_4 is waiting...
Thread_5 is waiting...
Thread_1 is now working!
Thread_1 is releasing resource.
Thread_2 is now working!
Thread_2 is releasing resource.
Thread_3 is now working!
Thread_3 is releasing resource.
Thread_4 is now working!
Thread_4 is releasing resource.
Thread_5 is now working!
Thread_5 is releasing resource.
```

In NetMutex, we construct a Mutex with a Boolean value indicating that the calling thread should have initial ownership of the Mutex, and a string that is the name of the Mutex. We then start a loop, creating five threads that call the Run() method. The Mutex is still owned by the Main thread. In the Run() function, the thread t has to wait until the main thread releases the ownership of the Mutex. Thus, the five threads wait at the call to WaitOne() in the Run() method. After sleeping for 5 seconds, the main thread releases the Mutex lock. The first of the five threads then gets the ownership of the Mutex lock, performs its work (simulated by a call to Thread.Sleep), and then releases the lock with a call to ReleaseMutex() on the Mutex instance. The next thread then acquires ownership of the Mutex. This continues until all the threads using the Mutex have released their locks and we return to the Console.ReadLine() method.

The Interlocked Class

Interlocked synchronizes access to a variable that is being shared by a number of threads. The operation is carried out in an atomic manner. This allows the developer to set a variable and retrieve its new value in one operation when using the Increment and Decrement methods of this class. For example, consider chatinterlocked.vb:

```
Imports System
Imports System.Threading

Class ChatApp
  Shared completeflag As New AutoResetEvent(False)
  Shared server As New ChatServer
  Shared users As Integer

  Public Shared Sub Main()
    Dim userNames() As String = New String() _
      {"Carol", "Karen", "Richard", "Ellie", _
      "Shayla", "Ruth", "Wilson", "Crissy"}
    For user As Integer = 0 To (userNames.Length - 1)
      ThreadPool.QueueUserWorkItem( _
        New WaitCallback( _
          AddressOf UserQuickChat), userNames(user))
      Interlocked.Increment(users)
    Next
    completeflag.WaitOne()
    Console.WriteLine("Everyone has had their say.")
    Console.ReadLine()
  End Sub

  Shared Sub UserQuickChat(ByVal user As Object)
    Dim userName As String
    userName = CType(user, String)

    server.Connect(userName)
    server.Say("Hello, Everyone!", userName)
    server.Disconnect(userName)
    If Interlocked.Decrement(users) = 0 Then
      completeflag.Set()
    End If
  End Sub
End Class

Class ChatServer
  Dim userCount As Integer = 0
  Public Sub Connect(ByVal username As String)
    SyncLock (Me)
      Console.WriteLine( _
        "-- {0} has joined. ({1} users ) -- ", _
```

```vb
        username, Interlocked.Increment(userCount))
      Thread.Sleep(500)
    End SyncLock
  End Sub
  Public Sub Say(ByVal message As String, _
    ByVal user As String)
      Console.WriteLine("{0} says:{2}{1}", _
        user, message, vbTab)
  End Sub

  Public Sub Disconnect(ByVal username As String)
    SyncLock (Me)
      Console.WriteLine( _
        "-- {0} has left. ({1} users ) --", _
        username, Interlocked.Decrement(userCount))
      Thread.Sleep(500)
    End SyncLock
  End Sub
End Class
```

The output for chatinterlocked is

```
-- Carol has joined. (1 users ) --
-- Karen has joined. (2 users ) --
Carol says:     Hello, Everyone!
-- Carol has left. (1 users ) --
Karen says:     Hello, Everyone!
-- Richard has joined. (2 users ) --
Richard says:   Hello, Everyone!
-- Karen has left. (1 users ) --
-- Shayla has joined. (2 users ) --
Shayla says:    Hello, Everyone!
-- Ruth has joined. (3 users ) --
Ruth says:      Hello, Everyone!
-- Crissy has joined. (4 users ) --
Crissy says:    Hello, Everyone!
-- Shayla has left. (3 users ) --
-- Ruth has left. (2 users ) --
-- Crissy has left. (1 users ) --
-- Ellie has joined. (2 users ) --
Ellie says:     Hello, Everyone!
-- Wilson has joined. (3 users ) --
-- Ellie has left. (2 users ) --
Wilson says:    Hello, Everyone!
-- Wilson has left. (1 users ) --
-- Richard has left. (0 users ) --
Everyone has had their say.
```

`chatinterlocked` attempts to put the use of the `Interlocked` class in context of a real-world scenario. We increment the value of the global variable (`users`) in an atomic manner. Like the `Increment()` method, a `Decrement()` method exists that reduces the value of a variable by one. In the same manner, the `Exchange()` method changes the value of two variables passed to it as `ByRef` parameters.

Synchronizing Shared Variables and Methods

Shared variables and methods are affected in a different way from instance variables and methods in a synchronization lock. Shared variables are class variables, whereas variables that belong to an object are object or instance variables. In other words, there will be only one instance of a Shared variable, a Shared method will be shared by multiple objects of the same class, and every object of the same class has its own set of instance variables and methods. So, if you synchronize a Shared variable or a Shared method, the lock is applied on the *entire class* of the objects created from that class. As a result, no other object will be allowed to use the Shared variables of the class.

The ThreadStaticAttribute Class

`ThreadStaticAttribute` is used on a Shared variable to create a separate variable for each thread executing it, rather than sharing (default behavior) the Shared variable across threads. This means that a Shared variable with the `ThreadStaticAttribute` is not shared across different threads accessing it. Each thread accessing it will have a separate copy of the same variable. If one thread modifies the variable, another thread accessing it will not be able to see the changes. This behavior is contrary to the default behavior of Shared variables. In short, `ThreadStaticAttribute` gives you the best of both worlds (Shared and instance).

Note The reason that the class is named `ThreadStaticAttribute` and not `ThreadSharedAttribute` comes from the fact that most OO (object-oriented) languages, such as C# and Java, use the keyword `Static` when VB .NET uses the keyword `Shared`.

The following listing shows the use of `ThreadStaticAttribute` in `NetShared.vb`:

```
Imports System
Imports System.Threading

Namespace NetShared
  Class ThreadStatic
    <ThreadStaticAttribute()> _
    Public Shared x As Integer = 1
    Public Shared y As Integer = 1

    Public Sub Run()
      Dim i As Integer
      For i = 1 To 10
        Dim t2 As Thread = Thread.CurrentThread
```

```vb
      x += 1
      y += 1
      Console.WriteLine( _
        "i={0} x={1} y={2} ThreadID={3}", _
        i, x, y, t2.GetHashCode)
      Thread.Sleep(1000)
    Next i
  End Sub
End Class
Public Class MainApp
  Public Shared Sub Main()
    Dim tS As New ThreadStatic
    Dim t1 As New Thread( _
      New ThreadStart(AddressOf tS.Run))
    Dim t2 As New Thread( _
      New ThreadStart(AddressOf tS.Run))
    t1.Start()
    t2.Start()
  End Sub
End Class
End Namespace
```

The output from NetShared is

```
i=1 ThreadID=2 x=1 y=2
i=1 ThreadID=3 x=1 y=3
i=2 ThreadID=2 x=2 y=4
i=2 ThreadID=3 x=2 y=5
i=3 ThreadID=3 x=3 y=6
i=3 ThreadID=2 x=3 y=7
i=4 ThreadID=3 x=4 y=8
i=4 ThreadID=2 x=4 y=9
i=5 ThreadID=3 x=5 y=10
i=5 ThreadID=2 x=5 y=11
i=6 ThreadID=3 x=6 y=12
i=6 ThreadID=2 x=6 y=13
i=7 ThreadID=3 x=7 y=14
i=7 ThreadID=2 x=7 y=15
i=8 ThreadID=3 x=8 y=16
i=8 ThreadID=2 x=8 y=17
i=9 ThreadID=3 x=9 y=18
i=9 ThreadID=2 x=9 y=19
i=10 ThreadID=3 x=10 y=20
i=10 ThreadID=2 x=10 y=21
```

As you know, a Shared class variable's value remains the same across multiple objects of the class. ThreadStaticAttribute allows each thread accessing a Shared variable to have its own copy. In ThreadStatic, variable x has ThreadStaticAttribute applied to it. As a result, each of the threads t1 and t2 will have separate copies of the Shared variable x, so changes made to x by thread t1 will not be visible to thread t2. On the other hand, changes made to the variable y by thread t1 will be visible to thread t2. If you observe the output of the program, variable x is incremented separately for threads t1 and t2.

Note The difference between a shared variable with a ThreadStaticAttribute and an instance variable is that the Shared variable does not require an object to access it, whereas a compiler exception will occur if you try to access an instance variable without creating the instance of an object.

Synchronization and Performance

Synchronization carries the overhead of the time required to acquire the synchronization lock. As a result, the performance is always poorer than the nonthread-safe version. Because multiple threads might be trying to access the objects at the same time to acquire the synchronization lock, the performance of the entire application might be affected inadvertently. This is a trade-off a developer must be aware of when designing larger applications. The important part is that these thread contentions are not visible until a thorough stress test is performed. Stress testing is extremely important in designing large-scale multithreaded applications. The developer has to decide whether to

- Be safe, and synchronize as much as possible. This makes the program slower, at worst no better than its single-threaded version.

- Consider performance, and synchronize as little as possible.

- Work within the multithreaded design as a continual trade-off between these two factors.

Beware of Deadlocks

Although synchronization is essential for thread-safety, you can cause deadlocks if it's not used properly. As such, you must understand deadlocks and how to avoid them. Deadlock occurs when one thread is waiting for a second thread to release a resource, and the second thread is waiting on the first thread to release a resource, resulting in a situation where neither thread will be freed. Figure 15-3 illustrates a typical deadlock scenario.

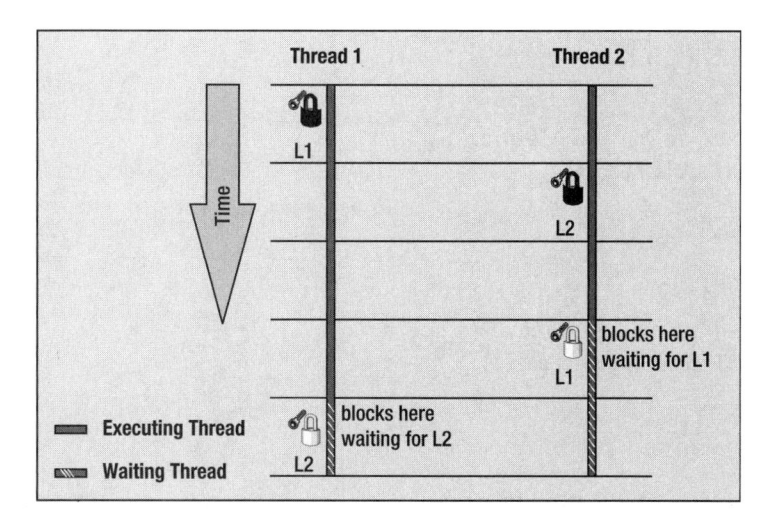

Figure 15-3. *Example of a typical deadlock scenario*

In this figure, Thread 1 acquires lock L1 on an object by entering its critical section. In this critical section, Thread 1 is supposed to acquire lock L2. Thread 2 acquires lock L2 and is supposed to acquire lock L1. So now Thread 1 cannot acquire lock L2 because Thread 2 owns it and Thread 2 cannot acquire lock L1 because Thread 1 owns it. As a result, both the threads enter into an infinite wait or deadlock. One of the best ways to prevent potential deadlocks is to avoid acquiring more than one lock at a time, which is often practical. However, if that is not possible, you need a strategy that ensures you acquire multiple locks in a consistent, defined order. Depending on each program design, the synchronization strategies to avoid deadlocks may vary. There is no standard strategy you can apply to avoid all deadlocks. Most of the time deadlocks are not detected until the application is deployed on a full-scale basis. You are fortunate if you can detect deadlocks in your program during the testing phase. A critical but often overlooked element of any locking strategy is documentation. Unfortunately, even when a good synchronization strategy is designed to avoid deadlocks, usually much less effort is made in documenting it. At the minimum, every method should have documentation associated with it that specifies the locks it acquires and explains the critical sections within that method.

Let's take a look at the `Deadlock.vb` example file:

```
Imports System
Imports System.Threading

Class Deadlock
  Private field_1 As Integer = 0
  Private field_2 As Integer = 0
  Private lock_1 As Object = New Object
  Private lock_2 As Object = New Object
```

```vbnet
    Public Sub First(ByVal val As Integer)
        SyncLock lock_1
            Console.WriteLine( _
              "First:Acquired lock_1: {0} Now Sleeping", _
              Thread.CurrentThread.GetHashCode())
            Thread.Sleep(1000)

            SyncLock lock_2
                Console.WriteLine( _
                    "First:Acquired lock_2: {0}", _
                    Thread.CurrentThread.GetHashCode())
                field_1 = val
                field_2 = val
            End SyncLock
        End SyncLock
    End Sub

    Public Sub Second(ByVal val As Integer)
        SyncLock lock_2
            Console.WriteLine( _
              "Second:Acquired lock_2: {0}", _
              Thread.CurrentThread.GetHashCode())
            SyncLock lock_1
                Console.WriteLine( _
                    "Second:Acquired lock_1: {0}", _
                    Thread.CurrentThread.GetHashCode())
                field_1 = val
                field_2 = val
            End SyncLock
        End SyncLock
    End Sub
End Class

Public Class MainApp
    Private d As New Deadlock
    Public Shared Sub Main()
        Dim m As New MainApp

        Dim t1 As New Thread( _
          New ThreadStart(AddressOf m.Run1))
        t1.Start()

        Dim t2 As New Thread( _
          New ThreadStart(AddressOf m.Run2))
        t2.Start()
    End Sub
    Public Sub Run1()
        Me.d.First(10)
```

```
        End Sub
        Public Sub Run2()
            Me.d.Second(10)
        End Sub
End Class
```

The output from `DeadLock` is

```
First:Acquired lock_1:2 Now Sleeping
Second:Acquired lock_2:3
```

In `DeadLock`, thread `t1` calls the `first()` method, acquires `lock_1`, and goes to sleep for 1 second. In the meantime, thread `t2` calls the `second()` method, acquires `lock_2`, and then tries to acquire `lock_1` in the same method. Thread `t` owns `lock_1`, however, so thread `t2` has to wait until thread `t1` releases `lock_1`. When thread `t1` wakes up, it tries to acquire `lock_2`. Now `lock_2` is owned by thread `t2` and thread `t1` cannot acquire it until thread `t2` releases `lock_2`. This results in a deadlock and a hang in the program. Commenting out the `Thread.Sleep()` line from the method `first()` may allow the code to run without a deadlock, at least temporarily, because thread `t1` acquires `lock_2` before thread `t2` in most cases. However, because you don't know when the thread execution switch will take place, you'll almost certainly run into this problem without the sleep as well. In real-world scenarios, instead of `Thread.Sleep()`, you might connect to a database resulting in thread `t2` acquiring `lock_2` before thread `t1`, and it will result in a deadlock. The example shows how important it is to carve out a good locking scheme in any multithreaded application. A good locking scheme can incorporate the acquisition of a lock by all the threads in a well-defined manner. In the preceding example, thread `t1` should not acquire `lock_2` until it is released by thread `t2` or thread `t2` should not acquire `lock_1` until thread `t1` releases it. These decisions depend on specific application scenarios and cannot be generalized in any way. Testing the locking scheme is equally important, because deadlocks usually occur in deployed systems due to lack of stress and functional testing.

End-to-End Examples

In this section, we'll look at two larger examples. First, we'll examine how to create thread-safe wrappers and then we'll move on to consider a database connection pool.

Writing Your Own Thread-Safe Wrappers

The general idea of writing your own wrapper comes from the fact that you might not want to make every class in your library thread-safe, as synchronization has performance penalties associated with it. Instead, you can give the application developer a choice of whether to use a synchronized class or not. The application developer might not want to take the risk of a deadlock nor pay the performance penalty of using thread-safe classes in a single-threaded environment; instead, he might prefer to have a choice of having a built-in synchronized wrapper for the same class in the library rather than writing a synchronized wrapper himself. Collection classes such as `ArrayList` and `Hashtable` in the `System.Collections` namespace already have this feature. You can decide whether you want to use a thread-safe `Hashtable` or not during initialization of the `Hashtable`. You can initialize a thread-safe `Hashtable` by calling the Shared `Synchronized()` method of the `Hashtable` class:

```
Dim h as Hashtable
h = Hashtable.Synchronized(New Hashtable())
```

In this example, we'll attempt to develop a class and a synchronized wrapper for the class. We'll develop a Book Collection library; Figure 15-4 shows the UML representation of the Book Collection library.

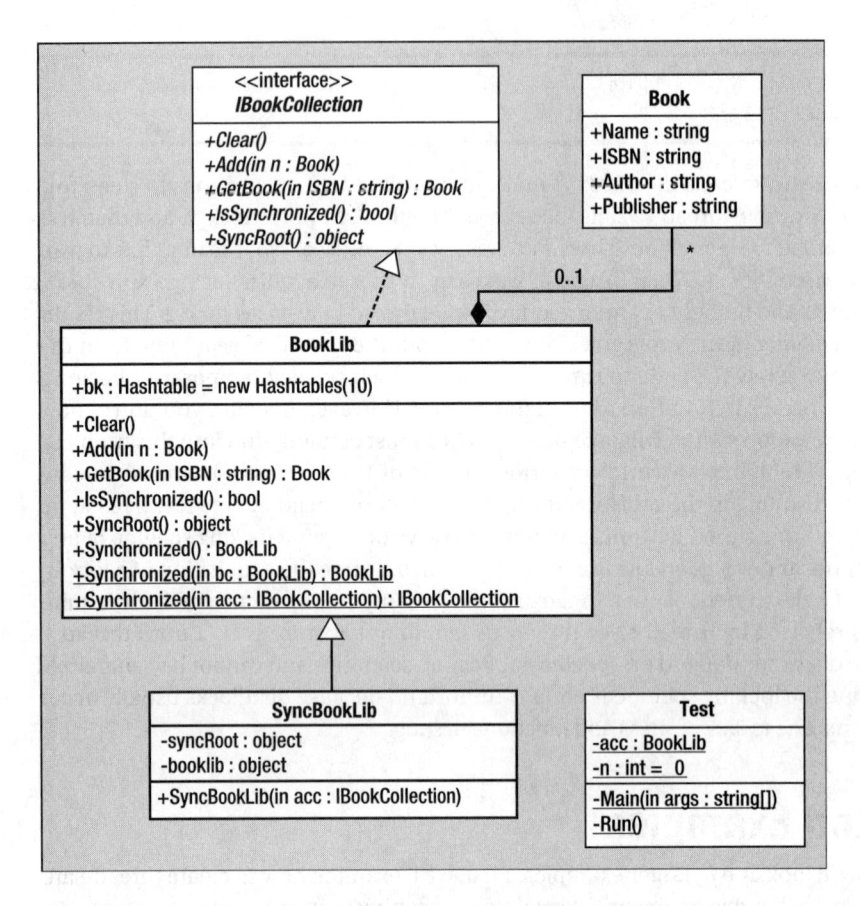

Figure 15-4. *A UML representation of the Book Collection library*

The program is very simple, but the concept of having intrinsic synchronization support is very important. By adding intrinsic synchronization support to your library, the developer can choose between a synchronized and nonsynchronized environment for the same class. For example, programmers who do not need synchronization can instantiate an object as follows:

```
Dim b As BookLib = New BookLib()
```

Whereas programmers who use your type in a thread-hot environment can use your thread-safe wrappers as follows:

```
Dim b As BookLib = New BookLib()
b = b.Synchronized()
```

The following is the complete BookLib.vb source along with its synchronized wrapper:

```vb
Imports System
Imports System.Threading
Imports System.Collections

' Interface for collections of books.
Interface IBookCollection
  Sub Clear()
  Sub Add(ByVal n As Book)
  Function GetBook(ByVal ISBN As String) As Book
  ReadOnly Property IsSynchronized() As Boolean
  ReadOnly Property SyncRoot() As Object
End Interface

Public Class Book
  ' Properties and private variables avoided
  ' for code simplicity. Real-World application
  ' should have private variables and
  ' properties accessing them.
  Public Name As String
  Public ISBN As String
  Public Author As String
  Public Publisher As String
End Class

' BookLib class. Non-Synchronized.
Class BookLib
  Implements IBookCollection
  Friend bk As New Hashtable(10)

  Public Overridable Sub Clear() _
    Implements IBookCollection.Clear
    Me.bk.Clear()
  End Sub

  Public Overridable Sub Add(ByVal b As Book) _
    Implements IBookCollection.Add
    Console.WriteLine( _
      "Adding Book for ThreadID: {0}", _
      AppDomain.GetCurrentThreadId)
      ' Sleep for 2 seconds to simulate work
      ' and demonstrate the synchronized wrapper.
      Thread.Sleep(2000)
      'Add ISBN as the Key
      bk.Add(b.ISBN, b)
  End Sub
```

```vb
Public Overridable Function GetBook( _
  ByVal ISBN As String) As Book _
  Implements IBookCollection.GetBook
  Console.WriteLine( _
    "Getting Book for ThreadID: {0}", _
    AppDomain.GetCurrentThreadId)
    Return CType(bk(ISBN), Book)
End Function

Public Overridable ReadOnly Property _
  IsSynchronized() As Boolean _
  Implements IBookCollection.IsSynchronized
    Get
      Return False
    End Get
End Property

Public Overridable ReadOnly Property SyncRoot() _
  As Object _
  Implements IBookCollection.SyncRoot
  Get
    Return Me
  End Get
End Property

Public Overloads Function Synchronized() As BookLib
  ' Return this instance in a thread-safe wrapper
  Return Synchronized(Me)
End Function

Public Overloads Shared Function Synchronized( _
  ByVal bc As BookLib) As BookLib
  ' Return the specified instance in a _
  ' thread-safe wrapper
  If bc Is Nothing Then
    Throw New ArgumentNullException("bc")
  End If

  If bc.GetType() Is GetType(SyncBookLib) Then
    Throw New InvalidOperationException( _
      "BookLib reference is already synchronized.")
  End If
  Return New SyncBookLib(bc)
End Function

Public Overloads Shared Function Synchronized( _
  ByVal acc As IBookCollection) As IBookCollection
  ' Return the specified instance in a thread-safe
  ' wrapper
```

```vb
      If acc Is Nothing Then
        Throw New ArgumentNullException("acc")
      End If
      If acc Is GetType(SyncBookLib) Then
        Throw New InvalidOperationException( _
          "BookLib reference is already synchronized.")
      End If

      Return New SyncBookLib(acc)
    End Function
End Class

' SyncBookLib is the Synchronized wrapper around the
' BookLib class. This class will allow us to
' instantiate a synchronized wrapper.
NotInheritable Class SyncBookLib
  Inherits booklib

  Shadows MsyncRoot As Object
  Private booklib As Object

  Friend Sub New(ByVal acc As IBookCollection)
    booklib = acc
    MsyncRoot = acc.SyncRoot
  End Sub

  Public Overrides Sub Clear()
    SyncLock SyncRoot
      MyBase.Clear()
    End SyncLock
  End Sub

  Public Overrides Sub Add(ByVal b As Book)
    SyncLock SyncRoot
      MyBase.Add(b)
    End SyncLock
  End Sub

  Public Overrides Function GetBook( _
    ByVal ISBN As String) As Book
    SyncLock SyncRoot
      Return CType(bk(ISBN), Book)
    End SyncLock
  End Function

  Public Overrides ReadOnly Property _
    IsSynchronized() As Boolean
```

```vbnet
      Get
        Return True
      End Get
    End Property

    Public Overrides ReadOnly Property _
      SyncRoot() As Object
      Get
        Return MsyncRoot
      End Get
    End Property
End Class

' This is the Main Application.
Class Test
  Private Shared acc As BookLib
  Private Shared n As Integer = 0
  ' bookNames and bookAuthors array used to
  ' simulate a datasource
  Private Shared bookNames As String() = { _
    "Visual Basic .NET Threading Handbook", _
    "Best Kept Secrets in .NET", _
    "Beginning C# Objects", _
    "Beginning C, Third Edition", _
    "Enterprise Development w/VS.NET,UML,and MSF", _
    "Comprehensive VB .NET Debugging", _
    "Moving To ASP.NET: Web Dev. w/ VB .NET"}
  Private Shared bookAuthors As String() = { _
    "Tobin Titus", _
    "Brian Bischof", _
    "Jacquie Barker", _
    "Ivor Horton", _
    "John Erik Hansen", _
    "Steve Harris", _
    "Mark Pearce"}

  Overloads Shared Sub Main(ByVal args() As String)
    acc = New BookLib
    ' If the any argument is passed from the
    ' command line, use a Synchronized Wrapper
    If args.Length > 0 Then
      acc = acc.Synchronized()
    End If
    Dim threads As Thread() = _
      {New Thread(New ThreadStart(AddressOf Run)), _
       New Thread(New ThreadStart(AddressOf Run)), _
       New Thread(New ThreadStart(AddressOf Run))}
```

```vbnet
    Dim t As Thread
    For Each t In threads
      t.Start()
    Next t
    For Each t In threads
      t.Join()
    Next t
    Dim i As Integer
    For i = 0 To n - 1
      Dim bk As Book = acc.GetBook(i.ToString())
      If Not (bk Is Nothing) Then
        Console.WriteLine("Book : " + bk.Name)
        Console.WriteLine("ISBN : " + bk.ISBN)
        Console.WriteLine("ISBN : " + bk.Publisher)
        Console.WriteLine("Author : " + bk.Author)
      End If
    Next i
    Console.WriteLine( _
      "Total Number of books added {0}", n)
    Console.ReadLine()
  End Sub
  Shared Sub Run()
    Dim i As Integer
    For i = 0 To 1
      Dim bk As New Book
      bk.Author = bookAuthors(n)
      bk.Name = bookNames(n)
      bk.Publisher = "APress"
      bk.ISBN = n  ' n simulates a unique ISBN number
      n += 1
      acc.Add(bk)
    Next i
  End Sub
End Class
```

In the preceding example, we first declare an interface `IBookCollection` that has the following methods and properties for handling the collection of books:

- **Clear()**: Method to clear the book collection.
- **Add()**: Method to add a book to the book collection.
- **GetBook()**: Method to get a book from the book collection.
- **IsSynchronized()**: Read-only property used to check whether the collection is synchronized or not.
- **SyncRoot()**: Read-only property used to get the synchronized root of the collection.

Next we declare a class called Book representing a book in the collection. For example, the collection might be a library or a book store, but the representation of the Book class is the same in both.

The BookLib class implements the IBookCollection interface. As a result, the BookLib class must implement all the methods and properties of the IBookCollection interface. We declare a Hashtable called bk as the collection that will contain the books. The Key of the Book object is its ISBN number. In the Add() method, we add a Book object to the Hashtable. In the GetBook() method, we retrieve the Book object if its ISBN number is supplied.

Now we must address any synchronization issues. In the Synchronized() method, we create an object of type SyncBookLib and return a reference to it. SyncBookLib is the synchronized version of the BookLib class. SyncBookLib inherits from the BookLib class, thus inheriting all the properties and methods that the BookLib class has already implemented. The difference between the SyncBookLib class and the BookLib class is that in the SyncBookLib class, we lock all the critical sections using monitors. For example, the Clear(), GetBook(), and Add() methods have locks in their implementations making them thread-safe, whereas in the BookLib class, there are no locks in any of the methods.

In the Test class, we create a synchronized BookLib if we pass any command-line argument. If no command-line arguments are passed, we create a nonthread-safe BookLib object. We then create three threads that add some books to the book library. When you run the application, the difference between the execution of synchronized BookLib and nonsynchronized BookLib will be clear. In the synchronized version, only one thread can access the library at any point of time. The other two threads have to wait until the first thread has finished adding books to the BookLib. This is not the case if we use the nonsynchronized version; all the threads are given concurrent access to the BookLib object instance.

The output from BookLib with a command-line argument (thread-safe) is as follows:

```
Adding Book for ThreadID: 3900
Adding Book for ThreadID: 3896
Adding Book for ThreadID: 3976
Adding Book for ThreadID: 3900
Adding Book for ThreadID: 3896
Adding Book for ThreadID: 3976
Book: Visual Basic .NET Threading Handbook
ISBN : 0
ISBN : Apress
Author : Tobin Titus
Book: Best Kept Secrets in .NET
ISBN : 1
ISBN : Apress
Author : Brian Bischof
Book: Beginning C# Objects: From Concepts to Code
ISBN : 2
ISBN : Apress
Author : Jacquie Barker
Book: Beginning C, Third Edition
ISBN : 3
ISBN : Apress
```

```
Author : Ivor Horton
Book: Enterprise Development with VS .NET,UML,and MSF
ISBN : 4
ISBN : Apress
Author : John Erik Hansen
Book: Comprehensive VB .NET Debugging
ISBN : 5
ISBN : Apress
Author : Steve Harris
Total Number of books added 6
```

The output from `BookLib` with no command-line argument (nonthread-safe) is the same:

```
Adding Book for ThreadID: 3704
Adding Book for ThreadID: 1168
Adding Book for ThreadID: 1560
Adding Book for ThreadID: 3704
Adding Book for ThreadID: 1168
Adding Book for ThreadID: 1560
Getting Book for ThreadID: 4032
Book: Visual Basic .NET Threading Handbook
ISBN : 0
ISBN : Apress
Author : Tobin Titus
Getting Book for ThreadID: 4032
Book: Best Kept Secrets in .NET
ISBN : 1
ISBN : Apress
Author : Brian Bischof
Getting Book for ThreadID: 4032
Book: Beginning C# Objects: From Concepts to Code
ISBN : 2
ISBN : Apress
Author : Jacquie Barker
Getting Book for ThreadID: 4032
Book: Beginning C, Third Edition
ISBN : 3
ISBN : Apress
Author : Ivor Horton
Getting Book for ThreadID: 4032
Book: Enterprise Development with VS .NET,UML,and MSF
ISBN : 4
ISBN : Apress
Author : John Erik Hansen
Getting Book for ThreadID: 4032
Book: Comprehensive VB .NET Debugging
```

```
ISBN : 5
ISBN : Apress
Author : Steve Harris
Total Number of books added 6
```

A Database Connection Pool

Object pools are common in enterprise software development where instantiation of objects has to be controlled to improve the performance of the application. For example, database connections are expensive objects to be created every time you need to connect to a database. So, instead of wasting resources in instantiating the database connection for every database call, you can pool and reuse some connection objects that you've already created and thus gain a performance advantage by saving the time and resources required to create a new connection object for every database call.

Object pooling can be thought of as similar to buying books. You check your list to see if you have the book already. If you do own that book already, you read the book you have, if not, you go buy it. Of course, if you don't have the funds to buy it, you wait until you have the money. After the money becomes available, if that book is still your major priority, you buy it and put it in your library. Similarly, in object pooling, you first check the pool to see whether the object has already been created and pooled. If the object is pooled, you get the pooled object; if it isn't pooled, you create a new object instance and pool it for future use. Object pooling is extensively used in large-scale application servers such as Enterprise Java Beans (EJB) servers, MTS/COM+, and even .NET Framework.

In this section, we'll develop a database connection pool for pooling database connections. Database connections are expensive to create. In a typical Web application, thousands of users might be trying to access the Web site at the same time. If most of these hits need database access to serve dynamic data and you create a new database connection for each user, you'll run out of the number of simultaneous connections supported by the database and, as a result, the Web site will either slow down considerably in delivering the dynamic content or crash altogether after a critical point is reached. Connection pooling helps you balance the number of simultaneous users trying to access the database with the number of simultaneous connections supported by the database. The pool also increases the performance of the Web site considerably because you won't have to create a new connection for every user. After data is served to one user, the connection is returned to the pool for future use.

■**Note** Keep in mind that ADO.NET, as well as other enterprise technologies, provides good mechanisms for connection pooling. This code is meant to demonstrate a thread pool. Other solutions might be considered for controlling database access.

Implementing the Pool

Let's start by looking at a UML diagram that depicts a database connection pool application. Figure 15-5 show the `ObjectPool` class and the `DBConnectionSingleton` class that inherits the `ObjectPool` class.

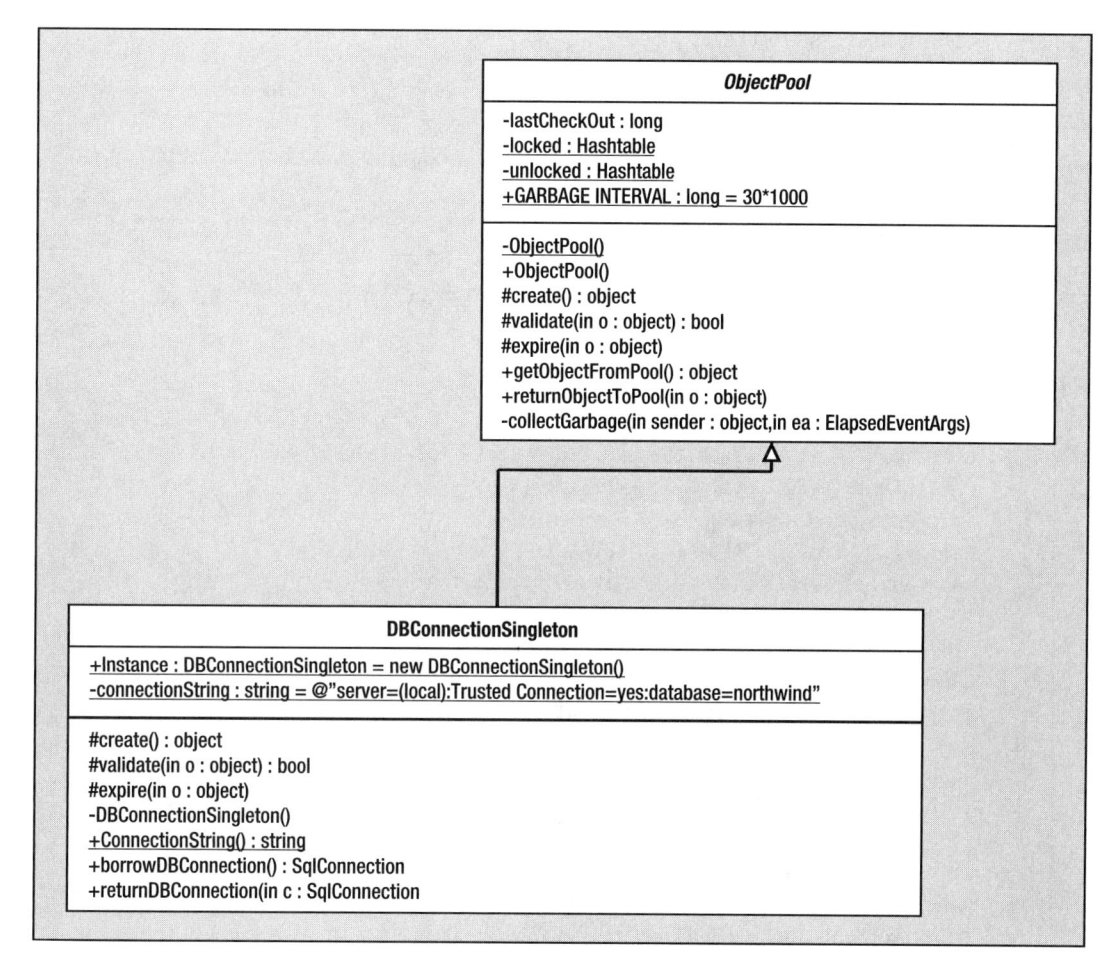

Figure 15-5. *UML diagram of a database connection pool application*

The `ObjectPool` **Class**

The following is the `ObjectPool` class in its entirety:

```
Imports System
Imports System.Collections
Imports System.Timers

Namespace ThreadVB

  Public MustInherit Class ObjectPool
    'Last Checkout time of any object from the pool.
    Private lastCheckOut As Long

    'Hashtable of the checked-out objects
    Private Shared locked As Hashtable
```

```vb
'Hashtable of available objects
Private Shared unlocked As Hashtable

'Clean-Up interval
Friend Shared GARBAGE_INTERVAL As Long = 30 * 1000

Shared Sub New()
  locked = Hashtable.Synchronized(New Hashtable())
  unlocked = Hashtable.Synchronized(New Hashtable())
End Sub

Friend Sub New()
  lastCheckOut = DateTime.Now.Ticks
  'Create a Time to track the expired objects for cleanup.
  Dim aTimer As New System.Timers.Timer()
  aTimer.Enabled = True
  aTimer.Interval = GARBAGE_INTERVAL
  AddHandler aTimer.Elapsed, AddressOf collectGarbage
End Sub

' The derived class should implement this method
Protected MustOverride Function create() As Object

' The derived class should implement this method
Protected MustOverride Function validate(ByVal o As Object) _
                                        As Boolean

' The derived class should implement this method
Protected MustOverride Sub expire(ByVal o As Object)

' Get the object from the pool
Friend Function getObjectFromPool() As Object
  Dim now As Long = DateTime.Now.Ticks
  lastCheckOut = now
  Dim o As Object = Nothing

  SyncLock Me
    Try
      Dim myEntry As DictionaryEntry
      For Each myEntry In unlocked
        o = myEntry.Key

        If validate(o) Then
          unlocked.Remove(o)
          locked.Add(o, now)
          Return o
        Else
          unlocked.Remove(o)
```

```vb
              expire(o)
              o = Nothing
            End If
          Next myEntry
        Catch
          ' Implement error handling
        End Try
        o = create()
        locked.Add(o, now)
      End SyncLock
      Return o
    End Function

    ' Return the object to the pool
    Friend Sub returnObjectToPool(ByVal o As Object)
      If Not (o Is Nothing) Then
        SyncLock Me
          locked.Remove(o)
          unlocked.Add(o, DateTime.Now.Ticks)
        End SyncLock
      End If
    End Sub

    ' Clean up the pool by deleting the expired objects.
    Private Sub collectGarbage(ByVal sender As Object, _
              ByVal ea As System.Timers.ElapsedEventArgs)
      SyncLock Me
        Dim o As Object
        Dim now As Long = DateTime.Now.Ticks
        Dim e As IDictionaryEnumerator = unlocked.GetEnumerator()

        Try
          While e.MoveNext()
            o = e.Key
            If now - CLng(unlocked(o)) > GARBAGE_INTERVAL Then
              unlocked.Remove(o)
              expire(o)
              o = Nothing
            End If
          End While
        Catch
          ' Implement error handling
        End Try
      End SyncLock
    End Sub
  End Class

End Namespace
```

The `ObjectPool` base class contains two important methods; `getObjectFromPool()`, which gets objects from the pool and `returnObjectToPool()`, which returns objects to the pool. The object pool is implemented as two hashtables, one called `locked` and the other called `unlocked`. The `locked` hashtable contains all the objects that are currently in use and `unlocked` contains all the objects that are free and available for use. The `ObjectPool` also contains three `MustOverride` methods that must be implemented by the derived classes: `create()`, `validate()`, and `expire()`.

In total, the `ObjectPool` class has three critical sections:

- **While getting an object to the pool, `getObjectFromPool()`**: A lock is needed while adding an object to the pool because the content of the `locked` and `unlocked` hashtables changes and you don't want any race condition here.

- **While returning an object to the pool, `returnObjectToPool()`**; Again, a lock is needed while returning an object to the pool because the content of the locked and unlocked hashtables changes and a new object becomes available for use. Here also you can't afford to have a race condition, because you don't want multiple threads accessing the same hashtable at the same time.

- **While cleaning up the expired objects from the pool**, `collectGarbage()`: In this method, you go over the `unlocked` hashtable to find and remove expired objects from the pool. The content of the `unlocked` hashtable may change and you need the removal of expired objects to be atomic.

In the `getObjectFromPool()` method, you iterate over the `unlocked` hashtable to get the first available object. The `validate()` method is used to validate the specific object. The `validate()` method can vary in specific implementations based on the type of the pooled object. For example, if the object is a database connection, the derived class of the object pool needs to implement the `validate()` method to check whether the connection to the database is open or closed. If the validation of the pooled object succeeds, you remove the object from the `unlocked` hashtable and put it in the `locked` hashtable. The `locked` hashtable contains the objects that are currently in use. If the validation fails, you kill the object with the `expire()` method. The `expire()` method also needs to be implemented by the derived class and is specific to the type of pooled object. For example, in case of a database connection, the expired object closes the database connection. If a pooled object is not found, that is, if the `unlocked` hashtable is empty, you create a new object using the `create()` method and put the object in the `locked` hashtable.

The `returnObjectToPool()` method implementation is much simpler. You just have to remove the object from the `locked` hashtable and put it back in the `unlocked` hashtable for recycling. In this whole recycling process, you have to take into consideration the memory usage of the application. Object pooling is directly proportional to memory usage. So the more objects you pool, the more memory you're using. To control memory usage, you should periodically garbage collect the objects that are pooled by assigning a timeout period to every pooled object. If the pooled object is not used within the timeout period, it is garbage collected. As a result, the memory usage of the object pool will vary depending on the load on the system.

The `collectGarbage()` method is used for handling the garbage collection of the pooled object. This method is called by the `aTimer` delegate that is initialized in the `ObjectPool` constructor. In our example, we keep the garbage collection interval to 30 seconds in the `GARBAGE_COLLECT` constant.

> **Note** We haven't implemented any database connection-specific code, so we can assume that the `ObjectPool` class can be used for the pooling any type of .NET Framework objects.

The DBConnectionSingleton Class

The `DBConnectionSingleton` class is the implementation of a database connection-specific object pool. The main purpose of this class is to provide database connection-specific implementations of the `create()`, `validate()`, and `expire()` methods inherited from the `ObjectPool` class. The class also provides methods called `borrowDBConnection()` and `returnDBConnection()` for borrowing and returning database connection objects from the object pool.

A complete listing of the `DBConnectionSingleton` class is as follows:

```
Imports System
Imports System.Data.SqlClient
Public NotInheritable Class DBConnectionSingleton
  Inherits ObjectPool

  ' Private Constructor of the Singleton
  Private Sub New()
  End Sub

  ' This is how you get the instance of a Singleton
  Public Shared Instance As New _
    DBConnectionSingleton()

  Private Shared _connectionString As String = _
      "server=(local); User ID=user;" + _
      "Password=password;database=northwind"

  Public Shared Property ConnectionString() _
    As String
    Get
      Return _connectionString
    End Get
    Set(ByVal Value As String)
      _connectionString = Value
    End Set
  End Property

  ' Implemented create function of the
  ' ObjectPool class
  Protected Overrides Function create() As Object
    Dim temp As New _
      SqlConnection(_connectionString)
```

```vbnet
      temp.Open()
      Return temp
    End Function

    ' Check whether the Connection is Open or Closed
    Protected Overrides Function validate( _
      ByVal o As Object) As Boolean
      Try
        Dim temp As SqlConnection = _
          CType(o, SqlConnection)
        Return Not _
          temp.State.Equals(ConnectionState.Closed)
      Catch
        ' Implement error handling
      End Try
    End Function

    ' Close the Database Connection
    Protected Overrides Sub expire(ByVal o As Object)
      Try
        CType(o, SqlConnection).Close()
      Catch
        ' Implement error handling
      End Try
    End Sub
    ' Borrow a Database Connection from the Pool
    Public Function borrowDBConnection() _
      As SqlConnection
      Try
        Return CType(MyBase.getObjectFromPool(), _
          SqlConnection)
      Catch e As Exception
        Throw e
      End Try
    End Function

    ' Return a Database Connection to the Pool
    Public Sub returnDBConnection( _
      ByVal c As SqlConnection)
      MyBase.returnObjectToPool(c)
    End Sub
End Class
```

Because we are dealing with the `SqlConnection` object, the `expire()` method closes the `SqlConnection`, the `create()` method creates the `SqlConnection`, and the `validate()` method checks whether the `SqlConnection` is open or not. The whole synchronization issue is hidden from the client application using the `DBConnectionSingleton` object instance.

Why Use a Singleton?

The Singleton is a popular creational design pattern, which is used when you need to have only one instance of an object. The intent of the Singleton pattern is to ensure a class has only one instance, and provide a global point of access to it. To implement a Singleton, you need a Private constructor so that the client application can't create a new object whenever it wants to. The Shared readonly property instance is used to create the only instance of the Singleton class. The .NET Framework, during the JIT process, initializes the Shared property when (and only when) any method uses this Shared property. If the property is not used, then the instance is not created. More precisely, the class gets constructed and loaded when *any* Shared member of the class is used by *any* caller. This feature is called *lazy initialization* and creates the object only on the first call to the instance property. The .NET Framework guarantees the thread-safety of Shared type initializations inherently. So, we do not have to worry about the thread-safety of the DBConnectionSingleton object because only one instance of it will ever be created during the lifetime of the application. The Shared variable instance holds the only instance of the DBConnectionSingleton class object.

Using the Database Connection Pool

The database connection pool is now ready for use and the ObjectPoolTester application in the code Downloads area for this chapter on the Apress Web site (http://www.apress.com) can be used to test it.

The following shows some code snippets of how to instantiate and use the database connection pool:

```
' Initialize the Pool
Dim pool As DBConnectionSingleton
pool = DBConnectionSingleton.Instance

' Set the ConnectionString of the DatabaseConnectionPool
DBConnectionSingleton.ConnectionString =
    " server=(local);User ID=sa;Password=;database=northwind"

' Borrow the SqlConnection object from the pool
Dim myConnection As SqlConnection = pool.borrowDBConnection()

' Return the Connection to the pool after using it
pool.returnDBConnection(myConnection)
```

In these examples, we initialize the DBConnectionSingleton object from the instance property of the DBConnectionSingleton class. As discussed earlier, we are assured that using the Singleton design pattern enables one and only one instance of the DBConnectionSingleton object. We set the ConnectionString property of the database connection to the Northwind database on the local SQL Server machine. Now, we can borrow database connections from the object pool using the borrowDBConnection() method of the pool object, and return the database connection by calling the returnDBConnection() method of the pool object. The following screenshot shows the ObjectPoolTester application in action. If you really want to explore how the pooling application works, the best way is to open the project in Visual Studio .NET and step through the ObjectPoolTester application in the Debug mode.

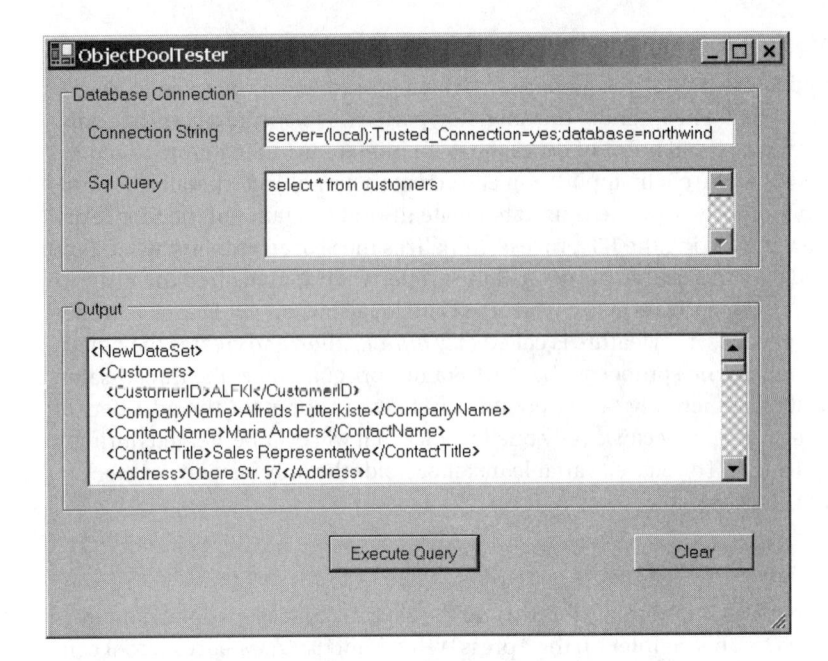

Summary

Synchronization is an extremely important concept in this multithreaded world of enterprise computing. It is extensively used in popular applications such as databases, messages queues, and even Web servers. Any developer developing multithreaded applications needs to completely understand the synchronization concepts. Rather than getting overwhelmed with the locking features and trying to make every object thread-safe, the developer should focus on deadlock scenarios and try to resolve as many deadlock conditions as possible right from the design stage of the application. Understanding the performance hit associated with synchronization and how it will affect the overall performance of your application is also important. In this chapter, along with the synchronization support in the .NET Framework, we also developed a couple of useful applications:

- **A custom thread-safe wrapper**: In this example, you learned how you can add intrinsic synchronization support to your library and give the application developer the choice of using synchronization or not. This helps the developer focus on the application rather than worrying about the thread-safety of your library.

- **A database connection pool**: In this example, you developed a generic object pool that can be used for pooling any type of similar objects. Following that, you developed a database connection pool inheriting from the object pool. The object pool can be reused to pool any kind of object.

These applications offer a good start in developing your own thread-safe APIs.

CHAPTER 16

Threading Models

Most highly scalable systems are highly concurrent (*concurrency* is the existence of more than one request for the same object at the same time). However, writing code that is highly concurrent and thread-safe (meaning when one or more threads are accessing shared data, there is no possibility that the data could be corrupted or made inconsistent) is a huge challenge.

If you use multithreading techniques with a formal threading model, you can write highly scalable code that can work in a concurrent fashion. In the previous chapters, you learned all about threading, including when to use threading and how to avoid the threading traps. In this chapter, you'll learn how to take advantage of the threading models supported by .NET, as well as some models you can impose on top of .NET to help you design your code.

By default, all the .NET applications are multithreaded, which was not the case in VB6. In WinForms, a special UI thread controls all the user interface-related functions such as keyboard activities and mouse activities. When you start running long-running, time-consuming processes on the UI thread, the application becomes unresponsive. If you can run tasks on a thread other than the UI thread, the application will behave better and the UI will respond well. In addition, creating numerous thread objects is not the only way to achieve this. You can use several techniques in addition to multithreading, including implementing asynchronous programming and using timer-based functions, as you saw in Chapter 14.

Multiple Threads in Applications

If you programmed in the earlier version of VB, you might know that VB supported multiple threads within a COM container, such as MTS or COM+. Although VB5/6 supported multiple threads, the threading model they supported was STA (Single Threaded Apartments). However, the .NET Framework does not have the concept of apartments and it manages all the threads within AppDomains. By default, all .NET applications are multithreaded and any code can access any object at any time, so you must be very careful with shared resources in the managed code.

The .NET Framework supports both managed and unmanaged threads and all the Win32 threading models. When you are trying to access COM components from managed code, unmanaged threads are created by the legacy COM components. Threads in the .NET Framework are created using the Thread object, whether managed or unmanaged.

If you have ever programmed multithreaded programs using Win32 APIs, you may remember that Win32 supported UI threads and worker threads. As you learned in Chapter 13, the threading names have now changed into Apartment Model Threading and Free Threading, respectively. The .NET Framework supports two basic threading models, which are Apartment

519

Model Threaded or Single Threaded Apartment (STA) components, and Free Threaded or Multiple Threaded Apartment (MTA) components. When you create a thread in .NET, by default it is an MTA thread.

Note You should only use the STA threading model when you're going to access STA-based COM components such as VB6 COM components. Otherwise, you shouldn't mark the current thread as STA because it involves a significant performance hit to the application.

To reiterate what you've learned earlier, an apartment is the logical container within the AppDomain for sharing threads in the same context. A context is an order of sequence. Objects reside inside an AppDomain and the context is created when an object is created during the activation process.

STA Threading Model

An STA thread apartment works on a concept called Object-per-Client model, meaning the code that creates the STA thread apartment owns its threads. There will only be one thread in any apartment as shown in Figure 16-1.

In STA threading, all the calls to a thread are placed in a queue and the calls are processed one by one. Therefore, the STA thread never executes multiple methods simultaneously. STA threads have their own private data and they don't share data between threads. This makes the threading model safe and avoids any data corruption and synchronization problems. However, this restricts the capabilities available to the developer, and performance suffers because data has to be copied with every thread created.

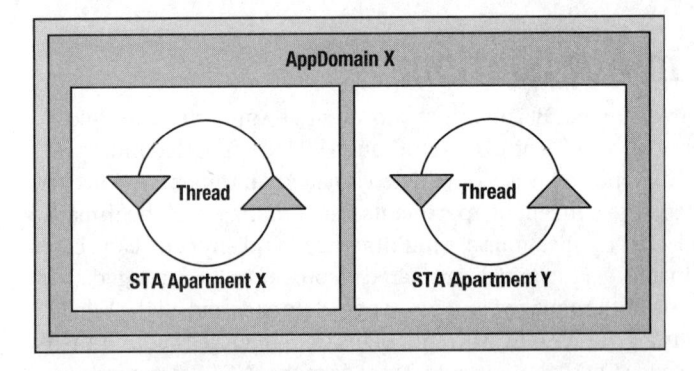

Figure 16-1. *STA thread apartments*

As you can see from the diagram, `AppDomain` X had two STA Threads, X and Y, running inside, and each of the STA apartments has only one thread. The term *thread affinity* is used when defining the relationship between the thread and the code that creates the thread. When a call is made to an STA apartment thread, then calls between the caller and the thread are handled by the contexts in the `AppDomain`, and the contexts maintain the thread affinity.

If your managed application is going to use unmanaged legacy COM components, then it's very important to know the threading model of the COM components before accessing them. The threading model information can be found in the Registry under:

`HKEY_CLASSES_ROOT\CLSID\{Class ID of the COM component}\InProcServer32`

If you want to specify that you are using the Apartment Threading model, then apply the `STAThreadAttribute` attribute on the `Main()` method:

```
<STAThreadAttribute> _
Sub Main()
    ...
End Sub
```

This attribute should only be used if you're trying to access legacy STA components from the managed code. Otherwise, mark `Main()` as `MTAThreadAttribute`:

```
<MTAThreadAttribute> _
Sub Main()
    ...
End Sub
```

The same principle applies for ASP.NET applications. If your ASP.NET page is accessing an STA COM component, then you have to use the `ASPCompact` directive at the top of the ASP.NET page:

`<%@ Page AspCompact="true" %>`

By default, all the ASP.NET pages are multithreaded, and when you use the `AspCompact` directive, the ASP.NET page is marked as STA. This ensures that the ASP.NET page is compatible with the threading model of a COM component.

Note When you mark the ASP.NET page to run under the STA threading model, the performance of the application suffers.

MTA Threading Model

The biggest difference between an STA and an MTA threaded apartment is that an MTA apartment can have more than one thread running simultaneously in the same apartment using all the shared data available in the apartment. This is illustrated in Figure 16-2.

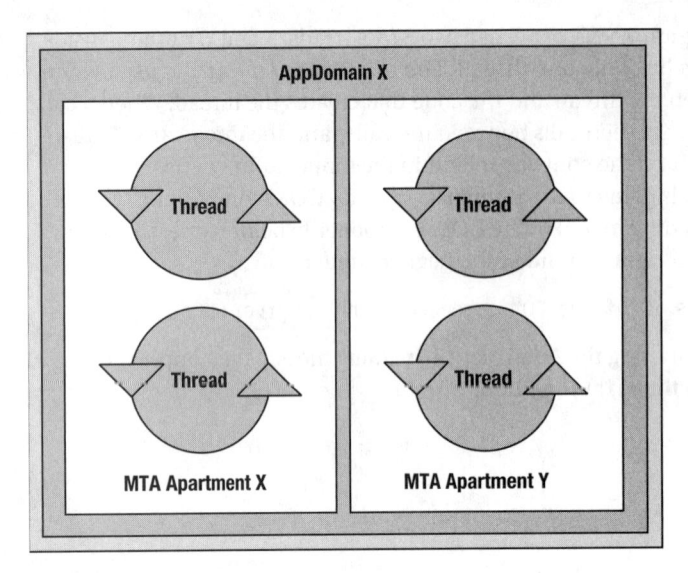

Figure 16-2. *MTA thread apartments*

Because the MTA model supports simultaneous multiple thread execution, it becomes the caller's responsibility to synchronize the global data between multiple threads. Many of these issues were covered in the previous chapter.

Specifying the Threading Model

The threading model for a thread can be set using the ApartmentState property of the Thread class. The ApartmentState enumeration defines the types of threading models supported by .NET.

Enumeration Value	Meaning
MTA	Creates a multithreaded apartment
STA	Creates a single-threaded apartment
Unknown	The apartment property of the Thread class is not set

As you've already learned, you should only mark the thread as an STA thread if you are going to access an STA-threaded legacy COM component. Otherwise, your threading model is in the default MTA threading model.

Designing Threaded Applications

A multithreaded program has two or more threads (flows of control). It can achieve significant performance gains with concurrency, with or without parallel thread execution. Concurrent thread execution means that two or more threads are executing at the same time. Parallelism occurs when two or more threads execute simultaneously across two or more processors.

In this section, we'll talk about real threading considerations and issues. Before you start developing applications, you should ask yourself these questions:

1. Is it possible to subdivide the application to run on different threads?

2. If it's possible to subdivide, how do I subdivide and what are the criteria for subdividing?

3. What would be the relationship between the main thread and the worker threads? (This defines how the tasks in the application will relate to each other.)

You can find out the answer to the first question by inspecting the application. For example, if your application does heavy I/O operation (such as reading an XML file or querying a database) that blocks the main thread, or it performs a lot of CPU-intensive processing (such as encrypting and decrypting data, hashing, and so on) that can also block the main thread.

If you've identified the parts of your application that are potential candidates for separate threads, then you should ask yourself the following questions:

- **Does each of the tasks identified use separate global resources?** For example, if you've identified two potential threads for your application and both will use the same global resource (such as a global variable or a DataSet object), then if both threads try to access the global resource at the same time, you could get inconsistent or corrupt data, as shown in the previous chapter. The only way to prevent this kind of problem is by using locks on the global resources, which could leave the other thread waiting. If both of the tasks will use the same global resource, then it isn't a good idea to break the task into two. For some resources, you could use the Monitor class to prevent the threads from locking up. Again, this was shown in Chapter 15.

- **How long could the thread be blocked?** It's not always possible to build applications that use independent global resources. For example, let's say both tasks in your application rely on a single global DataSet object. If the first task takes a lot of time to fill the DataSet object (it fills about 50,000 rows from the database), then you would ordinarily lock the DataSet object to prevent concurrency problems. Here is a pseudo code version of the first task.

    1. Open the Database connection.

    2. Lock the DataSet object.

    3. Perform the query.

    4. Fill the DataSet with 50,000 rows from the database.

    5. Unlock the DataSet object.

    In this case, the second task needs to wait for a long time to get access to the DataSet object, which happens only when the first task finishes its execution and releases the lock. This is a potential problem and it will likely remove the concurrency of your application. There is a better way to address this problem:

1. Open the Database connection.
2. Perform the query.
3. Fill the local DataSet with 50,000 rows from the database.
4. Lock the global DataSet object.
5. Set the local database to global dataset (DSGlobal = DSLocal).
6. Unlock the global DataSet object.

In this way, you're not locking the global DataSet object until you need to update it, which reduces the wait time for the lock on the global object to release.

- **Does the execution of one task depend on the other task?** For example, the tasks that you've identified could be querying the database and displaying the data in a DataGrid control. You can split the task into two by querying the database as the first task, and displaying the result in the DataGrid as the second task. The second task does not want to start until the first task is complete. Therefore, separating the querying and displaying the data in a DataGrid into two separate concurrently running tasks is not a viable option. One way around this is to have the first task raise an event when completed, and fire a new thread when this happens. Alternatively, you could use a timer that checks to see whether it has completed through a public field, and continues the execution of the thread when it has.

Threads and Relationship

The threads spun from a multithreaded application may or may not be related to each other. For example, in every application there is a main thread that spins other threads. The main thread becomes the controller of all other threads in the application. You can use a few common methods to define the relationship between the threads in a multithreaded application:

- Main and Worker thread model
- Peer thread model
- Pipeline thread model

The following sections provide details about each of these models, including some code so that you can see how they might be implemented in your applications

Main and Worker Thread Model

The Main and Worker thread model is the common model used throughout this book so far (see Figure 16-3).

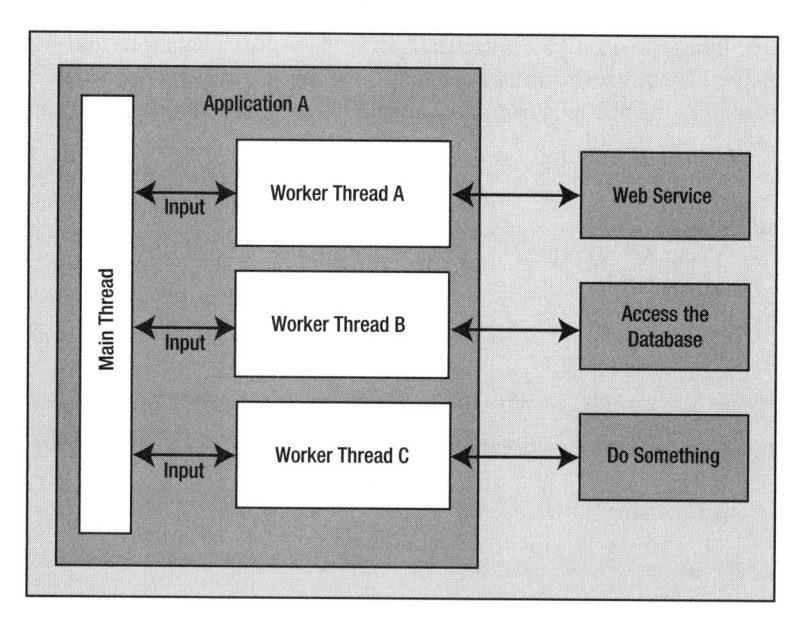

Figure 16-3. *The Main and Worker thread model*

In the Main and Worker thread model, the main thread receives all the input, which it passes to other threads to perform some task. The main thread may or may not wait for the worker threads to finish. In this model, the worker threads don't interact with the input sources; they read the input from the main thread to perform the task. For example, you could have three buttons on a WinForm application that trigger three events:

- Get data from a Web service.

- Get data from a database.

- Do something else when the last button is clicked such as parsing an XML file.

This is the simplest threading model. The main thread is contained within the Main() method, and is common in client GUI applications.

Following is some code to test this. The form used is shown in Figure 16-4.

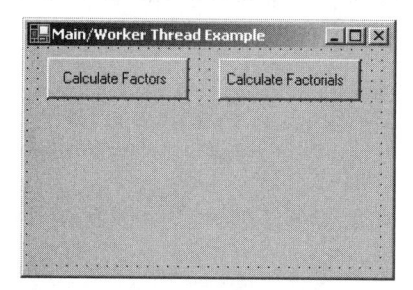

Figure 16-4. *Illustration of the form layout for the Main/Worker thread example*

If you click on a button, it fires off a worker thread that performs some calculations and returns the results in the space below the buttons. We'll just show the relative code sections here; however, you can download the full code from the Downloads section on the Apress Web site (*http://www.apress.com*).

```vb
Public Class MainWorker
  Public Function CalculateFactors( _
    ByVal number As Integer) As ArrayList
    If number < 3 Then Return Nothing
    Dim current As Integer
    Dim factors As New ArrayList()
    factors.Add("1")
    For current = 2 To number - 1
      If Math.Floor(number / current) * current = _
        number Then
        factors.Add(current.ToString())
      End If
    Next
    factors.Add(number.ToString())
    Return factors
  End Function

  Public Function CalculateFactorial( _
    ByVal number As Integer) As Long
    If number < 0 Then Return -1
    If number = 0 Then Return 1
    Dim returnValue As Long = 1
    Dim current As Integer
    For current = 1 To number
      returnValue *= current
    Next
    Return returnValue
  End Function
End Class
```

These methods are straightforward. They are wrapped in a class for modularity reasons. The first returns an `ArrayList` containing all the factors of the number passed in, whereas the second just returns a `Long`. Remember that factorials get very large very quickly. The factorial of 13 is 6,227,020,800. The factorial method doesn't tie up the processor for long, but it can be used to illustrate this model.

```vb
  Public Sub New()
    MyBase.New()

    ' This call is required by the Windows
    ' Form Designer.
    InitializeComponent()
```

```vb
    ' Add any initialization after the
    ' InitializeComponent() call
    threadMethods = New MainWorker()
End Sub
```

The constructor just contains an instantiation of a new `MainWorker` object that will be used in the methods. Following are the methods used for the button click events:

```vb
Private Sub cmdFactors_Click( _
  ByVal sender As System.Object, _
  ByVal e As System.EventArgs) _
  Handles cmdFactors.Click
    Dim calculateFactors As New _
      Threading.Thread( AddressOf _
        FactorsThread)
    calculateFactors.Start()
End Sub

Private Sub FactorsThread()
  Dim value As ArrayList = _
    threadMethods.CalculateFactors(200)
  lblResult.Visible = False
  lblResult.Text = String.Empty
  Dim count As Integer
  For count = 0 To value.Count - 1
    lblResult.Text &= CType( value.Item(count), _
      String)
    If count < value.Count - 1 Then
     lblResult.Text &= ", "
    End If
  Next
  lblResult.Visible = True
End Sub
```

The `cmdFactors_Click()` method instantiates a new thread with the next method, which formats and acts upon the result contained in `MainWorker.CalculateFactors()`. It needs to be wrapped because thread methods cannot have return values.

```vb
Private Sub cmdFactorial_Click( _
  ByVal sender As System.Object, _
  ByVal e As System.EventArgs) _
  Handles cmdFactorial.Click
  Dim calculateFactorial As New Thread( AddressOf _
      FactorialThread)
  calculateFactorial.Start()
End Sub
```

```
Private Sub FactorialThread()
  Dim value As Long = _
    threadMethods.CalculateFactorial(20)
  lblResult.Text = value.ToString()
End Sub
```

The preceding method is much simpler—whenever the `cmdFactorial` button is clicked, the `Main` thread fires off a new thread and updates the `lblResult` text label when the results have been achieved. This is a straightforward example of main/worker threads in actions. Obviously, this example can easily be changed to deal with connection to a database, or other more time-consuming activities.

You have to take care of issues relating to threads when you use this mode. You can have threads spawning threads, threads accessing the same resource, and threads going into an infinite loop. This is the simplest model, but also the one that requires the most work from the developer. In addition, the threads are completely independent of each other, all being controlled entirely by the parent, in this case, the `Main` thread.

Peer Thread Model

In the Peer thread model (see Figure 16-5), each thread receives its own input from the appropriate sources and processes the input accordingly. For example, the UI thread receives the input from the keyboard and mouse. On the other hand, `Worker Thread A` listens to a particular socket and processes the input as it comes in from the socket. In the same way, `Worker Thread B` waits for a system event and acts accordingly. In this model, all the threads execute concurrently without blocking or waiting for other threads.

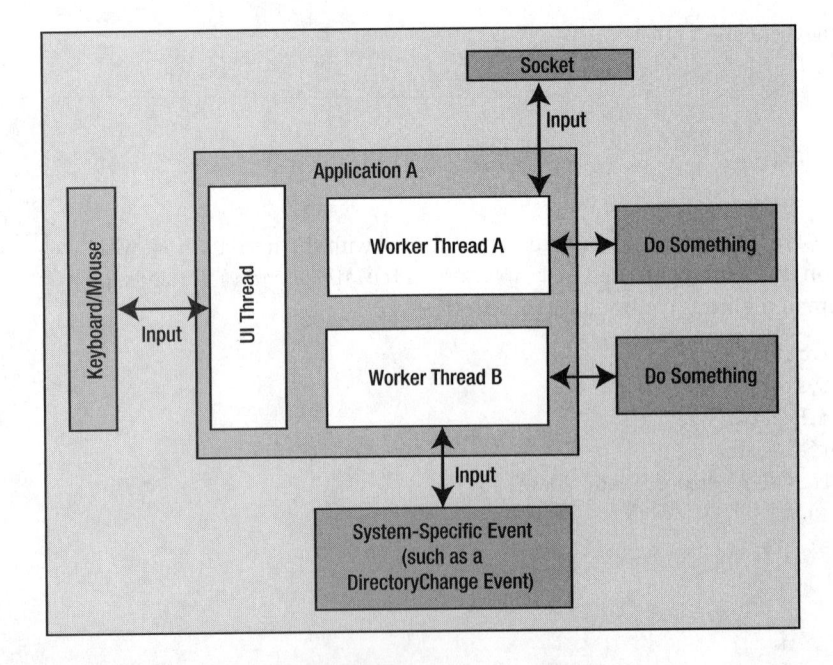

Figure 16-5. *The Peer thread model*

We can amend the previous example so that the `CalculateFactors()` method notices when the factorial thread finishes, and discovers the factorials of this number. We'll use the factorial of 8 in this example. In this example, however, we won't be using a socket, but just the setting of a variable. The principles are the same for sockets; you would either continuously listen, or to save processor cycles, sleep intermittently.

So, let's change the `WorkerThread` class first:

```
Public Class MainWorker2
Private factorial As Long
Public Overloads Function CalculateFactors( _
  ByVal number As Long) As ArrayList
  If number < 3 Then Return Nothing
    Dim current As Long
    Dim factors As New ArrayList
    factors.Add("1")
    For current = 2 To number - 1
      If Math.Floor(number / current) * current = _
        number Then
        factors.Add(current.ToString())
      End If
    Next
    factors.Add(number.ToString())
    Return factors
  End Function

  Public Overloads Function CalculateFactors() _
    As ArrayList
    Dim count As Integer
    For count = 1 To 10
      thread.CurrentThread.Sleep( _
      TimeSpan.FromSeconds(1))
      If factorial > 0 Then
        Exit For
      ElseIf count = 10 And factorial = 0 Then
        Return Nothing
      End If
    Next
    Dim returnValue As ArrayList = _
      CalculateFactors(factorial)
    Return returnValue
  End Function

  Public Function CalculateFactorial( _
    ByVal number As Long) As Long
    factorial = 0
    If number < 0 Then Return -1
    If number = 0 Then Return 1
    Dim returnValue As Long = 1
```

```vbnet
    Dim current As Integer
    For current = 1 To number
      returnValue *= current
    Next
    factorial = returnValue
    Return returnValue
  End Function
End Class
```

A private field has been created that will store the result of the factorial when created. In addition, a class has been added as `MainWorker2`. The `CalculateFactors()` method now has an overload, so that if it isn't passed an argument, it performs the business end of this model.

All that happens is that the thread monitors the state of the `factorial` field, as if it were a socket. It checks to see whether the field is anything other than 0, and if so, then calls the `CalculateFactors()` method with the value of `factorial` as its argument and returns the `ArrayList` that it produces. We have also reset the factorial field at the start of the `CalculateFactorial()` method so there will always be some work to do. At the end of this method, we set `factorial` to equal the factorial.

Now, the `frmCalculate` class needs altering also. Observe the following changes:

```vbnet
...
Private threadMethods As WorkerThread2
...
Public Sub New()
  MyBase.New()
  'This call is required by the Windows Form
  'Designer.
  InitializeComponent()

  'Add any initialization after the
  'InitializeComponent() call
  threadMethods = New WorkerThread2()
End Sub
...
Private Sub NewFactorsThread()
  Dim value As ArrayList = _
    threadMethods.CalculateFactors()
  lblResult.Visible = False
  lblResult.Text = String.Empty
  Dim count As Integer
  For count = 0 To value.Count - 1
    lblResult.Text &= CType( _
      value.Item(count), String)
    If count < value.Count - 1 Then
      lblResult.Text &= ", "
```

```vbnet
  Next
  lblResult.Visible = True
End Sub
...
Private Sub cmdFactorial_Click( _
  ByVal sender As System.Object, _
  ByVal e As System.EventArgs) _
  Handles cmdFactorial.Click
  Dim calculateFactors As New Thread( _
    AddressOf NewFactorsThread)
  Dim calculateFactorial As New Thread( _
    AddressOf FactorialThread)
  calculateFactors.Start()
  calculateFactorial.Start()
End Sub
```

Apart from defining the new `threadMethods` field as a new `MainWorker2` class, there are two main changes. We define a new method called `NewFactorsThread()` that calls the `MainWorker2`'s `CalculateFactors()` method with no arguments. The rest of this method is the same. In the `cmdFactorial_Click()` method, instead of just firing up the `FactorialThread` method in a thread, we fire up the `FactorsThread` too, and execute them out of sequence so that `FactorsThread` may have to wait for the factorial. You should be able to see how this can be tied into a network socket, and you'll see an example of monitoring such a socket in Chapter 19.

The common errors that could occur with this kind of model are deadlocks and blocking. If you have a thread continually listening at a socket and getting its parameters from that socket, then that socket may need to be locked from other threads. This means, therefore, that this is a very good model to use for manager classes. You could use a thread to monitor a socket and then fire off new threads to process the contents. Do not have more than one thread monitoring the same socket. In addition, if the thread is continually checking the socket or other resource, it may consume more processor cycles than necessary. As seen in the preceding example, you can use `Thread.Sleep()` to reduce the processor cycles.

As you'll see, this example is also similar to the Pipeline thread model in concept, but we are simulating a Peer thread model. If you click on the `Calculate Factorials` button, unless you have a very fast machine, you should have time to click on `Calculate Factors`, which will enable you to calculate and display the factors of 200 before it overwrites the text box with the factors of 8!, or 40320.

Pipeline Thread Model

The Pipeline thread model is based on a series of tasks and each of the tasks depends on the previous task (illustrated in Figure 16-6). For example, the main thread creates a series of threads and each other thread waits until the previous thread is finished executing.

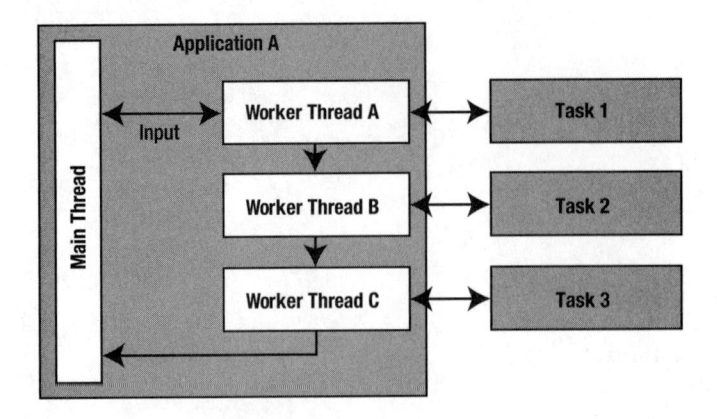

Figure 16-6. *The Pipeline thread model*

This kind of threading relationship is good if your task has certain stages and each of these stages depends on another. For example, your task could be processing input data and the process could have a few subtasks such as

- Filtering all the nonvalid characters, such as <, >, !, and so on

- Checking whether the data is formatted correctly

- Formatting all the numbers with currency signs and decimal points

- Processing the input

In this kind of situation, the next task can only be started if the previous task has finished. In the previous model, this is, in effect, what we were doing, as the factorial field was only set at the end of the thread. However, the proper way to implement the Pipeline thread model is to test explicitly that the thread has ended.

A few changes need to be made to the Peer thread model example to make it part of the Pipeline model. First, we'll show the code for frmCalculate:

```
...
Private threadMethods As PipelineThread
Private calculateFactorial As Thread
...
Public Sub New()
...
threadMethods = New PipelineThread()
...
Private Sub NewFactorsThread()
calculateFactors.Join()
...
```

As you can see, the changes are minimal here. The only interesting changes are the line that rescopes `calculateFactorial` and the `calculateFactors.Join()` line. This instructs the `calculateFactors` thread to wait until `calculateFactorial` has completed before executing. The `Join()` call has to be within the thread that you want to pause. It is called on the thread it is waiting for. This inevitably means that the thread variable has to be rescoped to be at least class-wide so that it can be accessed from other threads.

```
Class PipelineThread
   ...
   Public Overloads Function CalculateFactors() _
     As ArrayList
     Dim returnValue As ArrayList = _
       CalculateFactors(factorial)
     Return returnValue
   End Function
```

Again, the changes here are small. The preceding method no longer has to check whether `factorial` has been set, and can execute because it can assume the factorial has been calculated. This example could be useful when, for instance, you are waiting on a `DataSet` to fill before performing some further calculations. This would enable the thread to fire as soon as the thread that fills the `DataSet` is complete. Of course in a real application, error checking would have to be implemented as the thread could have completed but ended abruptly because of an error, or because of an `Abort()` instruction from another thread.

The traps you have to watch out for are the same traps that can occur with any thread. The first thread could be placed in an infinite loop, in which case, the second thread would never execute. By ensuring this can never happen in your first thread, you ensure that the second thread will execute and complete. In addition, you have to watch out for the thread ending unpredictably due to an error or otherwise, as mentioned in the previous paragraph.

This concludes the discussion of the three models that can be applied to threading. By modeling your application to one of these, you should become familiar with the structure of the code you would need to use.

Summary

In this chapter, we've discussed the various threading models that can be applied to your application, why you should use them, and how to implement them. You should now be confident in your knowledge of the following:

- Different types of basic threading models, such as STA and MTA apartments

- How to specify the threading model

- The different models of threads that can be applied and their relationships to each other

This chapter will help you design your threaded application because the application will fit into one or more of the models; the code examples given will also help you to build the code you need. With the .NET Framework, threads are far more powerful, but also far more prone to errors than they used to be. By being aware of which model your application fits into, you can look out for these potential errors.

CHAPTER 17

Scaling Threaded Applications

For situations in which the threads are short-lived, it's efficient to use a pool of threads for performing tasks rather than creating and then subsequently deleting an entirely new thread for each task. A task, in this chapter, could be a single method or a number of methods. The process of preallocating a collection, or pool, of threads prior to their actual usage in an application is known as **thread pooling**.

This chapter provides a detailed insight into thread pooling and covers the following topics:

- The concept of thread pooling

- The need for thread pooling

- The role of the CLR in thread pooling

- Glitches involved in thread pooling and their solutions

- The size of a thread pool

- The .NET `ThreadPool` class

- Thread pool programming in VB .NET

As you'll discover, the Common Language Runtime (CLR) of the .NET Framework plays a major role in the thread-pooling process.

What Is Thread Pooling?

Thread pooling is the process of creating a collection of threads during the initialization of a multithreaded application, and then reusing those threads for new tasks when required, instead of creating new threads. The number of threads for the process is usually fixed. However, you can increase the number of available threads. Each thread in the pool is given a task, and after that task has completed, the thread returns to the pool and waits for the next assignment.

The Need for Thread Pooling

Thread pooling is essential in multithreaded applications for the following reasons (it also makes their coding a lot easier and their execution more efficient):

- Thread pooling improves the response time of an application because threads are already available in the thread pool waiting for their next assignment and do not need to be created from scratch.

- Thread pooling saves the CLR from the overhead of creating an entirely new thread for every short-lived task and reclaiming its resources after it dies.

- Thread pooling optimizes the thread time-slices according to the current process running in the system.

- Thread pooling enables you to start several tasks without having to set the properties for each thread.

- Thread pooling enables you to more easily pass state information as an object to the procedure arguments of the task that is being executed.

- Thread pooling can be employed to fix the maximum number of threads for processing the client's request.

The Concept of Thread Pooling

One of the major problems affecting the responsiveness of a multithreaded application is the time involved in spawning threads for each task.

For example, a Web server is a multithreaded application that can service several client requests simultaneously. For example, suppose that 10 clients are accessing the Web server at the same time:

- If the server operates a thread per client policy, it spawns 10 new threads to service these clients, which entails the overhead of first creating those threads, managing them throughout their lifetime, and then destroying them. It's also possible that the machine will run out of resources at some point.

- Alternatively, if the server used a pool of threads to satisfy those requests, then it would save the time involved in the spawning of those threads each time a request from a client comes in. This is the concept behind thread pooling.

The Windows OS maintains a pool of threads for servicing requests. If an application requests a new thread, Windows tries to fetch it from the pool. If the pool is empty, it spawns a new thread and gives it to you. Windows dynamically manipulates the thread pool size to increase the response time of your applications.

To recap then, the factors affecting the threading design of a multithreaded application are

- Application responsiveness

- Thread-management resource allocation

- Resource sharing

- Thread synchronization

This chapter addresses responsiveness and resource sharing. The remaining factors have been covered in the previous chapters of this book.

The CLR and Threads

The CLR was designed with the aim of creating a managed code environment offering various services such as compiling, garbage collecting, memory managing, and, yes, thread pooling to applications targeted at the .NET platform.

A remarkable difference exists between how Win32 and the .NET Framework defines a process that hosts the threads that our applications use. In a traditional multithreaded Win32 application, each process is made up of collections of threads. Each thread in turn consists of Thread Local Storage (TLS) and call stacks for providing time slices for machines that have a single CPU. Single-processor machines allot time slices for each thread to execute based on the thread priority. When the time slice for a particular thread is exhausted, that thread is suspended and some other thread is allowed to perform its task. With the .NET Framework, each process can be subdivided into **application domains** that host the threads along with the TLS and call stack. It's worthwhile to note that interprocess communication is handled by a concept called **remoting** in .NET Framework.

Now that you have a basic understanding of thread pooling and the .NET process, let's dig into how the CLR provides the thread pooling functionality for .NET applications.

The Role of the CLR in Thread Pooling

The CLR forms the heart and soul of the .NET Framework by offering several services to managed applications, including thread pooling. For each task queued in the thread pool (work items), the CLR assigns a thread from the pool (a worker thread) and then releases the thread back to the pool after the task is done.

Thread pools are always implemented by the CLR using a multithreaded apartment (MTA) model, which employs high performance queues and dispatchers through preemptive multitasking. CPU time is split into several time slices; in each time slice, a particular thread executes while other threads wait. After the time slice is exhausted, other threads are allowed to use the CPU based on the highest priority of the remaining threads. The client requests are queued in the task queue and each item in this queue is dispatched to the first available thread in the thread pool.

After the thread completes its assigned task, it returns to the pool and waits for the next assignment from the CLR. The thread pool's size can be fixed or dynamic. If fixed, the number of threads doesn't change during the lifetime of the pool. Normally, you should use this type of pool when you're sure of the amount of resources available to your application, so that a fixed number of threads can be created when the pool is initialized. For example a fixed pool would be used when developing solutions for an intranet or even in applications where you can tightly define the system requirements of the target platform. Dynamic pool sizes are employed when you don't know the amount of resources available, as in the case of a Web server that will not know the number of client requests it will be asked to handle simultaneously.

Glitches Involved in Thread Pooling

Without doubt, thread pooling offers a lot of advantages when building multithreaded applications, but you should avoid thread pooling in some situations. The following lists the drawbacks and situations in which you should avoid using thread pooling:

- The CLR assigns the threads from the thread pool to the tasks and releases them to the pool after the task is completed. There is no direct way to cancel a task after it has been added to the queue.

- A thread pool should not be used for extensive or long tasks. Thread pooling is instead an effective solution for situations in which tasks are short lived, such as a Web server satisfying the client requests for a particular file.

- Thread pooling is a technique to employ threads in a cost-efficient manner, where cost efficiency is defined in terms of quantity and startup overhead. Care should be exercised to determine the utilization of threads in the pool. The size of the thread pool should be fixed accordingly.

- All the threads in the thread pool are in MTAs. If you want to place your threads in a single thread apartment, then a thread pool is not the way to go.

- If you need to identify the thread and perform various operations, such as starting it, suspending it, and aborting it, then a thread pool is not the way to do it.

- It isn't possible to set priorities for tasks employing thread pooling.

- Only one thread pool can be associated with any given process.

- If the task assigned to a thread in the thread pool becomes locked, then the thread is never released back to the pool for reuse. These situations can be avoided by employing effective programmatic skills.

The Size of a Thread Pool

The .NET Framework provides the `ThreadPool` class located in the `System.Threading` namespace for using thread pools in your applications. The number of tasks that can be queued into a thread pool is limited by the amount of memory in your machine. Likewise, the number of threads that can be active in a process is limited by the number of CPUs in your machine because, as you already know, each processor can only actively execute one thread at a time. By default, each thread in the thread pool uses the default task and runs at default priority in an MTA. The word default seems to be used rather vaguely here. That is no accident. Each system can have default priorities set differently. If, at any time, one of the threads is idle, then the thread pool will induce worker threads to keep all processors busy. If all the threads in the pool are busy and work is pending in the queue, then it will spawn new threads to complete the pending work. However, the number of threads created can't exceed the maximum number specified. By default, 25 thread pool threads can be created per processor. However, you can change this number by editing the CorSetMaxThreads member defined in the mscoree.h file. If additional threads are required, the requests are queued until some thread finishes its assigned task and returns to the pool. The .NET Framework uses thread pools for asynchronous calls, establishing socket connections and registered wait operations.

Exploring the ThreadPool Class

This section explores the various aspects of the ThreadPool class and shows how they can be employed to create thread pools in your .NET applications. The ThreadPool class provides a pool of threads that can be used for the following:

- Processing work items

- Processing asynchronous I/O calls

- Processing timers

- Waiting on behalf of other threads

The following table lists the methods of the ThreadPool class and their functionality.

Method Name	Functionality
BindHandle	This method binds the OS handle to the thread pool.
GetAvailableThreads	This method indicates the number of work items that can be added to the work items queue.
GetMaxThreads	This method indicates the number of requests that the thread pool can queue simultaneously.
QueueUserWorkItem	This method queues a work item to the thread pool.
RegisterWaitForSingleObject	This method registers a delegate that waits for a WaitHandle.
UnsafeQueueUserWorkItem	This is the unsafe version of the QueueUserWorkItem() method.
UnsafeRegisterWaitForSingleObject	This is the unsafe version of the RegisterWaitForSingleObject() method.

Of these methods, QueueUserWorkItem() and RegisterWaitForSingleObject() play the most important roles in thread pooling. Let's dig into the details of each method and consider both syntax and a sample call in VB .NET:

The BindHandle() method binds an OS handle to the thread pool:

```
Public Shared Function BindHandle(_
  ByVal osHandle As IntPtr) As Boolean
```

osHandle refers to the IntPtr type holding the OS handle. The return value is a Boolean where True indicates binding to the handle. This method throws a SecurityException if the caller does not have the required permission.

The GetAvailableThreads() method indicates the number of thread pool requests that can be added before reaching the maximum specified limit:

```
Public Shared Sub GetAvailableThreads( _
  ByRef workerThreads As Integer, _
  ByRef completionPortThreads As Integer)
```

workerThreads refers to the number of worker threads of the thread pool whereas completionPortThreads refers to the number of asynchronous I/O threads.

The GetMaxThreads() method returns the maximum number of concurrent requests that a thread pool can handle. Any requests above this limit are queued until some of the threads in the thread pool are freed up:

```
Public Shared Sub GetMaxThreads( _
  ByRef workerThreads As Integer, _
  ByRef completionPortThreads As Integer)
```

workerThreads refers to the number of worker threads of the thread pool whereas the completionPortThreads refers to the number of asynchronous I/O threads.

QueueUserWorkItem() is an overloaded method that queues a work item to the thread pool. It may be called in two forms. In the first form, the method queues the specified work item to the thread pool and calls the specified delegate associated with it:

```
Overloads Public Shared Function QueueUserWorkItem( _
  ByVal callBack As WaitCallback) As Boolean
```

Here callBack refers to the delegate to be invoked when the thread in the thread pool takes the work item. The return value true indicates the method succeeded and False indicates the method failed.

In the second form, the method queues the specified work item to the thread pool, invokes the specified delegate, and specifies the object to be passed to the delegate when the WorkItem is executed in the pool:

```
Overloads Public Shared Function QueueUserWorkItem( _
  ByVal callBack As WaitCallback, _
  ByVal state As Object) As Boolean
```

callBack refers to the delegate to be invoked when the thread in the thread pool services the work item, whereas state refers to the object containing the state that is being passed to the delegate when the servicing of the work item occurs. The return value True indicates the method succeeded and False indicates that the method failed.

RegisterWaitForSingleObject() is also an overloaded method. It registers a delegate that waits for a WaitHandle. This class encapsulates all the objects of the OS that wait for exclusive access to shared resources.

The method takes the following four forms. In the first form, the method registers a delegate and waits for the WaitHandle indicated by the timeout in milliseconds, which is given by a 32-bit signed integer. This overloaded form of the method has the following syntax in VB .NET:

```
Overloads Public Shared Function _
  RegisterWaitForSingleObject( _
  ByVal waitObject As WaitHandle, _
```

```
ByVal callBack As WaitOrTimerCallback, _
ByVal state As Object, _
ByVal millisecondsTimeOutInterval As Integer, _
ByVal executeOnlyOnce As Boolean) _
As  RegisteredWaitHandle
```

In the preceding syntax, the waitObject refers to the WaitHandle and the callBack refers to the WaitOrTimerCallback delegate to be invoked. The state parameter refers to the Object to be passed to the delegate. The millisecondsTimeOutInterval parameter refers to the timeout in milliseconds; if the timeout value is 0, then the function tests the object state and returns immediately; however, if the value is -1 the function waits forever. The executeOnlyOnce parameter indicates whether the thread has to wait on the waitObject parameter after the delegate has been invoked. The RegisteredWaitHandle parameter encapsulates the native handle.

This method throws an ArgumentOutOfRangeException if the millisecondsTimeOutInterval parameter is less than -1.

In the second form, the method does the same thing as specified in the first form but waits for the WaitHandle indicated by timeout in milliseconds that is given by the 32-bit unsigned integer. This overloaded form of the method has the following syntax:

```
Overloads Public Shared Function _
  RegisterWaitForSingleObject( _
  ByVal waitObject As WaitHandle, _
  ByVal callBack As WaitOrTimerCallback, _
  ByVal state As Object, _
  ByVal millisecondsTimeOutInterval As Long, _
  ByVal executeOnlyOnce As Boolean) As
RegisteredWaitHandle
```

In the third form, the method waits for the WaitHandle indicated by the timeout given by the TimeSpan value. This overloaded form of the method has the following syntax:

```
Overloads Public Shared Function _
  RegisterWaitForSingleObject( _
  ByVal waitObject As WaitHandle, _
  ByVal callBack As WaitOrTimerCallback, _
  ByVal state As Object, _
  ByVal timeout As TimeSpan, _
  ByVal executeOnlyOnce As Boolean) _
  As RegisteredWaitHandle
```

In the fourth form, the timeout is given in milliseconds by an unsigned integer; this method is not CLS compliant as given by the following syntax:

```
Overloads Public Shared Function RegisterWaitForSingleObject( _
        ByVal waitObject As WaitHandle, _
        ByVal callBack As WaitOrTimerCallback, _
        ByVal state As Object, _
        ByVal millisecondsTimeOutInterval As UInt32, _
        ByVal executeOnlyOnce As Boolean) As RegisteredWaitHandle
```

The `UnsafeQueueUserWorkItem()` method is the unsafe version of the `QueueUserWorkItem()` method and hence does not propagate the calling stack to the worker thread. This means that the code can lose the calling stack and, in doing so, elevate its security privileges. It has the following syntax:

```
Public Shared Function UnsafeQueueUserWorkItem( _
  ByVal callBack As WaitCallback, _
  ByVal state As Object) As Boolean
```

The `UnsafeRegisterWaitForSingleObject()` method is the unsafe version of the `RegisterWaitForSingleObject()` method and takes the following four forms:

```
Overloads Public Shared Function _
  UnsafeRegisterWaitForSingleObject( _
    WaitHandle, WaitOrTimerCallback, Object, Long, _
    Boolean) As RegisteredWaitHandle

Overloads Public Shared Function _
  UnsafeRegisterWaitForSingleObject( _
    WaitHandle, WaitOrTimerCallback, Object, Long, _
    Boolean) As RegisteredWaitHandle

Overloads Public Shared Function _
  UnsafeRegisterWaitForSingleObject( WaitHandle, _
    WaitOrTimerCallback, Object, TimeSpan, _
    Boolean) As RegisteredWaitHandle

Overloads Public Shared Function _
  UnsafeRegisterWaitForSingleObject( WaitHandle, _
    WaitOrTimerCallback, Object, UInt32, _
    Boolean) As RegisteredWaitHandle
```

Programming the Thread Pool in VB .NET

The previous sections of the chapter dealt with theoretical aspects of using thread pools in the .NET Framework. Now it's time to cover the programmatic aspects of creating and using thread pools in .NET applications from a VB .NET perspective. As described in the previous section, the `System.Threading` namespace contains the `ThreadPool` class that you can use to create a thread pool in .NET applications.

Before we start coding, you need to know three important rules concerning the `ThreadPool` class:

- There can be only one working thread per `ThreadPool` object.

- There can be only one `ThreadPool` object per process.

- A `ThreadPool` object is created for the first time when you call the `ThreadPool.QueueUserWorkItem()` method, or when a callback method is called through a timer or registered wait operation.

One common use of the `ThreadPool` class is to start many separate tasks without setting the properties of each thread. The following console example (ThreadModule.vb) shows how to add the tasks to a queue and how a `ThreadPool` object assigns the threads for each task currently waiting:

```
Imports System
Imports System.Threading

Module ThreadModule
  Public Sub longtask1(ByVal obj As Object)
    Dim i As Integer
    For i = 0 To 999
      Console.WriteLine( _
        "Long Task 1 is being executed")
    Next
  End Sub

  Public Sub longtask2(ByVal obj As Object)
    Dim i As Integer
    For i = 0 To 999
      Console.WriteLine( _
        "Long Task 2 is being executed")
    Next
  End Sub

  Sub Main()
    Dim thrPool As ThreadPool
    thrPool.QueueUserWorkItem( _
      New WaitCallback(AddressOf longtask1))
    thrPool.QueueUserWorkItem( _
      New WaitCallback(AddressOf longtask2))
    Console.Read()
  End Sub
End Module
```

Let's dissect the preceding example. It comprises two separate tasks called `longtask1` and `longtask2` that do the simple job of outputting a message to the console in a loop. A `ThreadPool` class can be employed to start these two tasks without setting the properties of threads for each individual task by passing the delegate of the procedure to the `WaitCallback()` method, as given by the following block of code:

```
Dim thrPool As ThreadPool
thrPool.QueueUserWorkItem( _
  New WaitCallback(AddressOf longtask1))
thrPool.QueueUserWorkItem( _
  New WaitCallback(AddressOf longtask2))
```

The example also has a `Console.Read()` statement that holds the input on the console until the user presses the Enter key (or any other key).

The next example (ThreadAppModule.vb) shows how to pass and return values from a thread in a thread pool. Note that only Sub procedures can be queued to a ThreadPool, hence we cannot return values directly, as in the case of functions. However, we can wrap up all these parameters into a class and pass an instance of that class as an argument to the QueueUserWorkItem() method:

```vb
Imports System
Imports System.Threading

Friend Class ObjState
   Friend inarg1 As String
   Friend inarg2 As String
   Friend outval As String
End Class

Module ThreadAppModule
   Sub Task1(ByVal StateObj As Object)
      Dim StObj As ObjState
      'cast the parameter object to the type ObjState
      StObj = CType(StateObj, ObjState)
      Console.WriteLine( _
         "Input Argument 1 in task 1:{0}", StObj.inarg1)
      Console.WriteLine( _
         "Input Argument 2 in task 1:{0}", StObj.inarg2)
      'The class variables can be employed
      'for returning values
      StObj.outval = "From Task1 {0} {1}", _
         StObj.inarg1, StObj.inarg2
   End Sub

   Sub Task2(ByVal StateObj As Object)
      Dim StObj As ObjState
      'cast the parameter object to the type ObjState
      StObj = CType(StateObj, ObjState)
      Console.WriteLine( _
         "Input Argument 1 in task 2:{0}", StObj.inarg1)
      Console.WriteLine( _
         "Input Argument 2 in task 2:{0}", StObj.inarg2)
      'The class variables can be employed for
      'returning values
      StObj.outval = String.Format("From Task2 {0} {1}", _
         StObj.inarg1, StObj.inarg2)
   End Sub

   Sub Main()
      Dim TPool As System.Threading.ThreadPool
      Dim StObj1 As New ObjState()
      Dim StObj2 As New ObjState()
      ' Set some fields that act like parameters in
      ' the state object.
```

```
    StObj1.inarg1 = "String Param1 of task 1"
    StObj1.inarg2 = "String Param2 of task 1"
    StObj2.inarg1 = "String Param1 of task 2"
    StObj2.inarg2 = "String Param2 of task 2"

    ' Queue a task
    TPool.QueueUserWorkItem( _
      New System.Threading.WaitCallback _
      (AddressOf Task1), StObj1)
    ' Queue another task
    TPool.QueueUserWorkItem( _
      New System.Threading.WaitCallback _
      (AddressOf Task2), StObj2)
    Console.Read()
  End Sub

End Module
```

The output from ThreadAppModule is

```
Input Argument 1 in task 1: String Param1 of task 1
Input Argument 2 in task 1: String Param2 of task 1
Input Argument 1 in task 2: String Param1 of task 2
Input Argument 2 in task 2: String Param2 of task 2
```

Let's explore the preceding example step by step. This example is similar to the previous example except for the passing of an object; we are passing the input and output parameters to tasks queued in the thread pool using the ObjState object.

The ObjState object contains two input parameters and one output parameter, all of type String, as given by the following code block:

```
Friend Class ObjState
  Friend inarg1 As String
  Friend inarg2 As String
  Friend outval As String
End Class
```

Next we define two procedures task1 and task2 and pass an instance of ObjState as a parameter to each of them. The procedures task1 and task2 concatenate the values of input parameters inarg1 and inarg2 of passed ObjState object and store the result in the outval class variable. This is given by the following code block:

```
  Sub Task1(ByVal StateObj As Object)
    Dim StObj As ObjState
    'cast the parameter object to the type ObjState
    StObj = CType(StateObj, ObjState)
    Console.WriteLine( _
      "Input Argument 1 in task1 {0}", StObj.inarg1)
    Console.WriteLine( _
      "Input Argument 2 in task1 {0}", StObj.inarg2)
```

```vbnet
    'The class variables can be employed for
    'returning values
    StObj.outval = "From Task1 {)} {1}", _
        StObj.inarg1, StObj.inarg2
End Sub

Sub Task2(ByVal StateObj As Object)
    Dim StObj As ObjState
    'cast the parameter object to the type ObjState
    StObj = CType(StateObj, ObjState)
    Console.WriteLine( _
        "Input Argument 1 in task 2 {0}", StObj.inarg1)
    Console.WriteLine( _
        "Input Argument 2 in task2 {0}", StObj.inarg2)
    'The class variables can be employed for
    'returning values
    StObj.outval = String.Format("From Task2 {0} {1}", _
        StObj.inarg1, StObj.inarg2)
End Sub
```

In the Sub Main() method, we queue these two tasks in the thread pool employing the QueueUserWorkItem() method of the ThreadPool class, as given by the following code block:

```vbnet
Sub Main()
    Dim thrPool As ThreadPool
    thrPool.QueueUserWorkItem( _
        New WaitCallback(AddressOf longtask1))
    thrPool.QueueUserWorkItem( _
        New WaitCallback(AddressOf longtask2))
    Console.Read()
End Sub
```

We can also queue work items that have wait operations involved with them to the thread pool by employing the RegisterWaitForSingleObject() to which WaitHandle is passed as an argument. This WaitHandle signals the method wrapped in a WaitOrTimerCallback delegate. In this case, the thread pool creates a background thread to invoke the callback method. The following example (vbThreadPool.vb) demonstrates this concept:

```vbnet
Imports System
Imports System.Threading

Public Class vbThreadPool
    Private Shared i As Integer = 0

    Public Shared Sub Main()
        Dim arev As New AutoResetEvent(False)
        ThreadPool.RegisterWaitForSingleObject(arev, _
            New WaitOrTimerCallback(AddressOf workitem), _
            Nothing, 2000, False)
```

```vbnet
    arev.Set()
    Console.Read()
  End Sub

  Public Shared Sub workitem(ByVal O As Object, _
    ByVal signaled As Boolean)
    i += 1
    Console.WriteLine( _
      "Thread Pool Work Item Invoked: {0}", i)
  End Sub
End Class
```

The output from the preceding example is something like the following:

```
Thread Pool Work Item Invoked: 1
Thread Pool Work Item Invoked: 2
Thread Pool Work Item Invoked: 3
Thread Pool Work Item Invoked: 4
.....
```

The output continues with a new line printed every 2 seconds and the value of i incremented by one until the user presses the Enter key to invoke the Console.Read() statement.

To start, an AutoResetEvent object called arev is created to signal the execution of queued work items:

```vbnet
Dim arev As New AutoResetEvent(False)
```

We invoke the RegisterWaitForSingleObject() method, which registers a delegate and signals the work item at the specified time interval. In our example, the interval is set to 2 seconds as given by the following piece of code:

```vbnet
ThreadPool.RegisterWaitForSingleObject(arev, _
  New WaitOrTimerCallback(AddressOf workitem), _
  Nothing, 2000, False)
```

To raise the event, we need to use the set() method of the AutoResetEvent object:

```vbnet
arev.Set()
```

This example concludes the practical session on using thread pools in VB .NET applications. The next section examines scalability and builds a thread pool manager application.

Scalability in .NET

If you have a multiprocessor system, then you'll see threads really show their worth. The Windows OS manages the allocation of threads to processors and, as you have seen throughout this book, firing any process automatically starts a thread. The .NET Framework does not provide fine-grained control of the processor allocation, preferring to allow the OS to control the scheduling, as it will have more information on the loading of the processors than the CLR would. The .NET Framework does, however, provide some control over which processor an entire process runs on. However, this applies to **all** of its threads, so its use is not applicable to this book.

If you have only one thread, the main thread, then every task within that thread will operate on the same processor. However, if a new thread is fired, then the OS schedules which processor it should be executed on. This decision as to which processor will run the thread consumes some processor resources, so for small tasks, it isn't generally worthwhile because the time to execute may be as long as the time it takes for the OS to allocate the task to a processor. However, this allocation has been taking less and less time in successive versions of Windows, so for anything other than the most trivial of tasks (when using threads), you should get a performance improvement by creating a new thread to execute your task. However, the benefits of threading are really shown in symmetric multiprocessor (SMP) systems in which the processors can be used to their full effect to distribute the load of the application.

The next section describes how to create a thread pool manager with which you can create and manage threads. This manager ensures that a maximum and minimum number of threads exist in a pool and that idle threads get reused.

A Thread Pool Manager

Throughout this book, you've seen different ways of creating threads; in this chapter, we've described the `ThreadPool` class to make use of the OS's own thread pool for short-lived threads. You can implement a halfway house between the two, however, by creating a class that keeps a pool of a specified number of threads to be supplied to any requesting application. This enables the threads to be managed more easily by your code, and allows for faster thread execution as you might be able to use a previously instantiated thread object. This class draws together much of the knowledge acquired so far, and you'll be able to use it in your own multithreaded applications. We will explain this class as we go along, and at the end provide an application to test that this assembly is working as expected.

So, let's get started by explaining the code of the thread pool manager contained in a file named `ThreadPool.vb`:

```
Imports System
Imports System.Collections
Imports System.Threading
Imports System.Text
Imports Microsoft.VisualBasic

Namespace GenThreadPool
```

The preceding declarations show that the only additional external assembly needed is `System.dll`. The `GenThreadPool` namespace is defined to contain all the relevant classes for this project. Next the interface called `IThreadPool` that will be used for the `GenThreadPoolImpl` class is shown:

```
Public Interface IThreadPool
    Sub AddJob(jobToRun As System.Threading.Thread)
    Function GetStats() As Stats
End Interface
```

This defines two methods for the thread pool, `AddJob()` and `GetStats()`, which will be detailed in the following definitions of the `GenThreadPoolImpl` class, which generates the thread pool that we will be using:

```
Public Class GenThreadPoolImpl
  Implements IThreadPool
  Private m_maxThreads As Integer
  Private m_minThreads As Integer
  Private m_maxIdleTime As Integer
  Private Shared m_debug As Boolean
  Private m_pendingJobs As ArrayList
  Private m_availableThreads As ArrayList
  Public Property PendingJobs As ArrayList
    Get
      Return m_pendingJobs
    End Get
    Set
      m_pendingJobs = value
    End Set
  End Property

  Public Property AvailableThreads As ArrayList
    Get
      Return m_availableThreads
    End Get
    Set
      m_availableThreads = value
    End Set
  End Property

  Public Property Debug() As Boolean
    Get
      Return m_debug
    End Get
    Set
      Me.m_debug = value
    End Set
  End Property

  Public Property MaxIdleTime() As Integer
    Get
      Return Me.m_maxIdleTime
    End Get
    Set
      Me.m_maxIdleTime = value
    End Set
  End Property

  Public Property MaxThreads() As Integer
    Get
      Return Me.m_maxThreads
    End Get
```

```
      Set
        Me.m_maxThreads = value
      End Set
    End Property

    Public Property MinThreads() As Integer
      Get
        Return Me.m_minThreads
      End Get
      Set
        Me.m_minThreads = value
      End Set
    End Property
```

This class implements the `IThreadPool` interface, which we defined earlier, and then goes on to define a few `Private` fields. The properties are just wrappers around the relevant `Private` members to prevent users from altering the values directly, in case further rules need to be added later. The fields `m_maxThreads`, `m_minThreads`, and `m_maxIdleTime` specify the maximum and minimum number of threads in the pool, and how long in milliseconds to allow a thread to become idle before removing it from the pool. There are three constructors for this class:

```
Public Sub New()
  m_maxThreads = 1
  m_minThreads = 0
  m_maxIdleTime = 300
  Me.m_pendingJobs = ArrayList.Synchronized( _
    New ArrayList())
  Me.m_availableThreads = ArrayList.Synchronized( _
    New ArrayList())
  m_debug = False
End Sub
```

The default constructor only permits one thread to be present in the pool, and destroys it after only 0.3 seconds. It also performs some lazy initialization, creating an array list to contain the jobs awaiting a thread, and the threads not yet allocated to a method call. The `m_debug` flag, when set to `True`, would allow further debugging information while testing:

```
Public Sub New( _
  maxThreads As Integer, minThreads As Integer, _
  maxIdleTime As Integer)
  m_maxThreads = maxThreads
  m_minThreads = minThreads
  m_maxIdleTime = maxIdleTime
  Me.m_pendingJobs = ArrayList.Synchronized( _
    New ArrayList())
  Me.m_availableThreads = ArrayList.Synchronized( _
    New ArrayList())
  m_debug = False
  InitAvailableThreads()
End Sub
```

When a `GenThreadPoolImpl` class is instantiated with three integers, we specify the minimum and maximum number of threads, and the idle time of the threads. It also fires off the `InitAvailableThreads()` method, detailed here:

```
Private Sub InitAvailableThreads()
If Me.m_maxThreads > 0 Then
  Dim i As Integer
  For i = 1 To (Me.m_maxThreads)
    Dim t As New Thread( _
      AddressOf (New GenPool(Me, Me)).run)
    Dim e As New ThreadElement(t)
    e.Idle = True
    Me.m_availableThreads.Add(e)
  Next
End If

End Sub
```

This creates the threads needed for the pool on instantiation. The default constructor only specified one thread, so it wasn't necessary before. This cycles through, creating the maximum amount of threads allowed by the pool, specified in m_maxThreads. Following is the constructor for four arguments:

```
Public Sub New(maxThreads As Integer, _
  minThreads As Integer, maxIdleTime As Integer, _
  debug_ As Boolean)
m_maxThreads = maxThreads
m_minThreads = minThreads
m_maxIdleTime = maxIdleTime
Me.m_pendingJobs = ArrayList.Synchronized( _
  New ArrayList())
Me.m_availableThreads = ArrayList.Synchronized( _
  New ArrayList())
Me.m_debug = debug_
InitAvailableThreads()
End Sub
```

This constructor does the same as the previous one, except this one allows us to set the debugging flag. The business end of this class is the `AddJob()` method:

```
Public Sub AddJob(job As Thread) _
  Implements IThreadPool.AddJob
  If job Is Nothing Then
    Return
  End If
  SyncLock Me
```

This subroutine actually adds a job to the pool. If the job passed as a parameter is nonexistent, then it exits the method. Otherwise, it provides a lock on the `GenThreadPoolImpl` instance to ensure that no other thread or process can add or remove a job:

```
m_pendingJobs.Add(job)
Dim index As Integer = FindFirstIdleThread()

If Me.m_debug Then
  Console.WriteLine( _
    "First Idle Thread is {0}",     index)
End If
If index = - 1 Then
  If m_maxThreads = - 1 Or _
    m_availableThreads.Count < m_maxThreads Then
    If Me.m_debug Then
      Console.WriteLine("Creating a new thread")
    End If

    Dim t As New Thread( _
      AddressOf (New GenPool(Me, Me)).Run)
```

The job is added to an `ArrayList`, which stores all the jobs awaiting execution and completion. The `FindFirstIdleThread()` function returns the index of a thread contained within `m_availableThreads` that is currently idle and so available for use. If the function returns -1, then there are no idle threads and the pool needs to attempt to create a new one. The `Run()` method of the `GenPool` class is fired inside this thread:

```
    Dim e As New ThreadElement(t)

    e.Idle = False
    e.GetMyThread().Start()
    Try
      m_availableThreads.Add(e)
    Catch ex As OutOfMemoryException
      Console.WriteLine("Out of memory: {0}", ex)
      Thread.Sleep(3000)
      m_availableThreads.Add(e)
      Console.WriteLine("Added Job again")
    End Try
    Return
  End If
If Me.m_debug Then
  Console.WriteLine( _
    "No Threads Available...{0}",  Me.GetStats())
End If
```

The `ThreadElement` class is another helper class (defined later) that adds some additional properties to a standard thread so that the pool can manage it effectively. The thread's `Start()` method is fired before it's added to the `m_availableThreads` collection:

```
Else
  Try
    If Me.m_debug Then
      Console.WriteLine( _
        "Using an existing thread...")
```

```
        End If
          CType(m_availableThreads(index), _
            ThreadElement).Idle = False
```

In the preceding code, we start to detail the condition whereby a thread is deemed idle and therefore free for allocation to a new job. First, we convert the thread explicitly into a `ThreadElement` and change its idle flag:

```
SyncLock CType(m_availableThreads(index), _
  ThreadElement).GetMyThread()
  Monitor.Pulse(CType(m_availableThreads(index), _
    ThreadElement).GetMyThread())
End SyncLock
```

Here we lock the thread so that it cannot be affected by any other process. We then alert all waiting threads that it is now available for use, so we issue a `Monitor.Pulse()` instruction, and then release the lock:

```
        Catch ex As Exception
          Console.WriteLine( _
            "Error while reusing thread {0}", _
          ex.Message)
          If Me.m_debug Then
            Console.WriteLine( _
              "Value of index is ", index)
            Console.WriteLine( _
              "Size of available threads is {0}", _
              Me.m_availableThreads.Count)
            Console.WriteLine( _
              "Available Threads is {0}", _
              Me.m_availableThreads.IsSynchronized)
          End If
        End Try
      End If
  End SyncLock
End Sub
```

Finally, we catch any exceptions and output the results to the command line, providing more useful debugging information if the `Me.Debug` flag has been set, which completes the `AddJob()` method.

Now let's look at the implementation of the `GetStats()` function:

```
Public Function GetStats() As Stats _
  Implements IThreadPool.GetStats
  Dim statsInstance As New Stats()
  statsInstance.MaxThreads = m_maxThreads
  statsInstance.MinThreads = m_minThreads
  statsInstance.MaxIdleTime = m_maxIdleTime
  statsInstance.PendingJobs = m_pendingJobs.Count
  statsInstance.NumThreads = m_availableThreads.Count
```

```
    statsInstance.JobsInProgress = _
       m_availableThreads.Count - FindIdleThreadCount()
    Return statsInstance
End Function
```

The `GetStats()` function returns a `Stats()` structure (defined later), which contains the minimum and maximum number of threads, as well as other values set in the constructor. Now let's look at the `FindIdleThreadCount()` function:

```
Public Function FindIdleThreadCount() As Integer
    Dim idleThreads As Integer = 0
    Dim i As Integer

    For i = 0 To m_availableThreads.Count - 1
      ' Check for ThreadElements that have their Idle
      ' Property true
      If CType(m_availableThreads(i), _
        ThreadElement).Idle Then
            idleThreads += 1
      End If
    Next
    Return idleThreads
End Function
```

This function was called earlier in the class and it simply goes through the array list of threads and returns how many of them are idle. We also used the `FindFirstIdleThread()` function:

```
Public Function FindFirstIdleThread() As Integer
    Dim i As Integer
    For i = 0 To m_availableThreads.Count - 1
      If CType(m_availableThreads(i), _
        ThreadElement).Idle Then
        Return i
      End If
    Next

    Return - 1
End Function
```

As you can see, the function returns the index of the first idle thread in the array list. We'll also need the following function:

```
Public Function FindThread() As Integer
    Dim i As Integer
    For i = 0 To m_availableThreads.Count - 1
      If CType(m_availableThreads(i), _
        ThreadElement).GetMyThread().Equals( _
          Thread.CurrentThread) Then
        Return i
      End If
```

```
      Next
      Return - 1
End Function
```

This method is used to determine in which index position in the array list the current thread is located. We'll also need the following method:

```
    Public Sub RemoveThread()
      Dim i As Integer
      For i = 0 To m_availableThreads.Count - 1
        If CType(m_availableThreads(i), _
          ThreadElement).GetMyThread().Equals( _
          Thread.CurrentThread) Then
            m_availableThreads.RemoveAt(i)
          Exit Sub
        End If
      Next
    End Sub
End Class
```

This removes the current thread from the array list of threads. This is, of course, used to remove a thread from the pool when it is finished and has been idle for longer than the time specified in Me.MaxIdleTime. Now we start to define the rest of the classes for this assembly:

```
Public Class GenPool
    Private m_lock As [Object]
    Private m_gn As GenThreadPoolImpl

    Public Sub New(lock_ As [Object], _
      gn As GenThreadPoolImpl)
      Me.m_lock = lock_
      Me.m_gn = gn
    End Sub
```

The GenPool class executes all the pending threads, and then removes them from the pool after the threads are complete and the period specified in idle time has elapsed. It checks to see whether any threads are available on the GenThreadPoolImpl passed as a reference to the constructor, and locks the values of the object passed as the first parameter. In general, this will be the same GenThreadPoolImpl object passed as the second argument:

```
Public Sub Run()
  Dim job As Thread
  While True
    While True
      SyncLock Me.m_lock
        If m_gn.PendingJobs.Count = 0 Then
          Dim index As Integer = m_gn.FindThread()
          If index = - 1 Then
            Exit Sub
          End If
```

```
            CType(m_gn.AvailableThreads(index), _
              ThreadElement).Idle = True
            Exit While
          End If
          job = CType(m_gn.PendingJobs(0), Thread)
          m_gn.PendingJobs.RemoveAt(0)
        End SyncLock
```

This `Run()` method starts a loop to attempt to find a thread in the pool that matches the current thread, and begin its execution. You can see in the preceding code that it locks the object passed in as a parameter to the constructor, and if there are no pending jobs, it just finds a thread in the pool that matches the current one, returning -1 if there isn't one. If there is a pending job, then the method retrieves the first one, and removes it from the queue.

```
        'run the job
        job.Start()
      End While
```

It then begins executing the method on the pending thread, and returns to the start of the loop:

```
      Try
        SyncLock Me
          If m_gn.MaxIdleTime = - 1 Then
            Monitor.Wait(Me)
          Else
            Monitor.Wait(Me, m_gn.MaxIdleTime)
          End If
        End SyncLock
      Catch

      End Try
```

In the next part of the loop (after it has no more pending jobs), the method locks the current object and waits for the thread to be free for execution for the period specified in `MaxIdleTime`:

```
      SyncLock m_lock
        If m_gn.PendingJobs.Count = 0 Then
          If m_gn.MinThreads <> - 1 And _
          m_gn.AvailableThreads.Count _
            > m_gn.MinThreads Then
            m_gn.RemoveThread()
            Return
          End If
        End If
      End SyncLock
    End While
  End Sub
End Class
```

Finally, it locks the object again, and if there are no pending jobs and there are more than the minimum required number of threads, then it removes the thread from the pool.

We now move on to the `ThreadElement` class:

```vb
Public Class ThreadElement
  Private m_idle As Boolean
  Private m_thread As Thread

  Public Sub New(th As Thread)
    Me.m_thread = th
    Me.m_idle = True
  End Sub
```

A `ThreadElement` is stored in the thread pool, and takes a thread as the parameter for its constructor. It sets the thread as idle on construction of this object:

```vb
  Public Property Idle() As Boolean
    Get
      Return Me.m_idle
    End Get
    Set
      Me.m_idle = value
    End Set
  End Property

  Public Function GetMyThread() As Thread
    Return Me.m_thread
  End Function
End Class
```

The preceding code is straightforward. The `Idle` property essentially defines when the thread's execution is complete, and the `GetMyThread()` method just returns the `Thread` object. Now look at the following structure:

```vb
Public Structure Stats
  Public MaxThreads As Integer
  Public MinThreads As Integer
  Public MaxIdleTime As Integer
  Public NumThreads As Integer
  Public PendingJobs As Integer
  Public JobsInProgress As Integer
```

Here we define the `Stats` structure that was mentioned earlier, which stores all the statistics of the thread pool. The fields are self-describing. `ToString()` is the only method:

```vb
  Public Overrides Function ToString() As String
    Dim lf as string = ControlChars.Lf
    Dim sb As New StringBuilder("MaxThreads = ")
    sb.Append(MaxThreads)
    sb.AppendFormat("{0}MinThreads = {1}", _
        lf, MinThreads)
    sb.AppendFormat("{0}MaxIdleTime = {1}", _
        lf, MaxIdleTime)
    sb.AppendFormat("{0}Pending Jobs = {1}", _
        lf, PendingJobs)
```

```
        sb.AppendFormat("{0}Jobs In Progress = {1}", _
            lf, JobsInProgress)
        Return sb.ToString()
      End Function
    End Structure
End Namespace
```

This `ToString()` method returns the structure in a string format using `StringBuilder` to build up the string. The 107 argument initiates the `StringBuilder`'s size to 107 characters, as it's fair to assume that there won't likely be more than 99,999 threads. If so, then `StringBuilder` resizes itself anyway. This capacity specification allows a small performance boost.

If you have an application that is firing methods repeatedly on different threads, this class can manage the process and help ensure that too many threads aren't spawned. Apart from containing a maximum and minimum number of threads, it also reuses existing threads if possible. You can now compile this project into a DLL, and use this class from within other projects. The following code (TestGenThreadPool.vb) allows you to test this thread pool class:

```
Imports System
Imports System.Threading
Imports GenThreadPool

Namespace TestGenThreadPool
  Public Class TestPerformance
    Public count As Integer
    Private m_lock As New [Object]()
    Public Sub New(pool As IThreadPool, _
      times As Integer)
      Console.WriteLine( _
        "Performance using Pool[in ms]: ")
      count = 0
      Dim start As Long = _
        System.DateTime.Now.Millisecond

      Console.WriteLine( _
        "Start Time for Job is {0}", _
        System.DateTime.Now)

      Dim i As Integer
      For i = 0 To times - 1
        Dim tl As New Thread( _
          AddressOf (New Job(Me)).Run)
        pool.AddJob(tl)
      Next
      While True
        SyncLock m_lock
          If count = times Then
            Exit While
          End If
        End SyncLock
```

```vb
      Try
        Thread.Sleep(5000)
      Catch
      End Try
    End While

    Console.WriteLine("{0}", _
      (System.DateTime.Now.Millisecond - start))
    Console.WriteLine( _
      "End Time for Job is {0}", _
      System.DateTime.Now)
      Console.WriteLine( _
        "Performance using no Pool[in ms]: ")
    count = 0
    start = System.DateTime.Now.Millisecond
    Console.WriteLine( _
      "Start Time for JobThread is {0}", _
      System.DateTime.Now)
    For i = 0 To times - 1
      Dim jt As New Thread( _
        AddressOf (New JobThread(Me)).Run)
      jt.Start()
    Next

    While True
      SyncLock m_lock
        If count = times Then
          Exit While
        End If
      End SyncLock
      Try
        Thread.Sleep(5000)
      Catch
      End Try
    End While
    Console.WriteLine("{0}", _
      (System.DateTime.Now.Millisecond - start))
    Console.WriteLine( _
      "End Time for JobThread is {0}", _
      System.DateTime.Now)
  End Sub
NotInheritable Class JobThread
  Private m_lock As New [Object]()
  Private tpf As TestPerformance
  Public Sub New(tpf_ As TestPerformance)
    Me.tpf = tpf_
  End Sub
```

```vbnet
      Public Sub Run()
        SyncLock m_lock
          tpf.count += 1
        End SyncLock
      End Sub
    End Class

    NotInheritable Class Job
      Private m_lock As New Object()
      Private tpf As TestPerformance
      Public Sub New(tpf_ As TestPerformance)
        Me.tpf = tpf_
      End Sub 'New
      Public Sub Run()
        SyncLock m_lock
          tpf.count += 1
        End SyncLock
      End Sub
    End Class
  End Class

  Class TestPool
    Private Shared i As Integer = 0
    Private j As Integer = 0
    Public Sub Run()
      i += 1
      j = i
      Console.WriteLine( _
        "Value of i in run is {0} ", j)
    End Sub
    Public Shared Sub Main(args() As String)
      Dim tp = New _
        GenThreadPoolImpl(1000, 1000, 300, True)
      Dim i As Integer
      For i = 0 To 99
        Dim td1 As New TestPool()
        Dim t1 As New Thread(AddressOf td1.Run)
        Dim td2 As New TestPool()
        Dim t2 As New Thread(AddressOf td2.Run)
        Dim td3 As New TestPool()
        Dim t3 As New Thread(AddressOf td3.Run)
        Dim td4 As New TestPool()
        Dim t4 As New Thread(AddressOf td4.Run)
        Dim td5 As New TestPool()
        Dim t5 As New Thread(AddressOf td5.Run)
        Dim td6 As New TestPool()
        Dim t6 As New Thread(AddressOf td6.Run)
        Dim td7 As New TestPool()
        Dim t7 As New Thread(AddressOf td7.Run)
```

```
            Dim td8 As New TestPool()
            Dim t8 As New Thread(AddressOf td8.Run)
            Dim td9 As New TestPool()
            Dim t9 As New Thread(AddressOf td9.Run)
            Dim td10 As New TestPool()
            Dim t10 As New Thread(AddressOf td10.Run)
            Dim td11 As New TestPool()
            Dim t11 As New Thread(AddressOf td11.Run)
            tp.AddJob(t1)
            tp.AddJob(t2)
            tp.AddJob(t3)
            tp.AddJob(t4)
            tp.AddJob(t5)

            tp.AddJob(t6)
            tp.AddJob(t7)
            tp.AddJob(t8)
            tp.AddJob(t9)
            tp.AddJob(t10)
            tp.AddJob(t11)
        Next

        Dim td12 As New TestPool()
        Dim t12 As New Thread(AddressOf td12.Run)
        tp.AddJob(t12)

        Dim p As New TestPerformance(tp, 1000)
    End Sub
  End Class
End Namespace
```

The preceding class mechanically attempts to add new threads to an instance of the thread pool, with the debug flag set to true. The best way to see this thread pool in action is to try it out in your own applications. You can use this class, after it is compiled.

Summary

In this chapter, you saw how thread pooling can be used when a thread is required for a relatively short duration. Thread pooling allows thread recycling. A thread is assigned a task and when that task has completed, the thread returns to the pool and waits for the next assignment. We also covered the various aspects of using thread pools in .NET applications. You learned the definition of a thread pool and then why you might choose to use one in your applications. The chapter also covered the role of CLR in creating the thread pool followed by the glitches involved in using a thread pool.

We later covered some more scalability issues, as the `ThreadPool` class isn't suitable for applications that may need to fire a number of long-lived threads. We discussed the creation of a `ThreadPool` manager class and mentioned how SMP systems can dramatically increase the performance of an application if it is threaded.

CHAPTER 18

Debugging and Tracing Threads

Debugging and tracing are two techniques frequently, and often necessarily, employed by developers. Debugging allows a developer to analyze an application's variables and code, and step through the program's code flow. Tracing allows a developer to trace the behavior of an application, displaying information in a *listener* (a log file, the Windows event log, or similar). These techniques are fundamental to creating robust applications because they provide an easy way to monitor and understand how an application is working. The big difference between the two techniques is that tracing can be done during an application's runtime, whereas the debugger is used at designtime, before releasing the final version of the application. During recent years, developers have suffered from the lack of a debugger for ASP applications. To understand a variable's value, code's flow, and every common task usually performed, ASP developers often had to populate their code with `Response.Write()` statements, echoing messages such as `Entered in the function`, `Exited from the loop`, and so on. When the developer had finished testing the ASP application, he needed to remove all the undesired statements. That's not the best way to debug a program.

Fortunately, .NET brings the debugging functionality to the next generation of ASP developers by providing four useful classes: `Trace`, `Debug`, `BooleanSwitch`, and `TraceSwitch`. In addition, any .NET language can use these classes; also, every developer that chooses to use Visual Studio .NET to create applications can perform debugging operations using its visual tools.

The various tracing and debugging techniques are especially useful for applications that use threads. If implemented well, these techniques allow developers to trace each thread's behavior to discover any applications' anomalies, such as unexpected resource consumption, bugs, and so on.

In this chapter, we'll analyze both tracing and debugging aspects in the following order:

- Using Visual Studio .NET debug analysis and its powerful tools
- Using the .NET tracing classes to implement these features in code
- Putting it all together by creating an application that uses tracing

For this chapter, Visual Studio .NET is necessary to make use of much of the tracing and debugging features shown. However, you can achieve some tracing functionality by using the `/d:TRACE=TRUE` switch.

Creating the Application Code

Usually, when you create an application (or part of one), you write the code and then try to run the application. Sometimes it works as expected, often it doesn't. When it doesn't, you try to discover what could be happening by examining more carefully the code that you wrote. In this case, you can use the debugger by choosing some breakpoints to stop the application's execution near or just before the guilty function, and then step through lines of code, examining (perhaps modifying) variable values to understand precisely what went wrong. Finally, when all is working, you can build the release version (a version without debugging components) of your application, and distribute it. In this type of program, you need to insert the tracing functionalities during the development history. In fact, even if the program works very well, often something unexpected will happen (especially when some external, possibly third party, com ponents fail). In that case, if you have filled the code with tracing instructions, you can turn on tracing and examine the resulting log file to understand what happened. Tracing functionalities are also useful in discovering where an application consumes resources or where it spends too much time to perform a task. Always use tracing functionalities in applications that use threads because it can be difficult to observe each thread's behavior.

Tracing, debugging, and performance techniques are often known as *instrumentation*. This term refers to the capacity to monitor an application's performance, and diagnose errors and bugs. An application that supports instrumentation must include the following:

- **Debugging**: Fixing errors and bugs during an application's development.

- **Code tracing**: Receiving information in a listening device during an application's execution.

- **Performance counters**: Using techniques to monitor an application's performance.

Let's examine what the .NET Framework provides that will enable you to add instrumentation to your applications.

Debugging Your Code

Usually, when you test your application and see that it's behaving in unexpected ways, you start examining the code more carefully. If you're using Visual Studio .NET to create your application, it provides many amazing tools to visually debug the application. In addition, no matter which language you choose to develop your application in, it will use the same debugger with the same tools. Moreover, the basic debugger's functionalities have been inherited from the Visual Basic 6 and Visual C++ IDEs, resulting in something that should be intuitive for most developers. However, we won't spend too much time on the debugger in general, and will focus this discussion mostly on those features directly relevant to threading.

The new debugger provides the following:

- The same tool to debug different applications created using different languages

- The capability to debug SQL Server stored procedures

- The capability to debug .NET Framework and Win32 native code, so that if you are debugging your Visual Basic .NET application and your thread uses a COM+ component, you can debug both the applications using the same debugger

- A more powerful and enhanced remote debugger

If you already have experience with the Visual Basic 6 debugger, you know that some functionality has been removed. The most relevant is the ability to change the code and continue with its execution. Using the Visual Studio .NET debugger, this feature is no longer available because each modification to the code requires a new compilation.

In this section, we'll analyze the debugging tools provided by the Visual Studio .NET IDE that can be especially useful during the testing and error discovery phase of thread application development.

Visual Studio .NET Debugger

By using the Visual Studio .NET debugger, as you know, you can break the execution of your application at a specified point simply by inserting a breakpoint near the line of the code you want to inspect. When the application is suspended, the debugger provides many tools to examine variables content, edit their value, examine the memory and call stack, and more.

Configuring Debugger Parameters

To use the Visual Studio .NET debugger, you have to build the application using the Debug project's configuration. In that way, you'll fill the application with symbolic debugging information rather than optimize the code. When everything appears to work fine, you would release your application after recompiling the code, choosing the Release project's configuration, which removes debugging information and optimizes the code.

When a new debugger session begins, a lot of resources are loaded into the memory. In fact, the debugger fills the memory with the various code to allow you to debug unmanaged code, SQL Server stored procedures, and more. You should remove these features when you don't need them. You can change the debugger's settings inside the Property Pages dialog box. The following dialog box appears.

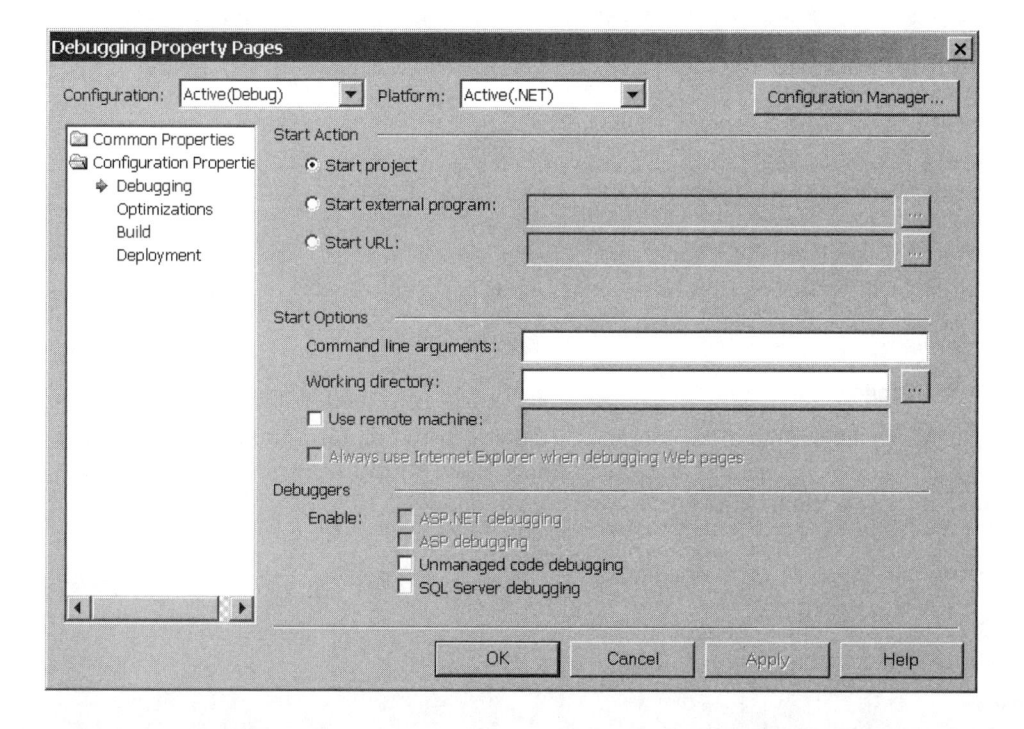

These configuration parameters are self explanatory, and not directly relevant to debugging threaded applications

After compiling a Debug configured project, the output directory contains the EXE or DLL file and a PDB (program database) file. Because IL (Intermediate Language) keeps the values of parameters and private members inside arrays, the original names of these variables are lost—as well as some other information relevant to debugging. When a project is compiled for debugging, or the /debug:full switch is used on the command-line compiler, a PDB file is generated at the same time. An absolute path pointing to the PDB file is contained within the EXE or DLL file. If the debugger doesn't find the program database file, it starts to search in the same application path and in the directory specified in the Property Pages dialog box. Finally, if the debugger can't find the PDB file in any directory, it generates a new one.

Using Debugger Tools

After you've loaded your project into Visual Studio .NET, you're ready to debug your application by pressing either the F10 or F11 key. If you aren't working with the release version of your application, you'll see the IDE showing many docked windows. During your debugging session, these windows will be filled with the variables' values, objects' dumps, call stack, disassembly code, and more. Let's start examining more closely these debugging tools, and how they can be used to assist in the debugging of your threaded application.

The Locals Window

This window allows you to examine and modify each variable's content defined locally in the function you are debugging. For example, debugging the following Main() method of TraceSwitchExample, you'll retrieve just the content of two variables: fs and t (see the following screenshot).

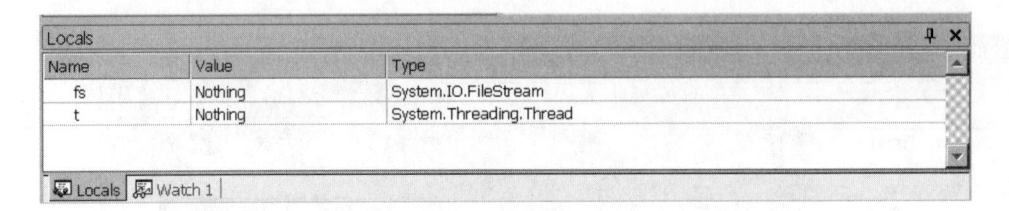

Name	Value	Type
fs	Nothing	System.IO.FileStream
t	Nothing	System.Threading.Thread

You can activate this window by selecting Debug ➤ Window ➤ Locals. Alternatively, you can press Ctrl+Alt+V, release those keys, and press L.

The Watch Window

You can drag variables from the source code, dropping them over this window to inspect their values and structure. In the following screenshot, a BooleanSwitch object (which you'll learn about in the next section) has been dropped into the window.

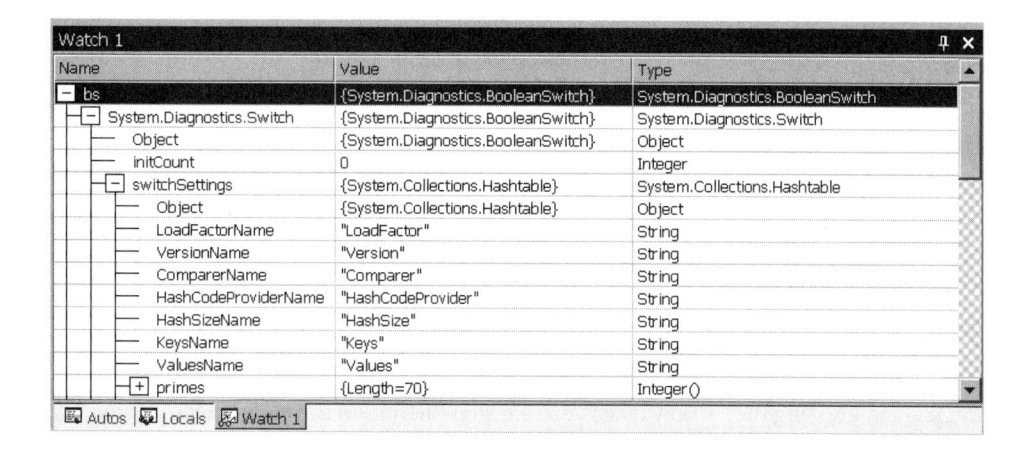

```
Watch 1                                                                    ᴨ ✕
Name                    Value                              Type
⊟ bs                    {System.Diagnostics.BooleanSwitch} System.Diagnostics.BooleanSwitch
  ⊟ System.Diagnostics.Switch {System.Diagnostics.BooleanSwitch} System.Diagnostics.Switch
      Object            {System.Diagnostics.BooleanSwitch} Object
      initCount         0                                  Integer
    ⊟ switchSettings    {System.Collections.Hashtable}     System.Collections.Hashtable
        Object          {System.Collections.Hashtable}     Object
        LoadFactorName  "LoadFactor"                       String
        VersionName     "Version"                          String
        ComparerName    "Comparer"                         String
        HashCodeProviderName "HashCodeProvider"            String
        HashSizeName    "HashSize"                         String
        KeysName        "Keys"                             String
        ValuesName      "Values"                           String
    ⊞ primes            {Length=70}                        Integer()
Autos | Locals | Watch 1
```

Expanding tree nodes by clicking the plus sign, you can examine and change object property values. You can activate up to four Watch windows by pressing Ctrl+Alt+W, releasing those keys, and pressing a key between 1 and 4.

Tip You can also add a variable to the Watch window by selecting it in the source code and choosing Add Watch from the context menu.

The Command Window – Immediate Window

This window provides a text field where you can query a variable's contents and change its values. When you need to retrieve the variable's content, you have to use a question mark before the expression. In the following screenshot, the Enabled property of the BooleanSwitch object has been examined, changed to False, and displayed again.

```
Command Window - Immediate                                                 ᴨ ✕
? bs.Enabled
True
bs.Enabled = false
? bs.Enabled
False
|
```

In addition, this window allows you to use various IDE commands, such as creating a new file, creating a new project, finding a string, and whatever else you can usually do within the Visual Studio .NET menu. To switch from Immediate mode to Command mode, you simply write the >cmd statement. After you are in Command mode, you'll be assisted by the IDE in finding the desired commands by the Intellisense functionality. To switch back to Immediate mode, the command is: >immed.

You can activate this window by selecting Debug ➤ Window ➤ Immediate, or you can press Ctrl+Alt+I.

Stepping Through the Code

Now that we've briefly described the more useful debug windows, we can focus our attention on code navigation. The Visual Studio .NET debugger allows developers to step between code lines, observing the program behavior at runtime. The debugger provides three different ways to step through the code:

- Step Into: Pressing the F11 key takes you through the code one step at a time, entering function bodies that you'll find on the way.
- Step Over: Pressing the F10 key takes you one step forward in the code, executing every function you encounter, but stepping over it (executing the function as one line).
- Step Out: Pressing Shift+F11 executes all the code within the function's body that you are currently stepped into.

Each time you step to the next line of code by pressing these keys, you are executing the highlighted code.

Note You cannot use the stepping features to step through a thread's execution. These are only relevant to see what the code is doing around the thread.

Another useful feature provided by the Visual Studio .NET debugger is the Run To Cursor functionality. Selecting it from the context menu over the source code, you can execute all the lines between the highlighted line and the line where the cursor is placed.

Finally, the Visual Studio .NET debugger provides a way to change the execution point of our application. You can decide to move your application's execution point by launching the debugger and choosing the Set Next Statement item in the context menu. Be careful when using this feature, because every line of code between the old and the new position will cease to be executed.

Setting Breakpoints

In large source code applications, you cannot easily step through all the code to get to the function you want to debug. The debugger enables you to set breakpoints in the code. The *breakpoint* is a point where the execution of your program is to be suspended. You can specify breakpoints both before and after launching the debugger session by placing the cursor on the line and pressing the F9 key. A red highlight appears on the line to signify that you've just added a breakpoint to the code, and a glyph is added to the left margin of the source window. To remove a breakpoint, you can either click on the glyph or press the F9 key again.

You can manage all the disseminated breakpoints from the Breakpoints window as shown in the following screenshot.

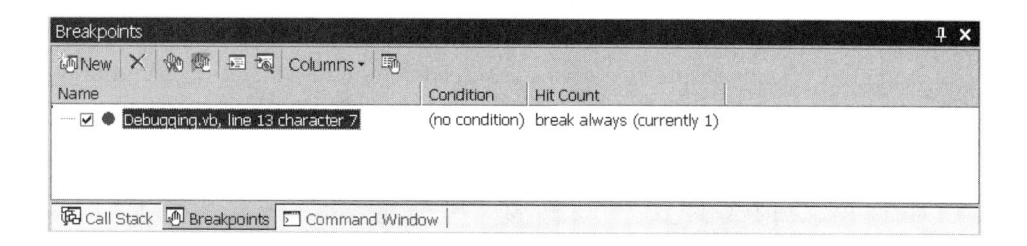

Using this window, you can add a new breakpoint, delete one or all breakpoints, disable all breakpoints, add and remove columns in the window, and view breakpoint properties.

Tip Breakpoints are the way you can suspend execution of a thread and examine its variables' contents.

You can specify to activate a breakpoint only when a specific variable changes its content. You have to specify the variable's name by choosing the Has Changed radio button in the breakpoint property pages. This again can be useful in threads, as you can detect when something unexpected occurs.

Finally, the Hit Count dialog box, accessed from the Breakpoints window (see the following screenshot), allows you to enable breakpoints when the breakpoint has reached the specified hit counter. Again this is useful in debugging threads as it allows you to see how often a thread is spawned.

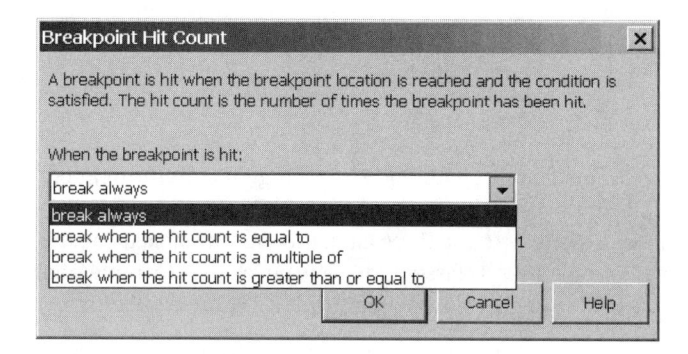

From the When the Breakpoint Is Hit combo box, you can select the condition that you want to assign to the breakpoint. For example, you can activate the breakpoint in a loop only when you are near to exiting from it. You can select the break when the hit count is equal to an item by assigning a value to the text field that will appear next to the combo.

To execute all the code's lines until the breakpoint is reached, you can press the F5 key; select Debug ➤ Start; or click the Start button on the standard toolbar.

Debugging Threads

The Visual Studio .NET debugger provides a special Threads window to manage threads during debugging sessions. You can display this window (as shown in the following diagram) by selecting Debug ➤ Windows ➤ Threads, or by pressing Ctrl+Alt+H.

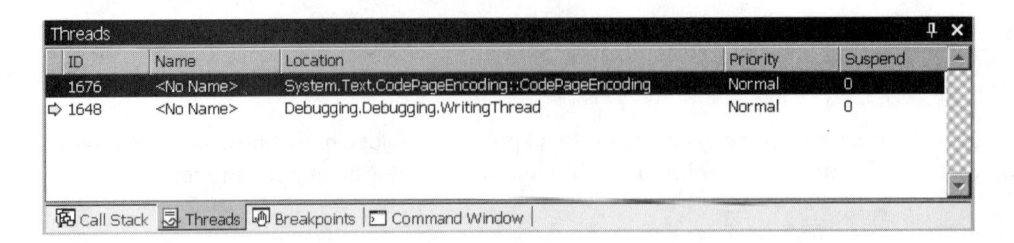

ID	Name	Location	Priority	Suspend
1676	<No Name>	System.Text.CodePageEncoding::CodePageEncoding	Normal	0
1648	<No Name>	Debugging.Debugging.WritingThread	Normal	0

The Threads window contains the following columns:

- **ID**: The thread's unique identifier assigned by the operating system.
- **Name**: The thread's name. You can specify it in the code using the Name property of the Thread object.
- **Location**: The function or memory address containing the thread.
- **Priority**: The thread's priority.
- **Suspend**: A counter for determining how often the thread has been suspended.

You can switch between threads by double-clicking on the item within the Threads window. You can also right-click on a thread and choose the Freeze menu item that will pause the thread's execution. To roll back the frozen thread state, you select the Thaw menu item.

Code Tracing

The next technique that we'll analyze to instrument your code is tracing. In a multithreaded application, this technique is especially important. You can trace a thread's behavior and interaction when more than one task has been started. As you'll see later, this isn't possible using the debugger. The .NET Framework provides some useful classes that allow developers to implement tracing functionality easily. Let's examine the tracing classes that the .NET Framework offers:

- **Trace**: This class has many shared methods that write messages to a listener. By default, the debug output windows are used as the listener application, but thanks to the Listeners collection, you can add different listeners as well, such as a text file listener or the Windows event log listener.
- **Debug**: This class has the same methods as the Trace class, writing information to a listener application. The largest difference between these two classes is when they are used. Trace is used at runtime; Debug is used at development time.
- **BooleanSwitch**: This class allows you to define a switch that turns on or off the tracing messages.
- **TraceSwitch**: This class provides four different tracing levels allowing developers to choose the severity of the messages to send to the listener.

The `System.Diagnostics.Trace` Class

In this section, we'll analyze the most frequently used methods of the .NET Framework Trace class, which encapsulates all the necessary methods to implement the tracing functionality easily. The Trace class is contained in the System.Diagnostics namespace and provides many shared methods for sending messages to the listener application. As you know, the Shared declaration means that you don't have to instantiate a new object from the Trace class and can use the method directly. For example:

```
Sub Main()
  Trace.WriteLine(t.ThreadState)
End Sub
```

This code snippet uses the WriteLine() method to output the thread state followed by a carriage return to the listener application. The following table lists all the shared methods provided by the Trace class:

- **Assert(condition, message)**: Displays the specified string message when the condition provided to the method evaluates to False. When you do not specify the message text, the Call Stack is displayed instead.

- **Fail(message)**: Similar to the Assert() method, this writes the specified text to the Call Stack when a failure occurs. The Assert() method differs because Fail() cannot specify a condition before displaying the error. In fact, the Fail() method is usually placed in the Catch statement of a Try-Catch-Finally instruction.

- **Write(message | object)**: Writes the specified text message, or object name, to the listener application.

- **WriteIf(condition, message)**: Writes the specified message text into the listener application if the specified condition is True.

- **WriteLine(message | object)**: Writes the specified message text, or object name, followed by a carriage return.

- **WriteLineIf(condition, message)**: Writes the specified message text followed by a carriage return if the specified condition is True.

The behavior of these methods depends on the listener application chosen. For example, the Assert() method displays a message box when the default listener is specified.

Default Listener Application

The Trace class provides a Listeners collection that allows you to add a new listener application. When no new listener object is added to the collection, the Trace class uses the default listener application: the Output debug window. This window is provided by the Visual Studio .NET IDE during debugging. For example, consider TraceExample1:

```
Sub Main()
  Trace.WriteLine("Entered in Main()")
  Dim i As Integer
  For i = 0 To 5
    Trace.WriteLine(i)
```

```
    Next
    Trace.WriteLine("Exiting from Main()")
    Console.ReadLine()
End Sub
```

The code is simple; it writes tracing information when entering and exiting from the `Main()` method, plus the variable's values into the loop. In the next screenshot, you can see how the Visual Studio .NET `Output` listener shows the information.

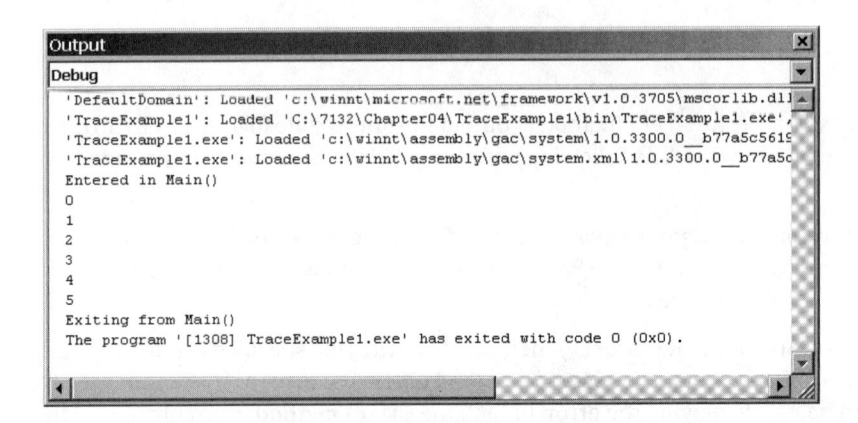

```
Output
Debug
'DefaultDomain': Loaded 'c:\winnt\microsoft.net\framework\v1.0.3705\mscorlib.dll'
'TraceExample1': Loaded 'C:\7132\Chapter04\TraceExample1\bin\TraceExample1.exe',
'TraceExample1.exe': Loaded 'c:\winnt\assembly\gac\system\1.0.3300.0__b77a5c5619
'TraceExample1.exe': Loaded 'c:\winnt\assembly\gac\system.xml\1.0.3300.0__b77a5c
Entered in Main()
0
1
2
3
4
5
Exiting from Main()
The program '[1308] TraceExample1.exe' has exited with code 0 (0x0).
```

The `Trace` class also provides two useful methods to assert error notification: `Assert()` and `Fail()`. `Assert()` allows developer to check a condition provided as parameter and write a message into the listener when this condition is `False`. `Fail()` writes a message into the listener each time a failure occurs. When no other listener is added to the collection, the `Assert()` method displays a message box to inform the user about an assertion. The following snippet of code, `TraceAssert.vb`, can be tested when the SQL Server service has been stopped deliberately to raise a connection exception:

```
Imports System. Threading;
Imports System.Data.SqlClient;
Public Class TraceAssert
  Public Sub DBThread()
    ' Create a connection object
    Dim connString as String
    connString = "server=.;database=pubs;uid=sa;pwd="
    Dim dbConn As New _
SqlConnection(connString)
    ' Create a command object to execute a
    ' SQL statement
    Dim dbQuery As New SqlCommand( _
        "SELECT * FROM authors", dbConn)
    Dim dr As SqlDataReader
    Trace.WriteLine( _
        DateTime.Now & " - Executing SQL statement")
    Try
```

```vbnet
      ' Open the connection to the database
      dbConn.Open()
      ' Execute the SQL statement
      dr = dbQuery.ExecuteReader( _
        CommandBehavior.CloseConnection)
      While (dr.Read())
        ' Reading records
      End While
    Catch ex As Exception
      ' Trace an assertion if connection fails
      Trace.Assert( dbConn.State = _
        ConnectionState.Open, "Error", _
        "Connection failed...")
      ' Trace an assertion if DataReader empty
      Trace.Assert(Not dr Is Nothing, "Error", _
        "The SqlDataReader is null!")
    Finally
      If (dr.IsClosed = False) And _
        (Not dr Is Nothing) Then
        dr.Close()
      End If
    End Try
  End Sub
  Public Shared Sub Main()
    Dim ta as New TraceAssert
    ' Create a thread
    Dim t As Thread
    t = New Thread( AddressOf ta.DBThread )
    ' Start the thread
    t.Start()
  End Sub
End Class
```

In the `Main()` method, a new thread is created and started. The new thread runs the code within the `DBThread()` subroutine. This code simply tries to contact the pubs SQL Server database, and retrieves all the data contained within the authors table. If the SQL Server service were not available, the error in the following screenshot would be displayed upon execution of the code.

The row that raises that assertion is

```
' Trace an assertion if something goes wrong
Trace.Assert(dbConn.State =_
   ConnectionState.Open, "Error", _
   "Connection failed...")
```

As you can see, the first parameter checks whether the state of the connection is Open. It will be set to False when the connection has not been opened, so the assertion will be displayed. As you'll see later in the section explaining the BooleanSwitch class, you can deactivate tracing messaging using the application configuration file. In that way, you can decide whether to display assert messages at runtime.

Using Different Listener Applications

In this section, you'll see how to change the default listener application. The Trace class (and the Debug class as you'll see later in the "The Debug Class" section) exposes the Listeners collection, which contains a collection of listener applications. Without adding any new listener classes, the DefaultTraceListener points to the Output debug window provided by Visual Studio .NET. However, the .NET Framework provides another two classes that can be used as listener applications:

- **EventLogTraceListener**: Using this class, you can redirect tracing messages to the Windows event log.

- **TextWriterTraceListener**: Using this class, you can redirect tracing messages to a text file or to a stream.

In a multithreaded application, you can change the default listener with one of the listed listeners if you need to trace an application's behavior during its execution outside of Visual Studio. Naturally, the Output debug window is available only during the debug. Using these two classes, you could choose whether trace messages are placed in the Windows event log or inside a text file. Usually, when you know that your application will run in an operating system equipped with the Windows event log, the EventLogTraceListener class is the best solution to choose for the following reasons:

- The event log is managed by the operating system.

- The event log allows administrators to specify security settings for the log.

- The event log has to be read with the Event Viewer. This displays with a better visual impact than a text file in Notepad.

Changing the default listener is simple, so consider TraceEventLog.vb:

```
Module TraceEventLog
  Sub Main()
    ' Create a trace listener for the event log.
    Dim eltl As New EventLogTraceListener("TraceLog")

    ' Add the event log trace listener to the
    ' collection.
    Trace.Listeners.Add(eltl)

    ' Write output to the event log.
    Trace.WriteLine("Entered in Main()")
    Console.ReadLine()
  End Sub
End Module
```

First, you have to create a new listener object. In the preceding example, a new EventLogTraceListener has been created to use the Windows event log as a listener application. The class constructor accepts a string where you can specify the source name that has written an entry. The constructor will instantiate a new EventLog object assigning the specified source name to the Source property of the EventLog class, automatically.

The next step is to add the new listener object to the Listeners collection using the Add() method and to provide the reference to the listener object. Finally, you can start to write tracing messages that will be redirected to the listener application.

Opening up the Windows event log using the Event Viewer application, you should see the new entry appearing in the Application Log section as shown in the following screenshot.

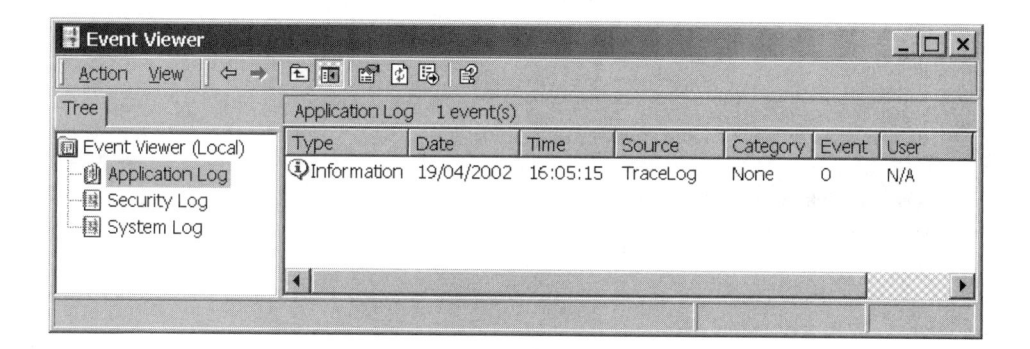

You can double-click the item inside the Application Log report to examine the message as shown in the next screenshot.

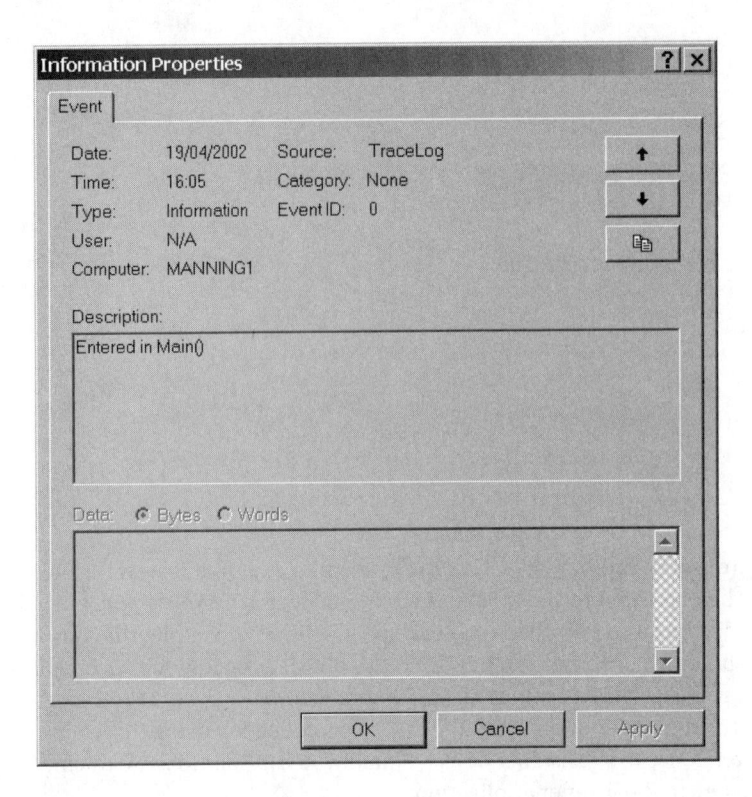

The preceding code adds a new listener to the `Listeners` collection so that you'll receive tracing messages both in the Output debug window and in the event log. If you want to remove the default listener to use just the event log application, you have to call the `RemoveAt()` method, as illustrated next:

```
Sub Main()
    ' Create a trace listener for the event log.
    Dim eltl As New EventLogTraceListener("TraceLog")
    ' Remove the default listener
    Trace.Listeners.RemoveAt(0)
    ' Add the event log trace listener to the
    ' collection.
    Trace.Listeners.Add(eltl)
    ' Write output to the event log.
    Trace.WriteLine("Entered in Main()")
End Sub
```

The `TextWriterTraceListener`

The `TextWriterTraceListener` class is useful when you have to write tracing messages to a text file or directly in a console application. In fact, during the `TextWriterTraceListener` object's creation, you can specify either a `TextWriter` object or a `Stream` object. Using a `Stream` object allows you to specify more details on how the file stream is handled. The following snippet of code, `TraceConsole.vb`, shows how to trace messages in a `Console` application:

```
Module TraceConsole
  Sub Main()
    ' Remove the default listener
    Trace.Listeners.RemoveAt(0)
    ' Add a console listener
    Trace.Listeners.Add( _
       New TextWriterTraceListener(Console.Out))
    ' Write a trace message
    Trace.WriteLine("Entered in Main()")
    Console.ReadLine()
  End Sub
End Module
```

Specifying the `Console.Out` streaming in the class's constructor, our Console application will display tracing messages:

Finally, let's add text log files as a listener. You have to add a new `TextWriterTraceListener` object, specifying a `FileStream` object in its constructor. When the application ends, you have to use the static `Close()` method provided by the `Trace` class to close the log writing all the tracing messages. In the following code, Debugging.vb, a thread is started that traces both main and secondary thread messages:

```
Private Sub WritingThread()
  ' Trace an info message
  Trace.WriteLine( _
    DateTime.Now & " - Entered in WritingThread()")
  ' Sleeping for one sec....
  Thread.CurrentThread.Sleep(1000)
  ' Trace an info message
  Trace.WriteLine( _
    DateTime.Now & " - Slept for 1 second...")
  Console.ReadLine()
End Sub
```

The `WritingThread()` method is simply used by the thread to sleep for a second and write some tracing messages.

Here, you create a new `FileStream` object, either creating or opening the Debugging.log file if it already exists. Then, you add the new listener into the `Listeners` collection by creating a new instance of the `TextWriterTraceListener` class within the `Add()` method:

```vb
Sub Main()
  ' Create a file listener
  Dim fs As New IO.FileStream("C:\Debugging.log", _
    IO.FileMode.OpenOrCreate)
  Trace.Listeners.Add( _
    New TextWriterTraceListener(fs))
```

After starting the thread, the code waits for the carriage return key from the user and then closes the listener application and flushes all the tracing messages to the log file:

```vb
  ' Write the line only when the switch is on
  Trace.WriteLine ( _
     DateTime.Now & " - Entered in Main()")
  ' Create a thread
  Dim newThread As Thread
  newThread = New Thread(AddressOf WritingThread)
  ' Start the thread
  newThread.Start()
  ' Wait for the user carriage return
  Console.Read()
  ' Close the file listener flushing the trace messages
  Trace.Close()
End Sub
```

The output of the code will be something similar to this:

```
30/04/2002 16:38:15 - Entered in Main()
30/04/2002 16:38:15 - Entered into WritingThread()
30/04/2002 16:38:16 - Slept for one second...
```

The Trace class provides a useful property called IndentLevel for indenting tracing messages. For instance, you could use different indent levels for tracing messages written by the main and secondary threads. Adding the following lines to the preceding code, you can accomplish this task easily:

```vb
Private Sub WritingThread()
  '  Setting indent level
  Trace.IndentLevel = 2
  ' Trace an info message
  Trace.WriteLine( _
    DateTime.Now & " - Entered in WritingThread()")
  ' Sleeping for one sec....
  Thread.CurrentThread.Sleep(1000)
  ' Trace an info message
  Trace.WriteLine( _
    DateTime.Now & " - Slept for 1 second...")
End Sub
```

The output of the modified code is

```
30/04/2002 16:40:07 - Entered in Main()
30/04/2002 16:40:07 - Entered into WritingThread()
30/04/2002 16:40:08 - Slept for one second...
```

Tip You can increment or decrement the level of the indentation using the `Indent()` and `Unindent()` methods.

Tracing Switches

When you're near to the application deployment phase, you'll probably want to remove all the tracing and debugging messages from the code. However, you don't have to look for every trace instruction and remove it. You can use compilation flags during the application building. From the Visual Studio .NET IDE, right-click on the project name within the Solution Explorer window, and select `Properties` from the context menu. The following dialog box appears.

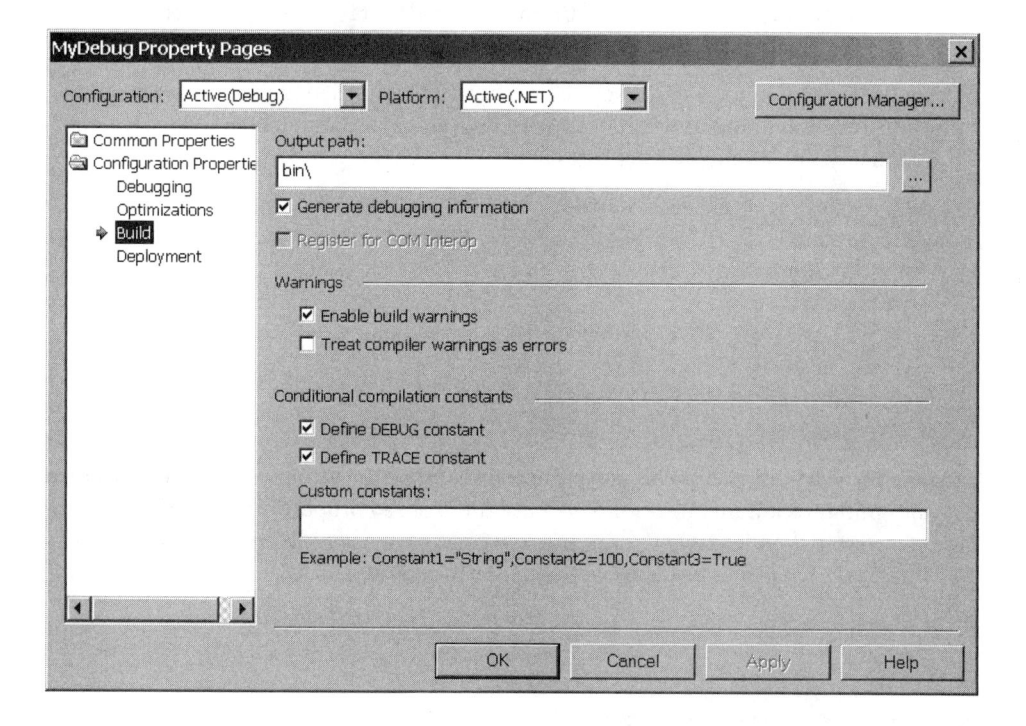

Now to strip all the Trace and Debug statements from the application, you just uncheck the `Define DEBUG Constant` and `Define TRACE Constant` check boxes, and recompile the solution.

> **Tip** To remove tracing functionalities, you can even use the vbc.exe command-line compiler. Simply use `/d:TRACE=FALSE /d:DEBUG=FALSE` switches when compiling.

Adding switches to the traced code allows you to activate/deactivate tracing messages at runtime. By simply declaring a value in the configuration file of your application, you can activate the trace functionality without rebuilding the entire solution. Naturally, you have to build the application to maintain tracing information, and this implicates a greater final application size and slower performance, even when the switches are turned off.

The `BooleanSwitch` and `TraceSwitch` classes are provided by the .NET Framework to implement these switches. Let's first examine the `BooleanSwitch` class.

The BooleanSwitch Class

By using this class in the traced code, you can decide to activate/deactivate messages by simply changing a value in the application configuration file. The `WriteLineIf()` and `WriteIf()` methods will be useful to write messages depending on the `Enabled` property provided by the `BooleanSwitch` class. To add switches to your application, you have to follow these steps:

1. Add an application configuration file either manually, or by selecting **Project ➤ Add New Item** from within Visual Studio .NET. Choose the `Application Configuration File` template from the dialog box.

2. Open the configuration file to insert the necessary XML tags to inform the application about the switch name and value. Specifying a value equal to 0 deactivates tracing functionality, and a value of 1 activates it:

   ```
   <?xml version="1.0" encoding="utf-8" ?>
   <configuration>
     <system.diagnostics>
       <switches>
         <add name="MySwitch" value="1" />
       </switches>
     </system.diagnostics>
   </configuration>
   ```

3. Create a new `BooleanSwitch` object in the code that has the same name as that specified in the configuration file. You could also use the `Enabled` property in conjunction with the `Trace` static methods. Let's continue the `Debugging` example by declaring a global `BooleanSwitch` object to be used everywhere in the code:

   ```
   Dim bs As BooleanSwitch
   Sub Main()
     ' Create a Boolean switch called MySwitch
     bs = New BooleanSwitch("MySwitch", _
       "Enable/Disable tracing functionalities")
     ' Create a file listener
     Dim fs As New FileStream("C:\Debugging.log", _
       FileMode.OpenOrCreate)
   ```

```
        Trace.Listeners.Add( _
          New TextWriterTraceListener(fs))
        ' Write the line only when the switch is on
        Trace.WriteLineIf( _
          bs.Enabled, DateTime.Now & _
          " - Entered in Main()")
        ...
    End Sub
```

The object is created in the `Main()` method and you specify the same name used in the configuration file plus a brief description. The `WriteLineIf()` method writes the message only if the `Enabled` property has been set to 1 in the configuration file.

The TraceSwitch Class

This class is an enhanced version of the `BooleanSwitch` class because it allows you to choose whether to deactivate tracing functionality or display messages using an importance-based hierarchy. Following are the trace levels:

- **0:** None—Tracing is deactivated.
- **1:** `TraceError`—Only the error messages will be written to the listener application.
- **2:** `TraceWarning`—Error and warning messages will be written to the listener application.
- **3:** `TraceInformation`—Error, warning, and information messages will be written to the listener application.
- **4:** `TraceVerbose`—All kind of messages will be written to the listener application.

So, when an error occurs, you can change the application configuration file to write just the error messages that you've added to the code to focus attention just on these kind of messages. The configuration file is the same you've seen for the `BooleanSwitch` example. What changes is the code, because you have to instantiate an object from the `TraceSwitch` class. You'll also use the enumeration values within the class to specify the level of the tracing messages. Consider the following `TraceSwitchExample.vb` example:

```
Public Class TraceSwitchExample
  Private Shared TSwitch As TraceSwitch
  Public Shared Sub Main()
    ' Create a Boolean switch called MySwitch
    TSwitch = New TraceSwitch("MySwitch", _
      "Four different trace levels")

    ' Create a file listener
    Dim fs As New FileStream( _
      "C:\Debugging.log", FileMode.OpenOrCreate)
    Trace.Listeners.Add( _
      New TextWriterTraceListener(fs))
    ' Write the line only when the switch is set
    Trace.WriteLineIf(TSwitch.TraceInfo, _
      DateTime.Now & " - Entered in Main()")
```

```vb
    ' Create a thread
    Dim threadInstance As Thread
    threadInstance = New Thread(AddressOf DBThread)
    ' Start the thread
    threadInstance.Start()
    ' Wait for the user carriage return
    Console.Read()
    ' Close the file listener flushing the trace
    ' messages
    Trace.Close()
End Sub
```

The code starts by declaring a global `TraceSwitch` object and then creates a new object, giving it the same name specified in the configuration file. We add a text file log listener to the application. We then start a new thread that contacts the `pubs` database within SQL Server to retrieve all the records from the `authors` table.

If the thread has been omitted, the `Open()` method raises an exception that generates a trace error message:

```vb
Imports System.Threading
Imports System.Data
Public Shared Sub DBThread()
    Dim connString as String
    connString = "server=.;database=pubs;uid=sa;pwd="
    ' Trace an info message
    Trace.WriteLineIf(TSwitch.TraceInfo, _
      DateTime.Now & " - Entered in DBThread()")
    ' Create a connection object
    Dim dbConn As New SqlConnection(connString)
    ' Create a command object to execute a SQL
    ' statement
    Dim dbQuery As New SqlCommand( _
        "SELECT * FROM authors", dbConn)
    Dim dr As SqlDataReader
    Try
      Trace.WriteLineIf(TSwitch.TraceInfo, _
        DateTime.Now & " - Executing SQL statement")
      ' Execute the SQL statement
      dr = dbQuery.ExecuteReader( _
        CommandBehavior.CloseConnection)
      While (dr.Read())
        ' Reading records
      End While
    Catch ex As Exception
      Trace.WriteLineIf(TSwitch.TraceError, _
        DateTime.Now & " - Error: " & ex.Message)
```

```
    Finally
        If (Not dr Is Nothing) AndAlso _
            (dr.IsClosed = False) Then
            dr.Close()
        End If
    End Try
  End Sub
End Class
```

Here is the output from the code when the value 1 is specified in the configuration file, which specifies `TraceError`:

```
19/04/2002 17:52:23 - Error: ExecuteReader requires an open and available
 Connection. The connection's current state is Closed.
Slept for 1 second...
```

Here is the output when the value 3 is specified in the configuration file, which specifies `TraceInformation`:

```
19/04/2002 17:54:23 - Entered in Main()
19/04/2002 17:54:23 - Entered in DBThread()
19/04/2002 17:54:24 - Executing SQL statement
19/04/2002 17:54:24 - Error: ExecuteReader requires an open and available
 Connection. The connection's current state is Closed.
```

The Debug Class

The `Debug` class provides the same functionality as the `Trace` class. You will find that it exposes the same methods and properties, with the same tracing results.

■**Tip** When you change the listener application using the `Listeners` collection provided by the `Trace` class, you'll change the listener application for `Debug` messages as well.

The big difference between these two classes is the context in which they should be used. The `Debug` class is useful when you need to add information during debugging sessions. Before deploying your application, you'll build the release version that removes debug information from the code automatically. Therefore, you would add `Trace` class functionalities when you need to check your application during the runtime phase.

The `DataImport` Example

At this point, we're ready to concentrate on a practical example that will demonstrate what you've seen thus far. The `DataImport` example is a typical application that waits for files to arrive in a specific directory before importing them into a SQL Server database. The code for this application, as with the rest of the code in this book, can be found in the Downloads section of the Apress Web site (http://www.apress.com). The classes used in this example are

- `FileSystemWatcher` allows developers to specify the directory to monitor, and to raise an event when something changes (a new file is created, removed, or otherwise). This class is contained in the `System.IO` namespace of the .NET Framework class library.
- `TextWriterTraceListener` implements our own tracing functionality.
- `Thread` allows you to start a new thread to import data into the database.
- Many classes from the `SqlClient` namespace necessary to manage the SQL Server database connection and update.

The first release of the `DataImport` application contains some logical errors that we'll discover using tracing functionality. In that way we can have a good example about log (trace) files and their importance.

The Code

Let's start analyzing the code of the `DataImport` example:

```
Imports System.IO
Imports System.Threading
Imports System.Data.SqlClient
Imports Microsoft.VisualBasic
Class DataImport
```

First of all, we added all the necessary namespaces to use the `FileSystemWatcher`, `Thread`, and SQL Server classes:

```
' Global Boolean switch used to activate/deactivate
' tracing functionality
Private Shared BS As BooleanSwitch

Public Shared Sub Main()
  ' Remove the default listener
  Trace.Listeners.RemoveAt(0)
  ' Create and add the new listener
  BS = New BooleanSwitch("DISwitch", _
      "DataImport switch")
  BS.Enabled = True
  Trace.Listeners.Add( _
    New TextWriterTraceListener( _
    New FileStream("C:\DataImport.log", _
    FileMode.OpenOrCreate)))
```

The code then removes the default listener and creates a new TextWriterTraceListener object that points to C:\DataImport.log:

```
' Create a FileSystemWatcher object used to
' monitor the specified directory
Dim fsw As New FileSystemWatcher()

' Set the path to watch and specify the file
' extension to monitor for
fsw.Path = "C:\temp"
fsw.Filter = "*.xml"

' No need to go into subdirs
fsw.IncludeSubdirectories = False

' Add the handler to manage the raised event
' when a new file is created
AddHandler fsw.Created, _
    New FileSystemEventHandler( _
    AddressOf OnFileCreated )

' Enable the object to raise the event
fsw.EnableRaisingEvents = True
```

Here the code creates a FileSystemWatcher object used to monitor the C:\temp directory specified in the Path property. The Filter property is useful to filter through each file within the directory looking for just the ones with the specified file extension. The IncludeSubdirectories property determines whether to extend the file monitoring to subdirectories. The AddHandler statement is used to specify the event that we want to manage in our code by providing the address of the function used as the event handler. In this case, we want to receive file-creation events, so we have to specify the Created event provided by the FileSystemWatcher class. Finally, the code enables the FileSystemWatcher object to raise events.

```
Try
    ' Call the WaitForChanged() method within an
    ' infinite loop. When the event is raised,
    ' OnFileCreated() will be called.
    Dim result As WaitForChangedResult
    Do
        result = fsw.WaitForChanged( _
            WatcherChangeTypes.Created)
        Trace.WriteLineIf(bs.Enabled, _
            DateTime.Now & " - Found: " & _
            result.Name & " file")
    Loop
```

The preceding code implements an infinite loop, which waits for the file-creation event to be raised. The WaitForChangedResult object will contain information about the file created. For example, the code uses the Name property to trace the name of the discovered file.

```
    Catch e As Exception
      Trace.WriteLineIf( bs.Enabled, DateTime.Now & _
      " - An exception occurred while waiting " & _
      "for file: ")
      Trace.Indent()
      Trace.WriteLineIf( bs.Enabled, DateTime.Now & _
      " - " &  e.ToString())
      Trace.Unindent()
    Finally
      fsw.EnableRaisingEvents = False
      Trace.WriteLineIf(bs.Enabled, DateTime.Now & _
        " - Directory monitoring stopped")
      Trace.Close()
    End Try
  End Sub
```

The preceding `Main()` subroutine ends by tracing some useful messages and any exceptions. The `OnFileCreated()` shared method is detailed here:

```
Private Shared Sub OnFileCreated( _
    ByVal source As Object, _
    ByVal eventArgs As FileSystemEventArgs)

    Try
      ' Create a new object from the ImportData class
      ' to process the incoming file
      Dim id As New DataImport()
      id.FileName = eventArgs.FullPath
      ' Create and start the thread
      Dim threadInstance As New Thread( _
        AddressOf id.Import)
      threadInstance.Name = "DataImportThread"
      threadInstance.Start()
```

Inside the `OnFileCreated` event handler, a new thread is started. This thread uses the `Import` method of the custom `ImportData` class used to import the XML file into the database. Because we know the full path of the discovered file (the `FileSystemEventArgs` parameter contains this information) and because we need it even in the `ImportData` class, we can use the `FileName` field provided by the class.

```
    Catch ex As Exception
      Trace.WriteLineIf(bs.Enabled, DateTime.Now & _
        " - An exception occurred while " & _
        " queuing file: ")
      Trace.Indent()
      Trace.WriteLineIf(bs.Enabled, DateTime.Now & _
        " - " & ex.ToString())
      Trace.Unindent()
```

```
    Finally
      Trace.Flush()
    End Try
  End Sub

  ' Path and file name of the retrieved file
  Public FileName As String = ControlChars.NullChar

  Public Sub Import()
    Dim connString as String
    connString = "server=.;database=pubs;uid=sa;pwd="
    ' Declare Sql objects to contact the database
    Dim dbConn As New SqlConnection(connString)
    Dim da As New SqlDataAdapter( _
        "SELECT * FROM authors", dbConn)
    Dim ds As New DataSet()
    Dim sa As New SqlCommandBuilder(da)
```

Inside the Import() method, the code starts by creating and setting all the necessary classes to contact the authors table within the SQL Server pubs database. The SqlConnection object allows us to specify database connection parameters. The SqlDataAdapter object connects to the database using the connection object executing the SQL statement specified as first parameter. Finally, the SqlCommandBuilder examines the SQL statement specified in the SqlDataAdapter constructor, creating INSERT, MODIFY, and DELETE statements automatically. They are needed when we use the Update() method exposed by the SqlDataAdapter class to physically change the database with new information.

```
    Try
      Trace.WriteLineIf(BS.Enabled, DateTime.Now & _
        " - Filling the DataSet.")
      ' Fill a dataset with data within
      ' the authors table
      da.Fill(ds)
```

Here the Fill() method from the SqlDataAdapter class is used to fill the DataSet object specified in its parameter, with the results of the SQL query specified earlier. The DataSet is an in-memory representation of the database data, so it will be formatted as the authors table and filled with every record contained in the table:

```
      ' Read the XML file filling another dataset
      Dim dsMerge As New DataSet()
      Trace.WriteLineIf(BS.Enabled, DateTime.Now & _
        " - Reading XML file.")
      dsMerge.ReadXml(FileName, _
        XmlReadMode.InferSchema)
      Trace.WriteLineIf(BS.Enabled, DateTime.Now & _
        " - DataSet filled with data.")
```

Here the code uses the discovered file to fill another `DataSet` object. This time, the `ReadXml()` method has been used. The power of the `DataSet` object is evident. You can manage data provided by both database and XML document in the same exact way. The `DataSet` object maintains an XML data representation of the records within itself.

```vb
' Update the database, tracing the total time
' needed to conclude the operation
Dim time As Date = DateTime.Now
Trace.WriteLineIf(BS.Enabled, time & _
  " - Updating database.")
da.Update(dsMerge)
Dim time2 As Date = DateTime.Now
Trace.WriteLineIf(BS.Enabled, time2 & _
  " - Database updated successfully.")
Trace.Indent()
Trace.WriteLineIf(BS.Enabled, DateTime.Now & _
  " - Total TIME: " & _
  DateDiff(DateInterval.Second, _
    time, time2) & " second/s")
Trace.Unindent()
```

Finally, the code uses the `Update()` method provided by the `SqlDataAdapter` class to write new records to the `authors` table. Note the tracing information used in this snippet of code; this provides detailed information by adding performance messages. The `DateTime` class has been used to retrieve the total time in seconds needed to update the database:

```vb
  Catch sqlEx As SqlException
    Trace.WriteLineIf(BS.Enabled, DateTime.Now & _
      " - A SQL exception occurred " & _
      " during file processing: ")
    Trace.Indent()
    Trace.WriteLineIf(BS.Enabled, DateTime.Now & _
      " - " & sqlEx.ToString())
    Trace.Unindent()
  Catch ex As Exception
    Trace.WriteLineIf(BS.Enabled, DateTime.Now & _
      " - A general exception occurred " & _
      " during file processing: ")
    Trace.Indent()
    Trace.WriteLineIf(BS.Enabled, DateTime.Now & _
      " - " & ex.ToString())
    Trace.Unindent()
  Finally
    Trace.Flush()
  End Try
 End Sub
End Class
```

Then, after writing the code for catching and dealing with any exceptions that may occur, the code is complete.

Testing the Application

To test the application, follow these steps:

1. Create a C:\temp directory to contain the XML file.

2. Run the DataImport application.

3. Copy the authors.xml file into the C:\temp directory.

As a result, you should find the DataImport.log file in the C:\ directory with content similar to this:

```
01/05/2002 12:23:01 - Found: authors.xml file
01/05/2002 12:23:01 - Filling the DataSet.
01/05/2002 12:23:02 - Reading XML file.
01/05/2002 12:23:02 - DataSet filled with data.
01/05/2002 12:23:02 - Updating database.
01/05/2002 12:23:02 - Database updated successfully.
01/05/2002 12:23:03 - Total TIME: 0 second/s
```

The authors.xml file is not that large so the total time is less than 1 second.

Logical Errors

All seems to be working well, but obviously, everything hasn't been accounted for. So far, we've tested the application with a very small file size, so when the application receives the file-creation event and opens the file, the process that copies it into the directory finishes its task of closing the file. What happens when we receive a huge file? When the thread tries to access the XML file and fill the DataSet object, it receives an access denied error caused by attempting to open a file already in use by the copier task. Try to test the application again by copying the huge_authors.xml file instead. Because we've used tracing messages, you may find the following error in the log file:

```
4/14/2002 1:29:00 PM - Found: huge_authors.xml file
4/14/2002 1:29:00 PM - Filling the DataSet.
4/14/2002 1:29:00 PM - Reading XML file.
4/14/2002 1:29:00 PM - A general exception occurred during file processing:
4/14/2002 1:29:00 PM - System.IO.IOException: The process cannot access
the file "C:\temp\huge_authors.xml" because it is being used by another
process.
at System.IO.__Error.WinIOError(Int32 errorCode, String str)
at System.IO.FileStream..ctor(String path, FileMode mode, FileAccess access,
FileShare share, Int32 bufferSize, Boolean useAsync, String msgPath, Boolean
bFromProxy)
at System.IO.FileStream..ctor(String path, FileMode mode, FileAccess access,
FileShare share)
at System.Xml.XmlDownloadManager.GetStream(Uri uri, ICredentials
credentials)
at System.Xml.XmlUrlResolver.GetEntity(Uri absoluteUri, String role, Type
```

ofObjectToReturn)
at System.Xml.XmlTextReader.CreateScanner()
at System.Xml.XmlTextReader.Init()
at System.Xml.XmlTextReader.Read()
at System.Xml.XmlReader.MoveToContent()
at System.Data.DataSet.ReadXml(XmlReader reader, XmlReadMode mode)
at System.Data.DataSet.ReadXml(String fileName, XmlReadMode mode)

The debugger often fails to catch this kind of error because the time used to launch it and the time to step through the code is often sufficient to copy the file. It may also not occur on your machine. It depends on the speed of your disk access and the amount of memory you have (in other words, how much the application is slowed down).

The error message suggests a possible solution to add to the application to resolve the error. Before calling the `ReadXml()` method, try to open the file with exclusive access. If an error occurs, then you can suspend the thread for a few seconds, trying again when the file can be processed. Let's see how the code changes, DataImport2, by adding the `GetFileAccess()` method:

```
Private Function GetFileAccess() As Boolean
  Trace.WriteLineIf(BS.Enabled, DateTime.Now & _
    " - Trying to get exclusive access to the " & _
    FileName & " file.")
  Dim checkFile As File

  Try
    Dim fs As FileStream = checkFile.Open( _
      m_strFileName, FileMode.Append, _
      FileAccess.Write, FileShare.None)
    fs.Close()
    Trace.WriteLineIf(BS.Enabled, DateTime.Now & _
      " - Access to the " & FileName & _
      " file allowed.")
    GetFileAccess = True
  Catch
    Trace.WriteLineIf(bs.Enabled, DateTime.Now & _
      " - Access denied to the " & m_strFileName _
      & " file.")
    GetFileAccess = False
  End Try
End Function
```

The `GetFileAccess()` function has been added to return a Boolean value indicating whether you can have exclusive access to the file or not. The function simply tries to open the file with the share access property set to None:

```
Public Sub Import()
  Dim connString as String
  connString = "server=.;database=pubs;uid=sa;pwd="
  ' Declare Sql objects to contact the database
  Dim dbConn As New SqlConnection(connString)
```

```
Dim da As New SqlDataAdapter( _
   "SELECT * FROM authors", dbConn)
Dim ds As New DataSet()
Dim sa As New SqlCommandBuilder(da)
Try
  Do While (GetFileAccess() = False)
    Thread.Sleep(3000)
    Trace.WriteLineIf(BS.Enabled, DateTime.Now & _
      " - Slept 5 seconds... Try to " & _
      " access to the " & FileName & _
      " file, again.")
  Loop
  Trace.WriteLineIf(bs.Enabled, DateTime.Now & _
    " - Filling the DataSet.")
  ' Fill a dataset with data within the
  ' authors table
  da.Fill(ds)
```

The Import() method provided by the ImportData class will try to get exclusive access to the file. If the file is still opened by the copier task, the thread will be suspended for 5 seconds. So, the GetFileAccess() function will be called until the source file can be opened:

Summary

In this chapter, you've seen how the Visual Studio .NET debugger can be used to observe an application's behavior during its execution. Also, you've seen which powerful tools the debugger provides to allow you to examine and change a variable's value, and more.

In the second part of the chapter, we covered the tracing functionality provided by .NET with three classes: Trace, Debug, and Switch. We started listing the most useful tracing functionalities, focusing on the ability to activate tracing techniques by modifying values within the application configuration file.

Finally, you saw a practical example where the tracing technique helps developers find and correct bugs and logical errors.

CHAPTER 19

Networking and Threading

In the previous chapters of this book, we've taken an in-depth look at threading in VB .NET and discussed the various concepts and techniques associated with programming multithreaded applications. Now that you are a threading expert, we'll build a simple multithreaded client-server application in VB .NET and put to use some of the concepts we've discussed thus far.

The effective use of threads and asynchronous programming is indispensable for certain applications' needs, such as network communication, effective UI, and disk IO, to just name a few. In all these cases, the application can freeze or appear to have crashed while it's waiting for an operation to complete. This is also true in the case of a network application where latency is often the most important criterion, especially with users that have low-speed connections. In the sample application showcased in this chapter, we'll use the System.Net namespace and briefly explore the networking capabilities of .NET, especially because the multiuser and asynchronous nature of network applications makes them ideal candidates for threading.

In particular, we'll discuss the following:

- Developing network applications in .NET using the System.Net namespace

- Developing a simple multithreaded client-server application based on TCP/IP

- Using intrinsic .NET functionality to implement asynchronous operations

- Using asynchronous message transfers between a client and a remote server

Networking in .NET

Prior to the advent of the .NET Framework, the ability to develop sophisticated Windows-based networking applications was limited to advanced C++ programmers using the convoluted WinSock library for the most part. There was, of course, the WinInet control that VB developers could use to accomplish relatively simple tasks. However, they did not have to attempt too much before facing functional impediments with the simple and limited services offered in that control.

Fortunately, the System.Net namespace within the .NET Framework brings a slew of effective functionality packaged in a simple and consistent object model. The ease of use of these classes does not compromise functionality, as almost all the core functions of WinSock 2.0 have been wrapped and abstracted in the System.Net namespace. Developers can easily develop at any level from sockets all the way up to HTTP. Also, unlike the raw use of the WinSock library, the System.Net namespace relieves developers from having the dubious pleasure of manually coding many imperative resource-management tasks, such as dealing with overlapped IO and completion ports.

So, without further delay, let's briefly explore the System.Net namespace.

System.Net Namespace

The System.Net namespace is actually compromised of two namespaces, System.Net and System.Net.Socket.

We'll primarily be using the System.Net.Sockets namespace in the sample application. The layered approach of the System.Net classes provides applications with the capability to access networks with various levels of control based on the demands of the application. In addition to the extensive support for sockets, System.Net classes also offer an impressive array of functionality to use with HTTP. For the most part, the System.Net offerings are categorized in three layers: application protocols, transport protocols, and Web protocols. The System.Net.Sockets namespace consists primarily of classes and utilities for dealing with the transport protocol. Let's look at some of the more important classes within the System.Net namespace:

- **Authorization**: Provides authentication messaging for a Web server.
- **Cookie**: Provides a set of properties and methods used to manage cookies. This class cannot be inherited.
- **Dns**: Simple domain name resolution functionality.
- **EndPoint**: Identifies a network address. This is a MustInherit class.
- **GlobalProxySelection**: Global default proxy instance for all HTTP requests.
- **HttpVersion**: Defines the HTTP version numbers supported by the HttpWebRequest and HttpWebResponse classes.
- **HttpWebRequest**: HTTP-specific implementation of the WebRequest class.
- **HttpWebResponse**: HTTP-specific implementation of the WebResponse class.
- **IPAddress**: Internet Protocol (IP) address.
- **IPEndPoint**: A network endpoint consisting of an IP address and a port number.
- **IPHostEntry**: Container class for Internet host address information.
- **NetworkCredential**: Provides credentials for password-based authentication schemes such as basic, digest, NTLM (New Technology LAN Manager), and Kerberos authentication.
- **SocketAddress**: Stores serialized information from EndPoint-derived classes.
- **SocketPermission**: Controls rights to make or accept socket connections.
- **WebClient**: Provides common methods for sending data to and receiving data from a resource identified by a URI.
- **WebException**: The exception that is thrown when an error occurs while accessing resources via HTTP.
- **WebPermission**: Controls rights to access HTTP Internet resources.
- **WebPermissionAttribute**: Specifies permission to access Internet resources.

- **WebProxy**: Contains HTTP proxy settings for the WebRequest class.
- **WebRequest**: Makes a request to a URI. This class must always be inherited (a MustInherit class).
- **WebResponse**: Provides a response from a URI. This class must always be inherited (a MustInherit class).

As you can see, the System.Net namespace contains a cornucopia of classes and utilities that are useful for a wide range of Web and network programming needs.

System.Net.Sockets Namespace

The System.Net.Sockets namespace primarily focuses on the transport layer, the socket layer for which it contains a comprehensive set of classes. These classes do an excellent job of abstracting much of the complexity associated with socket programming, while offering a powerful and productive socket stack that also adheres to the Berkeley socket. Lastly, built-in support for TCP and UDP is well integrated in the classes of the System.Net.Sockets. The classes of the System.Net.Sockets namespace are listed here:

- **LingerOption**: Contains information about the amount of time it will remain after closing with the presence of pending data (the socket's linger time).
- **MulticastOption**: Contains IP address values for IP multicast packets.
- **NetworkStream**: Provides the underlying stream of data for network access.
- **Socket**: Implements the Berkeley sockets interface.
- **SocketException**: The exception that is thrown when a socket error occurs.
- **TcpClient**: Provides client connections for TCP network services.
- **TcpListener**: Listens for connections from TCP network clients. This is essentially the TCP server class.
- **UdpClient**: Provides UDP network services.

A varying level of control is offered to the developer, including lower-level classes such as the Socket class, and higher-level classes, such as the TcpClient class that offers slightly less control with added productivity. An in-depth discussion of these classes would go beyond the scope of this book, but we'll take a closer look at some of these classes as we design and develop our sample application a little later in this chapter.

Creating the Sample Application

Now that you've had a brief introduction to networking in .NET, let's actually start discussing the application we're going to build in this chapter. The purpose of this example is to create a simple application to familiarize you with the use of threading in building networking applications in .NET. The application will actually consist of two small Windows Form applications; one acts as the server and the other acts as the client. We'll use VS .NET to design and implement these applications.

Design Goals

We want to create two autonomous and simple applications that interact with one another. The first application is a multithreaded/multiuser stock quote server program that looks up stock quotes from a database table and sends the data back to the requesting client asynchronously. The second application is the client and simply queries the server with a stock symbol for which it wants to get the quote information. All this will happen asynchronously, so that the client's UI is not paused while the server is responding to the request. The following list outlines and summarizes the basic requirements we'll abide by when building the applications:

- There will be two autonomous applications (one serving as the client and the other as the server) that can communicate with each other over the Internet.
- The UI of the client should not pause or freeze because of slow network connections, or any other delays, when querying the server for stock quotes.
- The server should be capable of handling numerous simultaneous client connections and queries and have the capability to communicate with the client in an asynchronous manner.
- Network settings must be abstracted away from the application and be modifiable.

To help you understand the typical user interaction within the application, let's look at a simple UML sequence diagram as shown in Figure 19-1.

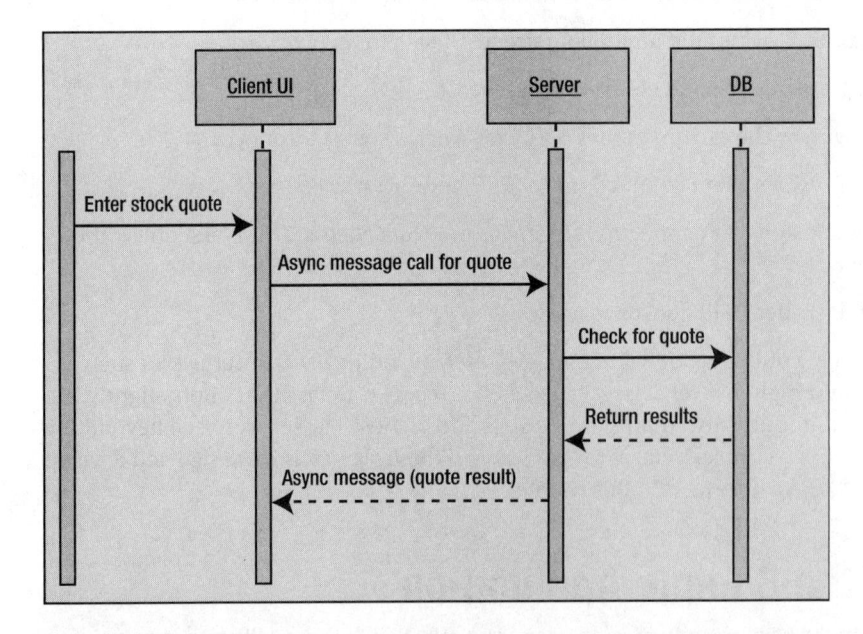

Figure 19-1. *UML diagram showing user interaction within a stock quote application*

So far, we've discussed the basic design guidelines for the applications from a very high level standpoint. If you are like most developers, you probably can't wait to see some code. So let's actually start building the two applications and examining code segments and concepts as we go along (as always, the code is available in the Downloads section of the Apress Web site at http://www.apress.com).

Building the Application

As mentioned before, the sample application in this chapter really consists of two autonomous applications: a client and a server. The two applications will communicate with each other via a specific TCP/IP port, which can be changed by altering the configuration file of the application (as you'll see later, both the client and the server need the same configuration file). Enough said, let's start by building the client application, which performs the simple task of querying the server for the result of a stock quote.

Creating the Client

Before we start building the application, let's take a moment or two to see the UML view of the client form class that is going to contain all the code for the client application (see Figure 19-2).

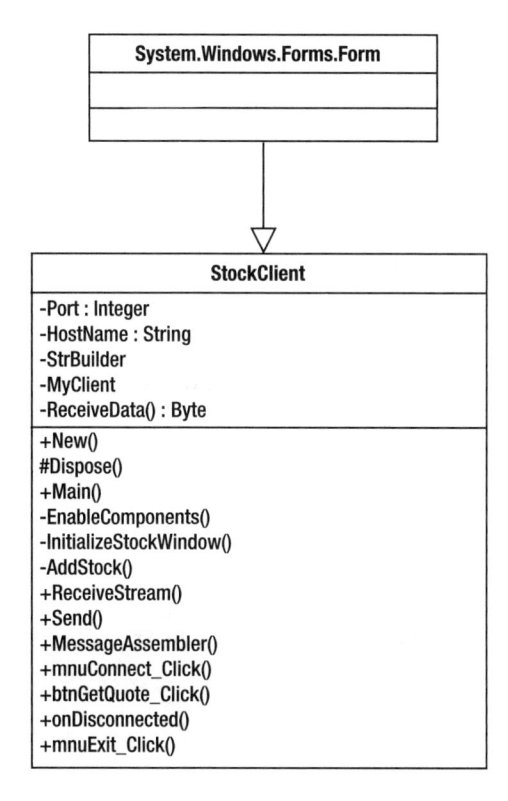

```
        System.Windows.Forms.Form
        ┌─────────────────────────┐
        │                         │
        │                         │
        └─────────────────────────┘
                    △
                    │
        ┌─────────────────────────┐
        │       StockClient       │
        ├─────────────────────────┤
        │ -Port : Integer         │
        │ -HostName : String      │
        │ -StrBuilder             │
        │ -MyClient               │
        │ -ReceiveData() : Byte   │
        ├─────────────────────────┤
        │ +New()                  │
        │ #Dispose()              │
        │ +Main()                 │
        │ -EnableComponents()     │
        │ -InitializeStockWindow()│
        │ -AddStock()             │
        │ +ReceiveStream()        │
        │ +Send()                 │
        │ +MessageAssembler()     │
        │ +mnuConnect_Click()     │
        │ +btnGetQuote_Click()    │
        │ +onDisconnected()       │
        │ +mnuExit_Click()        │
        └─────────────────────────┘
```

Figure 19-2. *UML view of the client form class*

The StockClient application simply inherits from the System.Windows.Forms.Form class and contains all the code for the client application, such as the Private member variables and the methods. To create the StockClient application, we start by creating a new Windows application project in VS .NET and naming it StockClient. On the default form, we create three controls on the page: a text box called txtStock, a button called btnGetQuote with its Text property set to Get Quote, and a new ListView control from the VS .NET toolbox called lstQuotes. Change the Name and Text properties of the form to StockClient. Also, add a MainMenu control to your form, and create a menu item &File with two subitems &Connect (called mnuConnect) and E&xit

(called `mnuExit`). Lastly, ensure that all the controls on the form, except the menu, have their `Enabled` property set to `False`; these will remain invisible until the user connects to the server. Your completed form should look like Figure 19-3.

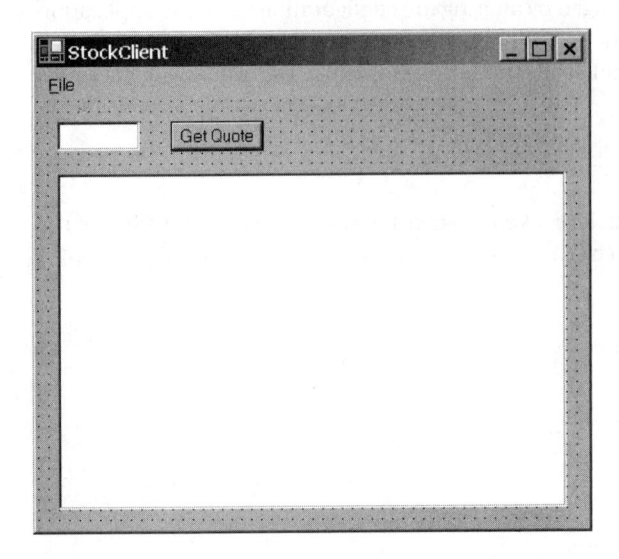

Figure 19-3. *The completed* `StockClient` *form*

We'll start with the set of `Imports` statements to reference the namespaces we need:

```
Imports System.Threading
Imports System.Net
Imports System.Net.Sockets
Imports System.Text
Imports System.IO
Imports System.Configuration
```

We also need some `Private` member variables that will be used throughout the `StockClient` application:

```
Private Port As Integer
Private HostName As String
Private Const PacketSize As Integer = 1024
Private ReceiveData(packetSize) As Byte
Private MyClient As TcpClient
Private StrBuilder As New StringBuilder()
```

We'll examine the variables and their uses later on, but for now let's amend our `ListView` control so that it can keep track of all the stock quotes that we enter. We need it to contain six columns: one column for each of the returned fields for the stock quote. The desired fields are Symbol, Price, Change, Bid, Ask, and Volume. Let's create a method called `InitializeStockWindow()` to add these columns to the `ListView` control as shown here:

```
Private Sub InitializeStockWindow()
  lstQuotes.View = System.Windows.Forms.View.Details
  lstQuotes.Columns.Add("Symbol", 60, _
      HorizontalAlignment.Left)
  lstQuotes.Columns.Add("Price", 50, _
      HorizontalAlignment.Left)
  lstQuotes.Columns.Add("Change", 60, _
      HorizontalAlignment.Left)
  lstQuotes.Columns.Add("Bid", 50, _
      HorizontalAlignment.Left)
  lstQuotes.Columns.Add("Ask", 50, _
      HorizontalAlignment.Left)
  lstQuotes.Columns.Add("Volume", 170, _
      HorizontalAlignment.Left)
End Sub
```

This code segment simply enables the grid lines of the `ListView` control, as well as assigning six columns of various widths to it. We'll call this function upon connecting to the server when the application is ready to start retrieving stock quotes from the server. We also need a method to enable and disable the controls as required, for instance upon the successful connection:

```
Private Sub EnableComponents(ByVal enable As Boolean)
  txtStock.Enabled = enable
  btnGetQuote.Enabled = enable
  lstQuotes.Enabled = enable
End Sub
```

Now we create a simple event called `Disconnected`, and an event handler for it called `OnDisconnected()`, which would be called after the event is actually raised. The `OnDisconnected()` method simply disables the connect option in the File menu as well as displaying an error message via a message box. It also disables the remaining input controls on the form:

```
Public Event Disconnected(ByVal sender As Object)
Private Sub OnDisconnected(ByVal sender As Object)
  mnuConnect.Enabled = True
  MessageBox.Show("The connection was lost!", _
    "Disconnected", MessageBoxButtons.OK, _
    MessageBoxIcon.Error)
  EnableComponents(False)
End Sub
```

To bind the `OnDisconnected()` method to the `Disconnected` event, we need to use an event handler:

```
AddHandler Disconnected, AddressOf OnDisconnected
```

As you may know, one of the greatest features of VB .NET is its capability to dynamically bind and unbind event handlers to events at runtime. You can use the `AddHandler` statement to assign a method to an event and, in much the same manner, use the `RemoveHandler` statement to detach an event handler method from an event. The ability to dynamically assign functionality to an event is very useful when you need to start or stop the event handler for an event or need to overwrite the behavior of an event handler. In the case of the `Disconnected` event, we assign it to the `OnDisconnected` delegate. Technically, we have the opportunity to accomplish this any time before the invocation of the event. However, it's usually best to declare all the event handlers early on in the application's execution, so we'll declare it in the `mnuConnect_Click` event soon after a connection to the server is established.

Speaking of the `mnuConnect_Click` event, double-click the Connect subitem of the File menu to enter code for the actual connection to the server. This is where we start to get our feet wet in network programming. First we need to instantiate a `TcpClient` object, which is a member of the `System.Net.Sockets` namespace. To do that, we need a host address and a port with which the client contacts the server. We'll abstract that information away from the core of the application by storing it in an external configuration file. .NET configuration files are well-formed XML files and are accompanied by a useful namespace in the .NET Framework, `System.Configuration`. With that in mind, let's look at the contents of the external configuration file that we can easily create in Notepad or VS .NET:

```
<configuration>
 <configSections>
  <section name="HostInfo"
type="System.Configuration.SingleTagSectionHandler"/>
 </configSections>
 <HostInfo hostname="localhost" port="6800" />
</configuration>
```

The XML contains an entry with two attributes storing the host information. We used `localhost`, and you can choose just about any port number between 1024 and 65000 (as long as it's not a reserved port). Save the file as `StockClient.exe.config`, and place it in the `bin` subdirectory where the compiled version of the application is going to reside.

Now add the following code to the `mnuConnect_Click` event handler:

```
Private Sub mnuConnect_Click( _
  ByVal sender As System.Object, _
  ByVal e As System.EventArgs) _
  Handles mnuConnect.Click

  Dim HostSettings As IDictionary
  Try
    HostSettings = _
      ConfigurationSettings.GetConfig("HostInfo")
    HostName = CType( HostSettings("hostname"), _
                    String)
    Port = CType(HostSettings("port"), Integer)
    MyClient = New TcpClient(HostName, Port)
    MyClient.GetStream.BeginRead(ReceiveData, 0, _
      PacketSize, AddressOf ReceiveStream, Nothing)
    EnableComponents(True)
    InitializeStockWindow()
    mnuConnect.Enabled = False
    AddHandler Disconnected, AddressOf onDisconnected
  Catch ex As Exception
```

```vb
    MessageBox.Show( _
      "Error: Unable to establish a connection!", _
      "Disconnected", MessageBoxButtons.OK, _
      MessageBoxIcon.Error)
  End Try
End Sub
```

The first portion of this code reads the host information from the configuration file. The `HostName`, `Port`, and `MyClient` fields have already been declared as `Private` at the start of the class. At this point, we just declare a local dictionary object to read in all the attributes of the `HostInfo` node in the configuration file.

An instance of the `TcpClient` class is instantiated by passing the DNS host name and a port number into the constructor. As you probably know, the host name maps to a specific host (or, more accurately, interface) on the network; the port number identifies the specific service on that host to connect to. The combination of host name and a service port is typically called an endpoint, which is represented in the .NET Framework by the `EndPoint` class. The `TcpClient` class constructor may take in an instance of the `IPEndPoint` class, but is also overloaded to accept a host name and a service port number.

Tip You can use the DNS class to resolve host names into IP addresses and then use a service port to construct an IPEndPoint class.

If we've done everything right and there is a server running on the same host name and port, a new connection will be established. Once connected, we must spawn a background thread to get data from the server asynchronously to enable the input controls for the user to receive stock symbols. Here's when things start to get a little interesting.

As mentioned previously, we need the receiving method of our application to be asynchronous. This is the only way the client can function without delays and serial user interaction. It is simply unacceptable to have the client application remain suspended while awaiting data to arrive from the server. Thanks to the .NET Framework, the solution is relatively simple and easy to implement. We first have to identify the `TcpClient`'s `NetworkStream` object. We can do that by calling the `GetStream()` method of the `TcpClient` object instance, which returns the underlying `NetworkStream` used to send and receive data. `GetStream()` creates an instance of the `NetworkStream` class using the underlying socket as its constructor parameter.

In addition, the instance of the `NetworkStream` class inherits from the `Stream` class, which provides a number of methods and properties used to facilitate network communications. After we have an underlying stream, we can use it to send and receive data over the network. Much like its cousin classes `FileStream` and `TextStream`, the `NetworkStream` class exposes read and write methods designed to send and receive data in a synchronous manner. `BeginRead()` and `BeginWrite()` are nothing more than the asynchronous versions of those methods. As a matter of fact, most of the methods in the .NET Framework classes beginning with `Begin`, such as `BeginRead()` and `BeginGetResponse()`, are intrinsically asynchronous without the programmer having to provide additional code when used with delegates. So we don't need to manually spawn new threads, and as the process reading the data is running on a background thread, the main thread of the application is free to remain attentive and responsive to UI interaction. Let's look at the signature of the `BeginRead()` method:

```
Overrides Public Function BeginRead( _
    ByVal buffer() As Byte, _
    ByVal offset As Integer, ByVal size As Integer, _
    ByVal callback As AsyncCallback, _
    ByVal state As Object) _
        As IAsyncResult
```

The following lists and explains each of the parameters of this method:

- **Buffer**: The data packet in which the data will arrive.
- **Offset**: The location in the buffer to begin storing the data to.
- **Size**: The size of the buffer.
- **Callback**: The delegate to call when the asynchronous call is complete.
- **State**: An object containing additional information supplied by the client.

Before we proceed further, let's take a moment to have a word or two about asynchronous calls, because it is a very important concept. As mentioned earlier, the problem with synchronous operations is that the working thread can be blocked until a certain operation is complete and that's not always desirable. Asynchronous calls run in a background thread and allow the initial thread (the calling thread) to continue as normal. .NET allows asynchronous calls via the help of delegates to just about any class and/or method. However, certain classes, such as the NetworkStream class, contain methods such as BeginRead() that have asynchronous capabilities built into them. Delegates are used to act as place holders for the functions against which asynchronous calls are made. In fact, delegates are nothing more than typesafe function pointers.

As you can see, the BeginRead() method requires byte arrays as opposed to string or text streams and, as such, is going to require a little more processing. We've already defined a variable named ReceiveData and another integer constant for the size of the byte array named PacketSize. Now we need to pass in the name of the method that will actually receive the data—the method that is going to be invoked by the callback delegate when the data arrives. Bear in mind that this method is going to be running in a background thread, so we have to be careful if we want to interact with the UI. Therefore, we simply spawn a background thread to receive the data as it arrives from the server over the network by just one line:

```
MyClient.GetStream.BeginRead( _
    receiveData, 0, packetSize, _
    AddressOf ReceiveStream, Nothing)
```

We create a method called ReceiveStream() that deals with the data in the byte packets as it arrives:

```vbnet
Private Sub ReceiveStream(ByVal ar As IAsyncResult)
  Dim ByteCount As Integer
  Try
    ByteCount = MyClient.GetStream.EndRead(ar)
    If ByteCount < 1 Then
      ' MessageBox.Show("Disconnected")
      RaiseEvent Disconnected(Me)
      Exit Sub
    End If
    MessageAssembler(ReceiveData, 0, ByteCount)
    MyClient.GetStream.BeginRead(ReceiveData, _
      0, PacketSize, AddressOf ReceiveStream, _
      Nothing)
  Catch ex As Exception
    'Display error message
    Dim Params() As Object = { _
      (String.Format("An error has occurred {0}", _
      ex.ToString))}
    Me.Invoke(New InvokeDisplay( _
      AddressOf Me.DisplayData), Params)
  End Try
End Sub
```

First, we have to check to see if there are any bytes in the byte array packet. There always has to be something in there. You can think of this as the pulse of the connection; as long as the client is connected to the server, there will be some data in that incoming packet, however small. We use the `EndRead()` method of the `Stream` object to check the current size of the byte array. We pass an instance of `IAsyncResult` into the `EndRead()` method. The `BeginRead()` method of the `GetStream()` method initiates an asynchronous call to the `ReceiveStream()` method, which is followed by a series of under-the-hood actions built in by the compiler to expedite the asynchronous operation. The `ReceiveStream()` method is then queued on a thread pool thread. If the delegate method, `ReceiveStream()`, throws an exception, then the newly created `Async` thread is terminated, and another exception is generated in the caller thread. Figure 19-4 further illustrates the situation.

If the number returned from the `EndRead()` method is anything less than 1, we know that the connection has been lost and we can raise the `Disconnected` event to take care of the appropriate work that needs to be done to handle that situation. However, if the number of bytes in the byte array is bigger than 0, we can start receiving the incoming data. At this point, we need the assistance of a helper method to help construct a string from the data that we retrieve from the server.

In fact, in .NET you can call almost any method asynchronously in much the same manner that we used the `BeginRead()` method. All you have to do is declare a delegate and call that delegate using the `BeginInvoke()` and the `EndInvoke()` methods. The intricacies of the asynchronous infrastructure are abstracted away so you don't have to worry about background threads and synchronization (not entirely, however).

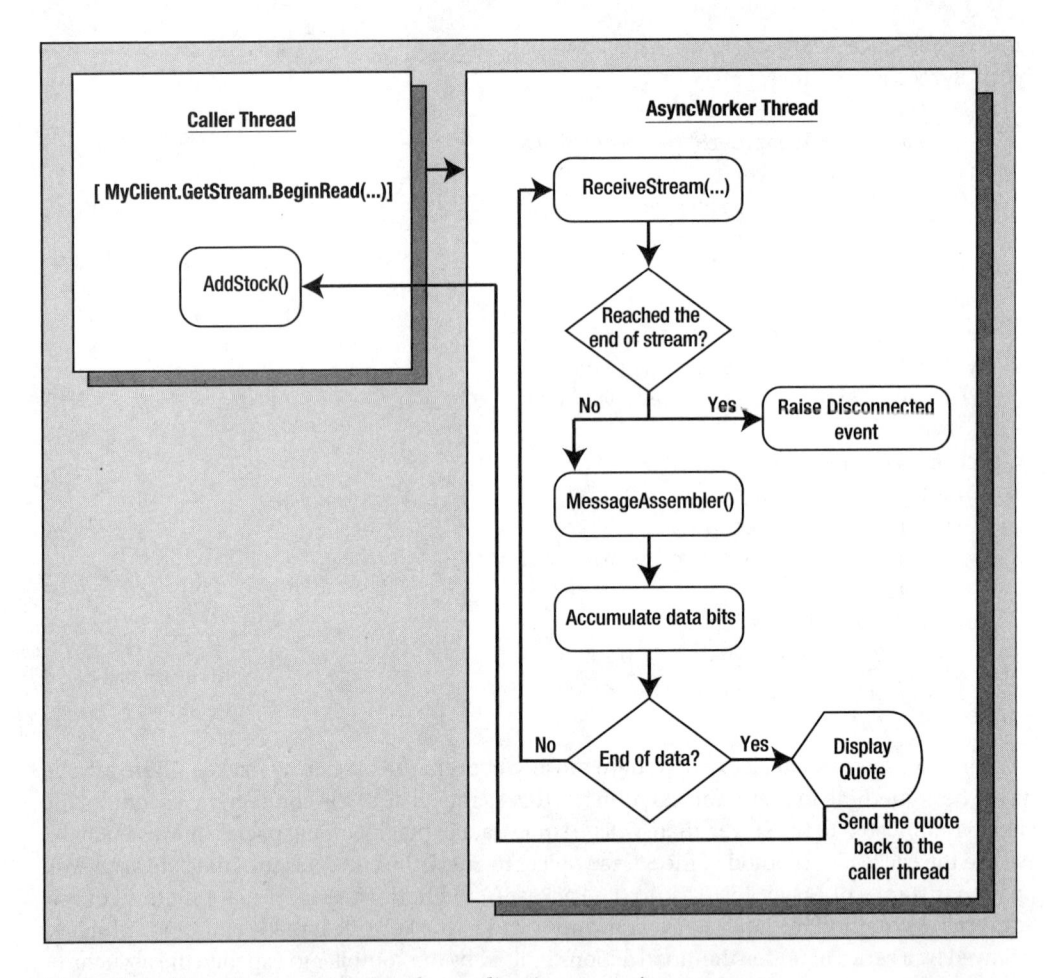

Figure 19-4. *Flow diagram showing the application execution sequence*

Now let's move on to the next portion of the code in which you see a call to the MessageAssembler() method. Due to the asynchronous nature of the BeginRead() method, we really have no way of knowing for sure when and in what quantity the data will arrive from the server. It could arrive all at once, or it could arrive in a hundred smaller pieces, each being only one or two characters long. So we have to perpetually read the data until we receive some sort of a signal indicating the end of the data for now. In this case, we will append a single character (#) to the end of our message that acts as a trigger agent for the MessageAssembler() method indicating the end of the incoming string, at which point the MessageAssembler class can stop waiting for more data and work with the data. In the meantime, we need assistance from the very useful StringBuilder class available in the System.Text namespace to help put together a whole string from the pieces of incoming byte arrays. This class provides a set of useful methods that make it ideal for string accumulation. In addition, tests have proven its performance to be significantly better than manual string concatenations when done in large iterations. Let's take a closer look at the MessageAssembler() method:

```
Private Sub MessageAssembler( _
    ByVal Bytes() As Byte, _
    ByVal offset As Integer, _
    ByVal count As Integer)
  Dim ByteCount As Integer
  For ByteCount = 0 To count - 1
    If Bytes(ByteCount) = 35 Then
      'Check for '#' to signal the end
      Dim Params() As Object = {StrBuilder.ToString}
      Me.Invoke(New InvokeDisplay( _
         AddressOf Me.DisplayData), Params)
      StrBuilder = New StringBuilder()
    Else
      StrBuilder.Append(ChrW(Bytes(ByteCount)))
    End If
  Next
End Sub
```

As you can see, the `MessageAssembler()` method loops through the byte array of data and accumulates the data as pieces of a string using the instance of the `StringBuilder` class until it encounters the # character. After it encounters that # character, signaling the end of the incoming string, it will stop and flush out the string by calling the `ToString()` method of the `StringBuilder` instance. We don't have to worry about manual conversion of bytes to strings at this point because the `StringBuilder` class takes care of that. It will then call the `DisplayData()` method to process the data:

```
Dim Params() As Object = {StrBuilder.ToString}
Me.Invoke(New InvokeDisplay( _
    AddressOf Me.DisplayData), Params)
```

This is the second time we've encountered something similar to this code, and you may be wondering what it is doing. Remember that this method is running in the background worker thread and is in the same thread that the UI form is. Although we can call the methods anywhere in the application, it is definitely not a good idea because that operation would not be thread-safe. Windows Forms are based on Win32 Single Threaded Apartments (STA) and thus are not thread-safe, which means that a form can't safely switch back and forth between operating threads (including the background threads spawned by an asynchronous operation) after it has been instantiated. You must call the methods of a form on the same thread in which the form is residing. To alleviate this issue, the CLR supports the `Invoke()` method, which marshals calls between the threads.

If you doubt this claim, you can always see for yourself by stepping through the code and looking at the Threads window to see the thread ID of the code that indicates the current thread in which the code is executing. By creating a delegate and calling it through the form's `Invoke()` method, it's executed in the form's thread and interaction with the form's controls is safely executed. Without marshalling, you often find that the code runs just fine and the desired functionality is accomplished initially, but you can run into problems later as this can cause instability in the application, with at times unpredictable behavior. This can get worse the more the application spawns threads. Therefore, don't talk to the GUI without marshalling the threads. In addition, the signature of the delegate must always match that of the `Invoke()` method, so we have to create an object array and insert the string in it; this is the only way we can use the `Invoke()` method. We call on the `DisplayData()` method to display the data as we want it:

```
Private Sub DisplayData(ByVal stockInfo As String)
  If stockInfo = "-1" Then
    MessageBox.Show("Symbol not found!", _
      "Invalid Symbol", _
      MessageBoxButtons.OK, MessageBoxIcon.Error)
  Else
    AddStock(stockInfo)
  End If
End Sub
```

In the `DisplayData()` method, we simply check the string to see whether its value is -1. As you'll see later, the server has been configured to simply return a -1 string if the requested stock quote cannot be returned because we've submitted an invalid symbol. Of course, in our case, an invalid symbol is any symbol that does not happen to be in our tiny database table of stocks, tbl_stocks (which you'll see later). Otherwise, we can go ahead and pass the `stockInfo` variable to the `AddStock()` method, which will gracefully add it to the `lstQuotes` control on the form:

```
Private Sub AddStock(ByVal stockInfo As String)
  Dim StockParameter() As String = _
      Split(stockInfo, ",")
  Dim Item As ListViewItem
  Item = New ListViewItem(StockParameter)
  If CDbl(StockParameter(2)) > 0 Then
    Item.ForeColor = Color.Green
  ElseIf CDbl(StockParameter(2)) < 0 Then
    Item.ForeColor = Color.Red
  End If
  lstQuotes.Items.Add(Item)
End Sub
```

We'll configure the server to return the data values in a string with the individual values being separated by a comma:

```
Symbol, Price, Change, Bid, Ask, Volume
```

So, the very first thing we have to do is to separate the individual values from one another by using the `Split()` method. We then create a new instance of the `ListViewItem` class and pass in the newly created string array as its constructor parameter. Finally, we want to be able to color code the stock quotes in the `lstQuotes` control so that if the price of a stock is down, the entire quote is displayed in red, and if the stock price is up, it is displayed in green. To accomplish this, we just have to convert the second value of the string array, which contains the current stock price, into a `Double` and check its value. After setting the color, we can just add a new entry into the `lstQuotes` control.

We're nearly done with the client code; we just need to create a few smaller methods to finish off. First, we need to add code to the `click` event of `btnGetQuote`:

```
Private Sub btnGetQuote_Click( _
  ByVal sender As System.Object, _
```

```
    ByVal e As System.EventArgs) _
    Handles btnGetQuote.Click
    Send(txtStock.Text.Trim + "#")
    txtStock.Text = ""
End Sub
```

This method simply gets the string value of the txtStock text box and appends a # character to the end of it to indicate the end of this string, and passes it to the Send() method. Remember that we needed the # character in the MessageAssembler() method to tell us when the end of the string was reached.

After the data is passed on to the Send() method, the Send() method creates a new instance of the StreamWriter class by passing the underlying TcpClient stream to it as its constructor and calling its Write() method, which sends the data across the socket in the form of a stream. We also call the Flush() method to ensure that the data is sent immediately and is not sitting in the buffer until some later point in the future:

```
Private Sub Send(ByVal sendData As String)
    Dim writer As New StreamWriter(MyClient.GetStream)
    writer.Write(sendData)
    writer.Flush()
End Sub
```

We're almost done here, but we have to do some minor cleanup code. For the most part, the Windows Form class does most of the cleanup by calling on the Dispose() method of itself and its base, but because .NET has nondeterministic garbage collection, it would a good idea to manually close the TcpClient connection. We can write a small function to do that, which would be called from the SocketClient_Closing() method, which is invoked when the user closes the form:

```
Private Sub StockClient_Closing( _
        ByVal sender As System.Object, _
        ByVal e As System.EventArgs) _
        Handles MyBase.Load
    closeConnection()
End Sub

Private Sub closeConnection()
    If Not MyClient Is Nothing Then
        MyClient.Close()
        MyClient = Nothing
    End If
End Sub
```

We also need to instantiate a copy of the StockClient form in the form's Main() method to kick start the application:

```
Public Shared Sub Main()
    Application.Run(New StockClient())
End Sub
```

Finally, we need to call the Application.Exit() method on the Click event of the exit menu item to shut down the application:

```
Private Sub mnuExit_Click( _
    ByVal sender As System.Object, _
    ByVal e As System.EventArgs) _
    Handles mnuExit.Click
  Application.Exit()
End Sub
```

We're done with the client portion of the application.

Creating the Server

Let's move on to creating the server application. Due to the multiclient nature of the target environment, we have to take a slightly different approach to create the StockServer application. We want to keep track of clients and know when they connect and disconnect. Client management would be far more effective with the use of a single class instance per client. Therefore, we'll create a separate client class that represents the clients that are connected to the server as you can see in the UML class diagram shown in Figure 19-5.

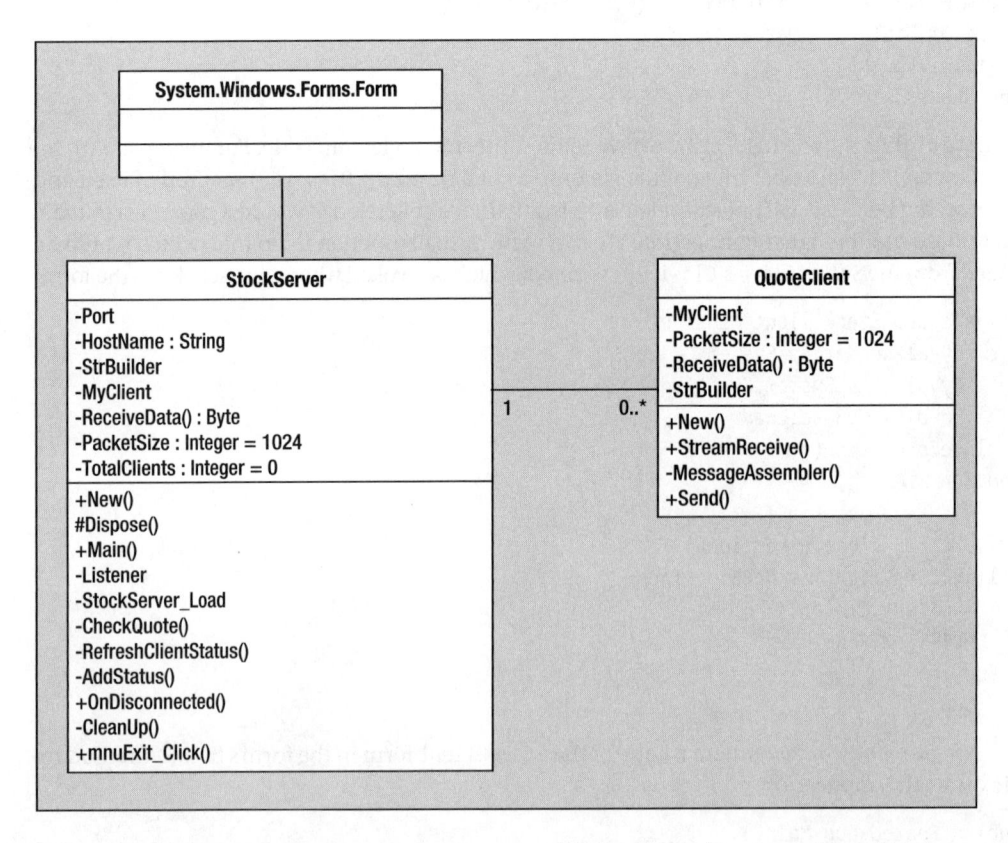

```
┌─────────────────────────────────────┐
│     System.Windows.Forms.Form       │
├─────────────────────────────────────┤
│                                     │
├─────────────────────────────────────┤
│                                     │
└─────────────────────────────────────┘
                  │
       ┌──────────┴──────────┐
       │                     │
┌──────────────────────┐   ┌──────────────────────────┐
│     StockServer      │   │      QuoteClient         │
├──────────────────────┤   ├──────────────────────────┤
│ -Port                │   │ -MyClient                │
│ -HostName : String   │   │ -PacketSize : Integer=1024│
│ -StrBuilder          │   │ -ReceiveData() : Byte    │
│ -MyClient            │ 1       0..*│ -StrBuilder              │
│ -ReceiveData() : Byte│◇─────────────│ +New()                   │
│ -PacketSize:Integer=1024│         │ +StreamReceive()         │
│ -TotalClients:Integer=0│          │ -MessageAssembler()      │
├──────────────────────┤   │ +Send()                  │
│ +New()               │   └──────────────────────────┘
│ #Dispose()           │
│ +Main()              │
│ -Listener            │
│ -StockServer_Load    │
│ -CheckQuote()        │
│ -RefreshClientStatus()│
│ -AddStatus()         │
│ +OnDisconnected()    │
│ -CleanUp()           │
│ +mnuExit_Click()     │
└──────────────────────┘
```

Figure 19-5. *Additon of a separate client class representing clients that are connected to the server*

A new instance of the QuoteClient class is created for each new client that connects to the server, so the StockServer class and the QuoteClient class have a one-to-many relationship. The QuoteClient class is always instantiated in a newly spawned thread made to handle the new client that has just connected. The QuoteClient class takes in a TcpClient object, responsible for the new client, as its constructor. We'll talk about the QuoteClient class a bit more later on. First, let's see what the UI is going to look like. The server application is a bit simpler than the client in terms of the UI. We need to have a single ListBox control to display some information along with the standard File menu with only the Exit subitem. In addition to those controls, drag and drop a new StatusBar and change its Anchor property to Bottom, Right, so that you can place it in the lower-right portion of the form. Be sure to change the name and the text property of the form to StockServer. Your form should now look something like the form shown in Figure 19-6.

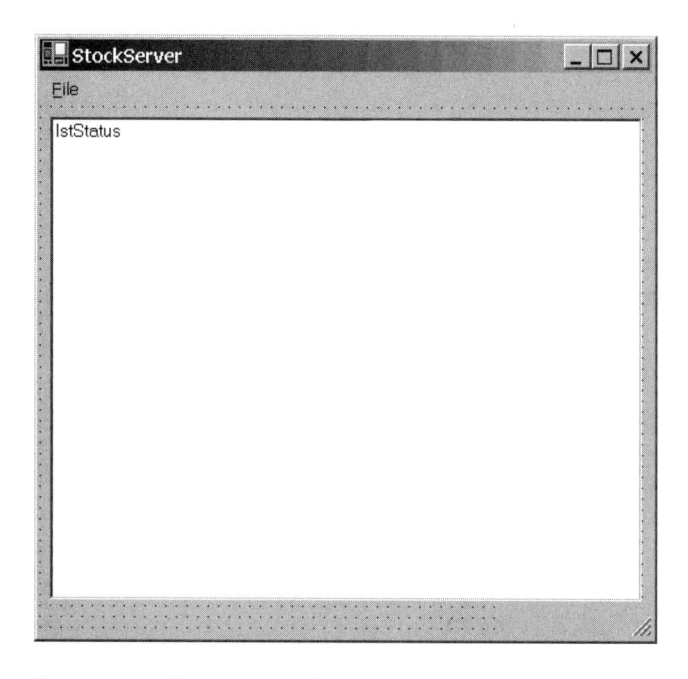

Figure 19-6. *Illustration of the* StockServer *form*

We also need a class module that we'll call QuoteClient.vb. This application will access a SQL Server database to get the stock quote information, so we need to make references to the necessary data namespaces in addition to the others shown here:

```
Imports System.Threading
Imports System.Net
Imports System.Net.Sockets
Imports System.Text
Imports System.Configuration
Imports System.Data
Imports System.Data.SqlClient
```

We also need some Private variables that will be used throughout the application. You'll see their use as we explore the code for this application:

```
Private ListenerThread As Thread
Private MyListener As TcpListener
Private Port As Integer
```

```vbnet
Private MyClient As TcpClient
Private TotalClients As Integer = 0
Private Const PacketSize As Integer = 1024
Private ReceiveData(PacketSize) As Byte
```

The server application starts running just as soon as it is opened, so we'll start by entering some code in the `StockServer_Load()` method of the application. We'll discuss the server's `Listener()` method, which is the core of the server itself, shortly; but first we start by spawning a new thread to run our `Listener()` method in the background:

```vbnet
Private Sub StockServer_Load( _
    ByVal sender As System.Object, _
    ByVal e As System.EventArgs) _
    Handles MyBase.Load
  Dim HostSettings As IDictionary
  Try
    HostSettings = _
      ConfigurationSettings.GetConfig("HostInfo")
    Port = CType(HostSettings("port"), Integer)
    ListenerThread = New Thread(AddressOf Listener)
    ListenerThread.Start()
    RefreshClientStatus()
  Catch ex As Exception
    AddStatus( _
      "An error has occurred. " & _
      "The server is not running." + _
      ex.ToString())
    CleanUp()
  Finally
    HostSettings = Nothing
  End Try
End Sub
```

Just as we did in the client application, we assign the port number from the configuration file into the `Port` variable, which we have already defined. We don't need the host name when creating server listeners because the server itself is the host. Because this application is really two autonomous parts running entirely independent of each other, be sure to use to the same configuration file for both the client and the server as nothing is going to work if the port number of the two applications don't match precisely. If an error occurs, we notify the user by using the `AddStatus()` method and do some manual cleaning up by calling the `CleanUp()` method, both of which you'll see later. But for now, let's look at the `Listener()` method:

```vbnet
Private Sub Listener()
  Try
    MyListener = New TcpListener(Port)
    MyListener.Start()
    Dim Message() As Object = _
      {"Server started. Awaiting new connections..."}
    Me.Invoke(New InvokeStatus( _
      AddressOf Me.AddStatus), Message)
```

```
      While (True)
        Dim NewClient As New QuoteClient( _
            MyListener.AcceptTcpClient())
        AddHandler NewClient.Disconnected, _
            AddressOf onDisconnected
        AddHandler NewClient.QuoteArrived, _
            AddressOf CheckQuote
        Dim ConnectMessage() As Object = _
            { String.Format( _
              "A new client just connected at {0}", _
              Now.ToShortTimeString() )}
        Me.Invoke(New InvokeStatus( _
            AddressOf Me.AddStatus), _
            ConnectMessage)
        TotalClients += 1
        RefreshClientStatus()
      End While
    Catch ex As Exception
      Dim Message() As Object = _
      { String.Format( _
        "The server stopped due to an unexpected error", _
        vbCrLf, ex.ToString() ) }
      Me.Invoke(
        New InvokeStatus( _
        AddressOf Me.AddStatus), Message)
    End Try
End Sub
```

This is a very important part of the server application because it represents the underlying engine of our server. As you can see, upon initialization of the port number, we called the `AcceptTcpClient()` method of the `TcpListener` class instance to accept incoming requests for connections. In essence, the `TcpListener` class is the server. It builds upon the `Socket` class to provide TCP services at a higher level of abstraction. However, the reason for spawning a new background thread to handle the `Listener()` method is the `AcceptClient()` method, which is a *synchronous* method that waits for connections while keeping the thread it's running on blocked—therefore we need to run it as a background thread. Once again, because this method is running in a background thread, we need to marshal between the current working thread and the thread in which the UI controls are running by using the `Invoke()` method of the form. We also start the *asynchronous* process of listening for incoming data, which in this case is going to be stock quote requests from the client. In much the same manner as we did in the client application, we'll use the `StreamReceive()` method that is located in the `QuoteClient` class:

```
Public Sub StreamReceive(ByVal ar As IAsyncResult)
  Dim ByteCount As Integer
  Try
    SyncLock MyClient.GetStream
      ByteCount = MyClient.GetStream.EndRead(ar)
    End SyncLock
```

```
      If ByteCount < 1 Then
        RaiseEvent Disconnected(Me)
        Exit Sub
      End If
      MessageAssembler(ReceiveData, 0, ByteCount)
      SyncLock MyClient.GetStream
        MyClient.GetStream.BeginRead( _
          ReceiveData, 0, PacketSize, _
          AddressOf StreamReceive, Nothing)
      End SyncLock
    Catch ex As Exception
      RaiseEvent Disconnected(Me)
    End Try
  End Sub
```

The major difference between this and its sister method in the client application arises from the fact that we are now in a multithreaded, multiuser environment and we can't just get the default stream and do whatever we want with it. There would be a very good chance of resource collisions, such as while we're reading data from it here, another thread in our server might attempt to send data to that same stream, so we need to use synchronization. For simple synchronization, we'll use the keyword `SyncLock` to lock the requested stream while we read from it. `SyncLock` is the most basic thread synchronization tool available. Don't forget to use good judgment when it comes to locking resources, as it can be detrimental to your application's performance if used in excess. For more sophisticated and custom tailored thread synchronizations, you can use some of the other classes available in the `System.Threading` namespace, such as `Interlocked`, which allows you to increment and decrement interlocks. Other than that, the `ReceiveStream()` method is more or less the same as the one in the client application.

The `MessageAssembler()` method also very closely resembles its counterpart defined in the client application. The only difference is that it calls the `CheckQuote()` method to connect to the database and retrieve the stock quote by raising the `QuoteArrived` event, which is dealt with in the `Listener()` method discussed previously.

```
Private Sub MessageAssembler( _
    ByVal Bytes() As Byte, _
    ByVal offset As Integer, _
    ByVal count As Integer)
  Dim ByteCount As Integer
  For ByteCount = 0 To count - 1
    If Bytes(ByteCount) = 35 Then
      'Check for '#' to signal the end
      RaiseEvent QuoteArrived( _
        Me, StrBuilder.ToString)
      StrBuilder = New StringBuilder()
    Else
      StrBuilder.Append(ChrW(Bytes(ByteCount)))
    End If
  Next
End Sub
```

Before we move on to the `CheckQuote()` method, let's briefly discuss the data source from which the server retrieves its quote information.

We need to start by creating a SQL Server database called StockDB, which will contain a single table called `tbl_stocks` with a structure as described in the following list:

Tip Database setup and population scripts (along with all the code from the book) are available in the Downloads section of the Apress Web site (http://www.apress.com).

- **Symbol**: The actual stock symbol.
- **Price**: The last price of the stock.
- **Change**: The price change of the stock.
- **Bid**: The last bid price of the stock.
- **Ask**: The last asking price of the stock.
- **Volume**: The total traded volume of the stock in a trading session.

That's all we need for the database, so back to the code and the `CheckQuote()` method. The `CheckQuote()` method resides in the class module attached to the main form of the application and is called by the local event handler when the `QuoteArrive()` method is triggered. The role of this method is to make a connection to the database, query it to retrieve the quote information, and pass the data back to the client. You can use the `SqlConnection` control in VS .NET and follow the wizards to generate a connection string to the database, or you can simply instantiate the `SqlConnection` class, which resides in the `System.Data.SqlClient` namespace, and manually assign it a connection string, as shown here:

```
Private Sub CheckQuote( _
    ByVal sender As QuoteClient, _
    ByVal stockSymbol As String)

  ' Connection string using SQL Server authentication
  Dim SqlConn As New SqlConnection( _
        "Initial Catalog=StockDB;" + _
        "Data Source=(local);User ID=sa;Password=")
  ' Alternative Connection string using Windows
  ' Integrated security
  ' Dim SqlConn As New SqlConnection("Initial
  ' Catalog=StockDB;" + _
  ' "Data Source=(local);Integrated Security=SSPI")
  Dim SqlStr As String = _
  "SELECT symbol, price, change, bid, ask, volume " _
    + "FROM tbl_stocks WHERE symbol='" _
    + stockSymbol + "'"
```

```vb
    Dim SqlCmd As SqlCommand = _
        New SqlCommand(SqlStr, SqlConn)
    Try
        SqlCmd.Connection.Open()
        Dim sqlDataRd As SqlDataReader = _
            SqlCmd.ExecuteReader()
        Dim FieldCount As Integer = 0
        Dim Records As Integer = 0
        Dim TempString As New StringBuilder()
        Do While sqlDataRd.Read()
            For FieldCount = 0 To 5
                TempString.Append( _
                    sqlDataRd.GetString(FieldCount) + ",")
                Records += 1
            Next
        Loop
            If Records = 0 Then
                sender.send("-1#")
            Else
                TempString.Replace(",", "#", _
                    TempString.Length - 1, 1)
                sender.send(TempString.ToString())
            End If
    Catch sqlEx As SqlException
        Dim Message() As Object = {sqlEx.ToString()}
        Me.Invoke(New InvokeStatus( _
            AddressOf Me.AddStatus), Message)
    Catch ex As Exception
        Dim Message() As Object = _
            {"Unable to retrieve quote information " _
            + " from the Database."}
        Me.Invoke(New InvokeStatus( _
            AddressOf Me.AddStatus), Message)
    Finally
        ' Close the Connection
        If SqlConn.State <> ConnectionState.Closed Then
            SqlConn.Close()
        End If
    End Try
End Sub
```

We also need a SQL query to return all six fields of the table for the individual stock the client has requested:

```vb
Dim SqlStr As String = _
"SELECT symbol, price, change, bid, ask, volume " _
+ "FROM tbl_stocks WHERE symbol='" _
+ stockSymbol + "'"
```

Now that we have the necessary SQL string and connection, we can instantiate the SqlCommand and SqlDataReader objects to read the data from the database server.

> **Tip** If you use any other database other than SQL Server 7.0/2000, you can't use the SqlConnection, SqlCommand, or the SqlDataReader objects because they have been specifically designed for use with the SQL Server. You should use the OleDB versions of those classes.

Finally, we execute the query by creating a new SqlDataReader class instance, and setting it to the result of the ExecuteReader() method of the SqlCommand object. After that, we iterate through each of the columns of returned data and append the values into a StringBuilder object, with a comma in between each value. If ExecuteReader() does not return any rows of data, then we have to send a string with a value of -1 back to notify the user of the nonexistence of the requested data. Otherwise, we replace the last comma in the string with a # (to indicate the end of string) and send it back to the client using the Send() method. Finally, we must ensure that the database connection is closed after we're finished with it. As you can see, the code in the Finally clause checks to see if the connection to the database is still open. If so, it will close the connection.

The Send() method of the server application resides in the QuoteClient class and requires slightly different code to the same method in the client application. The main difference is that we now are going to send the message asynchronously back to the client:

```
Public Sub send(ByVal sendData As String)
  Dim Buffer() As Byte = _
System.Text.ASCIIEncoding.ASCII.GetBytes(sendData)
  SyncLock MyClient.GetStream
    MyClient.GetStream.BeginWrite(Buffer, 0, _
      Buffer.Length, _
      Nothing, Nothing)
  End SyncLock
End Sub
```

The BeginWrite() method is similar to the BeginRead() method in terms of interface. We first have to convert the string message to a byte array, which can be easily accomplished by using the ASCII class in the System.Text namespace. Once again, we have to lock the stream to ensure that other threads are not writing to it as well. That's all that is required to asynchronously write the data to the client.

Running the Applications

Build each project in its own instance of VS .Net and don't forget to include the configuration files that we created earlier in the same directory as the application executables.

Let's now run the compiled applications. We need to run the StockServer.exe first so that it will start listening for clients as shown in Figure 19-7.

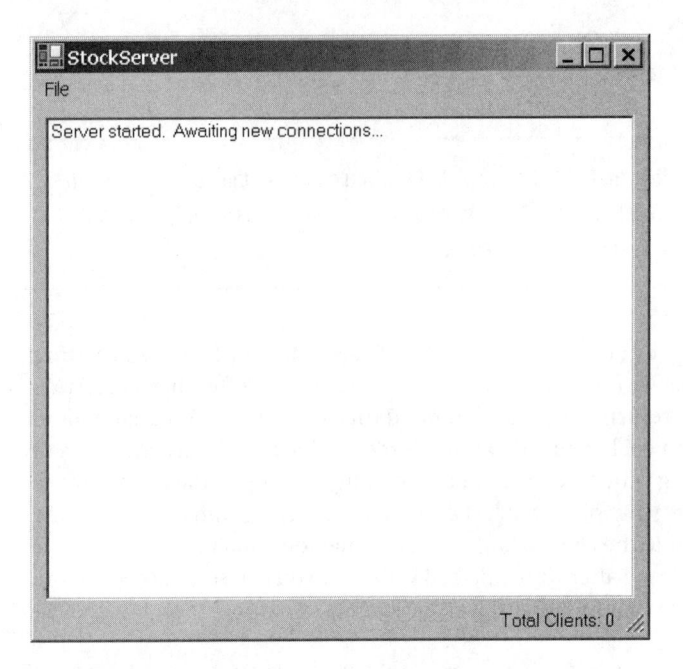

Figure 19-7. `StockServer` *application listening for clients*

Now run an instance of the client application. As you probably recall, we had disabled all the UI controls on the form until the user successfully connected to the server. So, let's go ahead and click on the Connect item in the File menu (see Figure 19-8).

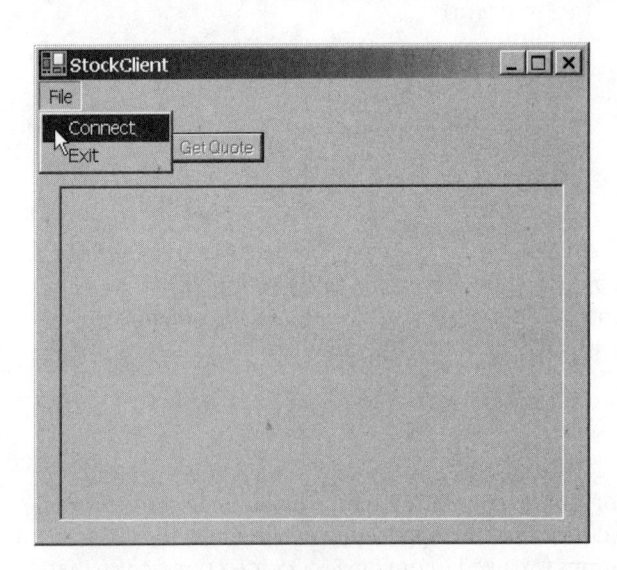

Figure 19-8. *Click* Connect *to connect* StockClient *to the server.*

All the controls (except the Connect option) are now enabled and the `ListView` control has been instantiated with all the right columns. Enter a valid stock symbol from the `tbl_stocks` table. Let's try `CSCO`, for example, as shown in Figure 19-9.

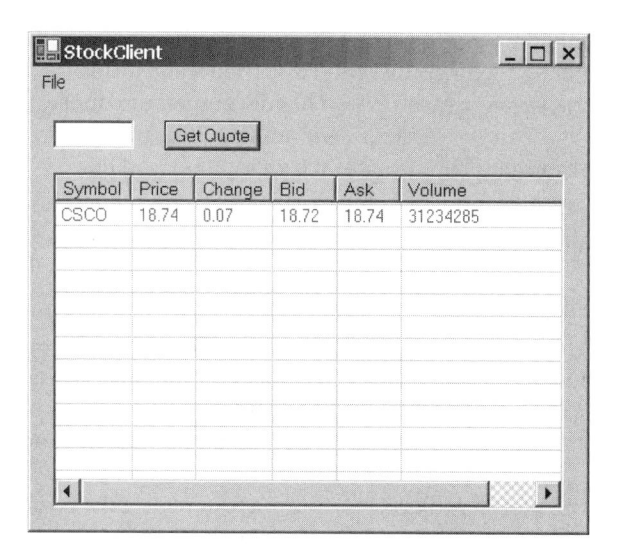

Figure 19-9. *Example of stock quote returned from the server*

The Stock Server successfully returned a quote and, because the change amount is positive, the entire row appears in the color green (as shown in Figure 19-10. Let's go ahead and create a few other instances of the StockClient class and see if they all function correctly.

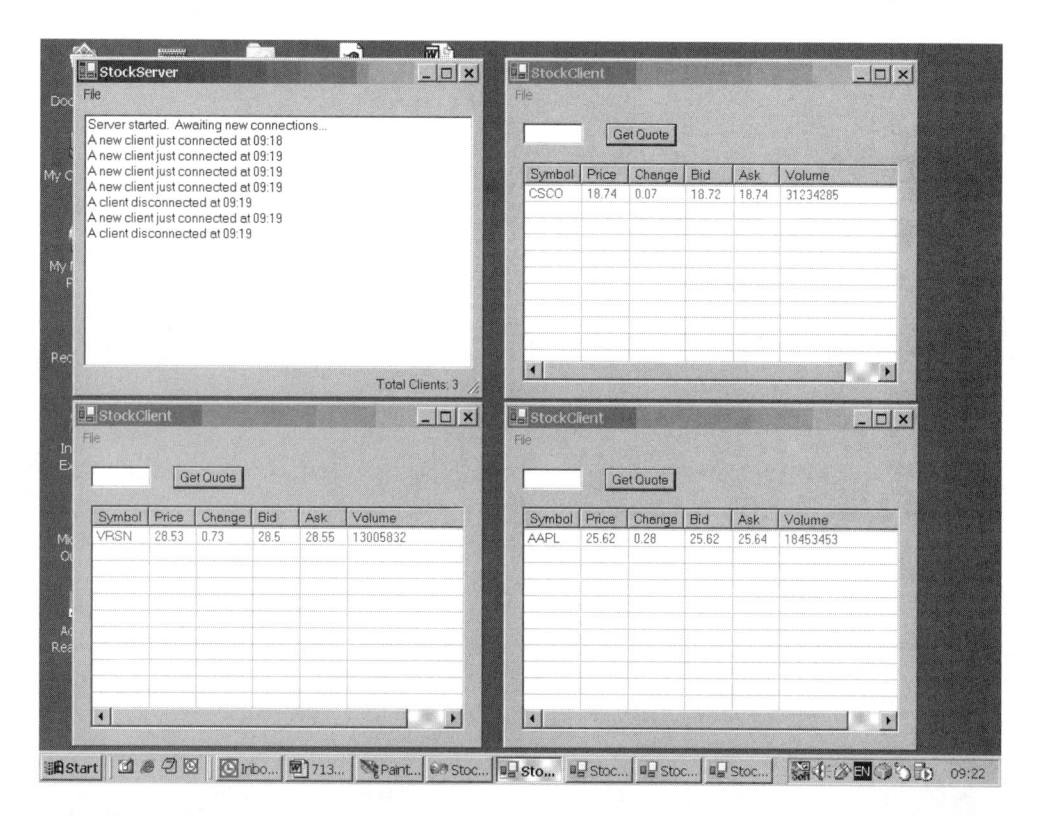

Figure 19-10. *Running multiple instances of the StockClient class*

As you can see, both the `StockClient` and the `StockServer` applications work very well with each other. The server keeps tracks of how many clients connect and disconnect and displays it in the `ListBox`. In addition, the multithreaded server is easily able to handle numerous connections, as well as send and receive data in an asynchronous fashion. You can step through the code for both the client and the server application and get a better feel for the application workflow.

Summary

As you've seen, developing multithreaded network applications with VS .NET is a straightforward process. Much of the plumbing and infrastructure has already been abstracted away in the form of a comprehensive and OO set of classes. For even greater control over the network sockets, the `System.Net.Socket` offers plenty of rich functionality. We also experienced how simple it is to use .NET's intrinsic support for asynchronous operations that run in the background worker thread without much code.

We hope that you found this book both helpful and enjoyable. The extra features in .NET give the VB developer more power than they have ever had—threading is just one of them.

Index

Symbols
.NET. *See* NET

A
Abort() method
   Thread class, 423, 442, 453, 454, 533
Abstract classes, 285
   compared to Concrete classes, 285
   description, 287
abstract classes
   EDI invoicing and billing system, 293
      Transformation abstract class, 293
      UploadNotify abstract class, 294
   implementing Abstract Factory Pattern, 286
   MustInherit keyword, 285, 287
Abstract Factory Pattern, 285
   data pipeline architecture, 288
   example of using, 287–288
   factory class, 291
   implementing, 285
   introduction, 285
   shared methods, 287, 289
   using with dynamic assembly loading, 286
      EDI invoicing and billing system, 289–300
Abstract value
   TypeAttributes enumeration, 311
AcceptTcpClient() method
   TcpListener class, 611
access modifiers
   building component classes, 360
accessor methods, invoking, 263
Account example
   attributes and SOAP, 304
      annotating Account class with NonSerializedAttribute class, 306
      annotating Account class with SerializableAttribute, 306
      custom attributes, 310
      defining Account class, 305
      deserializing data from XML file to recreate Account object in memory, 307
      imports statements, 304
      proving machine name not serialized, 310
      viewing metadata, 308–309
AcquireReaderLock() method
   ReaderWriterLock class, 484
AcquireWriterLock() method
   ReaderWriterLock class, 484, 487
<activated> element
   configuring CAOs, 101

Activator class
   creating or accessing objects of specific type, 30
   GetType() method, 30
Add() method
   Container class, 365
AddEventHandler() method
   EventInfo class, 246
AddressOf operator, 425
administrating priorities, threads, 409
ADO.NET classes
   System.Data.SqlClient namespace, 201
All field
   RefreshPropertiesAttribute class, 377, 388
All value
   AttributeTargets enumeration, 318
   MemberTypes enumeration, 235
AllocateDataSlot() method
   Thread class, 423
AllocateNamedDataSlot() method
   Thread class, 423
AllowMultiple property
   AttributeUsageAttribute class, 332
apartment threading model
   compared to free threading, 402
   running out of process, 403
   specifying, 521
ApartmentState enumeration
   defining threading models, 522
ApartmentState property
   Thread class, 424, 522
AppDomain class
   .NET Remoting and, 6
   and .NET remoting, 418
   executing code within, 416
   importing namespace, 414
   inheritance, 412
   lease manager, 9
   methods
      CreateDomain() method, 415, 417
      DoCallBack() method, 417
      GetAssemblies() method, 225
      SetData() method, 415, 417
   properties
      CurrentDomain property, 415, 418
      FriendlyName property, 417–418
      GetCurrentThreadId property, 416, 418
   setting AppDomain data, 413
   System namespace, 411, 425
application code, creating and debugging, 564

Application Configuration file
    configuring assembly binding, 280
    partially referencing assemblies, 282
application configuration files, 100
application domain. *See* AppDomain
<application> element
    <channels> child element, 103
    child element of <system.runtime.remoting>
        element, 101
    <customErrors> child element, 104
    <lifetime> child element, 104
    <service> child element, 101
ApplicationException class
    defining custom exception classes, 191
Application_Start() subroutine
    Global.asax file, 122
ArgumentNullException class, 481
    System namespace, 162, 169
ArgumentOutOfRangeException class
    System namespace, 162, 169, 541
arguments
    DllImportAttribute class example, 320
    passing into attributes, 319–322
ArrayEditor class
    System.ComponentModel.Design namespace, 379
ArrayList class
    inserting and removing items, 369
    System.Collections namespace, 526
ASCII class
    System.Text namespace, 615
ASP applications
    debugging, 563
ASP.NET
    reflection, 212
ASP.NET pages
    multi-threaded by default, 521
ASP.NET Web controls
    creating visual and non-visual controls, 345
ASPCompact directive, 521
aspect-oriented programming, 301
assemblies
    AssemblyVersionAttribute class, 303
    attributes insert metadata into, 301
    configuring assembly binding, 280
    defining for metadata for, 302
    dynamic assembly loading, 279
        creating assembly references, 280–282
        instantiating classes dynamically, 283–285
        methods, 282–283
assembly attributes, 327
    AssemblyVersion attribute, 123
    defining, 327, 329
    using, 327–328
    viewing assembly metadata with Windows
        Explorer, 331
Assembly class
    example of using, 284
    methods, 227
        CreateInstance() method, 283, 289
        Get . . . Assembly() methods, 225
        Load() method, 289
        dynamic assembly loading, methods for, 282
    obtaining, 225
    properties, 226
    System.Reflection namespace, 220, 223, 282
Assembly keyword, 327
assembly manifest, storing, 225
assembly metadata
    examining, 223, 225
        Assembly class, 225–227
        example, 228–230
Assembly property
    Type class, 225, 231
Assembly value
    AttributeTargets enumeration, 318
AssemblyDescriptionAttribute class
    Description property, 330
    retrieving using Attribute.GetCustomAttribute, 330
    System.Reflection namespace, 327
AssemblyName class
    properties
        CultureInfo property, 281
        Name property, 281
        Version property, 281
    specifying strong name, 281
    System.Reflection namespace, 227, 280–281
AssemblyQualifiedName property
    Type class, 231
AssemblyTitleAttribute class
    retrieving using Attribute.GetCustomAttribute, 330
    System.Reflection namespace, 327
    Title property, 330
AssemblyVersionAttribute class
    applies to assemblies, 303
    identifies assembly version to load, 304
    System.Reflection namespace, 303
    version number held in, 123
Assert() method
    Debug class, 187
    Trace class, 187, 571
        asserting error notification, 572
asynchronous callback example, 133
asynchronous calls
    via delegates, 602
asynchronous invocation, 130–131
    asynchronous callback, 133–134
    casting, 134
    result options
        frequent polling, 132
        running on separate thread, 132
        timeout used to check for completion, 133
asynchronous protocol
    session-oriented, 2
asynchronous remoting, 127
    call contexts, 154
        Teleconference Application example, 154–157
    event handlers, 127
    generating events in single application
        domains, 139–140
    multi-user asynchronous remote applications
        Conference example, 149–154
    multi-user remote applications, 149

no changes to the server, 130
passing events between remote applications, 141
   TickTock example, 141–143
remotely delegatable objects, 143
TickTock example, 143–149
slow asynchronous process, 130–131
   modifying Power example, 131–135
   schematic, 131
slow asynchronous remote process
   implementing Power example, 135–138
slow synchroneous process
   Power class library, 128–130
using events, 138
asynchronous session-oriented systems, 3
AsyncProcessMessage() method
   IMessageSink interface, 47
AsyncProcessRequest() method
   IClientChannelSink interface, 46
AsyncProcessResponse() method
   IClientChannelSink interface, 46
   IServerChannelSink interface, 46
ATM scenario
   achieving thread-safety, 470
Attribute class
   GetCustomAttribute() method, 311, 330, 332
   SerializableAttribute class inherits from, 317
   syntax, 316–317
   System namespace, 302
attribute classes
   .NET Framework, 302–304
   definitions, 316
   rules for defining, 302
   syntax, 316–319
attribute objects
   injecting into compiled MSIL code, 301
attributes, 220
   See also attribute classes
   .NET Framework attribute classes, 302–304
   assembly attributes, 327–332
   controlling the compiler using attributes, 322–327
   custom attributes, 332–340
   introduction, 301–302
   metadata, 301
   passing arguments into, 319–322
   syntax, 304
   testing data type for, 311–315
   using predefined attributes, 315
   using with SOAP, 304–311
Attributes property
   ParameterInfo class, 247
   Type class, 232, 314
AttributeTargets enumeration
   System namespace, 318
AttributeUsageAttribute class
   defining new custom attributes, 332
   properties
      AllowMultiple property, 332
      Inherited property, 332
   System namespace, 316
   using with SerializableAttribute class, 317
AuthorAttribute custom attribute, 334, 336

Authorization class
   System.Net namespace, 594
AutoResetEvent class
   compared to ManualResetEvent class, 491
   manual synchronization, 488, 491–492
   Set() method, 547
   synchronization support, 473
   System.Threading namespace, 422
   WaitOne() method, 492

B

Bank Application example
   client-side error checking, 183–185
   dealing with errors in the remote object, 185
      detecting errors at runtime, 188
      display Debug and Trace messages, 185–188
   defining Bank class library, 170–175
   defining BankClient application, 176–178
   defining custom exception classes, 191
      defining constructors, 194–196
      defining informational properties and methods, 197
      serialization, 192–194
   defining host for Bank remotable object, 175–176
   enabling remote debugging, 180–182
   improving application, 189–191
   logging error information at server, 198
      logging errors to a database, 200–203
      logging errors to a file, 198–199
      logging errors to Windows Event log, 203–207
   testing, 178–180
BaseChannelWithProperties class
   System.Runtime.Remoting.Channels namespace, 85
BaseType property
   Type class, 232
BeginInvoke() delegate method, 130, 134
BeginRead() method
   NetworkStream class, 601, 602, 615
BeginWrite() method
   NetworkStream class, 601, 615
BeginXXX methods, intrinsically asynchronous, 601
Berkeley socket
   System.Net.Sockets namespace, 595
best practice and Option Strict, 210
binary formatters, 10
BinaryClientFormatterSink class
   using TCP channel, 47
BinaryClientFormatterSinkProvider class
   System.Runtime.Remoting.Channels namespace, 48
BinaryFormatter class
   BinaryClientFormatterSink as implementation class, 47
   compared to SoapFormatter class, 308
   default formatter for TcpChannel class, 18
   speed of data transfer, 45
   System.Runtime.Serialization.Formatters.Binary namespace, 18, 44, 172, 308
BinaryServerFormatterSinkProvider class
   System.Runtime.Remoting.Channels namespace, 48

Binder class
    SelectMethod() method, 257
    System.Reflection namespace, 256
Binder property
    IRemotingFormatter interface, 66
BindHandle() method
    ThreadPool class, 539
binding, 213
    early binding, 213
    late binding, 215–218
    object-orientation, 214–215
    reflection, 212
    run-time binding, 214
BindingFlags enumeration
    example of value as a parameter, 236
    flag values, 235
        GetField flag, 267
        GetProperty flag, 262
        InvokeMethod flag, 256
        SetField flag, 267
        SetProperty flag, 262
    System.Reflection namespace, 283
    using with Type.GetFields/GetField, 239
    using with Type.GetMethods, 243
    using with Type.GetProperties, 241
    values, 283
Book Collection Library
    UML representation, 502
BookLib class, 508
BooleanSwitch class
    Enabled property, 580–581
    System.Diagnostics namespace, 570
    tracing switches, 580–581
breakpoints, setting, 568
Breakpoints window
    Hit Count dialog, 569
    Visual Studio .NET Debugger, 568
BrowsableAttribute class
    System.ComponentModel namespace, 375
Build property
    Version class, 281

C

call context, 8
    Teleconference Application example, 154–157
    using in asynchronous remoting, 154
Call Stacks, 537
callbacks, 434
    See also TimerCallback delegate
CanConvertFrom() method
    TypeConverter class, 389
CanConvertTo() method
    TypeConverter class, 384, 389
CanRead property
    PropertyInfo class, 240
CanWrite property
    PropertyInfo class, 240
CAO (Client-Activated Object), 30
    <activated> element, 101
    activation when appropriate, 30
    configuring with client element, 102–103
    registering, 30–31

casting
    asynchronous invocation, 134
Catch statement
    Trace.Fail usually placed within, 571
CategoryAttribute class
    System.ComponentModel namespace, 359, 375
channel classes, 17
    ChannelServices class, 18
    HTTP channel classes, 18
    TCP channel classes, 17
channel configuration, 103
    TCP protocol, 103
<channel> element
    attributes, 103
    displayName attribute, 103
channel interfaces, 83
channel sink
    See also sinks
    interfaces and classes, 45
ChannelData property
    IChannelReceiver interface, 84
ChannelName property
    IChannel interface, 84
ChannelPriority property
    IChannel interface, 84
channels, 10
    and formatters, choosing, 45
<channels> element, 101, 103–104
    <channel> child element, 103
Channels tab
    .NET Framework Configuration Tool, 109
ChannelServices class
    RegisterChannel() method, 30, 40
    System.Runtime.Remoting.Channels namespace, 18, 86
<channelSinkProviders> element
    child element of <system.runtime.remoting> element, 101
CharSet property
    DllImportAttribute class, 320
chatinterlocked example, 494–496
CheckQuote() method
    networking application example, 613
class member metadata, examining, 234
class type information. *See* metadata
Class value
    AttributeTargets enumeration, 318
    TypeAttributes enumeration, 311
CLI
    manual synchronization, 488
    synchronized code regions, 474
    synchronized contexts, 473
client application
    EDI invoicing and billing system, 299
client channel sink providers, 47–48
<client> element
    child of <application> element, 102
    configuration for client-activated objects, 103
client invocations on the server, 141
client-activated objects, 7–8
client-server systems
    asymmetric, 2
    introduction, 2–3

INDEX

client-side error checking
    recommendations, 184
<clientProviders> element
    template provided by <channelSinkProviders> element, 101
clients, server lacks knowledge of, 143
clock interrupts, 407
Close() method
    FileStream class, 196
    TextWriterTraceListener class, 577
CLR and threads, 537
    Invoke() method, 605
    Remoting in .NET Framework, 537
    thread pooling
        problems, 538
        role of CLR, 537
        size of thread pool, 538
co-operative systems
    common goals, 1
code debugging, 564
    See also debugging
code tracing, 564, 570
    See also tracing
    changing the default listener, 575–576
    classes, 570
    DataImport example, 584
    Debug class, 583
    TextWriterTraceListener class, 576–579
    Trace class, 571
        default listener application, 571–574
    tracing switches, 579–580
        BooleanSwitch class, 580–581
        TraceSwitch class, 581–583
    using different listener applications, 574–576
    Windows Event log, 574
CodeBase property
    Assembly class, 226
Collection classes
    synchronized wrappers, 501
collection protocol, 211
ColorEditor class
    System.ComponentModel.Design namespace, 380
COM, problems with, 4
COM components
    finding threading model of, 521
ComboBox class
    SelectedIndexChanged() method, 270
ComboxBox class
    SelectedItem property, 271
Command/immediate window, 567
Common Language Infrastructure. *See* CLI
common remoting errors, 159
    client application specifies an invalid host name, 166
    client application specifies an invalid object URI, 167
    client application specifies an invalid port, 166
    client application specifies an invalid protocol, 166
    miscellaneous error conditions, 167, 169
    server application isn't currently running, 165

CompareExchange() method
    Interlocked class, 473
compile-time type, 215
Compiler
    controlling compilation using attributes, 322–327
completionPortThreads, 540
Component class
    Control class inherits from, 345
    implementing IComponent interface, 359
Component Designer
    building components, 361
    generating constructors, 362
    InitializeComponent() method, 362
ComponentCollection class
    System.ComponentModel namespace, 365
components
    adding component objects to application, 373–375
    adding components from Toolbox, 362
    adding to ToolBox, 372
    building with System.ComponentModel namespace, 358
        Employee example, 358–395
    controls as type of component, 344
    creating component classes 343
    defining, 359
        access modifiers, 360
        as nested class, 360
        converter classes, 381
        custom container class to host components, 366–372
        properties and events, 375
        Visual Studio .NET, 360
    hosting in Container class, 364
        MySimpleContainer example, 364–366
    introduction, 344
    storing in a container, 364
    using in Visual Studio .NET, 372
Components property
    Container class, 365
Concrete classes, 285
    compared to Abstract classes, 285
    EDI invoicing and billing system, 297
        VendorTransform concrete classes, 297
        VendorUploadNotify concrete classes, 297
    implementing Abstract Factory Pattern, 286
concurrency, 519
    Mutex class, 173
ConditionalAttribute class, 302
    applies to methods, 303
    controlling compilation using attributes, 322
        viewing MSIL using Disassembler, 324, 326
    Debug preprocessor identifier and compiling without defining Debug preprocessor symbol, 324
        defining Debug preprocessor symbol, 325
    Debug preprocessor identifier and, 323–324
    decides whether method should be compiled or ignored, 304
    System.Diagnostics namespace, 303, 322

Conference example
    multi-user asynchronous remote applications
        implementing client code, 152
        implementing ConfAttendee class library, 150–151
        implementing Conference class library, 149–150
        implementing server code, 152
        running example, 153–154
configuration, 99
    channel implementation, 103
    file structure, 100
        <configuration> element, 101
        <system.runtime.remoting> element, 101
    loading files, 105
        Exchange example, 105–108
    registering client and server, 103
    standard configuration file types, 100
    viewing and modifying files with .NET Framework Configuration Tool, 108
configuration files
    EDI invoicing and billing system, 290
    information contained, 11
Configure() method
    RemotingConfiguration class, 19, 105, 122
Connect() method
    RemotingServices class, 16, 21
Console class
    Read() method, 543, 547
    ReadLine() method, 425
Constructor value
    AttributeTargets enumeration, 318
    MemberTypes enumeration, 235
ConstructorInfo class
    retrieving constructors of Employee class, 245–246
    System.Reflection namespace, 220, 234
Container class
    Components property, 365
    hosting components, 364
        MySimpleContainer example, 364
    implements IContainer interface, 364
    methods
        Add() method, 365
        Remove() method, 365
    System.ComponentModel namespace, 358
containers
    defining a custom container class to host components, 366–372
    definition, 344
    storing components in, 358, 364
context
    call context, 8
    context-bound objects, 8–9
    objects, 155
Context property
    IRemotingFormatter interface, 66
context switching
    time cost, 399
context-bound custom attributes, 338
    extending ContextAttribute class, 338
    LoggedAttribute context-bound custom attribute, 338

context-bound objects
    extension of transaction context, 8–9
ContextAttribute class
    extending to create context-bound custom attributes, 338
    System.Runtime.Remoting.Contexts namespace, 338
    using with ContextBoundObject class, 338
ContextBoundObject class
    synchronized contexts, 473
    System namespace, 338
    using with ContextAttribute class, 338
Control class
    extends Component class, 359
    implementing IComponent interface, 359
    inherits from Component, 345
    System.Web.UI namespace, 345
controls
    creating ASP.NET Web control, 345
    creating Windows Forms control, 345
    introduction, 344
    relationship between classes and interfaces, 345
converter classes
    defining for components, 381
ConvertFrom() method
    TypeConverter class, 389
ConvertTo() method
    TypeConverter class, 384, 389
Cookie class
    System.Net namespace, 594
cooperative multitasking, 398
CORBA, 4
Created event
    FileSystemWatcher class, 585
CreateDomain() method
    AppDomain class, 415, 417
CreateInstance flag value
    BindingFlags enumeration, 236
CreateInstance() method
    Assembly class, 227, 283–284, 289
CreateMessageSink() method
    IChannelSender interface, 84
CreateSink() method
    IClientChannelSinkProvider interface, 47
    IServerChannelSinkProvider interface, 47
CriticalSection() method
    synchronized code regions, 477–478
cryptography
    public key cryptography, 281
CultureInfo class
    System.Globalization namespace, 281, 283
CultureInfo property
    AssemblyName class, 281
CurDomain object
    SetData() method, 416
CurrentContext property
    Thread class, 424
CurrentCulture property
    Thread class, 424
CurrentDomain property
    AppDomain class, 415, 418
CurrentLeaseTime property
    ILease interface, 39

CurrentPrincipal property
    Thread class, 424
CurrentState property
    ILease interface, 39
CurrentThread property
    Thread class, 424
CurrentUICulture property
    Thread class, 424
custom attributes, 310, 332
    defining, 332–340
    testing for programmatically, 328–329
custom exception classes, 191
    defining constructors, 194–196
    defining informational properties and methods, 197
    Exception inheritance hierarchy, 191
    serialization, 192–194
custom remoting, 43
    See also custom serialization; custom transport protocols; custom transport sink
    channels with custom transport protocols, 83
    Invert example
        adding new client channel sink, 52–59
        basic, 48–52
    sink chain, 43
        adding custom formatter, 62–71
        channel sink interfaces and classes, 45
        client channel sink providers, 47–48
        customizing, 48
        formatter classes, 44
        replacing the formatter sink, 59–62
custom serialization, 71
    defining custom serialization format, 72
    Equation example, 71–83
custom transport protocols
    channel interfaces, 83
custom transport sink
    implementing, 83
    implementing a custom TCP/IP socket channel, 84–98
Custom value
    MemberTypes enumeration, 235
<customErrors> element
    child of <application> element, 104
Customize Toolbox dialog box, 372

D

data pipeline architecture
    Abstract Factory Pattern, 288
    EDI invoicing and billing system, 289
data source
    networking application example, 613
data types
    valid parameters for custom attribute, 333
database
    creating in SQL Server, 200
database connection pool example
    implementing the pool, 510, 514
        DBConnectionSingleton class, 515
        ObjectPool class, 511
        using the database connection pool, 517
        why use a singleton?, 517
database connection pool example, 510–517

Database load stage
    EDI invoicing and billing system, 289
DataImport example, 584
    classes used, 584
    code, 584–588
    logical errors, 589–591
    testing the application, 589
DateTimeEditor class
    System.ComponentModel.Design namespace, 377
DBConnectionSingleton class, 515
DCOM, 4
deadlocks, 498–499
Debug class
    Listeners collection, 186
    methods
        Assert() method, 187
        WriteLine() method, 186
    System.Diagnostics namespace, 185, 570, 583
<debug> element
    child of <system.runtime.remoting> element, 101
Debug preprocessor identifier
    ConditionalAttribute class and
        compiling without defining Debug preprocessor symbol, 324
        defining Debug preprocessor symbol, 325
    ConditionalAttribute class and, 323–324
Debug statements
    stripping from application, 579
Debug Users group, configuring, 181–182
debugging, 563–564
    .NET classes, 563
    ASP applications, 563
    creating application code, 564
debugging and error handling, 159
    dealing with errors in the client, 183–185
    dealing with errors in the remote object
        detecting errors at runtime, 188
        display Debug and Trace messages, 185–188
    defining custom exception classes, 191
    enabling remote debugging, 180–183
    exceptions, 159
    logging error information at server, 198
        logging errors to a database, 200–203
        logging errors to a file, 198–199
        logging errors to Windows event log, 203–207
    remote applications, 169
        Bank Application example, 169–191
DeclaredOnly flag value
    BindingFlags enumeration, 236
DeclaringType property
    MemberInfo class, 235
Decrement() method
    Interlocked class, 473, 496
Default flag value
    BindingFlags enumeration, 236
DefaultEventAttribute class
    defines default component event, 348
    System.ComponentModel namespace, 375
DefaultPropertyAttribute class
    defines default component property, 348
    System.ComponentModel namespace, 375

DefaultTraceListener class
    System.Diagnostics namespace, 574
DefaultValue property
    ParameterInfo class, 247
DefaultValueAttribute class
    System.ComponentModel namespace, 375
Delegate value
    AttributeTargets enumeration, 318
delegates
    alternative to reflection, 273
        example, 273–277
    asynchronous calls, 602
    event delegate cannot be accessed from a
        derived class, 146
    use in asynchronous callbacks, 133
    use with remotely delegatable objects, 146
DemoError example
    defining a host application, 163
    defining a remotable object, 160–163
    defining the client application, 163–165
    testing the remote application, 165
        client application specifies invalid host
            name, 166
        client application specifies invalid object
            URI, 167
        client application specifies invalid port, 166
        client application specifies invalid protocol,
            166
        miscellaneous error conditions, 167, 169
        server application isn't currently running,
            165
deploying metadata, 110
    interface only assemblies, 111
        advantages and limitations, 113
        Exchange example, 111–113
    Soapsuds tool, 113
Description property
    AssemblyDescriptionAttribute class, 330
DescriptionAttribute class
    System.ComponentModel namespace, 359,
        375
descriptor classes
    metadata defined with attributes, 352
deserialization, 10
    using SoapFormatter class, 305
Deserialize() method
    IFormatter interface, 44
    IRemotingFormatter interface, 66
design patterns, 519
Design View
    adding components from Toolbox, 362
designing threaded applications
    considerations, 523
destroying example, 453
destroying threads, 453
Disconnect() method
    RemotingServices class, 16
Disconnected event
    networking application example, 599
DisconnectedObject() method
    ITrackingHandler interface, 37
DisplayData() method
    networking application example, 606

displayName attribute
    <channel> element, 103
Dispose() method
    Component class, 362
    IContainer interface, 369
    IDisposable interface, 25
Dissassembler. *See* MSIL Disassembler
distributed garbage collection, 36
distributed systems, 1
    client-server systems, 2
    co-operative systems, 1
    evolution, 4–5
    multi-user systems, 3
    peer-to-peer systems, 2
    single-user systems, 3
    SOAP, 5
    Web Services, 5
DLL hell and .NET, 279
DllImportAttribute class
    System.Runtime.InteropServices namespace,
        320
Dns class
    resolving host names into IP address, 601
    System.Net namespace, 594, 601
DoCallBack() method
    AppDomain class, 417
Double class
    NaN field, 239
do_something_thread example, 426
dynamic assembly loading, 279–280
    benefits of using, 279
    configuring assembly binding, 280
    creating assembly references, 280
    defining AssemblyName, 280–282
    methods for dynamic class instantiation,
        283–285
    methods for dynamic loading, 282
    partially referencing assemblies, 282
    probing for assembly, 280
    using Abstract Factory Pattern, 286
    using with Abstract Factory Pattern
        EDI invoicing and billing system, 289–300
dynamic event handling
    remotely delegatable objects, 145
dynamic programming, 209
    See also reflection

E

early binding, 110, 213
EDI invoicing and billing system
    using dynamic assembly loading and Abstract
        Factory Pattern, 289–300
Employee example
    adding Employee component to ToolBox, 373
    adding properties and events, 359
    defining a delegate, 380
    defining converter classes, 381
        Address class, 387–388
        AddressConverter class, 388–391
        TelephoneNumber class, 381–382
        TelephoneNumberConverter class,
            382–385
        testing, 392–394

defining default event and default properties for
    Employee, 376–377
Dispose() method, 371
dragging and dropping component objects onto
    our applications, 373–375
dragging and dropping components onto Visual
    Designer, 358
Employee class
    adding some Addressfields and properties,
        391
    adding TelephoneNumber fields and
        properties, 385–386
    Age property, 377
    DateOfBirth property, 377
    Salary property, 378
    Skills property, 378
EmployeeContainer class
    Components property, 371
EmployeeEventArgs class, 380
equality test, 371
implementing IContainer interface, 369
implementing ISite interface, 367
retrieving
    class members, 236–237
    constructors, 245–246
    event metadata, 246–247
    method metadata, 243–244
    parameter metadata, 248–250
taxation, 381
using ArrayList to store Employee components,
    369–370
Enabled property
    BooleanSwitch class, 580–581
    ListView control, 597
encapsulation and versioning problems, 4
EndInvoke() delegate method, 130
EndPoint class
    System.Net namespace, 594, 601
EndRead() method
    NetworkStream class, 603
Enter() method
    Monitor class, 474–475, 481
        example, 475, 478
EntryPoint property
    Assembly class, 226
    DllImportAttribute class, 320
Enum value
    AttributeTargets enumeration, 318
Equals() method
    Thread class, 423
Equation example
    defining a custom serialization format, 72
        implementing a serializable MBV class,
            72–76
        implementing the client, 78–83
        implementing the host, 78
        implementing the remoting class, 76–77
        running example, 83
error notification
    Trace class, 572
EscapedCodeBase property
    Assembly class, 226
event delegates and derived classes, 146

event handlers
    asynchronous remoting, 127
    binding/unbinding to events at runtime,
        599
Event value
    AttributeTargets enumeration, 318
    MemberTypes enumeration, 235
Event Viewer application
    Application Log section, 575
Event Viewer utility, 204
EventArgs class
    System namespace, 150
EventDescriptor class
    System.ComponentModel namespace, 346
EventHandlerType property
    EventInfo class, 246
EventInfo class
    members, 246
    System.Reflection namespace, 220, 234
EventLog class
    Source property, 575
    System.Diagnostics namespace, 205
EventLogTraceListener class
    System.Diagnostics namespace, 574
events and asynchronous processss
    multi-user applications, 149–154
    single application domain events
        TickTock class library, 139
Evidence class
    System.Security.Policy namespace, 226
Evidence property
    Assembly class, 226
Exception class
    defining custom exception classes, 191
exception classes
    and serialization, 192–194
    annotating with Serializable attribute, 162
    custom exceptions for remote objects, 191
    defining informational properties and methods,
        197
exceptions, 159
    common remoting errors
        DemoError example, 160–169
    SerializationException class, 311
Exchange example
    hosting in IIS, 119
        IIS administration, 120–121
        IIS configuration, 120
    hosting in Windows Services, 115
        adding installation components, 118
        creating Windows Service project, 117
        installation, 119
        modifying the client, 116
        registering server object, 117–118
    loading files
        creating ExchangeClient, 106
        creating ExchangeClient.exe.config file,
            107
        creating ExchangeHost, 106
        creating ExchangeHost.exe.config file, 107
        creating ExchangeObjects class library,
            105–106
        running the example, 108

using interface only assemblies
    advantages and limitations of approach, 113
    creating the ExchangeInterface class library, 111
    modifying host and client applications, 112
    modifying the ExchangeObjects project, 111
  versioning
    assigning a version number, 123
    determining the version to use, 124
  versioning, 123–124
Exchange() method
  Interlocked class, 473
ExecuteReader() method
  SqlCommand class, 615
execution branching example, 427
ExecutionOrder example, 463–464
ExecutionOrder2 example, 464–465
Exit() method
  Monitor class, 474, 481
    example, 475, 478

F

factory class
  Abstract Factory Pattern, 291
  EDI invoicing and billing system, 291
Fail() method
  Trace class, 571, 572
Field value
  AttributeTargets enumeration, 318
  MemberTypes enumeration, 235
FieldInfo class
  invoking fields dynamically, 255–256
  methods, 238
    GetValue() method, 255
    SetValue() method, 255
  NaN field example, 239–240
  properties, 238
  System.Reflection namespace, 220, 234
fields
  definition, 213
  manipulating values with Type.InvokeMember, 267–272
  NonSerializedAttribute class, 303
FieldType() method
  FieldInfo class, 238
FileStream class
  Close() method, 196
FileSystemEventArgs class
  System.IO namespace, 586
FileSystemWatcher class
  Created event, 585
  DataImport example, 584
  IncludeSubdirectories property, 585
  properties
    Filter property, 585
    Path property, 585
Fill() method
  SqlDataAdapter class, 587
Filter property
  FileSystemWatcher class, 585
FindTypes() method
  Module class, 231
For Each statement, 211
For loop statement, 481

Form class
  properties
    Name property, 597
    Text property, 597
    System.Windows.Forms namespace, 597
Formatter class
  System.Runtime.Serialization namespace, 44
<formatter> element
  attributes, 125
formatters
  and channels, choosing, 45
  binary, 10
  SOAP, 10
free threading, 397, 404
  compared to apartment threading model, 402
  spawning new threads, 402
FreeNamedDataSlot() method
  Thread class, 423
Friend access modifiers, 360
FriendlyName property
  AppDomain class, 417–418
FromMinutes() method
  TimeSpan class, 445
FromSeconds() method
  TimeSpan class, 445
FullName property
  Assembly class, 227
  Type class, 231, 314

G

GAC
  dynamic assembly loading, 280
generic code
  using metadata to write, 352
  GenericProgramming example, 354–357
    components, 353
    dynamically modifying properties at run time, 353
GetAddMethod() method
  EventInfo class, 246
GetAssemblies() method
  AppDomain class, 225
GetAssembly() method
  Assembly class, 225–226
GetAttributes() method
  TypeDescriptor class, 348
GetAvailableThreads() method
  ThreadPool class, 539–540
GetCallingAssembly() method
  Assembly class, 225–226
GetConstructor() method
  Type class, 232, 245
GetConstructors() method
  Type class, 232
GetConstructors() method
  Type class, 245
GetCurrentThreadId property
  AppDomain class, 416, 418
GetCustomAttribute() method
  Attribute class, 311, 330, 332
GetCustomAttributes() method
  Assembly class, 227
  MemberInfo class, 311, 336
GetData() method
  Thread class, 423

GetDefaultEvent() method
    TypeDescriptor class, 347
GetDefaultProperty() method
    TypeDescriptor class, 348
GetDomain() method
    Thread class, 423
GetDomainID() method
    Thread class, 423
GetEditor() method
    TypeDescriptor class, 355
GetEntryAssembly() method
    Assembly class, 225–226
GetEvent() method
    Type class, 232, 246
GetEvents() method
    Type class, 232, 246
    TypeDescriptor class, 349
GetExecutingAssembly() method
    Assembly class, 225, 226
GetExportedTypes() method
    Assembly class, 227
GetField flag
    BindingFlags enumeration, 236, 267
GetField() method
    Type class, 232
        retrieving FieldInfo class, 239
GetFields() method
    Type class, 232
        retrieving FieldInfo class, 239
GetFile() method
    Assembly class, 227
GetFiles() method
    Assembly class, 227
GetGetMethod() method
    PropertyInfo class, 240
GetHashCode() method
    Thread class, 423
GetInterfaces() method
    Type class, 231
GetLifetimeService() method
    RemotingServices class, 41
GetLoadedModules() method
    Assembly class, 227
GetManifestResourceInfo() method
    Assembly class, 227
GetManifestResourceNames() method
    Assembly class, 227
GetManifestResourceStream() method
    Assembly class, 227
GetMaxThreads() method
    ThreadPool class, 539–540
GetMember() method
    Type class, 232, 235
GetMembers() method
    Type class, 232, 235–236
GetMethod() method
    Type class, 232
        obtaining MethodInfo class, 243
GetMethods() method
    Type class, 232
        obtaining MethodInfo class, 243
        using with BindingFlags enumeration, 243
GetModule() method
    Assembly class, 227
GetModules() method
    Assembly class, 227
GetName() method
    Assembly class, 227
GetNamedDataSlot() method
    Thread class, 423
GetNestedType() method
    Type class, 270
GetNestedTypes() method
    Type class, 270
GetObjectData() method
    ISerializable interface, 72, 194
GetParameters() method
    MethodBase class, 243
GetParameters() method
    ConstructorInfo class, 248
    MethodInfo class, 248
GetProperties() method
    Type class, 232
        retrieving PropertyInfo objects, 241
    TypeConverter class, 391
    TypeDescriptor class, 350
GetPropertiesSupported() method
    TypeConverter class, 391
GetProperty flag
    BindingFlags enumeration, 236, 262
GetProperty() method
    Type class, 232, 241, 255, 266
GetRaiseMethod() method
    EventInfo class, 246
GetReferencedAssemblies() method
    Assembly class, 227
GetRemoveMethod() method
    EventInfo class, 246
GetRequestStream() method
    IClientChannelSink interface, 46
GetResponseStream() method
    IServerChannelSink interface, 46
GetSatelliteAssembly() method
    Assembly class, 228
GetSetMethod() method
    PropertyInfo class, 240
GetStream() method
    TcpClient class, 601
GetType() method
    Activator class, 30
    Assembly class, 228
    Module class, 231
    Object class, 230
    Thread class, 423
    Type class, 230, 271
    TypeConverterAttribute class, 382, 388
GetType operator, 231
GetTypeInformation example, 346–352
GetTypes() method
    Assembly class, 228
    Module class, 231
GetUrlsForUri() method
    IChannelReceiver interface, 84
GetValue() method
    FieldInfo class, 238, 255
    PropertyInfo class, 240, 254, 266
Global Assembly Cache. *See* GAC
global attributes, 327

Global.asax file
    Application_Start() subroutine, 122
    registering objects programmatically, 122
GlobalAssemblyCache property
    Assembly class, 227
GlobalProxySelection class
    System.Net namespace, 594

H

Hashtable class
    Synchronized() method, 501
Hit Count dialog
    Breakpoints window, 569
hosting, 99, 115
    See also hosting components; hosting in
        Windows Services; hosting in IIS
    IIS (Internet Information Services), 119
    requirements, 115
hosting components
    using Container class, 364
hosting in IIS, 119
    advantages of using IIS, 122
    Exchange example
        IIS administration, 120–121
        IIS configuration, 120
        registering objects programmatically using
            Global.asax, 122
    Exchange example, 119–123
hosting in Windows Services
    Exchange example, 115–119
    VS .NET versions, 116
HTTP channel
    classes, 18
    terminology explained, 10
HttpApplication class
    implemementing IComponent interface, 359
HttpChannel class
    interfaces implemented, 18
    secure environments and maximum
        interoperability, 45
    SoapFormatter class, default formatter for, 18
HttpClientChannel class
    System.Runtime.Remoting.Channels.Http
        namespace, 18
HttpServerChannel class
    System.Runtime.Remoting.Channels.Http
        namespace, 18
HttpVersion class
    System.Net namespace, 594
HttpWebRequest class
    System.Net namespace, 594
HttpWebResponse class
    System.Net namespace, 594

I

IANA (Internet Assigned Numbers Authority)
    port numbers divided into groups, 18
IBookCollection interface
    methods and properties, 507
IChannel interface
    implemented by TcpChannel class, 17
    methods and properties, 83
    System.Runtime.Remoting.Channels
        namespace, 17
IChannelReceiver interface
    implemented by TcpChannel class, 17
    properties and methods, 84
    StartListening() method, 86
    StopListening() method, 86
    System.Runtime.Remoting.Channels
        namespace, 17
IChannelSender interface
    CreateMessageSink() method, 84
    implemented by TcpChannel class, 17
    System.Runtime.Remoting.Channels
        namespace, 17
IClientChannelSink interface
    properties and methods, 46
    System.Runtime.Remoting.Channels
        namespace, 45
IClientChannelSinkProvider interface
    properties and methods, 47
IClientFormatterSink interface
    implementation classes, 47
    System.Runtime.Remoting.Channels
        namespace, 46
IClientFormatterSinkProvider interface
    inheritance and implementation, 48
IComponent interface
    System.ComponentModel namespace, 344
    ways of implementing, 359
IContainer interface
    defining a class to implement, 367
    definition, 369
    Dispose() method, 369
    implemented by Container class, 364
    specifies requirements for container classes, 344
    System.ComponentModel namespace, 358
IDisposable interface
    user-defined MBR types, 25
IDL (Interface Definition Languages), 5
IFormatter interface
    classes that implement, 44
    methods, 44
    System.Runtime.Serialization namespace, 44, 66
IIS (Internet Information Services)
    hosting, 99, 119
ILease interface
    properties, 39
    Register() method, 41
    lease objects inherit from, 38
IlogicalThreadAffinative interface
    System.Runtime.Remoting.Messaging
        namespace, 154–155
IMessageSink interface
    properties and methods, 46
    System.Runtime.Remoting.Messaging
        namespace, 46, 60
ImportData() method
    UploadNotify abstract class, 295
Imports statements
    referencing namespaces, 598
IncludeSubdirectories property
    FileSystemWatcher class, 585
includeVersions attribute
    <formatter> element, 125
Increment() method
    Interlocked class, 473, 496

Indent() method
    Trace class, 579
IndentLevel property
    Trace class, 578
info classes
    class hierarchy, 234
    derivation, 234
    dynamically invoking members, 252–256
    examining class member metadata, 234
Inherited property
    AttributeUsageAttribute class, 332
inheritance
    AppDomain and Thread classes, 412
initial transformation stage
    EDI invoicing and billing system, 289
InitializeComponent() method
    Component Designer generated code, 362
InitializeLifetimeService() method
    MarshalByRefObject class, 38–39, 104
InitializeStockWindow() method
    networking application example, 598
InitialLeaseTime property
    ILease interface, 39
instance definition, 212
Instance flag value
    BindingFlags enumeration, 236, 283
InstanceDescriptor class
    System.ComponentModel.Design.Serialization namespace, 384
instrumentation, 564
Interface Definition Languages. See IDL
interface only assemblies
    advantages and limitations, 113
Interface value
    AttributeTargets enumeration, 319
    TypeAttributes enumeration, 311
Interlocked class
    chatinterlocked example, 494–496
    manual synchronization, 488, 494
    synchronization support, 473
    System.Threading namespace, 422, 612
Internet Assigned Numbers Authority. See IANA
Internet Information Server. See IIS
interprocess synchronization
    Mutex class, 492
Interrupt() method
    Thread class, 423, 445–446
interrupts, 405–406
    definition, 406
    process, 406
Interval property
    Timer class, 351
InvalidEnumArgumentException class
    System.ComponentModel namespace, 162
Invert example, 48
    adding a custom formatter
        implementing custom invert formatter, 66–69
        implementing invert server channel sink, 63–66
        implementing invert server channel sink provider, 62–63
        modifying InvertServer, 69–70
        modifying message sink, 70
        running example, 70–71
    adding new client channel sink, 52, 57–59
        implementing client channel sink, 54–56
        implementing client channel sink provider, 52–54
        modifying code to use invert client channel sink, 56–57
    basic version
        implementing Invert class library, 49
        implementing InvertClient, 51–52
        implementing InvertServer, 49–50
    implementing a custom TCP/IP socket channel, 84
        implementing the Invert Channel class, 84–90
        implementing the Invert client transport sink, 92–95
        implementing the Invert server sink, 90–91
        implementing the InvertClientTransportSinkProvider, 91–92
        modifying InvertClient to use InvertChannel, 96–97
        modifying InvertServer to use InvertChannel, 96
        running the example, 97–98
    replacing formatter sink, 59–61
        implementing, 60
        running the example, 62
Invoke() method
    MethodBase class, 243
    MethodInfo class, 252
        compared to Type.InvokeMember, 257
    supported by CLR, 605
InvokeMember() method
    Type class, 252
        advantages of using, 257
        compared to MethodInfo.Invoke(), 257
        invoking members dynamically, 256–272
        invoking methods, 257
        manipulating field values, 267–272
        manipulating property values, 262–266
        MethodInvocation example, 258–262
        passing BindingFlags.SetProperty as binding flag, 266
InvokeMethod flag
    BindingFlags enumeration, 236, 256–257
invoking members dynamically, 251–252
    cost, 272
    methods
        InvokeMember() method example, 258–262
    using Type.InvokeMember(), 256
        invoking methods, 257
        manipulating field values, 267–272
        manipulating property values, 262–266
InvokingFields example, 268–272
IOException class
    System.IO namespace, 199
IPAddress class
    System.Net namespace, 594
IPEndPoint class
    System.Net namespace, 594, 601

IPHostEntry class
    System.Net namespace, 594
IRemotingFormatter interface
    properties and methods, 66
    System.Runtime.Remoting.Messaging namespace
        properties and methods, 66
IsAbstract property
    MethodBase class, 243
IsAlive property
    Thread class, 424, 429
IsAssembly property
    FieldInfo class, 238
IsBackground property
    Thread class, 424
IsClass property
    Type class, 232
IsConstructor property
    MethodBase class, 243
IsDefined() method
    Assembly class, 228
ISerializable interface
    GetObjectData() method, 72, 194
    implementing, 74
    System.Runtime.Serialization namespace, 69, 71
ISerializationSurrogate interface
    System.Runtime.Serialization namespace, 69
IServerChannelSink interface
    defining a class to implement, 62
    properties and methods, 46
    System.Runtime.Remoting.Channels namespace, 45
IServerChannelSinkProvider interface
    defining a class to implement, 62
    properties and methods, 47
IServerFormatterSinkProvider interface
    inheritance and implementation, 48
IsFamily property
    FieldInfo class, 238
    MethodBase class, 243
IsFamilyAndAssembly property
    FieldInfo class, 238
    MethodBase class, 243
IsFamilyOrAssembly property
    FieldInfo class, 238
    MethodBase class, 243
IsFinal property
    MethodBase class, 243
IsIn property
    ParameterInfo class, 247
IsInitOnly property
    FieldInfo class, 238
IsInstanceOfType() method
    Type class, 232
ISite interface
    generic implementation, 367
    System.ComponentModel namespace, 367
IsLiteral property
    FieldInfo class, 238
IsMulticast property
    EventInfo class, 246
IsNotSerialized property
    FieldInfo class, 238

Isolation property
    TransactionAttribute class, 321
IsOptional property
    ParameterInfo class, 248
IsOut property
    ParameterInfo class, 247
ISponsor interface
    Renewal() method, 40
IsPrivate property
    FieldInfo class, 238
    MethodBase class, 243
IsPublic property
    FieldInfo class, 238
    MethodBase class, 243
IsRetval property
    ParameterInfo class, 247
IsStatic property
    FieldInfo class, 238
    MethodBase class, 243
IsSubclassOf() method
    Type class, 232
IsThreadPoolThread property
    Thread class, 424
IsVirtual property
    MethodBase class, 243
ITrackingHandler interface
    System.Runtime.Remoting.Services namespace, 37

J

Java Remote Method Invocations. *See* RMI
Join() method
    Thread class, 423, 442, 455, 457
joining threads, 455
Just-In-Time debugger, 183

L

Lapsed event
    Timer class, 351
late binding, 210, 215–218
    metadata, 218
    syntactic compared to reflective, 211
    VB .NET and reflection, 215–218
lazy initialization, 517
lease manager, 36
    AppDomains, 9
    sponsors, 36
lease manipulation, 38
    infinite lifetimes, 38
lease-based lifetimes, 9, 36–38
    lease manager, 36
    manipulating leases, 38
    renewing leases, 39
        creating sponsors, 40–41
    traffic handler implementation, 37
lifecycle of threads, 442
    destroying threads, 453–454
    interrupting a thread, 445–446
    joining threads, 455–457
    pausing and resuming threads, 447–453
    putting a thread to sleep, 443–445
<lifetime> element
    child of <application> element, 104

lifetime management. *See* leased-based lifetimes
LifetimeServices class
    SponsorshipTimeout property, 40
    System.Runtime.Remoting.Lifetime
        namespace, 40
LingerOption class
    System.Net.Sockets namespace, 595
ListBox control
    System.Web.UI.WebControls namespace, 609
Listener() method
    networking application example, 610
listeners
    tracing, 563
    using different listener applications, 574
Listeners collection
    Debug class, 186
    exposed by Trace class, 571, 574
    Trace class, 186
ListView control
    amending, 598–599
    Enabled property, 597
    System.Windows.Forms namespace, 597
ListViewItem class
    System.Windows.Forms namespace, 606
Load() method
    Assembly class, 225, 282, 284, 289
LoadFrom() method
    Assembly class, 225, 282
LoadModule() method
    Assembly class, 228
LoadWithPartialName() method
    Assembly class, 225, 282
Locals window, 566
Location property
    Assembly class, 227
Locking example, 483
LoggedAttribute context-bound custom attribute, 338
    using, 339
loosely-coupled pattern, 25

M

Machine configuration file, 100
    configuring assembly binding, 280
Machine Debug Manager tool. *See* MDM tool
machine.config
    <channels> element, 101
Main and Worker thread model, 524–528
MainMenu class
    System.Windows.Forms namespace, 597
Major property
    Version class, 281
managed threads, 418
manual synchronization
    AutoResetEvent class, 491–492
    classes used, 488
    Interlocked class, 494
    ManualResetEvent class, 488
    Mutex class, 492
    shared variables and methods, 496
ManualReset example, 490
ManualResetEvent class
    compared to AutoResetEvent class, 491
    example, 490
    inherits from the WaitHandle class, 488
    manual synchronization, 488
    methods
        Reset() method, 488
        Set() method, 488
        WaitOne() method, 490
    nonsignalled state example, 488–490
    synchronization support, 473
    System.Threading namespace, 422, 488
ManualSet example, 490
Marshal By Value objects
    versioning, 125
Marshal() method
    RemotingServices class, 16, 20, 36, 102
        publishing marshal by reference objects on
            server, 26
MarshalByRefObject class
    activation modes
        server-activated objects, 26
    activation modes, writing, 26
    class inheriting from can also have Serializable()
        attribute, 26
    inheriting from, 19
    InitializeLifetimeService() method, 38, 104
    lifetime management, 36
        leased-based lifetimes, 36–38
        renewing leases, 39–40
    System namespace, 16
MarshalByValueComponent class
    creating marshal-by-value component, 361
    implementing IComponent interface, 359
MarshaledObject() method
    ITrackingHandler interface, 37
marshaling, 11
    by reference or by value, 16
    user-defined objects, 22
marshaling classes
    MarshalByRefObject class, 16
    ObjRef class, 16
    RemotingServices class, 16
marshaling-by-reference
    activation modes, 26
        client activated objects, 30–31
        dynamically publishing SAOs, 31–36
        server activated objects, 26–30
    lifetime management, 36
        lease-based lifetimes, 36–38
        renewing leases, 39–40
    ObjRef class, 16
    user-defined objects, 25–26
    writing classes, 25
marshaling-by-value
    user-defined objects, 22
        accessing object behavior, 24
        passing MBV object, 24
        passing object state, 23
        tightly and loosely coupled solutions, 24–25
Math class
    Max() method, 257
MBR server object
    deploying metadata, 110

MDM tool
   Debug Users group, 181–182
   remote debugging, 181
MemberInfo class
   GetCustomAttributes() method, 311, 336
   properties, 235
   retrieving from a Type object, 235
   System.Reflection namespace, 220, 234
MemberType property
   MemberInfo class, 235
MemberTypes enumeration
   System.Reflection namespace, 235
   values, 235
message sink, 47
MessageAssembler() method
   networking application example, 604, 612
metadata
   See also deploying metadata; metadata assemblies
   accessing, 219–220
   attributes, 220
      defining with, 352
      inserting into assemblies, 301
   binding
      early binding, 110
      late binding, 218
   change the state of objects at run time, 352
   class type information, 110
   configuration and, 11
   defining for entire assembly, 302
   hierarchies, 219
   obtaining for types, properties and events, 346
   providing clients with, 99
   reflection, 212
   retrieving from running server with Soapsuds tool, 114
   run-time and design-time, 351
   using to write generic code, 352
   viewing with
      MSIL Disassembler, 308–309
      Windows Explorer, 331
metadata assemblies
   creating, 11
      advantages and disadvantages of approaches, 110
      and making available, 110
      interface only assemblies, 111
         advantages and limitations, 113
         Exchange example, 111
methods definition, 213
Method value
   AttributeTargets enumeration, 319
   MemberTypes enumeration, 235
MethodBase class
   methods, 243
   properties, 242–243
MethodInfo class
   invoking methods, 252–253
   obtaining, 243
   ReturnType property, 243
   System.Reflection namespace, 220, 226, 234
MethodInvocation example, 258–262
Minor property
   Version class, 281

mnuConnect_Click event handler
   networking application example, 600
mode attribute
   <customErrors> element, 104
   <wellknown> element, 101
<ModifiedAttribute> custom attribute, 334–336
Module class
   returned by Type.Module, 232
   System.Reflection namespace, 220, 231
Module property
   Type class, 232
Module value
   AttributeTargets enumeration, 319
Monitor class
   methods
      Enter() method, 474, 481
      Exit() method, 474, 481
      Pulse() method, 474, 478, 481
      PulseAll() method, 474
      TryEnter() method, 481
      Wait() method, 474, 478, 481
   synchronization
      code regions, 474
      support, 473
   System.Threading namespace, 422
MonitorEnterExit example, 475, 478
MonitorTryEnter example, 481
MSIL Disassembler
   code using Conditional attribute
      defining Debug preprocessor symbol, 326
      without defining Debug preprocessor symbol, 324
   viewing metadata, 308–309
MTA threading model, 520–521
   compared to STA threading model, 521
MTAThreadAttribute class, 521
multi-threaded applications
   additional processor overhead, 457
   thread pooling, 536
   threading design, 536
   use of memory, 457
multi-threading, 519
   processes, 402
   supported by VB6, 519
multi-user applications, 149
   configuring ports, 152
multi-user systems
   session-oriented, 3
MulticastOption class
   System.Net.Sockets namespace, 595
multifile assemblies, 224–225
Multiple Threaded Apartments. *See* MTA
multitasking, 398
multithreaded apartment model
   CLR implementation of thread pooling, 537
MustInherit classes, 595
MustInherit keyword
   Abstract classes, 285, 287
Mutex class
   concurrency issues, 173
   derived from the WaitHandle class, 492
   interprocess synchronization, 492
   manual synchronization, 488, 492

NetMutex example, 492–493
synchronization support, 473
System.Threading namespace, 422, 492
threadsafety, 174
WaitOne() method, 493
MyComplexContainer example, 367
MySimpleContainer example, 364–366

N

Name property
    AssemblyName class, 281
    FieldInfo class, 238
    Form class, 597
    MemberInfo class, 235
    PropertyInfo class, 240
    Thread class, 424
    Type class, 231
named arguments, 320–322
    using with DllImportAttribute class, 320
nested class
    defining component classes as, 360
NestedType value
    MemberTypes enumeration, 235
.NET
    component model built into framework, 5
    not procedural programming environment, 214
.NET applications
    designing threaded applications, 522–524
    multi-threading, 519
        by default, 519
.NET CLR LocksAndThreads
    performance counter information overview, 441
    table of categories, 441
.NET Component Model, 344
    See also System.ComponentModel namespace
    reflection, 345
        GenericProgramming example write, 353–357
        GetTypeInformation example, 346–352
        obtaining metadata, 346
        using metadata to write generic code, 352
.NET exception classes
    defining a remotable object, 162
.NET Framework
    AppDomain, 411
    attribute classes, 302–304
    creating objects, 279
    creating threads, 519
    dynamic assembly loading, 279
        creating assembly references, 280–282
        instantiating classes dynamically, 283–285
        methods, 282–283
    objects
        locking, 474
        waiting state, 474
    synchronization support, 472
    thread management and .NET runtime, 418
    threading supported, 519
        MTA threading model, 519
        STA threading model, 519
.NET Framework Configuration Tool, 99, 103
    overview, 108–110

.NET Remoting
    See also remoting
    benefits, 7
    context, 8
        call context, 8
        context-bound objects, 8–9
    first code example, 19
        creating client process, 20–21
        creating host process, 19
        creating shared class library, 19
        extending to illustrate MBV for user-defined objects, 22
        modifying to pass MBV object, 24
        running example, 21–22
        tightly and loosely coupled solutions, 24–25
    managing remote objects
        hosting, 9
        leased-based lifetime, 9
        marshaling, 11
        metadata and configuration, 11
    remote object types, 7
        client-activated objects, 8
        single call objects, 7
        singleton objects, 7
    remoting process
        formatters and serialization, 10
        samples, 11
        using channels, 10
        whole picture, 12–13
.NET Remoting classes, 15
    channel classes, 17
        ChannelServices class, 18
        HTTP channel classes, 18
        RemotingConfiguration class, 19
        TCP channel classes, 17
    marshaling classes, 16
        MarshalByRefObject class, 16
NetMutex example, 492–493
NetShared example, 496–498
NetworkCredential class
    System.Net namespace, 594
networking and threading, 593
    See also networking application example; networking in .NET
networking application example
    building, 597
    creating the client, 597–608
    creating the server, 608–615
    design goals, 596
        UML seqence diagram, 596
    running the applications, 615–618
networking in .NET, 593
    networking application example, 595–618
    System.Net namespace, 593
    System.Net.Sockets namespace, 595
NetworkStream class
    creating instance, 601
    inheriting from Stream class, 601
    methods
        BeginRead() method, 601, 615
        BeginWrite() method, 601, 615
        EndRead() method, 603
    System.Net.Sockets namespace, 595

Next property
    IClientChannelSinkProvider interface, 47
    IServerChannelSinkProvider interface, 47
NextChannelSink property
    IClientChannelSink interface, 46
    IServerChannelSink interface, 46
NextSink property
    IMessageSink interface, 47
no changes to the server, 130
NonCriticalSection() method
    synchronized code regions, 477–478
NonPublic flag value
    BindingFlags enumeration, 236
NonSerializedAttribute class, 74, 302
    annotating Account class, 306
    applies to fields, 303
    controls serialization and deserialization of objects, 304
    System namespace, 303, 305
nonsignalled state example, 488–490
NotInheritable declaration, 215
    SerializableAttribute class, 317

O

object pooling
    database connection pool example, 510
object state, passing, 23
object-oriented programming
    Abstract classes, 285
    Abstract Factory Pattern, 285
    Concrete classes, 285
    encapsulation, 4
    polymorphism, 286
Object-per-Client model, 520
ObjectPool class, 511
objects
    and reflection, 221
    creating objects in .NET, 279
    locking, 474
    waiting state, 474
objectUri attribute
    <wellknown> element, 101
ObjRef class
    System.Runtime.Remoting namespace, 16
OleDbCommand class
    System.Data.OleDb namespace, 202
OleDbConnection class
    System.Data.OleDb namespace, 202
OnDisconnected() method
    networking application example, 599
Option Strict
    best practice, 210
    late binding, 216
out-of-process
    apartment-threading concept, 403
Output debug window
    Visual Studio .NET, 571
Overridable keyword, 214
overusing threads, 457

P

Parameter value
    AttributeTargets enumeration, 319

ParameterAttributes enumeration
    System.Reflection namespace, 247
ParameterInfo class
    properties, 247
    System.Reflection namespace, 234
parameters, validity for custom attributes, 333
ParameterType property
    ParameterInfo class, 248
ParenthesizePropertyNameAttribute class
    System.ComponentModel namespace, 375
Parse() method
    IChannel interface, 84
Path property
    FileSystemWatcher class, 585
patterns
    Abstract Factory Pattern, 205
pausing and resuming threads, 447
Peer threading model end, 531
peer-to-peer systems
    information exchange, 2
performance counters, 564
Performance Monitor
    viewing threads inside CLR, 441
pipeline thread model, 531–533
PipeLineClassFactory class
    EDI invoicing and billing system, 291
pluggable software, writing, 352
PointerToProc instruction, 214
polymorphism, 286
    implementing Abstract Factory Pattern, 286
port attribute
    <channel> element, 103
port configuration, 152
port numbers, groups, 18
Position property
    ParameterInfo class, 248
positional arguments, 320–322
    using with DllImportAttribute class, 320
Power example
    slow asynchronous process, 130–131
        modifying client code, 131
        running the example, 134–135
    slow asynchronous remote process
        implementing server code, 135–136
        modifying client code, 137
        running example, 138
    slow synchronous process
        implementing the class library, 128
        implementing the client code, 128–130
        running the example, 130
preemptive multitasking, 398, 537
    problems, 399
Prime Number example, 447–450
    building UI, 448
    GeneratePrimeNumbers() method, 450, 451
        modifying, 452
    UpdateUI() method, 453
Priority property
    Thread class, 424
private fields
    accessing using reflection, 255
Process class
    ProcessorAffinity property, 404
    System.Diagnostics namespace, 404

ProcessMessage() method
  IClientChannelSink interface, 46
  IServerChannelSink interface, 46
processor overhead
  threads, 457
ProcessorAffinity property
  Process class, 404
Property Pages dialog
  changing debuggers settings, 565
Property value
  AttributeTargets enumeration, 319
  MemberTypes enumeration, 235
property values
  manipulating with Type.InvokeMember, 262–266
PropertyDescriptor class
  obtaining property information, 346
PropertyInfo class
  example, 241–242
  invoking properties dynamically, 254
    example, 254–255
  methods, 240
    GetValue() method, 254
    SetValue() method, 254
  properties, 240
  System.Reflection namespace, 220, 234
PropertyType property
  PropertyInfo class, 240
protocols
  introduction, 2
proxy objects, 13
  transparent and real, 13
Public access modifiers, 360
Public flag value
  BindingFlags enumeration, 236
public key cryptography
  description, 281
  strong naming, 281
Public value
  BindingFlags enumeration, 283
Publisher Policy file
  configuring assembly binding, 280
Pulse() method
  Monitor class, 474, 478, 481
PulseAll() method
  Monitor class, 474
pview
  administrating priorities, 409
pviewer
  administrating priorities, 409

Q

quantum. *See* time slices
Query Analyzer
  Query Pane, 200
QueueUserWorkItem() method
  ThreadPool class, 539–540, 542, 544, 546
QuoteClient.vb
  networking application example, 609

R

race conditions, 469
  ATM scenario, 470

read and write access
  ReaderWriterLock class, 487
Read() method
  Console class, 543, 547
ReaderWriterLock class
  example, 484, 486–487
  methods, 484
    AcquireWriterLock() method, 487
  read and write access, 487
  synchronized code regions, 474, 484
  System.Threading namespace, 422
ReadLine() method
  Console class, 425
ReadOnlyAttribute class
  System.ComponentModel namespace, 375
ReadWriteLock example, 484, 486–487
real proxy, 13
ReceiveStream() method
  networking application example, 602
Rectangle class
  System.Drawing namespace, 354
RectangleConverter class
  System.Drawing namespace, 354–355
ref attribute
  <channel> element, 103
references
  creating assembly references, 280
  partially referencing assemblies, 282
ReflectedType property
  MemberInfo class, 235
reflection
  and remoting, 221
  ASP.NET, 212
  binding, 213
    early binding, 213
    late binding, 215–218
    object-orientation, 214–215
    run-time binding, 214
  definition, 209–210
  dynamically modifying properties at run time
    GenericProgramming example, 353–357
  invocation at a price, 272–273
    delegates as alternative, 273–277
    type-safety, 272
  invoking members, 251
  metadata, 218
    accessing, 219–220
    attributes, 220
  .NET Component Model, 345
    GetTypeInformation example, 346–352
    obtaining metadata, 346
  type terminology, 212–213
  underlying theory, 212
  uses, 210–212
  using metadata to write generic code, 352
  using objects, 251
Reflection API, 209
  dynamically invoking members, 252
reflective invocation
  better alternatives, 272
reflective late binding
  compared to syntactic late binding, 211
ReflectProperties example, 263–267

RefreshPropertiesAttribute class
    All field, 377, 388
    System.ComponentModel namespace, 376
Register() method
    ILease interface, 41
RegisterActivatedClientType() method
    RemotingConfiguration class, 30
RegisterActivatedServiceType() method
    RemotingConfiguration class, 30
RegisterChannel() method
    ChannelServices class, 18, 30, 40
RegisteredWaitHandle class
    System.Threading namespace, 422
registering CAOs, 30–31
registering SAOs, 27
RegisterTrackingHandler() method
    TrackingServices class, 37
RegisterWaitForSingleObject() method
    ThreadPool class, 539–540, 546
RegisterWellKnownClientType() method
    creating proxy object, 29
    registering remote server activated object on client, 27
    RemotingConfiguration class, 122
RegisterWellKnownServiceType() method
    RemotingConfiguration class, 27, 103, 163
ReleaseMutex() method
    Mutex class, 173
ReleaseReaderLock() method
    ReaderWriterLock class, 484
ReleaseWriterLock() method
    ReaderWriterLock class, 484
Remote Applications tab
    .NET Framework Configuration Tool, 109
remote events, 141
    server lacks knowledge of client structure, 143
remote object types, 7
remote objects, managing
    hosting, 9
    leased-based lifetime, 9
    marshaling, 11
    metadata and configuration, 11
Remote Procedure Calls. *See* RPCs
remotely delegatable objects, 143
    dynamic event handling, 145
    removing static event handling, 145
remoting
    and AppDomain class, 418
    and .NET Framework, 537
    CLR and threads, 537
    common exceptions, 159–160
    debugging and error handling, 159
Remoting Services Properties dialog
    .NET Framework Configuration Tool, 109
RemotingConfiguration class
    Configure() method, 105, 122
    RegisterActivatedClientType() method, 30, 122
    RegisterWellKnownServiceType() method, 27, 103, 163
    System.Runtime.Remoting namespace, 19
RemotingConfiguration class
    RegisterWellKnownClientType() method, 27

RemotingException class, 36
    System.Runtime.Remoting namespace, 104, 166–167
RemotingServices class
    methods
        Connect() method, 16, 21
        Disconnect() method, 16
        GetLifetimeService() method, 41
        Marshal() method, 20, 36, 102
    marshalling methods, 16
    System.Runtime.Remoting namespace, 16
Remove() method
    Container class, 365
RemoveAt() method
    TraceListener collection class, 576
RemoveEventHandler() method
    EventInfo class, 246
Renewal() method
    ISponsor interface, 40
RenewOnCallTime property
    ILease interface, 39
RequiresNew value
    TransactionOption enumeration, 321
Reset() method
    ManualResetEvent class, 488, 490
ResetAbort() method
    Thread class, 423
Resume() method
    Thread class, 423, 447
resuming threads, 447
ReturnType property
    MethodInfo class, 243
ReturnValue value
    AttributeTargets enumeration, 319
Revision property
    Version class, 281
RMI, 4
RPCs (Remote Procedure Calls), 4
run time inefficiencies, 353
Run To Cursor feature
    Visual Studio .NET debugger, 568
run-time binding, 214
    PointerToProc instruction, 214
run-time type, 215

S

SAO (Server Activated Objects), 26
    dynamically publishing, 31
        defining the client application, 34
        defining the host application, 32–33
        defining the remoting class, 32
        testing application, 34–35
    registering, 27
    types, 26
    <wellknown> element, 101
scalability in .NET, 547
    thread pool manager, creating, 548
scaling threaded applications, 535
security configuration files, 100
SecurityException class
    System.Security namespace, 539
SelectedIndexChanged() method
    ComboBox class, 270

SelectedItem property
   ComboxBox class, 271
SelectMethod() method
   Binder class, 257
Serializable attribute
   adding to class definition, 71
   defining a remotable object, 161
   using pre-defined exception classes, 162
Serializable value
   TypeAttributes enumeration, 311, 314
Serializable() attribute, 23
   and classes inheriting from MarshalByRefObject class, 26
SerializableAttribute class, 302
   annotating Account class, 306
   applies to classes, structures, enums, and delegates, 303
   controls serialization and deserialization of objects, 304
   definition, 317
   inherits from Attribute class, 317
   NotInheritable declaration, 317
   rules for using attributes, 316
   System namespace, 303, 305
   using with AttributeUsageAttribute class, 317
serialization, 10, 23
   determining if object is serializable, 311
   time–stamped binary serialization, 62
   specifying binder, 68
   using SoapFormatter class, 305
SerializationException class
   System.Runtime.Serialization namespace, 169, 311
Serialize() method
   IFormatter interface, 44
   IRemotingFormatter interface, 66
server-activated objects, 7
server-activated single calls, 26
server-activated singletons, 26
   registering programmatically, 27
server
   invocations on the client, 141
   lacking knowledge of client structure, 143
<serverProviders> element
   template provided by <channelSinkProviders> element, 101
<service> element
   activating server objects, 102
   child of <application> element, 101
service node
   registering objects with remoting framework, 102
ServiceBase class
   ServiceName property, 117
ServiceName property
   ServiceBase class, 117
session-less systems
   typical example of, 2
session-oriented systems
   synchronous and asynchronous, 3
Set() method
   AutoResetEvent object, 547
   ManualResetEvent class, 488
      example, 490

SetData() method
   AppDomain class, 415, 417
   CurDomain object, 416
   Thread class, 423
SetField flag
   BindingFlags enumeration, 236, 267, 271
SetProperty flag
   BindingFlags enumeration, 236, 262
      passed by InvokeMember() method, 266
SetValue() method
   FieldInfo class, 238, 255
   PropertyInfo class, 240, 254
Shared access type
   invoking with MethodInfo class, 253
Shared declaration
   Trace class, 571
shared methods
   Abstract Factory Pattern, 287, 289
signature, definition, 213
Simple Object Access Protocol. *See* SOAP
simple_thread example, 424
   importing System.Threading namespace, 425
single application domains
   generating events, 139
      TickTock example, 139–140
single-call-objects, 7
single-file-assemblies, 224
Single-Threaded-Apartments. *See* STA
single-threaded-processes, 401
single-user-systems, 3
single-writer and multiple-reader
   ReaderWriterLock class, 484
Singleton class, 517
Singleton design pattern
   reason for using, 517
singleton objects, 7
singletons, use of, 142
singleton remoting service type
   registering class as, 175
sink chain, 43
   channel sink interfaces and classes, 45
   client channel sink providers, 47–48
   customizing, 48
      adding a custom formatter, 62–71
      replacing the formatter sink, 59–62
   formatter classes, 44
      choosing channels and formatters, 45
sinks, 13
Sleep() method
   Thread class, 423, 429, 442, 443, 493, 531
   deadlocks, 501
slow asynchronous process
   implementing, 131–135
SMP systems and benefits of threading, 548
SOAP (Simple Object Access Protocol), 5
   and Web Services, 5
   example of using with attributes, 304–311
   formatters, 10
   protocol overheads, 6
   support of non-NET clients, 7
<SOAP-ENV:Body> element, 310
<SOAP-ENV:Envelope> element, 310

SoapClientFormatterSink class
  System.Runtime.Remoting.Channels
    namespace, 47
SoapClientFormatterSinkProvider class
  System.Runtime.Remoting.Channels
    namespace, 48
SoapFormatter class
  compared to BinaryFormatter class, 308
  default formatter for HttpChannel class, 18
  human readable data, 45
  SoapClientFormatterSink provides client
    formatter sink that uses, 47
  System.Runtime.Serialization.Formatters.Soap
    namespace, 44, 172, 305
SoapServerFormatterSinkProvider class
  System.Runtime.Remoting.Channels
    namespace, 48
Soapsuds tool
  accessing in VS .NET, 113
  creating metadata assemblies, 110
  deploying metadata, 113
  generating WSDL files from server objects, 11
  options, 113
  retrieving metadata, 114
  versioning, 125
Socket class
  System.Net.Sockets namespace, 135, 595
socket programming
  System.Net.Sockets namespace, 595
SocketAddress class
  System.Net namespace, 594
SocketClient_Closing() method
  networking application example, 607
SocketException class
  System.Net.Sockets namespace, 165–167, 595
SocketPermission class
  System.Net namespace, 594
Source property
  EventLog class, 575
spinning threads with threads, 436
  performance considerations, 440
  with threads, 439
SpinWait() method
  Thread class, 423
sponsors, 10
  creating, 40–41
SponsorshipTimeout property
  LifetimeServices class, 40
SQL Server
  authentication, 202
  creating new database, 200
  debugging stored procedures, 564
SqlCommand class
  ExecuteReader() method, 615
  System.Data.SqlClient namespace, 202
SqlCommandBuilder class
  System.Data.SqlClient namespace, 587
SqlConnection class
  System.Data.SqlClient namespace, 202, 587, 613
SqlDataAdapter class
  Fill() method, 587
  System.Data.SqlClient namespace, 587
  Update() method, 587–588
SqlDataReader class
  System.Data.SqlClient namespace, 615
STA threading model, 519–520
  Object-per-Client model, 520
  safety of, 520
StackTrace class
  System.Diagnostics namespace, 226
Start() method
  Thread class, 423, 425, 443
StartListening() method
  IChannelReceiver interface, 84, 86
STAThreadAttribute class, 521
static binding. *See* early binding
static event handling, removing
  remotely delegatable objects, 145
Static flag value
  BindingFlags enumeration, 236
Step Into
  Visual Studio .NET Debugger, 568
Step Out
  Visual Studio .NET Debugger, 568
Step Over
  Visual Studio .NET Debugger, 568
StockClient form
  networking application example, 598
StockServer_Load() method
  networking application example, 610
StopListening() method
  IChannelReceiver interface, 84, 86
StreamReceive() method
  networking application example, 611
StreamWriter class
  creating new instance, 607
  System.IO namespace, 199
strictBinding attribute
  <formatter> element, 125
StringBuilder class
  System.Text namespace, 435, 604, 615
  ToString() method, 605
strong names
  public key cryptography, 281
  specifying in AssemblyName class, 281
  versioning, 124
Struct value
  AttributeTargets enumeration, 319
surrogate selector, specifying, 69
SurrogateSelector property
  IRemotingFormatter interface, 66
Suspend() method
  Thread class, 423, 447, 449
Suspend value
  ThreadState enumeration, 447, 450
SuspendRequested value
  ThreadState enumeration, 447, 450
symmetric multi-processor systems. *See* SMP systems
synchronization, 469
  .NET support, 472
  and performance, 498
  critical sections, 470–471
  database connection pool example, 510–517
  deadlocks, 498–501
  immutability, 471
  race conditions, 469

shared variables and methods, 496
    ThreadStaticAttribute class, 496–498
thread-safe wrappers example, 501–509
thread-safety, 469
synchronization strategies
    CLI, 473
    manual synchronization, 488
    synchronized code regions, 474
    synchronized contexts, 473
SynchronizationAttribute class
    synchronization support, 473
    System.EnterpriseServices namespace, 473
SynchronizationLockException class
    System.Threading namespace, 422
synchronized code regions
    CriticalSection() method, 477–478
    Monitor class, 474
    NonCriticalSection() method, 477–478
    ReaderWriterLock class, 474, 484
    SyncLock keyword, 482–483
    TryEnter() method
        Monitor class, 481
synchronized contexts
    ContextBoundObject class, 473
    SynchronizationAttribute class, 473
Synchronized() method
    Hashtable class, 501, 508
synchronized wrappers
    Collection classes, 501
synchronous invocation, 128
synchronous protocol, session-less, 2
synchronous session-oriented systems, 3
SyncLock keyword
    alternative to Monitor class methods, 482–483
    synchronized code regions, 482–483
SyncProcessMessage() method
    IMessageSink interface, 47
syntactic late binding
    compared to reflective late binding, 211
System namespace
    AppDomain class, 225, 411–413, 425
    ApplicationException class, 191
    ArgumentNullException class, 162, 169
    ArgumentOutOfRangeException class, 162, 169, 541
    Attribute class, 302, 311
    AttributeTargets enumeration, 318
    AttributeUsageAttribute class, 316
    ContextBoundObject class, 338, 473
    EventArgs class, 150
    Exception class, 191
    MarshalByRefObject class, 16
    Math class, 257
    NonSerializedAttribute class, 303, 305
    SerializableAttribute class, 303, 305, 316
    SystemException class, 191
    TimeSpan class, 434, 445
    Type class, 223
    UnauthorizedAccessException class, 199
    Version class, 281
System.Collections namespace
    ArrayList class, 369, 526
    Hashtable class, 501
System.ComponentModel namespace, 343
    attribute classes, 375
    benefit of reflection, 343
    CategoryAttribute class, 359
    ComponentCollection class, 365
    Container class, 358
    creating and using component classes, 343
    DefaultEventAttribute class, 348
    DefaultPropertyAttribute class, 348
    DescriptionAttribute class, 359
    EventDescriptor class, 346
    IComponent interface, 344
    IContainer interface, 344, 358
    InvalidEnumArgumentException class, 162
    ISite interface, 367
    PropertyDescriptor class, 346
    TypeConverter class, 354
    TypeDescriptor class, 346
System.ComponentModel.Design namespace
    ArrayEditor class, 379
    ColorEditor class, 380
    DateTimeEditor class, 377
System.ComponentModel.Design.Serialization namespace
    InstanceDescriptor class, 384
System.Configuration namespace, 600
System.Data.OleDb namespace
    classes, 201
System.Data.SqlClient namespace
    ADO.NET classes, 201
    classes used in DataImport example, 584, 587
    SqlCommand class, 202, 615
    SqlConnection class, 202, 613
    SqlDataReader class, 615
System.Diagnostics namespace
    BooleanSwitch class, 570
    ConditionalAttribute class, 303, 322
    Debug class, 185, 570, 583
    DefaultTraceListener class, 574
    EventLog class, 205, 575
    EventLogTraceListener class, 574
    Process class, 404
    StackTrace class, 226
    TextWriterTraceListener class, 574, 576, 584
    Trace class, 185, 570
    TraceSwitch class, 188, 570, 581
System.Drawing namespace
    Rectangle class, 354
    RectangleConverter class, 354–355
System.Drawing.Design namespace
    UITypeEditor class, 355
System.EnterpriseServices namespace
    .NET synchronization support, 472
    SynchronizationAttribute class, 473
    TransactionAttribute class, 306, 320
    TransactionOption enumeration, 321
System.Globalization namespace
    CultureInfo class, 281, 283
System.IO namespace
    FileStream class, 196
    FileSystemEventArgs class, 586
    FileSystemWatcher class, 584
    IOException class, 199

INDEX

standard file I/O classes, 305
StreamWriter class, 199
System.Net namespace
   functionality, 593
   networking in .NET, 593
   table of main classes, 594
System.Net.Sockets namespace, 594
   Socket class, 135
   SocketException class, 165–167
   TcpClient class, 600
   transport layer, 595
System.Net.Web namespace
   WebException class, 165–167
System.Reflection namespace
   Assembly class, 223, 225, 282
   AssemblyDescriptionAttribute class, 327
   AssemblyName class, 280
   AssemblyTitleAttribute class, 327
   AssemblyVersionAttribute class, 303
   Binder class, 256
   BindingFlags enumeration, 283
   classes, 220
   ConstructorInfo class, 234, 245
   EventInfo class, 234
   FieldInfo class, 234
   MemberInfo class, 234, 311, 336
   MemberTypes enumeration, 235
   MethodInfo class, 226, 234, 252
   Module class, 231
   ParameterInfo class, 234
   PropertyInfo class, 234
   TypeAttributes enumeration, 311
System.Runtime.InteropServices namespace
   DllImportAttribute class, 320
<system.runtime.remoting> element
   child elements, 101
System.Runtime.Remoting namespace
   ObjRef class, 16
   RemotingConfiguration class, 19, 105
   RemotingException class, 104, 166–167
   RemotingServices class, 16
   WellKnownObjectMode enumeration, 27
System.Runtime.Remoting.Activation namespace
   UrlAttribute class, 284
System.Runtime.Remoting.Channels namespace
   BaseChannelWithProperties class, 85
   channel sink interfaces and classes, 45
   ChannelServices class, 18
   classes and interfaces, 47–48
   interfaces, 17, 83
   SoapClientFormatterSink class, 47
System.Runtime.Remoting.Channels.Http namespace
   HttpChannel class, 18, 45
System.Runtime.Remoting.Channels.Tcp namespace, 17
   TcpChannel class, 17–18, 45
System.Runtime.Remoting.Contexts namespace
   ContextAttribute class, 338
System.Runtime.Remoting.Lifetime namespace
   ILease interface, 38
   ISponsor interface, 40
   LifetimeServices class, 40

System.Runtime.Remoting.Messaging namespace
   IlogicalThreadAffinative interface, 154–155
   IMessageSink interface, 46, 60
   IRemotingFormatter interface, 66
System.Runtime.Remoting.Services namespace
   ITrackingHandler interface, 37
   TrackingServices class, 37
System.Runtime.Serialization namespace
   Formatter class, 44
   IFormatter interface, 44, 66
   ISerializable interface, 69, 71
   ISerializationSurrogate interface, 69
   SerializationException class, 169, 311
System.Runtime.Serialization.Formatters.Binary namespace
   BinaryFormatter class, 18, 44, 172, 308
System.Runtime.Serialization.Formatters.Soap namespace
   SoapFormatter class, 18, 44, 172, 305
System.Security namespace
   SecurityException class, 539
System.Security.Policy namespace
   Evidence class, 226
System.ServiceProcess namespace
   ServiceBase class, 117
System.Text namespace
   ASCII class, 615
   StringBuilder class, 435, 604, 615
System.Threading namespace
   .NET synchronization support, 472
   classes, 421
   classes for manual synchronization, 488
   creating a thread, 424
   importing, 425
   Interlocked class, 612
   ManualResetEvent class, 488
   Mutex class, 492
   ReaderWriterLock class, 484
   spinning threads with threads, 436
   spinning threads with threads with threads, 439
   Thread class, 412, 418
   ThreadAbortException class, 442
   ThreadPool class, 538–539
   ThreadPriority enumeration, 431
   ThreadStart delegate, 425
      execution branching, 427
   ThreadState enumeration, 442
   Timer class, 434
   TimerCallback delegate, 434
   timers and callbacks, 434
   WaitCallback delegate, 543
   WaitOrTimerCallback delegate, 546
System.Timers namespace
   Timer class, 350
System.Web.Services namespace
   WebMethodAttribute class, 303
   WebServiceAttribute class, 303
System.Web.UI namespace
   Control class, 345
System.Web.UI.WebControls namespace
   ListBox control, 609
   WebControl class, 345

System.Windows.Forms namespace
   Form class, 597
   ListView control, 597
   ListViewItem class, 606
   MainMenu class, 597
SystemException class
   defining custom exception classes, 191

T

Task Manager
   administrating priorities, 409
      Excel example, 410
   CPU utilization
      threads, 400
   Thread Count option, 405
   viewing processes, 400
TCP channel
   classes, 17
   terminology explained, 10
TCP protocol
   channel configuration, 103
TcpChannel class
   BinaryFormatter is default formatter for, 18
   constructor overloads, 17
   executing within secure environments, 45
   System.Runtime.Remoting.Channels.Tcp namespace, 17
TcpClient class
   closing connection, 607
   instantiating, 600
   methods
      GetStream() method, 601
      Write() method, 607
   System.Net.Sockets namespace, 595
TcpListener class
   AcceptTcpClient() method, 611
   System.Net.Sockets namespace, 595
Teleconference Application example
   call contexts, 154
      creating a context object, 154–155
      getting call context, 155–156
      running example, 156–157
      setting call context, 155
Text property
   Form class, 597
TextWriterTraceListener class
   Close() method, 577
   creating new instance, 577
   DataImport example, 584
   System.Diagnostics namespace, 574, 576
thread abort, 408
thread affinity, 521
Thread class
   creating threads, 519
   DataImport example, 584
   inheritance, 412
   methods, 422
      Abort() method, 442, 453, 454, 533
      Join() method, 442, 455, 457
      Resume() method, 447
      Sleep() method, 429, 442, 493, 531
      Start() method, 425, 443
      Suspend() method, 447, 449
      Wait() method, 442
   properties, 423
      ApartmentState property, 522
      IsAlive property, 429
      ThreadState property, 431
   System.Threading namespace, 412, 418, 422
Thread Local Storage. *See* TLS
thread pool manager
   creating, 548
   FindFirstIdleThread() function, 552, 554
   FindIdleThreadCount() function, 554
   FindThread() function, 554
   GenPool class, 555
      Run() method, 552
   GenThreadPoolImpl class, 548, 555
      implements the IThreadPool interface, 550
      specifying min, max and idle time of threads, 551
   GetStats() function, 553
   IThreadPool interface, 548
      AddJob() method, 551
   Monitor class
      Pulse() method, 553
   RemoveThread() function, 555
   Stats structure, 557
   ThreadElement class, 552, 556–557
thread pooling, 535–538
thread priorities, 408–409
thread sleep, 407
thread-safe wrappers example, 501–509
thread-safety 469–472
ThreadAbortException class
   System.Threading namespace, 422, 442
ThreadAppModule example, 544–546
threaded applications
   design considerations, 522–524
ThreadExceptionEventArgs class
   System.Threading namespace, 422
threading, when to use, 421
threading defined
   clock interrupts, 407
   free threading, 397
   interrupts, 405
   multi-threaded processes, 402
   multitasking, 398
      cooperative, 398
      preemptive, 398
   multithreaded processes
      free threading, 402
   processes, 399
   setting AppDomain data, 413
   single threaded processes, 401
   thread abort, 408
   thread priorities, 408
   thread sleep, 407
   Threads Local Storage, 405
   time slices, 402
   unmanaged threads, 418
threading opportunities, 458
   accessing external resources, 461–462
   background processes, 458–460

threading traps
  execution order revisited, 463–465
  threads in a loop, 465, 467–468
ThreadInterruptedException class
  System.Threading namespace, 422
ThreadPool class
  methods, 539
    BindHandle() method, 539
    GetAvailableThreads() method, 540
    GetMaxThreads() method, 540
    QueueUserWorkItem() method, 540, 544, 546, 542
    RegisterWaitForSingleObject() method, 540, 546
    UnsafeQueueUserWorkItem() method, 542
    UnsafeRegisterWaitForSingleObject() method, 542
  programming in Visual Basic .NET, 542
    add tasks to queue, 543
    rules, 542
  System.Threading namespace, 422, 538
ThreadPriority enumeration
  System.Threading namespace, 431
threadpriority example, 432
threadpriority2 example, 433–434
threads
  blocking, 442
  callbacks, 434
  concurrency, 519
  creating
    multi-threading example, 426
  creating a simple example, 424
  designing threaded applications, 522–524
  lifecycle, 442
    destroying, 453–454
    interrupting, 445–446
    joining, 455–457
    pausing and resuming, 447–453
    putting thread to sleep, 443–445
  MTA threading model, 521
  opportunities for, 458
  overusing, 457
  priorities, 431
  scaling threaded applications, 535
  specifying threading model, 522
  spinning threads with threads, 436
    with threads, 439
  STA threading model, 519–520
  support in Visual Basic .NET, 410
  thread pooling, 535
  threading traps, 462
  TLS and Call Stacks, 537
  when to use, 457
threads and relationships, 524
  Main and Worker thread model, 524–528
  Peer threading model, 528–531
  pipeline thread model, 531–533
Threads Local Storage. See TLS
Threads window
  columns contained, 570
  Visual Studio .NET Debugger, 570

threadsafety
  Mutex class, 174
ThreadStart delegate
  execution branching, 427
  System.Threading namespace, 425, 427
ThreadStartBranching example, 427–429
ThreadState enumeration
  values, 442
  WaitSleepJoin state, 443, 445
threadstate example, 429–431
ThreadState property
  Thread class, 424, 431, 442
ThreadStateException class
  System.Threading namespace, 422, 449
ThreadStaticAttribute class
  NetShared example, 496–498
  shared variables and methods, 496
thread_interrupt example, 445–446
thread_joining example, 455, 457
thread_sleep example, 443–444
thread_spinning example, 436–438
thread_spinning2 example, 439–440
thread_timer example, 434–435
TickTock example
  generating events in a single application domain
    implementing class library, 139
    implementing client code, 139–140
    running example, 140
  passing events between remote applications
    implementing server code, 141–142
    modifying client code, 142–143
    running example, 143
  remotely delegatable objects, 143–144
    implementing class library, 144
    modifying class library, 145–148
    modifying client code, 145
    modifying server code, 148
    running example, 148–149
tightly-coupled solutions, 25
time slices, 402
time-stamped binary serialization, 62
Timeout class
  System.Threading namespace, 422
Timeout property
  TransactionAttribute class, 321
Timer class
  Elapsed event, 351
  Interval property, 351
  System.Threading namespace, 422, 434
  System.Timers namespace, 350
TimerCallback delegate
  System.Threading namespace, 434
timers, 434
TimeSpan class
  FromMinutes() method, 445
  FromSeconds() method, 445
  properties and methods, 445
  System namespace, 434
Title property
  AssemblyTitleAttribute class, 330

INDEX

TLS (Thread Local Storage), 400, 405, 537
Toolbox
    adding components to, 358
ToString() method
    Thread class, 423
    StringBuilder class, 605
Trace class
    IndentLevel property, 578
    Listeners collection, 186, 571
    methods, 571
        Assert() method, 187
        Indent() method, 579
        Unindent() method, 579
        WriteIf() method, 580
        WriteLine method, 186
        WriteLineIf() method, 580
    Shared declaration, 571
    System.Diagnostics namespace, 185, 570
Trace statements
    stripping from application, 579
TraceError property
    TraceSwitch class, 188
TraceInfo property
    TraceSwitch class, 188
TraceListener collection class
    RemoveAt() method, 576
TraceSwitch class
    example, 581
    properties, 188
    System.Diagnostics namespace, 188, 570
    table of hierarchical levels, 581
TraceVerbose property
    TraceSwitch class, 188
TraceWarning property
    TraceSwitch class, 188
tracing, 563
    listeners, 563
    switches, 579
        BooleanSwitch class, 580–581
        TraceSwitch class, 581–583
tracking handler, 36
    implementing, 37
TrackingServices class
    RegisterTrackingHandler() method, 37
    System.Runtime.Remoting.Services namespace, 37
transaction context
    context-bound objects, 8–9
TransactionAttribute class
    passing arguments into attributes, 320–322
    properties
        Isolation property, 321
        Timeout property, 321
    System.EnterpriseServices namespace, 306, 320
TransactionOption enumeration
    RequiresNew value, 321
    System.EnterpriseServices namespace, 321
Transformation abstract class
    EDI invoicing and billing system, 293
    VendorTransform concrete classes inherit from, 297
transparent proxy, 13

TryEnter() method
    Monitor class, 481
type, definition, 212
Type class
    dynamic invocation, 252
    members, 231–232
    methods
        GetConstructor() method, 245
        GetConstructors() method, 245
        GetEvent() method, 246
        GetEvents() method, 246
        GetField() method, 239
        GetFields() method, 239
        GetInterfaces() method, 231
        GetNestedType() method, 270
        GetNestedTypes() method, 270
        GetProperty() method, 255
        GetType() method, 230, 271
        InvokeMember() method, 252
    properties
        Assembly property, 225
        Attributes property, 314
        FullName property, 314
    retrieving Types, 230–231
    returned by FieldInfo.FieldType, 238
    System namespace, 220, 223, 228, 230
    using Info classes, 252
type conversion, 343
type member, definition, 212
type metadata
    accessing, 232–234
    examining, 230
        Module class methods, 231
        retrieving Types, 230–231
type terminology, reflection, 212
type-safety
    definition, 213
    delegates as alterative to reflective, 273
    reflective invocation, 272
TypeAttributes enumeration, 232
    Serializable value, 314
    System.Reflection namespace, 311
    table of values, 311
    testing for standard attributes, 312
TypeConverter class
    converter classes inherit from, 383
    methods
        CanConvertFrom() method, 389
        CanConvertTo() method, 384, 389
        ConvertFrom() method, 389
        ConvertTo() method, 384, 389
        GetProperties() method, 391
        GetPropertiesSupported() method, 391
    System.ComponentModel namespace, 354
TypeConverterAttribute class
    GetType() method, 382, 388
    System.ComponentModel namespace, 376
TypeDescriptor class
    methods
        GetAttributes() method, 348
        GetDefaultEvent() method, 348
        GetDefaultProperty() method, 348

GetEditor() method, 355
GetEvents() method, 349
GetProperties() method, 350
obtaining general metadata for data type, 346
TypeInfo value
    MemberTypes enumeration, 235

U

UDDI (Universal Description, Discovery and Integration), 5
UdpClient class
    System.Net.Sockets namespace, 595
UI threads
    in WinForms, 519
    supported by Win32, 519
UITypeEditor class
    System.Drawing.Design namespace, 355
UML
    class diagram for creating the server, 608
    view of client form class, 597
UnauthorizedAccessException class
    System namespace, 199
Unindent() method
    Trace class, 579
Universal Description, Discovery and Integration.
        See UDDI
unmanaged threads, 418
Unmarshal() method
    RemotingServices class, 16
UnmarshaledObject() method
    ITrackingHandler interface, 37
UnsafeQueueUserWorkItem() method
    ThreadPool class, 539, 542
UnsafeRegisterWaitForSingleObject() method
    ThreadPool class, 539, 542
Update() method
    SqlDataAdapter class, 587–588
UploadNotify abstract class
    EDI invoicing and billing system, 294
    ImportData() method, 295
    VendorUploadNotify concrete classes inherit from, 297
UrlAttribute class
    System.Runtime.Remoting.Activation namespace, 284
user-defined objects
    marshaling-by-reference, 25–26
    marshaling-by-value, 22

V

vbThreadPool example, 546
VendorTransform concrete classes
    EDI invoicing and billing system, 297
    inheriting from Transformation abstract class, 297
    overriding base class method, 298
VendorUploadNotify concrete classes
    EDI invoicing and billing system, 297
    inherit from UploadNotify abstract class, 297
    overriding base class method, 297
Version class
    Build property, 281
    Major property, 281
    Minor property, 281
    Revision property, 281
Version property
    AssemblyName class, 281
versioning, 99, 123
    assigning a version number, 123
    determining version to use, 124
    encapsulation and, 4
    Exchange example, 123
    Marshal By Value objects, 125
    Soapsuds tool, 125
    strong names must be assigned to assembly, 124
viewing processes, 400
Visual Basic .NET
    attribute names, 307
    late binding, 215–218
    not procedural programming language, 214
    programming the ThreadPool class, 542
    threads, support for, 410
Visual Designer
    interogating components at design time, 345
    property settings in Employee example, 393
    viewing events, 351
Visual Studio .NET
    adding component objects to application, 373–375
    adding components to Toolbox, 372
    building components, 360
        Component Designer, 361
    defining properties and events for a component, 375
    Just-In-Time debugger, 183
    Machine Debug Manager tool, 181
    ObjectPoolTester application, 517
    Output debug window, 571
    Solution Explorer window
        Properties, 579
    using components, 372
    Windows Application project, 597
        add ListView control, 597
Visual Studio .NET Debugger
    Breakpoints window, 568
        Hit Count dialog, 569
    Command/immediate window, 567
    compared to Visual Basic 6 debugger, 565
    configuring debugger parameters, 565–566
        building the application, 565
    debugger tools, 566
    debugging remoting objects, 180–182
    features, 564
    Locals window, 566
    Run To Cursor, 568
    setting breakpoints, 568–569
    stepping through the code, 568
    Threads window
        debugging threads, 570
    Watch window, 566

W

Wait and Pulse mechanism, 474, 478, 481
Wait() method
    Monitor class, 474, 478, 481
    Thread class, 442

INDEX

WaitAndPulse example, 478, 481
WaitCallback delegate
   System.Threading namespace, 543
WaitHandle class
   System.Threading namespace, 422
WaitOne() method
   AutoResetEvent class, 491–492
   ManualResetEvent class, 490
   Mutex class, 173, 493
WaitOrTimerCallback delegate
   System.Threading namespace, 546
WaitSleepJoin state
   ThreadState enumeration, 443, 445
Watch window, 566
Web Services
   defining with WSDL, 5
Web Services Definition Language. *See* WSDL
web sites
   Microsoft Knowledge Base, 143
web.config file
   Global.asax as alternative to, 122
WebClient class
   System.Net namespace, 594
WebControl class
   System.Web.UI.WebControls namespace, 345
WebException class
   System.Net namespace, 594
   System.Net.Web namespace, 165–167
WebMethodAttribute class
   applies to methods, 303
   facilitates Web Services, 304
   System.Web.Services namespace, 303
WebPermission class
   System.Net namespace, 594
WebPermissionAttribute class
   System.Net namespace, 594
WebProxy class
   System.Net namespace, 595
WebRequest class
   System.Net namespace, 595
WebResponse class
   System.Net namespace, 595
WebServiceAttribute class
   applies to classes, 303
   facilitates Web Services, 304
   System.Web.Services namespace, 303
well-known objects
   configuring with client element, 102–103
<wellknown> element
   configuring SAOs, 101

WellKnownObjectMode enumeration
   change to use single call mode, 29
   specifying singleton mode, 27
While loop and object creation, 137
Win32
   support for worker threads and UI threads, 519
Win32 API functions
   exposing using DllImport with named arguments, 320
   exposing using DllImport with positional arguments, 320
Windows authentication, 202
Windows Event log
   code tracing, 574
Windows event log
   logging errors to, 203–207
Windows Explorer
   viewing assembly metadata, 331
Windows Form Designer
   generated code, 81
Windows Forms control
   creating, 345
Windows Services
   hosting, 99
Windows Services. *See* hosting in Windows Services
Windows Task Manager. *See* Task Manager
WinForms
   UI threads, 519
WithEvents keyword, 139–140
worker threads, 402, 537
   supported by Win32, 519
workerThreads, 540
World Wide Web as session-less system, 2
Write() method
   TcpClient class, 607
   Trace class, 571
WriteIf() method
   Trace class, 571, 580
WriteLine() method
   Debug class, 186
   Trace class, 186–187, 571
WriteLineIf() method
   Trace class, 571, 580
WSDL (Web Services Definition Language), 5
   generalization of IDL, 5
   generating files from server objects, 11
   metadata descriptions, 114
      viewing in IE, 114

forums.apress.com
FOR PROFESSIONALS BY PROFESSIONALS™

JOIN THE APRESS FORUMS AND BE PART OF OUR COMMUNITY. You'll find discussions that cover topics of interest to IT professionals, programmers, and enthusiasts just like you. If you post a query to one of our forums, you can expect that some of the best minds in the business—especially Apress authors, who all write with *The Expert's Voice*™—will chime in to help you. Why not aim to become one of our most valuable participants (MVPs) and win cool stuff? Here's a sampling of what you'll find:

DATABASES
Data drives everything.
Share information, exchange ideas, and discuss any database programming or administration issues.

INTERNET TECHNOLOGIES AND NETWORKING
Try living without plumbing (and eventually IPv6).
Talk about networking topics including protocols, design, administration, wireless, wired, storage, backup, certifications, trends, and new technologies.

JAVA
We've come a long way from the old Oak tree.
Hang out and discuss Java in whatever flavor you choose: J2SE, J2EE, J2ME, Jakarta, and so on.

MAC OS X
All about the Zen of OS X.
OS X is both the present and the future for Mac apps. Make suggestions, offer up ideas, or boast about your new hardware.

OPEN SOURCE
Source code is good; understanding (open) source is better.
Discuss open source technologies and related topics such as PHP, MySQL, Linux, Perl, Apache, Python, and more.

PROGRAMMING/BUSINESS
Unfortunately, it is.
Talk about the Apress line of books that cover software methodology, best practices, and how programmers interact with the "suits."

WEB DEVELOPMENT/DESIGN
Ugly doesn't cut it anymore, and CGI is absurd.
Help is in sight for your site. Find design solutions for your projects and get ideas for building an interactive Web site.

SECURITY
Lots of bad guys out there—the good guys need help.
Discuss computer and network security issues here. Just don't let anyone else know the answers!

TECHNOLOGY IN ACTION
Cool things. Fun things.
It's after hours. It's time to play. Whether you're into LEGO® MINDSTORMS™ or turning an old PC into a DVR, this is where technology turns into fun.

WINDOWS
No defenestration here.
Ask questions about all aspects of Windows programming, get help on Microsoft technologies covered in Apress books, or provide feedback on any Apress Windows book.

HOW TO PARTICIPATE:
Go to the Apress Forums site at **http://forums.apress.com/**.
Click the New User link.